WORDS THAT MADE AMERICAN HISTORY
Since the Civil War

Words THAT MADE

AMERICAN HISTORY

❧ SINCE THE CIVIL WAR ❧

Third Edition, Abridged and Updated

Selected Readings Edited by

RICHARD N. CURRENT
The University of North Carolina at Greensboro

JOHN A. GARRATY
Columbia University

JULIUS WEINBERG
The Cleveland State University

Little, Brown and Company
BOSTON   TORONTO

LIBRARY OF CONGRESS CATALOG CARD NO. 77-91544
ISBN-0-316-165182

10   9   8   7   6   5

MV

*Published simultaneously in Canada
by Little, Brown & Company (Canada) Limited*

PRINTED IN THE UNITED STATES OF AMERICA

Edward A. Ross. From *The Old World in the New* by Edward A. Ross. Copyright 1914 by Edward Alsworth Ross. Reprinted by permission of Hawthorn Books, Inc. All rights reserved.

Randolph S. Bourne. From *The Atlantic Monthly,* Vol. 118, No. 1, 1916. Copyright © by The Atlantic Monthly Company, Boston, Mass. Reprinted with permission.

PREFACE

OUR TITLE, *Words That Made American History,* is not intended to suggest that American history has been made by words alone. We believe, however, that various speeches, pamphlets, books, and other writings have been quite literally epoch-making. Some have aroused people to immediate action. Some have rationalized and justified events after their occurrence. Others have exerted a lasting effect upon the thinking of the majority or of certain minorities. Still others, though not necessarily impelling people to thought or action, have reflected and recorded important aspects of the American character. Words that made American history in one or another of these senses form the substance of the present volume.

To include all such writings would require enough books to fill a good-sized library. Even to include only the most significant would take much more space than is available here. In preparing a book of readings appropriate for college history courses, we have had to choose between two selection procedures. One was to be as inclusive as possible, to gather excerpts from a great many documents and then pare the excerpts down to fit within our space limits. The other possibility was to be more selective, to choose a smaller number of items and present the whole, or at least an extensive part, of each one. We have adopted the second of these procedures. We think more is to be gained from longer, well-rounded pieces than from a profusion of snippets, and we trust that most students and teachers will agree with us. For this new edition, we have deleted a number of selections used in earlier editions that we found, through classroom experience, to be inappropriate for survey or introductory courses, and we have added several selections — on social reform prior to the Civil War, on the role of immigration in the American experience and the nativistic response to the new immigration at the turn of the century, and on the Watergate affair — in order to enhance the usefulness of our reader for the college classroom.

Our aim, then, is to present in fairly full detail a broadly representative collection of writings that have revealed or have influenced the thinking of Americans on important issues. We believe that supplementary readings of this kind, which stirred the minds and hearts of Americans in the past, will stir the interest of readers today and help bring history to life. Thus they will serve as a valuable supplement to the regular textbook.

In an introduction to each selection we have tried to supply essential information about the author and to place his work in its historical context, but we have deliberately avoided predigesting the author's words. We have tried not to give his message away in the introductions, and we have left the analysis to the student.

To guide undergraduates in their study of these materials and to provide a common basis for class discussions, we have, for this edition, retained the study guide that was incorporated into the previous edition. Our intent is that these guides be used as an integral part of each assignment, for they do not consist merely of lists of possible examination questions or of themes for discussion. They are designed, rather, to lead the student through the reading, to focus his attention on the course of each writer's argument, and to encourage him to evaluate that argument. The guides also call the student's attention to relations between certain selections, leading him to make comparisons, note trends, and observe how similar issues are expressed and treated in different periods of history. The stress is on independent evaluation combined with specificity — our hope being that each reader will do his own thinking about these essays — but we seek to direct his thinking toward the historically significant aspects of the material.

R. N. C.
J. A. G.
J. W.

CONTENTS

I. DIVISION AND REUNION

II. IMPLICATIONS OF INDUSTRIALISM

III. EXPANSION — BY LAND AND SEA

IV. THE SPIRIT OF PROGRESSIVISM

VII. CONTEMPORARY DOMESTIC CONCERNS

WORDS THAT MADE AMERICAN HISTORY
Since the Civil War

I. Division and Reunion

Abraham Lincoln

THE PEOPLE'S CONTEST

❧*1861, 1863, 1865*❧   ABRAHAM LINCOLN (1809-1865) used to be pictured, at times, as an appealing but quaint and rather pathetic figure who for the most part merely presided, at a distance, over the stirring and fateful events of his presidency. Only in recent years has historical scholarship made it possible to do full justice to him as an actual leader. It is now clear that he was the dominant and decisive American of his day. To summarize, he used rare political skill not only to gain and hold office but also to unite the North and thus reunite the nation. A statesman as well as a politician, he led the way cautiously but surely toward the emancipation of the slaves as well as the preservation of the Union. As commander in chief of the Army and the Navy, he took responsibility for making and seeing to the execution of the strategic plans that at last brought victory. And he gave point and meaning to all the bloodshed by symbolizing and putting into deathless words the ideals which, alone, were worth fighting for.

It would take more space than is available here to present adequately the words of his that have helped Americans make up their minds. The following selections provide a sampling of his more significant statements on the causes and the meaning of the Civil War.

MESSAGE TO CONGRESS

(July 4, 1861)

HAVING been convened on an extraordinary occasion, as authorized by the Constitution, your attention is not called to any ordinary subject of legislation.

At the beginning of the present Presidential term, four months ago, the functions of the Federal Government were found to be generally suspended within the several States of South Carolina, Georgia, Alabama, Mississippi, Louisiana, and Florida, excepting only those of the Post Office Department.

Within these States, all the Forts, Arsenals, Dock-yards, Customhouses, and the like, including the movable and stationary property in, and about them, had been seized, and were held in open hostility to this Government, excepting only Forts Pickens, Taylor, and Jefferson, on, and near the Florida coast, and Fort Sumter, in Charleston harbor, South Carolina. The Forts thus seized had been put in improved condition; new ones had been

3

built and armed forces had been organized, and were organizing, all avowedly with the same hostile purpose.

The forts remaining in the possession of the Federal government, in, and near, these States, were either besieged or menaced by warlike preparations; and especially Fort Sumter was nearly surrounded by well-protected hostile batteries, with guns equal in quality to the best of its own, and outnumbering the latter as perhaps ten to one. A disproportionate share, of the Federal muskets and rifles, had somehow found their way into these States, and had been seized, to be used against the government. Accumulations of the public revenue, lying within them, had been seized for the same object. The Navy was scattered in distant seas; leaving but a very small part of it within the immediate reach of the government. Officers of the Federal Army and Navy, had resigned in great numbers; and, of those resigning, a large proportion had taken up arms against the government. Simultaneously, and in connection, with all this, the purpose to sever the Federal Union, was openly avowed. In accordance with this purpose, an ordinance had been adopted in each of these States, declaring the States, respectively, to be separated from the National Union. A formula for instituting a combined government of these states had been promulgated; and this illegal organization, in the character of confederate States was already invoking recognition, aid, and intervention, from Foreign Powers.

Finding this condition of things, and believing it to be an imperative duty upon the incoming Executive, to prevent, if possible, the consummation of such attempt to destroy the Federal Union, a choice of means to that end became indispensable. This choice was made; and was declared in the Inaugural address. The policy chosen looked to the exhaustion of all peaceful measures, before a resort to any stronger ones. It sought only to hold the public places and property, not already wrested from the Government, and to collect the revenue; relying for the rest, on time, discussion, and the ballot-box. It promised a continuance of the mails at government expense, to the very people who were resisting the government; and it gave repeated pledges against any disturbance to any of the people, or any of their rights. Of all that which a president might constitutionally, and justifiably, do in such a case, everything was foreborne, without which, it was believed possible to keep the government on foot.

On the 5th of March, (the present incumbent's first full day in office) a letter of Major Anderson, commanding at Fort Sumter, written on the 28th of February, and received at the War Department on the 4th of March, was, by that Department, placed in his hands. This letter expressed the professional opinion of the writer, that re-inforcements could not be thrown into that Fort within the time for his relief, rendered necessary by the limited supply of provisions, and with a view of holding possession of the same, with a force of less than twenty thousand good, and well-disciplined men. This opinion was concurred in by all the officers of his command; and their *memoranda* on the subject, were made enclosures of Major Anderson's letter. The whole was immediately laid before Lieutenant General Scott, who at once concurred with Major Anderson in opinion. On reflection, however, he took full time consulting with other officers, both of the Army and the Navy; and, at the end of four days, came reluctantly, but decidedly, to the same conclusion as before. He also stated at the same time that no such sufficient force was then at the control of the Government, or could be raised, and brought to the ground, within the time when the provisions in the Fort would be exhausted. In a purely military point of view, this reduced the duty of the administration, in the case, to the mere matter of getting the garrison safely out of the Fort.

It was believed, however, that to so abandon that position, under the circumstances, would be utterly ruinous; that the *necessity* under which it was to be done, would not be fully understood — that, by many, it would be construed as a part of a *voluntary* policy — that, at home, it would discourage the friends of the Union, embolden its adversaries, and go far to insure to the latter, a recognition abroad — that, in fact, it would be our national destruction consummated. This could not be allowed. Starvation was not yet upon the garrison; and ere it would be reached, *Fort Pickens* might be re-inforced. This last, would be a clear indication of *policy,* and would better enable the country to accept the evacuation of Fort Sumter, as a military *necessity.* An order was at once directed to be sent for that landing of the troops from the Steamship Brooklyn, into Fort Pickens. This order could not go by land, but must take the longer, and slower route by sea. The first return news from the order was received just one week before the fall of Fort Sumter. The news itself was, that the officer commanding the Sabine, to which vessel the troops had been transferred from the Brooklyn, acting upon some *quasi* armistice of the late administration, (and of the existence of which, the present administration, up to the time the order was despatched, had only too vague and uncertain rumors, to fix attention) had refused to land the troops. To now re-inforce Fort Pickens, before a crisis would be reached at Fort Sumter was impossible — rendered so by the near exhaustion of provisions in the latter-named Fort. In precaution against such a conjuncture, the government had, a few days before, commenced preparing an expedition, as well adapted as might be, to relieve Fort Sumter, which expedition was intended to be ultimately used, or not, according to circumstances. The strongest anticipated case, for using it, was now presented; and it was resolved to send it forward. As had been intended, in this contingency, it was also resolved to notify the Governor of South Carolina, that he might expect an attempt would be made to provision the Fort; and that, if the attempt should not be resisted, there would be no effort to throw in men, arms, or ammunition, without further notice, or in case of an attack upon the Fort. This notice was accordingly given; whereupon the Fort was attacked, and bombarded to its fall, without even awaiting the arrival of the provisioning expedition.

It is thus seen that the assault upon, and reduction of, Fort Sumter, was, in no sense, a matter of self defence on the part of the assailants. They well knew that the garrison in the Fort could, by no possibility, commit aggression upon them. They knew — they were expressly notified — that the giving of bread to the few brave and hungry men of the garrison, was all which would on that occasion be attempted, unless themselves, by resisting so much, should provoke more. They knew that this Government desired to keep the garrison in the Fort, not to assail them, but merely to maintain visible possession, and thus to preserve the Union from actual, and immediate dissolution — trusting, as hereinbefore stated, to time, discussion, and the ballot-box, for final adjustment; and they assailed, and reduced the Fort, for precisely the reverse object — to drive out the visible authority of the Federal Union, and thus force it to immediate dissolution.

That this was their object, the Executive well understood; and having said to them in the inaugural address, "You can have no conflict without being yourselves the aggressors," he took pains, not only to keep this declaration good, but also to keep the case so free from the power of ingenious sophistry, as that the world should not be able to misunderstand it. By the affair at Fort Sumter, with its surrounding circumstances, that point was reached. Then, and thereby, the assailants of the Government, began the conflict of arms, without a gun in sight, or in expectancy, to return their fire, save only the few in the Fort, sent to that harbor, years before, for their own protection, and still ready to give that protecion, in whatever was lawful. In this act, discarding all else, they have forced upon the country, the distinct issue: "Immediate dissolution, or blood."

And this issue embraces more than the fate of these United States. It presents to the whole family of man, the question, whether a constitutional republic, or a democracy — a government of the people, by the same people — can, or cannot, maintain its territorial integrity, against its own domestic foes. It presents the question, whether discontented individuals, too few in numbers to control administration, according to organic law, in any case, can always, upon the pretences made in this case, or on any other pretences, or arbitrarily, without any pretence, break up their Government, and thus practically put an end to free government upon the earth. It forces us to ask: "Is there, in all republics, this inherent, and fatal weakness?" "Must a government, of necessity, be too *strong* for the liberties of its people, or too *weak* to maintain its own existence?"

So viewing the issue, no choice was left but to call out the war power of the Government; and so to resist force, employed for its destruction, by force, for its preservation. . . .

It might seem, at first thought, to be of little difference whether the present movement at the South be called "secession" or "rebellion." The movers, however, well understand the difference. At the beginning, they knew they could never raise their treason to any respectable magnitude, by any name which implies *violation* of law. They knew their people possessed as much of moral sense, as much of devotion to law and order, and as much pride in, and reverence for, the history, and government, of their common country, as any other civilized, and patriotic people. They knew they could make no advancement directly in the teeth of these strong and noble sentiments. Accordingly they commenced by an insidious debauching of the public mind. They invented an ingenious sophism, which, if conceded, was followed by perfectly logical steps, through all the incidents, to the complete destruction of the Union. The sophism itself is, that any state of the Union may, *consistently* with the national Constitution, and therefore *lawfully,* and *peacefully,* withdraw from the Union, without the consent of the Union, or of any other state. The little disguise that the supposed right is to be exercised only for just cause, themselves to be the sole judge of its justice, is too thin to merit any notice.

With rebellion thus sugar-coated, they have been drugging the public mind of their section for more than thirty years; and, until at length, they have brought many good men to a willingness to take up arms against the government the day *after* some assemblage of men have enacted the farcical pretence of taking their State out of the Union, who could have been brought to no such thing the day *before.*

This sophism derives much — perhaps the whole — of its currency, from the assumption, that there is some omnipotent, and sacred supremacy, pertaining to a *State* — to each State of our Federal Union. Our States have neither more, nor less power, than that reserved to them, in the Union, by the Constitution — no one of them ever having been a State out of the Union. The original ones passed into the Union even before they cast off their British colonial dependence; and the new ones each came into the Union directly from a condition of dependence, excepting Texas. And even Texas, in its temporary independence, was never designated a State. The new ones only took the designation of States, on coming into the Union, while that name was first adopted for the old ones, in, and by, the

Declaration of Independence. Therein the "United Colonies" were declared to be "Free and Independent States"; but, even then, the object plainly was not to declare their independence of *one another,* or of the *Union;* but directly the contrary, as their mutual pledge, and their mutual action, before, at the time, and afterwards, abundantly show. The express plighting of faith, by each and all of the original thirteen, in the Articles of Confederation, two years later, that the Union shall be perpetual, is most conclusive. Having never been States, either in substance, or in name, *outside* of the Union, whence this magical omnipotence of "State rights," asserting a claim of power to lawfully destroy the Union itself? Much is said about the "sovereignty" of the states; but the word, even, is not in the national Constitution; nor, as is believed, in any of the State constitutions. What is a "sovereignty," in the political sense of the term? Would it be far wrong to define it "A political community, without a political superior"? Tested by this, no one of our States, except Texas, ever was a sovereignty. And even Texas gave up the character on coming into the Union; by which act, she acknowledged the Constitution of the United States, and the laws and treaties of the United States made in pursuance of the Constitution, to be, for her, the supreme law of the land. The States have their *status* IN the Union, and they have no other *legal status.* If they break from this, they can only do so against law, and by revolution. The Union, and not themselves separately, procured their independence, and their liberty. By conquest, or purchase, the Union gave each of them, whatever of independence, and liberty, it has. The Union is older than any of the States; and, in fact, it created them as States. Originally, some dependent colonies made the Union; and, in turn, the Union threw off their old dependence, for them, and made them States, such as they are. Not one of them ever had a State constitution, independent of the Union. Of course, it is not forgotten that all the new States framed their constitutions, before they entered the Union; nevertheless, dependent upon, and preparatory to, coming into the Union.

Unquestionably the States have the powers, and rights, reserved to them in, and by the National Constitution; but among these, surely, are not included all conceivable powers, however mischievous, or destructive; but, at most, such only, as were known in the world, at the time, as governmental powers; and certainly, a power to destroy the government itself, had never been known as a governmental — as a merely administrative power. This relative matter of National power, and State rights, as a principle, is no other than the principle of *generality,* and *locality.* Whatever concerns the whole, should be confided to the whole — to the general government; while, whatever concerns *only* the State, should be left exclusively, to the

State. This is all there is of original principle about it. Whether the National Constitution, in defining boundaries between the two, has applied the principle with exact accuracy, is not to be questioned. We are all bound by that defining without question.

What is now combatted, is the position that secession is *consistent* with the Constitution — is *lawful,* and *peaceful.* It is not contended that there is any express law for it; and nothing should ever be implied as law, which leads to unjust, or absurd consequences. The nation purchased, with money, the countries out of which several of these States were formed. Is it just that they shall go off without leave, and without refunding? The nation paid very large sums (in the aggregate, I believe, nearly a hundred millions) to relieve Florida of the aboriginal tribes. Is it just that she shall now be off without consent, or without making any return? The nation is now in debt for money applied to the benefit of these so-called seceding States, in common with the rest. Is it just, either that creditors shall go unpaid, or the remaining States pay the whole? A part of the present national debt was contracted to pay the old debts of Texas. Is it just that she shall leave, and pay no part of this herself?

Again, if one State may secede, so may another; and when all shall have seceded, none is left to pay the debts. Is this quite just to creditors? Did we notify them on this sage view of ours, when we borrowed their money? If we now recognize this doctrine, by allowing the seceders to go in peace, it is difficult to see what we can do, if others choose to go, or to extort terms upon which they will promise to remain.

The seceders insist that our Constitution admits of secession. They have assumed to make a National Constitution of their own, in which, of necessity, they have either *discarded,* or *retained,* the right of secession, as they insist, it exists in ours. If they have discarded it, they thereby admit that, on principle, it ought not to be in ours. If they have retained it, by their own construction of ours they show that to be consistent they must secede from one another, whenever they shall find it the easiest way of settling their debts, or effecting any other selfish, or unjust object. The principle itself is one of disintegration, and upon which no government can possibly endure.

If all the States, save one, should assert the power to *drive* that one out of the Union, it is presumed the whole class of seceder politicians would at once deny the power, and denounce the act as the greatest outrage upon State rights. But suppose that precisely the same act, instead of being called "driving the one out," should be called "the seceding of the others from that one," it would be exactly what the seceders claim to do; unless, indeed, they make the point, that the one, because it is a minority, may rightfully do, what the others, because they are a majority, may not rightfully do. These politicians are subtle, and profound, on the rights of minorities. They are not partial to that power which made the Constitution, and speaks from the preamble, calling itself "We, the People." . . .

This is essentially a People's contest. On the side of the Union, it is a struggle for maintaining in the world, that form, and substance of government, whose leading object is, to elevate the condition of men — to lift artificial weights from all shoulders — to clear the paths of laudable pursuit for all — to afford all, an unfettered start, and a fair chance, in the race of life. Yielding to partial, and temporary departures, from necessity, this is the leading object of the government for whose existence we contend. . . .

GETTYSBURG ADDRESS

(November 20, 1863)

FOUR SCORE and seven years ago our fathers brought forth on this continent, a new nation, conceived in Liberty, and dedicated to the proposition that all men are created equal.

Now we are engaged in a great civil war, testing whether that nation, or any nation so conceived and so dedicated, can long endure. We are met on a great battle-field of that war. We have come here to dedicate a portion of that field, as a final resting place for those who here gave their lives that that nation might live. It is altogether fitting and proper that we should do this.

But, in a larger sense, we can not dedicate — we can not consecrate — we can not hallow — this ground. The brave men, living and dead, who struggled here, have consecrated it, far above our poor power to add or detract. The world will little note, nor long remember what we say here, but it can never forget what they did here. It is for us the living, rather, to be dedicated here to the unfinished work which they who fought here have thus far so nobly advanced. It is rather for us to be here dedicated to the great task remaining before us — that from these honored dead we take increased devotion to that cause for which they gave the last full measure of devotion — that we here highly resolve that these dead shall not have died in vain — that this nation, under God, shall have a new birth of freedom — and that government of the people, by the people, for the people, shall not perish from the earth.

SECOND INAUGURAL ADDRESS

(March 4, 1865)

AT THIS second appearing to take the oath of the presidential office, there is less occasion for an extended address than there was at the first. Then a statement, somewhat in detail, of a course to be pursued, seemed fitting and proper. Now, at the expiration of four years, during which public declarations have been constantly called forth on every point and phase of the great contest which still absorbs the attention, and engrosses the energies [*sic*] of the nation, little that is new could be presented. The progress of our arms, upon which all else chiefly depends, is as well known to the public as to myself; and it is, I trust, reasonably satisfactory and encouraging to all. With high hope for the future, no prediction in regard to it is ventured.

On the occasion corresponding to this four years ago, all thoughts were anxiously directed to an impending civil-war. All dreaded it — all sought to avert it. While the inaugural address was being delivered from this place, devoted altogether to *saving* the Union without war, insurgent agents were in the city seeking to *destroy* it without war — seeking to dissol[v]e the Union, and divide effects, by negotiation. Both parties deprecated war; but one of them would *make* war rather than let the nation survive; and the other would *accept* war rather than let it perish. And the war came.

One eighth of the whole population were colored slaves, not distributed generally over the Union, but localized in the Southern part of it. These slaves constituted a peculiar and powerful interest. All knew that this interest was, somehow, the cause of the war. To strengthen, perpetuate, and extend this interest was the object for which the insurgents would rend the Union, even by war; while the government claimed no right to do more than to restrict the territorial enlargement of it. Neither party expected for the war, the magnitude, or the duration, which it has already attained. Neither anticipated that the *cause* of the conflict might cease with, or even before, the conflict itself should cease. Each looked for an easier triumph, and a result less fundamental and astounding. Both read the same Bible, and pray to the same God; and each invokes His aid against the other. It may seem strange that any men should dare to ask a just God's assistance in wringing their bread from the sweat of other men's faces; but let us judge not that we be not judged. The prayers of both could not be answered; that of neither has been answered fully. The Almighty has His own purposes. "Woe unto the world because of offences! for it must needs be that offences come; but woe to that man by whom the offence cometh!" If we shall suppose that American Slavery is one of those offences which, in the providence of God, must needs come, but which, having continued through His appointed time, He now wills to remove, and that He gives to both North and South, this terrible war, as the woe due to those by whom the offence came, shall we discern therein any departure from those divine attributes which the believers in a Living God always ascribe to Him? Fondly do we hope—fervently do we pray—that this mighty scourge of war may speedily pass away. Yet, if God wills that it continue, until all the wealth piled by the bond-man's two hundred and fifty years of unrequited toil shall be sunk, and until every drop of blood drawn with the lash, shall be paid by another drawn with the sword, as was said three thousand years ago, so still it must be said "the judgments of the Lord, are true and righteous altogether."

With malice toward none; with charity for all; with firmness in the right, as God gives us to see the right, let us strive on to finish the work we are in; to bind up the nation's wounds; to care for him who shall have borne the battle, and for his widow, and his orphan — to do all which may achieve and cherish a just, and a lasting peace, among ourselves, and with all nations.

Study Guide

1. In his address to Congress in 1861 Lincoln sets forth the following:
   (a) his position on the crisis of the Union created by secession; and
   (b) a justification of his actions in response to this crisis. Let us analyze them.
       (1) What "condition of things" and choices does Lincoln indicate confronted him and the nation in 1861?
       (2) Note with care Lincoln's defense of his actions regarding the forts in the South — for a different interpretation of his actions will be set forth in the next selection, by Alexander Stephens, Vice President of the Confederacy.
       (3) Turning to the nature of the Union — and here, too, note carefully the differences in definition and in constitutional theory between Lincoln and Stephens (cf. pp. 6–9 and 14–18), what does Lincoln label a "sophism" (p. 7) and why?
       (4) In the last paragraph Lincoln somewhat defines the purpose of government. What is it?

2. The purposes of government are nowhere more exaltingly stated than in Lincoln's address at Gettysburg. Read it and answer the following:

(a) Where and under what circumstances did Lincoln pen these words?
(b) Why were they delivered at Gettysburg and why at this particular time?
(c) Can you account for the negligible response to this address by Lincoln's contemporaries or for its subsequent importance in American thought and literature?

3. While on the subject of Gettysburg, who was Edward Everett?

4. Like the Gettysburg Address, Lincoln's 1865 Inaugural Address is great literature; unlike that speech it is also an important practical document. Let us try to understand what Lincoln is saying.

(a) Has Lincoln altered his views regarding the justification for the war since his July 4, 1861, message to the Congress, and if so, how? What are his hopes for winning it?
(b) What is the purpose of the second paragraph on p. 11? Evaluate Lincoln's intent in uttering the following: "Both parties deprecated war; but one of them would *make* war rather than let the nation survive; and the other would *accept* war rather than let it perish. And the war came."
(c) Note that unlike his 1861 Message to Congress, Lincoln's address is now concerned with the institution of slavery. Can you account for this shift in his focus?
(d) From the paragraph on slavery, what can you glean about Lincoln's views toward slavery, its role in starting the war, and its future?

What can the following (p. 11) tell you about Lincoln's attitude toward the North and the South, the war, slavery, and God's purposes? "It may seem strange that any men should dare to ask a just God's assistance in wringing their bread from the sweat of other men's faces; but let us judge not that we be not judged. The prayers of both could not be answered; that of neither has been answered fully."

5. Relate the closing paragraph of Lincoln's address to the character and the purposes of his program for Reconstruction.

Alexander H. Stephens

THE WAR BETWEEN THE STATES

1868, 1870 As ABRAHAM LINCOLN (1809-1865) expressed the predominant Northern view before and during the Civil War, so Alexander H. Stephens (1812-1883), after the war was over, gave voice to the interpretation that came to prevail in the South. As a Whig from Georgia, Stephens once had been a congressional colleague and a close friend of Lincoln's. In 1860-1861 he at first opposed, then went along with, the secession of his state. Accepting office as Vice President of the Confederacy, he declared that the new government was built upon the "cornerstone" of slavery. During the war he disagreed with Jefferson Davis (1808-1889) when Davis took steps to increase the powers of the Confederate government as against the rights of the separate states. Stephens made himself the center of resistance to the Davis policies.

In 1865 he was imprisoned for several months in Fort Warren, in Boston harbor. In 1866 he was elected to the United States Senate but was excluded by the Republican majority, as were other senators and congressmen elected by the former Confederate states. In 1867, while Radical Reconstruction was getting under way, he began to write a work justifying the course of the South to secession and through the war. Like many Southerners, he now was much more wholeheartedly pro-Confederate than he ever had been.

The first volume of his work, significantly entitled *A Constitutional View of the Late War between the States,* was published in 1868, and the second volume in 1870. These volumes sold well and were read widely, especially in the South. Rationalizing the Lost Cause, Stephens played down the slavery question and played up the issue of state rights. He thus reflected and also helped to mold the opinions of his fellow Southerners. The conflict of 1861-1865, he argued, had been no "Civil War" but a "War between the States." Southerners adopted this designation and insisted upon it, though they had seldom if ever used it before 1868.

Stephens presented his case in the form of imaginary conversations, or "Colloquies," held at Liberty Hall, his Georgia plantation home. His guests (fictional characters, though based upon actual prototypes, he explained) were three Northerners: a War Democrat, a Conservative Republican, and a Radical Republican, "Judge Bynum," who appears in one of the selections reprinted below. Time and again, Stephens succeeds in demolishing the arguments of his visitors — at least to his own satisfaction.

COLLOQUY XII
(1868)

MR. STEPHENS. . . . In what you consider, then, the weakness of our Government, according to my idea of its nature, I repeat, its chief strength, its great beauty, its complete symmetry, its ultimate harmony, and, indeed, its very perfection, mainly consist; certainly, so long as the objects aimed at in its formation are the objects aimed at in its administration. And, on this principle, on the full recognition of the absolute ultimate Sovereignty of the several States, I did consider it the best, and the strongest, and the grandest Government on earth! My whole heart and soul were devoted to the Constitution, and the Union under it, with this understanding of its nature, charter, objects, and functions!

When, therefore, the State of Georgia seceded, against my judgment, viewing the measure in the light of *policy,* only, and not of right (for the causes, as we have seen, and shall see more fully, hereafter, were more than ample to justify the act, as a matter of right), I felt it to be my duty to go with her, not only from a sense of the obligations of allegiance, but from other high considerations of patriotism of not much less weight and influence. These considerations pressed upon the mind the importance of maintaining *this principle,* which *lies at the foundation of all Federal systems;* and to which we were mainly indebted, in ours, for all the great achievements of the past. It was under this construction of the nature of our system, that all these achievements had been attained. This was the essential and vital principle of the system, to which I was so thoroughly devoted. It was that which secured all the advantages of Confederation, without the risk of Centralism and Absolutism; and on its preservation depended, not only the safety and welfare, and even existence, of my own State, but the safety, welfare, and ultimate existence of all the other States of the Union! The States were older than the Union! They made it! It was but their own creation! Their preservation was of infinitely more importance than its continuance! The Union might cease to exist, and yet the States continue to exist, as before! Not so with the Union, in case of the destruction or annihilation of the States! With their extinction, the Union necessarily becomes extinct also! They may survive it, and form another, more perfect, if the lapse of time and changes of events show it to be necessary, for the same objects had in view when it was formed; but it can never survive them! What may be called a Union may spring from the common ruins, but it would not be the Union of the Constitution! — the Union of States! By whatever name it might be called, whether Union, Nation, Kingdom, or any thing else, according to the taste of its dupes or its devotees, it would, in reality, be nothing but that deformed and hideous Monster which rises from the decomposing elements of dead States, the world over, and which is well known by the friends of Constitutional Liberty, everywhere, as the Demon of Centralism, Absolutism, Despotism! This is the necessary reality of that result, whether the Imperial Powers be seized and wielded by the hands of many, of few, or of one!

The question, therefore, with me, assumed a magnitude and importance far above the welfare and destiny of my own State, it embraced the welfare and ultimate destiny of all the States, North as well as South; nay, more, it embraced, in its range, the general interest of mankind, so far, at least, as the oppressed of all other lands and climes were looking to this country, not only for a present asylum against the evils of misrule in their own, but were anxiously and earnestly looking forward to the Federative principles here established, as "the World's best hope," in the great future, for the regeneration, the *renaisance,* of the Nations of the Earth! Such, in my judgment, were the scope and bearing of the question and the principles involved.

Had this foundation principle of the system then been generally acknowledged — had no military force been called out to prevent the exercise of this right of withdrawal on the part of the seceding States — had no war been waged against Georgia and the other States, for their assertion and maintenance of this right, had not this primary law of our entire system of Government been violated in the war so waged, I cannot permit myself to entertain the shadow of a doubt, that the whole controversy, between the States and Sections, would, at no distant day, have been satisfactorily and harmoniously adjusted, under the peaceful and beneficent operation of this very law itself. Just as all perturbations and irregularities are adjusted in the solar system, by the simple law of gravitation, from which alone it sprung in the beginning, and on which alone its continuance, with its wonderfully harmonious workings, depends!

A brief illustration will more clearly unfold this view. Had the right of withdrawal not been denied or resisted, those States, which had openly, confessedly, and avowedly disregarded their obligations, under the Compact, in the matter of the rendition of fugitives from service, and fugitives from justice, appealing, as they did, to "a higher Law" than the Constitution, would have reconsidered their acts, and renewed their covenants under the bonds of Union, and the Federal administration would have abandoned its policy of taking charge of subjects not within the limits of its delegated powers. The first aberrations in the system; that is the disregard of plighted faith, which had caused the second, that is the secession movement, would themselves have been rectified by that very movement! This rectification on the one side would have been attended by a corresponding rectification on the other. This would have been a *necessary* and *inevitable* result, whatever parties, under the influence of passion at the time, may have thought of the nature and permanency of the separation. That is, it would necessarily and inevitably have been the result, if the assumption on which the Union was founded be correct, namely, that it was for the best interest of all the States to be united upon the terms set forth in the Constitution — each State faithfully performing all its obligations, and the Federal Head confining its action strictly to the subjects with which it was charged. On this point, that the Union was best for all, my own convictions were strong and thorough for many reasons, that may be given hereafter. If this postulate was correct, then the ultimate result of this action and reaction in the operation of the system in bringing about a re-adjustment of the parts to their original places, would have been as *inevitable* as the continued harmonious re-adjustment of continual disturbances in the material world is being produced by like action and counter-action continually going on throughout its entire organization, and the whole resulting from the same all-pervading and all-controlling law, the same law continuing the organization which brought it at first into existence.

But if, on the contrary, the whole assumption on which the Union was formed was wrong, — if it were not for the true and best interests of all the States, constituted as they were, to be so united, — if it were true, as asserted by the controlling spirits of the derelict States, that the Constitution itself as to them, was but a "covenant with death and an agreement with Hell," — then, of course, the re-adjustment would not have taken place, and ought not to have taken place. But I did not believe that the masses of the people in these States entertained any such sentiments towards the work of their Fathers!

My opinion was, that it only required those masses to see, feel, and appreciate the great advantages of that Union to them; and to realize the fact that a Compact, broken by them, could not longer be binding upon others, as Mr. Webster had said, to cause them to compel their officials to comply with the terms of an engagement, which, upon the whole, was of so great importance to their best interests. My convictions were equally strong that, when this was done, the masses of the people at the South, influenced by like considerations, would have controlled all opposition to their cheerful and cordial return to their proper places.

There would have been no war, no bloodshed, no sacking of towns and cities, no desolation, no billions of treasure expended, on either side, and no million of lives sacrificed in the unnatural and fraticidal strife; there would have been none of the present troubles about restoration, or reconstruction; but, instead of these lamentable scenes, a new spectacle of wonder would have been presented for the guide and instruction of the astonished Nations of the earth, greater than that exhibited after the Nullification pacification, of the matchless workings of our American Institutions of Self-Government by the people!

You readily perceive, therefore, how thoroughly, looking to the grand results, my entire feelings, heart, and soul, with every energy of mind and body, became enlisted in the success of this cause, when force was invoked, when war was waged to put it down. It was the cause, not only of the seceding States, but the cause of all the States, and in this view it became, to a great extent, the cause of Constitutional Liberty everywhere. It was the cause of the Federative principle of Government, against the principle of Empire! The cause of the Grecian type of

Civilization against the Asiatic! So, at least, I viewed it, with all the earnestness of the profoundest convictions.

The matter of Slavery, so-called, which was the proximate cause of these irregular movements on both sides, and which ended in the general collision of war, as we have seen, was of infinitely less importance to the Seceding States, than the recognition of this great principle. I say Slavery, so-called, because there was with us no such thing as Slavery in the full and proper sense of that word. No people ever lived more devoted to the principles of liberty, secured by free democratic institutions, than were the people of the South. None had ever given stronger proofs of this than they had done, from the day that Virginia moved in behalf of the assailed rights of Massachusetts, in 1774, to the firing of the first gun in Charleston Harbor, in 1861. What was called Slavery amongst us, was but a legal subordination of the African to the Caucasian race. This relation was so regulated by law as to promote, according to the intent and design of the system, the best interests of both races, the Black as well as the White, the Inferior, as well as the Superior. Both had rights secured, and both had duties imposed. It was a system of reciprocal service, and mutual bonds. But even the two thousand million dollars invested in the relation thus established, between private capital and the labor of this class of population, under the system, was but as the dust in the balance, compared with the vital attributes of the rights of Independence and Sovereignty on the part of the several States. For with these whatever changes and modifications, or improvements in this domestic institution, founded itself upon laws of nature, time, and experience, might have shown to be proper in the advancing progress of civilization, for the promotion of the great ends of society in all good Governments — that is the best interest of all classes, without wrong or injury to any — could, and would have been made by the superior race in these States, under the guidance of that reason, justice, philanthropy, and statemanship, which had ever marked their course, without the violent disruption of the entire social fabric, with all its attendant ills, and inconceivable wrongs, mischiefs, and sufferings; and especially without those terrible evils and consequences which must almost necessarily result from such disruptions and reorganizations as make a sudden and complete transfer of political power from the hands of the superior to the inferior race, in their present condition, intellectually and morally, in at least six States of the Union!

The system, as it existed, it is true, was not perfect. All admit this. No human systems are perfect. But great changes had been made in it, as this class of persons were gradually rising from their original barbarism, in their subordinate sphere, under the operation of the system, and from their contact, in this way, with the civilization of the superior race. Other changes would certainly have been made, even to the extinction of the system, if time, with its changes, and the progress of attainments on the part of those people had shown it to be proper — that is, best for both races. For if the system, as designed, was not really the best, or could not have been made the best for both races, or whenever it should have ceased to be so, it could and would have been thoroughly and radically changed, in due time, by the only proper and competent authority to act in the premises.

The erroneous dogma of the greatest good to the greatest number, was not the basis on which this Institution rested. Much less was it founded upon the dogma or principle of the sole interest or benefit of the white race to the exclusion of considerations embracing the interests and welfare of the other. It was erected upon no such idea as that *might,* barely, gives *right,* but it was organized and defended upon the immutable principles of justice to all, which is the foundation of all good Governments. This requires that society be so organized as to secure the greatest good possible, morally, intellectually, and politically, to all classes of persons within their jurisdictional control, without necessary wrong or detriment to any. This was the foundation principle on which this institution in these States was established and defended.

These questions are not now, however, before us. We are at present considering the workings of the Federal system, and not the wisdom or policy of the social systems of the several States, or the propriety of the *status* of their constituent elements respectively.

This whole question of Slavery, so-called, was but one relating to the proper *status* of the African as an element of a society composed of the Caucasian and African races, and the *status* which was best, not for the one race or the other, but best, upon the whole, for both.

Over these questions, the Federal Government had no rightful control whatever. They were expressly excluded, in the Compact of Union, from its jurisdiction or authority. Any such assumed control was a palpable violation of the Compact, which released all the parties to the Compact, affected by such action, from their obligations under the Compact. On this point there can be no shadow of doubt.

Waiving these questions, therefore, for the present, I repeat that this whole subject of Slavery, so-called, in any and every view of it, was, to the Seceding States, but a drop in the ocean compared with those other considerations involved in the issue. Hence, during the whole war, being thoroughly enlisted in it from these other and higher considerations, but being, at the same time, ever an earnest advocate for its speediest termination by an appeal from the arena of arms to the forum of reason, justice, and right, I was wedded to no idea as a basis of peace, but that of the recognition of the ultimate absolute Sovereignty of all the States as the essential basis of any permanent union between them, or any of them, consistent with the preservation of their ultimate existence and liberties. And I wanted, at no time, any recognition of Independence on the part of the Confederate States, but that of George III, of England. That is, the recognition of the Sovereignty and Independence of each, by name.

The Confederate States had made common cause for this great principle, as the original thirteen States had done in 1776. The recognition of this I regarded as essential to the future well-being, happiness, and prosperity of all the States, in existence and to be formed, as well as the countless millions of people who are hereafter to inhabit this half of the Western Hemisphere.

With this simple recognition I saw no formidable difficulty likely to arise in the future, from controversies between States or Sections. Whenever the passions of the day passed off, whatever Union or Unions were, or might be, really beneficial to all the States, would have resulted sooner or later, as inevitably as natural laws produce their natural effects. This they do in the moral and political world, if left to their proper and legitimate action, with as much certainty as they do in the material.

With this principle recognized, I looked upon it hereafter, and at no distant day, to become, by the natural law of political affinity — "mutual convenience and reciprocal advantage" — the great Continental Regulator of the Grand Federal Republic of "the United States of America," to whatever limits their boundaries might go, or to whatever extent their number might swell.

COLLOQUY XIII

(1870)

MR. STEPHENS. We have now, gentlemen, gone through with the preliminary questions; we have taken that historical review, which was necessary and essential for a correct understanding of the nature and character of the Government of the United States, from a violation of the organic principles of which, as I stated in the outset, the war had its origin. We have seen from this review that ours is a Federal Government. In other words, we have seen that it is a Government formed by a Convention, a *Foedus,* or Compact between distinct, separate, and Sovereign States. We have seen that this Federal or Conventional Government, so formed possesses inherently no power whatever. All its powers are held by delegation only, and by delegation from separate States. These powers are all enumerated and all limited to specific objects in the Constitution. Even the highest Sovereign Power it is permitted to exercise — the war power, for instance — is held by it by delegation only. Sovereignty itself — the great source of all political power — under the system, still resides where it did before the Compact was entered into, that is, in the States severally, or with the people of the several States respectively. By the Compact, the Sovereign Powers to be exercised by the Federal Head were not surrendered by the States — were not alienated or parted with by them. They were delegated only. The States by voluntary engagements, agreed only to abstain from their exercise themselves, and to confer this exercise by delegation upon common agents under the Convention, for the better security of the great objects aimed at by the formation of the Compact, which was the regulation of their external and inter-State affairs. . . .

Out of the million and a half, and more, of men in the Northern States who voted against Mr. Lincoln, in 1860, perhaps not ten thousand could be said, with truth, to be in favor of the Institution, or would have lived in a State where it existed. It was a subject with which they were thoroughly convinced they had nothing to do, and could have nothing to do under the terms of the Union by which the States were confederated, except to carry out and faithfully perform all the obligations of the Constitutional Compact in regard to it. In opposing the "Liberty Party," so-called, they enlisted under no banner of Slavery of any sort, but only arrayed themselves against that organization, which had virtually hoisted the banner of Consolidation. The struggle or conflict, therefore, from its rise to its culmination, was between those who, in whatever State they lived, were for maintaining our Federal system as it was established, and those who were for a consolidation of power in the Central Head.

But the great fact now to be considered in this investigation, is, that this Anti-Constitutional Party, in 1860, came into power upon this question in the Executive branch of the Federal Government.

This is the state of things which produced so much excitement and apprehension in the popular mind of the Southern States at that time. This Anti-Slavery Party had not only succeeded in getting a majority of the Northern States to openly violate their Constitutional faith in the avowed breach of the Compact, as stated; but had succeeded in electing a President and Vice-President pledged to principles which were not only at war with the domestic Institutions of the States of the South, but which must inevitably, if carried out, ultimately lead to the absorption of all power in the Central Government, and end sooner or later in Absolutism or Despotism. These were the principles then brought into conflict, which, as stated, resulted in the conflict of arms.

The Seceding States feeling no longer bound by a Compact which had been so openly violated, and a majority of their people being deeply impressed with the conviction that the whole frame-work of the Constitution would be overthrown by this Party which would soon have control of the Executive Department of the Government, determined to withdraw from the Union, for the very reasons which had induced them to enter it in the beginning. Seven of these States, South Carolina, Georgia, Florida, Alabama, Mississippi, Louisiana, and Texas, did withdraw. Conventions of their people, regularly called by the proper authorities in each of these States respectively — Conventions representing the Sovereignty of the States similar in all respects to those which by Ordinances had ratified the Constitution of the United States — passed Ordinances resuming the Sovereign Powers therein delegated. These were the Secession Ordinances, which we may hereafter have occasion to look into. These Conventions also appointed Delegates, to meet in Montgomery, Alabama, on the 4th of February, 1861, with a view to form a new Confederation among themselves, upon the same essential basis of the Constitution of the United States.

It was not in opposition to the principles of that Government that they withdrew from it. They quit the Union to save the principles of the Constitution, and to perpetuate, on this Continent, the liberties which it was intended to secure and establish. Mr. Buchanan was then President of the United States. He held that the Federal Government had no power to coërce a Seceding State to remain in the Union, but, strangely enough, at the same time held, that no State could rightfully withdraw from the Union. Mr. Lincoln came into power on the 4th of March, 1861. He held that the Federal Government did possess the Constitutional Power to maintain the Union of States by force, and it was in the maintenance of these views, the war was inaugurated by him.

Judge Bynum. Do you mean to say, Mr. Stephens, that the war was inaugurated by Mr. Lincoln?

Mr. Stephens. Most assuredly I do.

Judge Bynum. Why, how in the world, can you do that in the face of the well-known facts of the case? Did not General Beauregard in command of the Confederate forces, so-called, at Charleston, South Carolina, fire upon Fort Sumter in that Harbor? Did he not compel Major Anderson, the United States officer in command of that Fort, to capitulate and surrender? Was it not this outrage upon the American flag that caused such deep and universal excitement and indignation throughout the entire North? Was it not this that caused the great meetings in New York, Boston and every Northern city? Can you maintain in the face of these notorious facts, that the war was begun by Mr. Lincoln, or the Federal authorities? You rely mainly upon facts, as you say. Your whole argument professes to be based upon the facts of history. If there is any great fact that must go down to posterity forever, it is the fact that the Insurgents, or Confederates, if you please, began this war. This is a fact, which, as you have said of other matters, "can never be erased or obliterated."

Mr. Stephens. Not quite so fast, Judge. My whole argument is based upon facts, and upon facts that can never be erased or obliterated. It is a fact that the *first gun* was fired by the Confederates. It is a fact that General Beauregard did, on the 12th of April, 1861, bombard Fort Sumter, before any blow had actually been struck by the Federal authorities. That is not disputed at all. That is a fact which I have no disposition to erase or obliterate in any way. That is a great truth which will live forever. But did the firing of the first gun, or the reduction of Fort Sumter inaugurate or begin the war? That is a question to be first solved, before we can be agreed upon the fact as to who *inaugurated* the war; and in solving this question, you must allow me to say that in personal or national conflicts, it is not he who strikes the first blow, or fires the first gun that inaugurates or begins the conflict. Hallam has well said that "the *aggressor* in a war (that is, he who begins it,) is not the *first* who *uses force,* but the first who renders force *necessary."*

Which side, according to this high authority, (that only announces the common sentiments of mankind,) was the *aggressor* in this instance? Which side was it that provoked and rendered the first blow necessary? The true answer to that question will settle the fact as to which side began the war.

I maintain that it was inaugurated and begun, though no blow had been struck, when the hostile fleet, styled the "Relief Squadron," with eleven ships, carrying two hundred and eighty-five guns and two thousand four hundred men, was sent out from New York and Norfolk, with orders from the authorities at Washington, to re-enforce Fort Sumter peaceably, if permitted — "but forcibly if they must."

The war was then and there inaugurated and begun by the authorities at Washington. General Beauregard did not open fire upon Fort Sumter until this fleet was, to his knowledge, very near the harbor of Charleston, and until he had inquired of Major Anderson, in command of the Fort, whether he would engage to take no part in the expected blow, then coming down upon him from the approaching fleet. Francis W. Pickens, Governor of South Carolina, and General Beauregard, had both been notified that the fleet was coming, and of its objects, by a messenger from the authorities at Washington. This notice, however, was not given until it was near its destination. When Major Anderson, therefore, would make no such promise, it became necessary for General Beauregard to strike the first blow, as he did; otherwise the forces under his command might have been exposed to two fires at the same time — one in front, and the other in the rear.

To understand this fully, let us see how matters stood in Charleston Harbor at the time.

The Confederate States, then seven in number, had, as stated, all passed Ordinances of Secession. All of them, in regularly constituted Conventions, had withdrawn all their Sovereign powers previously delegated to the United States. They had formed a new Confederation, with a regularly constituted Government, at Montgomery, Alabama, as they had a perfect right to do, if our past conclusions were correct, and these you have not been able to assail. This new Confederation had sent a commission to the authorities at Washington, as we shall see, to settle all matters amicably and peacefully. War was by no means the wish or desire of the authorities at Montgomery. Very few of the public men in the Seceding States even expected war. All of them, it is true, held themselves in readiness for it, if it should be forced upon them against their wishes and most earnest protestations.

This is abundantly and conclusively apparent from the speeches and addresses of their leading public men at the time. It is apparent from the resolutions of the State Legislatures, and the State Conventions, before, and in their acts of Secession. It is apparent and manifest from their acts in their new Confederation at Montgomery. It is apparent from the inaugural address of President Davis. It is apparent from the appointment of commissioners to settle all matters involved in the separation from their former Confederates honorably, peaceably, amicably, and justly. It is apparent and manifest from every act that truly indicates the objects and motives of men, or from which their real aims can be justly arrived at. Peace not only with the States from which they had separated, but peace with all the world, was the strong desire of the Confederate States.

It was under these circumstances, that the Confederate commissioners were given to understand, that Fort Sumter would be peacefully evacuated. An assurance to this effect was given, though in an informal manner, by Mr. Seward, the Secretary of State under Mr. Lincoln. This pledge was most strangely violated by sending the armed squadron, as stated, to re-enforce and provision the Fort. The information that this fleet had put to sea with such orders, reached General Beauregard, when it was already near the offing, as I have stated. He immediately communicated the fact, by telegraph, to the authorities at Montgomery. In reply he received this order from the Secretary of War of the Confederate States Government:

"If you have no doubt of the authorized character of the agent who communicated to you the intention of the Washington Government to supply Fort Sumter by force, you will at once demand its evacuation; and if this is refused, proceed in such manner as you may determine, to reduce it."

Accordingly, on the 11th of April, General Beauregard made a demand on Major Anderson, in command of the Fort, for its evacuation.

In reply Major Anderson stated:

"I have the honor to acknowledge the receipt of your communication demanding the evacuation of this Fort, and to say in reply thereto, that it is a demand with which I regret that my sense of honor and my obligation to my Government prevent my compliance."

To this he added, verbally, to the messenger: "I will await the first shot, and, if you do not batter us to pieces, we will be starved out in a few days."

This written reply, as well as the verbal remark, were forthwith sent by General Beauregard to the Secretary of War at Montgomery, who immediately returned the following response:

"Do not desire needlessly to bombard Fort Sumter. If Major Anderson will state the time at which, as indicated by himself, he will evacuate, and agree that, in the meantime, he will not use his guns against us, unless ours should be employed against Fort Sumter, you are authorized thus to avoid the effusion of blood. If this or its equivalent be refused, reduce the Fort, as your judgment decides most practicable."

This was communicated to Major Anderson. He refused to comply with the terms. He would not consent to any such arrangement.

Whereupon, General Beauregard opened fire on the Fort at 4.30, on the morning of the 12th of April. The fire was returned. The bombardment lasted for thirty-two hours, when Major Anderson agreed to capitulate. General Beauregard exhibited no less of the magnanimity of the true soldier in the terms of capitulation, than he had of high military skill and genius in forming his plans, and in their execution for the reduction of the Fort. The entire garrison numbering eighty in all, officers and men, was permitted to be marched out with their colors and music. They were permitted to salute their flag with fifty guns. All private as well as company property was also allowed to be taken by those to whom it belonged. These were the same terms that General Beauregard had offered on the 11th, before he opened fire. As Providence ordered it, not a life was lost in this most memorable and frightful combat. The firing on both sides, at some times, particularly at night, was represented by those who witnessed it, as both "grand and terrific."

This was the first blow. It is true, the first gun was fired on the Confederate side. That is fully admitted. But all the facts show that, if force was thus first used by them, it was so first used only, because it was rendered necessary in self-defence on the part of those thus using it, and so rendered necessary by the opposite side. This first use of force, therefore, under the circumstances, cannot, in fact, be properly and justly considered as the beginning of the war.

What has been stated, also, shows how earnestly the authorities at Montgomery, had in every possible way, consistent with honor and safety, endeavored to avoid a collision of forces. The whole question of the right or wrong, therefore, in striking this first blow, as well as the right or wrong of the war, depends upon the Constitutional points we have been discussing. If the Seceding States were right on these points, then their first blow was perfectly justifiable, even if it had not been given, as it was, to avert one then impending over them.

JUDGE BYNUM. Please allow me to interrupt you for a moment. The views you express seem to me not only novel, but altogether unsuited to the facts, even as you state them. Allow me to ask, if the Fort did not belong to the United States? Was it not the property of the United States? Were not the officers and men in it attached to the service of the United States? What right, therefore, had General Beauregard, or any body else, to attempt to prevent the United States Government from provisioning the garrison then holding it, and re-enforcing it, if they thought proper? Was it not the duty of Mr. Lincoln to do it, as well as his right?

MR. STEPHENS. Not if South Carolina had the Sovereign right to demand the possession of the Fort. Rights, whether civil, moral, or political, never conflict. If South Carolina had this Sovereign right to demand the possession of the place, which was within her jurisdiction, then Mr. Lincoln could have had no right to continue to hold it against this demand; nor was it his duty, in any sense, to attempt, even, to provision it by force, under the circumstances.

The Fort was within the jurisdiction of South Carolina. It was built specially for her protection, and belonged to her in part as well as to the other States jointly. On the 11th of January, Governor Pickens, in behalf of the Sovereign Rights of the State, demanded its possession of Major Anderson for the use of the State. On his refusal to deliver it up, the Governor immediately sent I. W. Hayne, the Attorney General of the State, to

Washington, and made a like demand for its possession of Mr. Buchanan, the President, alleging that the possession of this Fort was necessary for the safety of the State for whose protection it had been erected. In this letter, Governor Pickens also stated, that a full valuation of the property would be accounted for, on settlement of the relations of South Carolina with the United States.

This whole question, relating to the right in this matter, and the side on which the right existed, depends, as I have said, upon the correctness of our conclusions on the points discussed. If South Carolina, after the resumption of her delegated powers, was a separate, Sovereign State (which is one of our established truths), then, of course, she had a perfect right to demand the possession of any landed property whatever, lying within the limits of her jurisdiction, if she deemed it of importance for her public use and benefit. This perfect right so to do, was subject to but one limitation, and that was the moral obligation to pay a fair and just compensation for the property so demanded for public use. There can be no question of the correctness of this principle. It is the foundation of the great right of Eminent domain, which ever accompanies Sovereignty. We have seen that this right of Eminent domain was never parted with by her, even under the Constitution. South Carolina, then, even before Secession, and while she held herself to be bound by the Constitution, had a perfect right to demand of the United States Government the possession of this identical property, on paying a just compensation for it, if she had deemed it essential for her public interests. This Fort never could have been erected on her soil without her consent, as we have seen. The title, therefore, of the United States to the land on which Fort Sumter was built, was in no essential respect different from the title of any other land-holder in the State. The tenure by which the United States claimed and held this property, differed in no essential respect from the tenure by which every other land-owner held similar property in the State; nor was this property of the United States, so purchased and held under grant from South Carolina, any less subject to the right of Eminent domain on the part of the State, than any other lands lying within her limits. If this was so even before Secession, (and no one can successfully assail the position,) then how much more clearly this right (by virtue of the principle of Eminent domain,) to demand the possession of this property for public use, for *her own protection,* appears after she had expressly resumed the exercise of all of her Sovereign powers? This right to demand the possession of this Fort, therefore, being unquestionably perfect in her as a Sovereign State after Secession, whether it was before or not, she had transferred to the Confederate States. Hence, their right to demand the evacuation of Fort Sumter, was perfect, viewed either morally, or politically.

The Confederate States had offered to come to a fair and just settlement with the United States, as to the value of this property, as well as all other public property belonging to all the States in common, at the time of their separation. This Fort, as well as all else that belonged to the United States, belonged in part to these seven Seceded States. They constituted seven of the United States, to which all this joint property belonged. All the Forts which lay within the limits of the Seceded States, had been turned over by these States, respectively, to the Confederacy, as we shall see. The Confederate States, therefore, through their authorities, had a right to demand, and take possession of all of these Forts, so lying within their limits, for their own public use, upon paying a just compensation for them to their former associates of the United States, who still adhered to that Union. These principles cannot be assailed. The offer so to pay whatever should be found to be due upon a general and just account, had been made. Mr. Lincoln, therefore, had no right under the circumstances, to hold any of these Forts by force, after the demand for the possession had been made; much less was it his duty either morally, or politically, when it was known that the attempt would inevitably lead to a war between the States. This is my answer to your property view.

Now, sir, I do stand upon facts, and these are the incontestable facts of this case, which will forever perpetuate the truth of my assertion, that upon the head of the Federal Government will forever rest the inauguration of this most terrible war which did ensue.

No part of its responsibility rests upon the Southern States. They were the aggressors in no instance. They were ever true to their plighted faith under the Constitution. No instance of a breach of its mutual covenants can be ever laid to their charge. The open and palpable breach was committed by a number of their Northern Confederates. No one can deny this. Those States at the North, which were untrue to their Constitutional engagements, claimed powers not delegated, and elected a Chief Magistrate pledged to carry out principles openly in defiance of the decision of the highest Judicial Tribunal known to the Constitution.

Their policy tended inevitably to a Centralized Despotism. It was under these circumstances that Secession was resorted to, as before stated; and, then, the war was begun and waged by the North to prevent the exercise of this Right. All that the Southern States did, was in defence, even in their firing the first gun. . . .

Study Guide

1. As you read Alexander Stephens, find the similarities and the differences between his views and those of Lincoln regarding:

(a) the nature of the Union;

(b) slavery;

(c) the causes of the Civil War; and

(d) the events and the responsibility for them that led to the outbreak of the war.

2. Beginning with the nature of the federal Union, what, according to Stephens, is the primary principle on which its formation rested? Elaborate on what implications Stephens draws from this basic assumption. List some salutary effects Stephens claims would have resulted from an acceptance of this view of the Union by the North. On the basis of the selections from Lincoln, would he have agreed?

3. Turning to Stephens's views regarding slavery, note at the outset his use of the phrase "slavery, so-called." What is his purpose in so doing? What is Stephens's evaluation of the extent of slavery, its character, and its future (had the Civil War not come)?

4. What role did slavery play, according to Stephens, in having caused the war?

5. Stephens's defense of the actions of the South just prior to the war can be best understood through his interpretations in Colloquy XIII of the following:

(a) the nature of the federal government;

(b) the character and the purposes of the Republican Party;

(c) the meaning of the election of 1860;

(d) the contrast in attitude and actions of James Buchanan and Lincoln;

(e) the roles played by Lincoln, Major Robert Anderson, and General Pierre Beauregard concerning the crisis at Fort Sumter;

(f) the immediate position and the ultimate aims of the seceding states; and

(g) finally, the actions of Lincoln and the government in Washington.

Charles Sumner

JUSTICE FOR THE FORMER SLAVE

≈§ 1872 §≈ As a UNITED STATES Senator, Charles Sumner (1811-1874) was almost unique in certain respects. For one thing, he was elected to the Senate with practically no previous experience in politics. For another, he was not the usual politician-type but was, instead, a "statesman doctrinaire" who took as his guide a set of inflexible moral principles rather than the shifting considerations of day-to-day expediency.

Sumner first won fame — or notoriety — with his 1856 "Crime against Kansas" speech, learnedly written and carefully rehearsed, in which he thoroughly damned slavery and the South. This philippic so enraged Southerners that one of them, Congressman Preston Brooks (1819-1857) of South Carolina, attacked Sumner with a cane and beat him almost senseless. Sumner thus became a martyr of the free-soil and antislavery cause.

His career touched upon most of the significant movements of his time. He was an advocate of international peace and of school and prison reform, one of the founders of the Republican Party, a leader of the Radical Republicans during and after the Civil War, and a promoter of the Liberal Republican campaign in 1872. As chairman of the Senate Committee on Foreign Relations, he made himself a powerful critic of American diplomacy during the Grant administration.

In opposing racial discrimination, Sumner was both consistent and persistent. As early as 1849 he challenged the legality of segregated schools in his home town, Boston. He maintained that both white and black children suffered from attending separate schools and that, no matter how good the facilities provided for blacks, "the separate school is not an equivalent." Six years later the Massachusetts legislature, dominated by his friends, outlawed racial segregation in all the public schools of the Commonwealth. During the Civil War and after, he was the foremost Senate champion of emancipation for the slaves and then of political and legal rights for the freedmen.

In 1870 he brought in, as a supplement to the Civil Rights Act of 1866, a bill to prohibit the assignment of blacks to separate facilities in public conveyances or public places, including schools. In 1871 he reintroduced his bill as an amendment to another bill for giving amnesty to leading ex-Confederates who had been deprived of political rights under the Fourteenth Amendment, and on January 15, 1872, he made a speech in favor of his amendment (most of this speech is included in the selection reprinted here). Not till 1875, after his death, did Congress finally pass his proposals, and even then they were not destined, for many years, to gain the popular and judicial support needed for their enforcement. But Sumner had been prophetic. A day was to come (in 1954) when the Supreme Court would adopt the very position he had held — that "separate but equal" is a contradiction in terms.

EQUAL RIGHTS

MR. PRESIDENT, Slavery, in its foremost pretensions, reappears in the present debate. Again the barbarous tyranny stalks into this Chamber, denying to a whole race the Equal Rights promised by a just citizenship. Some have thought Slavery dead. This is a mistake. If not in body, at least in spirit, or as a ghost making the country hideous, the ancient criminal yet lingers among us, insisting upon the continued degradation of a race.

Property in man has ceased to exist. The human auction-block has departed. No human being can call himself master, with impious power to separate husband and wife, to sell child from parent, to shut out the opportunities of religion, to close the gates of knowledge, and to rob another of his labor and all its fruits. These guilty prerogatives are ended. To this extent the slave is free. No longer a chattel, he is a man, — justly entitled to all that is accorded by law to any other man.

Such is the irresistible logic of his emancipation. Ceasing to be a slave, he became a man, whose foremost right is Equality of Rights. And yet Slavery has been strong enough to postpone his entry into the great possession. Cruelly, he was not permitted to testify in court; most unjustly, he was not allowed to vote. More than four millions of people, whose only offence was a skin once the badge of Slavery, were shut out from the courtroom, and also from the ballot-box, in open defiance of the great Declaration of our fathers, that all men are equal in rights, and that just government stands only on the consent of the governed. Such was the impudent behest of Slavery, prolonged after it was reported dead. At last these crying wrongs are overturned. The slave testifies; the slave votes. To this extent his equality is recognized.

Equality before the Law

But this is not enough. Much as it may seem, compared with the past, when all was denied, it is too little, because all is not yet recognized. The denial of any right is a wrong darkening the enjoyment of all the rest. Besides the right to testify and the right to vote, there are other rights without which Equality does not exist. The precise rule is Equality before the Law, nor more nor less; that is, that condition before the law in which all are alike, — being entitled, without discrimination, to the equal enjoyment of all institutions, privileges, advantages, and conveniences created or regulated by law, among which are the right to testify and the right to vote. But this plain requirement is not satisfied, logically or reasonably, by these two concessions, so that when they are recognized all others are trifles. The court-house and the ballot-box are not the only places for the rule. These two are not the only institutions for its operation. The rule is general; how, then, restrict it to two cases? It is, *All are equal before the law,* — not merely before the law in two cases, but before the law in all cases, without limitation or exception. Important as it is to testify and to vote, life is not all contained even in these possessions.

The new-made citizen is called to travel for business, for health, or for pleasure; but here his trials begin. His money, whether gold or paper, is the same as the white man's; but the doors of the public hotel, which from the earliest days of jurisprudence have always opened hospitably to the stranger, close against him, and the public conveyances, which the Common Law declares equally free to all alike, have no such freedom for him. He longs, perhaps, for respite and relaxation at some place of public amusement, duly licensed by law; and here also the same adverse discrimination is made. With the anxieties of a parent, seeking the welfare of his child, he strives to bestow upon him the inestimable blessings of education, and takes him affectionately to the common school, created by law, and supported by the taxation to which he has contributed; but these doors slam rudely in the face of the child where is garnered up the parent's heart. "Suffer little children, and forbid them not, to come unto me": such were the words of the Divine Master. But among us little children are turned away and forbidden at the door of the common school, because of the skin. And the same insulting ostracism shows itself in other institutions of science and learning, also in the church, and in the last resting-place on earth. . . .

Equality in rights is not only the first of rights, it is an axiom of political truth. But an axiom, whether of science or philosophy, is universal, and without exception or limitation; and this is according to the very law of its nature. Therefore it is not stating an axiom to announce grandly that only white men are equal in rights; nor is it stating an axiom to announce with the same grandeur that all persons are equal in rights, but that colored persons have no rights except to testify and vote. Nor is it a self-evident truth, as declared; for no truth is self-evident which is not universal. The asserted limitation destroys the original Declaration, making it a ridiculous sham, instead of that sublime Magna Charta before which kings, nobles, and all inequalities of birth must disappear as ghosts of night at the dawn.

Real Issue of the War

All this has additional force, when it is known that this very axiom or self-evident truth declared by our fathers was the real issue of the war, and was so publicly announced by the leaders on both sides. Behind the embattled armies were ideas, and the idea on our side was Equality in Rights, which on the other side was denied. The Nation insisted that all men are created equal; the Rebellion insisted that all men are created unequal. Here the evidence is explicit.

The inequality of men was an original postulate of Mr. Calhoun, which found final expression in the open denunciation of the self-evident truth as "a self-evident lie." Echoing this denunciation, Jefferson Davis, on leaving the Senate, January 21, 1861, in that farewell speech which some among you heard, but which all may read in the "Globe," made the issue in these words: —

> "It has been a belief that we are to be deprived in the Union of the rights which our fathers bequested to us, which has brought Mississippi into her present decision. *She has heard proclaimed the theory that all men are created free and equal, and this made the basis of an attack upon her social institutions; and the sacred Declaration of Independence has been invoked to maintain the position of the equality of the races.*"

The issue thus made by the chief Rebel was promptly joined. Abraham

Lincoln, the elected President, stopping at Independence Hall, February 22d, on his way to assume his duties at the National capital, in unpremeditated words thus interpreted the Declaration: —

"It was that which gave promise that in due time the weight should be lifted from the shoulders of all men, *and that all should have an equal chance.*"

Mark, if you please, the simplicity of this utterance. All are to have "an equal chance"; and this, he said, "is the sentiment embodied in the Declaration of Independence." Then, in reply to Jefferson Davis, he proceeded: —

"Now, my friends, can this country be saved upon that basis? If it can, I shall consider myself one of the happiest men in the world, if I can help to save it. If it cannot be saved upon that principle, it will be truly awful. But if this country cannot be saved without giving up that principle, I was about to say I would rather be assassinated on this spot than surrender it."

Giving these words still further solemnity, he added:

"I have said nothing but what I am willing to live by, and, if it be the pleasure of Almighty God, to die by."

And then, before raising the national banner over the historic Hall, he said: —

"It is on such an occasion as this that we can reason together, and reaffirm our devotion to the country and the principles of the Declaration of Independence."

Thus the gauntlet flung down by Jefferson Davis was taken up by Abraham Lincoln, who never forgot the issue.

The rejoinder was made by Alexander H. Stephens, Vice-President of the Rebellion, in a not-to-be forgotten speech at Savannah, March 21, 1861, when he did not hesitate to declare of the pretended Government, that —

"Its foundations are laid, its corner-stone rests, upon *the great truth that the Negro is not equal to the white man.*"

Then, glorying in this terrible shame, he added: —

"This, our new Government, is the first, in the history of the world, based upon this great physical, philosophical, and moral truth."
"This stone, which was rejected by the first builders, is become the chief stone of the corner."

To this unblushing avowal Abraham Lincoln replied in that marvelous, undying utterance at Gettysburg, — fit voice for the Republic, greater far than any victory:

> "Fourscore and seven years ago our fathers brought forth on this continent a new Nation, *conceived in Liberty, and dedicated to the proposition that all men are created equal."*

Thus, in precise conformity with the Declaration, was it announced that our Republic is dedicated to the Equal Rights of All; and then the prophet-President, soon to be a martyr, asked his countrymen to dedicate themselves to the great task remaining, highly resolving

> "that this Nation, under God, shall have a new birth of Freedom; and that Government of the people, by the people, and for the people shall not perish from the earth."

The victory of the war is vain without the grander victory through which the Republic is dedicated to the axiomatic, self-evident truth declared by our fathers, and reasserted by Abraham Lincoln. With this mighty truth as a guiding principle, the National Constitution is elevated, and made more than ever a protection to the citizen.

All this is so plain that it is difficult to argue it. What is the Republic, if it fails in this loyalty? What is the National Government, coextensive with the Republic, if fellow-citizens, counted by the million, can be shut out from equal rights in travel, in recreation, in education, and in other things, all contributing to human necessities? Where is that great promise by which "the pursuit of happiness" is placed, with life and liberty, under the safeguard of axiomatic, self-evident truth? Where is justice, if this ban of color is not promptly removed? Where is humanity? Where is reason?

Two Excuses

The two excuses show how irrational and utterly groundless is this pretension. They are on a par with the pretension itself. One is, that the question is of society, and not of rights, which is clearly a misrepresentation; and the other is, that the separate arrangements provided for colored persons constitute a substitute for equality in the nature of an equivalent, — all of which is clearly a contrivance, if not a trick: as if there could be any equivalent for equality.

No Question of Society

Of the first excuse it is difficult to speak with patience. It is a simple misrepresentation, and wherever it shows itself must be treated as such. There is no colored person who does not resent the imputation that he is seeking to intrude himself socially anywhere. This is no question of society, no question of social life, no question of social equality, if anybody knows what this means. The object is simply Equality before the Law, a term which explains itself. Now, as the law does not presume to create or regulate social relations, these are in no respect affected by the pending measure. Each person, whether Senator or citizen, is always free to choose who shall be his friend, his associate, his guest. And does not the ancient proverb declare that "a man is known by the company he keeps"? But this assumes that he may choose for himself. His house is his "castle"; and this very designation, borrowed from the Common Law, shows his absolute independence within its walls; nor is there any difference, whether it be palace or hovel. But when he leaves his "castle" and goes abroad, this independence is at an end. He walks the streets, but always subject to the prevailing law of Equality; nor can he appropriate the sidewalk to his own exclusive use, driving into the gutter all whose skin is less white than his own. But nobody pretends that Equality in the highway, whether on pavement or sidewalk, is a question of society. And permit me to say that Equality in all institutions created or regulated by law is as little a question of society.

In the days of Slavery it was an oft-repeated charge, that Emancipation was a measure of social equality; and the same charge became a cry at the successive efforts for the right to testify and the right to vote. At each stage the cry was raised, and now it makes itself heard again, as you are called to assure this crowning safeguard.

Equality not Found in Equivalents

Then comes the other excuse, which finds Equality in separation. Separate hotels, separate conveyances, separate theatres, separate schools and institutions of learning and science, separate churches, and separate cemeteries, — these are the artificial substitutes. And this is the contrivance by which a transcendent right, involving a transcendent duty, is evaded: for Equality is not only a right, but a duty.

How vain to argue that there is no denial of Equal Rights when this separation is enforced! The substitute is invariably an inferior article. Does any Senator deny it? Therefore, it is not Equality; at best it is an equivalent only. But no equivalent is Equality. Separation implies one thing for a white person and another thing for a colored person; but Equality is where all have the same alike. There can be no substitute for Equality, — nothing but itself. Even if accommodations are the same, as notoriously they are not, there is no Equality. In the process of substitution the vital elixir exhales and escapes: it is lost, and cannot be recovered; for Equality is found only in Equality. "Nought but itself can be its parallel"; but Senators undertake to find parallels in other things. . . .

Assuming — what is most absurd to assume, and what is contradicted by all experience — that a substitute can be an equivalent, it is so in form only, and not in reality. Every such assumption is an indignity to the colored race, instinct with the spirit of Slavery; and this decides its character. It is Slavery in its last appearance. Are you ready to prolong the hateful tyranny? Religion and reason condemn Caste as impious and unchristian making republican institutions and equal laws impossible; but here is Caste not unlike that which separates the Sudra from the Brahmin. Pray, Sir, who constitutes the white man a Brahmin? Whence his lordly title? Down to a recent period in Europe the Jews were driven to herd by themselves, separate from the Christians; but this discarded barbarism is revived among us in the ban of color. There are millions of fellow-citizens guilty of no offence except the dusky livery of the sun appointed by the Heavenly Father, whom you treat as others have treated the Jews, as the Brahmin treats the Sudra. But, pray, Sir, do not pretend that this is the great equality promised by our fathers.

In arraigning this attempt at separation as a Caste, I say nothing new. For years I have denounced it as such; and here I followed good authorities, as well as reason. Alexander von Humboldt, speaking of the negroes of New Mexico when Slavery prevailed, called them a Caste. A recent political and juridical writer of France uses the same term to denote not only the discrimination in India, but that in our own country, — especially referring to the exclusion of colored children from the common schools as among "the humiliating and brutal distinctions" by which their Caste is characterized. The principle of separation on the ground of hereditary inferiority is the distinctive essence of Caste; but this is the outrage which flaunts in our country, crying out, "I am better than thou, because I am white. Get away!"

The Remedy

Thus do I reject the two excuses. But I do not leave the cause here. I go further, and show how consistent is the pending measure with acknowledged principles, illustrated by undoubted law.

The bill for Equal Rights is simply supplementary to the existing Civil Rights Law, which is one of our great statutes of peace, and it stands on the same requirement of the National Constitution. If the Civil Rights Law is above question, as cannot be doubted, then also is this supplementary amendment; for it is only the complement of the other, and necessary to its completion. Without this amendment the original law is imperfect. It cannot be said, according to its title, that all persons are protected in their civil rights, so long as the outrages I expose continue to exist; nor is Slavery entirely dead.

Following reason and authority, the conclusion is easy. A Law Dictionary, of constant use as a repertory of established rules and principles, defines a "freeman" as "one in the possession of *the civil rights* enjoyed by the people generally." Happily, all are freemen now; but the colored people are still excluded from civil rights enjoyed by the people generally — and this, too, in the face of our new Bill of Rights intended for their especial protection.

By the Constitutional Amendment abolishing Slavery Congress is empowered "to enforce this article by appropriate legislation"; and in pursuance thereof the Civil Rights Law was enacted. That measure was justly accepted as "appropriate legislation." Without it Slavery would still exist in at least one of its most odious pretensions. By the Civil Rights Law colored persons were assured in the right to testify, which in most of the States was denied or abridged. So closely was this outrage connected with Slavery, that it was, indeed, part of this great wrong. Therefore its prohibition was "appropriate legislation" in the enforcement of the Constitutional Amendment. But the denial or abridgment of Equality on account of color is also part of Slavery. So long as it exists, Slavery is still present among us. Its prohibition is not only "appropriate," but necessary, to enforce the Constitional Amendment. Therefore it is strictly Constitutional, as if in the very text of the National Constitution.

The next Constitutional Amendment, known as the Fourteenth, contains two different provisions, which augment the power of Congress. The first furnishes the definition of "citizen," which down to this time had been left to construction only: —

> "*All persons* born or naturalized in the United States, and subject to the jurisdiction thereof, are *citizens* of the United States, and of the States wherever they reside."

Here, you will remark, are no words of race or color. "*All* persons," and not "*all white* persons," born or naturalized in the United States, and subject to the jurisdiction thereof, are "citizens." Such is the definition supplied by this Amendment. This is followed by another provision in aid of the definition: —

> "No State shall make or enforce any law which shall abridge the privileges or immunities of citizens of the United States; nor shall any State deprive any person of life, liberty, or property without due process of law, *nor deny to any person within its jurisdiction the equal protection of the laws.*"

And Congress is empowered to enforce this definition of Citizenship and this guaranty, by "appropriate legislation."

Here, then, are two Constitutional Amendments, each a fountain of power: the first, to enforce the Abolition of Slavery; and the second, to assure the privileges and immunities of citizens, and also the equal protection of the laws. If the Supplementary Civil Rights Bill, moved by me, is not within these accumulated powers, I am at a loss to know what is within those powers.

In considering these Constitutional provisions, I insist upon that interpretation which shall give them the most generous expansion, so that they shall be truly efficacious for human rights. Once Slavery was the animating principle in determining the meaning of the National Constitution: happily, it is so no longer. Another principle is now supreme, breathing into the whole the breath of a new life, and filling it in every part with one pervading, controlling sentiment, — being that great principle of Equality which triumphed at last on the battle-field, and, bearing the watchword of the Republic, now supplies the rule by which every word of the Constitution and all its parts must be interpreted, as much as if written in its text.

There is also an original provision of the National Constitution, not to be forgotten: —

> "The citizens of each State shall be entitled to all privileges and immunities of citizens in the several States."

Once a sterile letter, this is now a fruitful safeguard, to be interpreted, like all else, so that human rights shall most prevail. The term "privileges and immunities" was at an early day authoritatively defined by Judge Washington, who announced that they embraced "protection by the Government, the enjoyment of life and liberty, with the right to acquire and possess property of every kind, and to *pursue and obtain happiness and safety,* . . . the right of a citizen of one State to pass through or to reside in any other State, for purposes of trade, agricultue, professional pursuits, or otherwise." But these "privileges and immunities" are protected by the present measure.

No doubt the Supplementary Law must operate, not only in National jurisdiction, but also in the States, precisely as the Civil Rights Law; otherwise it will be of little value. Its sphere must be coextensive with the Republic, making the rights of the citizen uniform everywhere. But this can be only by one uniform safeguard sustained by the Nation. Citizenship is universal, and the same everywhere. It cannot be more or less in one State than in another.

But legislation is not enough. An enlightened public opinion must be invoked. Nor will this be wanting. The country will rally in aid of the law, more especially since it is a measure of justice and humanity. The law is needed now as a help to public opinion. It is needed by the very people whose present conduct makes occasion for it. Prompted by the law, leaning on the law, they will recognize the equal rights of all; nor do I despair of a public opinion which shall stamp the denial of these rights as an outrage not unlike Slavery itself. Custom and patronage will then be sought in obeying the law. . . .

In the absence of the law people please too often by inhumanity, but with the law teaching the lesson of duty they will please by humanity. Thus will the law be an instrument of improvement, necessary in precise proportion to the existing prejudice. Because people still please by inhumanity, therefore must there be a counteracting force. . . .

Common Schools

The Common School . . . must open to all, or its designation is a misnomer and a mockery. It is not a school for whites, or a school for blacks, but a school for all, — in other words, a common school. . . . Its object is the education of the young; and it is sustained by taxation, to which all contribute. Not only does it hold itself out to the public by its name . . . but it assumes the place of parent to all children within its locality, bound always to exercise a parent's watchful care and tenderness, which can know no distinction of child.

It is easy to see that the separate school, founded on an odious discrimination, and sometimes offered as an equivalent for the common school, is an ill-disguised violation of the principle of Equality, while as a pretended equivalent it is an utter failure, and instead of a parent is only a churlish step-mother.

A slight illustration will show how it fails; and here I mention an incident occurring in Washington, but which must repeat itself often on a larger scale, wherever separation is attempted. Colored children, living near what is called the common school, are driven from its doors, and compelled to walk a considerable distance — often troublesome, and in certain conditions of the weather difficult — to attend the separate school. One of these children has suffered from this exposure, and I have myself witnessed the emotion of the parent. This could not have occurred, had the child been received at the common schools in the neighborhood. Now it is idle to assert that children compelled to this exceptional journey to and fro are in the enjoyment of Equal Rights. The superadded pedestrianism and its attendant discomfort furnish the measure of Inequality in one of its forms, increased by the weakness or ill-health of the child. What must be the feelings of a colored father or mother daily witnessing this sacrifice to the demon of Caste?

This is an illustration merely, but it shows precisely how impossible it is for a separate school to be the equivalent of the common school. And yet it only touches the evil, without exhibiting its proportions. The indignity offered to the colored child is worse than any compulsory exposure; and here not only the child suffers, but the race to which he belongs is degraded, and the whole community is hardened in wrong.

The separate school wants the first requisite of the common school, inasmuch as it is not equally open to all; and since this is inconsistent with the declared rule of republican institutions, such a school is not republican in character. Therefore it is not a preparation for the duties of life. The child is not trained in the way he should go; for he is trained under the ban of Inequality. How can he grow up to the stature of equal citizenship? He is pinched and dwarfed while the stigma of color is stamped upon him. This is plain oppression, which you, Sir, would feel keenly, were it directed against you or your child. Surely the race enslaved for generations has suffered enough without being doomed to this prolonged proscription. Will not the Republic, redeemed by most costly sacrifice, insist upon justice to the children of the land, making the common school the benign example of republican institutions, where merit is the only ground of favor?

Nor is separation without evil to the whites. The prejudice of color is nursed, when it should be stifled. The Pharisaism of race becomes an element of character, when, like all other Pharisaisms, it should be cast out. Better even than knowledge is a kindly nature and the sentiment of equality. Such should be the constant lesson, repeated by the lips and inscribed on the heart; but the school itself must practise the lesson. Children learn by example more than by precept. How precious the example which teaches that all are equal in rights! But this can be only where all commingle in the common school as in common citizenship. There is no separate ballot-box: there should be no separate school. It is not enough that all should be taught alike; they must all be taught together. They are not only to receive equal quantities of knowledge; all are to receive it in the same way. But they cannot be taught alike, unless all are taught together; nor can they receive equal quantities of knowledge in the same way, except at the common school.

The common school is important to all; but to the colored child it is a necessity. Excluded from the common school, he finds himself too frequently without any substitute. But even where a separate school is planted, it is inferior in character, buildings, furniture, books, teachers: all are second-rate. No matter what the temporary disposition, the separate school will not flourish as the common school. It is but an offshoot or sucker, without the strength of the parent stem. That the two must differ is seen at once; and that this difference is adverse to the colored child is equally apparent. For him there is no assurance of education except in the common school, where he will be under the safeguard of all. White parents will take care not only that the common school is not neglected, but that its teachers and means of instruction are the best possible; and the colored child will have the benefit of this watchfulness. This decisive consideration completes the irresistible argument for the common school as the equal parent of all without distinction of color.

If to him that hath is given, according to the way of the world, it is not doubted that to him that hath not there is a positive duty in proportion to the necessity. Unhappily, our colored fellow-citizens are in this condition. But just in proportion as they are weak, and not yet recovered from the degradation in which they have been plunged, does the Republic owe its completest support and protection. Already a component part of our political corporation, they must become part of the educational corporation also, with Equality as the supreme law. . . .

Study Guide

1. Try to understand this address, a strong plea for full equality between the races, as a response to:
   (a) the zealousness and the goals of an abolitionist; and
   (b) the obduracy of Alexander Stephens.

2. What, in Sumner's view, is the unfulfilled task of the nation? What rights have been accorded to ex-slaves and why are they insufficient? "Important as it is to testify and to vote, life is not all contained even in these possessions" (p. 31). Explain and illustrate the above from Sumner's address. Explain also what Sumner is trying to say in the last paragraph of the portion entitled "Equality before the Law."

3. In the next section, "Real Issue of the War," Sumner contends that racial equality was the purpose of the war. How does he document this? On the basis of your readings of Lincoln and Stephens, would you agree? Compare and contrast, then, Sumner's conception of the purpose of the war with those of Lincoln (1861 and 1865) and Stephens.

4. What are the "two excuses" Sumner disposes of in his demand for full equality for blacks and *on what grounds* does he do so? Note especially his vehement denial of the possibility that facilities for whites and blacks can be "separate but equal" — arguments that have a logic and subtlety far in advance of his time. You will understand Sumner if you can explain the following excerpts:

    (a) "This is no question of society . . . if anybody knows what this means" (p. 35).

    (b) "There can be no substitute for Equality, — nothing but itself" (p. 35).

5. Sumner continues with constitutional arguments for his position. How does he employ the Thirteenth Amendment and the Fourteenth Amendment in support of his demands? What else, in his opinion, apart from legislation is required?

6. And, finally, Sumner turns to the role of the public schools in promoting equal rights for blacks. List the arguments he advances against segregation in education. What is the relevance of his arguments to current questions on the matter? Note carefully his perceptive appraisal of the impact segregation has on the whites.

7. In 1875, the Congress passed the Civil Rights Act, paying tribute to the memory of Charles Sumner. From your text, outline the provisions of the act and then relate them to this address by Sumner.

James S. Pike

SOUTH CAROLINA UNDER NEGRO GOVERNMENT

❧{1873}❧ As A CONDEMNATION of Radical Reconstruction, James S. Pike's *The Prostrate State: South Carolina under Negro Government* (1873) is a classic. The author, a Maine Republican and former abolitionist, appeared to be a most trustworthy witness because of his background. Contemporaries quoted and endorsed him as one "who, in view of his long and enthusiastic service in the anti-slavery cause, can hardly be accused of color-prejudice." Later historians cited him as a "Republican authority"; one of them praised his book as "the 'Uncle Tom's Cabin' of the redemption of the South." Certainly no other single work did so much to disillusion Northerners about Radical Reconstruction and prepare them for accepting the restoration of "white supremacy" in the South. Pike's description of rascality and misrule formed an image of the black and carpetbagger governments that still prevails in the popular mind.

Yet, as Robert F. Durden has recently shown, Pike (1811-1882) was by no means so disinterested as he seemed. Though indeed a veteran of the abolitionist crusade, he also was and always had been a Negrophobe. During the Civil War he had even proposed that the freed slaves be either deported or confined on a vast reservation, a "Negro pen," set aside for them within the conquered South. Moreover, when he made his reporting tour to South Carolina in 1873, he could hardly be described, without qualification, as a Republican. A friend of Horace Greeley (1811-1872), he had broken away from the regular party, denounced President U. S. Grant (1822-1885), and supported the Liberal Republican and Democratic candidate, Greeley, in the presidential campaign of 1872. After the failure of the Liberal Republican movement, Pike continued his attack on the Grant administration and its black and carpetbag following in the South. One way for him to discredit the Grant Republicans was to paint Radical Reconstruction in as bad a light as possible. His actual views, as he recorded them in the private journal of his travels, were far less severe than the strictures he published in a series of newspaper reports and then in his book.

The first four chapters of the book provide an adequate sampling of his published views.

THE PROSTRATE STATE

CHAPTER I

A Black Parliament. — Humiliation of the Whites. — Society Bottom-Side Up. — An Extraordinary Spectacle.

COLUMBIA, the capital of South Carolina, is charmingly situated in the heart of the upland country, near the geographical centre of the State. It has broad, open streets, regularly laid out, and fine, shady residences in and about the town. The opportunity for rides and drives can hardly be surpassed. There are good animals and good turnouts to be seen on the streets at all times; and now, in midwinter, the weather invites to such displays. It seems there was a little real winter here at Christmas and New Year's, when the whole country suffered such an excess of sudden cold. There was even skating and sleighing for a week. But now there is no frost, and the recollection of it is dispelled by the genial spring weather that prevails.

Yesterday, about 4 P.M., the assembled wisdom of the State, whose achievements are illustrated on that theatre, issued forth from the State-House. About three-quarters of the crowd belonged to the African race. They were of every hue, from the light octoroon to the deep black. They were such a looking body of men as might pour out of a market-house or a court-house at random in any Southern State. Every negro type and physiognomy was here to be seen, from the genteel serving-man to the rough-hewn customer from the rice or cotton field. Their dress was as varied as their countenances. There was the second-hand black frock-coat of infirm gentility, glossy and threadbare. There were the stove-pipe hat of many ironings and departed styles. There were also to be seen a total disregard of the proprieties of costume in the coarse and dirty garments of the field; the stub-jackets and slouch hats of soiling labor. In some instances, rough woolen comforters embraced the neck and hid the absence of linen. Heavy brogans, and short, torn trousers, it was impossible to hide. The dusky tide flowed out into the littered and barren grounds, and, issuing through the coarse wooden fence of the inclosure, melted away into the street beyond. These were the legislators of South Carolina.

In conspicuous base-relief over the door of exit, on the panels of the stately edifice, the marble visages of George McDuffie and Robert Y. Hayne overlooked the scene. Could they veritably witness it from their dread abode? What then? "I tremble," wrote Jefferson, when depicting the character of Southern slavery, "I tremble when I reflect that God is just." But did any of that old band of Southern Revolutionary patriots who wrestled in their souls with the curse of slavery ever contemplate such a descent into barbarism as this spectacle implied and typified? "My God, look at this!" was the unbidden ejaculation of a low-country planter, clad in homespun, as he leaned over the rail inside the House, gazing excitedly upon the body in session. "This is the first time I have been here. I thought I knew what we were doing when we consented to emancipation. I knew the negro, and I predicted much that has happened, but I never thought it would come to this. Let me go."

Here, then, is the outcome, the ripe, perfected fruit of the boasted civilization of the South, after two hundred years of experience. A white community, that had gradually risen from small beginnings, till it grew into wealth, culture, and refinement, and became accomplished in all the arts of civilization; that successfully asserted its resistance to a foreign tyranny by deeds of conspicuous valor, which achieved liberty and independence through the fire and tempest of civil war, and illustrated itself in the councils of the nation by orators and statesmen worthy of any age or nation — such a community is then reduced to this. It lies prostrate in the dust, ruled over by this strange conglomerate, gathered from the ranks of its own servile population. It is the spectacle of a society suddenly turned bottomside up. The wealth, the intelligence, the culture, the wisdom of the State, have broken through the crust of that social volcano on which they were contentedly reposing, and have sunk out of sight, consumed by the subterranean fires they had with such temerity braved and defied.

In the place of this old aristocratic society stands the rude form of the most ignorant democracy that mankind ever saw, invested with the functions of government. It is the dregs of the population habilitated in the robes of their intelligent predecessors, and asserting over them the rule of ignorance and corruption, through the inexorable machinery of a majority of numbers. It is barbarism overwhelming civilization by physical force. It is the slave rioting in the halls of his master, and putting that master under his feet. And, though it is done without malice and without vengeance, it is nevertheless none the less completely and absolutely done. Let us approach nearer and take a closer view. We will enter the House of Representatives. Here sit one hundred and twenty-four members. Of these, twenty-three are white men, representing the remains of the old civilization. These are good-looking, substantial citizens. They are men of weight and standing in the communities they represent. They are all from the hill country. The frosts of sixty and seventy winters whiten the heads of some among them. There they sit, grim and silent. They feel themselves to be but loose stones, thrown in to partially obstruct a current they are powerless to resist. They say little and do little as the days go by. They simply watch the rising tide, and mark the progressive steps of the inundation. They hold their places reluctantly. They feel themselves to be in some sort martyrs, bound stoically to suffer in behalf of that still great element in the State whose prostrate fortunes are becoming the sport of an unpitying Fate. Grouped in a corner of the commodious and well-furnished chamber, they stolidly survey the noisy riot that goes on in the great black Left and Centre, where the business and debates of the House are conducted, and where sit the strange and extraordinary guides of the fortunes of a once proud and haughty State. In this crucial trial of his pride, his manhood, his prejudices, his spirit, it must be said of the Southern Bourbon of the Legislature that he comports himself with a dignity, a reserve, and a decorum, that command admiration. He feels that the iron hand of Destiny is upon him. He is gloomy, disconsolate, hopeless. The gray heads of this generation openly profess that they look for no relief. They see no way of escape. The recovery of influence, of position, of control in the State, is felt by them to be impossible. They accept their position with a stoicism that promises no reward here or hereafter. They are the types of a conquered race. They staked all and lost all. Their lives remain, their property and their children do not. War, emancipation, and grinding taxation, have consumed them. Their struggle now is against complete confiscation. They endure, and wait for the night.

This dense negro crowd they confront do the debating, the squabbling, the law-making, and create all the clamor and disorder of the body. These twenty-three white men are but the observers, the enforced auditors of the dull and clumsy imitation of a deliberative body, whose appearance in their present capacity is at once a wonder and a shame to modern civilization.

Deducting the twenty-three members referred to, who comprise the entire strength of the opposition, we find one hundred and one remaining. Of this one hundred and one, ninety-four are colored, and seven are their white allies. Thus the blacks outnumber the whole body of whites in the House more than three to one. On the mere basis of numbers in the State the injustices of this disproportion is manifest, since the black population is relatively four to three of the whites. A just rectification of the disproportion, on the basis of population merely, would give fifty-four whites to seventy black members. And the line of race very nearly marks the line of hostile politics. As things stand, the body is almost literally a Black Parliament, and it is the only one on the face of the earth which is the representative of a white constituency and the professed exponent of an advanced type of modern civilization. But the reader will find almost any portraiture inadequate to give a vivid idea of the body, and enable him to comprehend the complete metamorphosis of the South Carolina Legislature, without observing its details. The Speaker is black, the Clerk is black, the door-keepers are black, the little pages are black, the chairman of the Ways and Means is black, and the chaplain is coal-black. At some of the desks sit colored men whose types it would be hard to find outside of Congo; whose costume, visages, attitudes, and expression, only befit the forecastle of a buccaneer. It must be remembered, also, that these men, with not more than half a dozen exceptions, have been themselves slaves, and that their ancestors were slaves for generations. Recollecting the report of the famous schooner Wanderer, fitted out by a Southern slave-holder twelve or fifteen years ago, in ostentatious defiance of the laws against the slave-trade, and whose owner and master boasted of having brought a cargo of slaves from Africa and safely landed them in South Carolina and Georgia, one thinks it must be true, and that some of these representatives are the very men then stolen from their African homes. If this be so, we will not now quarrel over their presence. It would be one of those extraordinary coincidences that would of itself almost seem to justify the belief of the direct interference of the hand of Providence in the affairs of men.

CHAPTER II

The Negro as a Legislator. — His Fluency in Debate. — Earnestness and Good-Humor his Characteristics. — The Future of the State.

ONE of the things that first strike a casual observer in this negro assembly is the fluency of debate, if the endless chatter that goes on there can be dignified with this term. The leading topics of discussion are all well understood by the members, as they are of a practical character, and appeal directly to the personal interests of every legislator, as well as to those of his constituents. When an appropriation bill is up to raise money to catch and punish the Ku-klux, they know exactly what it means. They feel it in their bones. So, too, with educational measures. The free school comes right home to them; then the business of arming and drilling the black militia. They are eager on this point. Sambo can talk on these topics and those of a kindred character, and their endless ramifications, day in and day out. There is no end to his gush and babble. The intellectual level is that of a bevy of fresh converts at a negro camp-meeting. Of course this kind of talk can be extended indefinitely. It is the doggerel of debate, and not beyond the reach of the lowest parts. Then the negro is imitative in the extreme. He can copy like a parrot or a monkey, and he is always ready for a trial of his skill. He believes he can do any thing, and never loses a chance to try, and is just as ready to be laughed at for his failure as applauded for his success. He is more vivacious than the white, and, being more volatile and good-natured, he is correspondingly more irrepressible. His misuse of language in his imitations is at times ludicrous beyond measure. He notoriously loves a joke or an anecdote, and will burst into a broad guffaw on the smallest provocation. He breaks out into an incoherent harangue on the floor just as easily, and being without practice, discipline, or experience, and wholly oblivious of Lindley Murray, or any other restraint on composition, he will go on repeating himself, dancing as it were to the music of his own voice, forever. He will speak half a dozen times on one question, and every time say the same things without knowing it. He answers completely to the description of a stupid speaker in Parliament, given by Lord Derby on one occasion. It was said of him that he did not know what he was going to say when he got up; he did not know what he was saying while he was speaking, and he did not know what he had said when he sat down.

But the old stagers admit that the colored brethren have a wonderful aptness at legislative proceedings. They are "quick as lightning" at detecting points of order, and they certainly make incessant and extraordinary use of their knowledge. No one is allowed to talk five minutes without interruption, and one interruption is the signal for another and another, until the original speaker is smothered under an avalanche of them. Forty questions of privilege will be raised in a day. At times, nothing goes on but alternating questions of order and of privilege. The inefficient colored friend who sits in the Speaker's chair cannot suppress this extraordinary element of the debate. Some of the blackest members exhibit a pertinacity of intrusion in raising these points of order and questions of privilege that few white men can equal. Their struggles to get the floor, their bellowings and physical contortions, baffle description. The Speaker's hammer plays a perpetual tattoo all to no purpose. The talking and the interruptions from all quarters go on with the utmost license. Every one esteems himself as good as his neighbor, and puts in his oar, apparently as often for love of riot and confusion as for any thing else. It is easy to imagine what are his ideas of propriety and dignity among a crowd of his own color, and these are illustrated without reserve. The Speaker orders a member whom he has discovered to be particularly unruly to take his seat. The member obeys, and with the same motion that he sits down, throws his feet on to his desk, hiding himself from the Speaker by the soles of his boots. In an instant he appears again on the floor. After a few experiences of this sort, the Speaker threatens, in a laugh, to call "the gemman" to order. This is considered a capital joke, and a guffaw follows. The laugh goes round, and then the peanuts are cracked and munched faster than ever; one hand being employed in fortifying the inner man with this nutriment of universal use, while the other enforces the views of the orator. This laughing propensity of the sable crowd is a great cause of disorder. They laugh as hens cackle — one begins and all follow.

But underneath all this shocking burlesque upon legislative proceedings, we must not forget that there is something very real to this uncouth and untutored multitude. It is not all sham, nor all burlesque. They have a genuine interest and a genuine earnestness in the business of the assembly which we are bound to recognize and respect, unless we would be accounted shallow critics. They have an earnest purpose, born of a conviction that their position and condition are not fully assured, which lends a sort of dignity to their proceedings. The barbarous, animated jargon in which they so often indulge is on occasion seen to be so transparently sincere and weighty in their own minds that sympathy supplants disgust. The whole thing is a wonderful novelty to them as well as to observers. Seven years ago these men were raising corn and cotton under the whip of the overseer. To-day they are raising points of order and questions of privilege. They find they can raise one as well as the other. They prefer the latter. It is easier, and better paid. Then, it is the evidence of an accomplished result.

It means escape and defense from old oppressors. It means liberty. It means the destruction of prison-walls only too real to them. It is the sunshine of their lives. It is their day of jubilee. It is their long-promised vision of the Lord God Almighty.

Shall we, then, be too critical over the spectacle? Perhaps we might more wisely wonder that they can do so well in so short a time. The barbarians overran Rome. The dark ages followed. But then the day finally broke, and civilization followed. The days were long and weary; but they came to an end at last. Now we have the printing-press, the railroad, the telegraph; and these denote an utter revolution in the affairs of mankind. Years may now accomplish what it formerly took ages to achieve. Under the new lights and influences shall not the black man speedily emerge? Who knows? We may fear, but we may hope. Nothing in our day is impossible. Take the contested supposition that South Carolina is to be Africanized. We have a Federal Union of great and growing States. It is incontestably white at the centre. We know it to possess vital powers. It is well abreast of all modern progress in ideas and improvements. Its influence is all-pervading. How can a State of the Union escape it? South Carolina alone, if left to herself, might fall into midnight darkness. Can she do it while she remains an integral part of the nation?

But will South Carolina be Africanized? That depends. Let us hear the judgment of an intelligent foreigner who has long lived in the South, and who was here when the war began. He does not believe it. White people from abroad are drifting in, bad as things are. Under freedom the blacks do not multiply as in slavery. The pickaninnies die off from want of care. Some blacks are coming in from North Carolina and Virginia, but others are going off farther South. The white young men who were growing into manhood did not seem inclined to leave their homes and migrate to foreign parts. There was an exodus after the war, but it has stopped, and many have come back. The old slave-holders still hold their lands. The negroes were poor and unable to buy, even if the land-owners would sell. This was a powerful impediment to the development of the negro into a controlling force in the State. His whole power was in his numbers. The present disproportion of four blacks to three whites in the State he believed was already decreasing. The whites seemed likely to more than hold their own, while the blacks would fall off. Cumulative voting would encourage the growth and add to the political power of the whites in the Legislature, where they were at present over-slaughed.

Then the manufacturing industry was growing in magnitude and vitality. This spread various new employments over the State, and every one became a centre to invite white immigration. This influence was already felt. Trade was increased in the towns, and this meant increase of white population. High taxes were a detriment and a drag. But the trader put them on to his goods, and the manufacturer on to his products, and made the consumer pay.

But this important question cannot be dismissed in a paragraph. It requires further treatment. It involves the fortunes of the State far too deeply, and the duties of the white people and the interests of the property holder, are too intimately connected with a just decision of it, to excuse a hasty or shallow judgment. We must defer its further consideration to another occasion. It is the question which is all in all to South Carolina.

CHAPTER III

Villainies of the State Government. — The Present Government no Improvement on the Last. — The Treasury Drained by the Thieves. — Venality of the Press.

THE corruption of the State government of South Carolina is a topic that has grown threadbare in the handling. The last administration stole right hand and left with a recklessness and audacity without parallel. The robbers under it embraced all grades of people. The thieves had to combine to aid one another. It took a combination of the principal authorities to get at the Treasury, and they had to share the plunder alike. All the smaller fry had their proportions, the legislators and lobbymen included. The principal men of the Scott administration are living in Columbia, and nobody undertakes to call them to account. They do not attempt even to conceal their plunder. If everybody was not implicated in the robberies of the Treasury, some way would be found to bring them to light. All that people know is, that the State bonded debt has been increased from five to fifteen millions, and that, besides this, there are all sorts of current obligations to pay afloat, issued by State officers who had authority to bind the Treasury. They are all tinctured with fraud, and some of them are such scandalous swindles that the courts have been able temporarily to stop their payment.

The whole of the late administration, which terminated its existence in November, 1872, was a morass of rottenness, and the present administration was born of the corruptions of that; but for the exhaustion of the State, there is no good reason to believe it would steal less than its predecessor. There seems to be no hope, therefore, that the villainies of the past will be speedily uncovered. The present Governor was Speaker of the last House, and he is credited with having issued during his term in office over $400,000 of pay "certificates" which are still unredeemed and for which there is no appropriation, but which must be saddled on the tax-payers sooner or later. The Blue Ridge Railroad scrip is another scandal embracing several millions of pure stealings. The case is briefly this: Some years ago a charter was obtained for a railroad across the southern end of the Blue Ridge from South Carolina into Kentucky. It was a difficult work, and the State promised it aid on certain conditions. The road was never made, and these conditions were never fulfilled, but since the restoration the State obligations were authorized to be issued. But this was not the worst of it. The sum authorized was $1,800,000. It turns out that on the strength of this authority over $5,000,000 of the scrip has been issued. It was rendered available to the holders by being made receivable for taxes, and in this way has got spread abroad. The whole scheme has been for the moment frustrated by a decision of the courts that the entire transaction is fraudulent and void from the start. With $5,000,000 of this stuff afloat, which the Legislature can legalize if the members are paid enough, what hope is there that the State will escape liability for the emission?

These are sample items of the corruptions of the late government outside of the increase of the bonded debt. The iniquity laps over into this administration, for the old Speaker has been chosen Governor, and the present Legislature has chosen Patterson Senator.

Yet the last canvass was carried on under the sting of the charges of corruption against the Scott administration, and it was hoped that the present would be an improvement upon that. The election of Patterson soon after the assembling of the Legislature, and the manner in which he was chosen, gave a sudden dash to those hopes. Then it has been found that some of the most unscrupulous white and black robbers who have, as members or lobbyists, long plied their nefarious trade at the capital still disfigure and disgrace the present Assembly. So tainted is the atmosphere with corruption, so universally implicated is everybody about the government, of such a character are the ornaments of society at the capital, that there is no such thing as an influential local opinion to be brought against the scamps. They plunder, and glory in it. They steal, and defy you to prove it. The legalization of fraudulent scrip is regarded simply as a smart operation. The purchase of a senatorship is considered only a profitable trade. Those who make the most out of the operation are the best fellows. "How did you get your money?" was asked of a prominent legislator and lobbyist. "I stole it," was the prompt reply. The same man pursues his trade today, openly and unabashed. A leading member of the last administration was told he had the credit of having robbed the State of his large fortune. "Let them prove it," was his only answer. Meanwhile, both of them openly revel in their riches under the very shadow of the lean and hungry Treasury whence their ill-gotten gains were filched. As has been already said, it is believed that the lank impoverishment of the Treasury and the total abasement and destruction of the State credit alone prevent the continuance of robbery on the old scale. As it is, taxation is not in the least diminished, and nearly two millions per annum are raised for State expenses where $400,000 formerly sufficed. This affords succulent pasturage for a large crowd. For it must be remembered that not a dollar of it goes for interest on the State debt. The barter and sale of the offices in which the finances of the State are manipulated, which are divided among the numerous small counties under a system offering unusual facilities for the business, go on with as much activity as ever. The new Governor has the reputation of spending $30,000 or $40,000 a year on a salary of $3,500, but his financial operations are taken as a matter of course, and only referred to with a slight shrug of the shoulders.

Not only are the residences of the white thieves who have stolen their half a million or more apiece, pointed out in Columbia, but here and there a comfortable abode of some sable ally, whose sole business is politics. But while the colored brother has had to be content hitherto with smaller sums than the white, which of itself would account for want of relative show, he is also more prodigal in his expenditures. Still his savings are not to be despised. Sambo takes naturally to stealing, for he is used to it. It was his notorious weakness in slavery, and in his unregenerate state he is far less culpable than the white. The only way he ever had to possess himself of any thing, was to steal it from somebody else. The white man is really the responsible party for his thefts. He may well turn and say to his former master, "The villainy you teach, I will execute." The narration I have given sufficiently shows how things have gone and are going in this State, but its effect would be much heightened if there were time and room for details. Here is one: The total amount of the stationery bill of the House for the twenty years preceding 1861 averaged $400 per annum. Last year it was $16,000. But the meanness of these legislative robberies is not less significant of the character of the legislation than their magnitude. Last year the Treasury was in great straits on one or two occasions for money to anticipate the taxes. Some of the banks came to its aid and advanced about $60,000. They were this year compelled to go before the Committee of Claims to get reimbursed. The shameless rascals refused to pay the claim unless they were allowed to bag some 15 or 20 per cent. of it for their share! Another class of men who are allowed to rob the State freely, comprises those who control the printing-offices. The influence of a free press is well understood in South Carolina. It was understood and dreaded under the old *régime,* and was muzzled accordingly. Nearly all the newspapers in the State are now subsidized. The State government employs and pays them *ad libitum*. One installment of $75,000 lately went to about twenty-five papers in sums ranging from $1,000 to $7,000 apiece, a list of which was published by order of a vote of the Legislature a short time ago. Down here these small weekly sheets can be pretty nearly kept going on these subsidies. Of course, none of the deviltry of the State government is likely to be exposed through them. The whole amount of the printing bills of the State last year, it is computed (for every thing here has to be in part guess-work), aggregated the immense sum of $600,000.

CHAPTER IV

*The Pure Blacks the Ruling Power. — Rivalries of Blacks and Yellows.
— Carpet-Bag Rule wellnigh over. — The State Governed
by its own Citizens.*

I<small>T</small> is something more than a question of mere curiosity, "Who rules this Legislature?" It is, to an overwhelming extent, as we have already seen, composed of colored men. They are of every hue, running from coal-black through all the intermediate shades, out to what seems pure white. There appears to be scarcely any limit to the variety of shades of the colored population of the State, and their representatives in the Legislature are hardly less various. There is really no way of knowing whether any given individual in South Carolina has black blood in his veins, except by tracing his descent. The specimens of the whitened-out colored men in the Legislature demonstrate this. But who leads among this assembly of blacks and yellows? Is it the white men? By no means; Sambo has already outgrown that.

There is a strong disposition, among the old whites of the State, to say and believe that it is the white blood in the negro race which is managing affairs in the new *régime*. The pure blacks have been set so low in the scale, that it would show great want of penetration or great misrepresentation on the part of the old masters for them to admit the capacity of the black to conduct civic affairs, even as well as they are conducted here. Hence, all credit is apt to be denied them, and given to the element of white blood that courses in the veins of their lighter-colored brethren. Let us look about the Legislature and see how this is. The man who uniformly discharges his duties in the most unassuming manner and in the best taste, is the chaplain of the House. He is coal-black. In the dignities and proprieties of his office, in what he says, and, still better, in what he omits to say, he might be profitably studied as a model by the white political parsons who so often officiate in Congress. Take the chairman of the House Committee of Ways and Means. He is another full-black man. By his position, he has charge of the most important business of the House. He was selected for his solid qualities, and he seems always to conduct himself with discretion. Two of the best speakers in the House are quite black. Their abilities are about equal. Their moral qualities differ. One appears to be honest, and the other to be a rascal. They are both leaders rather than led. Go into the Senate. It is not too much to say that the leading man of the Republican party in that body is Beverly Nash, a man wholly black. He is apparently consulted more and appealed to more, in the business of the body, than any man in it. It is admitted by his white opposition colleagues that he has more native ability than half the white men in the Senate. There is the Senator from Georgetown. He boasts of being a negro, and of having no fear of the white man in any respect. He evidently has no love for him. He is truculent and audacious, and has as much force and ability as any of the lighter-colored members of his race about him. He appears to be also one of the leading "strikers," and is not led, except through his interests. To say the least, none of the lighter-colored members of the race command any more consideration, or possess any more marked influence or talent, than these and other specimen blacks who might be named. So that there seems to be no reason for the conclusion that it is the white element in the negro race that is enabling this body of former slaves to discharge the functions of legislators. The full blacks are just as much entitled to the credit of what is done as the mulattoes.

The future results of this are yet to be developed in affairs here. History indicates that there is nearly as great an antagonism, when disputes of race begin, between blacks and yellows as between blacks and whites. The germs of this antagonism already begin to show themselves here. The white blood often takes on airs when it is commingled as well as when it is unmingled. The negro begins, as he did in Hayti, by getting rid of the white man. After he is disposed of, the mulatto may be pursued with equal persistence. If South Carolina should be Africanized, the same tendency to make it a pure black government would, it is likely, manifest itself here as in Hayti. So far, however, the tendency has only been to get rid of white local leaders; and, as they have been hitherto mostly carpet-baggers, there should be nobody to complain. It is such a merit to drive them out, that nobody stops to ask or care who follows them and fills their places. Wherever those places have been filled by colored men, the change has been advantageous to the State. This is notably the case in the important office of State Treasurer, who is a colored· man educated abroad by a rich father, who lived in Charleston. But, as the Treasury of South Carolina has been so thoroughly gutted by the thieves who have hitherto had possession of the State government, there is nothing left to steal. The note of any negro in the State is worth as much on the market as a South Carolina bond. It would puzzle even a Yankee carpet-bagger to make any thing out of the office of State Treasurer under such circumstances.

Three of these old carpet-bag leaders, now out of place, remain in Columbia; each, it is said, rolling in wealth. They, with a few remaining greedy legislative comrades, whom Sambo has not yet dismissed, together with the present Governor, constitute the chief ornaments of that privileged society. Speaking generally, then, we may say that the State government of South Carolina is no longer in the hands of the carpet-baggers. It is in the possession of her own people. The present State officers, legislative and executive, are all, or nearly all, South Carolinians. The Governor is a South Carolina white man, the Lieutenant-Governor, the President of the Senate, the Speaker of the House, the Treasurer, and other State officers, are all of the sable tint, and all are alike natives. South Carolina has, therefore, to all intents and purposes, the charge of her own affairs. The evils she suffers from the character of her rulers grow out of the nature of the constituency which chooses them.

That the State has been victimized, plundered, and robbed by audacious scoundrels from abroad is not to be denied. But at home she is mainly rescued from their clutches, and it is not they whom the people of the State will have much longer to contend with. Those who would reform South Carolina in the future, will have chiefly its native population only to deal with. The black man of the Legislature feels his oats, and considers that the time has already arrived when he can take care of himself. He is not going to throw away, however, his party relationships, or his party advantages. He will use these in the future as he is now using them, to advance his own purposes. He is familiar with the uses of the caucus and the league, and he feels strongly the advantages of combination and concentration, and he has learned the trick of using them as well as his white brethren. It is sometimes said that, in these caucuses and leagues, all legislative affairs are shaped, and that here the white man bears sway. The action of the Legislature does not bear out this view. There was a measure up for consideration the other day in the House, in which the negroes broke away and voted alone. It was a bill for a railroad very much needed, and to which there could be and was no honest objection. But some of the corrupt negro leaders thought the corporation could be forced to pay for the charter, and if the members opposed it they could get pay for their votes. Accordingly, the great body of the blacks combined, and the bill was refused a passage by a decisive majority, who chuckled over their achievement as they would have done if they had cornered a rabbit in a cotton-field. The opposition was so evidently corrupt and scandalous, that not a single white man on either side in the body would allow himself to be caught in opposing the measure, and not one white vote was given against it. This is one instance among many to show that Sambo is fast getting out of leading-strings, and is already his own leader in the Legislature.

Study Guide

1. Note, as indicated, that Pike is no Southerner — that although he had been an ardent abolitionist, he also believed blacks to be inferior to the whites. Focus, too, on the following:
   (a) the sharp contrast between his views of the ex-slave and those of Sumner, and
   (b) his decidedly negative opinions regarding the efficiency, honesty, and justice of the carpetbagger governments. (On this last subject, a strong controversy has raged among historians. The *traditional* interpretation that prevailed from the turn of the century until the 1940's labeled the Radical Reconstruction governments of the South vindictive, corrupt, and inefficient. The *revisionist* school that has come to the fore since the end of World War II has set forth totally opposing views. Pike obviously provided evidence for the first school. Amplify and illustrate.)

2. The easiest way to understand Pike's views (and, coincidentally, the traditional interpretation of Radical Reconstruction) is to *summarize* and *be able to document* his assessment of the following:
   (a) blacks, their competence, and their role in the Reconstruction governments;
   (b) the relationship between blacks and whites;
   (c) the roles of the "carpetbaggers" and "scalawags";
   (d) the officials, the administration, and the finances of the Reconstruction governments; and
   (e) Pike's fears and hopes for the future of the South.

Henry Grady
SECTIONAL HARMONY

❦ 1886 ❦ NEITHER victories on the battlefields, nor laws passed in Congress, nor even constitutional amendments could "settle" the sectional conflicts which had caused the Civil War. In some ways there was more bitterness and resentment between North and South during the Reconstruction Era than during the hate-filled years between the passage of the Kansas-Nebraska Act and Appo-

mattox. However, beneath the conflicts of Reconstruction, wounds were healing and new bonds were developing that would reunite the two regions in
fact as they had already been reunited in law. Industrial development of the
South and a moderate agricultural prosperity were important in this connection, and so was the gradual realization in the Southern states that the past was
truly dead beyond recall. Perhaps most important of all, the passage of time
dulled memories and brought forward new leaders. At any rate, by the 1880's
the old issues no longer seemed completely real. As Paul H. Buck says in *The
Road to Reunion,* "the South had buried its resentments and had entered a new
era of good feeling."

But this development was so gradual as to escape the notice of many observers. That is why the remarkable speech, "The New South," of Henry W.
Grady, delivered before the New England Society of New York City on December 21, 1886, was so influential. Other Southerners had said substantially
what Grady then enunciated, but only when phrased in his ornate but heartfelt language did the full impact of the changes taking place in the South hit
the nation as a whole. Grady's plea for sectional harmony struck deep and
hard. Newspapers all over the country commented upon it, and so did all the
influential magazines of the day. In the light of present sectional conflicts it
would be foolish to say that his speech marked the end of all bad feeling between North and South, but it was an exceptionally significant milestone along
the "road to reunion."

Grady (1850-1889), an editor of the influential Atlanta *Constitution,* was an
ideal spokesman for reconciliation, a man typical of the New South. Born into
a family of tradesmen, he had no ties with the old planter class. Being a newspaperman by profession, he had a wide circle of acquaintances North and South.
Finally, his oratorical style, "like a cannon ball in full flight fringed with
flowers," as one Northern lawyer put it, suited both the taste of his age and
also the particular needs of his topic, which called for both plain talk and
smooth.

THE NEW SOUTH

"THERE was a South of slavery and secession — that South is dead. There
is a South of union and freedom — that South, thank God, is living,
breathing, growing every hour." These words, delivered from the immortal lips of Benjamin H. Hill, at Tammany Hall, in 1866, true then
and truer now, I shall make my text to-night.

Mr. President and gentlemen: let me express to you my appreciation
of the kindness by which I am permitted to address you. I make this
abrupt acknowledgment advisedly, for I feel that if, when I raise my
provincial voice in this ancient and august presence, it could find courage
for no more than the opening sentence, it would be well if in that sentence I had met in a rough sense my obligation as a guest, and had
perished, so to speak, with courtesy on my lips and grace in my heart.

Permitted, through your kindness, to catch my second wind, let me say that I appreciate the significance of being the first Southerner to speak at this board, which bears the substance, if it surpasses the semblance, of original New England hospitality, and honors the sentiment that in turn honors you, but in which my personality is lost, and the compliment to my people made plain.

I bespeak the utmost stretch of your courtesy to-night. I am not troubled about those from whom I come. You remember the man whose wife sent him to a neighbor with a pitcher of milk, and who, tripping on the top step, fell with such casual interruptions as the landings afforded into the basement, and, while picking himself up, had the pleasure of hearing his wife call out, "John, did you break the pitcher?"

"No, I didn't," said John, "but I'll be dinged if I don't."

So, while those who call me from behind may inspire me with energy, if not with courage, I ask an indulgent hearing from you. I beg that you will bring your full faith in American fairness and frankness to judgment upon what I shall say. There was an old preacher once who told some boys of the Bible lesson he was going to read in the morning. The boys, finding the place, glued together the connecting pages. The next morning he read on the bottom of one page, "When Noah was one hundred and twenty years old he took unto himself a wife, who was" — then turning the page — "140 cubits long, 40 cubits wide, built of gopher wood, and covered with pitch inside and out." He was naturally puzzled at this. He read it again, verified it, and then said: "My friends, this is the first time I ever met this in the Bible, but I accept this as an evidence of the assertion that we are fearfully and wonderfully made." If I could get you to hold such faith to-night, I could proceed cheerfully to the task I otherwise approach with a sense of consecration.

Pardon me one word, Mr. President, spoken for the sole purpose of getting into the volumes that go out annually freighted with the rich eloquence of your speakers — the fact that the Cavalier as well as the Puritan was on the continent in its early days, and that he was "up and able to be about." I have read your books carefully, and I find no mention of this fact, which seems to me an important one for preserving a sort of historical equilibrium, if for nothing else.

Let me remind you that the Virginia Cavalier first challenged France on the continent — that Cavalier John Smith gave New England its very name, and was so pleased with the job that he has been handing his own name around ever since; and that while Myles Standish was cutting off men's ears for courting a girl without her parents' consent, and forbade men to kiss their wives on Sunday, the Cavalier was courting everything in sight, and that the Almighty had vouchsafed great increase to the Cavalier colonies, the huts in the wilderness being as full as the nests in the woods.

But having incorporated the Cavalier as a fact in your charming little books, I shall let him work out his own salvation, as he has always done, with engaging gallantry, and we will hold no controversy as to his merits. Why should we? Neither Puritan nor Cavalier long survived as such. The virtues and good traditions of both happily still live for the inspiration of their sons and the saving of the old fashion. But both Puritan and Cavalier were lost in the storm of the first Revolution, and the American citizen, supplanting both and stronger than either, took possession of the Republic bought by their common blood and fashioned to wisdom, and charged himself with teaching men government and establishing the voice of the people as the voice of God.

My friends, Dr. Talmage has told you that the typical American has yet to come. Let me tell you that he has already come. Great types, like valuable plants, are slow to flower and fruit. But from the union of these colonists, Puritans and Cavaliers, from the straightening of their purposes and the crossing of their blood, slow perfecting through a century, came he who stands as the first typical American, the first who comprehended within himself all the strength and gentleness, all the majesty and grace, of this Republic — Abraham Lincoln. He was the sum of Puritan and Cavalier, for in his ardent nature were fused the virtues of both, and in the depths of his great soul the faults of both were lost. He was greater than Puritan, greater than Cavalier, in that he was American, and that in his honest form were first gathered the vast and thrilling forces of his ideal government, charging it with such tremendous meaning and elevating it above human suffering, that martyrdom, though infamously aimed, came as a fitting crown to a life consecrated from the cradle to human liberty. Let us, each cherishing the traditions and honoring his fathers, build with reverent hands to the type of this simple but sublime life, in which all types are honored, and in our common glory as Americans there will be plenty and to spare for your forefathers and for mine.

Dr. Talmage has drawn for you, with a master's hand, the picture of your returning armies. He has told you how, in the pomp and circumstance of war, they came back to you, marching with proud and victorious tread, reading their glory in a nation's eyes! Will you bear with me while I tell you of another army that sought its home at the close of the late war? — an army that marched home in defeat and not in victory, in pathos and not in splendor, but in glory that equaled yours, and to hearts as loving as ever welcomed heroes home! Let me picture to you the foot-sore Confederate soldier, as, buttoning up in his faded gray jacket the parole which was to bear testimony to his children of his fidelity and faith, he turned his face southward from Appomattox in April, 1865. Think of him as, ragged, half-starved, heavy-hearted, enfeebled by want and wounds, having fought to exhaustion, he surrenders his gun, wrings the hands of his comrades in silence, and lifting his tear-stained and pallid face for the last time to the graves that dot old Virginia hills, pulls his gray cap over his brow and begins the slow and painful journey.

What does he find — let me ask you who went to your homes eager to find, in the welcome you had justly earned, full payment for four years' sacrifice — what does he find when, having followed the battle-stained cross against overwhelming odds, dreading death not half so much as surrender, he reaches the home he left so prosperous and beautiful? He finds his house in ruins, his farm devastated, his slaves free, his stock killed, his barns empty, his trade destroyed, his money worthless, his social system, feudal in its magnificence, swept away, his people without law or legal status, his comrades slain, and the burdens of others heavy on his shoulders. Crushed by defeat, his very traditions are gone; without money, credit, employment, material, or training; and besides all this, confronted with the gravest problem that ever met human intelligence — the establishment of a status for the vast body of his liberated slaves.

What does he do — this hero in gray with a heart of gold? Does he sit down in sullenness and despair? Not for a day. Surely God, who had stripped him of his prosperity, inspired him in his adversity. As ruin was never before so overwhelming, never was restoration swifter. The soldier stepped from the trenches into the furrow; horses that had charged federal guns marched before the plow, and fields that ran red with human blood in April were green with the harvest in June; women reared in luxury cut up their dresses and made breeches for their husbands, and, with a patience and heroism that fit women always as a garment, gave their hands to work. There was little bitterness in all this. Cheerfulness and frankness prevailed. "Bill Arp" struck the keynote when he said, "Well, I killed as many of them as they did of me, and now I'm going to work." So did the soldier returning home after defeat and roasting some corn on the roadside who made the remark to his comrades, "You may leave the South if you want to, but I'm going to Sandersville, kiss my wife, and raise a crop, and if the Yankees fool with me any more, I'll whip 'em again."

I want to say to General Sherman, who is considered an able man in our parts, though some people think he is a kind of careless man about fire, that from the ashes he left us in 1864 we have raised a brave and beautiful city; that somehow or other we have caught the sunshine in the bricks and mortar of our homes, and have builded therein not one ignoble prejudice or memory.

But what is the sum of our work? We have found out that in the summing up the free negro counts more than he did as a slave. We have planted the schoolhouse on the hilltop and made it free to white and black. We have sown towns and cities in the place of theories, and put business above politics. We have challenged your spinners in Massachusetts and your ironmakers in Pennsylvania. We have learned that the $400,000,000 annually received from our cotton crop will make us rich when the supplies that make it are home-raised. We have reduced the commercial rate of interest from 24 to 6 per cent, and are floating 4 per cent bonds. We have learned that one Northern immigrant is worth fifty foreigners, and have smoothed the path to Southward, wiped out the place where Mason and Dixon's line used to be, and hung out the latch-string to you and yours.

We have reached the point that marks perfect harmony in every household, when the husband confesses that the pies which his wife cooks are as good as those his mother used to bake; and we admit that the sun shines as brightly and the moon as softly as it did before the war. We have established thrift in city and country. We have fallen in love with work. We have restored comfort to homes from which culture and elegance never departed. We have let economy take root and spread among us as rank as the crab-grass which sprung from Sherman's cavalry camps, until we are ready to lay odds on the Georgia Yankee as he manufactures relics of the battlefield in a one-story shanty and squeezes pure olive oil out of his cotton seed, against any downeaster that ever swapped wooden nutmegs for flannel sausage in the valleys of Vermont. Above all, we know that we have achieved in these "piping times of peace" a fuller independence for the South than that which our fathers sought to win in the forum by their eloquence or compel in the field by their swords.

It is a rare privilege, sir, to have had part, however humble, in this work. Never was nobler duty confided to human hands than the uplifting and upbuilding of the prostrate and bleeding South — misguided, perhaps, but beautiful in her suffering, and honest, brave, and generous always. In the record of her social, industrial, and political illustration we await with confidence the verdict of the world.

But what of the negro? Have we solved the problem he presents or

progressed in honor and equity toward solution? Let the record speak to
the point. No section shows a more prosperous laboring population than
the negroes of the South, none in fuller sympathy with the employing
and land-owning class. He shares our school fund, has the fullest protection of our laws, and the friendship of our people. Self-interest, as well as
honor, demand that he should have this. Our future, our very existence,
depend upon our working out this problem in full and exact justice. We
understand that when Lincoln signed the Emancipation Proclamation,
your victory was assured, for he then committed you to the cause of
human liberty, against which the arms of man cannot prevail — while
those of our statesmen who trusted to make slavery the corner stone of
the Confederacy doomed us to defeat as far as they could, committing
us to a cause that reason could not defend or the sword maintain in sight
of advancing civilization.

Had Mr. Toombs said, which he did not say, "that he would call the
roll of his slaves at the foot of Bunker Hill," he would have been foolish,
for he might have known that whenever slavery became entangled in war
it must perish, and that the chattel in human flesh ended forever in
New England when your fathers — not to be blamed for parting with
what didn't pay — sold their slaves to our fathers — not to be praised for
knowing a paying thing when they saw it. The relations of the Southern
people with the negro are close and cordial. We remember with what
fidelity for four years he guarded our defenseless women and children,
whose husbands and fathers were fighting against his freedom. To his
eternal credit be it said that whenever he struck a blow for his own
liberty, he fought in open battle, and when at last he raised his black and
humble hands that the shackles might be struck off, those hands were
innocent of wrong against his helpless charges, and worthy to be taken
in loving grasp by every man who honors loyalty and devotion. Ruffians
have maltreated him, rascals have misled him, philanthropists established
a bank for him, but the South, with the North, protests against injustice
to this simple and sincere people.

To liberty and enfranchisement is as far as law can carry the negro.
The rest must be left to conscience and common sense. It must be left to
those among whom his lot is cast, with whom he is indissolubly connected, and whose prosperity depends upon their possessing his intelligent
sympathy and confidence. Faith has been kept with him, in spite of
calumnious assertions to the contrary by those who assume to speak for
us or by frank opponents. Faith will be kept with him in the future, if
the South holds her reason and integrity.

But have we kept faith with you? In the fullest sense, yes. When Lee surrendered — I don't say when Johnston surrendered, because I understand he still alludes to the time when he met General Sherman last as the time when he determined to abandon any further prosecution of the struggle — when Lee surrendered, I say, and Johnston quit, the South became, and has since been, loyal to this Union. We fought hard enough to know that we were whipped, and in perfect frankness accept as final the arbitrament of the sword to which we had appealed. The South found her jewel in the toad's head of defeat. The shackles that had held her in narrow limitations fell forever when the shackles of the negro slave were broken. Under the old régime the negroes were slaves to the South; the South was a slave to the system. The old plantation, with its simple police regulations and feudal habit, was the only type possible under slavery. Thus was gathered in the hands of a splendid and chivalric oligarchy the substance that should have been diffused among the people, as the rich blood, under certain artificial conditions, is gathered at the heart, filling that with affluent rapture, but leaving the body chill and colorless.

The old South rested everything on slavery and agriculture, unconscious that these could neither give nor maintain healthy growth. The new South presents a perfect democracy, the oligarchs leading in the popular movement; a social system compact and closely knitted, less splendid on the surface, but stronger at the core; a hundred farms for every plantation, fifty homes for every palace; and a diversified industry that meets the complex needs of this complex age.

The new South is enamored of her new work. Her soul is stirred with the breath of a new life. The light of a grander day is falling fair on her face. She is thrilling with the consciousness of growing power and prosperity. As she stands upright, full-statured and equal among the people of the earth, breathing the keen air and looking out upon the expanded horizon, she understands that her emancipation came because, through the inscrutable wisdom of God, her honest purpose was crossed and her brave armies were beaten.

This is said in no spirit of time-serving or apology. The South has nothing for which to apologize. She believes that the late struggle between the States was war and not rebellion, revolution and not conspiracy, and that her convictions were as honest as yours. I should be unjust to the dauntless spirit of the South and to my own convictions if I did not make this plain in this presence. The South has nothing to take back.

In my native town of Athens is a monument that crowns its central hill — a plain, white shaft. Deep cut into its shining side is a name dear to me above the names of men — that of a brave and simple man who died in brave and simple faith. Not for all the glories of New England, from Plymouth Rock all the way, would I exchange the heritage he left me in his soldier's death. To the foot of that shaft I shall send my children's children to reverence him who ennobled their name with his heroic blood. But, sir, speaking from the shadow of that memory which I honor as I do nothing else on earth, I say that the cause in which he suffered and for which he gave his life was adjudged by a higher and fuller wisdom than his or mine, and I am glad that the omniscient God held the balance of battle in His Almighty hand, and that human slavery was swept forever from American soil — that the American Union was saved from the wreck of war.

This message, Mr. President, comes to you from consecrated ground. Every foot of soil about the city in which I live is sacred as a battle ground of the Republic. Every hill that invests it is hallowed to you by the blood of your brothers who died for your victory, and doubly hallowed to us by the blood of those who died hopeless, but undaunted, in defeat — sacred soil to all of us, rich with memories that make us purer and stronger and better, silent but stanch witnesses in its red desolation of the matchless valor of American hearts and the deathless glory of American arms, speaking an eloquent witness in its white peace and prosperity to the indissoluble union of American States and the imperishable brotherhood of the American people.

Now, what answer has New England to this message? Will she permit the prejudice of war to remain in the hearts of the conquerors, when it has died in the hearts of the conquered? Will she transmit this prejudice to the next generation, that in their hearts, which never felt the generous ardor of conflict, it may perpetuate itself? Will she withhold, save in strained courtesy, the hand which straight from his soldier's heart Grant offered to Lee at Appomattox? Will she make the vision of a restored and happy people, which gathered above the couch of your dying captain, filling his heart with grace, touching his lips with praise, and glorifying his path to the grave — will she make the vision, on which the last sigh of his expiring soul breathed a benediction, a cheat and delusion?

If she does, the South, never abject in asking for comradeship, must accept with dignity its refusal; but if she does not refuse to accept in frankness and sincerity this message of good will and friendship, then will the prophecy of Webster, delivered in this very society forty years ago amid tremendous applause, be verified in its fullest sense, when he said: "Standing hand to hand and clasping hands, we should remain united as we have been for sixty years, citizens of the same country, members of the same government, united, all united now and united forever. There have been difficulties, contentions, and controversies, but I tell you that in my judgment, —

> Those opposed eyes,
> Which like the meteors of a troubled heaven,
> All of one nature, of one substance bred,
> Did lately meet in th' intestine shock,
> Shall now, in mutual well-beseeming ranks,
> March all one way.

Study Guide

1. Almost all the notions posited by Henry Grady for the postwar South are contained in this address: the need for sectional reconciliation; the myth of the Old South; the romanticization of the Civil War; the industrialization of the New South; the new role of the blacks; and, through all this, the regeneration of the entire nation.

2. Keep in mind *to whom,* and *where,* and *when* this speech is being made — to the New England Society, in New York City, only two decades after the end of the Civil War, which explains the opening quotation and much of what follows. What purpose, for example, can you see in his employment of the "Cavalier-Puritan" theme and how does he fit Lincoln into it? Ponder the purpose and impact of this (p. 59): "Let us, each cherishing the traditions and honoring his fathers, build with reverent hands to the type of this simple but sublime life, in which all types are honored, and in our common glory as Americans there will be plenty and to spare for your forefathers and for mine."

3. Note how skillfully Grady draws a portrait of the noble character and the high ideals of the Old South, its soldiers, its women, and even its slaves. Savor this (p. 60): "What does he do — this hero in gray with a heart of gold? Does he sit down in sullenness and despair? Not for a day. Surely God, who had stripped him of his prosperity, inspired him in his adversity."

4. As for the New South, note on what basis it will flourish — the new role for the black, the role of industry, and the role of the Northerner and Northern ways.

5. Speaking to the New England Society, a center of abolitionist sentiment, the subject of Southern slavery and its treatment of blacks was bound to be a touchy one. Pay special attention to the care and subtlety with

which he approaches the entire subject and how skillfully he removes it as an issue between the North and the South: his references to Lincoln and the Emancipation Proclamation, his comments on the slaves and their white masters during wartime, and his assertions about the future of blacks in the South.

6. The closing paragraphs of Grady's address are a classic of their kind. Astutely and movingly, Grady offers no apologies for the South and, at the same time, seeks to secure the friendship and the good will of its former enemy. Select the four or five key passages that, in your opinion, accomplish this purpose.

Booker T. Washington
THE NEGRO'S PLACE

❦1895❦ "IT WAS an ex-slave who eventually framed the *modus vivendi* of race relations in the New South," the historian C. Vann Woodward has written. "Booker T. Washington was more than the leader of his race. He was also a leader of white opinion with a national following, and he propounded not merely an educational theory but a social philosophy."

After working his way as a janitor through Hampton Institute, Booker T. Washington (1856–1915) studied and taught for several years and then, in 1881, founded the Tuskegee Institute in Alabama. Here he stressed practical training rather than liberal education for blacks. He assumed his position of national leadership, which he was to maintain until his death, with his speech at the opening of the Atlanta Cotton States and International Exposition in 1895. This was the first significant occasion on which a black addressed a mixed group of white and black people in the South. By that time, most of the blacks and their white friends were becoming disillusioned with the high hopes that had been born of emancipation and Reconstruction. Legal disfranchisement was beginning to be imposed, and the lines of segregation were being tightened. Washington did nothing to head off these trends. Instead, he proposed what came to be known as the "Atlanta Compromise," by which political rights and social privileges were to be sacrificed for economic opportunities. Full rights and privileges would, presumably, follow upon economic advance.

Ironically, this modest man, who foreswore social and political pretensions for his people, associated freely with Northern capitalists, advised Presidents on the disposal of Southern patronage, and influenced the distribution of Northern philanthropic funds. But his racial leadership did not go unchallenged. A growing minority of blacks looked to W. E. B. DuBois (1868–1964), a Massachusetts-born descendant of free blacks, a man who repudiated the Tuskegee program, demanded "aggressive action" for full equality, and became the first black official in the National Association for the Advancement of Colored People.

In his autobiography, *Up from Slavery* (1901), Washington quoted his famous Atlanta Exposition address and told of its reception and its significance.

THE ATLANTA EXPOSITION ADDRESS

THE Atlanta Exposition, at which I had been asked to make an address as a representative of the Negro race, . . . was opened with a short address from Governor Bullock. After other interesting exercises, including an invocation from Bishop Nelson, of Georgia, a dedicatory ode by Albert Howell, Jr., and addresses by the President of the Exposition and Mrs. Joseph Thompson, the President of the Woman's Board, Governor Bullock introduced me with the words, "We have with us to-day a representative of Negro enterprise and Negro civilization."

When I arose to speak, there was considerable cheering, especially from the coloured people. As I remember it now, the thing that was uppermost in my mind was the desire to say something that would cement the friendship of the races and bring about hearty coöperation between them. So far as my outward surroundings were concerned, the only thing that I recall distinctly now is that when I got up, I saw thousands of eyes looking intently into my face. The following is the address which I delivered: —

Mr. President and Gentlemen of the Board of Directors and Citizens:

One-third of the population of the South is of the Negro race. No enterprise seeking the material, civil, or moral welfare of this section can disregard this element of our population and reach the highest success. I but convey to you, Mr. President and Directors, the sentiment of the masses of my race when I say that in no way have the value and manhood of the American Negro been more fittingly and generously recognized than by the managers of this magnificent Exposition at every stage of its progress. It is a recognition that will do more to cement the friendship of the two races than any occurrence since the dawn of our freedom.

Not only this, but the opportunity here afforded will awaken among us a new era of industrial progress. Ignorant and inexperienced, it is not strange that in the first years of our new life we began at the top instead of at the bottom; that a seat in Congress or the state legislature was more sought than real estate or industrial skill; that the political convention or stump speaking had more attractions than starting a dairy farm or truck garden.

A ship lost at sea for many days suddenly sighted a friendly vessel. From the mast of the unfortunate vessel was seen a signal, "Water, water; we die of thirst!" The answer from the friendly vessel at once came back, "Cast down your bucket where you are." A second time the signal, "Water, water; send us water!" ran up from the distressed vessel, and was answered, "Cast down your bucket where you are." And a third and fourth signal for water was answered, "Cast down your bucket where you are." The captain of the distressed vessel, at last heeding the injunction, cast down his bucket, and it came up full of fresh, sparkling water from the mouth of the Amazon River. To those of my race who depend on bettering their condition in a foreign land or who underestimate the importance of cultivating friendly relations with the Southern white man, who is their next-door neighbour, I would say: "Cast down your bucket where you are" — cast it down in making friends, in every manly way, of the people of all races by whom we are surrounded.

Cast it down in agriculture, mechanics, in commerce, in domestic service, and in the professions. And in this connection it is well to bear in mind that whatever other sins the South may be called to bear, when it comes to business, pure and simple, it is in the South that the Negro is given a man's chance in the commercial world, and in nothing is this Exposition more eloquent than in emphasizing this chance. Our greatest danger is that in the great leap from slavery to freedom we may overlook the fact that the masses of us are to live by the productions of our hands, and fail to keep in mind that we shall prosper in proportion as we learn to dignify and glorify common labour and put brains and skill into the common occupations of life; shall prosper in proportion as we learn to draw the line between the superficial and the substantial, the ornamental gewgaws of life and the useful. No race can prosper till it learns that there is as much dignity in tilling a field as in writing a poem. It is at the bottom of life we must begin, and not at the top. Nor should we permit our grievances to overshadow our opportunities.

To those of the white race who look to the incoming of those of foreign birth and strange tongue and habits for the prosperity of the South, were I permitted I would repeat what I say to my own race, "Cast down your bucket where you are." Cast it down among the eight millions of Negroes whose habits you know, whose fidelity and love you have tested in days when to have proved treacherous meant the ruin of your firesides. Cast down your bucket among these people who have, without strikes and labour wars, tilled your fields, cleared your forests, builded your railroads and cities, and brought forth treasures from the bowels of the earth, and helped make possible this magnificent representation of the progress of the South. Casting down your bucket among my people, helping and encouraging them as you are doing on these grounds, and to education of head, hand, and heart, you will find that they will buy your surplus land, make blossom the waste places in your fields, and run your factories. While doing this, you can be sure in the future, as in the past, that you and your families will be surrounded by the most patient, faithful, law-abiding, and unresentful people that the world has seen. As we have proved our loyalty to you in the past, in nursing your children, watching by the sick-bed of your mothers and fathers, and often following them with tear-dimmed eyes to their graves, so in the future, in our humble way, we shall stand by you with a devotion that no foreigner can approach, ready to lay down our lives, if need be, in defence of yours, interlacing our industrial, commercial, civil, and religious life with yours in a way that shall make the interests of both races one. In all things that are purely social we can be as separate as the fingers, yet one as the hand in all things essential to mutual progress.

There is no defence or security for any of us except in the highest intelligence and development of all. If anywhere there are efforts tending to curtail the fullest growth of the Negro, let these efforts be turned into stimulating, encouraging, and making him the most useful and intelligent citizen. Effort or means so invested will pay a thousand per cent interest. These efforts will be twice blessed — "blessing him that gives and him that takes."

There is no escape through law of man or God from the inevitable: —

> The laws of changeless justice bind
> Oppressor with oppressed;
> And close as sin and suffering joined
> We march to fate abreast.

Nearly sixteen millions of hands will aid you in pulling the load upward, or they will pull against you the load downward. We shall constitute one-third and more of the ignorance and crime of the South, or one-third its intelligence and progress; we shall contribute one-third to the business and industrial prosperity of the South, or we shall prove a veritable body of death, stagnating, depressing, retarding every effort to advance the body politic.

Gentlemen of the Exposition, as we present to you our humble effort at an exhibition of our progress, you must not expect overmuch. Starting thirty years ago with ownership here and there in a few quilts and pumpkins and chickens (gathered from miscellaneous sources), remember the path that has led from these to the inventions and production of agricultural implements, buggies, steam-engines, newspapers, books, statuary, carving, paintings, the management of drug-stores and banks, has not been trodden without contact with thorns and thistles. While we take pride in what we exhibit as a result of our independent efforts, we do not for a moment forget that our part in this exhibition would fall far short of your expectations but for the constant help that has come to our educational life, not only from the Southern states, but especially from Northern philanthropists, who have made their gifts a constant stream of blessing and encouragement.

The wisest among my race understand that the agitation of questions of social equality is the extremest folly, and that progress in the enjoyment of all the privileges that will come to us must be the result of severe and constant struggle rather than of artificial forcing. No race that has anything to contribute to the markets of the world is long in any degree ostracized. It is important and right that all privileges of the law be ours, but it is vastly more important that we be prepared for the exercises of these privileges. The opportunity to earn a dollar in a factory just now is worth infinitely more than the opportunity to spend a dollar in an opera-house.

In conclusion, may I repeat that nothing in thirty years has given us more hope and encouragement, and drawn us so near to you of the white race, as this opportunity offered by the Exposition; and here bending, as it were, over the altar that represents the results of the struggles of your race and mine, both starting practically empty-handed three decades ago, I pledge that in your effort to work out the great and intricate problem which God has laid at the doors of the South, you shall have at all times the patient, sympathetic help of my race; only let this be constantly in mind, that, while from representations in these buildings of the product of field, of forest, of mine, of factory, letters, and art, much good will come, yet far above and beyond material benefits will be that higher good, that, let us pray God, will come, in a blotting out of sectional differences and racial animosities and suspicions, in a determination to administer absolute justice, in a willing obedience among all classes to the mandates of law. This, this, coupled with our material prosperity, will bring into our beloved South a new heaven and a new earth.

The first thing that I remember, after I had finished speaking, was that Governor Bullock rushed across the platform and took me by the hand,

and that others did the same. I received so many and such hearty congratulations that I found it difficult to get out of the building. I did not appreciate to any degree, however, the impression which my address seemed to have made, until the next morning, when I went into the business part of the city. As soon as I was recognized, I was surprised to find myself pointed out and surrounded by a crowd of men who wished to shake hands with me. This was kept up on every street on to which I went, to an extent which embarrassed me so much that I went back to my boarding-place. The next morning I returned to Tuskegee. At the station in Atlanta, and at almost all of the stations at which the train stopped between that city and Tuskegee, I found a crowd of people anxious to shake hands with me.

The papers in all parts of the United States published the address in full, and for months afterward there were complimentary editorial references to it. Mr. Clark Howell, the editor of the Atlanta *Constitution,* telegraphed to a New York paper, among other words, the following, "I do not exaggerate when I say that Professor Booker T. Washington's address yesterday was one of the most notable speeches, both as to character and as to the warmth of its reception, ever delivered to a Southern audience. The address was a revelation. The whole speech is a platform upon which blacks and whites can stand with full justice to each other."

The Boston *Transcript* said editorially: "The speech of Booker T. Washington at the Atlanta Exposition, this week, seems to have dwarfed all the other proceedings and the Exposition itself. The sensation that it has caused in the press has never been equalled."

I very soon began receiving all kinds of propositions from lecture bureaus, and editors of magazines and papers, to take the lecture platform, and to write articles. One lecture bureau offered me fifty thousand dollars, or two hundred dollars a night and expenses, if I would place my services at its disposal for a given period. To all these communications I replied that my life-work was at Tuskegee; and that whenever I spoke it must be in the interests of the Tuskegee school and my race, and that I would enter into no arrangements that seemed to place a mere commercial value upon my services.

Some days after its delivery I sent a copy of my address to the President of the United States, the Hon. Grover Cleveland. I received from him the following autograph reply:—

GRAY GABLES, BUZZARD'S BAY, MASS.,
October 6, 1895

BOOKER T. WASHINGTON, ESQ:

MY DEAR SIR: I thank you for sending me a copy of your address delivered at the Atlanta Exposition.

I thank you with much enthusiasm for making the address. I have read it with intense interest, and I think the Exposition would be fully justified if it did not do more than furnish the opportunity for its delivery. Your words cannot fail to delight and encourage all who wish well for your race; and if our coloured fellow-citizens do not from your utterances gather new hope and form new determinations to gain every valuable advantage offered them by their citizenship, it will be strange indeed.

Yours very truly,

GROVER CLEVELAND

Later I met Mr. Cleveland, for the first time, when, as President, he visited the Atlanta Exposition. At the request of myself and others he consented to spend an hour in the Negro Building, for the purpose of inspecting the Negro exhibit and of giving the coloured people in attendance an opportunity to shake hands with him. As soon as I met Mr. Cleveland I became impressed with his simplicity, greatness, and rugged honesty. I have met him many times since then, both at public functions and at his private residence in Princeton, and the more I see of him the more I admire him. When he visited the Negro Building in Atlanta he seemed to give himself up wholly, for that hour, to the coloured people. He seemed to be as careful to shake hands with some old coloured "auntie" clad partially in rags, and to take as much pleasure in doing so, as if he were greeting some millionnaire. Many of the coloured people took advantage of the occasion to get him to write his name in a book or on a slip of paper. He was as careful and patient in doing this as if he were putting his signature to some great state document.

Mr. Cleveland has not only shown his friendship for me in many personal ways, but has always consented to do anything I have asked of him for our school. This he has done, whether it was to make a personal donation or to use his influence in securing the donations of others. Judging from my personal acquaintance with Mr. Cleveland, I do not believe that he is conscious of possessing any colour prejudice. He is too great for that. In my contact with people I find that, as a rule, it is only the little, narrow people who live for themselves, who never read good books, who do not travel, who never open up their souls in a way to permit them to come into contact with other souls — with the great outside world. No man whose vision is bounded by colour can come into contact with what is highest and best in the world. In meeting men, in many places, I have found that the happiest people are those who do the most for others; the most miserable are those who do the least. I have also found that few things, if any, are capable of making one so blind and narrow as race prejudice. I often say to our students, in the course of my talks to them on Sunday evenings in the chapel, that the longer I live and the more experience I have of the world, the more I am convinced that, after all, the one thing that is most worth living for — and dying for, if need be — is the opportunity of making some one else more happy and more useful.

The coloured people and the coloured newspapers at first seemed to be greatly pleased with the character of my Atlanta address, as well as with its reception. But after the first burst of enthusiasm began to die away, and the coloured people began reading the speech in cold type, some of them seemed to feel that they had been hypnotized. They seemed to feel that I had been too liberal in my remarks toward the Southern whites, and that I had not spoken out strongly enough for what they termed the "rights" of the race. For a while there was a reaction, so far as a certain element of my own race was concerned, but later these reactionary ones seemed to have been won over to my way of believing and acting. . . .

I am often asked to express myself more freely than I do upon the political condition and the political future of my race. These recollections of my experience in Atlanta give me the opportunity to do so briefly. My own belief is, although I have never before said so in so many words, that the time will come when the Negro in the South will be accorded all the political rights which his ability, character, and material possessions entitle him to. I think, though, that the opportunity to freely exercise such political rights will not come in any large degree through outside or artificial forcing, but will be accorded to the Negro by the Southern white people themselves, and that they will protect him in the exercise of those rights. Just as soon as the South gets over the old feeling that it is being forced by "foreigners," or "aliens," to do something which it does not want to do, I believe that the change in the direction that I have indicated is going to begin. In fact, there are indications that it is already beginning in a slight degree.

Let me illustrate my meaning. Suppose that some months before the opening of the Atlanta Exposition there had been a general demand from the press and public platform outside the South that a Negro be given a place on the opening programme, and that a Negro be placed upon the board of jurors of award. Would any such recognition of the race have taken place? I do not think so. The Atlanta officials went as far as they did because they felt it to be a pleasure, as well as a duty, to reward what they considered merit in the Negro race. Say what we will, there is something in human nature which we cannot blot out, which makes one man, in the end, recognize and reward merit in another, re-gardless of colour or race.

I believe it is the duty of the Negro — as the greater part of the race is already doing — to deport himself modestly in regard to political claims, depending upon the slow but sure influences that proceed from the pos-session of property, intelligence, and high character for the full recogni-tion of his political rights. I think that the according of the full exercise of political rights is going to be a matter of natural, slow growth, not an over-night, gourd-vine affair. I do not believe that the Negro should cease voting, for a man cannot learn the exercise of self-government by ceasing to vote, any more than a boy can learn to swim by keeping out of the water, but I do believe that in his voting he should more and more be influenced by those of intelligence and character who are his next-door neighbours.

I know coloured men who, through the encouragement, help, and ad-vice of Southern white people, have accumulated thousands of dollars' worth of property, but who, at the same time, would never think of go-ing to those same persons for advice concerning the casting of their bal-lots. This, it seems to me, is unwise and unreasonable, and should cease. In saying this I do not mean that the Negro should truckle, or not vote from principle, for the instant he ceases to vote from principle he loses the confidence and respect of the Southern white man even.

I do not believe that any state should make a law that permits an ignorant and poverty-stricken white man to vote, and prevents a black man in the same condition from voting. Such a law is not only unjust, but it will react, as all unjust laws do, in time; for the effect of such a law is to encourage the Negro to secure education and property, and at the same time it encourages the white man to remain in ignorance and pov-erty. I believe that in time, through the operation of intelligence and friendly race relations, all cheating at the ballot-box in the South will cease. It will become apparent that the white man who begins by cheating a Negro out of his ballot soon learns to cheat a white man out of his, and that the man who does this ends his career of dishonesty by the theft of property or by some equally serious crime. In my opinion, the time will come when the South will encourage all of its citizens to vote. It will see that it pays better, from every standpoint, to have healthy, vigorous life than to have that political stagnation which always results when one-half of the population has no share and no interest in the Government.

As a rule, I believe in universal, free suffrage, but I believe that in the South we are confronted with peculiar conditions that justify the protection of the ballot in many of the states, for a while at least, either by an educational test, a property test, or by both combined; but whatever tests are required, they should be made to apply with equal and exact justice to both races.

Study Guide

1. Understand this address as the response of a black leader to the following developments: the failure of Radical Reconstruction; the death of Frederick Douglass; the "sectional harmony" at the expense of the blacks implicit in the words of Henry Grady; and the negation of black rights by the Supreme Court as stated by Joseph P. Bradley in the 1883 civil rights cases. Given the condition of blacks by the 1890's — social segregation, political disfranchisement, and economic subservience — there was little left for the ex-slaves but to develop a social philosophy akin to what Washington espoused at the Atlantic Exposition of 1895.

2. Explain the meanings Washington reads into "Cast down your bucket where you are" for blacks and for whites.

3. What, in this address, is the message Washington has for the Southern whites? Explain: "The wisest among my race understand that the agitation of questions of social equality is the extremest folly, and that progress in the enjoyment of all the privileges that will come to us must be the result of severe and constant struggle rather than of artificial forcing" (p. 70).

4. Account for the lack of enthusiasm of the state governor to the address, as well as that of Grover Cleveland. On the other hand, account for the enthusiasm for the address in the black community. Can you see why some blacks would be unhappy with this address? Explore.

5. What social philosophy for both blacks and whites does Washington espouse in his closing paragraphs? Would you call it elitist or egalitarian?

II. Implications of Industrialism

Edward Bellamy

A SOCIALIST UTOPIA

❖{*1888*}❖   By far the most popular of the attacks mounted against entrenched wealth and privilege in the post-Civil War years was that of Edward Bellamy (1850–1898). A reticent, bookish young man, son of a Baptist minister, Bellamy had engaged in newspaper work and written a number of interesting short stories when, in 1886, he began work on a novel describing a future society in which all production would be nationalized and every citizen would share equality in the fruits of the common labor. Two years later when this book, *Looking Backward,* appeared, it was an instant success. By 1890 over 200,000 copies had been sold and within another few years sales passed the million mark. Soon there were over 150 Nationalist Clubs in existence, dedicated to achieving the ideal system envisioned by Bellamy. During the 1890's several dozen utopian novels were published, many no doubt inspired by the success of *Looking Backward.* None, however, approached the popularity of that book.

The following selection, drawn from the opening chapters of the book, contains the clever literary device which had so much to do with the success of *Looking Backward* and illustrates the nature of Bellamy's criticism of nineteenth-century American capitalism. The remainder of the novel, which is enlivened by a typical Victorian romance between the hero and Dr. Leete's daughter, explains elaborately the character of the egalitarian socialism of the year 2000. Throughout there are frequent asides devoted to illustrating the futility and unreasonableness of the "old" system. Some of these, of course, might as well be applied to our own society, now much closer to Dr. Leete's day in time than to his way of thinking. A number of the good Doctor's remarks would not sound unusual in the mouths of modern thinkers like John K. Galbraith or the late President Kennedy. "We might, indeed, have much larger incomes, individually, if we chose so to use the surplus of our product," Leete says at one point. "[B]ut we prefer to expend it upon public works and pleasures in which all share. . . ."

Bellamy wrote another novel, *Equality,* and contributed many articles to Nationalist journals. But his health declined rapidly and he died long before the modern concept of the welfare state attracted much support.

LOOKING BACKWARD

I

I first saw the light in the city of Boston in the year 1857. "What!" you say "Eighteen fifty-seven? That is an odd slip. He means nineteen fifty-seven, of course." I beg your pardon, but there is no mistake. It was about four in the afternoon of December the 26th, one day after Christmas, in the year 1857, not 1957, that I first breathed the east wind of Boston, which,

I assure the reader, was at that remote period marked by the same penetrating quality characterizing it in the present year of grace, 2000.

These statements seem so absurd on their face, especially when I add that I am a young man apparently of about thirty years of age, that no person can be blamed for refusing to read another word of what promises to be a mere imposition upon his credulity. Nevertheless I earnestly assure the reader that no imposition is intended, and will undertake, if he shall follow me a few pages, to entirely convince him of this. If I may, then, provisionally assume, with the pledge of justifying the assumption, that I know better than the reader when I was born, I will go on with my narrative. As every schoolboy knows, in the latter part of the nineteenth century the civilization of today, or anything like it, did not exist, although the elements which were to develop it were already in ferment. Nothing had, however, occurred to modify the immemorial division of society into the four classes, or nations, as they may be more fitly called, since the differences between them were far greater than those between any nations nowadays, of the rich and the poor, the educated and the ignorant. I myself was rich and also educated, and possessed, therefore, all the elements of happiness enjoyed by the most fortunate in that age. Living in luxury, and occupied only with the pursuit of the pleasures and refinements of life, I derived the means of my support from the labor of others, rendering no sort of service in return. My parents and grandparents had lived in the same way, and I expected that my descendants, if I had any, would enjoy a like easy existence.

But how could I live without service to the world? you ask. Why should the world have supported in utter idleness one who was able to render service? The answer is that my great-grandfather had accumulated a sum of money on which his descendants had ever since lived. The sum, you will naturally infer, must have been very large not to have been exhausted in supporting three generations of idleness. This, however, was not the fact. The sum had been originally by no means large. It was, in fact, much larger now that three generations had been supported upon it in idleness, than it was at first. This mystery of use without consumption, of warmth without combustion, seems like magic, but was merely an ingenious application of the art now happily lost but carried to great perfection by your ancestors, of shifting the burden of one's support on the shoulders of others. The man who had accomplished this, and it was the end all sought, was said to live on the income of his investments. To explain at this point how the ancient methods of industry made this possible would delay us too much. I shall only stop now to say that interest on investments was a species of tax in perpetuity upon the product of those engaged in industry which a person possessing or inheriting money was able to levy. It must not be supposed that an arrangement which seems so unnatural and preposterous according to modern notions was never criticized by your ancestors. It had been the effort of lawgivers and prophets from the earliest ages to abolish interest, or at least to limit it to the smallest possible rate. All these efforts had, however, failed, as they necessarily must so long as the ancient social organizations prevailed. At the time of which I write, the latter part of the nineteenth century, governments had generally given up trying to regulate the subject at all.

By way of attempting to give the reader some general impression of the way people lived together in those days, and especially of the relations of the rich and poor to one another, perhaps I cannot do better than to compare society as it then was to a prodigious coach which the masses of humanity were harnessed to and dragged toilsomely along a very hilly and sandy road. The driver was hunger, and permitted no lagging, though the pace was necessarily very slow. Despite the difficulty of drawing the coach at all along so hard a road, the top was covered with passengers who never got down, even at the steepest ascents. These seats on top were very breezy and comfortable. Well up out of the dust, their occupants could enjoy the scenery at their leisure, or critically discuss the merits of the straining team. Naturally such places were in great demand and the competition for them was keen, every one seeking as the first end in life to secure a seat on the coach for himself and to leave it to his child after him. By the rule of the coach a man could leave his seat to whom he wished, but on the other hand there were so many accidents by which it might at any time be wholly lost. For all that they were so easy, the seats were very insecure, and at every sudden jolt of the coach persons were slipping out of them and falling to the ground, where they were instantly compelled to take hold of the rope and help to drag the coach on which they had before ridden so pleasantly. It was naturally regarded as a terrible misfortune to lose one's seat, and the apprehension that this might happen to them or their friends was a constant cloud upon the happiness of those who rode.

But did they think only of themselves? you ask. Was not their very luxury rendered intolerable to them by comparison with the lot of their brothers and sisters in the harness, and the knowledge that their own weight added to their toil? Had they no compassion for fellow beings from whom fortune only distinguished them? Oh, yes, commiseration was frequently expressed by those who rode for those who had to pull the coach, especially when the vehicle came to a bad place in the road, as it was constantly doing, or to a particularly steep hill. At such times, the desperate straining of the team, their agonized leaping and plunging under the pitiless lashing of hunger, the many who fainted at the rope and were trampled in the mire, made a very distressing spectacle, which often called forth highly creditable displays of feeling on the top of the coach. At such times the passengers would call down encouragingly to the toilers of the rope, exhorting them to patience, and holding out hopes of possible compensation in another world for the hardness of their lot, while others contributed to buy salves and liniments for the crippled and injured. It was agreed that it was a great pity that the coach should be so hard to pull, and there was a sense of general relief when the specially bad piece of road was gotten over. This relief was not, indeed, wholly on account of the team, for there was always some danger at these bad places of a general overturn in which all would lose their seats.

It must in truth be admitted that the main effect of the spectacle of the misery of the toilers at the rope was to enhance the passengers' sense of the value of their seats upon the coach, and to cause them to hold on to them more desperately than before. If the passengers could only have felt assured that neither they nor their friends would ever fall from the top, it is probable that, beyond contributing to the funds for liniments and bandages, they would have troubled themselves extremely little about those who dragged the coach.

I am well aware that this will appear to the men and women of the twentieth century as incredible inhumanity, but there are two facts, both very curious, which partly explain it. In the first place, it was firmly and sincerely believed that there was no other way in which Society could get along, except when the many pulled at the rope and the few rode, and not only this, but that no very radical improvement even was possible, either in the harness, the coach, the roadway, or the distribution of the toil. It had always been as it was, and it always would be so. It was a pity, but it could not be helped, and philosophy forbade wasting compassion on what was beyond remedy.

The other fact is yet more curious, consisting in a singular hallucination which those on the top of the coach generally shared, that they were not exactly like their brothers and sisters who pulled at the rope, but of finer clay, in some way belonging to a higher order of beings who might justly expect to be drawn. This seems unaccountable, but, as I once rode on this very coach and shared that very hallucination, I ought to be believed. The strangest thing about the hallucination was that those who had but just climbed up from the ground, before they had outgrown the marks of the rope upon their hands, began to fall under its influence.

As for those whose parents and grandparents before them had been so fortunate as to keep their seats on the top, the conviction they cherished of the essential difference between their sort of humanity and the common article was absolute. The effect of such a delusion in moderating fellow feeling for the sufferings of the mass of men into a distant and philosophical compassion is obvious. To it I refer as the only extenuation I can offer for the indifference which, at the period I write of, marked my own attitude toward the misery of my brothers.

In 1887 I came to my thirtieth year. Although still unmarried, I was engaged to wed Edith Bartlett. She, like myself, rode on the top of the coach. That is to say, not to encumber ourselves further with an illustration which has, I hope, served its purpose of giving the reader some general impression of how we lived then, her family was wealthy. In that age, when money alone commanded all that was agreeable and refined in life, it was enough for a woman to be rich, to have suitors, but Edith Bartlett was beautiful and graceful also.

My lady readers, I am aware, will protest at this. "Handsome she might have been," I hear them saying, "but graceful never, in the costumes which were the fashion at that period, when the head covering was a dizzy structure a foot tall, and the almost incredible extension of the skirt behind by means of artificial contrivances more thoroughly dehumanized the form than any former device of dressmakers. Fancy anyone graceful in such a costume!" The point is certainly well taken, and I can only reply that while the ladies of the twentieth century are lovely demonstrations of the effect of appropriate drapery in accenting feminine graces, my recollection of their great-grandmothers enables me to maintain that no deformity of costume can wholly disguise them.

Our marriage only waited on the completion of the house which I was building for our occupancy in one of the most desirable parts of the city, that is to say, a part chiefly inhabited by the rich. For it must be understood that the comparative desirability of different parts of Boston for residence depended then, not on natural features, but on the character of the neighboring population. Each class of nation lived by itself, in quarters of its own. A rich man living among the poor, an educated man among the uneducated, was like one living in isolation among a jealous and alien race. When the house had been begun, its completion by the winter of 1886 had been expected. The spring of the following year found it, however, yet incomplete, and my marriage still a thing of the future. The cause of a delay calculated to be particularly exasperating to an ardent lover was a series of strikes, that is to say, concerted refusals to work on the part of the bricklayers, masons, carpenters, painters, plumbers, and other trades concerned in house-building. What the specific causes of these strikes were I do not remember. Strikes had become so common at that period that people had ceased to inquire into their particular grounds. In one department of industry or another, they had been nearly incessant ever since the great business crisis of 1873. In fact, it had come to be the exceptional thing to see any class of laborers pursue their avocation steadily for more than a few months at a time.

The reader who observes the dates alluded to will of course recognize in these disturbances of industry the first and incoherent phase of the great movement which ended in the establishment of the modern industrial system with all its social consequences. This is all so plain in the retrospect that a child can understand it, but not being prophets, we of that day had no clear idea what was happening to us. What we did see was that industrially the country was in a very queer way. The relation between the workingman and the employer, between labor and capital, appeared in some unaccountable manner to have become dislocated. The working classes had quite suddenly and very generally become infected with a profound discontent with their condition, and an idea that it could be greatly bettered if they only knew how to go about it. On every side, with one accord, they preferred demands for higher pay, shorter hours, better dwellings, better educational advantages, and a share in the refinements and luxuries of life, demands which it was impossible to see the way to granting unless the world were to become a great deal richer than it then was. Though they knew something of what they wanted, they knew nothing of how to accomplish it, and the eager enthusiasm with which they thronged about anyone who seemed likely to give them any light on the subject lent sudden reputation to many would-be leaders, some of whom had little enough light to give. However chimerical the aspirations of the laboring classes might be deemed, the devotion with which they supported one another in the strikes, which were their chief weapon, and the sacrifices which they underwent to carry them out lent no doubt of their dead earnestness.

As to the final outcome of the labor troubles, which was the phrase by which the movement I have described was most commonly referred to, the opinions of the people of my class differed according to individual temperament. The sanguine argued very forcibly that it was in the very nature of things impossible that the new hopes of the workingmen could be satisfied, simply because the world had not the wherewithal to satisfy them. It was only because the masses worked very hard and lived on short commons that the race did not starve outright, and no considerable improvement in their condition was possible while the world, as a whole, remained so poor. It was not the capitalists whom the laboring men were contending with, these maintained, but the ironbound environment of humanity, and it was merely a question of the thickness of their skulls when they would discover the fact and make up their minds to endure what they could not cure.

The less sanguine admitted all this. Of course the workingmen's aspirations were impossible of fulfillment for natural reasons, but there were grounds to fear that they would not discover this fact until they had made a sad mess of society. They had the votes and the power to do so if they pleased, and their leaders meant they should. Some of these desponding observers went so far as to predict an impending social cataclysm. Humanity, they argued, having climbed to the top round of the ladder of civilization, was about to take a header into chaos, after which it would doubtless pick itself up, turn round, and begin to climb again. Repeated experiences of this sort in historic and prehistoric times possibly accounted for the puzzling bumps on the human cranium. Human history, like all great movements, was cyclical, and returned to the point of beginning. The idea of indefinite progress in a right line was a chimera of the imagination, with no analogue in nature. The parabola of a comet was perhaps a yet better illustration of the career of humanity. Tending upward and sunward from the aphelion of barbarism, the race attained the perihelion of civilization only to plunge downward once more to its nether goal in the regions of chaos.

This, of course, was an extreme opinion, but I remember serious men among my acquaintances who, in discussing the signs of the times, adopted a very similar tone. It was no doubt the common opinion of thoughtful men that society was approaching a critical period which might result in great changes. The labor troubles, their causes, course, and cure, took lead of all other topics in the public prints, and in serious conversation.

The nervous tension of the public mind could not have been more strikingly illustrated than it was by the alarm resulting from the talk of a small band of men who called themselves anarchists, and proposed to terrify the American people into adopting their ideas by threats of violence, as if a mighty nation which had but just put down a rebellion of half of its own numbers, in order to maintain its political system, were likely to adopt a new social system out of fear.

As one of the wealthy, with a large stake in the existing order of things, I naturally shared the apprehensions of my class. The particular grievance

I had against the working classes at the time of which I write, on account of the effect of their strikes in postponing my wedded bliss, no doubt lent a special animosity to my feeling toward them. . . .

II

. . . The house in which I lived had been occupied by three generations of the family of which I was the only living representative in the direct line. It was a large, ancient wooden mansion, very elegant in an old-fashioned way within, but situated in a quarter that had long since become undesirable for residence, from its invasion by tenement houses and manufactories. It was not a house to which I could think of bringing a bride, much less so dainty a one as Edith Bartlett. I had advertised it for sale, and meanwhile merely used it for sleeping purposes, dining at my club. One servant, a faithful colored man by the name of Sawyer, lived with me and attended to my few wants. One feature of the house I expected to miss greatly when I should leave it, and this was the sleeping chamber which I had built under the foundations. I could not have slept in the city at all, with its never-ceasing nightly noises, if I had been obliged to use an upstairs chamber. But to this subterranean room no murmur from the upper world ever penetrated. When I had entered it and closed the door, I was surrounded by the silence of the tomb. In order to prevent the dampness of the subsoil from penetrating the chamber the walls had been laid in hydraulic cement and were very thick, and the floor was likewise protected. In order that the room might serve also as a vault, equally proof against violence and flames, for the storage of valuables, I had roofed it with stone slabs hermetically sealed, and the outer door was of iron with a thick coating of asbestos. A small pipe, communicating with a windmill on top of the house, insured the renewal of air.

It might seem that the tenant of such a chamber ought to be able to command slumber, but it was rare that I slept well, even there, two nights in succession. So accustomed was I to wakefulness that I minded little the loss of one night's rest. A second night, however, spent in my reading chair instead of my bed, tired me out, and I never allowed myself to go longer than that without slumber, from fear of nervous disorder. From this statement it will be inferred that I had at my command some artificial means of inducing sleep in the last resort, and so in fact I had. If after two sleepless nights I found myself on the approach of the third without sensations of drowsiness, I called in Doctor Pillsbury.

He was a doctor by courtesy only, what was called in those days an "irregular" or "quack" doctor. He called himself a "Professor of Animal Magnetism." I had come across him in the course of some amateur investigations into the phenomena of animal magnetism. I don't think he knew anything about medicine, but he was certainly a remarkable mesmerist. It was for the purpose of being put to sleep by his manipulations that I used to send for him when I found a third night of sleeplessness impending. Let my nervous excitement or mental preoccupation be however great, Doctor Pillsbury never failed, after a short time, to leave me in a deep slumber, which continued till I was aroused by a reversal of the mesmerizing process. The process for awakening the sleeper was much simpler than that for putting him to sleep, and for convenience I had made Doctor Pillsbury teach Sawyer how to do it.

My faithful servant alone knew for what purpose Doctor Pillsbury visited me, or that he did so at all. Of course, when Edith became my wife I should have to tell her my secrets. I had not hitherto told her this, because there was unquestionably a slight risk in the mesmeric sleep, and I knew she would set her face against my practice. The risk, of course, was that it might become too profound and pass into a trance beyond the mesmerizer's power to break, ending in death. Repeated experiments had fully convinced me that the risk was next to nothing if reasonable precautions were exercised, and of this I hoped, though doubtingly, to convince Edith. I went directly home after leaving her, and at once sent Sawyer to fetch Doctor Pillsbury. Meanwhile I sought my subterranean sleeping chamber, and exchanging my costume for a comfortable dressing gown, sat down to read the letters by the evening mail which Sawyer had laid on my reading table.

One of them was from the builder of my new house, and confirmed what I had inferred from the newspaper item. The new strikes, he said, had postponed indefinitely the completion of the contract, as neither masters nor workmen would concede the point at issue without a long struggle. Caligula wished that the Roman people had but one neck that he might cut it off, and as I read this letter I am afraid that for a moment I was capable of wishing the same thing concerning the laboring classes of America. The return of Sawyer with the doctor interrupted my gloomy meditations.

It appeared that he had with difficulty been able to secure his services, as he was preparing to leave the city that very night. The doctor explained that since he had seen me last he had learned of a fine professional opening in a distant city, and decided to take prompt advantage of it. On my asking, in some panic, what I was to do for someone to put me to sleep, he gave me the names of several mesmerizers in Boston who, he averred, had quite as great powers as he.

Somewhat relieved on this point, I instructed Sawyer to rouse me at nine o'clock next morning, and, lying down on the bed in my dressing gown, assumed a comfortable attitude, and surrendered myself to the manipulations of the mesmerizer. Owing, perhaps, to my unusually nervous state, I was slower than common in losing consciousness, but at length a delicious drowsiness stole over me.

III and IV

"He is going to open his eyes, he had better see but one of us at first."

"Promise me, then, that you will not tell him."

The first voice was a man's, the second a woman's, and both spoke in whispers.

"I will see how he seems," replied the man.

"No, no, promise me," persisted the other.

"Let her have her way," whispered a third voice, also a woman.

"Well, well I promise, then," answered the man. "Quick, go! He is coming out of it."

There was a rustle of garments and I opened my eyes. A fine-looking man of perhaps sixty was bending over me, an expression of much benevolence mingled with great curiosity upon his features. He was an utter stranger. I raised myself on an elbow and looked around. The room was empty. I certainly had never been in it before, or one furnished like it. I looked back at my companion. He smiled.

"How do you feel?" he inquired.

"Where am I?" I demanded.

"You are in my house," was the reply.

"How came I here?"

"We will talk about that when you are stronger. Meanwhile, I beg you will feel no anxiety. You are among friends and in good hands. How do you feel?"

"A bit queerly," I replied, "but I am well, I suppose. Will you tell me how I came to be indebted to your hospitality? What has happened to me? How came I here? It was in my own house that I went to sleep."

"There will be time enough for explanations later," my unknown host replied, with a reassuring smile. "It will be better to avoid agitating talk until you are a little more yourself. Will you oblige me by taking a couple of swallows of this mixture? It will do you good. I am a physician."

I repelled the glass with my hand and sat up on the couch, although with an effort, for my head was strangely light.

"I insist upon knowing at once where I am and what you have been doing with me," I said.

"My dear sir," responded my companion, "let me beg that you will not agitate yourself. I would rather you did not insist upon explanations so soon, but if you do, I will try to satisfy you, provided you will first take this draught, which will strengthen you somewhat."

I thereupon drank what he offered me. Then he said, "It is not so simple a matter as you evidently suppose to tell you how you came here. You can tell me quite as much on that point as I can tell you. You have just been roused from a deep sleep, or, more properly, trance. So much I can tell you. You say you were in your own house when you fell into that sleep. May I ask you when that was?"

"When?" I replied. "When? Why, last evening, of course, at about ten o'clock. I left my man Sawyer orders to call me at nine o'clock. What has become of Sawyer?"

"I can't precisely tell you that," replied my companion, regarding me with a curious expression, "but I am sure that he is excusable for not being here. And now can you tell me a little more explicitly when it was that you fell into that sleep, the date, I mean?"

"Why, last night, of course. I said so, didn't I? That is, unless I have overslept an entire day. Great heavens! that cannot be possible, and yet I have an odd sensation of having slept a long time. It was Decoration Day that I went to sleep."

"Decoration Day?"

"Yes, Monday the 30th."

"Pardon me, the 30th of what?"

"Why, of this month, of course, unless I have slept into June, but that can't be."

"This month is September."

"September! You don't mean that I've slept since May! God in heaven! Why, it is incredible."

"We shall see," replied my companion. "You say that it was May 30th when you went to sleep?"

"Yes."

"May I ask of what year?"

I stared blankly at him, incapable of speech, for some moments.

"Of what year?" I feebly echoed at last.

"Yes, of what year, if you please? After you have told me that, I shall be able to tell you how long you have slept."

"It was the year 1887," I said.

My companion insisted that I should take another draught from the glass, and felt my pulse.

"My dear sir," he said, "your manner indicates that you are a man of culture, which I am aware was by no means the matter of course in your day it now is. No doubt, then, you have yourself made the observation that nothing in this world can be truly said to be more wonderful than anything else. The causes of all phenomena are equally adequate, and the results equally matter of course. That you should be startled by what I shall tell you is to be expected; but I am confident that you will not permit it to affect your equanimity unduly. Your appearance is that of a young man of barely thirty, and your bodily condition seems not greatly different from that of one just roused from a somewhat too long and profound sleep, and yet this is the tenth day of September in the year 2000, and you have slept exactly one hundred and thirteen years, three months, and eleven days." . . .

I had to admit that, if I were indeed the victim of a practical joke, its author had chosen an admirable agent for carrying out their imposition. The impressive and even eloquent manner of this man would have lent dignity to an argument that the moon was made of cheese. The smile with which I had regarded him as he advanced his trance hypothesis did not appear to confuse him in the slightest degree.

"Perhaps," I said, "you will go on and favor me with some particulars as to the circumstances under which you discovered this chamber of which you speak, and its contents. I enjoy good fiction."

"In this case," was the grave reply, "no fiction could be so strange as the truth. You must know that these many years I have been cherishing the idea of building a laboratory in the large garden beside this house, for the purpose of chemical experiments for which I have a taste. Last Thursday the excavation for the cellar was at last begun. It was completed by that night, and Friday the masons were to have come. Thursday night we had a tremendous deluge of rain, and Friday morning I found my cellar a frog pond and the walls quite washed down. My daughter, who had come out to view the disaster with me, called my attention to a corner of masonry laid bare by the crumbling away of one of the walls. I cleared a little earth from it, and, finding that it seemed part of a large mass, determined to investigate it. The workmen I sent for unearthed an oblong vault some eight feet below the surface, and set in the corner of what had evidently been the foundation walls of an ancient house. A layer of ashes and charcoal on the top of the vault showed that the house above had perished by fire. The vault itself was perfectly intact, the cement being as good as when first applied. It had a door, but this we could not force, and found entrance by removing one of the flagstones which formed the roof. The air which came up was stagnant but pure, dry and not cold. Descending with a lantern, I found myself in an apartment fitted up as a bedroom in the style of the nineteenth century. On the bed lay a young man. That he was dead and must have been dead a century was of course to be taken for granted; but the extraordinary state of preservation of the body struck me and the medical colleagues whom I had summoned with amazement. That the art of such embalming as this had ever been known we should not have believed, yet here seemed conclusive testimony that our immediate ancestors had possessed it. My medical colleagues, whose curiosity was highly excited, were at once for undertaking experiments to test the nature of the process employed, but I withheld them. My motive in so doing, at least the only motive I now need speak of, was the recollection of something I once had read about the extent to which your contemporaries had cultivated the subject of animal magnetism. It had occurred to me as just conceivable that you might be in a trance, and that the secret of your bodily integrity after so long a time was not the craft of an embalmer, but life. So extremely fanciful did this idea seem, even to me, that I did not risk the ridicule of my fellow physicians by mentioning it, but gave some other reason for postponing their experiments. No sooner, however, had they left me, than I set on foot a systematic attempt at resuscitation, of which you know the result." . . .

"I think you are going to be all right now," he said cheerily. "I should not have taken so abrupt a means to convince you of your position if your course, while perfectly excusable under the circumstances, had not rather obliged me to do so. I confess," he added, laughing, "I was a little apprehensive at one time that I should undergo what I believe you used to call a knockdown in the ninteenth century, if I did not act rather promptly. I remembered that the Bostonians of your day were famous pugilists, and thought best to lose no time. I take it you are now ready to acquit me of the charge of hoaxing you."

"If you had told me," I replied, profoundly awed, "that a thousand years instead of a hundred had elapsed since I last looked on this city, I should now believe you."

"Only a century has passed," he answered, "but many a millennium in the world's history has seen changes less extraordinary."

"And now," he added, extending his hand with an air of irresistible cordiality, "let me give you a hearty welcome to the Boston of the twentieth century and to this house. My name is Leete, Doctor Leete they call me."

"My name," I said as I shook his hand, "is Julian West."

"I am most happy in making your acquaintance, Mr. West," he responded. "Seeing that this house is built on the site of your own, I hope you will find it easy to make yourself at home in it."

After my refreshment Doctor Leete offered me a bath and a change of clothing, of which I gladly availed myself.

It did not appear that any very startling revolution in men's attire had been among the great changes my host had spoken of, for, barring a few details, my new habiliments did not puzzle me at all.

Physically, I was now myself again. But mentally, how it was with me, the reader will doubtless wonder. What were my intellectual sensations, he may wish to know, on finding myself so suddenly dropped as it were into a new world. In reply let me ask him to suppose himself suddenly, in the twinkling of an eye, transported from earth, say, to Paradise or Hades. What does he fancy would be his own experience? Would his thoughts return at once to the earth he had just left, or would he, after the first shock, well-nigh forget his former life for a while, albeit to be remembered later, in the interest excited by his new surroundings? All I can say is, that if his experience were at all like mine in the transition I am describing, the latter hypothesis would prove the correct one. The impressions of amazement and curiosity which my new surroundings produced occupied my mind, after the first shock, to the exclusion of all other thoughts. For the time the memory of my former life was, as it were, in abeyance.

No sooner did I find myself physically rehabilitated through the kind offices of my host, than I became eager to return to the housetop; and presently we were comfortably established there in easy chairs, with the city beneath and around us. After Doctor Leete had responded to numerous questions on my part, as to the ancient landmarks I missed and the new ones which had replaced them, he asked me what point of the contrast between the new and the old city struck me most forcibly.

"To speak of small things before great," I responded. "I really think that the complete absence of chimneys and their smoke is the detail that first impressed me."

"Ah!" ejaculated my companion with an air of much interest. "I had forgotten the chimneys, it is so long since they went out of use. It is nearly a century since the crude method of combustion on which you depended for heat became obsolete."

"In general," I said, "what impresses me most about the city is the material prosperity on the part of the people which its magnificence implies."

"I would give a great deal for just one glimpse of the Boston of your day," replied Doctor Leete. "No doubt, as you imply, the cities of that period were rather shabby affairs. If you had the taste to make them splendid, which I would not be so rude as to question, the general poverty resulting from your extraordinary industrial system would not have given you the means. Moreover, the excessive individualism which then prevailed was inconsistent with much public spirit. What little wealth you had seems almost wholly to have been lavished in private luxury. Nowadays, on the contrary, there is no destination of the surplus wealth so popular as the adornment of the city, which all enjoy in equal degree."

The sun had been setting as we returned to the housetop, and as we talked night descended upon the city.

"It is growing dark," said Doctor Leete. "Let us descend into the house. I want to introduce my wife and daughter to you." . . .

Doctor Leete, as well as the ladies, seemed greatly interested in my account of the circumstances under which I had gone to sleep in the underground chamber. All had suggestions to offer to account for my having been forgotten there, and the theory which we finally agreed on offers at least a plausible explanation, although whether it be in its details the true one, nobody, of course, will ever know. The layer of ashes found above the chamber indicated that the house had been burned down. Let it be supposed that the conflagration had taken place the night I fell asleep. It only remains to assume that Sawyer lost his life in the fire or by some accident connected with it, and the rest follows naturally enough. No one but he and Doctor Pillsbury either knew of the existence of the chamber or that I was in it, and Doctor Pillsbury, who had gone that night to New Orleans, had probably never heard of the fire at all. The conclusion of my friends, and of the public, must have been that I had perished in the flames. An excavation of the ruins, unless thorough, would not have disclosed the recess in the foundation walls connecting with my chamber. To be sure, if the site had been again built upon, at least immediately, such an excavation would have been necessary, but the troublous times and the undesirable character of the locality might well have prevented rebuilding. The size of the trees in the garden now occupying the site indicated, Doctor Leete said, that for more than half a century, at least, it had been open ground.

When, in the course of the evening the ladies retired, leaving Doctor Leete and myself alone, he sounded me as to my disposition for sleep, saying that if I felt like it my bed was ready for me; but if I was inclined to wakefulness nothing would please him better than to bear me company. "I am a late bird, myself," he said, "and, without suspicion of flattery, I may say that a companion more interesting than yourself could scarcely be imagined. It is decidedly not often that one has a chance to converse with a man of the nineteenth century."

Now I had been looking forward all the evening with some dread to the time when I should be alone, on retiring for the night. Surrounded by these most friendly strangers, stimulated and supported by their sympathetic interest, I had been able to keep my mental balance. Even then, however, in pauses of the conversation I had had glimpses, vivid as lightning flashes, of the horror of strangeness that was waiting to be faced when I could no longer command diversion. I knew I could not sleep that night, and as for lying awake and thinking, it argues no cowardice, I am sure, to confess that I was afraid of it. When, in reply to my host's question, I frankly told him this, he replied that it would be strange if I did not feel just so, but that I need have no anxiety about sleeping; whenever I wanted to go to bed, he would give me a dose which would insure me a sound night's sleep without fail. Next morning, no doubt, I would awake with the feeling of an old citizen.

"Before I acquire that," I replied, "I must know a little more about the sort of Boston I have come back to. You told me when we were upon the housetop that though a century only had elapsed since I fell asleep, it had been marked by greater changes in the conditions of humanity than many a previous millennium. With the city before me I could well believe that, but I am very curious to know what some of the changes have been. To make a beginning somewhere, for the subject is doubtless a large one, what solution, if any, have you found for the labor question? It was the Sphinx's riddle of the nineteenth century, and when I dropped out the Sphinx was threatening to devour society, because the answer was not forthcoming. It is well worth sleeping a hundred years to learn what the right answer was, if, indeed, you have found it yet."

"As no such thing as the labor question is known nowadays," replied Doctor Leete, "and there is no way in which it could arise, I suppose we may claim to have solved it. Society would indeed have fully deserved being devoured if it had failed to answer a riddle so entirely simple. In fact, to speak by the book, it was not necessary for society to solve the riddle at all. It may be said to have solved itself. The solution came as the result of a process of industrial evolution which could not have terminated otherwise. All that society had to do was to recognize and cooperate with that evolution, when its tendency had become unmistakable."

"I can only say," I answered, "that at the time I fell asleep no such evolution had been recognized."

"It was in 1887 that you fell into this sleep, I think you said."

"Yes, May 30, 1887."

My companion regarded me musingly for some moments. Then he observed, "And you tell me that even then there was no general recognition of the nature of the crisis which society was nearing? Of course, I fully credit your statement. The singular blindness of your contemporaries to the signs of the time is a phenomenon commented on by many of our historians, but few facts of history are more difficult for us to realize, so obvious and unmistakable as we look back seem the indications, which must also have come under your eyes, of the transformation about to come to pass. I should be intersted, Mr. West, if you would give me a little more definite idea of the view which you and men of your grade of intellect took of the state and prospects of society in 1887. You must, at least, have realized that the widespread industrial and social troubles, and the underlying dissatisfaction of all classes with the inequalities of society, and the general misery of mankind, were portents of great changes of some sort."

"We did, indeed, fully realize that," I replied. "We felt that society was dragging anchor and in danger of going adrift. Whither it would drift nobody could say, but all feared the rocks."

"Nevertheless," said Doctor Leete, "the set of the current was perfectly perceptible if you had but taken pains to observe it, and it was not toward the rocks, but toward a deeper channel."

"We had a popular proverb," I replied, "that 'hindsight is better than foresight,' the force of which I shall now, no doubt, appreciate more fully than ever. All I can say is, that the prospect was such when I went into that long sleep that I should not have been surprised had I looked down from your housetop today on a heap of charred and moss-grown ruins instead of this glorious city."

Doctor Leete had listened to me with close attention and nodded thoughtfully as I finished speaking. "What you have said," he observed, "will be regarded as a most valuable vindication of Storiot, whose account of your era has been generally thought exaggerated in its picture of the gloom and confusion of men's minds. That a period of transition like that should be full of excitement and agitation was indeed to be looked for; but seeing how plain was the tendency of the forces in operation, it was natural to believe that hope rather than fear would have been the prevailing temper of the popular mind."

"You have not yet told me what was the answer to the riddle which you found," I said. "I am impatient to know by what contradiction of natural sequence the peace and prosperity which you now seem to enjoy could have been the outcome of an era like my own."

"Excuse me," replied my host, "but do you smoke?" It was not till our cigars were lighted and drawing well that he resumed. "Since you are in the humor to talk rather than to sleep, as I certainly am, perhaps I cannot do better than to try to give you enough idea of our modern industrial system to dissipate at least the impression that there is any mystery about the process of its evolution. The Bostonians of your day had the reputation of being great askers of questions, and I am going to show my descent by asking you one to begin with. What should you name as the most prominent feature of the labor troubles of your day?"

"Why, the strikes, of course," I replied.

"Exactly. But what made the strikes so formidable?"

"The great labor organizations."

"And what was the motive of these great organizations?"

"The workmen claimed they had to organize to get their rights from the big corporations," I replied.

"That is just it," said Doctor Leete. "The organization of labor and the strikes were an effect, merely, of the concentration of capital in greater masses than had ever been known before. Before this concentration began, while as yet commerce and industry were conducted by innumerable petty concerns with small capital, instead of a small number of great concerns with vast capital, the individual workman was relatively important and independent in his relations to the employer. Moreover, when a little capital or a new idea was enough to start a man in business for himself, workingmen were constantly becoming employers and there was no hard and fast line between the two classes. Labor unions were needless then, and general strikes out of the question. But when the era of small concerns with small capital was succeeded by that of the great aggregations of capital, all this was changed. The individual laborer, who had been relatively important to the small employer, was reduced to insignificance and powerlessness over against the great corporation, while at the same time the way upward to the grade of employer was closed to him. Self-defense drove him to union with his fellows.

"The records of the period show that the outcry against the concentration of capital was furious. Men believed that it threatened society with a form of tyranny more abhorrent than it had ever endured. They believed that the great corporations were preparing for them the yoke of a baser servitude than had ever been imposed on the race, servitude not to men but to soulless machines incapable of any motive but insatiable greed. Looking back, we cannot wonder at their desperation, for certainly humanity was never confronted with a fate more sordid and hideous than would have been the era of corporate tyranny which they anticipated.

"Meanwhile, without being in the smallest degree checked by the clamor against it, the absorption of business by ever-larger monopolies continued. In the United States there was not, after the beginning of the last quarter of the century, any opportunity whatever for individual enterprise in any important field of industry, unless backed by a great capital. During the last decade of the century, such small businesses as still remained were fast-failing survivals of a past epoch, or mere parasites on the great corporations, or else existed in fields too small to attract the great capitalists. Small businesses, as far as they still remained, were reduced to the condition of rats and mice, living in holes and corners, and counting on evading notice for the enjoyment of existence. The railroads had gone on combining till a few great syndicates controlled every rail in the land. In manufactories, every important staple was controlled by a syndicate. These syndicates, pools, trusts, or whatever their name, fixed prices and crushed all competition except when combinations as vast as themselves arose. Then a struggle, resulting in a still greater consolidation, ensued. The great city bazaar crushed its country rivals with branch stores, and in the city itself absorbed its smaller rivals till the business of a whole quarter was concentrated under one roof, with a hundred former proprietors of shops serving as clerks. Having no business of his own to put his money in, the small capitalist, at the same time that he took service under the corporation, found no other investment for his money but its stocks and bonds, thus becoming doubly dependent upon it.

"The fact that the desperate popular opposition to the consolidation of business in a few powerful hands had no effect to check it proves that there must have been a strong economical reason for it. The small capitalists, with their innumerable petty concerns, had in fact yielded the field to the great aggregations of capital, because they belonged to a day of small things and were totally incompetent to the demands of an age of steam and telegraphs and the gigantic scale of its enterprises. To restore the former order of things, even if possible, would have involved returning to the day of stagecoaches. Oppressive and intolerable as was the regime of the great consolidations of capital, even its victims, while they cursed it, were forced to admit the prodigious increase of efficiency which had been imparted to the national industries, the vast economies effected by concentration of management and unity of organization, and to confess that since the new system had taken the place of the old the wealth of the world had increased at a rate before undreamed of. To be sure this vast increase had gone chiefly to make the rich richer, increasing the gap between them and the poor; but the fact remained that, as a means of producing wealth, capital had been proved efficient in proportion to its consolidation. The restoration of the old system with the subdivision of capital, if it were possible, might indeed bring back a greater equality of conditions, with more individual dignity and freedom, but it would be at the price of general poverty and the arrest of material progress.

"Was there, then, no way of commanding the services of the mighty wealth-producing principle of consolidated capital without bowing down to a plutocracy like that of Carthage? As soon as men began to ask themselves these questions, they found the answer ready for them. The movement toward the conduct of business by larger and larger aggregations of capital, the tendency toward monopolies, which had been so desperately and vainly resisted, was recognized at last, in its true significance, as a process which only needed to complete its logical evolution to open a golden future to humanity.

"Early in the last century the evolution was completed by the final consolidation of the entire capital of the nation. The industry and commerce of the country, ceasing to be conducted by a set of irresponsible corporations and syndicates of private persons at their caprice and for their profit, were entrusted to a single syndicate representing the people, to be conducted in the common interest for the common profit. The nation, that is to say, organized as the one great business corporation in which all other corporations were absorbed; it became the one capitalist in the place of all other capitalists, the sole employer, the final monopoly in which all previous and lesser monopolies were swallowed up, a monopoly in the profits and economies of which all citizens shared. The epoch of trusts had ended in The Great Trust. In a word, the people of the United States concluded to assume the conduct of their own business, just as one hundred-odd years before they had assumed the conduct of their own government, organizing now for industrial purposes on precisely the same grounds that they had then organized for political purposes. At last, strangely late in the world's history, the obvious fact was perceived that no business is so essentially the public business as the industry and commerce on which the people's livelihood depends, and that to entrust it to private persons to be managed for private profit is a folly similar in kind, though vastly greater in magnitude, to that of surrendering the functions of political government to kings and nobles to be conducted for their personal glorification."

"Such a stupendous change as you describe," said I, "did not, of course, take place without great bloodshed and terrible convulsions."

"On the contrary," replied Doctor Leete, "there was absolutely no violence. The change had been long foreseen. Public opinion had become fully ripe for it, and the whole mass of the people was behind it. There was no more possibility of opposing it by force than by argument. On the other hand the popular sentiment toward the great corporations and those identified with them had ceased to be one of bitterness, as they came to realize their necessity as a link, a transition phase, in the evolution of the true industrial system. The most violent foes of the great private monopolies were now forced to recognize how invaluable and indispensable had been their office in educating the people up to the point of assuming control of their own business. Fifty years before, the consolidation of the industries of the country under national control would have seemed a very daring experiment to the most sanguine. But by a series of object lessons, seen and studied by all men, the great corporations had taught the people an entirely new set of ideas on this subject. They had seen for many years syndicates handling revenues greater than those of states, and directing the labors of hundreds of thousands of men with an efficiency and economy unattainable in smaller operations. It had come to be recognized as an axiom that the larger the business the simpler the principles that can be applied to it; that, as the machine is truer than the hand, so the system, which in a great concern does the work of the master's eye in a small business, turns out more accurate results. Thus it came about that, thanks to the corporations themselves, when it was proposed that the nation should assume their functions, the suggestion implied nothing which seemed impracticable even to the timid. To be sure, it was a step beyond any yet taken, a broader generalization, but the very fact that the nation would be the sole corporation in the field would, it was seen, relieve the undertaking of many difficulties with which the partial monopolies had contended." . . .

Study Guide

1. In order to understand Bellamy, you must grasp two notions:
   (a) Bellamy's critique of the social and economic developments in the closing decades of the late nineteenth century; and
   (b) the device he employs (the utopian novel) in order to present his criticisms and his solutions. The first is well expressed in the imagery of the coach while the second will be found in his conversation with Doctor Leete.

2. Explain Bellamy's symbolism of the coach, the passengers, and the toilers and then proceed to follow Bellamy's attack on two cardinal tenets of late nineteenth-century conservative thought:
   (a) its fatalistic determinism; and
   (b) its commitment to the notion that the successful businessman represented "the survival of the fittest."

3. The remainder of the first chapter (pp. 82–86) is a sensitive portrayal of how many Americans in the 1880's felt about the growth of industrial

corporations, labor strife, and the variety of programs put forth in order to bring industrial peace.

4. In the fifth chapter, Bellamy offers his own program for reform, summed up in the following statement: "The solution came as the result of a process of industrial evolution which could not have terminated otherwise. All that society had to do was to recognize and cooperate with that evolution, when its tendency had become unmistakable." Note the optimism of Bellamy — that the ship (the course of historical development for the United States) will head "not toward the rocks" but "toward a deeper channel." How does Bellamy apply his optimistic view of the future to:

   (a) the conflicts between labor and capital; and
   (b) the concentration of wealth and the growth of trusts and monopoly?

5. Bellamy writes: "The epoch of trusts had ended in The Great Trust." Explain. Note also that all this will come about without strife, revolution, or violence. Can you explain why?

6. And finally:

   (a) Can you account for the immense popularity of Bellamy's book in the 1880's and 1890's? Explore.
   (b) What aspects of the current organization of American life (credit cards, social security numbers, zip codes, etc.) would Bellamy approve of and which would he disapprove of and why?

Terence V. Powderly and *Others*

LABOR UNIONS: PRINCIPLES AND TACTICS

❧{*1889, 1883, 1905*}❧   LATE NINETEENTH-CENTURY industrial development led to an enormous expansion of the number of mining, manufacturing, and construction workers in the United States — from about 3.2 million in 1870 to over 8.7 million in 1900 and some 11.5 million in 1910. Yet only a relative handful of these workers belonged to unions and most who did were skilled craftsmen, like carpenters, cigarmakers, and printers, whose work was really central to the new industrialization. Many reasons contribute to an explanation of the failure of workers to organize effectively, among them the American tradition of individualism and self-help, the lack of strong labor legislation, and the widespread resistance of manufacturers to bargaining with their employees collectively. But internal divisions within the labor movement were at least as important as any of these in holding back organization. The variety of opinion that flourished among labor leaders in these years is illustrated by the following selections. The first, drawn from *Thirty Years of Labor* (1889), the autobiography of Terence V. Powderly, describes the founding and philosophy of the Knights of Labor. Powderly, while in some respects remarkably forward-looking, represents the psychology of the pre-Civil War union leader — idealistic more than practical, concerned with a wide range of social reform rather than with the interests of wage earners narrowly conceived. The second, taken from a Senate investigation of the relations between labor and capital in 1883, presents the philosophy of the trade unionists who founded the American Federation of Labor, here articulated by Adolph Strasser, who was one of the founders of the AFL, and by Samuel Gompers, who became its first president in 1886 and guided it through most of its early history.

The inadequacies of both the Powderly and the AFL approaches from the viewpoint of unskilled workers in large industries help explain the creation of the radical Industrial Workers of the World in 1905. The ideas of the IWW are portrayed in a selection from the proceedings of the first IWW convention, held in 1905. Although not many workers accepted the anti-capitalistic doctrines of the IWW, its militancy, and still more, its insistence upon organizing workers on an industry-wide basis, had a profound long-range impact on the labor movement.

TERENCE V. POWDERLY, THE PATH I TROD

(1889)

THE FIRST committee on constitution of the order of the Knights of Labor, appointed by Mr. Stephens, consisted of representatives Robert Schilling, Chairman; Ralph Beaumont, Thomas King, T. V. Powderly, and George S. Boyle. Two members of this committee, Messrs. Schilling and Powderly, were members of the Industrial Brotherhood; and though neither one knew that the other would be present, both brought with them a sufficient supply of constitutions of the I. B. to supply the body. The adoption of the preamble was left to these two, and a glance at it will show what changes were made in the declaration of principles whose history has been traced down from year to year since it was first adopted by the National Labor Union of 1866.

The committee on constitution adopted the constitution of the Industrial Brotherhood so far as practicable. The constitution, when printed, bore the same legend on the title page as was adopted at the Rochester meeting in 1874. The following is the preamble adopted at Reading, January 3, 1878:

> "When bad men combine, the good must associate, else they will fall, one by one, an unpitied sacrifice in a contemptible struggle."

PREAMBLE

The recent alarming development and aggression of aggregated wealth, which, unless checked, will invariably lead to the pauperization and hopeless degradation of the toiling masses, render it imperative, if we desire to enjoy the blessings of life, that a check should be placed upon its power and upon unjust accumulation, and a system adopted which will secure to the laborer the fruits of his toil; and as this much-desired object can only be accomplished by the thorough unification of labor, and the united efforts of those who obey the divine injunction that "In the sweat of thy brow shalt thou eat bread," we have formed the * * * * with a view of securing the organization and direction, by co-operative effort, of the power of the industrial classes; and we submit to the world the objects sought to be accomplished by our organization, calling upon all who believe in securing "the greatest good to the greatest number" to aid and assist us: —

I. To bring within the folds of organization every department of productive industry, making knowledge a stand-point for action, and industrial and moral worth, not wealth, the true standard of individual and national greatness.

II. To secure to the toilers a proper share of the wealth that they create; more of the leisure that rightfully belongs to them; more societary advantages; more of the benefits, privileges, and emoluments of the world; in a word, all those rights and privileges necessary to make them capable of enjoying, appreciating, defending and perpetuating the blessings of good government.

III. To arrive at the true condition of the producing masses in their educational, moral, and financial condition, by demanding from the various governments the establishment of bureaus of Labor Statistics.

IV. The establishment of co-operative institutions, productive and distributive.

V. The reserving of the public lands — the heritage of the people — for the actual settler; — not another acre for railroads or speculators.

VI. The abrogation of all laws that do not bear equally upon capital and labor, the removal of unjust technicalities, delays, and discriminations in the administration of justice, and the adopting of measures providing for the health and safety of those engaged in mining, manufacturing, or building pursuits.

VII. The enactment of laws to compel chartered corporations to pay their employes weekly, in full, for labor performed during the preceding week, in the lawful money of the country.

VIII. The enactment of laws giving mechanics and laborers a first lien on their work for their full wages.

IX. The abolishment of the contract system on national, State, and municipal work.

X. The substitution of arbitration for strikes, whenever and wherever employers and employes are willing to meet on equitable grounds.

XI. The prohibition of the employment of children in workshops, mines and factories before attaining their fourteenth year.

XII. To abolish the system of letting out by contract the labor of convicts in our prisons and reformatory institutions.

XIII. To secure for both sexes equal pay for equal work.

XIV. The reduction of the hours of labor to eight per day, so that the laborers may have more time for social enjoyment and intellectual improvement, and be enabled to reap the advantages conferred by the labor-saving machinery which their brains have created.

XV. To prevail upon governments to establish a purely national circulating medium, based upon the faith and resources of the nation, and issued directly to the people, without the intervention of any system of banking corporations, which money shall be a legal tender in payment of all debts, public or private. . . .

In accepting the preamble of the Industrial Brotherhood, the convention fully realized that for the most part the reforms which were asked for in that 'preamble must one day come through political agitation and action. The chief aim of those who presented the document to the convention was to place something on the front page of the constitution which, it was hoped, every workingman would in time read and ponder over. It was their hope that by keeping those measures, so fraught with interest to the people, constantly before the eye of the worker, he would become educated in the science of politics to that extent that he would know that those things that were wrong in our political system were wrong simply because he did not attend to his political duties in a proper manner; that the righting of such things as were wrong would not be done by those who had the management of political affairs up to that time, but by himself. . . .

. . . The belief was prevalent until a short time ago among workingmen, that only the man who was engaged in manual toil could be called a workingman. The man who labored at the bench or anvil; the man who held the throttle of the engine, or delved in the everlasting gloom of the coal mine, did not believe that the man who made the drawings from which he forged, turned, or dug could be classed as a worker. The draughtsman, the time-keeper, the clerk, the school teacher, the civil engineer, the editor, the reporter, or the worst paid, most abused and illy appreciated of all toilers — woman — could not be called a worker. It was essential that the mechanics of America should know who were workers. A more wide-spread knowledge of the true definition of the word labor must be arrived at, and the true relations existing between all men who labor must be more clearly defined. Narrow prejudice, born of the injustice and oppressions of the past, must be overcome, and all who interest themselves in producing for the world's good must be made to understand that their interests are identical. All the way down the centuries of time in which the man who worked was held in bondage or servitude, either wholly or partially, he was brought directly in contact with the overseer, the superintendent, or the boss. From these he seldom received a word of kindness; indeed it was the recognized rule to treat all men who toiled as if they were of inferior clay.

The conditions which surrounded the laborer of past ages denied to him the right to dress himself and family in respectable garb. The coarsest material, made in the most untidy fashion, was considered good enough for him. Not only did his employer and overseer believe that his dress, habitation, furniture, and living should be of the coarsest, cheapest material or quality, but he also shared in that belief, and took it for granted that it was ordained of heaven; that the stay of the laborer on earth was only as a matter of convenience for his master, and that he must put up with every indignity, every insult, and privation rather than violate the rules of government, which were held up to him as being as sacred as the Ten Commandments. The holy Scriptures were quoted to show to the toiler that it was said in holy writ that he should be content with his slavish lot on earth in order that he might enjoy an eternity of bliss in a future world, through the portals of which those who held him in subjection could not get a glimpse of the happiness beyond. . . .

It was necessary to teach the laborer that it was not essential for him to grovel in the dust at the feet of a master in order to win his title deed to everlasting bliss in the hereafter; and it can not be wondered at that many who strove to better the condition of the toiler lost all respect for religion when they saw that those who affected to be the most devout worshipers at the foot of the heavenly throne, were the most tyrannical of task-masters when dealing with the poor and lowly, whose unfortunate lot was cast within the shadow of their heartless supervision. . . .

. . . Knowledge for the workingman meant that he should be able to detect the difference between the real and the sham. Whenever a learned man said that which did not appear to be just to labor, he was to be questioned, publicly questioned, as to his base of actual facts. All through the centuries toilers have erected the brass and granite monuments of the world's greatness, and have thrown up on hillside and plain the material for other homes than their own. The weary feet of toil have trodden the earth, and strong hands have formed the pillars of the bondage of old. All along the blood-stained march of the years that have flown, the struggling ones have given to earth more of richness in the sweat which fell to earth from their throbbing foreheads; the grain which lifted its head for long ages of time under the care of the toiler, has been enriched by the sweat, the blood, and the flesh of the poor, plodding men of toil. While the sun kissed to warmth and life the wheat and corn which their hands nurtured and cared for, they received the husks and stalks as their recompense for labor done. Their masters took the grain for themselves, but lifted no hand in its production. . . .

To make moral worth the standard of individual and national greatness, the men of toil had to be roused to a sense of duty; they had to be taught what their rights and duties were. To do this the hollow pretenses of the political parties, which every year came before the country and on platforms of "glittering generalities" appealed for the suffrages of the people, had to be exposed and shown to the people in their true light.

Legislation for labor came through the halls of Congress and State Legislature as a bone comes through the fingers of a stingy master to a half-starved dog, with the meat picked from it. The bone was there, but it only served the hungry one as a reminder that there should be something else. When tested before a tribunal of any kind, nearly all of the legislation of that day would be declared unconstitutional to grant a whole territory to a railroad company, or to grant a valuable franchise to a corporation, but the moment the well-picked bone that was bestowed upon the hungry dog, — Labor, — was taken to the Supreme Court, it was declared to be only a bone, nothing more. A knowledge of who his friends were in each Congress, in each session of the Legislature, was to be made the standpoint for action when the time rolled round to select new legislators. Moral worth was to be established as the future standard, and why should not the laborer do his own legislating, instead of letting it out to a second party?

This was a question which was debated long and earnestly in the councils of the workingmen, and attempt after attempt was made, with little or no success, at first, to elect workingmen to serve as representatives of the people. Those who represented, and those who were to be represented, were in need of education on the questions which concerned all alike, but it was evident that parties would never educate the people. They gave out their platforms each year, and before they were understood, they were exchanged for something else without accomplishing the reforms they aimed at.

Once every four years, in national contests, questions of political economy were brought before the people on public platform and in ward meeting, but with the sound of the candidate's voice went the thought of what he said, for it was understood that he talked for himself alone. A change had to come, and with it the placing of the preamble of the Knights of Labor in every man's hand every day of the year, to be studied not one day in every four years, but every day in every year, so that those things that were pointed out in it would be carefully bedded in the mind of man or discarded as untrue, and therefore worthless. . . .

ADOLPH STRASSER, TESTIMONY

(1883)

ADOLPH STRASSER sworn and examined.

SEN. JAMES L. PUGH: Question. Please state your residence and occupation. — Answer. I reside in New York. At present I am acting president and secretary of the Cigarmakers' International Union of America, and editor of the journal of the organization. I do not work at my trade now, but am simply acting as an officer of the Cigarmakers' International Union. . . .

SEN. HENRY W. BLAIR: It occurs to me to ask you whether it is in contemplation, as one of the ultimate purposes of the trades unions, that their funds shall be accumulated so that if, in order to prevent a panic by the excess of products being thrown upon the market, they can in future lessen production by suspending labor for a time, and maintain the laborers meanwhile out of the accumulated fund. Have your trades organizations any such idea as that? — A. The trades unions try to prevent panics, but in fact they cannot prevent them, because panics are governed by influences beyond their control.

Q. Panics result, do they not, largely from overproduction? — A. The trades unions try to make their members better consumers, thereby enlarging the home market, and at the same time to make them better producers. If we can make the working people generally better consumers we shall have no panics.

Q. But if the increase of the power of production goes on by the improvement of machinery and all that, will not your efforts be counteracted in that way? — A. Then we propose a reduction of the hours of labor. That will decrease production and will increase consumption. We hold that a man who works but eight hours a day will demand a better home than a man who works longer hours; he will not be willing to live in one or two squalid rooms; he will demand better clothes, better food, more books, more newspapers, more education, more of the commodities that labor provides, more of the world's wealth, and that will bring about a better distribution of wealth and will consequently check panics to a certain extent. I do not believe that it is possible for the trades unions to do away with panics altogether, because panics depend not merely upon the condition of the industries of the United States, but upon the condition of the industries of the whole civilized world.

Q. Do you not contemplate, in the end, the participation of all labor and of all men in the benefits of the trades unions? — A. Of course we try to extend the good of the trades unions as well as we can and as far as we can.

Q. You have some hope even of the Hottentot, have you not? — A. What do you mean by that?

Q. I mean this: That although it is a great way off, still some time every man is to be an intelligent man and an enlightened man? — A. Well, our organization does not consist of idealists.

Q. But how are you to limit the progress of civilization? It goes from land to land. Races improve continually and the elements of human nature are always the same. — A. Well, we do not control the production of the world. That is controlled by the employers, and that is a matter for them.

SEN. PUGH: Q. You are seeking to improve home matters first? — A. Yes, sir; I look to the trade I represent; I look first to cigars, to the interests of men who employ me to represent their interests.

SEN. BLAIR: I was only asking you in regard to your ultimate ends.

STRASSER: We have no ultimate ends. We are going on from day to day. We are fighting only for immediate objects — objects that can be realized in a few years.

SEN. CALL: Q. You want something better to eat and to wear, and better houses to live in? — A. Yes; we want to dress better and to live better, and become better off and better citizens generally.

SEN. BLAIR: I see that you are a little sensitive lest it should be thought that you are a mere theorizer. I do not look upon you in that light at all.

STRASSER: Well, we say in our constitution that we are opposed to theorists, and I have to represent the organization here. We are all practical men. . . .

SEN. PUGH: Q. You have furnished us with a very valuable fund of information. Have you any further statement to make of any other facts connected with this labor question? — A. Well, I have not yet proposed any remedies.

Q. We shall be glad to hear your views on that subject. — A. Well, we propose —

1. That trades unions shall be incorporated. At present there are a great many of the States that do not protect our funds. It is simply a breach of trust to use our funds improperly and we have lost considerable money in that way. . . . Therefore, we request that the Committee on Education and Labor of the Senate report . . . a bill for the incorporation of the trades unions, giving them legal rights and allowing them to have headquarters wherever they deem most fit or practicable. This, we hold, will give our organization more stability, and in that manner we shall be able to avoid strikes by perhaps settling with our employers, when otherwise we should be unable to do so, because when our employers know that we are to be legally recognized that will exercise such moral force upon them that they cannot avoid recognizing us themselves.

2. The next demand we make, one which we think will benefit labor, is the enforcement of the eight-hour law and its extension to the operation of all patents granted by the Government. By that I mean that if the Government grants a patent to anybody for any kind of invention, it shall be with the stipulation that the labor performed under that patent shall not be more than eight hours a day.

3. Our third demand is this: We claim that it is necessary to obtain information in regard to such questions as those which this committee is now investigating, and to that end we believe there is a necessity for a national bureau of labor statistics. . . . We hold that such a national bureau of labor statistics would give our legislators a great deal of information which will be very valuable to them as legislators, and we hold further that it would be a benefit, not only to labor, but, also, even greater benefit to capital, to have all this information compiled annually and distributed generally. . . .

SEN. JAMES Z. GEORGE: Q. I suppose you are aware that the power of Congress to pass acts of incorporation of the kind that you desire, outside of the District of Columbia and the Territories of the United States, is a matter of dispute? — A. Well, let Congress enact the law and let somebody who is opposed to it bring the question before the judiciary, and let it be submitted to the Supreme Court of the United States, and its constitutionality decided. I hold that it is constitutional. . . .

SEN. BLAIR: Q. The constitution of your union I suppose is similar to that of other unions in the country? — A. The difference in our organization is that it pays these various benefits which other organizations do not, because they do not accumulate the funds. We believe in the theory of accumulating a large fund, but some of the other trades do not. They have not had the experience that we have had.

Q. Capital is necessary to a successful strike, is it not? — A. Undoubtedly it is. You have to be equally as strong as the employers in order to be successful; you have to have means to hold out. . . .

SEN. GEORGE: Q. What is the feeling on the part of wage receivers generally towards their employers; is it a feeling of amity and confidence or is it a feeling of distrust? — A. In places where men receive good wages there is general good feeling; where they receive poor wages — starvation wages — there is generally bad feelings. The feeling between labor and capital depends largely on the employers. If they treat their men well and pay them fair wages, there is generally good feeling. If the employers treat their men badly and pay starvation wages, there is generally bad feeling. It depends wholly upon the employer. He has the power to encourage good feeling or the reverse.

Q. Mr. Lenz, the editor of a paper called Capital and Labor, expressed an opinion here that there was a growing socialistic feeling among the members of the trades unions; what is your observation in regard to that? — A. It is not so in the Cigar Makers' International Union. That organization does not inquire into the private opinions of a member; it takes in Democrats and Republicans, or anybody else so long as they are workers at the trade; that organization aims at practical measures, and will not allow any vague theories to be foisted upon it.

Q. Then you deny Mr. Lenz's statement so far as it relates to your organization? — A. As regards the Cigar Makers' International Union, I positively deny it. The members of that organization are simply practical men, going for practical objects that can be accomplished in a few years. . . .

SAMUEL GOMPERS, TESTIMONY
(1883)

MR. GOMPERS: . . . There is nothing in the labor movement that employers who have had unorganized laborers dread so much as organization; but organization alone will not do much unless the organization provides itself with a good fund, so that the operatives may be in a position, in the event of a struggle with their employers, to hold out. . . .

Modern industry evolves these organizations out of the existing conditions where there are two classes in society, one incessantly striving to obtain the labor of the other class for as little as possible, and to obtain the largest amount or number of hours of labor; and the members of the other class, being as individuals utterly helpless in a contest with their employers, naturally resort to combinations to improve their condition, and, in fact, they are forced by the conditions which surround them to organize for self-protection. Hence trades unions. Trades unions are not barbarous, nor are they the outgrowth of barbarism. On the contrary they are only possible where civilization exists. Trades unions cannot exist in China; they cannot exist in Russia; and in all those semi-barbarous countries they can hardly exist, if indeed they can exist at all. But they have been formed successfully in this country, in Germany, in England, and they are gradually gaining strength in France. In Great Britain they are very strong; they have been forming there for fifty years, and they are still forming, and I think there is a great future for them yet in America. Wherever trades unions have organized and are most firmly organized, there are the right [*sic*] of the people most respected. A people may be educated, but to me it appears that the greatest amount of intelligence exists in that country or that state where the people are best able to defend their rights, and their liberties as against those who are desirous of undermining them. Trades unions are organizations that instill into men a higher motive-power and give them a higher goal to look to. The hope that is too frequently deadened in their breasts when unorganized is awakened by the trades unions as it can be by nothing else. A man is sometimes reached by influences such as the church may hold out to him, but the conditions that will make him a better citizen and a more independent one are those that are evolved out of the trades union movement. That makes him a better citizen and a better man in every particular. There are only a few who can be reached by the church so as to affect their daily walk in life compared with the numbers reached by these organizations.

SEN. BLAIR: The outside public, I think, very largely confound the conditions out of which the trades union grows or is formed, with the, to the general public mind, somewhat revolutionary ideas that are embraced under the names of socialism and communism. Before you get through, won't you let us understand to what extent the trades union is an outgrowth or an evolution of those ideas, and to what extent it stands apart from them and is based on different principles? — A. The trades unions are by no means an outgrowth of socialistic or communistic ideas or principles, but the socialistic and communistic notions are evolved from some of the trades unions' movements. As to the question of the principles of communism or socialism prevailing in trades unions, there are a number of men who connect themselves as workingmen with the trades unions who may have socialistic convictions, yet who never gave them currency; who say, "Whatever ideas we may have as to the future state of society, regardless of what the end of the labor movement as a movement between classes may be, they must remain in the background, and we must subordinate our convictions, and our views and our acts to the general good that the trades-union movement brings to the laborer."

A large number of them think and act in that way. On the other hand, there are men — not so numerous now as they have been in the past — who are endeavoring to conquer the trades-union movement and subordinate it to those doctrines, and in a measure, in a few such organizations that condition of things exists, but by no means does it exist in the largest, most powerful, and best organized trades unions. There the view of which I spoke just now, the desire to improve the condition of the workingmen by and through the efforts of the trades union, is fully lived up to. I do not know whether I have covered the entire ground of the question.

SEN. GEORGE: You state, then, that the trades unions generally are not propagandists of socialistic views? — A. They are not. On the contrary, the endeavors of which I have spoken, made by certain persons to conquer the trades unions in certain cases, are resisted by the trades unionists; in the first place for the trades unions' sake, and even persons who have these convictions perhaps equally as strong as the others will yet subordinate them entirely to the good to be received directly through the trades unions. These last help those who have not such convictions to resist those who seek to use the trades unions to propagate their socialistic ideas.

Q. Do you think the trades unions have impeded or advanced the spread of socialistic views? — A. I believe that the existence of the trades-union movement, more especially where the unionists are better organized, has evoked a spirit and a demand for reform, but has held in check the more radical elements in society. . . .

INDUSTRIAL WORKERS OF THE WORLD, FIRST CONVENTION

(1905)

MR. A. M. SIMONS, of Chicago, then read the Manifesto calling for the convention, as follows:

MANIFESTO

Social relations and groupings only reflect mechanical and industrial conditions. The *great facts* of present industry are the displacement of human skill by machines and the increase of capitalist power through concentration in the possession of the tools with which wealth is produced and distributed.

Because of these facts trade divisions among laborers and competition among capitalists are alike disappearing. Class divisions grow ever more fixed and class antagonisms more sharp. Trade lines have been swallowed up in a common servitude of all workers to the machines which they tend. New machines, ever replacing less productive ones, wipe out whole trades and plunge new bodies of workers into the ever-growing army of tradeless, hopeless unemployed. As human beings and human skill are displaced by mechanical progress, the capitalists need use the workers only during that brief period when muscles and nerves respond most intensely. The moment the laborer no longer yields the maximum of profits, he is thrown upon the scrap pile, to starve alongside the discarded machine. A *dead line* has been drawn, and an age-limit established, to cross which, in this world of monopolized opportunities, means condemnation to industrial death.

The worker, wholly separated from the land and the tools, with his skill of craftsmanship rendered useless, is sunk in the uniform mass of wage slaves. He sees his power of resistance broken by craft divisions, perpetuated from out-grown industrial stages. His wages constantly grow less as his hours grow longer and monopolized prices grow higher. Shifted hither and thither by the demands of profit-takers the laborer's home no longer exists. In this helpless condition he is forced to accept whatever humiliating conditions his master may impose. He is submitted to a physical and intellectual examination more searching than was the chattel slave when sold from the auction block. Laborers are no longer classified by differences in trade skill, but the employer assigns them according to the machines to which they are attached. These divisions, far from representing differences in skill or interests among the laborers, are imposed by the employers that workers may be pitted against one another and spurred to greater exertion in the shop, and that all resistance to capitalist tyranny may be weakened by artificial distinctions.

While encouraging these outgrown divisions among the workers the capitalists carefully adjust themselves to the new conditions. They wipe out all differences among themselves and present a united front in their war upon labor. Through employers' associations, they seek to crush, with brutal force, by the injunctions of the judiciary, and the use of military power, all efforts at resistance. Or when the other policy seems more profitable, they conceal their daggers beneath the Civic Federation and hoodwink and betray those whom they would rule and exploit. Both methods depend for success upon the blindness and internal dissensions of the working class. The employers' line of battle and methods of warfare correspond to the solidarity of the mechanical and industrial concentration, while laborers still form their fighting organizations on lines of long-gone trade divisions. The battles of the past emphasize this lesson. The *textile* workers of Lowell, Philadelphia and Fall River; the *butchers* of Chicago, weakened by the disintegrating effects of trade divisions; the *machinists* on the Santa Fe, unsupported by their fellow-workers subject to the same masters; the long-struggling *miners* of Colorado, hampered by lack of unity and solidarity upon the industrial battle-field, all bear witness to the helplessness and impotency of labor as at present organized.

This worn-out and corrupt system offers no promise of improvement and adaptation. There is no silver lining to the clouds of darkness and despair settling down upon the world of labor.

This system offers only a perpetual struggle for slight relief within wage slavery. It is blind to the possibility of establishing an industrial democracy, wherein there shall be no wage slavery, but where the workers will own the tools which they operate, and the product of which they alone will enjoy.

It shatters the ranks of the workers into fragments, rendering them helpless and impotent on the industrial battle-field.

Separation of craft from craft renders industrial and financial solidarity impossible.

Union men scab upon union men; hatred of worker for worker is engendered, and the workers are delivered helpless and disintegrated into the hands of the capitalists.

Craft jealousy leads to the attempt to create trade monopolies.

Prohibitive initiation fees are established that force men to become scabs against their will. Men whom manliness or circumstances have driven from one trade are thereby fined when they seek to transfer membership to the union of a new craft.

Craft divisions foster political ignorance among the workers, thus dividing their class at the ballot box, as well as in the shop, mine and factory.

Craft unions may be and have been used to assist employers in the establishment of monopolies and the raising of prices. One set of workers are thus used to make harder the conditions of life of another body of laborers.

Craft divisions hinder the growth of class consciousness of the workers, foster the idea of harmony of interests between employing exploiter and employed slave. They permit the association of the misleaders of the workers with the capitalists in the Civic Federations, where plans are made for the perpetuation of capitalism, and the permanent enslavement of the workers through the wage system.

Previous efforts for the betterment of the working class have proven abortive because limited in scope and disconnected in action.

Universal economic evils afflicting the working class can be eradicated only by a universal working class movement. Such a movement of the working class is impossible while separate craft and wage agreements are made favoring the employer against other crafts in the same industry, and while energies are wasted in fruitless jurisdiction struggles which serve only to further the personal aggrandizement of union officials.

A movement to fulfill these conditions must consist of one great industrial union embracing all industries, — providing for craft autonomy locally, industrial autonomy internationally, and working class unity generally.

It must be founded on the class struggle, and its general administration must be conducted in harmony with the recognition of the irrepressible conflict between the capitalist class and the working class.

It should be established as the economic organization of the working class, without affiliation with any political party.

All power should rest in a collective membership.

Local, national and general administration, including union labels, buttons, badges, transfer cards, initiation fees, and per capita tax should be uniform throughout.

All members must hold membership in the local, national or international union covering the industry in which they are employed, but transfers of membership between unions, local, national or international, should be universal.

Workingmen bringing union cards from industrial unions in foreign countries should be freely admitted into the organization.

The general administration should issue a publication representing the entire union and its principles which should reach all members in every industry at regular intervals.

A *central defense fund,* to which all members contribute equally, should be established and maintained.

All workers, therefore, who agree with the principles herein set forth, will meet in convention at Chicago the 27th day of June, 1905, for the purpose of forming an economic organization of the working class along the lines marked out in this Manifesto. . . .

DEL. RICHTER: Mr. Chairman and Fellow Delegates: If the sending of delegates to this convention indicates anything, it shows that there is a desire among the working class to free itself from oppression, and the response to the call for this convention shows that it expects that this convention will express through its declaration of principles the situation as it exists to-day as far as the capitalist class and the working class are concerned, and that it will point out a policy by which it may generate strength enough to free itself from wage slavery. Now, fellow workmen, the Preamble offered by your committee starts out, "The working class and the employing class have nothing in common." It appears to me that the paragraph as it stands has no sense and is untrue. It does not say anything about such matters as we should expect in the Preamble of this new organization which has set itself the task of freeing the working class. For this reason I move that we strike out that clause and substitute the following: "Labor is necessary to satisfy the needs of society. Therefore every able person should do some useful work for its maintenance. The means of production and distribution have grown to such a size and have become so costly that only a few can own them, as long as private ownership thereof exists, condemning the rest of mankind to obtain an existence by selling their labor power to those few. The private ownership of the land and modern tools of production has turned them into means of oppression and exploitation, forcing the wage earning class to suffer want and misery and insecurity of employment, while the increasing profit of the capitalist class secures to them a life of idleness and luxury." I move that this be substituted for the first paragraph of the Preamble as submitted by the Committee.

DEL. SCHATKE: Mr. Chairman and Fellow Delegates —

THE CHAIRMAN: Just a moment. There is no second to the substitute offered for paragraph one. The debate occurs on the original motion, which is to adopt paragraph one as reported by the Committee on Constitution.

DEL. SCHATKE: Mr. Chairman and Fellow Delegates: There has been objection offered against this paragraph which says that the capitalist class and the working class have nothing in common. Have we anything in common? I was once in a mining town and I came to the post office. There were two little children playing out of doors. They enjoyed their play very much. A man came out from the post office and grabbed one child by the hand and said, "You have no business to play with this child." The child commenced to cry, and said, "Why, I love that child." "Well," said the man, "don't you know that that child's father was a miner and your father is a business man and also the postmaster?" Now, haven't those two classes something in common? Isn't it frightful when the miners and the workingmen down in the gutter live in those hovels and they have got to pay rent for them? Haven't they got something in common when the little children have to go to work in the cotton mills in the eastern cities and work long hours watching the looms and get $2.80 in two weeks, and the children of the rich spend thousands of dollars in luxuries and for flowers, while the workingmen who produce all wealth that these people enjoy have to live in poverty and degradation? Isn't that a beautiful communism? How do you like that kind of communism. I ask that this motion shall be adopted.

DEL. GILBERT: I would like to say, Mr. Chairman and Fellow Delegates, that it is quite impossible for us to split hairs and to analyze with fine accuracy the scientific interpretation of this or any other document. But one of the things that pleased me particularly about that Preamble was this, that while possibly it was not stated in absolutely scientific terms, it seems to me it was stated in the terse, ordinary language of the plain people, and that is what we want. We do not want to put out from this convention an academic statement. We want simply to put out a statement that will carry conviction to the mind of the humble toiler, and when you talk about there being nothing in common between them the average common horse sense knows that. Therefore I would move you the adoption of that first clause, without wasting the time of the convention. (Seconded.)

THE CHAIRMAN: The motion is out of order.

DEL. WHITE: I have heard a good many Preambles read, and this is the first time I have seen a Preamble that has not got the ear marks of too many professors. The language sounds good to me. I believe we can go before the working class of this country with it and that they can understand the report without having to get dictionaries and find out what is meant. What we want is to go before the common people with a Preamble so plain that every honest Tom, Dick and Harry, including ourselves, can understand it. I am in favor of the entire Preamble as reported by the Committee. . . .

DEL. DE LEON: The paragraph, if you will let me read it over again, says: "Between these two classes a struggle must go on until all the toilers come together on the political as well as the industrial field and take and hold that which they produce by their labor, through an economic organization of the working class without affiliation with any political party." That is the language as offered. I wish to speak for the clause as a member of that committee, and against the proposed substitute. The argument has been made by Delegate Simons that that is contradictory; that this clause proposes political action without a political party. Now, let me invite your attention to the Manifesto, to the promise and invitation under which this convention is gathered, and under the terms of which it is convened. You will find on page four of this issue of this form of the Manifesto (holding up a copy), this passage: "Craft divisions foster political ignorance among the workers, thus DIVIDING THAT CLASS AT THE BALLOT BOX as well as in shop, mine and factory";

and on the next page of the Manifesto you find this clause: "It (this organization) should be established as the economic organization of the working class WITHOUT AFFILIATION WITH ANY POLITICAL PARTY." If to recognize the necessity of uniting the working people on the political field, and in the same breath to say that the taking and the holding of the things that the people produce can be done without affiliation with any political party — if that is a contradiction; if it can be said that these two clauses in this proposed paragraph are contradictory, then the contradiction was advocated by Delegate Simons himself, who was one of the signers of this Manifesto, (Applause). Here you have his signature (holding up the page of the Manifesto with Simon's signature). But, delegates, there is no contradiction, none whatever; and I consider that these two passages in the Manifesto, if any one thing was to be picked out more prominent than any other, are indeed significant of the stage of development, genuine capitalistic development in America. This Manifesto enumerates a series of evils that result from the present craft division: — it shatters the ranks of the workers and renders industrial and financial solidarity impossible; union men scab it upon one another; jealousy is created, and prohibitive initiation fees are adopted; "craft divisions foster political ignorance among the working class, thus dividing them at the ballot box." If this, the division of the working class on the political field, is an evil, then it follows that unity of the working people on the political field is a thing to be desired. And so it is; and this clause in the Preamble correctly so states it. . . .

I know not a single exception of any party candidate, ever elected upon a political platform of the emancipation of the working class, who did not sell them out as fast as elected. (Applause). Now, it may be asked, "that being so, why not abolish altogether the political movement? Why, at all, unite the workers on the political field?" The aspiration to unite the workers upon the political field is an aspiration in line and in step with civilization. Civilized man, when he argues with an adversary, does not start with clenching his fist and telling him, "smell this bunch of bones." He does not start by telling him, "feel my biceps." He begins with arguing; physical force by arms is the last resort. That is the method of the civilized man, and the method of civilized man is the method of civilized organization. The barbarian begins with physical force; the civilized man ends with that, when physical force is necessary. (Applause). Civilized man will always here in America give a chance to peace; he will, accordingly, proceed along the lines that make peace possible. But civilized man, unless he is a visionary, will know that unless there is Might behind your Right, your Right is something to laugh at.

And the thing to do, consequently, is to gather behind that ballot, behind that united political movement, the Might which is alone able, when necessary, to "take and hold." Without the working people are united on the political field; without the delusion has been removed from their minds that any of the issues of the capitalist class can do for them anything permanently, or even temporarily; without the working people have been removed altogether from the mental thraldom of the capitalist class, from its insidious influence, there is no possibility of your having those conditions under which they can really organize themselves economically in such a way as to "take and hold." And after those mental conditions are generally established, there needs something more than the statement to "take and hold"; something more than a political declaration, something more than the permission of the capitalist political inspectors to allow this or that candidate to filter through. You then need the industrial organization of the working class, so that, if the capitalist should be foolish enough in America to defeat, to thwart the will of the workers expressed by the ballot — I do not say "the will of the workers, as returned by the capitalist election inspectors," but the will of the people as expressed at the ballot box — then there will be a condition of things by which the working class can absolutely cease production, and thereby starve out the capitalist class, and render their present economic means and all their preparations for war absolutely useless. . . .

DEL. BARTLETT: I am in favor of referring back to the Committee for this reason: I think the working class has been sufficiently hypnotized in regard to what true working class politics are. The prevailing opinion exists among the workingmen that going up to a capitalist ballot box and dropping a piece of paper in it means working class politics. I want to tell you that that is the most contemptible lie that was ever told you, for this reason: To imagine that you could go into a capitalist hall of Congress and by a vote take possession of their property. Isn't that a piece of rank nonsense? You might just as well go over to the Board of Directors' room of the North Western Railway Company and cast a vote to take possession of their property. Do you think they would hand it over to you? No. They will never do anything like that. So get that microbe out of your head. What we are up against you all know pretty well. There are certain reasons why we can't tell the truth right here.

A DELEGATE: No, sir, none.

DEL. BARTLETT: But the fact that stares us in the face is that we have a struggle ahead of us, and this struggle is going to be a bitter one, and the clearer we can get, the nearer to the earth we can get, the better it will be for your carcasses. Now, what are true working class politics? Is it that you are voting at a capitalist ballot box? No. True, working class politics means this? That in so far as the working class is organized to take possession and enforce their demands on the economic field, working class politics grows co-extensively with this economic power, and all the voting that you fellows have to do is among yourselves as to what plan of action you will take against this capitalist class, and time will reveal to you fellows the rank nonsense of voting at a capitalist ballot box. You can vote better probably with machine guns and hand grenades in the course of time.

(Manifestations of disapproval in various parts of the hall.)

DEL. BARTLETT: I am in favor of referring that resolution back to the Committee in order that they can strike out all of that confusing language about political action at the capitalist ballot box and all that stuff, and bring back in place of that clause a plain statement of what the working class is going to do on the economic field. I thank you. . . .

THE CHAIRMAN: It has been regularly moved and seconded that the Preamble be adopted in its entirety.

A DELEGATE: As amended?

THE CHAIRMAN: Yes, the whole Preamble. Those in favor of adopting this Preamble as amended will signify it by saying aye. Contrary, no. The Preamble is adopted as amended. (Great applause.)

PREAMBLE

The working class and the employing class have nothing in common. There can be no peace so long as hunger and want are found among millions of working people and the few, who make up the employing class, have all the good things of life.

Between these two classes a struggle must go on until all the toilers come together on the political, as well as on the industrial field, and take and hold that which they produce by their labor, through an economic organization of the working class without affiliation with any political party.

The rapid gathering of wealth and the centering of the management of industries into fewer and fewer hands make the trades union unable to cope with the ever-growing power of the employing class, because the trades unions foster a state of things which allows one set of workers to be pitted against another set of workers in the same industry, thereby helping defeat one another in wage wars. The trades unions aid the employing class to mislead the workers into the belief that the working class have interests in common with their employers.

These sad conditions can be changed and the interests of the working class upheld by an organization formed in such a way that all its members in any one industry, or in all industries, if necessary, cease work whenever a strike or lockout is on in any department thereof, thus making an injury to one an injury to all. . . .

Study Guide

1. Read the introduction and pay particular attention to the variations in union philosophy represented by the Knights of Labor (pp. 101–106); the American Federation of Labor (pp. 106–111); and the International Workers of the World (pp. 111–120). The selections document in greater detail these basic differences in labor philosophy.

2. Take note, at the outset, of the history of the Knights, going back to the National Labor Union and the Industrial Brotherhood. Note, too, the dualistic view of society in the quotation preceding the preamble — an important theme in the Knights's social philosophy and why certain professions (stockbrokers and liquor salesmen, for example) were not permitted to join the organization.

3. The preamble of the Knights' constitution contains some fifteen principles (means and goals) of the movement — some more consequential than others. Of particular importance in the operational aspects of the organization were Nos. IV and X, although the latter was not always adhered to. Otherwise, what evidence in these principles is there that the Knights's program was broadly idealistic and reformist in character?

4. Continuing, summarize the attitudes of the Knights toward:
   (a) politics;
   (b) the "brotherhood" of laborers;
   (c) the laborer's status in society; and
   (d) the need for the Knights of Labor.

5. Adolph Strasser and Samuel Gompers, of course, do not share Powderly's labor philosophy. Begin by summarizing Strasser's views on the following:
   (a) the role of workers in either causing or solving financial depressions;
   (b) the future of labor unions;
   (c) social and economic problems in foreign countries;
   (d) the "ultimate ends" of labor unions; and
   (e) the role of abstract theory in labor unions.

6. In reviewing Strasser's list of demands, do the following:
   (a) outline them; and
   (b) relate them to the labor philosophy he enunciated in his previous testimony.

7. Strasser's closing testimony reveals the hardheaded practicality that dominated the leaders of the American Federation of Labor. Explore and illustrate.

8. Shrewdly and sincerely, Gompers stresses a particular view of labor unionism in his testimony. Summarize his views on:
   (a) the purpose of trade unions;
   (b) their relationship to society generally;
   (c) their influence on their membership; and
   (d) their relationship to and impact upon radicalism and utopianism.

9. Turning to the International Workers of the World, note, throughout the selection, the sharp differences in their conceptualization of the problem of labor with that of the Knights, Strasser, and Gompers. Find evidence in their manifesto for their belief in:
   (a) the growing concentration of industry;
   (b) class conflict;
   (c) the need for *industrial* unionism;
   (d) the growing plight of the workingman;
   (e) the inadequacy of craft unions; and
   (f) a need for a revolutionary solution to the problems of labor.

10. What kind of organization do they envisage? How many of these notions would the Knights or the leadership of the American Federation of Labor accept?

11. Turning to the debate on the manifesto, answer the following:
   (a) What appears to be the purpose of Delegate Richter's proposed amendment and what comments on it are made by Delegates Schatke, Gilbert, and White?
   (b) What position is taken by Delegate (Daniel) De Leon (later the head of the Marxist Socialist Workers Party) on the unity of the labor movement and on the efficacy of political action?
   (c) What is the position of Delegate Bartlett on political action?

12. What stand is taken in the preamble on:
   (a) class conflict;
   (b) political action;
   (c) economic action; and
   (d) trade unions?

13. The very last paragraph contains the essence of what the IWW would substitute for trade unions. Explain.

14. In review:
   (a) Where in a spectrum of varying degrees of liberalism would you put each of these labor organizations?

(b) What is the attitude of each toward the following:
(1) capitalism;
(2) strikes;
(3) arbitration and conciliation;
(4) political action; and
(5) class struggle?

Andrew Carnegie

RESPONSIBILITIES OF THE RICH

{1889} THE popularity of works of protest like *Looking Backward* indicates clearly the extent to which there was a deep public concern about the tremendous changes that were rocking the foundations of American society in the last decades of the nineteenth century. Thoughtful persons were deeply disturbed by the concentration of so much economic power in huge corporations and the resulting concentrations of wealth and social influence in the hands of new multimillionaire business and financial tycoons. Masses of ordinary citizens, moved by a complex mixture of jealousy, fear, admiration, and awe, were confused and irritated when they thought about these new institutions and the men who ran them.

However, it would be wrong to assume that wealth and individual power were without defenders. The traditional American faith in freedom and individual enterprise of course played into the hands of those who wished to let well enough alone. The vogue of the British philosopher Herbert Spencer (1820-1903), who opposed even such minor interferences with the operation of "natural" forces as the public school system and the government-operated post office, reflects the continuing influence of this point of view. The relatively high standard of living in the United States and the continuing belief that America was the land of opportunity *par excellence* also encouraged people to look tolerantly on the power and wealth of the great leaders of business. When the Baptist preacher Russell Conwell (1843-1925) pointed out, in his oft-repeated address, *Acres of Diamonds,* that the accumulation of wealth was a Christian duty, he never lacked an appreciative audience.

But the most striking defense of the new order was that of Andrew Carnegie (1835-1919), himself one of the new economic potentates. His essay "Wealth," which appeared in the *North American Review* in 1889, took actually a compromise position. The millionaire's unquestioned right to accumulate a great fortune he argued, was balanced by his obligation to arrange for its disposition in socially useful ways. Although the *Review's* circulation was tiny, the message of this essay soon reached a gigantic audience. It was published in England, and in a short time magazines and newspapers all over the western world were discussing it. One may almost trace the history of modern philanthropy from this article.

THE GOSPEL OF WEALTH

THE PROBLEM OF THE ADMINISTRATION OF WEALTH

THE problem of our age is the proper administration of wealth, that the ties of brotherhood may still bind together the rich and poor in harmonious relationship. The conditions of human life have not only been changed, but revolutionized, within the past few hundred years. In former days there was little difference between the dwelling, dress, food, and environment of the chief and those of his retainers. The Indians are today where civilized man then was. When visiting the Sioux, I was led to the wigwam of the chief. It was like the others in external appearance, and even within the difference was trifling between it and those of the poorest of his braves. The contrast between the palace of the millionaire and the cottage of the laborer with us to-day measures the change which has come with civilization. This change, however, is not to be deplored, but welcomed as highly beneficial. It is well, nay, essential, for the progress of the race that the houses of some should be homes for all that is highest and best in literature and the arts, and for all the refinements of civilization, rather than that none should be so. Much better this great irregularity than universal squalor. Without wealth there can be no Maecenas. The "good old times" were not good old times. Neither master nor servant was as well situated then as to-day. A relapse to old conditions would be disastrous to both — not the least so to him who serves — and would sweep away civilization with it. But whether the change be for good or ill, it is upon us, beyond our power to alter, and, therefore, to be accepted and made the best of. It is a waste of time to criticize the inevitable.

It is easy to see how the change has come. One illustration will serve for almost every phase of the cause. In the manufacture of products we have the whole story. It applies to all combinations of human industry, as stimulated and enlarged by the inventions of this scientific age. Formerly, articles were manufactured at the domestic hearth, or in small shops which formed part of the household. The master and his apprentices worked side by side, the latter living with the master, and therefore subject to the same conditions. When these apprentices rose to be masters, there was little or no change in their mode of life, and they, in turn, educated succeeding apprentices in the same routine. There was, substantially, social equality, and even political equality, for those engaged in industrial pursuits had then little or no voice in the State.

The inevitable result of such a mode of manufacture was crude articles at high prices. To-day the world obtains commodities of excellent quality at prices which even the preceding generation would have deemed incredible. In the commercial world similar causes have produced similar results, and the race is benefited thereby. The poor enjoy what the rich could not before afford. What were the luxuries have become the necessaries of life. The laborer has now more comforts than the farmer had a few generations ago. The farmer has more luxuries than the landlord had, and is more richly clad and better housed. The landlord has books and pictures rarer and appointments more artistic than the king could then obtain.

The price we pay for this salutary change is, no doubt, great. We assemble thousands of operatives in the factory, and in the mine, of whom the employer can know little or nothing, and to whom he is little better than a myth. All intercourse between them is at an end. Rigid castes are formed, and, as usual, mutual ignorance breeds mutual distrust. Each caste is without sympathy with the other, and ready to credit anything disparaging in regard to it. Under the law of competition, the employer of thousands is forced into the strictest economies, among which the rates paid to labor figure prominently, and often there is friction between the employer and the employed, between capital and labor, between rich and poor. Human society loses homogeneity.

The price which society pays for the law of competition, like the price it pays for cheap comforts and luxuries, is also great; but the advantages of this law are also greater still than its cost — for it is to this law that we owe our wonderful material development, which brings improved conditions in its train. But, whether the law be benign or not, we must say of it, as we say of the change in the conditions of men to which we have referred: It is here; we cannot evade it; no substitutes for it have been found; and while the law may be sometimes hard for the individual, it is best for the race, because it insures the survival of the fittest in every department. We accept and welcome, therefore, as conditions to which we must accommodate ourselves, great inequality of environments; the concentration of business, industrial and commercial, in the hands of a few; and the law of competition between these, as being not only beneficial, but essential to the future progress of the race. Having accepted these, it follows that there must be great scope for the exercise of special ability in the merchant and in the manufacturer who has to conduct affairs upon a great scale. That this talent for organization and management is rare among men is proved by the fact that it invariably secures enormous rewards for its possessor, no matter where or under what laws or conditions. The experienced in affairs always rate the MAN whose services can be obtained as a partner as not only the first consideration, but such as render the question of his capital scarcely worth considering: for able men soon create capital; in the hands of those without the special talent required, capital soon takes wings. Such men become interested in firms or corporations using millions; and, estimating only simple interest to be made upon the capital invested, it is inevitable that their income must exceed their expenditure and that they must, therefore, accumulate wealth. Nor is there any middle ground which such men can occupy, because the great manufacturing or commercial concern which does not earn at least interest upon its capital soon becomes bankrupt. It must either go forward or fall behind; to stand still is impossible. It is a condition essential to its successful operation that it should be thus far profitable, and even that, in addition to interest on capital, it should make profit. It is a law, as certain as any of the others named, that men possessed of this peculiar talent for affairs, under the free play of economic forces must, of necessity, soon be in receipt of more revenue than can be juiciously expended upon themselves; and this law is as beneficial for the race as the others.

Objections to the foundations upon which society is based are not in order, because the condition of the race is better with these than it has been with any other which has been tried. Of the effect of any new substitutes proposed we cannot be sure. The Socialist or Anarchist who seeks to overturn present conditions is to be regarded as attacking the foundation upon which civilization itself rests, for civilization took its start from the day when the capable, industrious workman said to his incompetent and lazy fellow, "If thou dost not sow, thou shalt not reap," and thus ended primitive Communism by separating the drones from the bees. One who studies this subject will soon be brought face to face with the conclusion that upon the sacredness of property civilization itself depends — the right of the laborer to his hundred dollars in the savings-bank, and equally the legal right of the millionaire to his millions. Every man must be allowed "to sit under his own vine and fig-tree, with none to make afraid," if human society is to advance, or even to remain so far advanced as it is. To those who propose to substitute Communism for this intense Individualism, the answer therefore is: The race has tried that. All progress from that barbarous day to the present time has resulted from its displacement. Not evil, but good, has come to the race from the accumulation of wealth by those who have had the ability and energy to produce it. But even if we admit for a moment that it might be better for the race to discard its present foundation, Individualism, — that is a nobler ideal that man should labor, not for himself alone, but in and for a brotherhood of his fellows, and share with them all in common, realizing Swedenborg's idea of heaven, where, as he says, the angels derive their happiness, not from laboring for self, but for each other, — even admit all this, and a sufficient answer is, This is not evolution, but revolution. It necessitates the changing of human nature itself — a work of eons, even if it were good to change it, which we cannot know.

It is not practicable in our day or in our age. Even if desirable theoretically, it belongs to another and long-succeeding sociological stratum. Our duty is with what is practicable now — with the next step possible in our day and generation. It is criminal to waste our energies in endeavoring to uproot, when all we can profitably accomplish is to bend the universal tree of humanity a little in the direction most favorable to the production of good fruit under existing circumstances. We might as well urge the destruction of the highest existing type of man because he failed to reach our ideal as to favor the destruction of Individualism, Private Property, the Law of Accumulation of Wealth, and the Law of Competition; for these are the highest result of human experience, the soil in which society, so far, has produced the best fruit. Unequally or unjustly, perhaps, as these laws sometimes operate, and imperfect as they appear to the Idealist, they are, nevertheless, like the highest type of man, the best and most valuable of all that humanity has yet accomplished.

We start, then, with a condition of affairs under which the best interests of the race are promoted, but which inevitably gives wealth to the few. Thus far, accepting conditions as they exist, the situation can be surveyed and pronounced good. The question then arises, — and if the foregoing be correct, it is the only question with which we have to deal, — What is the proper mode of administering wealth after the laws upon which civilization is founded have thrown it into the hands of the few? And it is of this great question that I believe I offer the true solution. It will be understood that fortunes are here spoken of, not moderate sums saved by many years of effort, the returns from which are required for the comfortable maintenance and education of families. This is not wealth, but only competence, which it should be the aim of all to acquire, and which it is for the best interests of society should be acquired.

There are but three modes in which surplus wealth can be disposed of. It can be left to the families of the decedents; or it can be bequeathed for public purposes; or, finally, it can be administered by its possessors during their lives. Under the first and second modes most of the wealth of the world that has reached the few has hitherto been applied. Let us in turn consider each of these modes. The first is the most injudicious. In monarchical countries, the estates and the greatest portion of the wealth are left to the first son, that the vanity of the parent may be gratified by the thought that his name and title are to descend unimpaired to succeeding generations. The condition of this class in Europe to-day teaches the failure of such hopes or ambitions. The successors have become impoverished through their follies, or from the fall in the value of land. Even in Great Britain the strict law of entail has been found inadequate to maintain an hereditary class. Its soil is rapidly passing into the hands of the stranger. Under republican institutions the division of property among the children is much fairer; but the question which forces itself upon thoughtful men in all lands is, Why should men leave great fortunes to their children? If this is done from affection, is it not misguided affection? Observation teaches that, generally speaking, it is not well for the children that they should be so burdened. Neither is it well for the State. Beyond providing for the wife and daughters moderate sources of income, and very moderate allowances indeed, if any, for the sons, men may well hesitate; for it is no longer questionable that great sums bequeathed often work more for the injury than for the good of the recipients. Wise men will soon conclude that, for the best interests of the members of their families, and of the State, such bequests are an improper use of their means.

It is not suggested that men who have failed to educate their sons to earn a livelihood shall cast them adrift in poverty. If any man has seen fit to rear his sons with a view to their living idle lives, or, what is highly commendable, has instilled in them the sentiment that they are in a position to labor for public ends without reference to pecuniary considerations, then, of course, the duty of the parent is to see that such are provided for in moderation. There are instances of millionaires' sons unspoiled by wealth, who, being rich, still perform great services to the community. Such are the very salt of the earth, as valuable as, unfortunately, they are rare. It is not the exception, however, but the rule that men must regard; and, looking at the usual result of enormous sums conferred upon legatees, the thoughtful man must shortly say, "I would as soon leave to my son a curse as the almighty dollar," and admit to himself that it is not the welfare of the children, but family pride, which inspires these legacies.

As to the second mode, that of leaving wealth at death for public uses, it may be said that this is only a means for the disposal of wealth, provided a man is content to wait until he is dead before he becomes of much good in the world. Knowledge of the results of legacies bequeathed is not calculated to inspire the brightest hopes of much posthumous good being accomplished by them. The cases are not few in which the real object sought by the testator is not attained, nor are they few in which his real wishes are thwarted. In many cases the bequests are so used as to become only monuments of his folly. It is well to remember that it requires the exercise of not less ability than that which acquires it, to use wealth so as to be really beneficial to the community. Besides this, it may fairly be said that no man is to be extolled for doing what he cannot help doing, nor is he to be thanked by the community to which he only leaves wealth at death. Men who leave vast sums in this way may fairly be thought men who would not have left it at all had they been able to take it with them. The memories of such cannot be held in grateful remembrance, for there is no grace in their gifts. It is not to be wondered at that such bequests seem so generally to lack the blessing.

The growing disposition to tax more and more heavily large estates left at death is a cheering indication of the growth of a salutary change in public opinion. The State of Pennsylvania now takes — subject to some exceptions — one tenth of the property left by its citizens. The budget presented in the British Parliament the other day proposes to increase the death duties; and, most significant of all, the new tax is to be a graduated one. Of all forms of taxation this seems the wisest. Men who continue hoarding great sums all their lives, the proper use of which for public ends would work good to the community from which it chiefly came, should be made to feel that the community, in the form of the State, cannot thus be deprived of its proper share. By taxing estates heavily at death the State marks its condemnation of the selfish millionaire's unworthy life.

It is desirable that nations should go much further in this direction. Indeed, it is difficult to set bounds to the share of a rich man's estate which should go at his death to the public through the agency of the State, and by all means such taxes should be graduated, beginning at nothing upon moderate sums to dependents, and increasing rapidly as the amounts swell, until of the millionaire's hoard, as of Shylock's, at least

> The other half
> Comes to the privy coffer of the State.

This policy would work powerfully to induce the rich man to attend to the administration of wealth during his life, which is the end that society should always have in view, as being by far the most fruitful for the people. Nor need it be feared that this policy would sap the root of enterprise and render men less anxious to accumulate, for, to the class whose ambition it is to leave great fortunes and be talked about after their death, it will attract even more attention, and, indeed, be a somewhat nobler ambition, to have enormous sums paid over to the State from their fortunes.

There remains, then, only one mode of using great fortunes; but in this we have the true antidote for the temporary unequal distribution of wealth, the reconciliation of the rich and the poor — a reign of harmony, another ideal, differing, indeed, from that of the Communist in requiring only the further evolution of existing conditions, not the total overthrow of our civilization. It is founded upon the present most intense Individualism, and the race is prepared to put it in practice by degrees whenever it pleases. Under its sway we shall have an ideal State, in which the surplus wealth of the few will become, in the best sense, the property of the many, because administered for the common good; and this wealth, passing through the hands of the few, can be made a much more potent force for the elevation of our race than if distributed in small sums to the people themselves. Even the poorest can be made to see this, and to agree that great sums gathered by some of their fellow-citizens and spent for public purposes, from which the masses reap the principal benefit, are more valuable to them than if scattered among themselves in trifling amounts through the course of many years.

If we consider the results which flow from the Cooper Institute, for instance, to the best portion of the race in New York not possessed of means, and compare these with those which would have ensued for the good of the masses from an equal sum distributed by Mr. Cooper in his lifetime in the form of wages, which is the highest form of distribution, being for work done and not for charity, we can form some estimate of the possibilities for the improvement of the race which lie embedded in the present law of the accumulation of wealth. Much of this sum, if distributed in small quantities among the people, would have been wasted in the indulgence of appetite, some of it in excess, and it may be doubted whether even the part put to the best use, that of adding to the comforts of the home, would have yielded results for the race, as a race, at all comparable to those which are flowing and are to flow from the Cooper Institute from generation to generation. Let the advocate of violent or radical change ponder well this thought.

We might even go so far as to take another instance — that of Mr. Tilden's bequest of five millions of dollars for a free library in the city of New York; but in referring to this one cannot help saying involuntarily: How much better if Mr. Tilden had devoted the last years of his own life to the proper administration of this immense sum; in which case neither legal contest nor any other cause of delay could have interfered with his aims. But let us assume that Mr. Tilden's millions finally become the means of giving to this city a noble public library, where the treasures of the world contained in books will be open to all forever, without money and without price. Considering the good of that part of the race which congregates in and around Manhattan Island, would its permanent benefit have been better promoted had these millions been allowed to circulate in small sums through the hands of the masses? Even the most strenuous advocate of Communism must entertain a doubt upon this subject. Most of those who think will probably entertain no doubt whatever.

Poor and restricted are our opportunities in this life, narrow our horizon, our best work most imperfect; but rich men should be thankful for one inestimable boon. They have it in their power during their lives to busy themselves in organizing benefactions from which the masses of their fellows will derive lasting advantage, and thus dignify their own lives. The highest life is probably to be reached, not by such imitation of the life of Christ as Count Tolstoi gives us, but, while animated by Christ's spirit, by recognizing the changed conditions of this age, and adopting modes of expressing this spirit suitable to the changed conditions under which we live, still laboring for the good of our fellows, which was the essence of his life and teaching, but laboring in a different manner.

This, then, is held to be the duty of the man of wealth: To set an example of modest, unostentatious living, shunning display or extravagance; to provide moderately for the legitimate wants of those dependent upon him; and, after doing so, to consider all surplus revenues which come to him simply as trust funds, which he is called upon to administer, and strictly bound as a matter of duty to administer in the manner which, in his judgment, is best calculated to produce the most beneficial results for the community — the man of wealth thus becoming the mere trustee and agent for his poorer brethren, bringing to their service his superior wisdom, experience, and ability to administer, doing for them better than they would or could do for themselves.

We are met here with the difficulty of determining what are moderate sums to leave to members of the family; what is modest, unostentatious living; what is the test of extravagance. There must be different standards for different conditions. The answer is that it is as impossible to name exact amounts or actions as it is to define good manners, good taste, or the rule of propriety; but, nevertheless, these are verities, well known, although indefinable. Public sentiment is quick to know and to feel what offends these. So in the case of wealth. The rule in regard to good taste in the dress of men or women applies here. Whatever makes one conspicuous offends the canon. If any family be chiefly known for display, for extravagance in home, table, or equipage, for enormous sums ostentatiously spent in any form upon itself — if these be its chief distinctions, we have no difficulty in estimating its nature or culture. So likewise in regard to the use or abuse of its surplus wealth, or to generous, free-handed coöperation in good public uses, or to unabated efforts to accumulate and hoard to the last, or whether they administer or bequeath. The verdict rests with the best and most enlightened public sentiment. The community will surely judge, and its judgments will not often be wrong.

The best uses to which surplus wealth can be put have already been indicated. Those who would administer wisely must, indeed, be wise; for one of the serious obstacles to the improvement of our race is indiscriminate charity. It were better for mankind that the millions of the rich were thrown into the sea than so spent as to encourage the slothful, the drunken, the unworthy. Of every thousand dollars spent in so-called charity to-day, it is probable that nine hundred and fifty dollars is unwisely spent — so spent, indeed, as to produce the very evils which it hopes to mitigate or cure. A well-known writer of philosophic books admitted the other day that he had given a quarter of a dollar to a man who approached him as he was coming to visit the house of his friend. He knew nothing of the habits of this beggar, knew not the use that would be made of this money, although he had every reason to suspect that it would be spent improperly. This man professed to be a disciple of Herbert Spencer; yet the quarter-dollar given that night will probably work more injury than all the money will do good which its thoughtless donor will ever be able to give in true charity. He only gratified his own feelings, saved himself from annoyance — and this was probably one of the most selfish and very worst actions of his life, for in all respects he is most worthy.

In bestowing charity, the main consideration should be to help those who will help themselves; to provide part of the means by which those who desire to improve may do so; to give those who desire to rise the aids by which they may rise; to assist, but rarely or never to do all. Neither the individual nor the race is improved by almsgiving. Those worthy of assistance, except in rare cases, seldom require assistance. The really valuable men of the race never do, except in case of accident or sudden change. Every one has, of course, cases of individuals brought to his own knowledge where temporary assistance can do genuine good, and these he will not overlook. But the amount which can be wisely given by the individual for individuals is necessarily limited by his lack of knowledge of the circumstances connected with each. He is the only true reformer who is as careful and as anxious not to aid the unworthy as he is to aid the worthy, and, perhaps, even more so, for in almsgiving more injury is probably done by rewarding vice than by relieving virtue.

The rich man is thus almost restricted to following the examples of Peter Cooper, Enoch Pratt of Baltimore, Mr. Pratt of Brooklyn, Senator Stanford, and others, who know that the best means of benefiting the community is to place within its reach the ladders upon which the aspiring can rise -- free libraries, parks, and means of recreation, by which men are helped in body and mind; works of art, certain to give pleasure and improve the public taste; and public institutions of various kinds, which will improve the general condition of the people; in this manner returning their surplus wealth to the mass of their fellows in the forms best calculated to do them lasting good.

Thus is the problem of rich and poor to be solved. The laws of accumulation will be left free, the laws of distribution free. Individualism will continue, but the millionaire will be but a trustee for the poor, intrusted for a season with a great part of the increased wealth of the community, but administering it for the community far better than it could or would have done for itself. The best minds will thus have reached a stage in the development of the race in which it is clearly seen that there is no mode of disposing of surplus wealth creditable to thoughtful and earnest men into whose hands it flows, save by using it year by year for the general good. This day already dawns. Men may die without incurring the pity of their fellows, still sharers in great business enterprises from which their capital cannot be or has not been withdrawn, and which is left chiefly at death for public uses; yet the day is not far distant when the man who dies leaving behind him millions of available wealth, which was free for him to administer during life, will pass away "unwept, unhonored, and unsung," no matter to what uses he leaves the dross which he cannot take with him. Of such as these the public verdict will then be: "The man who dies thus rich dies disgraced."

Such, in my opinion, is the true gospel concerning wealth, obedience to which is destined some day to solve the problem of the rich and the poor, and to bring "Peace on earth, among men good will."

Study Guide

1. Before Carnegie offers advice on "the administration of wealth" (pp. 126–132), he takes great pains to establish the clear superiority of the capitalistic system over any other economic system (pp. 123–126).

   (a) What specific benefits does Carnegie see as a result of mass production?

   (b) What are the drawbacks so far as Carnegie is concerned, and is he willing to pay the price?

2. Continuing with his assessment of the capitalistic system:

   (a) How does Carnegie justify the accumulation of wealth by the few?

   (b) What are Carnegie's views of the following:

      (1) individualism;

      (2) private property;

    (3) the Law of the Accumulation of Wealth; and
    (4) the Law of Competition?

3. Explain these truisms of late nineteenth-century conservative thought:
    (a) "Without wealth there can be no Maecenas."
    (b) "The price which society pays for the law of competition, like the price it pays for cheap comforts and luxuries, is also great; but the advantages of this law are also greater still than its cost — for it is to this law that we owe our wonderful material development, which brings improved conditions in its train."

4. In the second half of his essay (pp. 126–132), Carnegie explores the responsibilities of the man of wealth and the options open to him for the disposition of his property, and, in the end, he formulates his doctrine of "The Gospel of Wealth."
    (a) Begin by outlining the three alternatives open, according to Carnegie, to the possessor of surplus wealth.
    (b) What reasons does he advance *in opposition* to the first two?
    (c) What reasons does he set forth *in support* of the third alternative?
    (d) What does Carnegie mean by this: "Even the poorest can be made to see this, and to agree that great sums gathered by some of their fellow-citizens and spent for public purposes, from which the masses reap the principal benefit, are more valuable to them than if scattered among themselves in trifling amounts through the course of many years" (p. 129).
    (e) What point does Carnegie intend to make by citing Cooper Union and the Tilden gift?
    (f) Note, too, the following excerpts:
        (1) ". . . The man of wealth thus becoming a mere trustee and agent for his poorer brethren, bringing to their service his superior wisdom, experience, and ability to administer, doing for them better than they would or could do for themselves."
        (2) ". . . One of the serious obstacles to the improvement of our race is indiscriminate charity." Illustrate.
        (3) "In bestowing charity, the main consideration should be to help those who will help themselves. . . ."

5. Some general thoughts:
    (a) Relate Carnegie's "gospel of wealth" to the Presbyterian notion of the "stewardship of wealth" and the more general concept of the "Protestant Ethic."
    (b) Did Carnegie ever act upon the "gospel of wealth" concept? How?
    (c) Dozens of major universities, libraries, and art galleries in the nation grew out of the generosity of late nineteenth-century philanthropists. How did the tax laws of that time favor the accumulation of wealth? Through what financial instrument is this done today?

Jacob A. Riis
URBAN BLIGHT

⊰⊱*1890*⊰⊱   Jacob Riis was born in Denmark and migrated to the United States in 1870, when he was twenty-one. For a number of years he lived from hand to mouth in New York City, finally obtaining a job as a newspaperman. While serving as a police reporter for *The New York Sun* he became familiar with the noxious conditions prevalent in the slums, and in 1890 he published *How the Other Half Lives,* an exposé of these conditions illustrated with graphic photographs, taken by himself. The book, a bestseller, was chiefly an attack on slum tenement houses and a call for the reform of housing laws. Housing conditions in 1890 were indeed terrible, far worse than in any American city today. But Riis also discussed many other urban evils — crime, disease, immorality, and the mistreatment of minorities — where little progress has been made in the eighty-odd years since his book appeared. Although not without prejudices of his own, Riis was a genuine reformer and something of an idealist. His view of America, typical of that of many immigrants and of native reformers, was that its very virtues demanded that its weaknesses be exposed and corrected. This tone supplies a special flavor of urgency to his book which helps explain its immediate impact and also its enduring influence.

HOW THE OTHER HALF LIVES

Long ago it was said that "one half of the world does not know how the other half lives." That was true then. It did not know because it did not care. The half that was on top cared little for the struggles, and less for the fate of those who were underneath, so long as it was able to hold them there and keep its own seat. There came a time when the discomfort and crowding below were so great, and the consequent upheavals so violent, that it was no longer an easy thing to do, and then the upper half fell to inquiring what was the matter. Information on the subject has been accumulating rapidly since, and the whole world has had its hands full answering for its old ignorance.

In New York, the youngest of the world's great cities, that time came later than elsewhere, because the crowding had not been so great. There were those who believed that it would never come; but their hopes were vain. Greed and reckless selfishness wrought like results here as in the cities of older lands. . . .

To-day three-fourths of its people live in the tenements, and the nineteenth century drift of the population to the cities is sending ever-increas-

ing multitudes to crowd them. The fifteen thousand tenant houses that
were the despair of the sanitarian in the past generation have swelled
into thirty-seven thousand, and more than twelve hundred thousand
persons call them home. . . . In the tenements all the influences make
for evil; because they are the hot-beds of the epidemics that carry death
to rich and poor alike; the nurseries of pauperism and crime that fill our
jails and police courts; that throw off a scum of forty thousand human
wrecks to the island asylums and workhouses year by year; that turned
out in the last eight years a round half million beggars to prey upon our
charities; that maintain a standing army of ten thousand tramps with all
that that implies; because, above all, they touch the family life with
deadly moral contagion. This is their worst crime, inseparable from the
system. That we have to own it the child of our own wrong does not
excuse it, even though it gives it claim upon our utmost patience and
tenderest charity.

What are you going to do about it? is the question of to-day. . . . The
remedy that shall be an effective answer to the coming appeal for justice
must proceed from the public conscience. Neither legislation nor charity
can cover the ground. The greed of capital that wrought the evil must
itself undo it, as far as it can now be undone. Homes must be built for
the working masses by those who employ their labor; but tenements
must cease to be "good property" in the old, heartless sense. . . .

The first tenement New York knew bore the mark of Cain from its
birth, though a generation passed before the writing was deciphered. It
was the "rear house," infamous ever after in our city's history. There
had been tenant-houses before, but they were not built for the purpose.
Nothing would probably have shocked their original owners more than
the idea of their harboring a promiscuous crowd; for they were the
decorous homes of the old Knickerbockers, the proud aristocracy of Manhattan in the early days.

It was the stir and bustle of trade, together with the tremendous immigration that followed upon the war of 1812 that dislodged them. In
thirty-five years the city of less than a hundred thousand came to harbor
half a million souls, for whom homes had to be found. Within the
memory of men not yet in their prime, Washington had moved from
his house on Cherry Hill as too far out of town to be easily reached.
Now the old residents followed his example; but they moved in a different direction and for a different reason. Their comfortable dwellings in
the once fashionable streets along the East River front fell into the hands
of real-estate agents and boarding-house keepers; and here, says the
report to the Legislature of 1857, when the evils engendered had excited

just alarm, "in its beginning, the tenant-house became a real blessing to that class of industrious poor whose small earnings limited their expenses, and whose employment in workshops, stores, or about the warehouses and thoroughfares, render a near residence of much importance." Not for long, however. As business increased, and the city grew with rapid strides, the necessities of the poor became the opportunity of their wealthier neighbors, and the stamp was set upon the old houses, suddenly become valuable, which the best thought and effort of a later age has vainly struggled to efface. Their "*large* rooms were partitioned into *several smaller ones,* without regard to light or ventilation, the rate of rent being lower in proportion to space or height from the street; and they soon became filled from cellar to garret with a class of tenantry living from hand to mouth, loose in morals, improvident in habits, degraded, and squalid as beggary itself." It was thus the dark bedroom, prolific of untold depravities, came into the world. It was destined to survive the old houses. In their new role, says the old report, eloquent in its indignant denunciation of "evils more destructive than wars," "they were not intended to last. Rents were fixed high enough to cover damage and abuse from this class, from whom nothing was expected, and the most was made of them while they lasted. Neatness, order, cleanliness, were never dreamed of in connection with the tenant-house system, as it spread its localities from year to year; while reckless slovenliness, discontent, privation, and ignorance were left to work out their invariable results, until the entire premises reached the level of tenant-house dilapidation, containing, but sheltering not, the miserable hordes that crowded beneath smouldering, water-rotted roofs or burrowed among the rats of clammy cellars." Yet so illogical is human greed that, at a later day, when called to account, "the proprietors frequently urged the filthy habits of the tenants as an excuse for the condition of their property, utterly losing sight of the fact that it was the tolerance of those habits which was the real evil, and that for this they themselves were alone responsible."

Still the pressure of the crowds did not abate, and in the old garden where the stolid Dutch burgher grew his tulips or early cabbages a rear house was built, generally of wood, two stories high at first. Presently it was carried up another story, and another. Where two families had lived ten moved in. The front house followed suit, if the brick walls were strong enough. The question was not always asked, judging from complaints made by a contemporary witness, that the old buildings were "often carried up to a great height without regard to the strength of the foundation walls." It was rent the owner was after; nothing was said in the contract about either the safety or the comfort of the tenants. The garden gate no longer swung on its rusty hinges. The shell-paved walk had become an alley; what the rear house had left of the garden, a "court." Plenty such are yet to be found in the Fourth Ward, with here and there one of the original real tenements.

Worse was to follow. It was "soon perceived by estate owners and agents of property that a greater percentage of profits could be realized by the conversion of houses and blocks into barracks, and dividing their space into smaller proportions capable of containing human life within four walls. . . . Blocks were rented of real estate owners, or 'purchased on time,' or taken in charge at a percentage, and held for under-letting." With the appearance of the middleman, wholly irresponsible, and utterly reckless and unrestrained, began the era of tenement building which turned out such blocks as Gotham Court, where, in one cholera epidemic that scarcely touched the clean wards, the tenants died at the rate of one hundred and ninety-five to the thousand of population; which forced the general mortality of the city up from 1 in 41.83 in 1815, to 1 in 27.33 in 1855, a year of unusual freedom from epidemic disease, and which wrung from the early organizers of the Health Department this wail: "There are numerous examples of tenement-houses in which are lodged several hundred people that have a *pro rata* allotment of ground area scarcely equal to two square yards upon the city lot, court-yards and all included." The tenement-house population had swelled to half a million souls by that time, and on the East Side, in what is still the most densely populated district in all the world, China not excluded, it was packed at the rate of 290,000 to the square mile, a state of affairs wholly unexampled. The utmost cupidity of other lands and other days had never contrived to herd much more than half that number within the same space. The greatest crowding of Old London was at the rate of 175,816. Swine roamed the streets and gutters as their principal scavengers.[1] The death of a child in a tenement was registered at the Bureau of Vital Statistics as "plainly due to suffocation in the foul air of an unventilated apartment," and the Senators, who had come down from Albany to find out what was the matter with New York, reported that "there are annually cut off from the population by disease and death enough human beings to people a city, and enough human labor to sustain it." . . .

Lest anybody flatter himself with the notion that these were evils of a day that is happily past and may safely be forgotten, let me mention here three very recent instances of tenement-house life that came under

---

[1] It was not until the winter of 1867 that owners of swine were prohibited by ordinance from letting them run at large in the built-up portions of the city.

my notice. One was the burning of a rear house in Mott Street, from appearances one of the original tenant-houses that made their owners rich. The fire made homeless ten families, who had paid an average of $5 a month for their mean little cubby-holes. The owner himself told me that it was *fully* insured for $800, though it brought him in $600 a year rent. He evidently considered himself especially entitled to be pitied for losing such valuable property. Another was the case of a hard-working family of man and wife, young people from the old country, who took poison together in a Crosby Street tenement because they were "tired." There was no other explanation, and none was needed when I stood in the room in which they had lived. It was in the attic with sloping ceiling and a single window so far out on the roof that it seemed not to belong to the place at all. With scarcely room enough to turn around in they had been compelled to pay five dollars and a half a month in advance. There were four such rooms in that attic, and together they brought in as much as many a handsome little cottage in a pleasant part of Brooklyn. The third instance was that of a colored family of husband and wife, and baby in a wretched rear rookery in West Third Street. Their rent was eight dollars and a half for a single room on the top-story, so small that I was unable to get a photograph of it even by placing the camera outside the open door. Three short steps across either way would have measured its full extent. . . .

To-day, what is a tenement? The law defines it as a house "occupied by three or more families, living independently and doing their cooking on the premises; or by more than two families on a floor, so living and cooking and having a common right in the halls, stairways, yards, etc." That is the legal meaning, and includes flats and apartment-houses, with which we have nothing to do. In its narrower sense the typical tenement was thus described when last arraigned before the bar of public justice: "It is generally a brick building from four to six stories high on the street, frequently with a store on the first floor which, when used for the sale of liquor, has a side opening for the benefit of the inmates and to evade the Sunday law; four families occupy each floor, and a set of rooms consists of one or two dark closets, used as bedrooms, with a living room twelve feet by ten. The staircase is too often a dark well in the centre of the house, and no direct through ventilation is possible, each family being separated from the other by partitions. Frequently the rear of the lot is occupied by another building of three stories high with two families on a floor." The picture is nearly as true to-day as ten years ago, and will be for a long time to come. The dim light admitted by the air-shaft shines upon greater crowds than ever. Tenements are still "good property," and the poverty of the poor man his destruction. A barrack down town where he *has to live* because he is poor brings in a third more rent than a decent flat house in Harlem. The statement once made a sensation that between seventy and eighty children had been found in one tenement. It no longer excites even passing attention, when the sanitary police report counting 101 adults and 91 children in a Crosby Street house, one of twins, built together. The children in the other, if I am not mistaken, numbered 89, a total of 180 for two tenements! Or when a midnight inspection in Mulberry Street unearths a hundred and fifty "lodgers" sleeping on filthy floors in two buildings. Spite of brown-stone trimmings, plate-glass and mosaic vestibule floors, the water does not rise in summer to the second story, while the beer flows unchecked to the all-night picnics on the roof. The saloon with the side-door and the landlord divide the prosperity of the place between them, and the tenant, in sullen submission, foots the bills.

Where are the tenements of to-day? Say rather: where are they not? In fifty years they have crept up from the Fourth Ward slums and the Five Points the whole length of the island, and have polluted the Annexed District to the Westchester line. Crowding all the lower wards, wherever business leaves a foot of ground unclaimed; strung along both rivers, like ball and chain tied to the foot of every street, and filling up Harlem with their restless, pent-up multitudes, they hold within their clutch the wealth and business of New York, hold them at their mercy in the day of mob-rule and wrath. The bullet-proof shutters, the stacks of hand-grenades, and the Gatling guns of the Sub-Treasury are tacit admissions of the fact and of the quality of the mercy expected. The tenements to-day are New York, harboring three-fourths of its population. When another generation shall have doubled the census of our city, and to that vast army of workers, held captive by poverty, the very name of home shall be as a bitter mockery, what will the harvest be?

The color line must be drawn through the tenements to give the picture its proper shading. The landlord does the drawing, does it with an absence of pretence, a frankness of despotism, that is nothing if not brutal. The Czar of all the Russias is not more absolute upon his own soil than the New York landlord in his dealings with colored tenants. Where he permits them to live, they go; where he shuts the door, stay out. By his grace they exist at all in certain localities; his ukase banishes them from others. He accepts the responsibility, when laid at his door, with unruffled complacency. It is business, he will tell you. And it is. He makes the prejudice in which he traffics pay him well, and that, as he thinks it quite superfluous to tell you, is what he is there for. . . .

Ever since the war New York has been receiving the overflow of colored population from the Southern cities. In the last decade this migration has grown to such proportions that it is estimated that our Blacks have quite doubled in number since the Tenth Census. Whether the exchange has been of advantage to the negro may well be questioned. Trades of which he had practical control in his Southern home are not open to him here. I know that it may be answered that there is no industrial prescription of color; that it is a matter of choice. Perhaps so. At all events he does not choose then. How many colored carpenters or masons has anyone seen at work in New York? In the South there are enough of them and, if the testimony of the most intelligent of their people is worth anything, plenty of them have come here. As a matter of fact the colored man takes in New York, without a struggle, the lower level of menial service for which his past traditions and natural love of ease perhaps as yet fit him best. Even the colored barber is rapidly getting to be a thing of the past. Along shore, at any unskilled labor, he works unmolested; but he does not appear to prefer the job. His sphere thus defined, he naturally takes his stand among the poor, and in the homes of the poor. Until very recent times — the years since a change was wrought can be counted on the fingers of one hand — he was practically restricted in the choice of a home to a narrow section on the West Side, that nevertheless had a social top and bottom to it — the top in the tenements on the line of Seventh Avenue as far north as Thirty-second Street, where he was allowed to occupy the houses of unsavory reputation which the police had cleared and for which decent white tenants could not be found; the bottom in the vile rookeries of Thompson Street and South Fifth Avenue, the old "Africa" that is now fast becoming a modern Italy. To-day there are black colonies in Yorkville and Morrisania. The encroachment of business and the Italian below, and the swelling of the population above, have been the chief agents in working out his second emancipation, a very real one, for with his cutting loose from the old tenements there has come a distinct and gratifying improvement in the tenant, that argues louder than the theories or speeches the influence of vile surroundings in debasing the man. The colored citizen whom this year's census man found in his Ninety-ninth Street "flat" is a very different individual from the "nigger" his predecessor counted in the black-and-tan slums of Thompson and Sullivan Streets. There is no more clean and orderly community in New York than the new settlement of colored people that is growing up on the East Side from Yorkville to Harlem.

Cleanliness is the characteristic of the negro in his new surroundings, as it was his virtue in the old. In this respect he is immensely the superior of the lowest of the whites, the Italians and the Polish Jews, below whom he has been classed in the past in the tenant scale. Nevertheless, he has always had to pay higher rents than even these for the poorest and most stinted rooms. . . . When a fair share of prosperity is his, he knows how to make life and home very pleasant to those about him. Pianos and parlor furniture abound in the uptown homes of colored tenants and give them a very prosperous air. But even where the wolf howls at the door, he makes a bold and gorgeous front. The amount of "style" displayed on fine Sundays on Sixth and Seventh Avenues by colored holiday-makers would turn a pessimist black with wrath. The negro's great ambition is to rise in the social scale to which his color has made him a stranger and an outsider, and he is quite willing to accept the shadow for the substance where that is the best he can get. The claw-hammer coat and white tie of a waiter in a first-class summer hotel, with the chance of taking his ease in six months of winter, are to him the next best thing to mingling with the white quality he serves, on equal terms. His festive gatherings, pre-eminently his cake-walks, at which a sugared and frosted cake is the proud prize of the couple with the most aristocratic step and carriage, are comic mixtures of elaborate ceremonial and the joyous abandon of the natural man. With all his ludicrous incongruities, his sensuality and his lack of moral accountability, his superstition and other faults that are the effect of temperament and of centuries of slavery, he has his eminently good points. He is loyal to the backbone, proud of being an American and of his new-found citizenship. He is at least as easily moulded for good as for evil. His churches are crowded to the doors on Sunday nights when the colored colony turns out to worship. His people own church property in this city upon which they have paid a half a million dollars out of the depth of their poverty, with comparatively little assistance from their white brethren. He is both willing and anxious to learn, and his intellectual status is distinctly improving. If his emotions are not very deeply rooted, they are at least sincere while they last, and until the tempter gets the upper hand again.

Of all the temptations that beset him, the one that troubles him and the police most is his passion for gambling. The game of policy is a kind of unlawful penny lottery specially adapted to his means, but patronized extensively by poor white players as well. It is the meanest of swindles, but reaps for its backers rich fortunes wherever colored people congregate. Between the fortune-teller and the policy shop, closely allied frauds always, the wages of many a hard day's work are wasted by the negro; but the loss causes him few regrets. Penniless, but with undaunted faith in his ultimate "luck," he looks forward to the time when he shall once more be able to take a hand at "beating policy." When periodically the negro's lucky numbers, 4–11–44, come out on the slips of the alleged daily drawings, that are supposed to be held in some far-off Western town, intense excitement reigns in Thompson Street and along the Avenue, where someone is always the winner. An immense impetus is given then to the bogus business that has no existence outside of the cigar stores and candy shops where it hides from the law, save in some cunning Bowery "broker's" back office, where the slips are printed and the "winnings" apportioned daily with due regard to the backer's interests.

It is a question whether "Africa" has been improved by the advent of the Italian, with the tramp from the Mulberry Street Bend in his train. The moral turpitude of Thompson Street has been notorious for years, and the mingling of the three elements does not seem to have wrought any change for the better. The border-land where the white and black races meet in common debauch, the aptly-named black-and-tan saloon, has never been debatable ground from a moral stand-point. It has always been the worst of the desperately bad. Than this commingling of the utterly depraved of both sexes, white and black, on such ground, there can be no greater abomination. Usually it is some foul cellar dive, perhaps run by the political "leader" of the district, who is "in with" the police. In any event it gathers to itself all the lawbreakers and all the human wrecks within reach. When a fight breaks our during the dance a dozen razors are handy in as many boot-legs, and there is always a job for the surgeon and the ambulance. The black "tough" is as handy with the razor in a fight as his peaceably inclined brother is with it in pursuit of his honest trade. As the Chinaman hides his knife in his sleeve and the Italian his stiletto in the bosom, so the negro goes to the ball with a razor in his boot-leg, and on occasion does as much execution with it as both of the others together. More than three-fourths of the business the police have with the colored people in New York arises in the black-and-tan district, now no longer fairly representative of their color.

I have touched briefly upon such facts in the negro's life as may serve to throw light on the social condition of his people in New York. If, when the account is made up between the races, it shall be claimed that he falls short of the result to be expected from twenty-five years of freedom, it may be well to turn to the other side of the ledger and see how much of the blame is borne by the prejudice and greed that have kept him from rising under a burden of responsibility to which he could hardly be equal. And in this view he may be seen to have advanced much farther and faster than before suspected, and to promise, after all, with fair treatment, quite as well as the rest of us, his white-skinned fellow-citizens, had any right to expect.

Of the harvest of tares, sown in iniquity and reaped in wrath, the police returns tell the story. The pen that wrote the "Song of the Shirt" is needed to tell of the sad and toil-worn lives of New York's working-women. The cry echoes by night and by day through its tenements:

> Oh, God! that bread should be so dear,
> And flesh and blood so cheap!

Six months have not passed since at a great public meeting in this city, the Working Women's Society reported: "It is a known fact that men's wages cannot fall below a limit upon which they can exist, but woman's wages have no limit, since the paths of shame are always open to her. It is simply impossible for any woman to live without assistance on the low salary a saleswoman earns, without depriving herself of real necessities. . . . It is inevitable that they must in many instances resort to evil." It was only a few brief weeks before that verdict was uttered, that the community was shocked by the story of a gentle and refined woman who, left in direst poverty to earn her own living alone among strangers, threw herself from her attic window, preferring death to dishonor. "I would have done my honest work, even to scrubbing," she wrote, drenched and starving, after a vain search for work in a driving storm. She had tramped the streets for weeks on her weary errand, and the only living wages that were offered her were the wages of sin. The ink was not dry upon her letter before a woman in an East Side tenement wrote down her reason for self-murder: "Weakness, sleeplessness, and yet obliged to work. My strength fails me. Sing at my coffin: 'Where does the soul find a home and rest?'" Her story may be found as one of two typical "cases of despair" in one little church community, in the *City Mission Society's Monthly* for last February. It is a story that has many parallels in the experience of every missionary, every police reporter and every family doctor whose practice is among the poor.

It is estimated that at least one hundred and fifty thousand women and girls earn their own living in New York; but there is reason to believe that this estimate falls far short of the truth when sufficient account is taken of the large number who are not wholly dependent upon their own labor, while contributing by it to the family's earnings. These alone constitute a large class of the women wage-earners, and it is characteristic of the situation that the very fact that some need not starve on their wages condemns the rest to that fate. The pay they are willing to accept all have to take. What the "everlasting law of supply and demand," that serves as such a convenient gag for public indignation, has to do with it, one learns from observation all along the road of inquiry into these real woman's wrongs. To take the case of the saleswomen for illustration: The investigation of the Working Women's Society disclosed the fact that wages averaging from $2 to $4.50 a week were reduced by excessive fines, the employers placing a value upon time lost that is not given to services rendered. A little girl, who received two dollars a week, made cash-sales amounting to $167 in a single day, while the receipts of a fifteen-dollar male clerk in the same department footed up only $125; yet for some trivial mistake the girl was fined sixty cents out of her two dollars. The practice prevailed in some stores of dividing the fines between the superintendent and the time-keeper at the end of the year. In one instance they amounted to $3,000, and "the superintendent was heard to charge the time-keeper with not being strict enough in his duties." One of the causes for fine in a certain large store was sitting down. The law requiring seats for saleswomen, generally ignored, was obeyed faithfully in this establishment. The seats were there, but the girls were fined when found using them. . . .

These facts give a slight idea of the hardships and the poor pay of a business that notoriously absorbs child-labor. The girls are sent to the store before they have fairly entered their teens, because the money they can earn there is needed for the support of the family. If the boys will not work, if the street tempts them from home, among the girls at least there must be no drones. To keep their places they are told to lie about their age and to say that they are over fourteen. The precaution is usually superfluous. The Women's Investigating Committee found the majority of the children employed in the stores to be under age, but heard only in a single instance of the truant officers calling. In that case they came once a year and sent the youngest children home; but in a month's time they were all back in their places, and were not again disturbed. When it comes to the factories, where hard bodily labor is added to long hours, stifling rooms, and starvation wages, matters are even worse. The Legislature has passed laws to prevent the employment of children, as it has forbidden saloon-keepers to sell them beer, and it has provided means of enforcing its mandate, so efficient, that the very number of factories in New York is *guessed* at as in the neighborhood of twelve thousand. Up till this summer, a single inspector was charged with the duty of keeping the run of them all, and of seeing to it that the law was respected by the owners.

Sixty cents is put as the average day's earnings of the 150,000, but into this computation enters the stylish "cashier's" two dollars a day, as well as the thirty cents of the poor little girl who pulls threads in an East Side factory, and, if anything, the average is probably too high. Such as it is, however, it represents board, rent, clothing, and "pleasure" to this army of workers. Here is the case of a woman employed in the manufacturing department of a Broadway house. It stands for a hundred like her own. She averages three dollars a week. Pays $1.50 for her room; for breakfast she has a cup of coffee; lunch she cannot afford. One meal a day is her allowance. This woman is young, she is pretty. She has "the world before her." Is it anything less than a miracle if she is guilty of nothing worse than the "early and improvident marriage," against which moralists exclaim as one of the prolific causes of the distress of the poor? Almost any door might seem to offer welcome escape from such slavery as this. . . .

A case was brought to my notice recently by a woman doctor, whose heart as well as her life-work is with the poor, of a widow with two little children she found at work in an East Side attic, making paper-bags. Her father, she told the doctor, had made good wages at it; but she received only five cents for six hundred of the little three-cornered bags, and her fingers had to be very swift and handle the paste-brush very deftly to bring her earnings up to twenty-five and thirty cents a day. She paid four dollars a month for her room. The rest went to buy food for herself and the children. The physician's purse, rather than her skill, had healing for their complaint.

I have aimed to set down a few dry facts merely. They carry their own comment. Back of the shop with its weary, grinding toil — the home in the tenement, of which it was said in a report of the State Labor Bureau: "Decency and womanly reserve cannot be maintained there — what wonder so many fall away from virtue?" Of the outlook, what? Last Christmas Eve my business took me to an obscure street among the West Side tenements. An old woman had just fallen on the doorstep, stricken with paralysis. The doctor said she would never again move her right hand or foot. The whole side was dead. By her bedside, in their cheerless room, sat the patient's aged sister, a hopeless cripple, in dumb despair. Forty years ago the sisters had come, five in number then, with their mother, from the North of Ireland to make their home and earn a living among strangers. They were lace embroiderers and found work easily at good wages. All the rest had died as the years went by. The two remained and, firmly resolved to lead an honest life, worked on though wages fell and fell as age and toil stiffened their once nimble fingers and dimmed their sight. Then one of them dropped out, her hands palsied and her courage gone. Still the other toiled on, resting neither by night nor by day, that the sister might not want. Now that she too had been stricken, as she was going to the store for the work that was to keep them through the holidays, the battle was over at last. There was before them starvation, or the poor-house. And the proud spirits of the sisters, helpless now, quailed at the outlook.

These were old, with life behind them. For them nothing was left but to sit in the shadow and wait. But of the thousands, who are travelling the road they trod to the end, with the hot blood of youth in their veins, with the love of life and of the beautiful world to which not even sixty cents a day can shut their eyes — who is to blame if their feet find the paths of shame that are "always open to them?" The very paths that have effaced the saving "limit," and to which it is declared to be "inevitable that they must in many instances resort." Let the moralist answer. Let the wise economist apply his rule of supply and demand, and let the answer be heard in this city of a thousand charities where justice goes begging.

To the everlasting credit of New York's working-girl let it be said that, rough though her road be, all but hopeless her battle with life, only in the rarest instances does she go astray. As a class she is brave, virtuous, and true. New York's army of profligate women is not, as in some foreign cities, recruited from her ranks. She is as plucky as she is proud. That "American girls never whimper" became a proverb long ago, and she accepts her lot uncomplainingly, doing the best she can and holding her cherished independence cheap at the cost of a meal, or of half her daily ration, if need be. The home in the tenement and the traditions of her childhood have neither trained her to luxury nor predisposed her in favor of domestic labor in preference to the shop. So, to the world she presents a cheerful, uncomplaining front that sometimes deceives it. Her courage will not be without its reward. Slowly, as the conviction is thrust upon society that woman's work must enter more and more into its planning, a better day is dawning. The organization of working girls' clubs, unions, and societies with a community of interests, despite the obstacles to such a movement, bears testimony to it, as to the devotion of the unselfish women who have made their poorer sisters' cause their own, and will yet wring from an unfair world the justice too long denied her.

Study Guide

1. These selections on urban life taken from Jacob Riis's *How the Other Half Lives* treat the following subtopics:

    (a) the tenements;

    (b) the blacks; and

    (c) the conditions of labor for the working girl.

2. Summarize (pp. 134–135) Riis's assessment of the prevalence of tenements in New York City and the problems they create.

3. Trace the development of tenements as follows:

   (a) What served initially as the source of tenement housing?

   (b) Summarize the economic, social, hygienic, and other consequences of the growth of tenements for their owners and their inhabitants.

4. Turning to the blacks in New York, summarize Riis's conclusions about:

   (a) the attitudes of their landlords;

   (b) economic conditions; and

   (c) social habits and values.

5. Riis's last topic is the urban working girl.

   (a) How many working girls does Riis estimate there are in New York City, what wages are they paid, and what factor determines their wages?

   (b) How does the problem of the working girl relate to the problem of child labor? What is the rate of pay in this latter instance?

   (c) What virtue does Riis ascribe to the working girl?

Omaha Convention

THE POPULIST PROGRAM

❦*1892*❦ FOR American farmers, particularly those living in the South or in the Plains states west of the Mississippi, the early 1890's was a time of desperation. With the prices of staples like wheat and cotton falling to all-time lows and with the transportation and marketing facilities that they depended upon controlled by monopolistic corporations, many farmers found it impossible to operate at a profit. Since many were also burdened with heavy mortgage payments and other fixed costs, bankruptcy was a common occurrence. Such conditions led to the rise of the Alliance movement and then, in 1892, to the organization of the Populist party, for the farmers were convinced that both the Democratic and the Republican parties were controlled by heartless capitalists eager only to exploit the rural areas.

Much has been written by historians about the Populists. To some students populism has seemed a forerunner of the 20th-century liberal reform movements, to others an essentially reactionary effort of property-conscious citizens to overthrow the forces of modern industrial society that were usurping the dominant position in American society formerly held by agriculturalists. Were the Populists idealists trying to form a farmer-labor coalition against predatory capitalism, or were they merely selfish, embittered men resistant to all outside influence and paranoiacally suspicious of city life, immigrants, bankers, and anyone better off at the moment than themselves?

A completely satisfactory answer to this question will probably never be found. But it is instructive to study the first platform of the party, fashioned at the Populist convention at Omaha, Nebraska, in 1892. On this platform the party carried Kansas and elected a large number of local officials in other states. Its presidential candidate, James B. Weaver, polled over a million popular votes.

THE PLATFORM OF THE POPULIST PARTY

ASSEMBLED upon the 116th anniversary of the Declaration of Independence, the People's Party of America, in their first national convention, invoking upon their action the blessing of Almighty God, put forth in the name and on behalf of the people of this country, the following preamble and declaration of principles:

PREAMBLE

The conditions which surround us best justify our co-operation; we meet in the midst of a nation brought to the verge of moral, political, and material ruin. Corruption dominates the ballot-box, the Legislatures, the Congress, and touches even the ermine of the bench. The people are demoralized; most of the States have been compelled to isolate the voters at the polling places to prevent universal intimidation and bribery. The newspapers are largely subsidized or muzzled, public opinion silenced, business prostrated, homes covered with mortgages, labor impoverished, and the land concentrating in the hands of capitalists. The urban workmen are denied the right to organize for self-protection, imported pauperized labor beats down their wages, a hireling standing army, unrecognized by our laws, is established to shoot them down, and they are rapidly degenerating into European conditions. The fruits of the toil of millions are boldly stolen to build up colossal fortunes for a few, unprecedented in the history of mankind; and the possessors of these, in turn, despise the Republic and endanger liberty. From the same prolific womb of governmental injustice we breed the two great classes — tramps and millionaires.

The national power to create money is appropriated to enrich bondholders; a vast public debt payable in legal-tender currency has been funded into gold-bearing bonds, thereby adding millions to the burdens of the people.

Silver, which has been accepted as coin since the dawn of history, has been demonetized to add to the purchasing power of gold by decreasing the value of all forms of property as well as human labor, and the supply of currency is purposely abridged to fatten usurers, bankrupt enterprise, and enslave industry. A vast conspiracy against mankind has been organized on two continents, and it is rapidly taking possession of the world. If not met and overthrown at once it forebodes terrible social convulsions, the destruction of civilization, or the establishment of an absolute despotism.

We have witnessed for more than a quarter of a century the struggles of the two great political parties for power and plunder, while grievous wrongs have been inflicted upon the suffering people. We charge that the controlling influences dominating both these parties have permitted the existing dreadful conditions to develop without serious effort to prevent or restrain them. Neither do they now promise us any substantial reform. They have agreed together to ignore, in the coming campaign, every issue but one. They propose to drown the outcries of a plundered people with the uproar of a sham battle over the tariff, so that capitalists, corporations, national banks, rings, trusts, watered stock, the demonetization of silver and the oppressions of the usurers may all be lost sight of. They propose to sacrifice our homes, lives, and children on the altar of mammon; to destroy the multitude in order to secure corruption funds from the millionaires.

Assembled on the anniversary of the birthday of the nation, and filled with the spirit of the grand general and chief who established our independence, we seek to restore the government of the Republic to the hands of the "plain people," with which class it originated. We assert our purposes to be identical with the purposes of the National Constitution; to form a more perfect union and establish justice, insure domestic tranquillity, provide for the common defence, promote the general welfare, and secure the blessings of liberty for ourselves and our posterity.

We declare that this Republic can only endure as a free government while built upon the love of the people for each other and for the nation; that it cannot be pinned together by bayonets; that the Civil War is over, and that every passion and resentment which grew out of it must die with it, and that we must be in fact, as we are in name, one united brotherhood of free men.

Our country finds itself confronted by conditions for which there is no precedent in the history of the world; our annual agricultural productions amount to billions of dollars in value, which must, within a few weeks or months, be exchanged for billions of dollars' worth of commodities consumed in their production; the existing currency supply is wholly inadequate to make this exchange; the results are falling prices, the formation of combines and rings, the impoverishment of the producing class. We pledge ourselves that if given power we will labor to correct these evils by wise and reasonable legislation, in accordance with the terms of our platform.

We believe that the power of government — in other words, of the people — should be expanded (as in the case of the postal service) as rapidly and as far as the good sense of an intelligent people and the teachings of experience shall justify, to the end that oppression, injustice, and poverty shall eventually cease in the land.

While our sympathies as a party of reform are naturally upon the side of every proposition which will tend to make men intelligent, virtuous, and temperate, we nevertheless regard these questions, important as they are, as secondary to the great issues now pressing for solution, and upon which not only our individual prosperity but the very existence of free institutions depend; and we ask all men to first help us to determine whether we are to have a republic to administer before we differ as to the conditions upon which it is to be administered, believing that the forces of reform this day organized will never cease to move forward until every wrong is righted and equal rights and equal privileges securely established for all the men and women of this country.

PLATFORM

We declare, therefore —

First. — That the union of the labor forces of the United States this day consummated shall be permanent and perpetual; may its spirit enter into all hearts for the salvation of the Republic and the uplifting of mankind.

Second. — Wealth belongs to him who creates it, and every dollar taken from industry without an equivalent is robbery. "If any will not work, neither shall he eat." The interests of rural and civil labor are the same; their enemies are identical.

Third. — We believe that the time has come when the railroad corporations will either own the people or the people must own the railroads; and should the government enter upon the work of owning and managing all railroads, we should favor an amendment to the constitution by which all persons engaged in the government service shall be placed under a civil-service regulation of the most rigid character, so as to prevent the increase of the power of the national administration by the use of such additional government employes.

FINANCE. — We demand a national currency, safe, sound, and flexible issued by the general government only, a full legal tender for all debts, public and private, and that without the use of banking corporations; a just, equitable, and efficient means of distribution direct to the people, at a tax not to exceed 2 percent, per annum, to be provided as set forth in the sub-treasury plan of the Farmers' Alliance, or a better system; also by payments in discharge of its obligations for public improvements.

1. We demand free and unlimited coinage of silver and gold at the present legal ratio of 16 to 1.
2. We demand that the amount of circulating medium be speedily increased to not less than $50 per capita.

3. We demand a graduated income tax.

4. We believe that the money of the country should be kept as much as possible in the hands of the people, and hence we demand that all State and national revenues shall be limited to the necessary expenses of the government, economically and honestly administered.

5. We demand that postal savings banks be established by the government for the safe deposit of the earnings of the people and to facilitate exchange.

TRANSPORTATION. — Transportation being a means of exchange and a public necessity, the government should own and operate the railroads in the interest of the people. The telegraph and telephone, like the post-office system, being a necessity for the transmission of news, should be owned and operated by the government in the interest of the people.

LAND. — The land, including all the natural sources of wealth, is the heritage of the people, and should not be monopolized for speculative purposes, and alien ownership of land should be prohibited. All land now held by railroads and other corporations in excess of their actual needs, and all lands now owned by aliens should be reclaimed by the government and held for actual settlers only.

EXPRESSION OF SENTIMENTS

Your Committee on Platform and Resolutions beg leave unanimously to report the following:

Whereas, Other questions have been presented for our consideration, we hereby submit the following, not as a part of the Platform of the People's Party, but as resolutions expressive of the sentiment of this Convention.

1. RESOLVED, That we demand a free ballot and a fair count in all elections, and pledge ourselves to secure it to every legal voter without Federal intervention, through the adoption by the States of the unperverted Australian or secret ballot system.

2. RESOLVED, That the revenue derived from a graduated income tax should be applied to the reduction of the burden of taxation now levied upon the domestic industries of this country.

3. RESOLVED, That we pledge our support to fair and liberal pensions to ex-Union soldiers and sailors.

4. RESOLVED, That we condemn the fallacy of protecting American labor under the present system, which opens our ports to the pauper and criminal classes of the world and crowds out our wage-earners; and we denounce the present ineffective laws against contract labor, and demand the further restriction of undesirable emigration.

5. RESOLVED, That we cordially sympathize with the efforts of organized workingmen to shorten the hours of labor, and demand a rigid enforcement of the existing eight-hour law on Government work, and ask that a penalty clause be added to the said law.

6. RESOLVED, That we regard the maintenance of a large standing army of mercenaries, known as the Pinkerton system, as a menace to our liberties, and we demand its abolition; and we condemn the recent invasion of the Territory of Wyoming by the hired assassins of plutocracy, assisted by Federal officers.

7. RESOLVED, That we commend to the favorable consideration of the people and the reform press the legislative system known as the initiative and referendum.

8. RESOLVED, That we favor a constitutional provision limiting the office of President and Vice-President to one term, and providing for the election of Senators of the United States by a direct vote of the people.

9. RESOLVED, That we oppose any subsidy or national aid to any private corporation for any purpose.

10. RESOLVED, That this convention sympathizes with the Knights of Labor and their righteous contest with the tyrannical combine of clothing manufacturers of Rochester, and declare it to be a duty of all who hate tyranny and oppression to refuse to purchase the goods made by the said manufacturers, or to patronize any merchants who sell such goods.

Study Guide

1. This statement by the Populists is in three parts: a preamble, the platform, and an "expression of sentiments." What views do the Populists have of the following aspects of American life:
   (a) its political institutions and processes;
   (b) the media;
   (c) labor;
   (d) creditors and bankers; and
   (e) currency?

2. Also in the preamble, you will find a strongly dualistic view of the American people: rich and poor, creditors and debtors, nonvirtuous and virtuous, plunderers and the plundered, and nonproductive and productive. Find evidence in the preamble (pp. 148–150) *for each* dualism.

3. The preamble offers evidence for other Populist themes:
   (a) a nostalgic view of the past;
   (b) hostility to the functioning of the market;

(c) a belief in positive government; and

(d) a desire for an egalitarian social structure. Identify and amplify.

4. What does the platform have to say about the following:

(a) wealth and labor;

(b) the railroads;

(c) financial matters;

(d) the ratio of silver to gold and the currency;

(e) an income tax;

(f) government expenditures;

(g) postal savings; and

(h) transportation and the ownership of land?

5. The "sentiments" expressed cover a number of peripheral, yet not inconsequential, issues that agitated the nation in the 1890's. Outline them.

6. In retrospect: on the basis of this platform, to which view of the Populists mentioned in the introduction would you subscribe? Explain.

W. H. Harvey

THE COMMON MAN'S MONEY

❧1894❧ IN THE controversy between gold and silver advocates in the 1890's, the nearest thing to a bible for the silver men was the work of William Hope ("Coin") Harvey (1851-1936), an amateur economist of Chicago. His first tract, *Coin's Financial School* (1894), took the form of a series of imaginary lectures, in which Coin, like a schoolmaster, set forth the essential facts of the currency question, answered questions from "gold bugs" in his audience, and handily disposed of the case that was put up for gold as the nation's money. The book sold 400,000 copies in less than a year. It was followed by three other Harvey books, *The Tale of Two Nations, Coin's Financial School up to Date,* and *Coin's Handbook,* all of which developed a similar theme and sold almost as well as the first. The maligned gold men replied with heat. In an actual debate with Harvey, the University of Chicago economist J. Laurence Laughlin (1850–1933) denounced *Coin's Financial School* as "an avowed appeal to class prejudice," full of "unmistakable dishonesty, untruths, inaccuracies, and misleading arguments." Nevertheless, Harvey's books kept on selling.

Encouraged by his literary success, Harvey founded an organization which he called "The Patriots of America" and through which he intended to rout the gold-minded bankers from their citadels of power. But he had no real organizing ability. The Populists and then the Democrats capitalized upon the sentiment his pamphleteering had helped to arouse. Finally, William Jennings Bryan (1860-1925) captured the leadership of the silverites with his "Cross of Gold" speech at the Chicago convention of the Democratic party in 1896.

Reprinted here is all of the first and most of the last chapter of *Coin's Financial School.*

COIN'S FINANCIAL SCHOOL

So MUCH uncertainty prevailing about the many facts connected with the monetary question, very few are able to intelligently understand the subject.

Hard times are with us; the country is distracted; very few things are marketable at a price above the cost of production; tens of thousands are out of employment; the jails, penitentiaries, workhouses and insane asylums are full; the gold reserve at Washington is sinking; the government is running at a loss with a deficit in every department; a huge debt hangs like an appalling cloud over the country; taxes have assumed the importance of a mortgage, and 50 per cent of the public revenues are likely to go delinquent; hungered and half-starved men are banding into armies and marching toward Washington; the cry of distress is heard on every hand; business is paralyzed; commerce is at a standstill; riots and strikes prevail throughout the land; schemes to remedy our ills when put into execution are smashed like box-cars in a railroad wreck, and Wall street looks in vain for an excuse to account for the failure of prosperity to return since the repeal of the silver purchase act.

It is a time for wisdom and sound sense to take the helm, and Coin, a young financier living in Chicago, acting upon such a suggestion, established a school of finance to instruct the youths of the nation, with a view to their having a clear understanding of what has been considered an abstruse subject; to lead them out of the labyrinth of falsehoods, heresies and isms that distract the country.

THE FIRST DAY

The school opened on the 7th day of May, 1894.

There was a good attendance, and the large hall selected in the Art Institute was comfortably filled. Sons of merchants and bankers, in fact all classes of business, were well represented. Journalists, however, predominated. Coin stepped on to the platform, looking the smooth little financier that he is, and said:

"I am pleased to see such a large attendance. It indicates a desire to learn and master a subject that has baffled your fathers. The reins of the government will soon be placed in your hands, and its future will be molded by your honesty and intelligence.

"I ask you to accept nothing from me that does not stand the analysis of reason; that you will freely ask questions and pass criticisms, and if there is any one present who believes that all who differ from *him* are lunatics and fools, he is requested to vacate his seat and leave the room."

The son of Editor Scott of the *Chicago Herald,* here arose and walked out. Coin paused a moment, and then continued: "My object will be to teach you the A, B, C of the questions about money that are now a matter of every-day conversation."

The Money Unit

"In money there must be a unit. In arithmetic, as you are aware, you are taught what a unit is. Thus, I make here on the blackboard the figure 1. That, in arithmetic, is a unit. All countings are sums or multiples of that unit. A unit, therefore, in mathematics, was a necessity as a basis to start from. In making money it was equally as necessary to establish a unit. The constitution gave the power to Congress to 'coin money and regulate the value thereof.' Congress adopted silver and gold as money. It then proceeded to fix the unit.

"That is, it then fixed what should constitute one dollar, the same thing that the mathematician did when he fixed one figure from which all others should be counted. Congress fixed the monetary unit to consist of $371\frac{1}{4}$ grains of pure silver, and provided for a certain amount of alloy (baser metals) to be mixed with it to give it greater hardness and durability. This was in 1792, in the days of Washington and Jefferson and our revolutionary forefathers, who had a hatred of England, and an intimate knowledge of her designs on this country.

"They had fought eight long years for their independence from British domination in this country, and when they had seen the last red-coat leave our shores, they settled down to establish a permanent government, and among the first things they did was to make $371\frac{1}{4}$ grains of silver the unit of values. That much silver was to constitute a dollar. And each dollar was a unit. They then provided for all other money to be counted from this unit of a silver dollar. Hence, dimes, quarters and half-dollars were exact fractional parts of the dollar so fixed.

"Gold was made money, but its value was counted from these silver units or dollars. The ratio between silver and gold was fixed at 15 to 1, and afterward at 16 to 1. So that in making gold coins their relative weight was regulated by this ratio.

"This continued to be the law up to 1873. During that long period, the unit of values was never changed and always contained $371\frac{1}{4}$ grains of pure silver. While that was the law it was impossible for any one to say that the silver in a silver dollar was only worth 47 cents, or any other number of cents less than 100 cents, or a dollar. For it was itself the unit of values. While that was the law it would have been as absurd to say that the silver in a silver dollar was only worth 47 cents, as it would be to say that this figure 1 which I have on the blackboard is only forty-seven one-hundredths of one.

"When the ratio was changed from 15 to 16 to 1 the silver dollar or unit was left the same size and the gold dollar was made smaller. The latter was changed from 24.7 grains to 23.2 grains pure gold, thus making it smaller. This occurred in 1834. The silver dollar still remained the unit and continued so until 1873.

"Both were legal tender in the payment of all debts, and the mints were open to the coinage of all that came. So that up to 1873, we were on what was known as a bimetallic basis, but what was in fact a silver basis, with gold as a companion metal enjoying the same privileges as silver, except that silver fixed the unit, and the value of gold was regulated by it. This was bimetallism.

"Our forefathers showed much wisdom in selecting silver, of the two metals, out of which to make the unit. Much depended on this decision. For the one selected to represent the unit would thereafter be unchangeable in value. That is, the metal in it could never be worth less than a dollar, for it would be the unit of value itself. The demand for silver in the arts or for money by other nations might make the quantity of silver in a silver dollar sell for more than a dollar, but it could never be worth less than a dollar. Less than itself.

"In considering which of these two metals they would thus favor by making it the unit, they were led to adopt silver because it was the most reliable. It was the most favored as money by the people. It was scattered among all the people. Men having a design to injure business by making money scarce, could not so easily get hold of all the silver and hide it away, as they could gold. This was the principal reason that led them to the conclusion to select silver, the more stable of the two metals, upon which to fix the unit. It was so much handled by the people and preferred by them, that it was called the people's money.

"Gold was considered the money of the rich. It was owned principally by that class of people, and the poor people seldom handled it, and the very poor people seldom ever saw any of it."

Here young Medill, of the *Chicago Tribune,* held up his hand, which indicated that he had something to say or wished to ask a question. Coin paused and asked him what he wanted.

He arose in his seat and said that his father claimed that we had been on a gold basis ever since 1837, that prior to 1873 there never had been but eight million dollars of silver coined. Here young Wilson, of the *Farm, Field and Fireside,* said he wanted to ask, who owns the *Chicago Tribune?*

Coin tapped the little bell on the table to restore order, and ruled the last question out, as there was one already before the house by Mr. Medill.

"Prior to 1873," said Coin, "there were one hundred and five millions of silver coined by the United States and eight million of this was in silver dollars. When your father said that 'only eight million dollars in silver' had been coined, he meant to say that 'only eight million silver dollars had been coined.' He also neglected to say — that is — he forgot to state, that ninety-seven millions had been coined into dimes, quarters and halves.

"About one hundred millions of foreign silver had found its way into this country prior to 1860. It was principally Spanish, Mexican and Canadian coin. It had all been made legal tender in the United States by act of Congress. We needed more silver than we had, and Congress passed laws making all foreign silver coins legal tender in this country. I will read you one of these laws — they are scattered all through the statutes prior to 1873." Here Coin picked up a copy of the laws. . . .

The Crime of 1873

"We now come to the act of 1873," continued Coin. "On February 12, 1873, Congress passed an act purporting to be a revision of the coinage laws. The law covers 15 pages of our statutes. It repealed the *unit* clause in the law of 1792, and in its place substituted a law in the following language:

"That the gold coins of the United States shall be a one-dollar piece which at the standard weight of twenty-five and eight-tenths grains *shall be the unit of value.*

"It then deprived silver of its right to unrestricted free coinage, and destroyed it as legal tender money in the payment of debts, except to the amount of five dollars.

"At that time we were all using paper money. No one was handling silver and gold coins. It was when specie payments were about to be resumed that the country appeared to realize what had been done. The newspapers on the morning of February 13, 1873, and at no time in the vicinity of that period, had any account of the change. General Grant, who was President of the United States at that time, said afterwards, that he had no idea of it, and would not have signed the bill if he had known that it demonetized silver.

"In the language of Senator Daniel of Virginia, it seems to have gone through Congress 'like the silent tread of a cat.'

"An army of a half million of men invading our shores, the warships of the world bombarding our coasts, could not have made us surrender the money of the people and substitute in its place the money of the rich.

A few words embraced in fifteen pages of statutes put through Congress in the rush of bills did it. The pen was mightier than the sword.

"But we are not here to deal with sentiment. We are here to learn facts. Plain, blunt facts.

"The law of 1873 made gold the *unit* of values. And that is the law to-day. When the silver was the unit of value, gold enjoyed *free coinage,* and was legal tender in the payment of all debts. Now things have changed. Gold is the unit and silver does not enjoy free coinage. It is refused at the mints. We might get along with gold as the *unit,* if silver enjoyed the same right gold did prior to 1873. But that right is now denied to silver. When silver was the unit, the unlimited demand for gold to coin into money, made the demand as great as the supply, and this held up the value of gold bullion."

Here Victor F. Lawson, Jr., of the Chicago *Evening News,* interrupted the little financier with the statement that his paper, the *News,* had stated time and again that silver had become so plentiful it had ceased to be a precious metal. And that this statement believed by him to be a fact had more to do with his prejudice to silver than anything else. And he would like to know if that was not a fact?

"There is no truth in the statement," replied Coin. "On page 21 of my Handbook you will find a table on this subject, compiled by Mulhall, the London statistician. It gives the quantity of gold and silver in the world both coined and uncoined at six periods — at the years 1600, 1700, 1800, 1848, 1880, and 1890. It shows that in 1600 there were 27 tons of silver to one ton of gold. In 1700, 34 tons of silver to one ton of gold. In 1800, 32 tons of silver to one ton of gold. In 1848, 31 tons of silver to one ton of gold. In 1880, 18 tons of silver to one ton of gold. In 1890, 18 tons of silver to one ton of gold.

"The United States is producing more silver than it ever did, or was until recently. But the balance of the world is producing much less. They are fixing the price on our silver and taking it away from us, at their price. The report of the Director of the Mint shows that since 1850 the world has produced less silver than gold, while during the first fifty years of the century the world produced 78 per cent more silver than gold. Instead of becoming more plentiful, it is less plentiful. So it is less, instead of more.

"Any one can get the official statistics by writing to the treasurer at Washington, and asking for his official book of statistics. Also write to the Director of the Mint and ask him for his report. If you get no answer write to your Congressman. These books are furnished free and you will get them.

"At the time the United States demonetized silver in February, 1873, silver as measured in gold was worth $1.02. The argument of depreciated silver could not then be made. Not one of the arguments that are now made against silver was then possible. They are all the bastard children of the crime of 1873.

"It was demonetized secretly, and since then a powerful money trust has used deception and misrepresentations that have led tens of thousands of honest minds astray."

William Henry Smith, Jr., of the Associated Press, wanted to know if the size of the gold dollar was ever changed more than the one time mentioned by Coin, viz., in 1834.

"Yes," said Coin. "In 1837 it was changed from 23.3 to 23.22. This change of 2/100ths was for convenience in calculation, but the change was made in the gold coin — never in the silver dollar (the *unit*) till 1873.

Adjourned. . . .

THE SIXTH DAY

The manner in which the little lecturer had handled his subject on the fifth day had greatly enhanced his popularity. What he had said, had been in the nature of a revelation to nearly all that heard it, and his grouping of facts had made a profound impression.

What created the most comment, was his statement as to the space in which all the gold and silver of the world could be placed. In all the hotel lobbies it was the subject of conversation. The bare statement that all the gold in the world could be put in a cube of 22 feet appeared ridiculous — absurd.

Few that had entertained the single gold standard view of the monetary question were willing to believe it. They argued that it was impossible; that the business of the world could not be transacted on such an insignificant amount of property for primary money. They said, "Wait till the morning papers come out; the *Tribune* would puncture it, the *Inter Ocean, Herald,* in fact, all of the papers would either admit it by their silence, contradict it or give the facts."

At the Grand Pacific Hotel the cashier was kept busy answering requests to see a twenty-dollar gold piece. They wanted to measure it — to get its diameter and thickness. As none was to be had, they had to content themselves with measuring up silver dollars and figuring out how much space all the silver in the world would occupy. This resulted in confirming Coin's statement.

Mr. George Sengel, a prominent citizen of Fort Smith, Arkansas, while discussing the subject with a large party in the rotunda of the Palmer House, stood up in a chair and addressed the crowd, saying:

"Gentlemen, I have just been up in Coin's room and examined the government reports as to the amount of gold and silver in the world, and have made the calculation myself as to the quantity of it, and I find that the statements made are true. All the gold and silver in the world obtainable for money can be put in the office of this hotel, and all the gold can be put in this office and not materially interfere with the comfort of the guests of the house.

"I have been until to-day in favor of a single gold standard, but hard times, and this fact that all the gold in the world available for money can be put in a space of twenty-two feet each way, has knocked it out of me. Count on me and old Arkansas for bimetallism."

Mr. Sengel's speech was greeted with applause, and he was followed by others expressing similar views.

The morning papers gave full reports of the previous day's lecture. All editorially confirmed Coin's statement as to the quantity of gold and silver in the world, and the space it would occupy, except the *Herald* and *Tribune*; they were silent on the subject.

It was generally known that Coin would discuss independent action of the United States on the last day, and from the number that tried to gain admission, a hall many times as large could have been easily filled.

At the hour for opening the hall large crowds surrounded the entrance to the Art Institute, and the corridors were filled with people. In the large hall where the lectures were delivered the walls had been decorated with the American colors. This had been seen to by a committee of bimetallists; they had given special attention to the decorations around the platform, and though assuming many forms, each piece had been made from United States' flags. The scene presented was striking and patriotic.

When the doors were opened the hall was soon filled and thousands were turned away.

Coin was escorted by a committee of bimetallists in carriages from his hotel to the Art Institute, each carriage used by the committee being draped in the American colors. It was the first demonstration of the kind made in honor of the little financier of the people, since the lectures had begun.

The evidences of his popularity were now to be seen on every hand. Many, however, had reserved their judgment to hear from him on the United States taking independent action, and all were anxious to listen to what he would say on that subject.

His appearance upon the platform was the signal for an ovation. He had grown immensely popular in those last five days.

He laid his silk hat on the table, and at once stepped to the middle of the platform. He raised his eyes to the audience; slowly turned his head to the right and left, and looked into the sea of faces that confronted him.

Independent Free Coinage

"In the midst of plenty, we are in want," he began.

"Helpless children and the best womanhood and manhood of America appeal to us for release from a bondage that is destructive of life and liberty. All the nations of the Western Hemisphere turn to their great sister republic for assistance in the emancipation of the people of at least one-half the world.

"The Orient, with its teeming millions of people, and France, the cradle of science and liberty in Europe, look to the United States to lead in the struggle to roll back the accumulated disasters of the last twenty-one years. What shall our answer be? [Applause.]

"If it is claimed we must adopt for our money the metal England selects, and can have no independent choice in the matter, let us make the test and find out if it is true. It is not American to give up without trying. If it is true, let us attach England to the United States and blot her name out from among the nations of the earth. [Applause.]

"A war with England would be the most popular ever waged on the face of the earth. [Applause.] If it is true that she can dictate the money of the world, and thereby create world-wide misery, it would be the most just war ever waged by man. [Applause.]

"But fortunately this is not necessary. Those who would have you think that we must wait for England, either have not studied this subject, or have the same interest in continuing the present conditions as England. It is a vain hope to expect her voluntarily to consent. England is the creditor nation of the globe, and collects hundreds of millions of dollars in interest annually in gold from the rest of the world. We are paying her two hundred millions yearly in interest. She demands it in gold; the contracts call for it in gold. Do you expect her to voluntarily release any part of it? It has a purchasing power twice what a bimetallic currency would have. She knows it.

"The men that control the legislation of England are citizens of that country with fixed incomes. They are interest gatherers to the amount annually of over one thousand millions of dollars. The men over there holding bimetallic conventions, and passing resolutions, have not one-fifth the influence with the law-making power that the bimetallists in the United States have with our Congress and President. No; nothing is to be expected from England.

"Whenever property interests and humanity have come in conflict, England has ever been the enemy of human liberty. All reforms with those so unfortunate as to be in her power have been won with the sword. She yields only to force. [Applause.]

"The money lenders in the United States, who own substantially all of our money, have a selfish interest in maintaining the gold standard. They, too, will not yield. They believe that if the gold standard can survive for a few years longer, the people will get used to it — get used to their poverty — and quietly submit.

"To that end they organize international bimetallic committees and say, 'Wait on England, she will be forced to give us bimetallism.' Vain hope! Deception on this subject has been practiced long enough upon a patient and outraged people.

"With silver remonetized, and gold at a premium, not one-tenth the hardships could result that now afflict us. Why? First: it would double the value of all property. Second: only 4 per cent of the business of the people of this nation is carried on with foreign countries; and a part of this 4 per cent would be transactions with silver using nations; while 96 per cent of the business of our people is domestic transactions. Home business. Is it not better to legislate in the interest of 96 per cent of our business, than the remaining 4 per cent? . . .

"In the impending struggle for the mastery of the commerce of the world, the financial combat between England and the United States cannot be avoided if we are to retain our self-respect, and our people their freedom and prosperity. [Applause.]

"The gold standard will give England the commerce and wealth of the world. The bimetallic standard will make the United States the most prosperous nation on the globe. [Applause.]

"To avoid the struggle means a surrender to England. It means more — it means a tomb raised to the memory of the republic. Delay is dangerous. At any moment an internecine war may break out among us. Wrongs and outrages will not be continuously endured. The people will strike at the laws that inflict them.

"To wait on England is puerile and unnecessary. Her interests are not our interests. 'But,' you ask me, 'how are we to do it?' It will work itself. We have been frightened at a shadow. We have been as much deceived in this respect as we have about other matters connected with this subject.

"Free coinage by the United States will at once establish a parity between the two metals. Any nation that is big enough to take all the silver in the world, and give back merchandise and products in payment for it, will at once establish the parity between it and gold. [Applause.] . . .

"When it is considered that we are giving two dollars worth of property now, in payment for one dollar in gold, you will realize that we are now paying 100 per cent premium on gold. [Applause.]

"And this applies not only to our foreign business, but to our home business.

"With silver remonetized, and a just and equitable standard of values, we can, if necessary, by act of Congress, reduce the number of grains in a gold dollar till it is of the same value as the silver dollar. [Applause.] We can legislate the premium out of gold. [Applause.] Who will say that this is not an effective remedy? I pause for a reply!"

Coin waited for a reply. No one answering him, he continued:

"Until an answer that will commend itself to an unbiased mind is given to this remedy, that guarantees a parity between the metals, write upon the character of every 'international bimetallist' the words 'gold monometallist.'"

Pausing for a moment, as if still waiting for his position to be attacked, he proceeded:

"Give the people back their favored primary money! Give us two arms with which to transact business! Silver the right arm and gold the left arm! Silver the money of the people, and gold the money of the rich.

"Stop this legalized robbery, that is transferring the property of the debtors to the possession of the creditors!

"Citizens! the integrity of the government has been violated. A Financial Trust has control of your money, and with it, is robbing you of your property. Vampires feed upon your commercial blood. The money in the banks is subject to the check of the money lenders. They expect you to quietly submit, and leave your fellow citizens at their mercy. Through the instrumentality of law they have committed a crime that overshadows all other crimes. And yet they appeal to law for their protection. If the starving workingman commits the crime of trespass, they appeal to the law they have contaminated, for his punishment. Drive these money-changers from your temples. Let them discover by your aspect, their masters — the people." [Applause.]

"The United States commands the situation, and can dictate bimetallism to the world at the ratio she is inclined to fix.

"Our foreign ministers sailing out of the New York harbor past the statue of 'Liberty Enlightening the World' should go with instructions to educate the nations of the earth upon the American Financial Policy. We should negative the self-interested influence of England, and speak for industrial prosperity.

"We are now the ally of England in the most cruel and unjust persecution against the weak and defenseless people of the world that was ever waged by tyrants since the dawn of history. [Applause.]

"Our people are losing each year hundreds of millions of dollars; incalculable suffering exists throughout the land; we have begun the work of cutting each other's throats; poor men crazed with hunger are daily shot down by the officers of the law; want, distress and anxiety pervades the entire Union.

"If we are to act let us act quickly.

"It has been truthfully said:

" 'It is at once the result and security of oppression that its victim soon becomes incapable of resistance. Submission to its first encroachments is followed by the fatal lethargy that destroys every noble ambition, and converts the people into cowardly poltroons and fawning sycophants, who hug their chains and lick the hand that smites them!'

"Oppression now seeks to enslave this fair land. Its name is greed. Surrounded by the comforts of life, it is unconscious of the condition of others. Despotism, whether in Russia marching its helpless victims to an eternal night of sorrow, or in Ireland where its humiliating influences are ever before the human eye, or elsewhere; it is the same.

"It is already with us. It has come in the same form that it has come everywhere — by regarding the interests of property as paramount to the interests of humanity. That influence extends from the highest to the lowest. The deputy sheriff regards the $4 a day he gets as more important to him than the life or cause of the workmen he shoots down.

"The Pullman Palace Car Company recently reduced the already low wages of its employees 33⅓ per cent. Unable to make a living, they laid down their tools. A few days later the company declared a quarterly dividend of 2 per cent on watered capital of $30,000,000. This quarterly dividend was $600,000.

"Had this company sent for the committee of the workmen and said, 'We were about to declare our regular quarterly dividend of 2 per cent; it amounts to $600,000; we have concluded to make it 1½ per cent; this will give us $475,000 for three months, or one quarter's profits, and we are going to use the other $125,000 to put back the wages of the men. There would have been no strike. The men would have hailed it as generosity, and the hearts of 4,000 workmen would have been made glad.

"It was not done. It was not to be thought of. These stockholders living in comfort with all their wants provided for, think more of their property interests than they do of humanity, and will see men starve or reduced to the condition of serfs rather than concede an equitable distribution of the profits of their business.

"This has occurred here in the city of your homes; in the World's Fair city; a city supposed to be as patriotic as any we have; if this is human nature here, what do you expect from the men in England who hold our bonds, notes and mortgages payable in gold.

"We are forced to take independent action. To hesitate is cowardly! Shall we wait while the cry of the helpless is heard on every hand? Shall we wait while our institutions are crumbling?" (Cries of "No — no — no!")

"This is a struggle for humanity. For our homes and firesides. For the purity and integrity of our government.

"That all the people of this country sufficiently intelligent to vote cannot understand that the reduction of our primary money to one half its former quantity reduces the value of property proportionately, is one of the inexplainable phenomena in human history.

"Those who do understand it should go among the people and awake them to the situation of peril, in which they are placed. Awake them as you would with startling cries at the coming of flood and fires.

"Arouse them as did Paul Revere as he rode through the streets shouting: 'The British are on our shores.'" . . .

Study Guide

1. This selection may be divided into two major segments:
   (a) W. H. ("Coin") Harvey's view of the history of the American monetary system (pp. 155–159); and
   (b) Harvey's assessment of the nation's financial and monetary plight and his solution for it (pp. 161–165).

You can understand the first section — Harvey's insistence that silver rather than gold was the basic "unit" of American currency — if you keep in mind (contrary to Harvey's assertion) that in the United States in the decades between the end of the Civil War and 1897, silver, not gold, was in increasing supply. The basic division between Harvey and his followers, those who favored the use of gold *and* silver — a position called bimetallism — and his opponents was, to a large extent, a division between debtors, who wanted to pay their debts with an inflated, soft currency; and creditors, who profited from a deflated, hard currency. The Coinage Act of 1873, called by Harvey and other bimetallists "the Crime of 1873," omitted the standard silver dollar from coinage — a deliberate attempt, according to the silverites, to deflate the currency and to cause hardships to those debtors, farmers, and others who needed a more plentiful currency with which to pay off their debts. These essential facts should be kept firmly in mind as you read Harvey's analysis of the currency and the economy during the depression of the 1890's.

2. In the light of the above, turn now to some of the details of Harvey's history of American currency and explain why he insists on:

   (a) considering silver as the basic "unit" of the American dollar (pp. 155–156);
   (b) limiting the role of gold to merely "a companion metal" (p. 156);
   (c) calling gold "the money of the rich" (p. 156); and
   (d) asserting that as a result of the Coinage Act of 1873, "gold is the unit and silver does not enjoy free coinage" and that this is a "crime" against a segment of the American people (pp. 157–158).

3. In his closing arguments (pp. 161–165), Harvey focuses on the sinister role of the English and the American bankers. What, according to Harvey, is their position on bimetallism and why is this harmful to "the people"? What does Harvey propose as the course of action for America?

4. In retrospect, it is well to remember the following: while commodity prices did decline greatly in the late 1880's and early 1890's, causing much hardship and suffering to many Americans, bimetallism, the coinage of all the silver and gold mined in the United States, had its dangers as well, particularly with almost all of the European nations moving towards a gold standard. The gold-silver controversy was, at the insistence of William Jennings Bryan, the principal issue in the presidential election of 1896. Explore.

III. Expansion — by Land and Sea

Helen Hunt Jackson

JUSTICE FOR THE INDIAN

◆{ *1881* }◆   By 1880 nearly all the American Indians had been confined on reservations, most of them west of the Mississippi River. Here they often were defrauded by corrupt government agents and victimized by unscrupulous traders. The sufferings of one tribe, the Ponca, were told to Eastern audiences in 1879 by a brave and a girl, Standing Bear and Bright Eyes. Their story prompted Helen Hunt Jackson to write a book about the wrongs done the Indian by the white man — a book that aroused passionate and partly successful efforts to right the wrongs.

Born in Massachusetts, twice married and once divorced, Mrs. Jackson (1830–1885) spent a part of her mature life in the West, especially in Colorado and California. Under the name H. H. (Helen Hunt) she wrote numerous poems and stories, among them the sentimental tale of Indian life and love, *Ramona* (1884). Her most influential work, the one inspired by Standing Bear and Bright Eyes, was *A Century of Dishonor: A Sketch of the United States Government's Dealings with Some of the Indian Tribes* (1881).

Widely read, this book stirred President Grover Cleveland and many Eastern humanitarians to an interest in reforming Indian affairs. Two organizations were established for appealing to the public and lobbying with the government — the Indian Rights Association in 1882 and the annual Lake Mohonk Conference of Friends of the Indians in 1883. The Eastern reformers urged, among other things, that the Indians be given an opportunity to acquire individual landholdings and American citizenship. Western frontiersmen, most of whom thought the only good Indian was a dead Indian, agreed with the reformers to the extent of favoring a division of reservation lands among the Indians; the frontiersmen hoped to get the leftover lands for themselves. The result was the passage, in 1887 (after Mrs. Jackson's death), of the Dawes Severalty Act, which with some exaggeration has been called the "Indian Emancipation Act." This law authorized the President, at his discretion, to end tribal government and divide the lands among the tribesmen, who were to become citizens immediately and outright owners after twenty-five years.

The conclusion and part of the appendix of *A Century of Dishonor* follow.

A CENTURY OF DISHONOR

THE FOLLOWING letters were printed in the *New York Tribune* in the winter of 1879. They are of interest, not only as giving a minute account of one of the most atrocious massacres ever perpetrated, but also as showing the sense of justice which is to be found in the frontiersman's mind today. That men, exasperated by atrocities and outrages, should have avenged themselves with hot haste and cruelty, was, perhaps, only human;

but that men should be found, fifteen years later, apologizing for, nay, justifying the cruel deed, is indeed a matter of marvel.

LETTER I

In June, 1864, Governor Evans, of Colorado, sent out a circular to the Indians of the Plains, inviting all friendly Indians to come into the neighborhood of the forts, and be protected by the United States troops. Hostilities and depredations had been committed by some bands of Indians, and the Government was about to make war upon them. This circular says:

"In some instances they (the Indians) have attacked and killed soldiers, and murdered peaceable citizens. For this the Great Father is angry, and will certainly hunt them out and punish them; but he does not want to injure those who remain friendly to the whites. He desires to protect and take care of them. For this purpose I direct that all friendly Indians keep away from those who are at war, and go to places of safety. Friendly Arapahoes and Cheyennes belonging to the Arkansas River will go to Major Colby, United States Agent at Fort Lyon, who will give them provisions and show them a place of safety."

In consequence of this proclamation of the governor, a band of Cheyennes, several hundred in number, came in and settled down near Fort Lyon. After a time they were requested to move to Sand Creek, about forty miles from Fort Lyon, where they were still guaranteed "perfect safety" and the protection of the Government. Rations of food were issued to them from time to time. On the 27th of November, Colonel J. M. Chivington, a member of the Methodist Episcopal Church in Denver, and Colonel of the First Colorado Cavalry, led his regiment by a forced march to Fort Lyon, induced some of the United States troops to join him, and fell upon this camp of friendly Indians at daybreak. The chief, White Antelope, always known as friendly to the whites, came running toward the soldiers, holding up his hands and crying "Stop! stop!" in English. When he saw that there was no mistake, that it was a deliberate attack, he folded his arms and waited till he was shot down. The United States flag was floating over the lodge of Black Kettle, the head chief of the tribe; below it was tied also a small white flag as additional security — a precaution Black Kettle had been advised by United States officers to take if he met troops on the Plains. In Major Wynkoop's testimony, given before the committee appointed by Congress to investigate this massacre, is the following passage:

"Women and children were killed and scalped, children shot at their

mothers' breasts, and all the bodies mutilated in the most horrible manner. . . . The dead bodies of females profaned in such a manner that the
recital is sickening, Colonel J. M. Chivington all the time inciting his
troops to their diabolical outrages."

Another man testified as to what he saw on the 30th of November,
three days after the battle, as follows:

"I saw a man dismount from his horse and cut the ear from the body
of an Indian, and the scalp from the head of another. I saw a number of
children killed; they had bullet-holes in them; one child had been cut
with some sharp instrument across its side. I saw another that both ears
had been cut off. . . . I saw several of the Third Regiment cut off fingers
to get the rings off them. I saw Major Sayre scalp a dead Indian. The
scalp had a long tail of silver hanging to it."

Robert Bent testified:

"I saw one squaw lying on the bank, whose leg had been broken. A
soldier came up to her with a drawn sabre. She raised her arm to protect
herself; he struck, breaking her arm. She rolled over, and raised her other
arm; he struck, breaking that, and then left her without killing her. I
saw one squaw cut open, with an unborn child lying by her side."

Major Anthony testified:

"There was one little child, probably three years old, just big enough
to walk through the sand. The Indians had gone ahead, and this little
child was behind, following after them. The little fellow was perfectly
naked, travelling in the sand. I saw one man get off his horse at a distance of about seventy-five yards and draw up his rifle and fire. He
missed the child. Another man came up and said, 'Let me try the son of
a b — —. I can hit him.' He got down off his horse, kneeled down, and
fired at the child, but he missed him. A third man came up, and made a
similar remark, and fired, and the little fellow dropped."

The Indians were not able to make much resistance, as only a part of
them were armed, the United States officers having required them to
give up their guns. Luckily they had kept a few.

When this Colorado regiment of demons returned to Denver they
were greeted with an ovation. *The Denver News* said: "All acquitted
themselves well. Colorado soldiers have again covered themselves with
glory"; and at a theatrical performance given in the city, these scalps
taken from Indians were held up and exhibited to the audience, which
applauded rapturously.

After listening, day after day, to such testimonies as these I have
quoted, and others so much worse that I may not write and *The Tribune*

could not print the words needful to tell them, the committee reported: "It is difficult to believe that beings in the form of men, and disgracing the uniform of United States soldiers and officers, could commit or countenance the commission of such acts of cruelty and barbarity"; and of Colonel Chivington: "He deliberately planned and executed a foul and dastardly massacre, which would have disgraced the veriest savage among those who were the victims of his cruelty."

This was just fifteen years ago, no more. Shall we apply the same rule of judgment to the white men of Colorado that the Government is now applying to the Utes? There are 130,000 inhabitants of Colorado; hundreds of them had a hand in this massacre, and thousands in cool blood applauded it when it was done. There are 4000 Utes in Colorado. Twelve of them, desperate, guilty men, have committed murder and rape, and three or four hundred of them did, in the convenient phrase of our diplomacy, "go to war against the Government"; *i.e.*, they attempted, by force of arms, to restrain the entrance upon their own lands — lands bought, owned and paid for — of soldiers that the Government had sent there, to be ready to make war upon them, in case the agent thought it best to do so! This is the plain English of it. This is the plain, naked truth of it.

And now the Secretary of the Interior has stopped the issue of rations to 1000 of these helpless creatures; rations, be it understood, which are not, and never were, a charity, but are the Utes' rightful dues, on account of lands by them sold; dues which the Government promised to pay "annually forever." Will the American people justify this? There is such a thing as the conscience of a nation — as a nation's sense of justice. Can it not be roused to speak now? Shall we sit still, warm and well fed, in our homes, while five hundred women and little children are being slowly starved in the bleak, barren wilderness of Colorado? Starved, not because storm, or blight, or drouth has visited their country and cut off their crops; not because pestilence has laid its hand on them and slain the hunters who brought them meat, but because it lies within the promise of one man, by one word, to deprive them of one-half their necessary food for as long a term of years as he may please; and "the Secretary of the Interior cannot consistently feed a tribe that has gone to war against the Government."

We read in the statutes of the United States that certain things may be done by "executive order" of the President. Is it not time for a President to interfere when hundreds of women and children are being starved in his Republic by the order of one man? Colonel J. M. Chivington's method was less inhuman by far. To be shot dead is a mercy, and a grace for which we would all sue, if to be starved to death were our only other alternative.

H. H.

New York, Jan. 31st, 1880

This letter drew from the former editor of the *Rocky Mountain News,* a Denver newspaper, the following reply:

LETTER II

To the Editor of the Tribune:

Sir, — In your edition of yesterday appears an article, under the above caption, which arraigns the people of Colorado as a community of barbarous murderers, and finally elevates them above the present Secretary of the Interior, thereby placing the latter gentleman in a most unenviable light if the charges averred be true. "The Sand Creek Massacre" of 1864 is made the text and burden of the article; its application is to the present condition of the White River band of Utes in Colorado. Quotations are given from the testimony gathered, and the report made thereon by a committee of Congress charged with a so-called investigation of the Sand Creek affair. That investigation was made for a certain selfish purpose. It was to break down and ruin certain men. Evidence was taken upon one side only. It was largely false, and infamously partial. There was no answer for the defence.

The Cheyenne and Arapahoe Indians assembled at Sand Creek were not under the protection of a United States fort. A few of them had been encamped about Fort Lyon and drawing supplies therefrom, but they had gradually disappeared and joined the main camp on Dry Sandy, forty miles from the fort, separated from it by a waterless desert, and entirely beyond the limit of its control or observation. While some of the occupants were still, no doubt, occasional visitors at the fort, and applicants for supplies and ammunition, most of the warriors were engaged in raiding the great Platte River Road, seventy-five miles farther north, robbing and burning trains, stealing cattle and horses, robbing and destroying the United States mails, and killing white people. During the summer and fall they had murdered over fifty of the citizens of Colorado. They had stolen and destroyed provisions and merchandise, and driven away stock worth hundreds of thousands of dollars. They had interrupted the mails, and for thirty-two consecutive days none were allowed to pass their lines. When satiated with murder and arson, and loaded with plunder, they would retire to their sacred refuge on Sand Creek to rest and refresh themselves, recruit their wasted supplies of ammunition from Fort Lyon — begged under the garb of gentle, peaceful savages — and then return to the road to relieve their tired comrades, and riot again in carnage and robbery. These are facts; and when the "robbers' roost" was cleaned out, on that sad but glorious 27th day of November, 1864, they were sufficiently proven. Scalps of white men not yet dried; letters and photographs stolen from the mails; bills of lading and invoices of goods; bales and bolts of the goods themselves, addressed to merchants in Denver; half-worn clothing of white women and children, and many other articles of like character, were found in that poetical Indian camp, and recovered by the Colorado soldiers. They were brought to Denver, and those were the scalps exhibited in the theatre of that city. There was also an Indian saddle-blanket entirely fringed around the edges with white women's scalps, with the long, fair hair attached. There was an Indian saddle over the pommel of which was stretched skin stripped from the body of a white woman. Is it any wonder that soldiers flushed with victory, after one of the hardest campaigns ever endured by men, should indulge — some of them — in unwarranted atrocities after finding such evidence of barbarism, and while more than forty of their comrades were weltering in their own blood upon the field?

If "H. H." had been in Denver in the early part of that summer, when the bloated, festering bodies of the Hungate family — father, mother, and two babes — were drawn through the streets naked in an ox-wagon, cut, mutilated, and scalped — the work of those same red fiends who were so justly punished at Sand Creek; if, later, "H. H." had seen an upright and most estimable business man go crazy over the news of his son's being tortured to death a hundred miles down the Platte, as I did; if "H. H." had seen one-half the Colorado homes made desolate that fateful season and a tithe of the tears that were caused to flow. I think there would have been one little word of excuse for the people of Colorado — more than a doubtful comparison with an inefficient and culpable Indian policy. Bear in mind that Colorado had no railroads then. Her supplies reached her by only one road — along the Platte — in wagons drawn by oxen, mules, or horses. That line was in full possession of the enemy. Starvation stared us in the face. Hardly a party went or came without some persons being killed. In some instances whole trains were cut off and destroyed. Sand Creek saved Colorado, and taught the Indians the most salutary lesson they had ever learned. And now, after fifteen years, and here in the shadow of the Nation's Capitol, with the spectre of "H. H.'s" condemnation staring me in the face, I am neither afraid nor ashamed to repeat the language then used by *The Denver News:* "All acquitted themselves well. Colorado soldiers have again covered themselves with glory."

Thus much of history is gone over by "H. H." to present in true dramatic form the deplorable condition of the White River Utes, 1000 in number, who are now suffering the pangs of hunger and the discomfort of cold in the wilds of Western Colorado, without any kind agent to issue rations, provide blankets, or build fires for them. It is really too bad. A painful dispensation of Providence has deprived them of their best friend, and they are desolate and bereaved. He placed his life and its best efforts, his unbounded enthusiasm for their good, his great Christian heart — all at their service. But an accident befell him, and he is no more. The coroner's jury that sat upon his remains found that his dead body had a barrel stave driven into his mouth, a log-chain around his neck, by which it had been dragged about like a dead hog, and sundry bullet-holes through his body. The presumption was that from the effect of some one of these accidents he died; and alas! he is no longer to serve out weekly rations to his flock of gentle Utes. There is no sorrow over his death or the desolation it wrought, but there is pity, oceans of pity, for the Indians who are hungry and cold. True, at the time he died they took the flour, the pork, and salt, and coffee, and sugar, and tobacco, and blankets, and all the other supplies that he would have issued to them through all this long winter had he lived. With his care these would have lasted until spring, and been sufficient for their wants; but without it, "H. H." is suspicious that they are all gone, and yet it is but just past the middle of winter. Can "H. H." tell why this is thus? It is also true that they drove away the large herd of cattle from the increase of which that same unfortunate agent and his predecessors had supplied them with beef for eleven years past, and yet the consumption did not keep pace with the natural increase. They took them all, and are presumed to have them now. True, again, they had at the beginning of winter, or at the period of the melancholy loss of their best friend, about 4000 horses that were rolling fat, and three acres of dogs — not bad food in an emergency, or for an Indian thanksgiving feast — some of which should still remain.

The Whole White River Band Guilty

But "H. H." intimates that there is an alleged excuse for withholding rations from these poor, persecuted red angels. "Twelve" of them have been bad, and the tyrant at the head of the Interior Department is systematically starving all of the 1000 who constitute the band, and their 4000 horses, and 1800 cattle, and three acres of dogs, and six months' supplies, because those twelve bad Indians cannot conscientiously pick themselves out and be offered up as a burnt-offering and a sacrifice to appease the wrath of an outraged and partly civilized nation. This the present indictment, and the Secretary and the President are commanded to stand up and plead "Guilty or not guilty, but you know you are guilty, d — — n you." Now I challenge and defy "H. H.," or any other person living, to pick out or name twelve White River male Utes, over sixteen years of age, who were *not* guilty, directly or indirectly, as principals or accomplices before the fact, in the Thornburgh attack or in the Agency massacre. I know these Indians well enough to know that these attacks were perfectly understood and deliberately planned. I cannot be made to believe that a single one of them, of common-sense and intelligence, was ignorant of what was to take place, and that knowledge extended far beyond the White River band. There were plenty of recruits from both the Los Pinos and the Uintah bands. In withholding supplies from the White River Utes the Secretary of the Interior is simply obeying the law. He cannot, except upon his own personal responsibility, issue supplies to a hostile Indian tribe, and the country will hold him accountable for a departure from his line of duty. Inferentially the Indians are justified by "H. H." in their attack upon Thornburgh's command. Their object was to defend "their own lands — lands bought, owned, and paid for." Bought of whom, pray? Paid for by whom? To whom was payment made? The soldiers were making no attack; they contemplated none. The agent had no authority to order an attack. He could not proclaim war. He could have no control whatever over the troops. But his life was in danger. The honor of his family was at stake. He asked for protection. "H. H." says he had no right to it. His life and the honor of his aged wife and of his virgin daughter are gone, and "H. H." is the champion of fiends who wrought the ruin.

Wm. N. Byers

Washington, D.C., Feb. 6th, 1880

CONCLUSION

There are within the limits of the United States between two hundred and fifty and three hundred thousand Indians, exclusive of those in Alaska. The names of the different tribes and bands, as entered in the statistical tables of the Indian Office Reports, number nearly three hundred. One of the most careful estimates which have been made of their numbers and localities gives them as follows: "In Minnesota and States east of the Mississippi, about 32,500; in Nebraska, Kansas, and the Indian Territory, 70,650; in the Territories of Dakota, Montana, Wyoming, and Idaho, 65,000; in Nevada and the Territories of Colorado, New Mexico, Utah, and Arizona, 84,000; and on the Pacific slope, 48,000."

Of these, 130,000 are self-supporting on their own reservations, "receiving nothing from the Government except interest on their own moneys, or annuities granted them in consideration of the cession of their lands to the United States." [1]

This fact alone would seem sufficient to dispose forever of the accusation, so persistently brought against the Indian, that he will not work.

Of the remainder, 84,000 are partially supported by the Government — the interest money due them and their annuities, as provided by treaty, being inadequate to their subsistence on the reservations where they are confined. In many cases, however, these Indians furnish a large part of their support — the White River Utes, for instance, who are reported by the Indian Bureau as getting sixty-six per cent of their living by "root-digging, hunting, and fishing"; the Squaxin band, in Washington Territory, as earning seventy-five per cent, and the Chippewas of Lake Superior as earning fifty per cent in the same way. These facts also would seem to dispose of the accusation that the Indian will not work.

There are about 55,000 who never visit an agency, over whom the Government does not pretend to have either control or care. These 55,000 "subsist by hunting, fishing, on roots, nuts, berries, etc., and by begging and stealing"; and this also seems to dispose of the accusation that the Indian will not "work for a living." There remains a small portion, about 31,000, that are entirely subsisted by the Government.

There is not among these three hundred bands of Indians one which has not suffered cruelly at the hands either of the Government or of white settlers. The poorer, the more insignificant, the more helpless the band, the more certain the cruelty and outrage to which they have been subjected. This is especially true of the bands on the Pacific slope. These Indians found themselves of a sudden surrounded by and caught up in the great influx of gold-seeking settlers, as helpless creatures on a shore are caught up in a tidal wave. There was not time for the Government to make treaties; not even time for communities to make laws. The tale of the wrongs, the oppressions, the murders of the Pacific-slope Indians in the last thirty years would be a volume by itself, and is too monstrous to be believed.

It makes little difference, however, where one opens the record of the history of the Indians; every page and every year has its dark stain. The story of one tribe is the story of all, varied only by differences of time and place; but neither time nor place makes any difference in the main facts. Colorado is as greedy and unjust in 1880 as was Georgia in 1830, and Ohio in 1795; and the United States Government breaks promises now as deftly as then, and with an added ingenuity from long practice.

[1] Annual Report of Indian Commissioner for 1872.

One of its strongest supports in so doing is the wide-spread sentiment among the people of dislike to the Indian, of impatience with his presence as a "barrier to civilization," and distrust of it as a possible danger. The old tales of the frontier life, with its horrors of Indian warfare, have gradually, by two or three generations' telling, produced in the average mind something like an hereditary instinct of questioning and unreasoning aversion which it is almost impossible to dislodge or soften.

There are hundreds of pages of unimpeachable testimony on the side of the Indian; but it goes for nothing, is set down as sentimentalism or partisanship, tossed aside and forgotten.

President after president has appointed commission after commission to inquire into and report upon Indian affairs, and to make suggestions as to the best methods of managing them. The reports are filled with eloquent statements of wrongs done to the Indians, of perfidies on the part of the Government; they counsel, as earnestly as words can, a trial of the simple and unperplexing expedients of telling truth, keeping promises, making fair bargains, dealing justly in all ways and all things. These reports are bound up with the Government's Annual Reports, and that is the end of them. It would probably be no exaggeration to say that not one American citizen out of ten thousand ever sees them or knows that they exist, and yet any one of them, circulated throughout the country, read by the right-thinking, right-feeling men and women of this land, would be of itself a "campaign document" that would initiate a revolution which would not subside until the Indians' wrongs were, so far as is now left possible, righted.

In 1869 President Grant appointed a commission of nine men, representing the influence and philanthropy of six leading States, to visit the different Indian reservations, and to "examine all matters appertaining to Indian affairs."

In the report of this commission are such paragraphs as the following: "To assert that 'the Indian will not work' is as true as it would be to say that the white man will not work.

"Why should the Indian be expected to plant corn, fence lands, build houses, or do anything but get food from day to day, when experience has taught him that the product of his labor will be seized by the white man tomorrow? The most industrious white man would become a drone under similar circumstances. Nevertheless, many of the Indians" (the commissioners might more forcibly have said 130,000 of the Indians) "are already at work, and furnish ample refutation of the assertion that 'the Indian will not work.' There is no escape from the inexorable logic of facts.

"The history of the Government connections with the Indians is a shameful record of broken treaties and unfulfilled promises. The history of the border white man's connection with the Indians is a sickening record of murder, outrage, robbery, and wrongs committed by the former, as the rule, and occasional savage outbreaks and unspeakably barbarous deeds of retaliation by the latter, as the exception.

"Taught by the Government that they had rights entitled to respect, when those rights have been assailed by the rapacity of the white man, the arm which should have been raised to protect them has ever been ready to sustain the aggressor.

"The testimony of some of the highest military officers of the United States is on record to the effect that, in our Indian wars, almost without exception, the first aggressions have been made by the white man; and the assertion is supported by every civilian of reputation who has studied the subject. In addition to the class of robbers and outlaws who find impunity in their nefarious pursuits on the frontiers, there is a large class of professedly reputable men who use every means in their power to bring on Indian wars for the sake of the profit to be realized from the presence of troops and the expenditure of Government funds in their midst. They proclaim death to the Indians at all times in words and publications, making no distinction between the innocent and the guilty. They irate the lowest class of men to the perpetration of the darkest deeds against their victims, and as judges and jurymen shield them from the justice due to their crimes. Every crime committed by a white man against an Indian is concealed or palliated. Every offence committed by an Indian against a white man is borne on the wings of the post or the telegraph to the remotest corner of the land, clothed with all the horrors which the reality or imagination can throw around it. Against such influences as these the people of the United States need to be warned."

To assume that it would be easy, or by any one sudden stroke of legislative policy possible, to undo the mischief and hurt of the long past, set the Indian policy of the country right for the future, and make the Indians at once safe and happy, is the blunder of a hasty and uninformed judgment. The notion which seems to be growing more prevalent, that simply to make all Indians at once citizens of the United States would be a sovereign and instantaneous panacea for all their ills and all the Government's perplexities, is a very inconsiderate one. To administer complete citizenship of a sudden, all round, to all Indians, barbarous and civilized alike, would be as grotesque a blunder as to dose them all round with any one medicine, irrespective of the symptoms and needs of their diseases. It would kill more than it would cure. Nevertheless, it is true, as was well stated by one of the superintendents of Indian Affairs in 1857, that, "so long as they are not citizens of the United States, their rights of property must remain insecure against invasion. The doors of the federal tribunals being barred against them while wards and dependents, they can only partially exercise the rights of free government, or give to those who make, execute, and construe the few laws they are allowed to enact, dignity sufficient to make them respectable. While they continue individually to gather the crumbs that fall from the table of the United States, idleness, improvidence, and indebtedness will be the rule, and industry, thrift, and freedom from debt the exception. The utter absence of individual title to particular lands deprives every one among them of the chief incentive to labor and exertion — the very mainspring on which the prosperity of a people depends."

All judicious plans and measures for their safety and salvation must embody provisions for their becoming citizens as fast as they are fit, and must protect them till then in every right and particular in which our laws protect other "persons" who are not citizens.

There is a disposition in a certain class of minds to be impatient with any protestation against wrong which is unaccompanied or unprepared with a quick and exact scheme of remedy. This is illogical. When pioneers in a new country find a tract of poisonous and swampy wilderness to be reclaimed, they do not withhold their hands from fire and axe till they see clearly which way roads should run, where good water will spring, and what crops will best grow on the redeemed land. They first clear the swamp. So with this poisonous and baffling part of the domain of our national affairs — let us first "clear the swamp."

However great perplexity and difficulty there may be in the details of any and every plan possible for doing at this late day anything like justice to the Indian, however, hard it may be for good statesmen and good men to agree upon the things that ought to be done, there certainly is, or ought to be, no perplexity whatever, no difficulty whatever, in agreeing upon certain things that ought not to be done, and which must cease to be done before the first steps can be taken toward righting the wrongs, curing the ills, and wiping out the disgrace to us of the present condition of our Indians.

Cheating, robbing, breaking promises — these three are clearly things which must cease to be done. One more thing, also, and that is the refusal of the protection of the law to the Indian's rights of property, "of life, liberty, and the pursuit of happiness."

When these four things have ceased to be done, time, statesmanship, philanthropy, and Christianity can slowly and surely do the rest. Till these four things have ceased to be done, statesmanship and philanthropy alike must work in vain, and even Christianity can reap but small harvest.

Study Guide

1. This chapter contains five selections — all concerned with the expansionist thrust of the American nation in the late nineteenth century. The first (Helen Hunt Jackson) documents the destruction of the Indian and his culture as the white man moved West; the second (Frederick Jackson Turner) expresses a feeling common to many Americans in the 1890's — the notion that the frontier had come to an end; two essays (Alfred Thayer Mahan, and Albert J. Beveridge), differing in emphasis and somewhat in purpose, are united by a common call for expansion overseas; and one (Mark Twain) is in opposition to that expansion. Let us begin with the controversy over the justice (or lack of justice) done to the Indian.

2. In her introductory paragraph, Helen Hunt Jackson provides the rationale for the publication of her letter (pp. 170–173) and the publication of a counter view from the editor of the *Rocky Mountain News* (pp. 173–176). What prompted the exchange?

3. For what purpose does Mrs. Jackson, in her letter in the *New York Tribune,* recite the details of the Chivington Massacre? What action does she urge on the federal government and how does she justify it?

4. Outline the grounds, both in fact and in principle, upon which William N. Byers disagrees?

5. The conclusions to which Mrs. Jackson comes regarding federal Indian policy and her recommendations will be found on pp. 176–181. What are her comments on:
   (a) the work habits of the Indian;
   (b) the federal benefits received by them; and
   (c) the record of the United States government?

   What are her recommendations? Can you see how in these closing paragraphs the basis was laid for the passage, a few years later, of the Dawes Severalty Act? Explain.

Frederick Jackson Turner

WHAT THE WEST HAS MEANT

1893 IN 1893, at the World's Columbian Exposition in Chicago, there was much to attract the fair-goer's attention. There were, for example, side shows such as "Little Egypt" with its naughty belly-dancers. Also at the fair — but this attracted little attention at the time — was an assemblage of sober professors who belonged to the American Historical Association. One of the younger members, on this occasion, read a paper which was to be remembered long after the exposition as a whole had been pretty much forgotten. This essay was, indeed, to revolutionize the thinking of historians, and through them the thinking of the schools and of the public, about the meaning of the American past.

The young historian was Frederick Jackson Turner (1861–1932). He had graduated from the University of Wisconsin, earned a Ph.D. at Johns Hopkins (where he was a friend and fellow student of Woodrow Wilson), and returned to Wisconsin to teach. Afterwards he was to be for many years a professor of history at Harvard.

His famous essay was entitled "The Significance of the Frontier in American History." In it he viewed the American past from the standpoint of his native ground, the Middle West, whereas most historians before him had looked at the subject from the perspective of the Atlantic coast. He was interested in basic questions, such as the origin of the national character and of American democracy. Older historians had traced the "germs" of democratic institutions as far as the forests of ancient Germany. Turner found the roots of American democracy as well as other American ways in the forests of his own country.

For nearly forty years the frontier interpretation prevailed. Then critics arose to point out that Turner had been vague regarding some matters and confused or contradictory regarding others. Few scholars today accept the Turner hypothesis without qualification, but even fewer dare to deny that "there must be something to it."

THE SIGNIFICANCE OF THE FRONTIER IN AMERICAN HISTORY

IN A RECENT bulletin of the superintendent of the census for 1890 appear these significant words: "Up to and including 1880 the country had a frontier of settlement, but at present the unsettled area has been so broken into by isolated bodies of settlement that there can hardly be said to be a frontier line. In the discussion of its extent, its westward movement, etc., it cannot, therefore, any longer have a place in the census reports." This brief official statement marks the closing of a great historic movement. Up to our own day American history has been in a large degree the history of the colonization of the Great West. The existence of an area of free land, its continuous recession, and the advance of American settlement westward explain American development.

Behind institutions, behind constitutional forms and modifications, lie the vital forces that call these organs into life and shape them to meet changing conditions. The peculiarity of American institutions is the fact that they have been compelled to adapt themselves to the changes of an expanding people — to the changes involved in crossing a continent, in winning a wilderness, and in developing at each area of this progress, out of the primitive economic and political conditions of the frontier, the complexity of city life. Said Calhoun in 1817, "We are great, and rapidly — I was about to say fearfully — growing!" So saying, he touched the distinguishing feature of American life. All peoples show development: the germ theory of politics has been sufficiently emphasized. In the case of most nations, however, the development has occurred in a limited area; and if the nation has expanded, it has met other growing peoples whom it has conquered. But in the case of the United States we have a different phenomenon. Limiting our attention to the Atlantic coast, we have the familiar phenomenon of the evolution of institutions in a limited area, such as the rise of representative government; the differentiation of simple colonial governments into complex organs; the progress from primitive industrial society, without division of labor, up to manufacturing civilization. But we have in addition to this *a recurrence of the process of evolution in each Western area reached in the process of expansion.* Thus American development has exhibited not merely advance along a single line but a return to primitive conditions on a continually advancing frontier line, and a new development for that area. American social development has been continually beginning over again on the frontier. This perennial rebirth, this fluidity of American life, this expansion westward with its new opportunities, its continuous touch with the simplicity of primitive society, furnish the forces dominating American character. The true point of view in the history of this nation is not the Atlantic coast, it is the Great West. Even the slavery struggle, which is made so exclusive an object of attention by writers like Professor von Holst, occupies its important place in American history because of its relation to westward expansion.

In this advance the frontier is the outer edge of the wave — the meeting point between savagery and civilization. Much has been written about the frontier from the point of view of border warfare and the chase, but as a field for the serious study of the economist and the historian it has been neglected.

What is the [American] frontier? It is not the European frontier — a fortified boundary line running through dense populations. The most significant thing about it is that it lies at the hither edge of free land. In the census reports it is treated as the margin of that settlement which has a density of two or more to the square mile. The term is an elastic one, and for our purpose does not need sharp definition. We shall consider the whole frontier belt, including the Indian country and the outer margin of the "settled area" of the census reports. This paper will make no attempt to treat the subject exhaustively; its aim is simply to call attention to the frontier as a fertile field for investigation, and to suggest some of the problems which arise in connection with it.

In the settlement of America we have to observe how European life entered the continent, and how America modified and developed that life, and reacted on Europe. Our early history is the study of European germs developing in an American environment. Too exclusive attention has been paid by institutional students to the Germanic origins, too little to the American factors. The frontier is the line of most rapid and effective Americanization. The wilderness masters the colonist. It finds him a European in dress, industries, tools, modes of travel, and thought. It takes him from the railroad car and puts him in the birch canoe. It strips off the garments of civilization, and arrays him in the hunting shirt and the moccasin. It puts him in the log cabin of the Cherokee and the Iroquois, and runs an Indian palisade around him. Before long he has gone to planting Indian corn and plowing with a sharp stick; he shouts the war cry and takes the scalp in orthodox Indian fashion. In short, at the frontier the environment is at first too strong for the man. He must accept the conditions which it furnishes, or perish, and so he fits himself into the Indian clearings and follows the Indian trails. Little by little he transforms the wilderness, but the outcome is not the old Europe, not simply the development of Germanic germs, any more than the first phenomenon was a case of reversion to the Germanic mark. The fact is that here is a new product that is American. At first the frontier was the Atlantic coast. It was the frontier of Europe in a very real sense. Moving westward, the frontier became more and more American. *As successive terminal moraines result from successive glaciations, so each frontier leaves its traces behind it, and when it becomes a settled area the region still partakes of the frontier characteristics.* Thus the advance of the frontier has meant a steady movement away from the influence of Europe, a steady growth of independence on American lines. And to study this advance, the men who grew up under these conditions, and the political, economic, and social results of it, is to study the really American part of our history.

THE STAGES OF FRONTIER ADVANCE

In the course of the seventeenth century the frontier was advanced up the Atlantic river courses, just beyond the fall line, and the tidewater region became the settled area. In the first half of the eighteenth century another advance occurred. Traders followed the Delaware and Shawnese Indians to the Ohio as early as the end of the first quarter of the century.

Governor Spotswood of Virginia made an expedition in 1714 across the Blue Ridge. The end of the first quarter of the century saw the advance of the Scotch-Irish and the Palatine Germans up the Shenandoah Valley into the western part of Virginia, and along the Piedmont region of the Carolinas. The Germans in New York pushed the frontier of settlement up the Mohawk to German Flats. In Pennsylvania the town of Bedford indicates the line of settlement. Settlements had begun on New River, a branch of the Kanawha, and on the sources of the Yadkin and French Broad. The king attempted to arrest the advance by his proclamation of 1763 forbidding settlements beyond the sources of the rivers flowing into the Atlantic; but in vain. In the period of the Revolution the frontier crossed the Alleghenies into Kentucky and Tennessee, and the upper waters of the Ohio were settled. When the first census was taken in 1790, the continuous settled area was bounded by a line which ran near the coast of Maine, and included New England except a portion of Vermont and New Hampshire, New York along the Hudson and up the Mohawk about Schenectady, eastern and southern Pennsylvania, Virginia well across the Shenandoah Valley, and the Carolinas and eastern Georgia. Beyond this region of continuous settlement were the small settled areas of Kentucky and Tennessee and the Ohio, with the mountains inter-vening between them and the Atlantic area, thus giving a new and im-portant character to the frontier. The isolation of the region increased its peculiarly American tendencies, and the need for transportation facilities to connect it with the East called out important schemes of internal im-provement, which will be noted farther on. The "West," as a self-con-scious section, began to evolve.

From decade to decade distinct advances of the frontier occurred. By the census of 1820 the settled area included Ohio, southern Indiana and Illinois, southeastern Missouri, and about one-half of Louisiana. This settled area had surrounded Indian areas, and the management of these tribes became an object of political concern. The frontier region of the time lay along the Great Lakes, where Astor's American Fur Company operated in the Indian trade, and beyond the Mississippi, where Indian traders extended their activity even to the Rocky Mountains; Florida also furnished frontier conditions. The Mississippi River region was the scene of typical frontier settlements.

The rising steam navigation on Western waters, the opening of the Erie Canal, and the westward extension of cotton culture added five frontier states to the Union in this period. Grund, writing in 1836, de-clares: "It appears, then, that the universal disposition of Americans to emigrate to the western wilderness, in order to enlarge their dominion over inanimate nature, is the actual result of an expansive power, which is inherent in them, and which, by continually agitating all classes of society, is constantly throwing a large portion of the whole population on the extreme confines of the state, in order to gain space for its development. Hardly is a new state or territory formed before the same principle manifests itself again, and gives rise to a further emigration; and so it is destined to go on until a physical barrier must finally obstruct its progress."

In the middle of this century the line indicated by the present eastern boundary of Indian Territory, Nebraska, and Kansas marked the frontier of the Indian country. Minnesota and Wisconsin still exhibited frontier conditions, but the distinctive frontier of the period is found in California, where the gold discoveries had sent a sudden tide of adventurous miners, and in Oregon and the settlements in Utah. As the frontier had leaped over the Alleghenies, so now it skipped the Great Plains and the Rocky Mountains; and in the same way that the advance of the frontiersmen beyond the Alleghenies had caused the rise of important questions of transportation and internal improvement, so now the settlers beyond the Rocky Mountains needed means of communication with the East, and in the furnishing of these arose the settlement of the Great Plains and the development of still another kind of frontier life. Railroads, fostered by land grants, sent an increasing tide of immigrants into the far West. The United States Army fought a series of Indian wars in Minnesota, Dakota, and the Indian Territory.

By 1880 the settled area had been pushed into northern Michigan, Wisconsin, and Minnesota, along Dakota rivers, and into the Black Hills region, and was ascending the rivers of Kansas and Nebraska. The development of mines in Colorado had drawn isolated frontier settlements into that region, and Montana and Idaho were receiving settlers. The frontier was found in these mining camps and the ranches of the Great Plains. The superintendent of the census for 1890 reports, as previously stated, that the settlements of the West lie so scattered over the region that there can no longer be said to be a frontier line.

In these successive frontiers we find natural boundary lines which have served to mark and to affect the characteristics of the frontiers, namely: the "fall line"; the Allegheny Mountains; the Mississippi; the Missouri where its direction approximates north and south; the line of the arid lands, approximately the ninety-ninth meridian; and the Rocky Mountains. The fall line marked the frontier of the seventeenth century; the Alleghenies that of the eighteenth; the Mississippi that of the first quarter of the nineteenth; the Missouri that of the middle of this century (omitting the California movement); and the belt of the Rocky Mountains and the arid tract, the present frontier. Each was won by a series of Indian wars.

THE FRONTIER FURNISHES A FIELD
FOR COMPARATIVE STUDY OF SOCIAL DEVELOPMENT

At the Atlantic frontier one can study the germs of processes repeated at each successive frontier. We have the complex European life, sharply precipitated by the wilderness into the simplicity of primitive conditions. The first frontier had to meet its Indian question, its question of the disposition of the public domain, of the means of intercourse with the older settlements, of the extension of political organization, of religious and educational activity. And the settlement of these and similar questions for one frontier served as a guide for the next. The American student need not go to the "prim little townships of Sleswick" for illustrations of the law of continuity and development. For example, he may study the origin of our land-policies in the colonial land policy; he may see how the system grew by adapting the statutes to the customs of the successive frontiers. He may see how the mining experience in the lead regions of Wisconsin, Illinois, and Iowa was applied to the mining laws of the Sierras, and how our Indian policy has been a series of experimentations on successive frontiers. Each tier of new states has found, in the older ones, material for its constitutions. Each frontier has made similar contributions to American character, as will be discussed farther on.

But with all these similarities there are essential differences, due to the place element and the time element. It is evident that the farming frontier of the Mississippi Valley presents different conditions from the mining frontier of the Rocky Mountains. The frontier reached by the Pacific Railroad, surveyed into rectangles, guarded by the United States Army, and recruited by the daily immigrant ship, moves forward at a swifter pace and in a different way than the frontier reached by the birch canoe or the pack horse. The geologist traces patiently the shores of ancient seas, maps their areas, and compares the older and the newer. It would be a work worth the historian's labors to mark these various frontiers and in detail compare one with another. Not only would there result a more adequate conception of American development and characteristics, but invaluable additions would be made to the history of society.

Loria, the Italian economist, has urged the study of colonial life as an aid in understanding the stages of European development, affirming that colonial settlement is for economic science what the mountain is for geology, bringing to light primitive stratifications. "America," he says, "has the key to the historical enigma which Europe has sought for centuries in vain, and the land which has no history reveals luminously the course of universal history." He is right. The United States lies like a huge page in the history of society. Line by line as we read from west to east we find the record of social evolution. It begins with the Indian and the hunter; it goes on to tell of the disintegration of savagery by the entrance of the trader, the pathfinder of civilization; we read the annals of the pastoral stage in ranch life; the exploitation of the soil by the raising of unrotated crops of corn and wheat in sparsely settled farming communities; the intensive culture of the denser farm settlement; and finally the manufacturing organization with city and factory system. This page is familiar to the student of census statistics, but how little of it has been used by our historians.

Each of these areas has had an influence in our economic and political history; the evolution of each into a higher stage has worked political transformations. But what constitutional historian has made any adequate attempt to interpret political facts by the light of these social areas and changes?

The Atlantic frontier was compounded of fisherman, fur-trader, miner, cattle-raiser, and farmer. Excepting the fisherman, each type of industry was on the march toward the West, impelled by an irresistible attraction. Each passed in successive waves across the continent. Stand at Cumberland Gap and watch the procession of civilization, marching single file — the buffalo, following the trail to the salt springs, the Indian, the fur-trader and hunter, the cattle-raiser, the pioneer farmer — and the frontier has passed by. Stand at South Pass in the Rockies a century later and see the same procession with wider intervals between. The unequal rate of advance compels us to distinguish the frontier into the trader's frontier, the rancher's frontier or the miner's frontier, and the farmer's frontier. When the mines and the cowpens were still near the fall line, the traders' pack trains were tinkling across the Alleghenies, and the French on the Great Lakes were fortifying their posts, alarmed by the British trader's birch canoe. When the trappers scaled the Rockies, the farmer was still near the mouth of the Missouri.

THE INDIAN TRADER'S FRONTIER

Why was it that the Indian trader passed so rapidly across the continent? What effects followed from the trader's frontier? The trade was coeval with American discovery. The Norsemen, Vespucius, Verrazano, Hudson, John Smith, all trafficked for furs. The Plymouth pilgrims settled in Indian cornfields, and their first return cargo was of beaver and lumber. The records of the various New England colonies show how steadily exploration was carried into the wilderness by this trade. What is true for New England is, as would be expected, even plainer for the rest of the colonies. All along the coast from Maine to Georgia the Indian trade opened up the river courses. Steadily the trader passed westward, utilizing the older lines of French trade. The Ohio, the Great Lakes, the Mississippi, the Missouri, and the Platte, the lines of westward advance, were ascended by traders. They found the passes in the Rocky Mountains and guided Lewis and Clark, Frémont, and Bidwell.

The explanation of the rapidity of this advance is bound up with the effects of the trader on the Indian. The trading post left the unarmed tribes at the mercy of those that had purchased firearms — a truth which the Iroquois Indians wrote in blood, and so the remote and unvisited tribes gave eager welcome to the trader. "The savages," wrote La Salle, "take better care of us French than of their own children; from us only can they get guns and goods." This accounts for the trader's power and the rapidity of his advance. Thus the disintegrating forces of civilization entered the wilderness. Every river valley and Indian trail became a fissure in Indian society, and so that society became honeycombed. Long before the pioneer farmer appeared on the scene, primitive Indian life had passed away. The farmers met Indians armed with guns. The trading frontier, while steadily undermining Indian power by making the tribes ultimately dependent on the whites, yet through its sale of guns gave to the Indian increased power of resistance to the farming frontier. French colonization was dominated by its trading frontier, English colonization by its farming frontier. There was an antagonism between the two frontiers as between the two nations. Said Duquesne to the Iroquois, "Are you ignorant of the difference between the king of England and the king of France? Go see the forts that our king has established and you will see that you can still hunt under their very walls. They have been placed for your advantage in places which you frequent. The English, on the contrary, are no sooner in possession of a place than the game is driven away. The forest falls before them as they advance, and the soil is laid bare so that you can scarce find the wherewithal to erect a shelter for the night."

And yet, in spite of this opposition of the interests of the trader and the farmer, the Indian trade pioneered the way for civilization. The buffalo trail became the Indian trail, and this became the trader's "trace"; the trails widened into roads, and the roads into turnpikes, and these in turn were transformed into railroads. The same origin can be shown for the railroads of the South, the far West, and the Dominion of Canada.

The trading posts reached by these trails were on the sites of Indian villages which had been placed in positions suggested by nature; and these trading posts, situated so as to command the water systems of the country, have grown into such cities as Albany, Pittsburgh, Detroit, Chicago, St. Louis, Council Bluffs, and Kansas City. Thus civilization in America has followed the arteries made by geology, pouring an ever richer tide through them, until at last the slender paths of aboriginal intercourse have been broadened and interwoven into the complex mazes of modern commercial lines; the wilderness has been interpenetrated by lines of civilization, growing ever more numerous. It is like the steady growth of a complex nervous system for the originally simple, inert continent. If one would understand why we are today one nation rather than a collection of isolated states, he must study this economic and social consolidation of the country. In this progress from savage conditions lie topics for the evolutionist.

The effect of the Indian frontier as a consolidating agent in our history is important. From the close of the seventeenth century various intercolonial congresses have been called to treat with the Indians and establish common measures of defense. Particularism was strongest in colonies with no Indian frontier. This frontier stretched along the western border like a cord of union. The Indian was a common danger, demanding united action. Most celebrated of these conferences was the Albany Congress of 1754, called to treat with the Six Nations, and to consider plans of union. Even a cursory reading of the plan proposed by the Congress reveals the importance of the frontier. The powers of the general council and the officers were, chiefly, the determination of peace and war with the Indians, the regulation of Indian trade, the purchase of Indian lands, and the creation and government of new settlements as a security against the Indians. It is evident that the unifying tendencies of the Revolutionary period were facilitated by the previous co-operation in the regulation of the frontier. In this connection may be mentioned the importance of the frontier, from that day to this, as a military training school, keeping alive the power of resistance to aggression, and developing the stalwart and rugged qualities of the frontiersman.

THE RANCHER'S FRONTIER

It would not be possible in the limits of this paper to trace the other frontiers across the continent. Travelers of the eighteenth century found the "cowpens" among the canebrakes and peavine pastures of the South, and the "cow drivers" took their droves to Charleston, Philadelphia, and New York. Travelers at the close of the War of 1812 met droves of more than a thousand cattle and swine from the interior of Ohio going to Pennsylvania to fatten for the Philadelphia market. The ranges of the Great Plains, with ranch and cowboy and nomadic life, are things of yesterday and of today. The experience of the Carolina cowpens guided the ranchers of Texas. One element favoring the rapid extension of the rancher's frontier is the fact that in a remote country lacking transportation facilities the product must be in small bulk, or must be able to transport itself, and the cattle-raiser could easily drive his product to market. The effect of these great ranches on the subsequent agrarian history of the localities in which they existed should be studied.

THE FARMER'S FRONTIER

The maps of the census reports show an uneven advance of the farmer's frontier, with tongues of settlement pushed forward and with indentations of wilderness. In part this is due to Indian resistance, in part to the location of river valleys and passes, in part to the unequal force of the centers of frontier attraction. Among the important centers of attraction may be mentioned the following: fertile and favorably situated soils, salt springs, mines, and army posts.

ARMY POSTS

The frontier army post, serving to protect the settlers from the Indians, has also acted as a wedge to open the Indian country, and has been a nucleus for settlement. In this connection mention should also be made of the government military and exploring expeditions in determining the lines of settlement. But all the more important expeditions were greatly indebted to the earliest pathmakers, the Indian guides, the traders and trappers, and the French voyageurs, who were inevitable parts of governmental expeditions from the days of Lewis and Clark. Each expedition was an epitome of the previous factors in western advance.

SALT SPRINGS

In an interesting monograph Victor Hehn has traced the effect of salt upon early European development and has pointed out how it affected the lines of settlement and the form of administration. A similar study might be made for the salt springs of the United States. The early settlers were tied to the coast by the need of salt, without which they could not preserve their meats or live in comfort. Writing in 1752, Bishop Spangenburg says of a colony for which he was seeking lands in North Carolina, "They will require salt & other necessaries which they can neither manufacture nor raise. Either they must go to Charleston, which is 300 miles distant . . . or else they must go to Boling's Point in V^a on a branch of the James, & is also 300 miles from here . . . or else they must go down the Roanoke — I know not how many miles — where salt is brought up from the Cape Fear." This may serve as a typical illustration. An annual pilgrimage to the coast for salt thus became essential. Taking flocks of furs and ginseng root, the early settlers sent their pack trains after seeding time each year to the coast. This proved to be an important educational influence, since it was almost the only way in which the pioneer learned what was going on in the East. But when discovery was made of the salt springs of the Kanawha, and the Holston, and Kentucky, and central New York, the West began to be freed from dependence on the coast. It was in part the effect of finding these salt springs that enabled settlement to cross the mountains.

From the time the mountains rose between the pioneer and the seaboard, a new order of Americanism arose. The West and the East began to get out of touch with each other. The settlements from the sea to the mountains kept connection with the rear and had a certain solidarity. But the overmountain men grew more and more independent. The East took a narrow view of American advance, and nearly lost these men. Kentucky and Tennessee history bears abundant witness to the truth of this statement. The East began to try to hedge and limit westward expansion. Though Webster could declare that there were no Alleghenies in his politics, yet in politics in general they were a very solid factor.

LAND

The exploitation of the beasts took hunter and trader to the West, the exploitation of the grasses took the rancher West, and the exploitation of the virgin soil of the river valleys and prairies attracted the farmer. Good soils have been the most continuous attraction to the farmer's frontier. The land hunger of the Virginians drew them down the rivers into Carolina, in early colonial days; the search for soils took the Massachusetts men to Pennsylvania and to New York. As the Eastern lands were taken up, migration flowed across them to the West. Daniel Boone, the great backwoodsman, who combined the occupations of hunter, trader, cattle-raiser, farmer, and surveyor — learning, probably from the traders, of the fertility of the lands on the upper Yadkin, where the traders were wont to rest as they took their way to the Indians — left his Pennsylvania home with his father, and passed down the Great Valley road to that stream. Learning from a trader of its game and the rich pastures of Kentucky, he pioneered the way for the farmers to that region. Thence he passed to the frontier of Missouri, where his settlement was long a landmark on the frontier. Here again he helped to open the way for civilization, finding salt licks, and trails, and land. His son was among the earliest trappers in the passes of the Rocky Mountains, and his party are said to have been the first to camp on the present site of Denver. His grandson, Colonel A. J. Boone of Colorado, was a power among the Indians of the Rocky Mountains, and was appointed an agent by the government. Kit Carson's mother was a Boone. Thus this family epitomizes the backwoodsman's advance across the continent.

The farmer's advance came in a distinct series of waves. In Peck's *New Guide to the West,* published in Cincinnati in 1837, occurs this suggestive passage:

Generally, in all the western settlements, three classes, like the waves of the ocean, have rolled one after the other. First, comes the pioneer, who depends for the subsistence of his family chiefly upon the natural growth of vegetation, called the "range," and the proceeds of hunting. His implements of agriculture are rude, chiefly of his own make, and his efforts directed mainly to a crop of corn and a "truck patch." The last is a rude garden for growing cabbage, beans, corn for roasting ears, cucumbers and potatoes. A log cabin and, occasionally, a stable and corn-crib, and a field of a dozen acres, the timber girdled or "deadened," and fenced, are enough for his occupancy. It is quite immaterial whether he ever becomes the owner of the soil. He is the occupant for the time being, pays no rent, and feels as independent as the "lord of the manor." With a horse, cow, and one or two breeders of swine, he strikes into the woods with his family, and becomes the founder of a new country, or perhaps state. He builds his cabin, gathers around him a few other families of similar tastes and habits, and occupies till the range is somewhat subdued, and hunting a little precarious, or, which is more frequently the case, till neighbors crowd around, roads, bridges, and fields annoy him, and he lacks elbow room. The pre-emption law enables him to dispose of his cabin and corn-field to the next class of emigrants, and, to employ his own figures, he "breaks for the high timber," "clears out for the New Purchase," or migrates to Arkansas, or Texas, to work the same process over.

The next class of emigrants purchase the lands, add field to field, clear out the roads, throw rough bridges over the streams, put up hewn log houses, with glass windows, and brick or stone chimneys, occasionally plant orchards, build mills, school-houses, courthouses, etc., and exhibit the picture and forms of plain, frugal, civilized life.

Another wave rolls on. The men of capital and enterprise come. The "settler" is ready to sell out, and take the advantage of the rise of property — push farther into the interior, and become, himself, a man of capital and enterprise in turn. The small village rises to a spacious town or city; substantial edifices of brick, extensive fields, orchards, gardens, colleges and churches are seen. Broadcloths, silks, leg-horns, crapes, and all the refinements, luxuries, elegancies, frivolities and fashions are in vogue. Thus wave after wave is rolling westward: — the real *El dorado* is still farther on.

A portion of the two first classes remain stationary amidst the general movement, improve their habits and condition, and rise in the scale of society.

The writer has traveled much amongst the first class — the real pioneers. He has lived many years in connection with the second grade; and now the third wave is sweeping over large districts of Indiana, Illinois and Missouri. Migration has become almost a habit in the West. Hundreds of men can be found, not over fifty years of age, who have settled for the fourth, fifth or sixth time on a new spot. To sell out, and remove only a few hundred miles, makes up a portion of the variety of backwoods life and manners.

Omitting those of the pioneer farmers who move from the love of adventure, the advance of the more steady farmer is easy to understand. Obviously the immigrant was attracted by the cheap lands of the frontier, and even the native farmer felt their influence strongly. Year by year the farmers who lived on soil, whose returns were diminished by unrotated crops, were offered the virgin soil of the frontier at nominal prices. Their growing families demanded more lands, and these were dear. The competition of the unexhausted, cheap, and easily tilled prairie lands compelled the farmer either to go West and continue the exhaustion of the soil on a new frontier or to adopt intensive culture. Thus the census of 1890 shows, in the Northwest, many counties in which there is an absolute, or a relative, decrease of population. These states have been sending farmers to advance the frontier on the plains, and have themselves begun to turn to intensive farming and to manufacture. A decade before this, Ohio had shown the same transition stage. Thus the demand for land and the love of wilderness freedom drew the frontier ever onward.

Having now roughly outlined the various kinds of frontiers, and their modes of advance, chiefly from the point of view of the frontier itself, we may next inquire what were the influences on the East and on the Old World. A rapid enumeration of some of the more noteworthy effects is all that I have time for.

COMPOSITE NATIONALITY

First, we note that the frontier promoted the formation of a composite nationality for the American people. The coast was preponderantly English, but the later tides of continental immigration flowed across to the free lands. This was the case from the early colonial days. The Scotch-Irish and the Palatine Germans, or "Pennsylvania Dutch," furnished dominant elements in the stock of the colonial frontier. With these peoples were also the freed indented servants, or redemptioners, who at the expiration of their time of service passed to the frontier. Governor Alexander Spotswood of Virginia writes in 1717, "The Inhabitants of our frontiers are composed generally of such as have been transported hither as Servants, and being out of their time, and settle themselves where Land is to be taken up and that will produce the necessarys of Life with little Labour." Very generally these redemptioners were of non-English stock. In the crucible of the frontier immigrants were Americanized, liberated, and fused into a mixed race, English in neither nationality nor characteristics. The process has gone on from the early days to our own. Burke and other writers in the middle of the eighteenth century believed that Pennsylvania was threatened with the "danger of being wholly foreign in language, manners, and perhaps even inclinations." The German and Scotch-Irish elements in the frontier of the South were only less great. In the middle of the present century the German element in Wisconsin was already so considerable that leading publicists looked to the creation of a German state out of the commonwealth by concentrating their colonization. Such examples teach us to beware of misinterpreting the fact that there is a common English speech in America into a belief that the stock is also English.

INDUSTRIAL INDEPENDENCE

In another way the advance of the frontier decreased our dependence on England. The coast, particularly of the South, lacked diversified industries and was dependent on England for the bulk of its supplies. In the South there was even a dependence on the Northern colonies for articles of food. Governor James Glen of South Carolina writes in the middle of the eighteenth century: "Our trade with New York and Philadelphia was of this sort, draining us of all the little money and bills that we could gather from other places, for their bread, flour, beer, hams, bacon, and other things of their produce, all which except beer, our new townships begin to supply us with, which are settled with very industrious and consequently thriving Germans. This no doubt diminishes the number of shipping, and the appearance of our trade, but is far from being a detriment to us."

Before long the frontier created a demand for merchants. As it retreated from the coast it became less and less possible for England to bring her supplies directly to the consumer's wharfs. and carry away staple crops; and staple crops began to give way to diversified agriculture for a time. The effect of this phase of the frontier action upon the northern section is perceived when we realize how the advance of the frontier aroused seaboard cities like Boston, New York, and Baltimore to engage in rivalry for what Washington called "the extensive and valuable trade of a rising empire."

EFFECTS ON NATIONAL LEGISLATION

The legislation which most developed the powers of the national government, and played the largest part in its activity, was conditioned on the frontier. Writers have discussed the subjects of tariff, land, and internal improvement as pendants to the slavery question. But when American history comes to be rightly viewed it will be seen that the slavery question is an incident. In the period from the end of the first half of the present century to the close of the Civil War, slavery rose to primary but far from exclusive importance. But this does not justify Professor von Holst, to take an example, in treating our constitutional history in its formative period down to 1828 in a single volume, giving six volumes chiefly to the history of slavery from 1828 to 1861, under the title of a *Constitutional History of the United States*. The growth of nationalism and the evolution of American political institutions were dependent on the advance of the frontier. Even so recent a writer as Rhodes, in his *History of the United States since the Compromise of 1850*, has treated the legislation called out by the western advance as incidental to the slavery struggle.

This is a wrong perspective. The pioneer needed the goods of the coast, and so the grand series of internal improvements and railroad legislation began, with potent nationalizing effects. But the West was not content with bringing the farm to the factory. Under the lead of Clay — "Harry of the West" — protective tariffs were passed, with the cry of bringing the factory to the farm.

THE PUBLIC DOMAIN

The public domain has been a force of profound importance in the nationalization and development of the government. The effects of the struggle of the landed and the landless states, and of the Ordinance of 1787, need no discussion. Administratively the frontier called out some of the highest and most vitalizing activities of the general government. The purchase of Louisiana was perhaps the constitutional turning point in the history of the republic, inasmuch as it afforded both a new area for national legislation, and the occasion of the downfall of the policy of strict construction. But the purchase of Louisiana was called out by frontier needs and demands. As frontier states accrued to the Union, the national power grew. In a speech on the dedication of the Calhoun monument, Mr. Lamar explained: "In 1789 the states were the creators of the federal government; in 1861 the federal government was the creator of a large majority of the states."

When we consider the public domain from the point of view of the sale and disposal of the public lands, we are again brought face to face with the frontier. The policy of the United States in dealing with its lands is in sharp contrast with the European system of scientific administration. Efforts to make this domain a source of revenue, and to withhold it from emigrants in order that settlement might be compact, were in vain. The jealousy and the fears of the East were powerless in the face of the demands of the frontiersmen. John Quincy Adams was obliged to confess: "My own system of administration, which was to make the national domain the inexhaustible fund for progressive and unceasing internal improvement, has failed." The reason is obvious; systems of administration were not what the West demanded; it wanted land. Adams states the situation as follows:

"The slave-holders of the South have bought the cooperation of the Western country by the bribe of the Western lands, abandoning to the new Western States their own proportion of this public property, and aiding them in the design of grasping all the lands into their own hands. Thomas H. Benton was the author of this system, which he brought forward as a substitute for the American system of Mr. Clay, and to supplant him as the leading statesman of the West. Mr. Clay, by his tariff compromise with Mr. Calhoun, abandoned his own American system. At the same time he brought forward a plan for distributing among all the States of the Union the proceeds of the sales of the public lands. His bill for that purpose passed both houses of Congress, but was vetoed by President Jackson, who, in his annual message of December, 1832, formally recommended that all the public lands should be gratuitously given away to individual adventurers and to the States in which the lands are situated."

"No subject," said Henry Clay, "which has presented itself to the present, or perhaps any preceding, congress, is of greater magnitude than that of the public lands." When we consider the far-reaching effects of the government's land policy upon political, economic, and social aspects of American life, we are disposed to agree with him. But this legislation was framed under frontier influences, and under the lead of Western statesmen like Benton and Jackson. Said Senator Scott of Indiana in 1841: "I consider the pre-emption law merely declaratory of the custom or common law of the settlers."

NATIONAL TENDENCIES OF THE FRONTIER

It is safe to say that the legislation with regard to land, tariff, and internal improvements — the American system of the nationalizing Whig Party — was conditioned on frontier ideas and needs. But it was not merely in legislative action that the frontier worked against the sectionalism of the coast. The economic and social characteristics of the frontier worked against sectionalism. The men of the frontier had closer resemblances to the Middle region than to either of the other sections. Pennsylvania had been the seed plot of frontier emigration, and, although she passed on her settlers along the Great Valley into the west of Virginia and the Carolinas, yet the industrial society of these Southern frontiersmen was always more like that of the Middle region than like that of the tidewater portion of the South, which later came to spread its industrial type throughout the South.

The Middle region, entered by New York harbor, was an open door to all Europe. The tidewater part of the South represented typical Englishmen, modified by a warm climate and servile labor, and living in baronial fashion on great plantations; New England stood for a special English movement — Puritanism. The Middle region was less English than the other sections. It had a wide mixture of nationalities, a varied society, the mixed town and county system of local government, a varied economic life, many religious sects. In short, it was a region mediating between New England and the South, and the East and the West. It represented that composite nationality which the contemporary United States exhibits, that juxtaposition of non-English groups, occupying a valley or a little settlement, and presenting reflections of the map of Europe in their variety. It was democratic and nonsectional, if not national; "easy, tolerant, and contented"; rooted strongly in material prosperity. It was typical of the modern United States. It was at least sectional not only because it lay between North and South but also because with no barriers to shut out its frontiers from its settled region, and with a system of connecting waterways, the Middle region mediated between East and West as well as between North and South. Thus it became the typically American region. Even the New Englander, who was shut out from the frontier by the Middle region, tarrying in New York or Pennsylvania on his westward march, lost the acuteness of his sectionalism on the way.

Until the spread of cotton culture into the interior gave homogeneity to the South, the western part of it showed tendencies to fall away from the faith of the fathers into internal improvement legislation and nationalism. In the Virginia convention of 1829–30, called to revise the constitution, Mr. Leigh, of Chesterfield, one of the tidewater counties, declared:

"One of the main causes of discontent which led to this convention, that which had the strongest influence in overcoming our veneration for the work of our fathers, which taught us to contemn the sentiments of Henry and Mason and Pendleton, which weaned us from our reverence for the constituted authorities of the state, was an overweening passion for internal improvement. I say this with perfect knowledge; for it has been avowed to me by gentleman from the West over and over again. And let me tell the gentleman from Albemarle (Mr. Gordon) that it has been another principal object of those who set this ball of revolution in motion, to overturn the doctrine of state rights, of which Virginia has been the very pillar, and to remove the barrier she has interposed to the interference of the federal government in that same work of internal improvement, by so reorganizing the legislature that Virginia, too, may be hitched to the federal car."

It was this nationalizing tendency of the West that transformed the democracy of Jefferson into the national republicanism of Monroe and the democracy of Andrew Jackson. The West of the War of 1812, the West of Clay, and Benton, and Harrison, and Andrew Jackson, shut off by the Middle states and the mountains from the coast sections, had a solidarity of its own with national tendencies. On the tide of the Father of Waters, North and South met and mingled into a nation. Interstate migration went steadily on — a process of cross-fertilization of ideas and institutions. The fierce struggle of the sections over slavery on the western frontier does not diminish the truth of this statement; it proves the truth of it. Slavery was a sectional trait that would not down, but in the West it could not remain sectional. It was the greatest of frontiersmen who declared: "I believe this government cannot endure permanently half slave and half free. It will become all of one thing, or all of the other." Nothing works for nationalism like intercourse within the nation. Mobility of population is death to localism, and the western frontier worked irresistibly in unsettling population. The effects reached back from the frontier and affected profoundly the Atlantic Coast, and even the Old World.

GROWTH OF DEMOCRACY

But the most important effect of the frontier has been in the promotion of democracy here and in Europe. As has been pointed out, the frontier is productive of individualism. Complex society is precipitated by the wilderness into a kind of primitive organization based on the family. The tendency is anti-social. It produces antipathy to control, and particularly to any direct control. The tax-gatherer is viewed as a representative of oppression. Professor Osgood, in an able article, has pointed out that the frontier conditions prevalent in the colonies are important factors in the explanation of the American Revolution, where individual liberty was sometimes confused with absence of all effective government. The same conditions aid in explaining the difficulty of instituting a strong government in the period of the confederacy. The frontier individualism has from the beginning promoted democracy.

The frontier states that came into the Union in the first quarter of a century of its existence came in with democratic suffrage provisions, and had reactive effects of the highest importance upon the older states whose peoples were being attracted there. It was *western* New York that forced an extension of suffrage in the constitutional convention of that state in 1821; and it was *western* Virginia that compelled the tidewater region to put a more liberal suffrage provision in the constitution framed in 1830, and to give to the frontier region a more nearly proportionate representation with the tidewater aristocracy. The rise of democracy as an effective force in the nation came in with Western preponderance under Jackson and William Henry Harrison, and it meant the triumph of the frontier — with all of its good and with all of its evil elements.

An interesting illustration of the tone of frontier democracy in 1830 comes from the debates in the Virginia convention already referred to. A representative from western Virginia declared: "But, sir, it is not the increase of population in the West which this gentlemen ought to fear. It is the energy which the mountain breeze and western habits impart to those emigrants. They are regenerated, politically I mean, sir. They soon become *working politicians;* and the difference, sir, between a *talking* and a *working* politician is immense. The Old Dominion has long been celebrated for producing great orators; the ablest metaphysicians in policy; men that can split hairs in all abstruse questions of political economy. But at home, or when they return from congress, they have negroes to fan them asleep. But a Pennsylvania, a New York, an Ohio, or a western Virginia statesman, though far inferior in logic, metaphysics and rhetoric to an old Virginia statesman, has this advantage, that when he returns home he takes off his coat and takes hold of the plough. This gives him bone and muscle, sir, and preserves his republican principles pure and uncontaminated."

So long as free land exists, the opportunity for a competency exists, and economic power secures political power. But the democracy born of free land, strong in selfishness and individualism, intolerant of administrative experience and education, and pressing individual liberty beyond its proper bounds, has its dangers as well as its benefits. Individualism in America has allowed a laxity in regard to governmental affairs which has rendered possible the spoils system, and all the manifest evils that follow from the lack of a highly developed civic spirit. In this connection may be noted also the influence of frontier conditions in permitting lax business honor, inflated paper currency, and wildcat banking. The colonial and Revolutionary frontier was the region whence emanated many of the worst forms of an evil currency. The West in the War of 1812 repeated the phenomenon on the frontier of that day, while the speculation and wildcat banking of the period of the crisis of 1837 occurred on the new frontier belt of the next tier of states. Thus each one of the periods of lax financial integrity coincides with periods when a new set of frontier communities had arisen, and coincides in area with these successive frontiers, for the most part. The recent Populist agitation is a case in point. Many a state that now declines any connection with the tenets of the Populists itself adhered to such ideas in an earlier stage of the development of the state. A primitive society can hardly be expected to show the intelligent appreciation of the complexity of business interests in a developed society. The continual recurrence of these areas of paper-money agitation is another evidence that the frontier can be isolated and studied as a factor in American history of the highest importance.

ATTEMPTS TO CHECK AND REGULATE THE FRONTIER

The East has always feared the result of an unregulated advance of the frontier, and has tried to check and guide it. The English authorities would have checked settlement at the headwaters of the Atlantic tributaries and allowed the savages to enjoy their deserts in quiet lest the peltry trade should decrease. This called out Burke's splendid protest:

"[If] you stopped your grants, what would be the consequence? The people would occupy without grants. They have already so occupied in many places. You cannot station garrisons in every part of these deserts. If you drive the people from one place, they will carry on their annual tillage, and remove with their flocks and herds to another. Many of the people in the back settlements are already little attached to particular situations. Already they have topped the Appalachian mountains. From thence they behold before them an immense plain, one vast, rich, level meadow; a square of five hundred miles. Over this they would wander without a possibility of restraint; they would change their manners with their habits of life; would soon forget a government by which they were disowned; would become hordes of English Tartars; and, pouring down upon your unfortified frontiers a fierce and irresistible cavalry, become masters of your governors and your counselors, your collectors and comptrollers, and of all the slaves that adhered to them. Such would, and in no long time must, be the effect of attempting to forbid as a crime, and to suppress as an evil, the command and blessing of Providence, 'Increase and multiply.' Such would be the happy result of an endeavor to keep as a lair of wild beasts that earth which God by an express charter has given to the children of men."

But the English government was not alone in its desire to limit the advance of the frontier, and guide its destinies. Tidewater Virginia and South Carolina gerrymandered those colonies to ensure the dominance of the coast in their legislatures. Washington desired to settle a state at a time in the Northwest; Jefferson would have reserved from settlement the territory of his Louisiana purchase north of the thirty-second parallel, in order to offer it to the Indians in exchange for their settlement east of the Mississippi. "When we shall be full on this side," he writes, "we may lay off a range of states on the western bank from the head to the mouth, and so range after range, advancing compactly as we multiply." Madison went so far as to argue to the French minister that the United States had no interest in seeing population extend itself on the right bank of the Mississippi, but should rather fear it. When the Oregon question was under debate, in 1824, Smyth of Virginia would have drawn an unchangeable line for the limits of the United States at the outer limit of two tiers of states beyond the Mississippi, complaining that the seaboard states were being drained of the flower of their population by the bringing of too much land into market. Even Thomas Benton, the man of widest views of the destiny of the West, at this stage of his career declared that along the ridge of the Rocky Mountains "the western limits of the republic should be drawn, and the statue of the fabled god Terminus should be raised upon its highest peak, never to be thrown down." But the attempts to limit our boundaries, to restrict land sales and settlement, and to deprive the West of its share of political power were all in vain. Steadily that frontier of settlement advanced and carried with it individualism, democracy, and nationalism, and powerfully affected the East and the Old World.

MISSIONARY ACTIVITY

The most effective efforts of the East to regulate the frontier came through its educational and religious activity, exerted by interstate migration and by organized societies. Speaking in 1835, Dr. Lyman Beecher declared: "It is equally plain that the religious and political destiny of our nation is to be decided in the West," and he pointed out that the population of the West "is assembled from all the states of the Union, and from all the nations of Europe, and is rushing in like the waters of the flood, demanding for its moral preservation the immediate and universal action of those institutions which discipline the mind, and arm the conscience and the heart. And so various are the opinions and habits, and so recent and imperfect is the acquaintance, and so sparse are the settlements of the West, that no homogeneous public sentiment can be formed to legislate immediately into being the requisite institutions. And yet they are all needed immediately, in their utmost perfection and power. A nation is being 'born in a day'. . . . But what will become of the West, if her prosperity rushes up to such a majesty of power, while those great institutions linger which are necessary to form the mind, and the conscience, and the heart of that vast world. It must not be permitted. . . . Let no man at the East quiet himself, and dream of liberty, whatever may become of the West. . . . Her destiny is our destiny."

With this appeal to the conscience of New England, he adds appeals to her fears lest other religious sects anticipate her own. The New England preacher and schoolteacher left their mark on the West. The dread of Western emancipation from New England's political and economic control was paralleled by fears lest the West cut loose from her religion. Commenting in 1850 on reports that settlement was rapidly extending northward in Wisconsin, the editor of the *Home Missionary* writes: "We scarcely know whether to rejoice or to mourn over this extension of our settlements. While we sympathize in whatever tends to increase the physical resources and prosperity of our country, we cannot forget that with all these dispersions into remote and still remoter corners of the land, the supply of the means of grace is becoming relatively less and less." Acting in accordance with such ideas, home missions were established and Western colleges were erected. As seaboard cities like Philadelphia, New York, and Baltimore strove for the mastery of Western trade, so the various denominations strove for the possession of the West. Thus an intellectual stream from New England sources fertilized the West. On the other hand, the contest for power and the expansive tendency furnished to the various sects by the existence of a moving frontier must have had important results on the character of religious organization in the United States. The religious aspects of the frontier make a chapter in our history which needs study.

INTELLECTUAL TRAITS

From the conditions of frontier life came intellectual traits of profound importance. The works of travelers along each frontier from colonial days onward describe for each certain traits, and these traits have, while softening down, still persisted as survivals in the place of their origin, even when a higher social organization succeeded. The result is that to the frontier the American intellect owes its striking characteristics. That coarseness and strength combined with acuteness and inquisitiveness, that practical, inventive turn of mind, quick to find expedients, that masterful grasp of material things, lacking in the artistic but powerful to effect great ends, that restless, nervous energy, that dominant individualism, working for good and for evil, and withal that buoyancy and exuberance which comes with freedom, these are traits of the frontier, or traits called out elsewhere because of the existence of the frontier. Since the days when the fleet of Columbus sailed into the waters of the New World, America has been another name for opportunity, and the people of the United States have taken their tone from the incessant expansion which has not only been open but has even been forced upon them. He would be a rash prophet who should assert that the expansive character of American life has now entirely ceased. Movement has been its dominant fact, and, unless this training has no effect upon a people, the American intellect will continually demand a wider field for its exercise. But never again will such gifts of free land offer themselves. For a moment at the frontier the bonds of custom are broken, and unrestraint is triumphant. There is not *tabula rasa*. The stubborn American environment is there with its imperious summons to accept its conditions; the inherited ways of doing things are also there; and yet, in spite of environment, and in spite of custom, each frontier did indeed furnish a new field of opportunity, a gate of escape from the bondage of the past; and freshness, and confidence, and scorn of older society, impatience of its restraints and its ideas, and indifference to its lessons, have accompanied the frontier. What the Mediterranean Sea was to the Greeks, breaking the bond of custom, offering new experiences, calling out new institutions and activities, that, and more, the ever retreating frontier has been to the United States directly, and to the nations of Europe more remotely. And now, four centuries from the discovery of America, at the end of a hundred years of life under the Constitution, the frontier has gone, and with its going has closed the first period of American history.

Study Guide

1. Turner's influential essay contains the following themes:
   (a) his basic thesis (pp. 182–184);
   (b) a chronological conceptualization of the American frontier (pp. 184–187);

(c) the variety of frontiers (pp. 187–195);

(d) the influence of the frontier (pp. 195–201);

(e) the interaction between East and West (pp. 201–203); and

(f) conclusion (pp. 203–204).

Note, at the outset, Turner's basic theme: "The true point of view in the history of this nation is not the Atlantic coast, it is the Great West." Elaborate on what point of view Turner is opposing and the meaning of his basic proposition.

2. On pp. 185–187, Turner outlines the principal frontier stages; use this outline and work your way through "The Stages of Frontier Advance," summarizing illustratively as you go.

3. Try to understand the point Turner is making on pp. 187–188: the notion that the study of frontier history can teach the historian much about social evolution and its political, economic, and constitutional implications. How does Turner go about trying to confirm this point?

4. Summarize Turner's views on the impact of the frontier on ethnic differences, industry, national legislation, the nationalization of the country, and the growth of democratic institutions.

5. What is the nature of East-West interaction according to Turner? Amplify.

6. What contributions to the intellectual character of the American people does Turner claim for the frontier?

7. Looking back, can you account for the usefulness and the popularity of the "Turner thesis" on a generation of American historians who followed and built upon Turner's ideas? Why, after 1890, would the notion of the importance of the frontier in American history attract both historians and laymen? (A clue will be found in the first paragraph of the Turner essay.)

8. And in conclusion:

(a) Would you say that Turner's treatment of the frontier is a balanced one? Does he find many negative characteristics on the frontier?

(b) Can you think of any as a consequence of *your* studies in American history?

(c) One historian has suggested that the "Turner thesis" came to be one of the causes of American imperialism in the closing years of the 1890's. Can you see how and why? Explain.

(d) All in all, what would you say is of lasting value for a student of American history in this essay?

Alfred Thayer Mahan

SEA POWER AND IMPERIALISM

◆§{*1890*}§◆ OF ALL American historical writings, those of Alfred T. Mahan had the greatest practical importance. The son of a West Point professor, Mahan (1840-1914) chose a career in the navy, graduated from the Naval Academy at Annapolis, served as a Union officer during the Civil War, and eventually rose to the rank of rear admiral. In 1894 he was appointed lecturer on history, strategy, and tactics and president of the Naval War College at Newport, R.I. During the Spanish-American War he was a member of the naval board of strategy.

Meanwhile he wrote numerous books and articles on the role of sea power in history. Sea power, he argued, had been and continued to be decisive in the national struggles of the modern world. As means to greatness for the United States, he advocated the construction of a big navy, the building of an Isthmian canal, the acquisition of overseas bases, the promotion of foreign trade and investment, and the cultivation of friendship with Great Britain. His writings were used by American proponents of navalism and expansion, among them his friends Theodore Roosevelt and Henry Cabot Lodge. His arguments appealed also to big-navy men abroad; his books were placed, at the direction of Kaiser William II, in the ships' libraries of the German Navy.

Mahan's views are well summarized in his essay "The United States Looking Outward," originally published as a magazine article in 1890 and republished in *The Interest of America in Sea Power* (1897).

THE UNITED STATES LOOKING OUTWARD

INDICATIONS are not wanting of an approaching change in the thoughts and policy of Americans as to their relations with the world outside their own borders. For the past quarter of a century, the predominant idea, which has asserted itself successfully at the polls and shaped the course of the government, has been to preserve the home market for the home industries. The employer and the workman alike have been taught to look at the various economical measures proposed from this point of view, to regard with hostility any step favoring the intrusion of the foreign producer upon their own domain, and rather to demand increasingly rigorous measures of exclusion than to acquiesce in any loosening of the chain that binds the consumer to them. The inevitable consequence has followed, as in all cases when the mind or the eye is exclusively fixed in one direction, that the danger of loss or the prospect of advantage in another quarter has been overlooked; and although the abounding resources of the country have maintained the exports at a high figure, this flattering result has been due more to the superabundant bounty of Nature than to the demand of other nations for our protected manufactures.

For nearly the lifetime of a generation, therefore, American industries have been thus protected, until the practice has assumed the force of a tradition, and is clothed in the mail of conservatism. In their mutual relations, these industries resemble the activities of a modern ironclad that has heavy armor, but inferior engines and guns; mighty for defence, weak for offence. Within, the home market is secured; but outside, beyond the broad seas, there are the markets of the world, that can be entered and controlled only by a vigorous contest, to which the habit of trusting to protection by statute does not conduce.

At bottom, however, the temperament of the American people is essentially alien to such a sluggish attitude. Independently of all bias for or against protection, it is safe to predict that, when the opportunities for gain abroad are understood, the course of American enterprise will cleave a channel by which to reach them. Viewed broadly, it is a most welcome as well as significant fact that a prominent and influential advocate of protection, a leader of the party committed to its support, a keen reader of the signs of the times and of the drift of opinion, has identified himself with a line of policy which looks to nothing less than such modifications of the tariff as may expand the commerce of the United States to all quarters of the globe. Men of all parties can unite on the words of Mr. Blaine, as reported in a recent speech: "It is not an ambitious destiny for so great a country as ours to manufacture only what we can consume, or produce only what we can eat." In face of this utterance of so shrewd and able a public man, even the extreme character of the recent tariff legislation seems but a sign of the coming change, and brings to mind that famous Continental System, of which our own is the analogue, to support which Napoleon added legion to legion and enterprise to enterprise, till the fabric of the Empire itself crashed beneath the weight.

The interesting and significant feature of this changing attitude is the turning of the eyes outward, instead of inward only, to seek the welfare of the country. To affirm the importance of distant markets, and the relation to them of our own immense powers of production, implies logically the recognition of the link that joins the products and the markets, — that is, the carrying trade; the three together constituting that chain of maritime power to which Great Britain owes her wealth and greatness. Further, is it too much to say that, as two of these links, the shipping and the markets, are exterior to our own borders, the acknowledgment of them carries with it a view of the relations of the United States to the world radically distinct from the simple idea of self-sufficingness? We shall not follow far this line of thought before there will dawn the realization of America's unique position, facing the older worlds of the East and West, her shores washed by the oceans which touch the one or the other, but which are common to her alone.

Coincident with these signs of change in our own policy there is a restlessness in the world at large which is deeply significant, if not ominous. It is beside our purpose to dwell upon the internal state of Europe, whence, if disturbances arise, the effect upon us may be but partial and indirect. But the great seaboard powers there do not stand on guard against their continental rivals only; they cherish also aspirations for commercial extension, for colonies, and for influence in distant regions, which may bring, and, even under our present contracted policy, already have brought them into collision with ourselves. The incident of the Samoa Islands, trivial apparently, was nevertheless eminently suggestive of European ambitions. America then roused from sleep as to interests closely concerning her future. At this moment internal troubles are imminent in the Sandwich Islands, where it should be our fixed determination to allow no foreign influence to equal our own. All over the world German commercial and colonial push is coming into collision with other nations: witness the affair of the Caroline Islands with Spain; the partition of New Guinea with England; the yet more recent negotiation between these two powers concerning their share in Africa, viewed with deep distrust and jealousy by France; the Samoa affair; the conflict between German control and American interests in the islands of the western Pacific; and the alleged progress of German influence in Central and South America. It is noteworthy that, while these various contentions are sustained with the aggressive military spirit characteristic of the German Empire, they are credibly said to arise from the national temper more than from the deliberate policy of the government, which in this matter does not lead, but follows, the feeling of the people, — a condition much more formidable.

There is no sound reason for believing that the world has passed into a period of assured peace outside the limits of Europe. Unsettled political conditions, such as exist in Haïti, Central America, and many of the Pacific islands, especially the Hawaiian group, when combined with great military or commercial importance as is the case with most of these positions, involve, now as always, dangerous germs of quarrel, against which it is prudent at least to be prepared. Undoubtedly, the general temper of nations is more averse from war than it was of old. If no less selfish and grasping than our predecessors, we feel more dislike to the discomforts and sufferings attendant upon a breach of peace; but to retain that highly valued repose and the undisturbed enjoyment of the returns of commerce, it is necessary to argue upon somewhat equal terms of strength with an adversary. It is the preparedness of the enemy, and not acquiescence in the existing state of things, that now holds back the armies of Europe.

On the other hand, neither the sanctions of international law nor the justice of a cause can be depended upon for a fair settlement of differences, when they come into conflict with a strong political necessity on the one side opposed to comparative weakness on the other. In our still-pending dispute over the seal-fishing of Bering Sea, whatever may be thought of the strength of our argument, in view of generally admitted principles of international law, it is beyond doubt that our contention is reasonable, just, and in the interest of the world at large. But in the attempt to enforce it we have come into collision not only with national susceptibilities as to the honor of the flag, which we ourselves very strongly share, but also with a state governed by a powerful necessity, and exceedingly strong where we are particularly weak and exposed. Not only has Great Britain a mighty navy and we a long defenceless seacoast, but it is a great commercial and political advantage to her that her larger colonies, and above all Canada, should feel that the power of the mother country is something which they need, and upon which they can count. The dispute is between the United States and Canada, not the United States and Great Britain; but it has been ably used by the latter to promote the solidarity of sympathy between herself and her colony. With the mother country alone an equitable arrangement, conducive to well-understood mutual interests, could be reached readily; but the purely local and peculiarly selfish wishes of Canadian fishermen dictate the policy of Great Britain, because Canada is the most important link uniting her to her colonies and maritime interests in the Pacific. In case of a European war, it is possible that the British navy will not be able to hold open the route through the Mediterranean to the East; but having a strong naval station at Halifax, and another at Esquimalt, on the Pacific, the two connected by the Canadian Pacific Railroad, England possesses an alternate line of communication far less exposed to maritime aggression than the former, or than the third route by the Cape of Good Hope, as well as two bases essential to the service of her commerce, or other naval operations, in the North Atlantic and the Pacific. Whatever arrangement of this question is finally reached, the fruit of Lord Salisbury's attitude scarcely can fail to be a strengthening of the sentiments of attachment to, and reliance upon, the mother country, not only in Canada, but in the other great colonies. These feelings of attachment and mutual dependence supply the living spirit, without which the nascent schemes for Imperial Federation are but dead mechanical contrivances; nor are they without influence upon such generally unsentimental considerations as those of buying and selling, and the course of trade.

This dispute, seemingly paltry yet really serious, sudden in its appearance and dependent for its issue upon other considerations than its own merits, may serve to convince us of many latent and yet unforeseen dangers to the peace of the western hemisphere, attendant upon the opening of a canal through the Central American Isthmus. In a general way, it is evident enough that this canal, by modifying the direction of trade routes, will induce a great increase of commercial activity and carrying trade throughout the Caribbean Sea; and that this now comparatively deserted nook of the ocean will become, like the Red Sea, a great thoroughfare of shipping, and will attract, as never before in our day, the interest and ambition of maritime nations. Every position in that sea will have enhanced commercial and military value, and the canal itself will become a strategic centre of the most vital importance. Like the Canadian Pacific Railroad, it will be a link between the two oceans; but, unlike it, the use, unless most carefully guarded by treaties, will belong wholly to the belligerent which controls the sea by its naval power. In case of war, the United States will unquestionably command the Canadian Railroad, despite the deterrent force of operations by the hostile navy upon our seaboard; but no less unquestionably will she be impotent, as against any of the great maritime powers, to control the Central American canal. Militarily speaking, and having reference to European complications only, the piercing of the Isthmus is nothing but a disaster to the United States, in the present state of her military and naval preparation. It is especially dangerous to the Pacific coast; but the increased exposure of one part of our seaboard reacts unfavorably upon the whole military situation.

Despite a certain great original superiority conferred by our geographical nearness and immense resources, — due, in other words, to our natural advantages, and not to our intelligent preparations, — the United States is woefully unready, not only in fact but in purpose, to assert in the Caribbean and Central America a weight of influence proportioned to the extent of her interests. We have not the navy, and, what is worse, we are not willing to have the navy, that will weigh seriously in any disputes with those nations whose interests will conflict there with our own. We have not, and we are not anxious to provide, the defence of the seaboard which will leave the navy free for its work at sea. We have not, but many other powers have, positions, either within or on the borders of the Caribbean, which not only possess great natural advantages for the control of that sea, but have received and are receiving that artificial strength of fortification and armament which will make them practically inexpugnable. On the contrary, we have not on the Gulf of Mexico even the beginning of a navy yard which could serve as the base of our operations. Let me not be misunderstood. I am not regretting that we have not the means to meet on terms of equality the great navies of the Old World. I recognize, what few at least say, that, despite its great surplus revenue, this country is poor in proportion to its length of seaboard and its exposed points. That which I deplore, and which is a sober, just, and reasonable cause of deep national concern, is that the nation neither has nor cares to have its sea frontier so defended, and its navy of such power, as shall suffice, with the advantages of our position, to weight seriously when inevitable discussions arise, — such as we have recently had about Samoa and Bering Sea, and which may at any moment come up about the Caribbean Sea or the canal. Is the United States, for instance, prepared to allow Germany to acquire the Dutch stronghold of Curaçao, fronting the Atlantic outlet of both the proposed canals of Panama and Nicaragua? Is she prepared to acquiesce in any foreign power purchasing from Haïti a naval station on the Windward Passage, through which pass our steamer routes to the Isthmus? Would she acquiesce in a foreign protectorate over the Sandwich Islands, that great central station of the Pacific, equidistant from San Francisco, Samoa, and the Marquesas, and an important post on our lines of communication with both Australia and China? Or will it be maintained that any one of these questions, supposing it to arise, is so exclusively one-sided, the arguments of policy and right so exclusively with us, that the other party will at once yield his eager wish, and gracefully withdraw? Was it so at Samoa? Is it so as regards Bering Sea? The motto seen on so many ancient cannon, *Ultima ratio regum*, is not without its message to republics.

It is perfectly reasonable and legitimate, in estimating our needs of military preparation, to take into account the remoteness of the chief naval and military nations from our shores, and the consequent difficulty of maintaining operations at such a distance. It is equally proper, in framing our policy, to consider the jealousies of the European family of states, and their consequent unwillingness to incur the enmity of a people so strong as ourselves; their dread of our revenge in the future, as well as their inability to detach more than a certain part of their forces to our shores without losing much of their own weight in the councils of Europe. In truth, a careful determination of the force that Great Britain or France could probably spare for operations against our coasts, if the latter were suitably defended, without weakening their European position or unduly exposing their colonies and commerce, is the starting-point from which to calculate the strength of our own navy. If the latter be superior to the force that thus can be sent against it, and the coast be so defended as to leave the navy free to strike where it will, we can maintain our rights; not merely the rights which international law concedes, and which the moral sense of nations now supports, but also those equally real rights which, though not conferred by law, depend upon a clear preponderance of interest, upon obviously necessary policy, upon self-preservation, either total or partial. Were we so situated now in respect of military strength, we could secure our perfectly just claim as to the seal fisheries; not by seizing foreign ships on the open sea, but by the evident fact that, our cities being protected from maritime attack, our position and superior population lay open the Canadian Pacific, as well as the frontier of the Dominion, to do with as we please. Diplomats do not flourish such disagreeable truths in each other's faces; they look for a *modus vivendi,* and find it.

While, therefore, the advantages of our own position in the western hemisphere, and the disadvantages under which the operations of a European state would labor, are undeniable and just elements in the calculations of the statesman, it is folly to look upon them as sufficient alone for our security. Much more needs to be cast into the scale that it may incline in favor of our strength. They are mere defensive factors, and partial at that. Though distant, our shores can be reached; being defenceless, they can detain but a short time a force sent against them. With a probability of three months' peace in Europe, no maritime power would fear to support its demands by a number of ships with which it would be loath indeed to part for a year.

Yet, were our sea frontier as strong as it now is weak, passive self-defence, whether in trade or war, would be but a poor policy, so long as this world continues to be one of struggle and vicissitude. All around us now is strife; "the struggle of life," "the race of life," are phrases so familiar that we do not feel their significance till we stop to think about them. Everywhere nation is arrayed against nation; our own no less than others. What is our protective system but an organized warfare? In carrying it on, it is true, we have only to use certain procedures which all states now concede to be a legal exercise of the national power, even though injurious to themselves. It is lawful, they say, to do what we will with our own. Are our people, however, so unaggressive that they are likely not to want their own way in matters where their interests turn on points of disputed right, or so little sensitive as to submit quietly to encroachment by others, in quarters where they long have considered their own influence should prevail?

Our self-imposed isolation in the matter of markets, and the decline of our shipping interest in the last thirty years, have coincided singularly with an actual remoteness of this continent from the life of the rest of the world. The writer has before him a map of the North and South Atlantic oceans, showing the direction of the principal trade routes and the proportion of tonnage passing over each; and it is curious to note what deserted regions, comparatively, are the Gulf of Mexico, the Caribbean Sea, and the adjoining countries and islands. A broad band stretches from our northern Atlantic coast to the English Channel; another as broad from the British Islands to the East, through the Mediterranean and Red Sea, overflowing the borders of the latter in order to express the volume of trade. Around either cape — Good Hope and Horn — pass strips of about one-fourth this width, joining near the equator, midway between Africa and South America. From the West Indies issues a thread, indicating the present commerce of Great Britain with a region which once, in the Napoleonic wars, embraced one-fourth of the whole trade of the Empire. The significance is unmistakable: Europe has now little mercantile interest in the Caribbean Sea.

When the Isthmus is pierced, this isolation will pass away, and with it the indifference of foreign nations. From wheresoever they come and whithersoever they afterward go, all ships that use the canal will pass through the Caribbean. Whatever the effect produced upon the prosperity of the adjacent continent and islands by the thousand wants attendant upon maritime activity, around such a focus of trade will centre large commercial and political interests. To protect and develop its own, each nation will seek points of support and means of influence in a quarter where the United States always has been jealously sensitive to the intrusion of European powers. The precise value of the Monroe Doctrine is understood very loosely by most Americans, but the effect of the familiar phrase has been to develop a national sensitiveness, which is a more frequent cause of war than material interests; and over disputes caused by such feelings there will preside none of the calming influence due to the moral authority of international law, with its recognized principles, for the points in dispute will be of policy, of interest, not of conceded right. Already France and Great Britain are giving to ports held by them a degree of artificial strength uncalled for by their present importance. They look to the near future. Among the islands and on the mainland there are many positions of great importance, held now by weak or unstable states. Is the United States willing to see them sold to a powerful rival? But what right will she invoke against the transfer? She can allege but one, — that of her reasonable policy supported by her might.

Whether they will or no, Americans must now begin to look outward. The growing production of the country demands it. An increasing volume of public sentiment demands it. The position of the United States, between the two Old Worlds and the two great oceans, makes the same claim, which will soon be strengthened by the creation of the new link joining the Atlantic and Pacific. The tendency will be maintained and increased by the growth of the European colonies in the Pacific, by the advancing civilization of Japan, and by the rapid peopling of our Pacific States with men who have all the aggressive spirit of the advanced line of national progress. Nowhere does a vigorous foreign policy find more favor than among the people west of the Rocky Mountains.

It has been said that, in our present state of unpreparedness, a trans-isthmian canal will be a military disaster to the United States, and especially to the Pacific coast. When the canal is finished, the Atlantic seaboard will be neither more nor less exposed than it now is; it will merely share with the country at large the increased danger of foreign complications with inadequate means to meet them. The danger of the Pacific coast will be greater by so much as the way between it and Europe is shortened through a passage which the stronger maritime power can control. The danger will lie not merely in the greater facility for despatching a hostile squadron from Europe, but also in the fact that a more powerful fleet than formerly can be maintained on that coast by a European power, because it can be called home so much more promptly in case of need. The greatest weakness of the Pacific ports, however, if wisely met by our government, will go far to insure our naval superiority there. The two chief centres, San Francisco and Puget Sound, owing to the width and the great depth of the entrances, cannot be effectively protected by torpedoes; and consequently, as fleets can always pass batteries through an unobstructed channel, they cannot obtain perfect security by means of fortifications only. Valuable as such works will be to them, they must be further garrisoned by coast-defence ships, whose part in repelling an enemy will be co-ordinated with that of the batteries. The sphere of action of such ships should not be permitted to extend far beyond the port to which they are allotted, and of whose defence they form an essential part; but within that sweep they will always be a powerful reinforcement to the sea-going navy, when the strategic conditions of a war cause hostilities to centre around their port. By sacrificing power to go long distances, the coast-defence ship gains proportionate weight of armor and guns; that is, of defensive and offensive strength. It therefore adds an element of unique value to the fleet with which it for a time acts. No foreign states, except Great Britain, have ports so near our Pacific coast as to bring it within the radius of action of their coast-defense ships; and it is very doubtful whether even Great Britain will put such ships at Vancouver Island, the chief value of which will be lost to her when the Canadian Pacific is severed, — a blow always in the power of this country. It is upon our Atlantic seaboard that the mistress of Halifax, of Bermuda, and of Jamaica will now defend Vancouver and the Canadian Pacific. In the present state of our seaboard defence she can do so absolutely. What is all Canada compared with our exposed great cities? Even were the coast fortified, she still could do so, if our navy be no stronger than is designed as yet. What harm can we do Canada proportionate to the injury we should suffer by the interruption of our coasting trade, and by a blockade of Boston, New York, the Delaware, and the Chesapeake? Such a blockade Great Britain certainly could make technically efficient, under the somewhat loose definitions of international law. Neutrals would accept it as such.

The military needs of the Pacific States, as well as their supreme importance to the whole country, are yet a matter of the future, but of a future so near that provision should begin immediately. To weigh their importance, consider what influence in the Pacific would be attributed to a nation comprising only the States of Washington, Oregon, and California, when filled with such men as now people them and still are pouring in, and which controlled such maritime centres as San Francisco, Puget Sound, and the Columbia River. Can it be counted less because they are bound by the ties of blood and close political union to the great communities of the East? But such influence, to work without jar and friction, requires underlying military readiness, like the proverbial iron hand under the velvet glove. To provide this, three things are needful: First, protection of the chief harbors, by fortifications and coast-defence ships, which gives defensive strength, provides security to the community within, and supplies the bases necessary to all military operations. Secondly, naval force, the arm of offensive power, which alone enables a country to extend its influence outward. Thirdly, it should be an inviolable resolution of our national policy, that no foreign state should henceforth acquire a coaling position within three thousand miles of San Francisco, — and a distance which includes the Hawaiian and Galapagos islands and the coast of Central America. For fuel is the life of modern naval war; it is the food of the ship; without it the modern monsters of the deep die of inanition. Around it, therefore, cluster some of the most important considerations of naval strategy. In the Caribbean and in the Atlantic we are confronted with many a foreign coal depot, bidding us stand to our arms, even as Carthage bade Rome; but let us not acquiesce in an addition to our dangers, a further diversion of our strength, by being forestalled in the North Pacific.

In conclusion, while Great Britain is undoubtedly the most formidable of our possible enemies, both by her great navy and by the strong positions she holds near our coasts, it must be added that a cordial understanding with that country is one of the first of our external interests. Both nations doubtless, and properly, seek their own advantage; but both, also, are controlled by a sense of law and justice, drawn from the same sources, and deep-rooted in their instincts. Whatever temporary aberration may occur, a return to mutual standards of right will certainly follow. Formal alliance between the two is out of the question, but a cordial recognition of the similarity of character and ideas will give birth to sympathy, which in turn will facilitate a co-operation beneficial to both; for if sentimentality is weak, sentiment is strong.

Study Guide

1. Alfred T. Mahan offers a rationale for American expansion overseas; his views are those of a naval officer and historian. In essence, he advances the argument that an expanded naval presence by the United States will promote the economic and strategic interests of the American nation.

2. Turning to Mahan's economic analysis, take up the following:

    (a) How does Mahan account for the prosperity of the United States in the nineteenth century and why is he fearful that this will not continue in the future?

    (b) Explain (pp. 206–207): "The inevitable consequence has followed, as in all cases when the mind or the eye is exclusively fixed in one direction, that the danger of loss or the prospect of advantage in another quarter has been overlooked; and although the abounding resources of the country have maintained the exports at a high figure, this flattering result has been due more to the superabundant bounty of Nature than to the demand of other nations for our protected manufactures."

    (c) Do you understand his reference to Napoleon's "Continental System"? Define.

    (d) What connection does he establish between "the products," "the market," and "the carrying trade"?

3. In the middle section of his essay (pp. 208–215), Mahan ranges over a number of areas of the world, takes up a number of problems between nations, and renders an opinion on the relationship of the United States to these areas and their international problems.

    (a) What does Mahan see as the relationship between the United States and Europe and, more specifically, Germany? For what reasons does he consider Germany a "formidable" problem?

    (b) What are his views on the possibility of war? How astute, in the light of the twentieth century, do you consider this observation? "It is the preparedness of the enemy, and not acquiescence in the existing state of things, that now holds back the armies of Europe."

(c) Summarize in outline form Mahan's views of the relationship between the United States, England, and Canada.

(d) Turning to Central America, Mahan focuses strongly and at great length upon the implications of a canal across Panama — on our military position, on our strategic needs, on the Monroe Doctrine, and on our economic well-being. Summarize the problems he raises and his assessment of each. (What evidence did Mahan have, by the way, that a canal in Panama was a distinct possibility?)

4. Mahan's essay closes with a demand for three things in order to preserve the prosperity and the security of the United States. What are they? What does Mahan make a plea for in the last paragraph of the selection and how prophetic are his remarks on this subject in the light of later developments?

Albert J. Beveridge

THE PHILIPPINES

❧{1900}❧   THE Spanish-American War transformed the issue of imperialism. In the first place it brought a string of island possessions under the American flag—Puerto Rico, Guam, the Philippines. The future isthmian canal demanded by Mahan and other imperialists thereupon became an urgent necessity. But the war also brought economic imperialism to the fore. ~~Men like Mahan had argued that colonies would stimulate trade, but businessmen in general had opposed overseas ventures, which they feared would unsettle the domestic economy and lead to higher taxes.~~ After the defeat of Spain, however, a massive shift of business sentiment occurred and there was much talk of colonies as markets and as sources of raw materials for American industry.

The most attractive region from the point of view of the economic imperialists was the Philippine archipelago, both for itself and for the supposed entree it provided to "the markets of China." However, the Filipinos, ardently nationalistic, had expected the United States to withdraw from their lands after defeating the Spanish, as the nation had promised to do in Cuba. When it did not, they took up arms against their "liberators" and a bloody guerrilla war ensued. This provoked a great debate in the United States between those who wished to hold the Islands and those who felt that the United States had no business imposing its will on any people who did not wish to be part of the American empire.

One of the key figures in this debate was Albert J. Beveridge of Indiana (1862-1927). A man of fierce enthusiasms and immense industry, Beveridge had been elected to the Senate in 1899, when only 36. He fastened upon the issue of imperialism as a means of making his reputation. Before taking his Senate seat he set out on a tour of the Philippines, determined to make himself an expert on the region. While in the Islands he talked to hundreds of persons, visited the battlefronts, and explored remote areas, cramming his notebook with facts and opinions. Then, when Congress met, he seized the first opportunity to make an elaborate speech on the subject, despite the fact that tradition required that freshmen senators ordinarily remain silent for a year before addressing their colleagues. Such was the interest in his views that the galleries were packed, when, on January 9, 1900, he rose to speak in defense of the proposition: "*Resolved* . . . that the Philippines Islands are territory belonging to the United States; that it is the intention of the United States to retain them as such and to establish and maintain such governmental control throughout the archipelago as the situation may demand."

SPEECH IN THE SENATE, 1900

MR. BEVERIDGE: Mr. President, I address the Senate at this time because Senators and Members of the House on both sides have asked that I give to Congress and the country my observations in the Philippines and the far East, and the conclusions which those observations compel; and because of hurtful resolutions introduced and utterances made in the Senate, every word of which will cost and is costing the lives of American soldiers.

Mr. President, the times call for candor. The Philippines are ours forever, "territory belonging to the United States," as the Constitution calls them. And just beyond the Philippines are China's illimitable markets. We will not retreat from either. We will not repudiate our duty in the archipelago. We will not abandon our opportunity in the Orient. We will not renounce our part in the mission of our race, trustee, under God, of the civilization of the world. And we will move forward to our work, not howling out regrets like slaves whipped to their burdens, but with gratitude for a task worthy of our strength, and thanksgiving to Almighty God that He has marked us as His chosen people, henceforth to lead in the regeneration of the world.

This island empire is the last land left in all the oceans. If it should prove a mistake to abandon it, the blunder once made would be irretrievable. If it proves a mistake to hold it, the error can be corrected when we will. Every other progressive nation stands ready to relieve us.

But to hold it will be no mistake. Our largest trade henceforth must be with Asia. The Pacific is our ocean. More and more Europe will manufacture the most it needs, secure from its colonies the most it consumes. Where shall we turn for consumers of our surplus? Geography answers the question. China is our natural customer. She is nearer to us than to England, Germany, or Russia, the commercial powers of the present and the future. They have moved nearer to China by securing permanent bases on her borders. The Philippines give us a base at the door of all the East. . . .

But if they did not command China, India, the Orient, the whole Pacific for purposes of offense, defense, and trade, the Philippines are so valuable in themselves that we should hold them. I have cruised more than 2,000 miles through the archipelago, every moment a surprise at its loveliness and wealth. I have ridden hundreds of miles on the islands, every foot of the way a revelation of vegetable and mineral riches.

No land in America surpasses in fertility the plains and valleys of Luzon. Rice and coffee, sugar and cocoanuts, hemp and tobacco, and many products of the temperate as well as the tropic zone grow in various sections of the archipelago. I have seen hundreds of bushels of Indian corn lying in a road fringed with banana trees. The forests of Negros, Mindanao, Mindoro, Paluan, and parts of Luzon are invaluable and intact. The wood of the Philippines can supply the furniture of the world for a century to come. At Cebu the best informed man in the island told me that 40 miles of Cebu's mountain chain are practically mountains of coal. Pablo Majia, one of the most reliable men on the islands, confirmed the statement. Some declare that the coal is only lignite; but ship captains who have used it told me that it is better steamer fuel than the best coal of Japan.

I have a nugget of pure gold picked up in its present form on the banks of a Philippine creek. I have gold dust washed out by crude processes of careless natives from the sands of a Philippine stream. Both indicate great deposits at the source from which they come. In one of the islands great deposits of copper exist untouched. The mineral wealth of this empire of the ocean will one day surprise the world. I base this statement partly on personal observation, but chiefly on the testimony of foreign merchants in the Philippines, who have practically investigated the subject, and upon the unanimous opinion of natives and priests. And the mineral wealth is but a small fraction of the agricultural wealth of these islands.

And the wood, hemp, copra, and other products of the Philippines supply what we need and can not ourselves produce. And the markets they will themselves afford will be immense. Spain's export and import trade, with the islands undeveloped, was $11,534,731 annually. Our trade with the islands developed will be $125,000,000 annually, for who believes that we can not do ten times as well as Spain? Consider their imperial dimensions. Luzon is larger and richer than New York, Pennsylvania, Illinois, or Ohio. Mindanao is larger and richer than all New England, exclusive of Maine. Manila, as a port of call and exchange, will, in the time of men now living, far surpass Liverpool. Behold the exhaustless markets they command. It is as if a half dozen of our States were set down between Oceania and the Orient, and those States themselves undeveloped and unspoiled of their primitive wealth and resources. . . .

It will be hard for Americans who have not studied them to understand the people. They are a barbarous race, modified by three centuries of contact with a decadent race. The Filipino is the South Sea Malay, put through a process of three hundred years of superstition in religion, dishonesty in dealing, disorder in habits of industry, and cruelty, caprice, and corruption in government. It is barely possible that 1,000 men in all the archipelago are capable of self-government in the Anglo-Saxon sense. My own belief is that there are not 100 men among them who comprehend what Anglo-Saxon self-government even means, and there are over 5,000,000 people to be governed. . . . Aguinaldo is a clever, popular leader, able, brave, resourceful, cunning, ambitious, unscrupulous, and masterful. He is full of decision, initiative, and authority, and had the confidence of the masses. He is a natural dictator. His ideas of government are absolute orders, implicit obedience, or immediate death. He understands the character of his countrymen. He is a Malay Sylla; not a Filipino Washington.

These conclusions were forced upon me by observing the people in all walks of life in the different islands, and by conversations with foreign merchants, priests, mestizos, pure Filipinos, and every variety of mind, character, and opinion from San Fernando, in Luzon, on down through the entire archipelago to the interior of Sulu. . . .

Senators, it would be better to abandon this combined garden and Gibraltar of the Pacific, and count our blood and treasure already spent a profitable loss, than to apply any academic arrangement of self-government to these children. They are not capable of self-government. How could they be? They are not of a self-governing race. They are Orientals, Malays, instructed by Spaniards in the latter's worst estate.

They know nothing of practical government except as they have witnessed the weak, corrupt, cruel, and capricious rule of Spain. What magic will anyone employ to dissolve in their minds and characters those impressions of governors and governed which three centuries of misrule has created? What alchemy will change the oriental quality of their blood and set the self-governing currents of the American pouring through their Malay veins? How shall they, in the twinkling of an eye, be exalted to the heights of self-governing peoples which required a thousand years for us to reach, Anglo-Saxon though we are?

Let men beware how they employ the term "self-government." It is a sacred term. It is the watchword at the door of the inner temple of liberty, for liberty does not always mean self-government. Self-government is a method of liberty — the highest, simple, best — and it is acquired only after centuries of study and struggle and experiment and instruction and all the elements of the progress of man. Self-government is no base and common thing, to be bestowed on the merely audacious. It is the degree which crowns the graduate of liberty, not the name of liberty's infant class, who have not yet mastered the alphabet of freedom. Savage blood, oriental blood, Malay blood, Spanish example — are these the elements of self-government?

We must act on the situation as it exists, not as we would wish it. I have talked with hundreds of these people, getting their views as to the practical workings of self-government. The great majority simply do not understand any participation in any government whatever. The most enlightened among them declare that self-government will succeed because the employers of labor will compel their employees to vote as their employer wills and that this will insure intelligent voting. I was assured that we could depend upon good men always being in office because the officials who constitute the government will nominate their successors, choose those among the people who will do the voting, and determine how and where elections will be held.

The most ardent advocate of self-government that I met was anxious that I should know that such a government would be tranquil because, as he said, if anyone criticised it, the government would shoot the offender. A few of them have a sort of verbal understanding of the democratic theory, but the above are the examples of the ideas of the practical workings of self-government entertained by the aristocracy, the rich planters and traders, and heavy employers of labor, the men who would run the government.

Example for decades will be necessary to instruct them in American ideas and methods of administration. Example, example; always example —this alone will teach them. As a race, their general ability is not excellent. Educators, both men and women, to whom I have talked in Cebu and Luzon, were unanimous in the opinion that in all solid and useful education they are, as a people, dull and stupid. In showy things, like carving and painting or embroidery or music, they have apparent aptitude, but even this is superficial and never thorough. They have facility of speech, too.

The three best educators on the island at different times made to me the same comparison, that the common people in their stupidity are like their caribou bulls. They are not even good agriculturists. Their waste of cane is inexcusable. Their destruction of hemp fiber is childish. They are incurably indolent. They have no continuity or thoroughness of industry.

They will quit work without notice and amuse themselves until the money they have earned is spent. They are like children playing at men's work.

No one need fear their competition with our labor. No reward could beguile, no force compel, these children of indolence to leave their trifling lives for the fierce and fervid industry of high-wrought America. The very reverse is the fact. One great problem is the necessary labor to develop these islands — to build the roads, open the mines, clear the wilderness, drain the swamps, dredge the harbors. The natives will not supply it. A lingering prejudice against the Chinese may prevent us from letting them supply it. Ultimately, when the real truth of the climate and human conditions is known, it is barely possible that our labor will go there. Even now young men with the right moral fiber and a little capital can make fortunes there as planters.

But the natives will not come here. Let all men dismiss that fear. . . .

The Declaration of Independence does not forbid us to do our part in the regeneration of the world. If it did, the Declaration would be wrong, just as the Articles of Confederation, drafted by the very same men who signed the Declaration, was found to be wrong. The Declaration has no application to the present situation. It was written by self-governing men for self-governing men.

It was written by men who, for a century and a half, had been experimenting in self-government on this continent, and whose ancestors for hundreds of years before had been gradually developing toward that high and holy estate. The Declaration applies only to people capable of self-government. How dare any man prostitute this expression of the very elect of self-governing peoples to a race of Malay children of barbarism, schooled in Spanish methods and ideas? And you, who say the Declaration applies to all men, how dare you deny its application to the American Indian? And if you deny it to the Indian at home, how dare you grant it to the Malay abroad?

The Declaration does not contemplate that all government must have the consent of the governed. It announces that man's "inalienable rights are life, liberty, and the pursuit of happiness; that to secure these rights governments are established among men deriving their just powers from the consent of the governed; that when any form of government becomes destructive of those rights, it is the right of the people to alter or abolish it." "Life, liberty, and the pursuit of happiness" are the important things; "consent of the governed" is one of the means to those ends. . . .

Self-government, when that will best secure these ends, as in the case of people capable of self-government; other appropriate forms when people are not capable of self-government. And so the authors of the Declaration themselves governed the Indian without his consent; the inhabitants of Louisiana without their consent; and ever since the sons of the makers of the Declaration have been governing not by theory, but by practice, after the fashion of our governing race, now by one form, now by another, but always for the purpose of securing the great eternal ends of life, liberty, and the pursuit of happiness, not in the savage, but in the civilized meaning of those terms — life according to orderly methods of civilized society; liberty regulated by law; pursuit of happiness limited by the pursuit of happiness by every other man.

If this is not the meaning of the Declaration, our Government itself denies the Declaration every time it receives the representative of any but a republican form of government, such as that of the Sultan, the Czar, or other absolute autocrats, whose governments, according to the opposition's interpretation of the Declaration, are spurious governments, because the people governed have not "consented" to them. . . .

Mr. President, this question is deeper than any question of party politics; deeper than any question of the isolated policy of our country even; deeper even than any question of constitutional power. It is elemental. It is racial. God has not been preparing the English-speaking and Teutonic peoples for a thousand years for nothing but vain and idle self-contemplation and self-admiration. No! He has made us the master organizers of the world to establish system where chaos reigns. He has given us the spirit of progress to overwhelm the forces of reaction throughout the earth. He has made us adepts in government that we may administer government among savage and senile peoples. Were it not for such a force as this the world would relapse into barbarism and night. And of all our race He has marked the American people as His chosen nation to finally lead in the regeneration of the world. This is the divine mission of America, and it holds for us all the profit, all the glory, all the happiness possible to man. We are trustees of the world's progress, guardians of its righteous peace. The judgment of the Master is upon us: "Ye have been faithful over a few things; I will make you ruler over many things."

What shall history say of us? Shall it say that we renounced that holy trust, left the savage to his base condition, the wilderness to the reign of waste, deserted duty, abandoned glory, forget our sordid profit even, because we feared our strength and read the charter of our powers with the doubter's eye and the quibbler's mind? Shall it say that, called by events to captain and command the proudest, ablest, purest race of history in history's noblest work, we declined that great commission? Our fathers would not have had it so. No! They founded no paralytic government, incapable of the simplest acts of administration. They planted no sluggard people, passive while the world's work calls them. They established no reactionary nation. They unfurled no retreating flag.

That flag has never paused in its onward march. Who dares halt it now — now, when history's largest events are carrying it forward; now, when we are at last one people, strong enough for any task, great enough for any glory destiny can bestow? How comes it that our first century closes with the process of consolidating the American people into a unit just accomplished, and quick upon the stroke of that great hour presses upon us our world opportunity, world duty, and world glory, which none but a people welded into an indivisible nation can achieve or perform?

Blind indeed is he who sees not the hand of God in events so vast, so harmonious, so benign. Reactionary indeed is the mind that perceives not that this vital people is the strongest of the saving forces of the world; that our place, therefore, is at the head of the constructing and redeeming nations of the earth; and that to stand aside while events march on is a surrender of our interests, a betrayal of our duty as blind as it is base. Craven indeed is the heart that fears to perform a work so golden and so noble; that dares not win a glory so immortal.

Do you tell me that it will cost us money? When did Americans ever measure duty by financial standards? Do you tell me of the tremendous toil required to overcome the vast difficulties of our task? What mighty work for the world, for humanity, even for ourselves, has ever been done with ease? Even our bread must we eat by the sweat of our faces. Why are we charged with power such as no people ever knew, if we are not to use it in a work such as no people ever wrought? Who will dispute the divine meaning of the fable of the talents?

Do you remind me of the precious blood that must be shed, the lives that must be given, the broken hearts of loved ones for their slain? And this is indeed a heavier price than all combined. And yet as a nation every historic duty we have done, every achievement we have accomplished, has been by the sacrifice of our noblest sons. Every holy memory that glorifies the flag is of those heroes who have died that its onward march might not be stayed. It is the nation's dearest lives yielded for the flag that makes it dear to us; it is the nation's most precious blood poured out for it that makes it precious to us. That flag is woven of heroism and grief, of the bravery of men and women's tears, of righteousness and battle, of sacrifice and anguish, of triumph and of glory. It is these which make our flag a holy thing. Who would tear from that sacred banner the glorious legends of a single battle where it has waved on land or sea? What son of a soldier of the flag whose father fell beneath it on any field would surrender that proud record for the heraldry of a king? In the cause of civilization, in the service of the Republic anywhere on earth, Americans consider wounds the noblest decorations man can win, and count the giving of their lives a glad and precious duty.

Pray God that spirit never fails. Pray God the time may never come when Mammon and the love of ease shall so debase our blood that we will fear to shed it for the flag and its imperial destiny. Pray God the time may never come when American heroism is but a legend like the story of the Cid, American faith in our mission and our might a dream dissolved, and the glory of our mighty race departed.

And that time will never come. We will renew our youth at the fountain of new and glorious deeds. We will exalt our reverence for the flag by carrying it to a noble future as well as by remembering its ineffable past. Its immortality will not pass, because everywhere and always we will acknowledge and discharge the solemn responsibilities our sacred flag, in its deepest meaning, puts upon us. And so, Senators, with reverent hearts, where dwells the fear of God, the American people move forward to the future of their hope and the doing of His work. ...

Study Guide

1. This peroration in the Senate favoring the acquisition of the Philippines by the United States can be divided into several parts:
   (a) the wealth of the islands and the contribution they can make to our economy (pp. 218–220);
   (b) the kind of government the Filipinos need, and how we can fulfill their political requirements without sacrificing our own (pp. 220–222);
   (c) and, consequently, a reinterpretation of the Declaration of Independence (pp. 222–223); and
   (d) finally, a vision of what role the United States is destined to play on the world's stage (pp. 223–224).

2. Note why Beveridge is able to speak so knowledgeably about the national resources and wealth of the Islands; proceed then to outline the economic assets he feels would accrue to the United States by their acquisition.

3. Turning to the political aspects of annexation:
   (a) How does Beveridge portray American rule as a positive good for the Philippines?
   (b) What do the following quotations tell you about Beveridge's sense of Anglo-Saxon superiority as well as the rationale he developed for it?
      (1) "They are a barbarous race, modified by three centuries of contact with a decadent race";

(2) "My own belief is that there are not 100 men among them who comprehend what Anglo-Saxon self-government even means . . .";

(3) "He [Aguinaldo] is a Malay Sylla; not a Filipino Washington";

(4) "What alchemy will change the oriental quality of their blood and set the self-governing currents of the American pouring through their Malay veins?"; and

(5) "Example for decades will be necessary to instruct them in American ideas and methods of administration. Example, example; always example — this alone will teach them."

4. How is Beveridge able to justify the annexation of the Philippines under the Declaration of Independence? How does he rationalize our failure to offer the Filipinos a form of government that derives from the "consent of the governed"?

5. Beveridge's closing paragraph can stand as a paradigm of the American imperialistic fervor of the 1890's: his arrogant references to the English-speaking "Teutons," his invocation of history, the symbols of patriotism and the Deity, and his vision of the future. Explain and illustrate each of the above.

Mark Twain

THE CASE AGAINST IMPERIALISM

1901 THE arguments of men like Beveridge unquestionably converted a majority of the American people to the idea of colonial expansion. Supposed economic advantages were important in this respect, but the appeal of purely emotional arguments was probably much greater. Suddenly conscious of their strength as a nation, the people were fascinated by the idea of empire, of the United States taking its place among the great powers of the world.

On the other hand, a vocal minority looked upon imperialism and especially upon the use of force to subjugate the Philippines, as a violation of the finest American traditions, a denial of the values so powerfully expressed in the Declaration of Independence. Some of these anti-imperialists were narrow isolationists, but others were men of the broadest interests—intellectuals, writers, old-fashioned statesmen, labor leaders, and businessmen. The steelmaster Andrew Carnegie and Samuel Gompers of the American Federation of Labor opposed keeping the Philippines. So did Grover Cleveland, former Speaker of the House of Representatives Thomas B. Reed, the philosopher William James, and many others. No one attacked imperialism more sharply than Mark Twain.

By 1900 Twain was world-famous as a humorist and widely regarded as one of the great literary geniuses of the day. But his original buoyant optimism had turned to the blackest, most sardonic pressimism; he was becoming a bitter critic of American society. No aspect of the times aroused his ire more than the new imperialism. The following selection is taken from an essay he published in the *North American Review* in 1901.

TO THE PERSON SITTING IN DARKNESS

SHALL WE? That is, shall we go on conferring our Civilization upon the peoples that sit in darkness, or shall we give those poor things a rest? Shall we bang right ahead in our old-time, loud, pious way, and commit the new century to the game; or shall we sober up and sit down and think it over first? Would it not be prudent to get our Civilization tools together, and see how much stock is left on hand in the way of Glass Beads and Theology, and Maxim Guns and Hymn Books, and Trade Gin and Torches of Progress and Enlightenment (patent adjustable ones, good to fire villages with, upon occasion), and balance the books, and arrive at the profit and loss, so that we may intelligently decide whether to continue the business or sell out the property and start a new Civilization Scheme on the proceeds?

Extending the Blessings of Civilization to our Brother who Sits in Darkness has been a good trade and has paid well, on the whole; and there is money in it yet, if carefully worked — but not enough, in my judgment, to make any considerable risk advisable. The People that Sit in Darkness are getting to be too scarce — too scarce and too shy. And such darkness as is now left is really of but an indifferent quality, and not dark enough for the game. The most of those People that Sit in Darkness have been furnished with more light than was good for them or profitable for us. We have been injudicious.

The Blessings-of-Civilization Trust, wisely and cautiously administered, is a Daisy. There is more money in it, more territory, more sovereignty, and other kinds of emolument, than there is in any other game that is played. But Christendom has been playing it badly of late years, and must certainly suffer by it, in my opinion. She has been so eager to get every stake that appeared on the green cloth, that the People who Sit in Darkness have noticed it — they have noticed it, and have begun to show alarm. They have become suspicious of the Blessings of Civilization. More— they have begun to examine them. This is not well. The Blessings of Civilization are all right, and a good commercial property; there could not be a better, in a dim light. In the right kind of a light, and at a proper distance, with the goods a little out of focus, they furnish this desirable exhibit to the Gentlemen who Sit in Darkness:

LOVE,	LAW AND ORDER,
JUSTICE,	LIBERTY,
GENTLENESS,	EQUALITY,
CHRISTIANITY,	HONORABLE DEALING,
PROTECTION TO THE WEAK,	MERCY,
TEMPERANCE,	EDUCATION,

—and so on.

There. Is it good? Sir, it is pie. It will bring into camp any idiot that sits in darkness anywhere. But not if we adulterate it. It is proper to be emphatic upon that point. This brand is strictly for Export — apparently. *Apparently.* Privately and confidentially, it is nothing of the kind. Privately and confidentially, it is merely an outside cover, gay and pretty and attractive, displaying the special patterns of our Civilization which we reserve for Home Consumption, while *inside* the bale is the Actual Thing that the Customer Sitting in Darkness buys with his blood and tears and land and liberty. That Actual Thing is, indeed, Civilization, but it is only for Export. Is there a difference between the two brands? In some of the details, yes.

We all know that the Business is being ruined. The reason is not far to seek. It is because our Mr. McKinley, and Mr. Chamberlain, and the Kaiser, and the Tsar and the French have been exporting the Actual Thing *with the outside cover left off.* This is bad for the Game. It shows that these new players of it are not sufficiently acquainted with it. . . .

Our Master of the Game plays it badly — plays it as Mr. Chamberlain was playing it in South Africa. It was a mistake to do that; also, it was one which was quite unlooked for in a Master who was playing it so well in Cuba. In Cuba, he was playing the usual and regular *American* game, and it was winning, for there is no way to beat it. The Master, contemplating Cuba, said: "Here is an oppressed and friendless little nation which is willing to fight to be free; we go partners, and put up the strength of seventy million sympathizers and the resources of the United States: play!" Nothing but Europe combined could call that hand: and Europe cannot combine on anything. There, in Cuba, he was following our great traditions in a way which made us very proud of him, and proud of the deep dissatisfaction which his play was provoking in continental Europe. Moved by a high inspiration, he threw out those stirring words which proclaimed that forcible annexation would be "criminal aggression"; and in that utterance fired another "shot heard round the world." The memory of that fine saying will be outlived by the remembrance of no act of his but one — that he forgot it within the twelvemonth, and its honorable gospel along with it.

For, presently, came the Philippine temptation. It was strong; it was too strong, and he made that bad mistake: he played the European game, the Chamberlain game. It was a pity; it was a great pity, that error; that one grievous error, that irrevocable error. For it was the very place and time to play the American game again. And at no cost. Rich winnings to be gathered in, too; rich and permanent; indestructible; a fortune transmissible forever to the children of the flag. Not land, not money, not dominion — no, something worth many times more than that dross: our share, the spectacle of a nation of long harassed and persecuted slaves set free through our influence; our posterity's share, the golden memory of that fair deed. The game was in our hands. If it had been played according to the American rules, Dewey would have sailed away from Manila as soon as he had destroyed the Spanish fleet — after putting up a sign on shore guaranteeing foreign property and life against damage by the Filipinos, and warning the Powers that interference with the emancipated patriots would be regarded as an act unfriendly to the United States. The Powers cannot combine, in even a bad cause, and the sign would not have been molested.

Dewey could have gone about his affairs elsewhere, and left the competent Filipino army to starve out the little Spanish garrison and send it home, and the Filipino citizens to set up the form of government they might prefer, and deal with the friars and their doubtful acquisitions according to Filipino ideas of fairness and justice—ideas which have since been tested and found to be of as high an order as any that prevail in Europe or America.

But we . . . lost the chance to add another Cuba and another honorable deed to our good record. . . .

Now, my plan is: . . . let us audaciously present the whole of the facts, shirking none. . . . This daring truthfulness will astonish and dazzle the Person Sitting in Darkness, and he will take the Explanation down before his mental vision has had time to get back into focus. Let us say to him:

"Our case is simple. On the 1st of May, Dewey destroyed the Spanish fleet. This left the Archipelago in the hands of its proper and rightful owners, the Filipino nation. Their army numbered 30,000 men, and they were competent to whip out or starve out the little Spanish garrison; then the people could set up a government of their own devising. Our traditions required that Dewey should now set up his warning sign, and go away. But the Master of the Game happened to think of another plan —

the European plan. He acted upon it. This was, to send out an army — ostensibly to help the native patriots put the finishing touch upon their long and plucky struggle for independence, but really to take their land away from them and keep it. That is, in the interest of Progress and Civilization. The plan developed, stage by stage, and quite satisfactorily. We entered into a military alliance with the trusting Filipinos, and they hemmed in Manila on the land side, and by their valuable help the place, with its garrison of 8,000 or 10,000 Spaniards, was captured — a thing which we could not have accomplished unaided at that time. We got their help by — by ingenuity. We knew they were fighting for their independence, and that they had been at it for two years. We knew they supposed that we also were fighting in their worthy cause — just as we had helped the Cubans fight for Cuban independence — and we allowed them to go on thinking so. *Until Manila was ours and we could get along without them.* Then we showed our hand. Of course, they were surprised — that was natural; surprised and disappointed; disappointed and grieved. To them it looked un-American; uncharacteristic; foreign to our established traditions. And this was natural, too; for we were only playing the American Game in public — in private it was the European. It was neatly done, very neatly, and it bewildered them. They could not understand it; for we had been so friendly — so affectionate, even — with those simple-minded patriots! We, our own selves, had brought back out of exile their leader, their hero, their hope, their Washington — Aguinaldo; brought him in a warship, in high honor, under the sacred shelter and hospitality of the flag; brought him back and restored him to his people, and got their moving and eloquent gratitude for it. Yes, we had been so friendly to them, and had heartened them up in so many ways! We had lent them guns and ammunition; advised with them; exchanged pleasant courtesies with them; placed our sick and wounded in their kindly care; intrusted our Spanish prisoners to their humane and honest hands; fought shoulder to shoulder with them against "the common enemy" (our own phrase); praised their courage, praised their gallantry, praised their mercifulness, praised their fine and honorable conduct; borrowed their trenches, borrowed strong positions which they had previously captured from the Spaniards; petted them, lied to them — officially proclaiming that our land and naval forces came to give them their freedom and displace the bad Spanish Government — fooled them, used them until we needed them no longer; then derided the sucked orange and threw it away. We kept the positions which we had beguiled them of; by and by, we moved a force forward and overlapped patriot ground — a clever thought, for we needed trouble, and this would produce it. A Filipino soldier, crossing the ground, where no one had a right to forbid him, was shot by our sentry. The badgered patriots resented this with arms, without waiting to know whether Aguinaldo, who was absent, would approve or not. Aguinaldo did not approve; but that availed nothing. What we wanted, in the interest of Progress and Civilization, was the Archipelago, unencumbered by patriots struggling for independence; and War was what we needed. We clinched our opportunity. . . .

At this point in our frank statement of fact to the Person Sitting in Darkness, we should throw in a little trade taffy about the Blessings of Civilization — for a change, and for the refreshment of his spirit — then go on with our tale:

"We and the patriots having captured Manila, Spain's ownership of the Archipelago and her sovereignty over it were at an end — obliterated — annihilated — not a rag or shred of either remaining behind. It was then that we conceived the divinely humorous idea of *buying* both of these specters from Spain! [It is quite safe to confess this to the Person Sitting in Darkness, since neither he nor any other sane person will believe it.] In buying those ghosts for twenty millions, we also contracted to take care of the friars and their accumulations. I think we also agreed to propagate leprosy and smallpox, but as to this there is doubt. But it is not important; persons afflicted with the friars do not mind other diseases.

"With our Treaty ratified, Manila subdued, and our Ghosts secured, we had no further use for Aguinaldo and the owners of the Archipelago. We forced a war, and we have been hunting America's guest and ally through the woods and swamps ever since."

At this point in the tale, it will be well to boast a little of our war work and our heroisms in the field, so as to make our performance look as fine as England's in South Africa; but I believe it will not be best to emphasize this too much. We must be cautious. . . .

Having now laid all the historical facts before the Person Sitting in Darkness, we should bring him to again, and explain them to him. We should say to him:

"They look doubtful, but in reality they are not. There have been lies; yes, but they were told in a good cause. We have been treacherous; but that was only in order that real good might come out of apparent evil. True, we have crushed a deceived and confiding people; we have turned against the weak and the friendless who trusted us; we have stamped out a just and intelligent and well-ordered republic; we have stabbed an ally in the back and slapped the face of a guest; we have bought a Shadow from an enemy that hadn't it to sell; we have robbed a trusting friend of his land and his liberty; we have invited our clean young men to shoulder a discredited musket and do bandits' work under a flag which bandits have been accustomed to fear, not to follow; we have debauched America's honor and blackened her face before the world; but each detail was for the best. We know this. The Head of every State and Sovereignty in Christendom and 90 per cent of every legislative body in Christendom, including our Congress and our fifty state legislatures, are members not only of the church, but also of the Blessings-of-Civilization Trust. This world-girdling accumulation of trained morals, high principles, and justice cannot do an unright thing, an unfair thing, an ungenerous thing, an unclean thing. It knows what it is about. Give yourself no uneasiness; it is all right."

Now then, that will convince the Person. You will see. It will restore the Business. Also, it will elect the Master of the Game to the vacant place in the Trinity of our national gods; and there on their high thrones the Three will sit, age after age, in the people's sight, each bearing the Emblem of his service: Washington, the Sword of the Liberator; Lincoln, the Slave's Broken Chains; the Master, the Chains Repaired.

It will give the Business a splendid new start. You will see.

Everything is prosperous, now; everything is just as we should wish it. We have got the Archipelago, and we shall never give it up. Also, we have every reason to hope that we shall have an opportunity before very long to slip out of our congressional contract with Cuba and give her something better in the place of it. It is a rich country, and many of us are already beginning to see that the contract was a sentimental mistake. But now — right now — is the best time to do some profitable rehabilitating work — work that will set us up and make us comfortable, and discourage gossip. We cannot conceal from ourselves that, privately, we are a little troubled about our uniform. It is one of our prides; it is acquainted with honor; it is familiar with great deeds and noble; we love it, we revere it; and so this errand it is on makes us uneasy. And our flag — another pride of ours, our chiefest! We have worshiped it so; and when we have seen it in far lands — glimpsing it unexpectedly in that strange sky, waving its welcome and benediction to us — we have caught our breaths, and uncovered our heads, and couldn't speak, for a moment, for the thought of what it was to us and the great ideals it stood for. Indeed, we *must* do something about these things; it is easily managed. We can have a special one — our states do it: we can have just our usual flag, with the white stripes painted black and the stars replaced by the skull and crossbones. . . .

By help of these suggested amendments, Progress and Civilization in that country can have a boom, and it will take in the Persons who are Sitting in Darkness, and we can resume Business at the old stand.

Study Guide

1. The bitter sarcasm of Twain can make this literary tour de force difficult to understand — unless you watch out for it. Twain begins by commenting on imperialism generally, and then proceeds to discuss American imperialism in particular, how and why the United States got into the Spanish-American War, how and why we acquired Cuba and the Philippines, and what a horrible mistake was committed by the Congress and President of the United States.

2. First: Who is "our Brother who Sits in Darkness"? Does Twain really believe he does so?

3. What distinction does Twain draw between older and more recent forms of imperialism? (He makes another reference to this on p. 230 when he distinguishes between the American tradition vs. "the European plan.") His feelings about the older American form can be gleaned from this: "In the right kind of light, and at a proper distance, with the goods a little out of focus, they furnish this desirable exhibit to the Gentlemen who Sit in Darkness . . ." (p. 227). Note, also, the distinction he draws between "Civilization" for Americans at home and the "Civilization" we offer for the native populations overseas, a mere cover over "the Actual Thing that the Customer Sitting in Darkness buys with his blood and tears and land and liberty." What does Twain mean when he criticizes the imperialistic nations for running "Business" by "exporting the Actual Thing *with the outside cover left off*"?

4. Twain goes on to apply the distinction he drew between the older and newer forms of imperialism to the relationship we established with Cuba and the one we were about to establish with the Philippines. In line with this, explain the following:

    (a) "There, in Cuba, he was following our great traditions in a way which made us very proud of him, and proud of the deep dissatisfaction which his play was provoking in continental Europe."

    (b) "For, presently, came the Philippine temptation. It was strong; it was too strong, and he made that bad mistake: he played the European game, the Chamberlain game" (a reference to Joseph Chamberlain, Colonial Secretary of Great Britain during the Boer War).

5. Twain concludes with:

    (a) a tale told to "the Person Sitting in Darkness" — a devastatingly critical recital of the United States's behavior in recent years in our relations with Spain, Cuba, and Aguinaldo and the Filipinos; and

    (b) a brilliant tirade against our entire imperialistic posture. Read both carefully and try, as best as you can, to understand all the symbolism, references, and allusions he has set down in these closing paragraphs:

(1) his reference to "the Ghosts";
(2) his listing of those to whom we were unfaithful;
(3) the three "Emblems"; and
(4) his closing comments on the flag and its desecration.

6. In a review of the chapter, summarize the varieties of imperialistic motivation and rhetoric: the strategic (Mahan), the economic (Mahan and Beveridge), and the patriotic (Beveridge).

(a) What beliefs do all these men have in common?
(b) How do their ideas differ?
(c) What, in essence, would Twain say to them?
(d) Does Twain oppose the goal of a prosperous and powerful American nation or is his quarrel with them more one of *procedure* rather than *substance?*
(e) Does the unit on the pros and cons of imperialism have any parallels to the debate over our role in Southeast Asia in the 1960's and 1970's? Elaborate.

IV. The Spirit of Progressivism

W. E. B. DuBois, BLACK MILITANCY (*1903*)

Lincoln Steffens, MUNICIPAL CORRUPTION (*1904*)

Upton Sinclair, POISONED MEAT AND POISONED LIVES (*1906*)

Charlotte Perkins Gilman, THE EQUALITY OF WOMEN (*1912*)

Theodore Roosevelt, SOCIAL JUSTICE (*1910*)

Woodrow Wilson, BACK TO LIBERTY (*1913*)

E. A. Ross, IMMIGRATION RESTRICTION (*1914*)

Randolph Bourne, A PLURALISTIC NATION (*1916*)

W. E. B. DuBois

BLACK MILITANCY

◄{1903}►   BLACK LEADER Booker T. Washington's policy of accommodation to white prejudices brought him wide fame but did little to improve the actual treatment of his people. As a result, a number of black leaders (and eventually some white reformers as well) began to criticize the Washington approach and to mount forceful attacks on racial prejudice and discrimination. Prominent among these critics was W. E. Burghardt DuBois, a northern-born historian of black and French Huguenot ancestry. DuBois was a leader of the Niagara Movement, which, in 1905, called for an end to all racial segregation, the guarantee of the right to vote and all civil rights to blacks, and a massive effort to improve black education. He was also in 1909 a founder of the National Association for the Advancement of Colored People. Himself well-educated — he held a Ph.D. from Harvard — he had far less understanding of the feelings and problems of the mass of American blacks than Washington, but he clearly represented the wave of the future in the fight for racial equality. The following selections from his book, *The Souls of Black Folk* (1903), describe his attitude toward Washington's way of dealing with the race issue and his own views of black education.

THE SOULS OF BLACK FOLK

OF MR. BOOKER T. WASHINGTON AND OTHERS

EASILY THE MOST striking thing in the history of the American Negro since 1876 is the ascendancy of Mr. Booker T. Washington. It began at the time when war memories and ideals were rapidly passing; a day of astonishing commercial development was dawning; a sense of doubt and hesitation overtook the freedmen's sons, — then it was that his leading began. Mr. Washington came, with a simple definite programme, at the psychological moment when the nation was a little ashamed of having bestowed so much sentiment on Negroes, and was concentrating its energies on Dollars. His programme of industrial education, conciliation of the South, and submission and silence as to civil and political rights, was not wholly original; the Free Negroes from 1830 up to war-time had striven to build industrial schools, and the American Missionary Association had from the first taught various trades; and Price and others had sought a way of honorable alliance with the best of the Southerners. But Mr. Washington first indissolubly linked these things; he put enthusiasm, unlimited energy, and perfect faith into this programme, and changed it from a by-path into a veritable Way of Life. And the tale of the methods by which he did this is a fascinating study of human life.

It startled the nation to hear a Negro advocating such a programme after many decades of bitter complaint; it startled and won the applause of the South, it interested and won the admiration of the North; and after a confused murmur of protest, it silenced if it did not convert the Negroes themselves.

To gain the sympathy and cooperation of the various elements comprising the white South was Mr. Washington's first task; and this, at the time Tuskegee was founded, seemed, for a black man, well-nigh impossible. And yet ten years later it was done in the word spoken at Atlanta; "In all things purely social we can be as separate as the five fingers, and yet one as the hand in all things essential to mutual progress." This "Atlanta Compromise" is by all odds the most notable thing in Mr. Washington's career. The South interpreted it in different ways: the radicals received it as a complete surrender of the demand for civil and political equality; the conservatives, as a generously conceived working basis for mutual understanding. So both approved it, and to-day its author is certainly the most distinguished Southerner since Jefferson Davis, and the one with the largest personal following.

Next to this achievement comes Mr. Washington's work in gaining place and consideration in the North. Others less shrewd and tactful had formerly essayed to sit on these two stools and had fallen between them; but as Mr. Washington knew the heart of the South from birth and training, so by singular insight he intuitively grasped the spirit of the age which was dominating the North. And so thoroughly did he learn the speech and thought of triumphant commercialism, and the ideals of material prosperity, that the picture of a lone black boy poring over a French grammar amid the weeds and dirt of a neglected home soon seemed to him the acme of absurdities. One wonders what Socrates and St. Francis of Assisi would say to this.

And yet this very singleness of vision and thorough oneness with his age is a mark of the successful man. It is as though Nature must needs make men narrow in order to give them force. So Mr. Washington's cult has gained unquestioning followers, his work has wonderfully prospered, his friends are legion, and his enemies are confounded. To-day he stands as the one recognized spokesman of his ten million fellows, and one of the most notable figures in a nation of seventy millions. One hesitates, therefore, to criticise a life which, beginning with so little, has done so much. And yet the time is come when one may speak in all sincerity and utter courtesy of the mistakes and shortcomings of Mr. Washington's career, as well as of his triumphs, without being thought captious or envious, and without forgetting that it is easier to do ill than well in the world.

The criticism that has hitherto met Mr. Washington has not always been of this broad character. In the South especially has he had to walk warily to avoid the harshest judgments, — and naturally so, for he is dealing with the one subject of deepest sensitiveness to that section. Twice — once when at the Chicago celebration of the Spanish-American War he alluded to the color-prejudice that is "eating away the vitals of the South," and once when he dined with President Roosevelt — has the resulting Southern criticism been violent enough to threaten seriously his popularity. In the North the feeling has several times forced itself into words, that Mr. Washington's counsels of submission overlooked certain elements of true manhood, and that his educational programme was unnecessarily narrow. Usually, however, such criticism has not found open expression, although, too, the spiritual sons of the Abolitionists have not been prepared to acknowledge that the schools founded before Tuskegee, by men of broad ideals and self-sacrificing spirit, were wholly failures or worthy of ridicule. While, then, criticism has not failed to follow Mr. Washington, yet the prevailing public opinion of the land has been but too willing to deliver the solution of a wearisome problem into his hands, and say, "If that is all you and your race ask, take it."

Among his own people, however, Mr. Washington has encountered the strongest and most lasting opposition, amounting at times to bitterness, and even to-day continuing strong and insistent even though largely silenced in outward expression by the public opinion of the nation. Some of this opposition is, of course, mere envy; the disappointment of displaced demagogues and the spite of narrow minds. But aside from this, there is among educated and thoughtful colored men in all parts of the land a feeling of deep regret, sorrow, and apprehension at the wide currency and ascendancy which some of Mr. Washington's theories have gained. These same men admire his sincerity of purpose, and are willing to forgive much to honest endeavor which is doing something worth the doing. They cooperate with Mr. Washington as far as they conscientiously can; and, indeed, it is no ordinary tribute to this man's tact and power that, steering as he must between so many diverse interests and opinions, he so largely retains the respect of all.

But the hushing of the criticism of honest opponents is a dangerous thing. It leads some of the best of the critics to unfortunate silence and paralysis of effort, and others to burst into speech so passionately and intemperately as to lose listeners. Honest and earnest criticism from those whose interests are most nearly touched, — criticism of writers by readers, of government by those governed, of leaders by those led, — this is the soul of democracy and the safeguard of modern society. If the best of the American Negroes receive by outer pressure a leader whom they had not recognized before, manifestly there is here a certain palpable gain. Yet there is also irreparable loss, — a loss of that peculiarly valuable education which a group receives when by search and criticism it finds and commissions its own leaders. The way in which this is done is at once the most elementary and the nicest problem of social growth. History is but the record of such group-leadership; and yet how infinitely changeful is its type and character! And of all types and kinds, what can be more instructive than the leadership of a group within a group? — that curious double movement where real progress may be negative and actual advance be relative retrogression. All this is the social student's inspiration and despair.

Now in the past the American Negro has had instructive experience in the choosing of group leaders, founding thus a peculiar dynasty which in the light of present conditions is worth while studying. When sticks and stones and beasts form the sole environment of a people, their attitude is largely one of determined opposition to and conquest of natural forces. But when to earth and brute is added an environment of men and ideas, then the attitude of the imprisoned group may take three main forms, — a feeling of revolt and revenge; an attempt to adjust all thought and action to the will of the greater group; or, finally, a determined effort at self-realization and self-development despite environing opinion. The influence of all of these attitudes at various times can be traced in the history of the American Negro, and in the evolution of his successive leaders. . . .

Mr. Washington represents in Negro thought the old attitude of adjustment and submission; but adjustment at such a peculiar time as to make his programme unique. This is an age of unusual economic development, and Mr. Washington's progamme naturally takes an economic cast, becoming a gospel of Work and Money to such an extent as apparently almost completely to overshadow the higher aims of life. Moreover, this is an age when the more advanced races are coming in closer contact with the less developed races, and the race-feeling is therefore intensified; and Mr. Washington's programme practically accepts the alleged inferiority of the Negro races. Again, in our own land, the reaction from the sentiment of war time has given impetus to race-prejudice against Negroes, and Mr. Washington withdraws many of the high demands of Negroes as men and American citizens. In other periods of intensified prejudice all the Negro's tendency to self-assertion has been called forth; at this period a policy of submission is advocated. In the history of nearly all other races and peoples the doctrine preached at such crises has been that manly self-respect is worth more than lands and houses, and that a people who voluntarily surrender such respect, or cease striving for it, are not worth civilizing.

In answer to this, it has been claimed that the Negro can survive only through submission. Mr. Washington distinctly asks that black people give up, at least for the present, three things, —

First, political power,
Second, insistence on civil rights,
Third, higher education of Negro youth, — and concentrate all their energies on industrial education, the accumulation of wealth, and the conciliation of the South. This policy has been courageously and insistently advocated for over fifteen years, and has been triumphant for perhaps ten years. As a result of this tender of the palm-branch, what has been the return? In these years there have occurred:

1. The disfranchisement of the Negro.
2. The legal creation of a distinct status of civil inferiority for the Negro.
3. The steady withdrawal of aid from institutions for the higher training of the Negro.

These movements are not, to be sure, direct results of Mr. Washington's teachings; but his propaganda has, without a shadow of a doubt, helped their speedier accomplishment. The question then comes: Is it possible, and probable, that nine millions of men can make effective progress in economic lines if they are deprived of political rights, made a servile caste, and allowed only the most meagre chance for developing their exceptional men? If history and reason give any distinct answer to these questions, it is an emphatic *No*. And Mr. Washington thus faces the triple paradox of his career:

1. He is striving nobly to make Negro artisans business men and property-owners; but it is utterly impossible, under modern competitive methods, for workingmen and property-owners to defend their rights and exist without the right of suffrage.
2. He insists on thrift and self-respect, but at the same time counsels a silent submission to civic inferiority such as is bound to sap the manhood of any race in the long run.

3. He advocates common-school and industrial training, and depreciates institutions of higher learning; but neither the Negro common-schools, nor Tuskegee itself, could remain open a day were it not for teachers trained in Negro colleges, or trained by their graduates.

This triple paradox in Mr. Washington's position is the object of criticism by two classes of colored Americans. One class is spiritually descended from Toussaint the Savior, through Gabriel, Vesey, and Turner, and they represent the attitude of revolt and revenge; they hate the white South blindly and distrust the white race generally, and so far as they agree on definite action, think that the Negro's only hope lies in emigration beyond the borders of the United States. And yet, by the irony of fate, nothing has more effectually made this programme seem hopeless than the recent course of the United States toward weaker and darker peoples in the West Indies, Hawaii, and the Philippines, — for where in the world may we go and be safe from lying and brute force?

The other class of Negroes who cannot agree with Mr. Washington has hitherto said little aloud. They deprecate the sight of scattered counsels, of internal disagreement; and especially they dislike making their just criticism of a useful and earnest man an excuse for a general discharge of venom from small-minded opponents. Nevertheless, the questions involved are so fundamental and serious that it is difficult to see how men like the Grimkes, Kelly Miller, J. W. E. Bowen, and other representatives of this group, can much longer be silent. Such men feel in conscience bound to ask of this nation three things:

1. The right to vote.
2. Civic equality.
3. The education of youth according to ability.

They acknowledge Mr. Washington's invaluable service in counselling patience and courtesy in such demands; they do not ask that ignorant black men vote when ignorant whites are debarred, or that any reasonable restrictions in the suffrage should not be applied; they know that the low social level of the mass of the race is responsible for much discrimination against it, but they also know, and the nation knows, that relentless color-prejudice is more often a cause than a result of the Negro's degradation; they seek the abatement of this relic of barbarism, and not its systematic encouragement and pampering by all agencies of social power from the Associated Press to the Church of Christ. They advocate, with Mr. Washington, a broad system of Negro common schools supplemented by thorough industrial training; but they are surprised that a man of Mr. Washington's insight cannot see that no such educational system ever has rested or can rest on any other basis than that of the well-equipped college and university, and they insist that there is a demand for a few such institutions throughout the South to train the best of the Negro youth as teachers, professional men, and leaders.

This group of men honor Mr. Washington for his attitude of conciliation toward the white South; they accept the "Atlanta Compromise" in its broadest interpretation; they recognize, with him, many signs of promise, many men of high purpose and fair judgment, in this section; they know that no easy task has been laid upon a region already tottering under heavy burdens. But, nevertheless, they insist that the way to truth and right lies in straightforward honesty, not in indiscriminate flattery; in praising those of the South who do well and criticising uncompromisingly those who do ill; in taking advantage of the opportunities at hand and urging their fellows to do the same, but at the same time in remembering that only a firm adherence to their higher ideals and aspirations will ever keep those ideals within the realm of possibility. They do not expect that the free right to vote, to enjoy civic rights, and to be educated, will come in a moment; they do not expect to see the bias and prejudices of years disappear at the blast of a trumpet; but they are absolutely certain that the way for a people to gain their reasonable rights is not by voluntarily throwing them away and insisting that they do not want them; that the way for a people to gain respect is not by continually belittling and ridiculing themselves; that, on the contrary, negroes must insist continually, in season and out of season, that voting is necessary to modern manhood, that color discrimination is barbarism, and that black boys need education as well as white boys.

In failing thus to state plainly and unequivocally the legitimate demands of their people, even at the cost of opposing an honored leader, the thinking classes of American Negroes would shirk a heavy responsibility, — a responsibility to themselves, a responsibility to the struggling masses, a responsibility to the darker races of men whose future depends so largely on this American experiment, but especially a responsibility to this nation, — this common Fatherland. It is wrong to encourage a man or a people in evil-doing; it is wrong to aid and abet a national crime simply because it is unpopular not to do so. The growing spirit of kindliness and reconciliation between the North and South after the frightful differences of a generation ago ought to be a source of deep congratulation to all, and especially to those whose mistreatment caused the war; but if that reconciliation is to be marked by the industrial slavery and civic death of those same black men, with permanent legislation into a position of inferiority, then those black men, if they are really men, are called upon by every consideration of patriotism and loyalty to oppose such a course by all civilized methods, even though such opposition involves disagreement with Mr. Booker T. Washington. We have no right to sit silently by while the inevitable seeds are sown for a harvest of disaster to our children, black and white.

First, it is the duty of black men to judge the South discriminatingly. The present generation of Southerners are not responsible for the past, and they should not be blindly hated or blamed for it. Furthermore, to no class is the indiscriminate endorsement of the recent course of the South toward Negroes more nauseating than to the best thought of the South. The South is not "solid"; it is a land in the ferment of social change, wherein forces of all kinds are fighting for supremacy; and to praise the ill the South is to-day perpetrating is just as wrong as to condemn the good. Discriminating and broad-minded criticism is what the South needs, — needs it for the sake of her own white sons and daughters, and for the insurance of robust, healthy mental and moral development. . . .

It would be unjust to Mr. Washington not to acknowledge that in several instances he has opposed movements in the South which were unjust to the Negro; he sent memorials to the Louisiana and Alabama constitutional conventions, he has spoken against lynching, and in other ways has openly or silently set his influence against sinister schemes and unfortunate happenings. Notwithstanding this, it is equally true to assert that on the whole the distinct impression left by Mr. Washington's propaganda is, first, that the South is justified in its present attitude toward the Negro because of the Negro's degradation; secondly, that the prime cause of the Negro's failure to rise more quickly is his wrong education in the past; and, thirdly, that his future rise depends primarily on his own efforts. Each of these propositions is a dangerous half-truth. The supplementary truths must never be lost sight of: first, slavery and race-prejudice are potent if not sufficient causes of the Negro's position; second, industrial and common-school training were necessarily slow in planting because they had to await the black teachers trained by higher institutions, — it being extremely doubtful if any essentially different development was possible, and certainly a Tuskegee was unthinkable before 1880; and, third, while it is a great truth to say that the Negro must strive and strive mightily to help himself, it is equally true that unless his striving be not simply seconded, but rather aroused and encouraged, by the initiative of the richer and wiser environing group, he cannot hope for great success.

In his failure to realize and impress this last point, Mr. Washington is especially to be criticised. His doctrine has tended to make the whites, North and South, shift the burden of the Negro problem to the Negro's shoulders and stand aside as critical and rather pessimistic spectators; when in fact the burden belongs to the nation, and the hands of none of us are clean if we bend not our energies to righting these great wrongs.

The South ought to be led, by candid and honest criticism, to assert her better self and do her full duty to the race she has cruelly wronged and is still wronging. The North — her co-partner in guilt — cannot salve her conscience by plastering it with gold. We cannot settle this problem by diplomacy and suaveness, by "policy" alone. If worse come to worst, can the moral fibre of this country survive the slow throttling and murder of nine millions of men?

The black men of America have a duty to perform, a duty stern and delicate, — a forward movement to oppose a part of the work of their greatest leader. So far as Mr. Washington preaches Thrift, Patience, and Industrial Training for the masses, we must hold up his hands and strive with him, rejoicing in his honors and glorying in the strength of this Joshua called of God and of man to lead the headless host. But so far as Mr. Washington apologizes for injustice, North or South, does not rightly value the privilege and duty of voting, belittles the emasculating effects of caste distinctions, and opposes the higher training and ambition of our brighter minds, — so far as he, the South, or the North, does this, — we must unceasingly and firmly oppose them. By every civilized and peaceful method we must strive for the rights which the world accords to men, clinging unwaveringly to those great words which the sons of the Fathers would fain forget: "We hold these truths to be self-evident: That all men are created equal; that they are endowed by their Creator with certain unalienable rights; that among these are life, liberty, and the pursuit of happiness."

OF THE TRAINING OF BLACK MEN

From the shimmering swirl of waters where many, many thoughts ago the slave-ship first saw the square tower of Jamestown, have flowed down to our day three streams of thinking: one swollen from the larger world here and over-seas, saying, the multiplying of human wants in culture-lands calls for the world-wide cooperation of men in satisfying them. Hence arises a new human unity, pulling the ends of earth nearer, and all men, black, yellow, and white. The larger humanity strives to feel in this contact of living Nations and sleeping hordes a thrill of new life in the world, crying, "If the contact of Life and Sleep be Death, shame on such Life." To be sure, behind this thought lurks the afterthought of force and dominion, — the making of brown men to delve when the temptation of beads and red calico cloys.

The second thought streaming from the deathship and the curving river is the thought of the older South, — the sincere and passionate belief that somewhere between men and cattle, God created a *tertium quid,* and called it a Negro, — a clownish, simple creature, at times even lovable within its limitations, but straitly foreordained to walk within the Veil. To be sure, behind the thought lurks the afterthought, — some of them with favoring chance might become men, but in sheer self-defence we dare not let them, and we build about them walls so high, and hang between them and the light a veil so thick, that they shall not even think of breaking through.

And last of all there trickles down that third and darker thought, — the thought of the things themselves, the confused, half-conscious mutter of men who are black and whitened, crying "Liberty, Freedom, Opportunity — vouchsafe to us, O boastful World, the chance of living men!" To be sure, behind the thought lurks the afterthought, — suppose after all, the World is right and we are less than men? Suppose this mad impulse within is all wrong, some mock mirage from the untrue?

So here we stand among thoughts of human unity, even through conquest and slavery; the inferiority of black men, even if forced by fraud; a shriek in the night for the freedom of men who themselves are not yet sure of their right to demand it. This is the tangle of thought and afterthought wherein we are called to solve the problem of training men for life.

Behind all its curiousness, so attractive alike to sage and *dilettante,* lie its dim dangers, throwing across us shadows at once grotesque and awful. Plain it is to us that what the world seeks through desert and wild we have within our threshold, — a stalwart laboring force, suited to the semitropics; if, deaf to the voice of the Zeitgeist, we refuse to use and develop these men, we risk poverty and loss. If, on the other hand, seized by the brutal afterthought, we debauch the race thus caught in our talons, selfishly sucking their blood and brains in the future as in the past, what shall save us from national decadence? Only that saner selfishness, which Education teaches men, can find the rights of all in the whirl of work. . . .

But when we have vaguely said that Education will set this tangle straight, what have we uttered but a truism? Training for life teaches living; but what training for the profitable living together of black men and white? . . . No secure civilization can be built in the South with the Negro as an ignorant, turbulent proletariat. Suppose we seek to remedy this by making them laborers and nothing more: they are not fools, they have tasted of the Tree of Life, and they will not cease to think, will not cease attempting to read the riddle of the world. By taking away their best equipped teachers and leaders, by slamming the door of opportunity in the faces of their bolder and brighter minds, will you make them satisfied with their lot? or will you not rather transfer their leading from the hands of men taught to think to the hands of untrained demagogues? We ought not to forget that despite the pressure of poverty, and despite the active discouragement and even ridicule of friends, the demand for higher training steadily increases among Negro youth: there were, in the years from 1875 to 1880, 22 Negro graduates from Northern colleges; from 1885 to 1890 there were 43, and from 1895 to 1900, nearly 100 graduates. From Southern Negro colleges there were, in the same three periods, 143, 413, and over 500 graduates. Here, then, is the plain thirst for training; by refusing to give this Talented Tenth the key to knowledge, can any sane man imagine that they will lightly lay aside their yearning and contentedly become hewers of wood and drawers of water?

No. The dangerously clear logic of the Negro's position will more and more loudly assert itself in that day when increasing wealth and more intricate social organization preclude the South from being, as it so largely is, simply an armed camp for intimidating black folk. Such waste of energy cannot be spared if the South is to catch up with civilization. And as the black third of the land grows in thrift and skill, unless skilfully guided in its larger philosophy, it must more and more brood over the red past and the creeping, crooked present, until it grasps a gospel of revolt and revenge and throws its new-found energies athwart the current of advance. Even to-day the masses of the Negroes see all too clearly the anomalies of their position and the moral crookedness of yours. You may marshal strong indictments against them, but their counter-cries, lacking though they be in formal logic, have burning truths within them which you may not wholly ignore, O Southern Gentlemen! If you deplore their presence here, they ask, Who brought us? When you cry, Deliver us from the vision of intermarriage, they answer that legal marriage is infinitely better than systematic concubinage and prostitution. And if in just fury you accuse their vagabonds of violating women, they also in fury quite as just may reply: The wrong which your gentlemen have done against helpless black women in defiance of your own laws is written on the foreheads of two millions of mulattoes, and written in ineffaceable blood. And finally, when you fasten crime upon this race as its peculiar trait, they answer that slavery was the arch-crime, and lynching and lawlessness its twin abortion; that color and race are not crimes, and yet they it is which in this land receives most unceasing condemnation, North, East, South, and West.

I will not say such arguments are wholly justified,—I will not insist that there is no other side to the shield; but I do say that of the nine millions of Negroes in this nation, there is scarcely one out of the cradle to whom these arguments do not daily present themselves in the guise of terrible truth. I insist that the question of the future is how best to keep these millions from brooding over the wrongs of the past and the difficulties of the present, so that all their energies may be bent toward a cheerful striving and co-operation with their white neighbors toward a larger, juster, and fuller future. That one wise method of doing this lies in the closer knitting of the Negro to the great industrial possibilities of the South is a great truth. And this the common schools and the manual training and trade schools are working to accomplish. But these alone are not enough. The foundations of knowledge in this race, as in others, must be sunk deep in the college and university if we would build a solid, permanent structure. Internal problems of social advance must inevitably come,—problems of work and wages, of families and homes, of morals and the true valuing of the things of life; and all these and other inevitable problems of civilization the Negro must meet and solve largely for himself, by reason of his isolation; and can there be any possible solution other than by study and thought and an appeal to the rich experience of the past? Is there not, with such a group and in such a crisis, infinitely more danger to be apprehended from half-trained minds and shallow thinking than from over-education and over-refinement? Surely we have wit enough to found a Negro college so manned and equipped as to steer successfully between the *dilettante* and the fool. We shall hardly induce black men to believe that if their stomachs be full, it matters little about their brains. They already dimly perceive that the paths of peace winding between honest toil and dignified manhood call for the guidance of skilled thinkers, the loving, reverent comradeship between the black lowly and the black men emancipated by training and culture.

The function of the Negro college, then, is clear: it must maintain the standards of popular education, it must seek the social regeneration of the Negro, and it must help in the solution of problems of race contact and co-operation. And finally, beyond all this, it must develop men. Above our modern socialism, and out of the worship of the mass, must persist and evolve that higher individualism which the centres of culture protect; there must come a loftier respect for the sovereign human soul that seeks to know itself and the world about; that seeks a freedom for expansion and self-development; that will love and hate and labor in its own way, untrammeled alike by old and new. Such souls aforetime have inspired and guided worlds, and if we be not wholly bewitched by our Rhine-gold, they shall again. ~~Herein the longing of black men must have respect;~~ the rich and bitter depth of their experience, the unknown treasures of their inner life, the strange rendings of nature they have seen, may give the world new points of view and make their loving, living, and doing precious to all human hearts. And to themselves in these the days that try their souls, the chance to soar in the dim blue air above the smoke is to their finer spirits boon and guerdon for what they lose on earth by being black. . . .

Study Guide

1. This selection, a direct refutation by a rising black leader of the conciliatory program offered by Booker T. Washington in the "Atlanta Compromise" (1895), is atypical of the progressive thrust — a movement that generally avoided the problem of race prejudice in its search for reform. More typical of reformist thought in the Progressive Era are the selections that follow: corruption in city government (Lincoln Steffens); the adulteration of foods (Upton Sinclair); and the equality of women (Charlotte Perkins Gilman).

2. The first essay by DuBois can be divided thus:
   (a) his review of the career of Booker T. Washington (pp. 237–238); and
   (b) his critique of Washington's leadership and program (pp. 238–245).
   The key sentence in DuBois's analysis of Washington's rise to fame and influence is the following: "Mr. Washington came, with a simple definite programme, at the psychological moment when the nation was a little ashamed of having bestowed so much sentiment on Negroes, and was concentrating its energies on Dollars." DuBois then proceeds to document this conclusion by explaining Washington's popularity in the South, in the North, and among blacks. Follow his reasoning by answering the following questions:
   (a) How does DuBois account for the appeal of Washington's message to both Southern (white) radicals and conservatives?
   (b) What, to DuBois, appears to be the appeal of Washington's "Atlanta Compromise" to the North?
   (c) What is he willing to concede concerning Washington's leadership of the black community?
   (d) Is DuBois's reaction critical or enthusiastic? Explain.

3. On pp. 240–241, DuBois outlines the varieties of leadership available to black Americans and then categorizes that of Washington. Explain.

4. Turning to DuBois's critique of Washington's political, social, and educational philosophy:

    (a) He begins with Washington's views and then outlines the developments in the South, indicating that there exists between the two a causal relationship. Explain.

    (b) On what grounds does DuBois find Washington's threefold program inadequate?

    (c) What two black groups is DuBois counting on to criticize the position and the program offered by Washington?

    (d) What group does DuBois stand with and what (pp. 242–243) would it substitute for Washington's program?

5. What "half-truths," implicit if not explicit in Washington's program, does DuBois attack in his closing arguments? Outline and amplify.

6. DuBois's essay on "The Training of Black Men" opens with a poetic, and somewhat difficult to understand, triad of visions defining the relationship between races and peoples:

    (a) the brotherhood of man on a universal scale, a dream that can be shared by all, yet potentially hazardous to "brown men";

    (b) the racism of the Southern whites; and

    (c) the black's hope for equality and opportunity — albeit unsure of his right to them.

    Education, according to DuBois, must surmount and deal with these disparate visions and goals. This educational program must grow out of "thoughts of human unity, even through conquest and slavery; the inferiority of black men, even if forced by fraud; [and] a shriek in the night for the freedom of men who themselves are not yet sure of their right to demand it" (p. 246).

7. DuBois talks about the growth in the demand for higher education among blacks and a role for the "Talented Tenth." Explain what he means by the phrase and what role he envisages for this group.

8. What boon does DuBois offer the South should blacks be given educational opportunity?

9. DuBois finally concludes that education must be directed toward the "social regeneration of the Negro." Explain and amplify on the basis of the last paragraph.

Lincoln Steffens
MUNICIPAL CORRUPTION

❧{*1904*}❧ THE STORY of that particular type of journalism which Theodore Roosevelt (1858-1919) called "muckraking" and which has been defined as "the exposing of evils and corruption for the real or ostensible purpose of promoting righteousness and social justice," can be told from two quite different points of view. Seen one way, it was the inevitable outgrowth of certain economic and social trends in American life, the result of the rise of industrial monopolies, the festering expansion of vast cities, the migration of millions of people previously inexperienced with democracy, and the dislocation of most aspects of life in a time of rapid change. The development of the cheap mass-circulation magazine provided, when muckraking is placed in this context, the catalyst in which these trends were precipitated and called to the attention of an indignant public.

From a different point of view, however, muckraking can be said to have developed haphazardly; those responsible for it did not foresee the results of their activities. S. S. McClure, an authentic genius of early-twentieth century journalism, wanted to sell copies of his magazine. To accomplish this end, Lincoln Steffens, who worked for McClure, hired a St. Louis reporter named Claude H. Wetmore to write an article about a crusading St. Louis attorney who was trying to break up a ring of corrupt politicians. The article, when written, seemed too tame so Steffens revised it. The author, alarmed by the changes, demanded that Steffens add his own name to the piece. Steffens agreed. Thus he became a great celebrity in reform journalism and *McClure's Magazine* the leading publication in its field. "The era of the muckrakers had begun."

For the response to "Tweed Days in St. Louis" when it appeared in October 1902 was tremendous. Steffens, "to make sure that the process was identical everywhere," rushed off to Minneapolis, Pittsburgh, Philadelphia, and other cities to study local corruption. The results appeared in *McClure's* (its circulation zoomed to half a million) and then, in 1904, in Steffens' remarkable book, *The Shame of the Cities.* Thus a major addition was made to the accumulating forces of protest and reform. "Tweed Days in St. Louis" and Steffens's later adventures, the significance of which he summarized in the preface to his book, helped to shape the frame of mind that we characterize as "progressive."

Steffens (1866–1936) went on to a long, interesting, and somewhat controversial career in journalism. His *Autobiography* (1931) is one of the finest in the English language.

THE SHAME OF THE CITIES

. . . WHEN I set out on my travels, an honest New Yorker told me honestly that I would find that the Irish, the Catholic Irish, were at the bottom of it all everywhere. The first city I went to was St. Louis, a German city. The next was Minneapolis, a Scandinavian city, with a leadership of New Englanders. Then came Pittsburg, Scotch Presbyterian, and that was what my New York friend was. "Ah, but they are all foreign populations," I heard. The next city was Philadelphia, the purest American community of all, and the most hopeless. And after that came Chicago and New York, both mongrel-bred, but the one a triumph of reform, the other the best example of good government that I had seen. The "foreign element" excuse is one of the hypocritical lies that save us from the clear sight of ourselves.

Another such conceit of our egotism is that which deplores our politics and lauds our business. This is the wail of the typical American citizen. Now, the typical American citizen is the business man. The typical business man is a bad citizen; he is busy. If he is a "big business man" and very busy, he does not neglect, he is busy with politics, oh, very busy and very businesslike. I found him buying boodlers in St. Louis, defending grafters in Minneapolis, originating corruption in Pittsburg, sharing with bosses in Philadelphia, deploring reform in Chicago, and beating good government with corruption funds in New York. He is a self-righteous fraud, this big business man. He is the chief source of corruption, and it were a boon if he would neglect politics. But he is not the business man that neglects politics; that worthy is the good citizen, the typical business man. He is too busy, he is the one that has no use and therefore no time for politics. When his neglect has permitted bad government to go so far that he can be stirred to action, he is unhappy, and he looks around for a cure that shall be quick, so that he may hurry back to the shop. Naturally, too, when he talks politics, he talks shop. His patent remedy is quack; it is business.

"Give us a business man," he says ("like me," he means). "Let him introduce business methods into politics and government; then I shall be left alone to attend to my business."

There is hardly an office from United States Senator down to Alderman in any part of the country to which the business man has not been elected; yet politics remains corrupt, government pretty bad, and the selfish citizen has to hold himself in readiness like the old volunteer firemen to rush forth at any hour, in any weather, to prevent the fire; and he goes out sometimes and he puts out the fire (after the damage is done) and he goes back to the shop sighing for the business man in politics. The business man has failed in politics as he has in citizenship. Why?

Because politics is business. That's what's the matter with it. That's what's the matter with everything, — art, literature, religion, journalism, law, medicine,—they're all business, and all—as you see them. Make politics a sport, as they do in England, or a profession, as they do in Germany, and we'll have—well, something else than we have now,—if we want it, which is another question. But don't try to reform politics with the banker, the lawyer, and the dry-goods merchant, for these are business men and there are two great hindrances to their achievement of reform: one is that they are different from, but no better than, the politicians; the other is that politics is not "their line." . . .

But there is hope, not alone despair, in the commercialism of our politics. If our political leaders are to be always a lot of political merchants, they will supply any demand we may create. All we have to do is to establish a steady demand for good government. The bosses have us split up into parties. To him parties are nothing but means to his corrupt ends. He "bolts" his party, but we must not; the bribe-giver changes his party, from one election to another, from one county to another, from one city to another, but the honest voter must not. Why? Because if the honest voter cared no more for his party than the politician and the grafter, then the honest vote would govern, and that would be bad—for graft. It is idiotic, this devotion to a machine that is used to take our sovereignty from us. If we would leave parties to the politicians, and would vote not for the party, not even for men, but for the city, and the State, and the nation, we should rule parties, and cities, and States, and nation. If we would vote in mass on the more promising ticket, or, if the two are equally bad, would throw out the party that is in, and wait till the next election and then throw out the other party that is in—then, I say, the commercial politican would feel a demand for good government and he would supply it. That process would take a generation or more to complete, for the politicians now really do not know what good government is. But it has taken as long to develop bad government, and the politicians know what that is. If it would not "go," they would offer something else, and, if the demand were steady, they, being so commercial, would "deliver the goods."

But do the people want good government? Tammany says they don't. Are the people honest? Are the people better than Tammany? Are they better than the merchant and the politician? Isn't our corrupt government, after all, representative?

President Roosevelt has been sneered at for going about the country preaching, as a cure for our American evils, good conduct in the individual, simple honesty, courage, and efficiency. "Platitudes!" the sophisticated say. Platitudes? If my observations have been true, the literal adoption of Mr. Roosevelt's reform scheme would result in a revolution, more radical and terrible to existing institutions, from the Congress to the Church, from the bank to the ward organization, than socialism or even than anarchy. Why, that would change all of us — not alone our neighbors, not alone the grafters, but you and me.

No, the contemned methods of our despised politics are the master methods of our braggart business, and the corruption that shocks us in public affairs we practice ourselves in our private concerns. There is no essential difference between the pull that gets your wife into society or for your book a favorable review, and that which gets a heeler into office, a thief out of jail, and a rich man's son on the board of directors of a corporation; none between the corruption of a labor union, a bank, and a political machine; none between a dummy director of a trust and the caucus-bound member of a legislature; none between a labor boss like Sam Parks, a boss of banks like John D. Rockefeller, a boss of railroads like J. P. Morgan, and a political boss like Matthew S. Quay. The boss is not a political, he is an American institution, the product of a freed people that have not the spirit to be free.

And it's all a moral weakness; a weakness right where we think we are strongest. Oh, we are good — on Sunday, and we are "fearfully patriotic" on the Fourth of July. But the bribe we pay to the janitor to prefer our interests to the landlord's, is the little brother of the bribe passed to the alderman to sell a city street, and the father of the air-brake stock assigned to the president of a railroad to have this life-saving invention adopted on his road. And as for graft, railroad passes, saloon and bawdy-house blackmail, and watered stock, all these belong to the same family. We are pathetically proud of our democratic institutions and our republican form of government, of our grand Constitution and our just laws. We are a free and sovereign people, we govern ourselves and the government is ours. But that is the point. We are responsible, not our leaders, since we follow them. We *let* them divert our loyalty from the United States to some "party"; we *let* them boss the party and turn our municipal democracies into autocracies and our republican nation into a plutocracy. We cheat our government and we let our leaders loot it, and we let them wheedle and bribe our sovereignty from us. . . .

. . . When I set out to describe the corrupt systems of certain typical cities, I meant to show simply how the people were deceived and betrayed. But in the very first study — St. Louis — the startling truth lay bare that corruption was not merely political; it was financial, commercial, social; the ramifications of boodle were so complex, various, and far-reaching, that one mind could hardly grasp them, and not even

Joseph W. Folk, the tireless prosecutor, could follow them all. This state of things was indicated in the first article which Claude H. Wetmore and I compiled together, but it was not shown plainly enough. Mr. Wetmore lived in St. Louis, and he had respect for names which meant little to me. But when I went next to Minneapolis alone, I could see more independently, without respect for persons, and there were traces of the same phenomenon. The first St. Louis article was called "Tweed Days in St. Louis," and though the "better citizen" received attention the Tweeds were the center of interest. In "The Shame of Minneapolis," the truth was put into the title; it was the Shame of Minneapolis; not of the Ames administration, not of the Tweeds, but of the city and its citizens. And yet Minneapolis was not nearly so bad as St. Louis; police graft is never so universal as boodle. It is more shocking, but it is so filthy that it cannot involve so large a part of society. So I returned to St. Louis, and I went over the whole ground again, with the people in mind, not alone the caught and convicted boodlers. And this time the true meaning of "Tweed Days in St. Louis" was made plain. The article was called "The Shamelessness of St. Louis," and that was the burden of the story. In Pittsburg also the people was the subject, and though the civic spirit there was better, the extent of the corruption throughout the social organization of the community was indicated. But it was not till I got to Philadelphia that the possibilities of popular corruption were worked out to the limit of humiliating confession. That was the place for such a study. There is nothing like it in the country, except possibly, in Cincinnati. Philadelphia certainly is not merely corrupt, but corrupted, and this was made clear. Philadelphia was charged up to — the American citizen.

It was impossible in the space of a magazine article to cover in any one city all the phases of municipal government, so I chose cities that typified most strikingly some particular phase or phases. Thus as St. Louis exemplified boodle; Minneapolis, police graft; Pittsburg, a political and industrial machine; and Philadelphia, general civic corruption; so Chicago was an illustration of reform, and New York of good government. All these things occur in most of these places. There are, and long have been, reformers in St. Louis, and there is to-day police graft there. Minneapolis has had boodling and council reform, and boodling is breaking out there again. Pittsburg has general corruption, and Philadelphia a very perfect political machine. Chicago has police graft and a low order of administrative and general corruption which permeates business, labor, and society generally. As for New York, the metropolis might exemplify almost anything that occurs anywhere in American cities, but no city has had for many years such a good administration as was that of Mayor Seth Low.

That which I have made each city stand for, is that which it had most highly developed. It would be absurd to seek for organized reform in St. Louis, for example, with Chicago next door; or for graft in Chicago with Minneapolis so near. After Minneapolis, a description of administrative corruption in Chicago would have seemed like a repetition. Perhaps it was not just to treat only the conspicuous element in each situation. But why should I be just? I was not judging; I arrogated to myself no such function. I was not writing about Chicago for Chicago, but for the other cities, so I picked out what light each had for the instruction of the others. But, if I was never complete, I never exaggerated. Every one of those articles was an understatement, especially where the conditions were bad, and the proof thereof is that while each article seemed to astonish other cities, it disappointed the city which was its subject. Thus my friends in Philadelphia, who knew what there was to know, and those especially who knew what I knew, expressed surprise that I reported so little. And one St. Louis newspaper said that "the facts were thrown at me and I fell down over them." There was truth in these flings. I cut twenty thousand words out of the Philadelphia article and then had not written half my facts. I know a man who is making a history of the corrupt construction of the Philadelphia City Hall, in three volumes, and he grieves because he lacks space. You can't put all the known incidents of the corruption of an American city into a book.

This is all very unscientific, but then, I am not a scientist. I am a journalist. I did not gather with indifference all the facts and arrange them patiently for permanent preservation and laboratory analysis. I did not want to preserve, I wanted to destroy the facts. My purpose was no more scientific than the spirit of my investigation and reports; it was, as I said above, to see if the shameful facts, spread out in all their shame, would not burn through our civic shamelessness and set fire to American pride. That was the journalism of it. I wanted to move and to convince. That is why I was not interested in all the facts, sought none that was new, and rejected half those that were old. I often was asked to expose something suspected. I couldn't; and why should I? Exposure of the unknown was not my purpose. The people: what they will put up with, how they are fooled, how cheaply they are bought, how dearly sold, how easily intimidated, and how led, for good or for evil—that was the inquiry, and so the significant facts were those only which everybody in each city knew, and of these, only those which everybody in every other town would recognize, from their common knowledge of such things, to be probable. But these, understated, were charged always to the guilty persons when individuals were to blame, and finally brought home to the people themselves, who, having the power, have also the responsibility, they and those they respect, and those that guide them. . . .

But of course the tangible results are few. The real triumph of the year's work was the complete demonstration it has given, in a thousand little ways, that our shamelessness is superficial, that beneath it lies a pride which, being real, may save us yet. And it is real. The grafters who said you may put the blame anywhere but on the people, where it belongs, and that Americans can be moved only by flattery,—they lied. They lied about themselves. They, too, are American citizens; they too, are of the people; and some of them also were reached by shame. The great truth I tried to make plain was that which Mr. Folk insists so constantly upon: that bribery is no ordinary felony, but treason, that the "corruption which breaks out here and there and now and then" is not an occasional offense, but a common practice, and that the effect of it is literally to change the form of our government from one that is representative of the people to an oligarchy, representative of special interests. Some politicians have seen that this is so, and it bothers them. I think I prize more highly than any other of my experiences the half-dozen times when grafting politicians I had "roasted," as they put it, called on me afterwards to say, in the words of one who spoke with a wonderful solemnity:

"You are right. I never thought of it that way, but it's right. I don't know whether you can do anything, but you're right, dead right. And I'm all wrong. We're all, all wrong. I don't see how we can stop it now; I don't see how I can change. I can't, I guess. No, I can't, not now. But, say, I may be able to help you, and I will if I can. You can have anything I've got."

So you see, they are not such bad fellows, these practical politicians. I wish I could tell more about them: how they have helped me; how candidly and unselfishly they have assisted me to facts and an understanding of the facts, which, as I warned them, as they knew well, were to be used against them. If I could—and I will some day—I should show that one of the surest hopes we have is the politician himself. Ask him for good politics; punish him when he gives bad, and reward him when he gives good; make politics pay. Now, he says, you don't know and you don't care, and that you must be flattered and fooled—and there, I say, he is wrong. I did not flatter anybody; I told the truth as near as I could get it, and instead of resentment there was encouragement.

After "The Shame of Minneapolis," and "The Shamelessness of St. Louis," not only did citizens of these cities approve, but citizens of other cities, individuals, groups, and organizations, sent in invitations, hundreds of them, "to come and show us up; we're worse than they are."

We Americans may have failed. We may be mercenary and selfish. Democracy with us may be impossible and corruption inevitable, but these articles, if they have proved nothing else, have demonstrated beyond doubt that we can stand the truth; that there is pride in the character of American citizenship; and that this pride may be a power in the land. So this little volume, a record of shame and yet of self-respect, a disgraceful confession, yet a declaration of honor, is dedicated, in all good faith, to the accused — to all the citizens of all the cities in the United States.

TWEED DAYS IN ST. LOUIS

St. Louis, the fourth city in size in the United States, is making two announcements to the world: one that it is the worst-governed city in the land; the other that it wishes all men to come there (for the World's Fair) and see it. It isn't our worst-governed city; Philadelphia is that. But St. Louis is worth examining while we have it inside out.

There is a man at work there, one man, working all alone, but he is the Circuit (district or State) Attorney, and he is "doing his duty." That is what thousands of district attorneys and other public officials have promised to do and boasted of doing. This man has a literal sort of mind. He is a thin-lipped, firm-mouthed, dark little man, who never raises his voice, but goes ahead doing, with a smiling eye and a set jaw, the simple thing he said he would do. The politicians and reputable citizens who asked him to run urged him when he declined. When he said that if elected he would have to do his duty, they said, "Of course." So he ran, they supported him, and he was elected. Now some of these politicians are sentenced to the penitentiary, some are in Mexico. The Circuit Attorney, finding that his "duty" was to catch and convict criminals, and that the biggest criminals were some of these same politicians and leading citizens, went after them. It is magnificent, but the politicians declare it isn't politics.

The corruption of St. Louis came from the top. The best citizens — the merchants and big financiers — used to rule the town, and they ruled it well. They set out to outstrip Chicago. The commercial and industrial war between these two cities was at one time a picturesque and dramatic spectacle such as is witnessed only in our country. Business men were not mere merchants and the politicians were not mere grafters; the two kinds of citizens got together and wielded the power of banks, railroads, factories, the prestige of the city, and the spirit of its citizens to gain business and population. And it was a close race. Chicago, having the start, always led, but St. Louis had pluck, intelligence, and tremendous energy. It pressed Chicago hard. It excelled in a sense of civic beauty and good government; and there are those who think yet it might have won. But a change occurred. Public spirit became private spirit, public enterprise became private greed.

Along about 1890, public franchises and privileges were sought, not only for legitimate profit and common convenience, but for loot. Taking but slight and always selfish interest in the public councils, the big men misused politics. The riffraff, catching the smell of corruption, rushed into the Municipal Assembly, drove out the remaining respectable men, and sold the city — its streets, its wharves, its markets, and all that it had — to the now greedy business men and bribers. In other words, when the leading men began to devour their own city, the herd rushed into the trough and fed also.

So gradually has this occurred that these same citizens hardly realize it. Go to St. Louis and you will find the habit of civic pride in them; they still boast. The visitor is told of the wealth of the residents, of the financial strength of the banks, and of the growing importance of the industries, yet he sees poorly paved, refuse-burdened streets, and dusty or mud-covered alleys; he passes a ramshackle fire-trap crowded with the sick, and learns that it is the City Hospital; he enters the "Four Courts," and his nostrils are greeted by the odor of formaldehyde used as a disinfectant, and insect powder spread to destroy vermin; he calls at the new City Hall, and finds half the entrance boarded with pine planks to cover up the unfinished interior. Finally, he turns a tap in the hotel, to see liquid mud flow into wash-basin or bath-tub.

The St. Louis charter vests legislative power of great scope in a Municipal Assembly, which is composed of a council and a House of Delegates. Here is a description of the latter by one of Mr. Folk's grand juries:

"We have had before us many of those who have been, and most of those who are now, members of the House of Delegates. We found a number of these utterly illiterate and lacking in ordinary intelligence, unable to give a better reason for favoring or opposing a measure than a desire to act with the majority. In some, no trace of mentality or morality could be found; in others, a low order of training appeared, united with base cunning, groveling instincts, and sordid desires. Unqualified to respond to the ordinary requirements of life, they are utterly incapable of comprehending the significance of an ordinance, and are incapacitated, both by nature and training, to be the makers of laws. The choosing of such men to be legislators makes a travesty of justice, sets a premium on incompetency, and deliberately poisons the very source of the law."

These creatures were well organized. They had a "combine" — a legislative institution — which the grand jury described as follows:

"Our investigation, covering more or less fully a period of ten years, shows that, with few exceptions, no ordinance has been passed wherein valuable privileges or franchises are granted until those interested have paid the legislators the money demanded for action in the particular case. Combines in both branches of the Municipal Assembly are formed by members sufficient in number to control legislation. To one member of this combine is delegated the authority to act for the combine, and to receive and to distribute to each member the money agreed upon as the price of his vote in support of, or opposition to, a pending measure. So long has this practice existed that such members have come to regard the receipt of money for action on pending measures as a legitimate perquisite of a legislator."

One legislator consulted a lawyer with the intention of suing a firm to recover an unpaid balance on a fee for the grant of a switch-way. Such difficulties rarely occurred, however. In order to insure a regular and indisputable revenue, the combine of each house drew up a schedule of bribery prices for all possible sorts of grants, just such a list as a commercial traveler takes out on the road with him. There was a price for a grain elevator, a price for a short switch; side tracks were charged for by the linear foot, but at rates which varied according to the nature of the ground taken; a street improvement cost so much; wharf space was classified and precisely rated. As there was a scale for favorable legislation, so there was one for defeating bills. It made a difference in the price if there was opposition, and it made a difference whether the privilege asked was legitimate or not. But nothing was passed free of charge. Many of the legislators were saloon-keepers — it was in St. Louis that a practical joker nearly emptied the House of Delegates by tipping a boy to rush into a session and call out, "Mister, your saloon is on fire," — but even the saloon-keepers of a neighborhood had to pay to keep in their inconvenient locality a market which public interest would have moved.

From the Assembly, bribery spread into other departments. Men empowered to issue peddlers' licenses and permits to citizens who wished to erect awnings or use a portion of the sidewalk for storage purposes charged an amount in excess of the prices stipulated by law, and pocketed the difference. The city's money was loaned at interest, and the interest was converted into private bank accounts. . . .

The blackest years were 1898, 1899, and 1900. Foreign corporations came into the city to share in its despoliation, and home industries were driven out by blackmail. Franchises worth millions were granted without one cent of cash to the city, and with provision for only the smallest future payment; several companies which refused to pay blackmail had to leave; citizens were robbed more and more boldly; pay-rolls were padded with the names of non-existent persons; work on public improvements was neglected, while money for them went to the boodlers.

Some of the newspapers protested, disinterested citizens were alarmed, and the shrewder men gave warnings, but none dared make an effective stand. Behind the corruptionists were men of wealth and social standing, who, because of special privileges granted them, felt bound to support and defend the looters. Independent victims of the far-reaching conspiracy submitted in silence, through fear of injury to their business. Men whose integrity was never questioned, who held high positions of trust, who were church members and teachers of Bible classes, contributed to the support of the dynasty, — became blackmailers, in fact, — and their excuse was that others did the same, and that if they proved the exception it would work their ruin. The system became loose through license and plenty till it was as wild and weak as that of Tweed in New York.

Then the unexpected happened — an accident. There was no uprising of the people, but they were restive; and the Democratic party leaders, thinking to gain some independent votes, decided to raise the cry "reform" and put up a ticket of candidates different enough from the usual offerings of political parties to give color to their platform. These leaders were not in earnest. There was little difference between the two parties in the city; but the rascals that were in had been getting the greater share of the spoils, and the "outs" wanted more than was given to them. "Boodle" was not the issue, no exposures were made or threatened, and the bosses expected to control their men if elected. Simply as part of the game, the Democrats raised the slogan, "reform" and "no more Ziegenheinism."

Mayor Ziegenhein, called "Uncle Henry," was a "good fellow," "one of the boys," and though it was during his administration that the city grew ripe and went to rot, his opponents talked only of incompetence and neglect, and repeated such stories as that of his famous reply to some citizens who complained because certain street lights were put out: "You have the moon yet — ain't it?"

When somebody mentioned Joseph W. Folk for Circuit Attorney the leaders were ready to accept him. They didn't know much about him. He was a young man from Tennessee; had been President of the Jefferson Club, and arbitrated the railroad strike of 1898. But Folk did not want the place. He was a civil lawyer, had had no practice at the criminal bar, cared little about it, and a lucrative business as counsel for corporations was interesting him. He rejected the invitation. The committee called again and again, urging his duty to his party, and the city, etc.

"Very well," he said, at last, "I will accept the nomination, but if elected I will do my duty. There must be no attempt to influence my actions when I am called upon to punish lawbreakers."

The committeemen took such statements as the conventional platitudes of candidates. They nominated him, the Democratic ticket was elected, and Folk became Circuit Attorney for the Eighth Missouri District.

Three weeks after taking the oath of office his campaign pledges were put to the test. A number of arrests had been made in connection with the recent election, and charges of illegal registration were preferred against men of both parties. Mr. Folk took them up like routine cases of ordinary crime. Political bosses rushed to the rescue. Mr. Folk was reminded of his duty to his party, and told that he was expected to construe the law in such a manner that repeaters and other election criminals who had hoisted Democracy's flag and helped elect him might be either discharged or receive the minimum punishment. The nature of the young lawyer's reply can best be inferred from the words of that veteran political leader, Colonel Ed Butler who, after a visit to Mr. Folk, wrathfully exclaimed, "D—n Joe! he thinks he's the whole thing as Circuit Attorney."

The election cases were passed through the courts with astonishing rapidity; no more mercy was shown Democrats than Republicans, and before winter came a number of ward heelers and old-time party workers were behind the bars in Jefferson City. He next turned his attention to grafters and straw bondsmen with whom the courts were infested, and several of these leeches are in the penitentiary to-day. The business was broken up because of his activity. But Mr. Folk had made little more than the beginning.

One afternoon, late in January, 1903, a newspaper reporter, known as "Red" Galvin, called Mr. Folk's attention to a ten-line newspaper item to the effect that a large sum of money had been placed in a bank for the purpose of bribing certain Assemblymen to secure the passage of a street railroad ordinance. No names were mentioned, but Mr. Galvin surmised that the bill referred to was one introduced on behalf of the Suburban Railway Company. An hour later Mr. Folk sent the names of nearly one hundred persons to the sheriff, with instructions to subpoena them before the grand jury at once. The list include Councilmen, members of the House of Delegates, officers and directors of the Suburban Railway, bank presidents and cashiers. In three days the investigation was being pushed with vigor, but St. Louis was laughing at the "huge joke." Such things had been attempted before. The men who had been ordered to appear before the grand jury jested as they chatted in the anterooms, and newspaper accounts of these preliminary examinations were written in the spirit of burlesque.

It has developed since that Circuit Attorney Folk knew nothing, and was not able to learn much more during the first days; but he says he saw here and there puffs of smoke and he determined to find the fire. It was not an easy job. The first break into such a system is always difficult. Mr. Folk began with nothing but courage and a strong personal conviction. He caused peremptory summons to be issued, for the immediate attendance in the grand jury room of Charles H. Turner, president of the Suburban Railway, and Philip Stock, a representative of brewers' interests, who, he had reason to believe, was the legislative agent in this deal.

"Gentlemen," said Mr. Folk, "I have secured sufficient evidence to warrant the return of indictments against you for bribery, and I shall prosecute you to the full extent of the law and send you to the penitentiary unless you tell to this grand jury the complete history of the corruptionist methods employed by you to secure the passage of Ordinance No. 44. I shall give you three days to consider the matter. At the end of that time, if you have not returned here and given us the information demanded, warrants will be issued for your arrest."

They looked at the audacious young prosecutor and left the Four Courts building without uttering a word. He waited. Two days later, ex-Lieutenant Governor Charles P. Johnson, the veteran criminal lawyer, called, and said that his client, Mr. Stock, was in such poor health that he would be unable to appear before the grand jury.

"I am truly sorry that Mr. Stock is ill," replied Mr. Folk, "for his presence here is imperative, and if he fails to appear he will be arrested before sundown."

That evening a conference was held in Governor Johnson's office, and the next day this story was told in the grand jury room by Charles H. Turner, millionaire president of the Suburban Railway, and corroborated by Philip Stock, man-about-town and a good fellow: The Suburban, anxious to sell out a large profit to its only competitor, the St. Louis Transit Co., caused to be drafted the measure known as House Bill No. 44. So sweeping were its grants that Mr. Turner, who planned and executed the document, told the directors in his confidence that its enactment into law would enhance the value of the property from three to six million dollars. The bill introduced, Mr. Turner visited Colonel Butler, who had long been known as a legislative agent, and asked his price for securing the passage of the measure. "One hundred and forty-five thousand dollars will be my fee," was the reply. The railway president demurred. He would think the matter over, he said, and he hired a cheaper man, Mr. Stock. Stock conferred with the representative of the combine in the House of Delegates and reported that $75,000 would be necessary in this branch of the Assembly. Mr. Turner presented a note indorsed by two of the directors whom he could trust, and secured a loan from the German American Savings Bank.

Bribe funds in pocket, the legislative agent telephoned John Murrell, at that time a representative of the House combine, to meet him in the office of the Lincoln Trust Company. There the two rented a safe-deposit box. Mr. Stock placed in the drawer the roll of $75,000, and each subscribed to an agreement that the box should not be opened unless both were present. Of course the conditions spread upon the bank's daybook made no reference to the purpose for which this fund had been deposited, but an agreement entered into by Messrs. Stock and Murrell was to the effect that the $75,000 should be given Mr. Murrell as soon as the bill became an ordinance, and by him distributed to the members of the combine. Stock turned to the Council, and upon his report a further sum of $60,000 was secured. These bills were placed in a safe-deposit box of the Mississippi Valley Trust Co., and the man who held the key as representative of the Council combine was Charles H. Kratz.

All seemed well, but a few weeks after placing these funds in escrow, Mr. Stock reported to his employer that there was an unexpected hitch due to the action of Emil Meysenburg, who, as a member of the Council Committee on Railroads, was holding up the report on the bill. Mr. Stock said that Mr. Meysenburg held some worthless shares in a defunct corporation and wanted Mr. Stock to purchase this paper at its par value of $9,000. Mr. Turner gave Mr. Stock the money with which to buy the shares.

Thus the passage of House Bill 44 promised to cost the Suburban Railway Co. $144,000, only one thousand dollars less than that originally named by the political boss to whom Mr. Turner had first applied. The bill, however, passed both houses of the Assembly. The sworn servants of the city had done their work and held out their hands for the bribe money.

Then came a court mandate which prevented the Suburban Railway Co. from reaping the benefit of the vote-buying, and Charles H. Turner, angered at the check, issued orders that the money in safe-deposit boxes should not be touched. War was declared between bribe-givers and bribe-takers, and the latter resorted to tactics which they hoped would frighten the Suburban people into submission — such as making enough of the story public to cause rumors of impending prosecution. It was that first item which Mr. Folk saw and acted upon.

When Messrs. Turner and Stock unfolded in the grand jury room the details of their bribery plot, Circuit Attorney Folk found himself in possession of verbal evidence of a great crime; he needed as material exhibits the two large sums of money in safe-deposit vaults of two of the largest banking institutions of the West. Had this money been withdrawn? Could he get it if it was there? Lockboxes had always been considered sacred and beyond the power of the law to open. "I've always held," said Mr. Folk, "that the fact that a thing never had been done was no reason for thinking it couldn't be done." He decided in this case that the magnitude of the interests involved warranted unusual action, so he selected a committee of grand jurors and visited one of the banks. He told the president, a personal friend, the facts that had come into his possession, and asked permission to search for the fund.

"Impossible," was the reply. "Our rules deny anyone the right."

"Mr. ——," said Mr. Folk, "a crime has been committed, and you hold concealed the principal evidence thereto. In the name of the State of Missouri I demand that you cause the box to be opened. If you refuse, I shall cause a warrant to be issued, charging you as an accessory."

For a minute not a word was spoken by anyone in the room; then the banker said in almost inaudible tones:

"Give me a little time, gentlemen. I must consult with our legal adviser before taking such a step."

"We will wait ten minutes," said the Circuit Attorney. "By that time we must have access to the vault or a warrant will be applied for."

At the expiration of that time a solemn procession wended its way from the president's office to the vaults in the sub-cellar — the president, the cashier, and the corporation's lawyer, the grand jurors, and the Circuit Attorney. All bent eagerly forward as the key was inserted in the lock. The iron drawer yielded, and a roll of something wrapped in brown paper was brought to light. The Circuit Attorney removed the rubber bands, and national bank notes of large denomination spread out flat before them. The money was counted, and the sum was $75,000!

The boodle fund was returned to its repository, officers of the bank were told they would be held responsible for it until the courts could act. The investigators visited the other financial institution. They met with more resistance there. The threat to procure a warrant had no effect until

Mr. Folk left the building and set off in the direction of the Four Courts. Then a messenger called him back, and the second box was opened. In this was found $60,000. The chain of evidence was complete.

From that moment events moved rapidly. Charles Kratz and John K. Murrell, alleged representatives of Council and House combines, were arrested on bench warrants and placed under heavy bonds. Kratz was brought into court from a meeting at which plans were being formed for his election to the National Congress. Murrell was taken from his undertaking establishment. Emil Meysenburg, millionaire broker, was seated in his office when a sheriff's deputy entered and read a document that charged him with bribery. The summons reached Henry Nicolaus while he was seated at his desk, and the wealthy brewer was compelled to send for a bondsman to avoid passing a night in jail. The cable flashed the news to Cairo, Egypt, that Ellis Wainwright, many times a millionaire, proprietor of the St. Louis brewery that bears his name, had been indicted. Julius Lehmann, one of the members of the House of Delegates, who had joked while waiting in the grand jury's anteroom, had his laughter cut short by the hand of a deputy sheriff on his shoulder and the words, "You are charged with perjury." He was joined at the bar of the criminal court by Harry Faulkner, another jolly good fellow.

Consternation spread among the boodle gang. Some of the men took night trains for other States and foreign countries; the majority remained and counseled together. Within twenty-four hours after the first indictments were returned, a meeting of bribe-givers and bribe-takers was held in South St. Louis. The total wealth of those in attendance was $30,000,000, and their combined political influence sufficient to carry any municipal election under normal conditions.

This great power was aligned in opposition to one man, who still was alone. It was not until many indictments had been returned that a citizens' committee was formed to furnish funds, and even then most of the contributors concealed their identity. Mr. James L. Blair, the treasurer, testified in court that they were afraid to be known lest "it ruin their business."

At the meeting of corruptionists three courses were decided upon. Political leaders were to work on the Circuit Attorney by promise of future reward, or by threats. Detectives were to ferret out of the young lawyer's past anything that could be used against him. Witnesses would be sent out of town and provided with money to remain away until the adjournment of the grand jury.

Mr. Folk at once felt the pressure, and it was of a character to startle one. Statesmen, lawyers, merchants, clubmen, churchmen — in fact, men prominent in all walks of life — visited him at his office and at his home, and urged that he cease such activity against his fellow-townspeople. Political preferment was promised if he would yield; a political grave if he persisted. Threatening letters came, warning him of plots to murder, to disfigure, and to blackguard. Word came from Tennessee that detectives were investigating every act of his life. Mr. Folk told the politicians that he was not seeking political favors, and not looking forward to another office; the others he defied. Meantime he probed the deeper into the municipal sore. With his first successes for prestige and aided by the panic among the boodlers, he soon had them suspicious of one another, exchanging charges of betrayal, and ready to "squeal" or run at the slightest sign of danger. One member of the House of Delegates became so frightened while under the inquisitorial cross-fire that he was seized with a nervous chill; his false teeth fell to the floor, and the rattle so increased his alarm that he rushed from the room without stopping to pick up his teeth, and boarded the next train.

It was not long before Mr. Folk had dug up the intimate history of ten years of corruption, especially of the business of the North and South and the Central Traction franchise grants, the last-named being even more iniquitous than the Suburban.

Early in 1898 a "promoter" rented a bridal suite at the Planters' Hotel, and having stocked the rooms with wines, liquors, and cigars until they resembled a candidate's headquarters during a convention, sought introduction to members of the Assembly and to such political bosses as had influence with the city fathers. Two weeks after his arrival the Central Traction bill was introduced "by request" in the Council. The measure was a blanket franchise, granting rights of way which had not been given to old-established companies, and permitting the beneficiaries to parallel any track in the city. It passed both Houses despite the protests of every newspaper in the city, save one, and was vetoed by the mayor. The cost to the promoter was $145,000.

Preparations were made to pass the bill over the executive's veto. The bridal suite was restocked, larger sums of money were placed on deposit in the banks, and the services of three legislative agents were engaged. Evidence now in the possession of the St. Louis courts tells in detail the disposition of $250,000 of bribe money. Sworn statements prove that $75,000 was spent in the House of Delegates. The remainder of the $250,000 was distributed in the Council, whose members, though few in number, appraised their honor at a higher figure on account of their higher positions in the business and social world. Finally, but one vote was needed to complete the necessary two-thirds in the upper Chamber. To secure this a councilman of reputed integrity was paid $5,000 in consideration that he vote aye when the ordinance should come up for final passage. But the promoter did not dare risk all upon the vote of one man, and he made this novel proposition to another honored member, who accepted it:

"You will vote on roll call after Mr. ——. I will place $45,000 in the hands of your son, which amount will become yours, if you have to vote for the measure because of Mr. ——'s not keeping his promise. But if he stands out for it you can vote against it, and the money shall revert to me."

On the evening when the bill was read for final passage the City Hall was crowded with ward heelers and lesser politicians. These men had been engaged by the promoter, at five and ten dollars a head, to cheer on the boodling Assemblymen. The bill passed the House with a rush, and all crowded into the Council Chamber. While the roll was being called the silence was profound, for all knew that some men in the Chamber whose reputations had been free from blemish, were under promise and pay to part with honor that night. When the clerk was two-thirds down the list those who had kept count knew that but one vote was needed. One more name was called. The man addressed turned red, then white, and after a moment's hesitation he whispered "Aye"! The silence was so death-like that his vote was heard throughout the room, and those near enough heard also the sigh of relief that escaped from the member who could now vote "no" and save his reputation.

The Central Franchise bill was a law, passed over the mayor's veto. The promoter had expended nearly $300,000 in securing the legislation, but within a week he sold his rights of way to "Eastern capitalists" for $1,250,000. The United Railways Company was formed, and without owning an inch of steel rail, or a plank in a car, was able to compel every street railroad in St. Louis, with the exception of the Suburban, to part with stock and right of way and agree to a merger. Out of this grew the St. Louis Transit Company of to-day. . . .

Pitiful? Yes, but typical. Other cities are today in the same condition as St. Louis before Mr. Folk was invited in to see its rottenness. Chicago is cleaning itself up just now, so is Minneapolis, and Pittsburg recently had a bribery scandal; Boston is at peace, Cincinnati and St. Paul are satisfied, while Philadelphia is happy with the worst government in the world. As for the small towns and the villages, many of these are busy as bees at the loot.

St. Louis, indeed, in its disgrace, has a great advantage. It was exposed late; it has not been reformed and caught again and again, until its citizens are reconciled to corruption. But, best of all, the man who has turned St. Louis inside out, turned it, as it were, upside down, too. In all cities, the better classes — the business men — are the sources of corruption; but they are so rarely pursued and caught that we do not fully realize whence the trouble comes. Thus most cities blame the politicians and the ignorant and vicious poor.

Mr. Folk has shown St. Louis that its bankers, brokers, corporation officers, — its business men are the sources of evil, so that from the start it will know the municipal problem in its true light. With a tradition for public spirit, it may drop Butler and its runaway bankers, brokers, and brewers, and pushing aside the scruples of the hundreds of men down in blue book, and red book, and church register, who are lying hidden behind the statutes of limitations, the city may restore good government. Otherwise the exposures by Mr. Folk will result only in the perfection of the corrupt system. For the corrupt can learn a lesson when the good citizens cannot. The Tweed régime in New York taught Tammany to organize its boodle business; the police exposure taught it to improve its method of collecting blackmail. And both now are almost perfect and safe. The rascals of St. Louis will learn in like manner; they will concentrate the control of their bribery system, excluding from the profit-sharing the great mass of weak rascals, and carrying on the business as a business in the interest of a trustworthy few. District Attorney Jerome cannot catch the Tammany men, and Circuit Attorney Folk will not be able another time to break the St. Louis ring. This is St. Louis' one great chance.

But, for the rest of us, it does not matter about St. Louis any more than it matters about Colonel Butler *et al*. The point is, that what went on in St. Louis is going on in most of our cities, towns, and villages. The problem of municipal government in America has not been solved. The people may be tired of it, but they cannot give it up — not yet.

Study Guide

1. This selection can be divided into several parts:
   (a) introductory comments on the state of city governments (pp. 251–254);
   (b) a rationale for Steffens's investigations (pp. 254–258); and
   (c) a detailed narrative-analysis of what happened in St. Louis when municipal reform was attempted (pp. 258–269).

2. What do you make of Steffens's introductory remarks — intended as an assessment of the reasons for municipal corruption — and his suggested

solution? What role, in Steffens's analysis of the problem, do the following play:

(a) the immigrant;

(b) the businessman;

(c) the politician; and

(d) the average citizen?

What *similarities* and what *differences* in the quality and degree of municipal corruption does Steffens find among the various cities he visited?

3. How does Steffens characterize his efforts and what results does he hope to see as a result of them?

4. Before you read about the "Tweed Days in St. Louis," identify Tweed. Then proceed to analyze the exposé of conditions in St. Louis:

(a) *When,* and *how,* and *over what does* political corruption begin to flourish?

(b) Whom does Steffens blame for corruption in St. Louis and what groups does he hold relatively blameless?

(c) Who is Joseph W. Folk and what role does Steffens hope he and others like him will play in the reform process?

(d) How optimistic does Steffens appear to be about the possibilities of reform?

5. A final question to ponder: Some historians have suggested that Steffens was an objective social scientist; others consider him a subjective moralist. On the basis of this excerpt from his writings, offer an opinion.

Upton Sinclair

POISONED MEAT AND POISONED LIVES

❧ *1906* ❧   No ONE reflects the crusading spirit of the Progressive Era better than Upton Sinclair. From the time of his graduation from the City College of New York in 1897 he was temperamentally committed to improving the world. A socialist, he was early convinced not only that capitalism was wrong but that all of its weaknesses could be quickly cured by drastic economic and political reforms. Quick to become indignant at evil and deceit, he resolved to try to "make it impossible for joy and tenderness and rapture and awe to be lashed at and spit upon and trampled and smashed into annihilation."

Sinclair was determined to be a great writer as well as a reformer. Early in his career he made a quiet study of the lives of Chicago stockyard workers. Dressed in old clothes and carrying a dinner pail, he spent seven weeks wandering through the meat packing plants observing all their gruesome horrors. Then he began to write a novel describing in vivid detail everything that he had seen. For months he worked away, living in a small shack he had built with his own hands near Princeton, New Jersey. He published parts of his story in a socialist weekly called *Appeal to Reason* (which is ironic, since his tale was so obviously aimed at men's emotions). He also wrote two muckraking articles on the slaughterhouses for *Collier's*. Finally, after much controversy and a change of publishers, *The Jungle* appeared in 1906. In Sinclair's own words, it "became a sensation overnight." For months it was a best seller; soon it was being translated into many languages. President Theodore Roosevelt ordered an investigation of the packers and within the year Congress had passed the Pure Food and Drug Act and a stiff meat-inspection act.

The Jungle thus accomplished the author's immediate objectives. It sold over 150,000 copies within a generation, and is still widely read. It made Sinclair famous. But like that other reform tract, *Looking Backward,* it did not accomplish its ultimate goal of changing the basic structure of society. The thousands who read Sinclair's melodramatic, sentimental and diffuse story of the Lithuanian worker, Jurgis Rudkus and his wife Ona Lukoszaite, were properly indignant about the evils it described, but they did not follow Jurgis along the path to socialism.

Upton Sinclair (1878–1968) is one of the most prolific and widely read novelists of the twentieth century. His *Dragon's Teeth* (1942) won a Pulitzer prize. He had also been frequently a Socialist candidate for political office, and in 1934, he was the unsuccessful Democratic candidate for Governor of California.

THE JUNGLE

A FULL hour before the party reached the city they had begun to note the perplexing changes in the atmosphere. It grew darker all the time, and upon the earth the grass seemed to grow less green. Every minute, as the train sped on, the colors of things became dingier; the fields were grown parched and yellow, the landscape hideous and bare. And along with the thickening smoke they began to notice another circumstance, a strange, pungent odor. They were not sure that it was unpleasant, this odor; some might have called it sickening, but their taste in odors was not developed, and they were only sure that it was curious. Now, sitting in the trolley car, they realized that they were on their way to the home of it — that they had travelled all the way from Lithuania to it. It was now no longer something far off and faint, that you caught in whiffs; you could literally taste it, as well as smell it — you could take hold of it, almost, and examine it at your leisure. They were divided in their opinions about it. It was an elemental odor, raw and crude; it was rich, almost rancid, sensual, and strong. There were some who drank it in as if it were an intoxicant; there were others who put their handkerchiefs to their faces. The new emigrants were still tasting it, lost in wonder, when suddenly the car came to a halt, and the door was flung open, and a voice shouted —"Stockyards!"

They were left standing upon the corner, staring; down a side street there were two rows of brick houses, and between them a vista: half a dozen chimneys, tall as the tallest of buildings, touching the very sky — and leaping from them half a dozen columns of smoke, thick, oily, and black as night. It might have come from the center of the world, this smoke, where the fires of the ages still smoulder. It came as if self-impelled, driving all before it, a perpetual explosion. It was inexhaustible; one stared, waiting to see it stop, but still the great streams rolled out. They spread in vast clouds overhead, writhing, curling; then, uniting in one giant river, they streamed away down the sky, stretching a black pall as far as the eye could reach.

Then the party became aware of another strange thing. This, too, like the odor, was a thing elemental; it was a sound, a sound made up of ten thousand little sounds. You scarcely noticed it at first — it sunk into your consciousness, a vague disturbance, a trouble. It was like the murmuring of the bees in the spring, the whisperings of the forest; it suggested endless activity, the rumblings of a world in motion. It was only by an effort that one could realize that it was made by animals, that it was the distant lowing of ten thousand cattle, the distant grunting of ten thousand swine. . . .

There is over a square mile of space in the yards, and more than half of it is occupied by cattle pens; north and south as far as the eye can reach there stretches a sea of pens. And they were all filled — so many cattle no one had ever dreamed existed in the world. Red cattle, black, white, and yellow cattle; old cattle and young cattle; great bellowing bulls and little calves not an hour born; meek-eyed milch cows and fierce, long-horned Texas steers. The sound of them here was as of all the barnyards of the universe; and as for counting them — it would have taken all day simply to count the pens. . . .

"And what will become of all these creatures?" cried Teta Elzbieta.

"By tonight," Jokubas answered, "they will all be killed and cut up; and over there on the other side of the packing houses are more railroad tracks, where the cars come to take them away."

There were two hundred and fifty miles of track within the yards, their guide went on to tell them. They brought about ten thousand head of cattle every day, and as many hogs, and half as many sheep — which meant some eight or ten million live creatures turned into food every year. One stood and watched, and little by little caught the drift of the tide, as it set in the direction of the packing houses. There were groups of cattle being driven to the chutes, which were roadways about fifteen feet wide, raised high above the pens. In these chutes the stream of animals was continuous; it was quite uncanny to watch them, pressing on to their fate, all unsuspicious — a very river of death. Our friends were not poetical, and the sight suggested to them no metaphors of human destiny; they thought only of the wonderful efficiency of it all. The chutes into which the hogs went climbed high up — to the very top of the distant buildings, and Jokubas explained that the hogs went up by the power of their own legs, and then their weight carried them back through all the processes necessary to make them into pork.

"They don't waste anything here," said the guide, and then he laughed and added a witticism, which he was pleased that his unsophisticated friends should take to be his own: "They use everything about the hog except the squeal." . . .

They climbed a long series of stairways outside of the building, to the top of its five or six stories. Here were the chute, with its river of hogs, all patiently toiling upward; there was a place for them to rest to cool off, and then through another passageway they went into a room from which there is no returning for hogs.

It was a long, narrow room, with a gallery along it for visitors. At the head there was a great iron wheel, about twenty feet in circumference, with rings here and there along its edge. Upon both sides of this wheel there was a narrow space, into which came the hogs at the end of their journey; in the midst of them stood a great burly Negro, bare-armed and bare-chested. He was resting for the moment, for the wheel had stopped while men were cleaning up. In a minute or two, however, it began slowly to revolve, and then the men upon each side of it sprang to work. They had chains which they fastened about the leg of the nearest hog, and the other end of the chain they hooked into one of the rings upon the wheel. So, as the wheel turned, a hog was suddenly jerked off his feet and borne aloft.

At the same instant the ear was assailed by a most terrifying shriek; the visitors started in alarm, the women turned pale and shrank back. The shriek was followed by another, louder and yet more agonizing — for once started upon that journey, the hog never came back; at the top of the wheel he was shunted off upon a trolley, and went sailing down the room. And meantime another was swung up, and then another, and another, until there was a double line of them, each dangling by a foot and kicking in frenzy — and squealing. The uproar was appalling, perilous to the eardrums; one feared there was too much sound for the room to hold — that the walls must give way or the ceiling crack. There were high squeals and low squeals, grunts, and wails of agony; there would come a momentary lull, and then a fresh outburst, louder than ever, surging up to a deafening climax. It was too much for some of the visitors — the men would look at each other, laughing nervously, and the women would stand with hands clenched, and the blood rushing to their faces, and the tears starting in their eyes.

Meantime, heedless of all these things, the men upon the floor were going about their work. Neither squeals of hogs nor tears of visitors made any difference to them; one by one they hooked up the hogs, and one by one with a swift stroke they slit their throats. There was a long line of hogs, with squeals and life-blood ebbing away together, until at last each started again, and vanished with a splash into a huge vat of boiling water.

It was all so very businesslike that one watched it fascinated. It was pork-making by machinery, pork-making by applied mathematics. And yet somehow the most matter-of-fact person could not help thinking of the hogs; they were so innocent, they came so very trustingly; and they were so very human in their protests — and so perfectly within their rights! They had done nothing to deserve it, and it was adding insult to injury, as the thing was done here, swinging them up in this cold-blooded, impersonal way, without a pretence at apology, without the homage of a tear. Now and then a visitor wept, to be sure; but this slaughtering machine ran on, visitors or no visitors. It was like some horrible crime committed in a dungeon, all unseen and unheeded, buried out of sight and of memory.

One could not stand and watch very long without becoming philosophical, without beginning to deal in symbols and similes, and to hear the hog-squeal of the universe. Was it permitted to believe that there was nowhere upon the earth, or above the earth, a heaven for hogs, where they were requited for all this suffering? Each one of these hogs was a separate creature. Some were white hogs, some were black; some were brown, some were spotted; some were old, some were young; some were long and lean, some were monstrous. And each of them had an individuality of his own, a will of his own, a hope and a heart's desire; each was full of self-confidence, of self-importance, and a sense of dignity. And trusting and strong in faith he had gone about his business, the while a black shadow hung over him and a horrid Fate waited in his pathway. Now suddenly it had swooped upon him, and had seized him by the leg. Relentless, remorseless, it was; all his protests, his screams, were nothing to it — it did its cruel will with him, as if his wishes, his feelings, had simply no existence at all; it cut his throat and watched him gasp out his life. And now was one to believe that there was nowhere a god of hogs, to whom this hog-personality was precious, to whom these hog-squeals and agonies had a meaning? Who would take this hog into his arms and comfort him, reward him for his work well done, and show him the meaning of his sacrifice? Perhaps some glimpse of all this was in the thoughts of our humble-minded Jurgis, as he turned to go on with the rest of the party, and muttered: *"Dieve* — but I'm glad I'm not a hog!"

The carcass hog was scooped out of the vat by machinery, and then it fell to the second floor, passing on the way through a wonderful machine with numerous scrapers, which adjusted themselves to the size and shape of the animal, and sent it out at the other end with nearly all of its bristles removed. It was then again strung up by machinery, and sent upon another trolley ride; this time passing between two lines of men, who sat upon a raised platform, each doing a certain single thing to the carcass as it came to him. One scraped the outside of a leg; another scraped the inside of the same leg. One with a swift stroke cut the throat; another with two swift strokes severed the head, which fell to the floor and vanished through a hole. Another made a slit down the body; a second opened the body wider; a third with a saw cut the breastbone; a fourth loosened the entrails; a fifth pulled them out — and they also slid through a hole in the floor. There were men to scrape each side and men to scrape the back; there were men to clean the carcass inside, to trim it and wash it. Looking down this room, one saw, creeping slowly, a line of dangling hogs a hundred yards in length; and for every yard there was a man, working as if a demon were after him. At the end of this hog's progress every inch of the carcass had been gone over several times, and then it was rolled into the chilling room, where it stayed for twenty-four hours, and where a stranger might lose himself in a forest of freezing hogs.

Before the carcass was admitted here, however, it had to pass a government inspector, who sat in the doorway and felt of the glands in the neck for tuberculosis. This government inspector did not have the manner of a man who was worked to death; he was apparently not haunted by a fear that the hog might get by him before he had finished his testing. If you were a sociable person, he was quite willing to enter into conversation with you, and to explain to you the deadly nature of the ptomaines which are found in tubercular pork; and while he was talking with you you could hardly be so ungrateful as to notice that a dozen carcasses were passing him untouched. This inspector wore an imposing silver badge, and he gave an atmosphere of authority to the scene, and, as it were, put the stamp of official approval upon the things which were done in Durham's.

Jurgis went down the line with the rest of the visitors, staring open-mouthed, lost in wonder. He had dressed hogs himself in the forest of Lithuania; but he had never expected to live to see one hog dressed by several hundred men. It was like a wonderful poem to him, and he took it all in guilelessly — even to the conspicuous signs demanding immaculate cleanliness of the employees. Jurgis was vexed when the cynical Jokubas translated these signs with sarcastic comments, offering to take them to the secret rooms where the spoiled meats went to be doctored.

The party descended to the next floor, where the various waste materials were treated. Here came the entrails, to be scraped and washed clean for sausage casings; men and women worked here in the midst of a sickening stench, which caused the visitors to hasten by, gasping. To another room came all the scraps to be "tanked," which meant boiling and pumping off the grease to make soap and lard; below they took out the refuse, and this, too, was a region in which the visitors did not linger. In still other places men were engaged in cutting up the carcases that had been through the chilling rooms. First there were the "splitters," the most expert workmen in the plant, who earned as high as fifty cents an hour, and did not a thing all day except chop hogs down the middle. Then there were "cleaver men," great giants with muscles of iron; each had two men to attend him — to slide the half carcass in front of him on the table, and hold it while he chopped it, and then turn each piece so that he might chop it once more. His cleaver had a blade about two feet long, and he never made but one cut; he made it so neatly, too, that his implement did not smite through and dull itself — there was just enough force for a perfect cut, and no more. So through various yawning holes there slipped to the floor below — to one room hams, to another forequarters, to another sides of pork. One might go down to this floor and see the pickling rooms, where the hams were put into vats, and the great smoke rooms, with their airtight iron doors. In other rooms they prepared salt pork — there were whole cellars full of it, built up in great towers to the ceiling. In yet other rooms they were putting up meat in boxes and barrels, and wrapping hams and bacon in oiled paper, sealing and labeling and sewing them. From the doors of these rooms went men with loaded trucks, to the platform where freight cars were waiting to be filled; and one went out there and realized with a start that he had come at last to the ground floor of this enormous building. . . .

. . . No tiniest particle of organic matter was wasted in Durham's. Out of the horns of the cattle they made combs, buttons, hairpins, and imitation ivory; out of the shin bones and other big bones they cut knife and tooth brush handles, and mouthpieces for pipes; out of the hoofs they cut hairpins and buttons, before they made the rest into glue. From such things as feet, knuckles, hide clippings, and sinews came such strange and unlikely products as gelatin, isinglass, and phosphorus, bone black, shoe blacking, and bone oil. They had curled-hair works for the cattle tails, and a "wool pullery" for the sheep skins; they made pepsin from the stomachs of the pigs, and albumen from the blood, and violin strings from the ill-smelling entrails. When there was nothing else to be done with a thing, they first put it into a tank and got out of it all the tallow and grease, and then they made it into fertilizer. All these industries were gathered into buildings near by, connected by galleries and railroads with the main establishment, and it was estimated that they had handled nearly a quarter of a billion of animals since the founding of the plant by the elder Durham a generation and more ago. If you counted with it the other big plants — and they were now really all one — it was, so Jakubas informed them, the greatest aggregation of labor and capital ever gathered in one place. It employed thirty thousand men; it supported directly two hundred and fifty thousand people in its neighborhood, and indirectly it supported half a million. It sent its products to every country in the civilized world, and it furnished the food for no less than thirty million people! . . .

Now Antanas Rudkus was the meekest man that God ever put on earth, and so Jurgis found it a striking confirmation of what the men all said, that his father had been at work only two days before he came home as bitter as any of them, and cursing Durham's with all the power of his soul. For they had set him to cleaning out the traps; and the family sat round and listened in wonder while he told them what that meant. It seemed that he was working in the room where the men prepared the beef for canning, and the beef had lain in vats full of chemicals, and men with great forks speared it out and dumped it into trucks, to be taken to the cooking room. When they had speared out all they could reach, they emptied the vat on the floor, and then with shovels scraped off the balance and dumped it into the truck. This floor was filthy, yet they set Antanas with his mop slopping the "pickle" into a hole that connected with a sink, where it was caught and used over again forever; and if that was not enough, there was a trap in the pipe, where all the scraps of meat and odds and ends of refuse were caught, and every few days it was the old man's task to clean these out, and shovel their contents into one of the trucks with the rest of the meat!

This was the experience of Antanas; and then there came also Jonas and Marija with tales to tell. Marija was working for one of the independent packers, and was quite beside herself and outrageous with triumph over the sums of money she was making as a painter of cans. But one day she walked home with a pale-faced little woman who worked opposite to her, Jadvyga Marcinkus by name, and Jadvyga told her how she, Marija, had chanced to get her job. She had taken the place of an Irish woman who had been working in that factory ever since anyone could remember, for over fifteen years, so she declared. Mary Dennis was her name, and a long time ago she had been seduced, and had a little boy; he was a cripple, and an epileptic, but still he was all that she had in the world to love, and they had lived in a little room alone somewhere back of Halsted Street, where the Irish were. Mary had had consumption, and all day long you might hear her coughing as she worked; of late she had been going all to pieces, and when Marija came, the "forelady" had suddenly decided to turn her off. The forelady had to come up to a certain standard herself, and could not stop for sick people, Jadvyga explained. The fact that Mary had been there so long had not made any difference to her — it was doubtful if she even knew that, for both the forelady and the superintendent were new people, having only been there two or three years themselves. Jadvyga did not know what had become of the poor creature; she would have gone to see her, but had been sick herself. She had pains in her back all the time, Jadvyga explained, and feared that she had womb trouble. It was not fit work for a woman, handling fourteen-pound cans all day.

It was a striking circumstance that Jonas, too, had gotten his job by the misfortune of some other person. Jonas pushed a truck loaded with hams from the smoke rooms on to an elevator, and thence to the packing rooms. The trucks were all of iron, and heavy, and they put about threescore hams on each of them, a load of more than a quarter of a ton. On the uneven floor it was a task for a man to start one of these trucks, unless he was a giant; and when it was once started he naturally tried his best to keep it going. There was always the boss prowling about, and if there was a second's delay he would fall to cursing; Lithuanians and Slovaks and such, who could not understand what was said to them, the bosses were wont to kick about the place like so many dogs. Therefore these trucks went for the most part on the run; and the predecessor of Jonas had been jammed against the wall by one and crushed in a horrible and nameless manner.

All of these were sinister incidents; but they were trifles compared to what Jurgis saw with his own eyes before long. One curious thing he had noticed, the very first day, in his profession of shoveler of guts; which was the sharp trick of the floor bosses whenever there chanced to come a "slunk" calf. Any man who knows anything about butchering knows that the flesh of a cow that is about to calve, or has just calved, is not fit for food. A good many of these came every day to the packing houses — and, of course, if they had chosen, it would have been an easy matter for the packers to keep them till they were fit for food. But for the saving of time and fodder, it was the law that cows of that sort came along with the others, and whoever noticed it would tell the boss, and the boss would start up a conversation with the government inspector, and the two would stroll away. So, in a trice the carcass of the cow would be cleaned out, and the entrails would have vanished; it was Jurgis' task to slide them into the trap, calves and all, and on the floor below they took out these "slunk" calves, and butchered them for meat, and used even the skins of them.

One day a man slipped and hurt his leg; and that afternoon, when the last of the cattle had been disposed of, and the men were leaving, Jurgis was ordered to remain and do some special work which this injured man had usually done. It was late, almost dark, and the government inspectors had all gone, and there were only a dozen or two of men on the floor. That day they had killed about four thousand cattle, and these cattle had come in freight trains from far states, and some of them had got hurt. There were some with broken legs, and some with gored sides; there were some that had died, from what cause no one could say; and they were all to be disposed of, here in the darkness and silence. "Downers," the men called them; and the packing house had a special elevator upon which they were raised to the killing beds, where the gang proceeded to handle them, with an air of businesslike nonchalance which said plainer than any words that it was a matter of everyday routine. It took a couple of hours to get them out of the way, and in the end Jurgis saw them go into the chilling rooms with the rest of the meat, being carefully scattered here and there so that they could not be identified. When he came home that night he was in a very somber mood, having begun to see at last how those might be right who had laughed at him for his faith in America. . . .

. . . "Bubbly Creek" is an arm of the Chicago River, and forms the southern boundary of the yards; all the drainage of the square mile of packing houses empties into it, so that it is really a great open sewer a hundred or two feet wide. One long arm of it is blind, and the filth stays there forever and a day. The grease and chemicals that are poured into it undergo all sorts of strange transformations, which are the cause of its name; it is constantly in motion, as if huge fish were feeding in it, or great leviathans were disporting themselves in its depths. Bubbles of carbonic acid gas will rise to the surface and burst, and make rings two or three feet wide. Here and there the grease and filth have caked solid, and the creek looks like a bed of lava; chickens walk about on it, feeding, and many times an unwary stranger has started to stroll across, and vanished temporarily. The packers used to leave the creek that way, till every now and then the surface would catch on fire and burn furiously, and the fire department would have to come and put it out. Once, however, an ingenious stranger came and started to gather this filth in scows, to make lard out of; then the packers took the cue, and got out an injunction to stop him, and afterwards gathered it themselves. The banks of "Bubbly Creek" are plastered thick with hairs, and this also the packers gather and clean.

And there were things even stranger than this, according to the gossip of the men. The packers had secret mains, through which they stole billions of gallons of the city's water. The newspapers had been full of this scandal — once there had even been an investigation, and an actual uncovering of the pipes; but nobody had been punished, and the thing went right on. And then there was the condemned meat industry, with its endless horrors. The people of Chicago saw the government inspectors in Packingtown, and they all took that to mean that they were protected from diseased meat; they did not understand that these hundred and sixty-three inspectors had been appointed at the request of the packers, and that they were paid by the United States government to certify that all the diseased meat was kept in the state. They had no authority beyond that; for the inspection of meat to be sold in the city and state the whole force in Packingtown consisted of three henchmen of the local political machine! And shortly afterward one of these, a physician, made the discovery that the carcasses of steers which had been condemned as tubercular by the government inspectors, and which therefore contained ptomaines, which are deadly poisons, were left upon an open platform and carted away to be sold in the city; and so he insisted that these carcasses be treated with an injection of kerosene — and was ordered to resign the same week! So indignant were the packers that they went farther, and compelled the mayor to abolish the whole bureau of inspection; so that since then there has not been even a pretence of any interference with the graft. There was said to be two thousand dollars a week hush money from the tubercular steers alone, and as much again from the hogs which had died of cholera on the trains, and which you might see any day being loaded into box cars and hauled away to a place called Globe, in Indiana, where they made a fancy grade of lard.

Jurgis heard of these things little by little, in the gossip of those who were obliged to perpetrate them. It seemed as if every time you met a person from a new department, you heard of new swindles and new crimes. There was, for instance, a Lithuanian who was a cattle butcher for the plant where Marija had worked, which killed meat for canning only; and to hear this man describe the animals which came to his place would have been worthwhile for a Dante or a Zola. It seemed that they must have agencies all over the country, to hunt out old and crippled and diseased cattle to be canned. There were cattle which had been fed on "whiskey malt," the refuse of the breweries, and had become what the men called "steerly" — which means covered with boils. It was a nasty job killing these, for when you plunged your knife into them they would burst and splash foul-smelling stuff into your face; and when a man's sleeves were smeared with blood, and his hands steeped in it, how was he ever to wipe his face, or to clear his eyes so that he could see? It was stuff such as this that made the "embalmed beef" that had killed several times as many United States soldiers as all the bullets of the Spaniards; only the army beef, besides, was not fresh canned, it was old stuff that had been lying for years in the cellars.

Then one Sunday evening, Jurgis sat puffing his pipe by the kitchen stove, and talking with an old fellow whom Jonas had introduced, and who worked in the canning-rooms at Durham's; and so Jurgis learned a few things about the great and only Durham canned goods, which had become a national institution. They were regular alchemists at Durham's; they advertised a mushroom-catsup, and the men who made it did not know what a mushroom looked like. They advertised "potted chicken" — and it was like the boarding-house soup of the comic papers, through which a chicken had walked with rubbers on. Perhaps they had a secret process for making chickens chemically — who knows? said Jurgis's friend; the things that went into the mixture were tripe, and the fat of pork, and beef suet, and hearts of beef, and finally the waste ends of veal, when they had any. They put these up in several grades, and sold them at several prices; but the contents of the cans all came out of the same hopper. And then there was "potted game" and "potted grouse," "potted ham," and "deviled ham" — de-vyled, as the men called it. "Devyled" ham was made out of the waste ends of smoked beef that were too small to be sliced by the machines; and also tripe, dyed with chemicals so that it would not show white, and trimmings of hams and corned beef, and potatoes, skins and all, and finally the hard cartilaginous gullets of beef, after the tongues had been cut out. All this ingenious mixture was ground up and flavored with spices to make it taste like something. Anybody who could invent a new imitation had been sure of a fortune from old Durham, said Jurgis's informant, but it was hard to think of anything new in a place where so many sharp wits had been at work for so long; where men welcomed tuberculosis in the cattle they were feeding, because it made them fatten more quickly; and where they bought up all the old rancid butter left over in the grocery stores of a continent, and "oxidized" it by a forced-air process, to take away the odor, rechurned it with skim milk, and sold it in bricks in the cities! Up to a year or two ago it had been the custom to kill horses in the yards — ostensibly for fertilizer; but after long agitation the newspapers had been able to make the public realize that the horses were being canned. Now it was against the law to kill horses in Packingtown, and the law was really complied with — for the present, at any rate. Any day, however, one might see sharp-horned and shaggy-haired creatures running with the sheep — and yet what a job you would have to get the public to believe that a good part of what it buys for lamb and mutton is really goat's flesh!

There was another interesting set of statistics that a person might have gathered in Packingtown — those of the various afflictions of the workers. When Jurgis had first inspected the packing plants with Szedvilas, he had marveled while he listened to the tale of all the things that were made out of the carcasses of animals, and of all the lesser industries that were maintained there; now he found that each one of these lesser industries was a separate little inferno, in its way as horrible as the killing-beds, the source and fountain of them all. The workers in each of them had their own peculiar diseases. And the wandering visitor peering down through the damp and the steam, and as old Durham's architects had not built the killing room for the convenience of the hoisters, at every few feet they would have to stoop under a beam, say four feet above the one they ran on, which got them into the habit of stooping, so that in a few years they would be walking like chimpanzees. Worst of any, however, were the fertilizer men, and those who served in the cooking rooms. These people could not be shown to the visitor — for the odor of a fertilizer man would scare any ordinary visitor at a hundred yards, and as for the other men, who worked in tank rooms full of steam, and in some of which there were open vats near the level of the floor, their peculiar trouble was that they fell into the vats; and when they were fished out, there was never enough of them left to be worth exhibiting — sometimes they would be overlooked for days, till all but the bones of them had gone out to the world as Durham's Pure Leaf Lard! . . .

With one member trimming beef in a cannery, and another working in a sausage factory, the family had a first-hand knowledge of the great majority of Packingtown swindles. For it was the custom, as they found, whenever meat was so spoiled that it could not be used for anything else, either to can it or else to chop it up into sausage. With what had been told them by Jonas, who had worked in the pickle rooms, they could now study the whole of the spoiled-meat industry on the inside, and read a new and grim meaning into that old Packingtown jest — that they use everything of the pig except the squeal.

Jonas had told them how the meat that was taken out of pickle would often be found sour, and how they would rub it up with soda to take away the smell, and sell it to be eaten on free-lunch counters; also of all the miracles of chemistry which they performed, giving to any sort of meat, fresh or salted, whole or chopped, any color and any flavor and any odor they chose. In the pickling of hams they had an ingenious apparatus, by which they saved time and increased the capacity of the plant — a machine consisting of a hollow needle attached to a pump; by plunging this needle into the meat and working with his foot a man could fill a ham with pickle in a few seconds. And yet, in spite of this, there would be hams found spoiled, some of them with an odor so bad that a man could hardly bear to be in the room with them. To pump into these the packers had a second and much stronger pickle which destroyed the odor — a process known to the workers as "giving them thirty per cent." Also, after the hams had been smoked, there would be found some that had gone to the bad. Formerly these had been sold as "Number Three Grade," but later on some ingenious person had hit upon a new device, and now they would extract the bone, about which the bad part generally lay, and insert in the hole a white-hot iron. After this invention there was no longer Number One, Two, and Three Grade — there was only Number One Grade. The packers were always originating such schemes — they had what they called "boneless hams," which were all the odds and ends of pork stuffed into casings; and "California hams," which were the shoulders, with big knuckle joints, and nearly all the meat cut out; and fancy "skinned hams," which were made of the oldest hogs, whose skins were so heavy and coarse that no one would buy them — that is, until they had been cooked and chopped fine and labelled "head cheese"!

It was only when the whole ham was spoiled that it came into the department of Elzbieta. Cut up by the two-thousand-revolutions-a-minute flyers, and mixed with half a ton of other meat, no odor that ever was in a ham could make any difference. There was never the least attention paid to what was cut up for sausage; there would come all the way back from Europe old sausage that had been rejected, and that was mouldy and white — it would be dosed with borax and glycerine, and dumped into the hoppers, and made over again for home consumption. There would be meat that had tumbled out on the floor, in the dirt and sawdust, where the workers had tramped and spit uncounted billions of consumption germs. There would be meat stored in great piles in rooms; and the water from leaky roofs would drip over it, and thousands of rats would race about on it. It was too dark in these storage places to see well, but a man could run his hand over these piles of meat and sweep off handfuls of the dried dung of rats. These rats were nuisances, and the packers would put poisoned bread out for them, they would die, and then rats, bread, and meat would go into the hoppers together. This is no fairy story and no joke; the meat would be shovelled into carts, and the man who did the shoveling would not trouble to lift out a rat even when he saw one — there were things that went into the sausage in comparison with which a poisoned rat was a tidbit. There was no place for the men to wash their hands before they ate their dinner, and so they made a practice of washing them in the water that was to be ladled into the sausage. There were the butt-ends of smoked meat, and the scraps of corned beef, and all the odds and ends of the waste of the plants, that would be dumped into old barrels in the cellar and left there. Under the system of rigid economy which the packers enforced, there were some jobs that it only paid to do once in a long time, and among these was the cleaning out of the waste barrels. Every spring they did it; and in the barrels would be dirt and rust and old nails and stale water — and cart load after cart load of it would be taken up and dumped into the hoppers with fresh meat, and sent out to the public's breakfast. Some of it they would make into "smoked" sausage — but as the smoking took time, and was therefore expensive, they would call upon their chemistry department, and preserve it with borax and color it with gelatine to make it brown. All of their sausage came out of the same bowl, but when they came to wrap it they would stamp some of it "special," and for this they would charge two cents more a pound. . . .

Poor Jurgis was not very happy in his home life. Elzbieta was sick a good deal now, and the boys were wild and unruly, and very much the worse for their life upon the streets. But he stuck by the family nevertheless, for they reminded him of his old happiness; and when things went wrong he could solace himself with a plunge into the Socialist movement. Since his life had been caught up into the current of this great stream, things which had before been the whole of life to him came to seem of relatively slight importance; his interests were elsewhere, in the world of ideas. His outward life was commonplace and uninteresting; he was just a hotel porter, and expected to remain one while he lived; but meantime, in the realm of thought, his life was a perpetual adventure. There was so much to know — so many wonders to be discovered! Never in all his life did Jurgis forget the day before election, when there came a telephone message from a friend of Harry Adams, asking him to bring Jurgis to see him that night; and Jurgis went, and met one of the minds of the movement.

The invitation was from a man named Fisher, a Chicago millionaire who had given up his life to settlement work, and had a little home in the heart of the city's slums. He did not belong to the party, but he was in sympathy with it; and he said that he was to have as his guest that night the editor of a big Eastern magazine, who wrote against Socialism, but really did not know what it was. The millionaire suggested that Adams bring Jurgis along, and then start up the subject of "pure food," in which the editor was interested.

Young Fisher's home was a little two-story brick house, dingy and weather-beaten outside, but attractive within. The room that Jurgis saw was half lined with books, and upon the walls were many pictures, dimly visible in the soft, yellow light; it was a cold, rainy night, so a log fire was crackling in the open hearth. Seven or eight people were gathered about it when Adams and his friend arrived, and Jurgis saw to his dismay that three of them were ladies. He had never talked to people of this sort before, and he fell into an agony of embarrassment. He stood in the doorway clutching his hat tightly in his hands, and made a deep bow to each of the persons as he was introduced; then, when he was asked to have a seat, he took a chair in a dark corner, and sat down upon the edge of it, and wiped the perspiration off his forehead with his sleeve. He was terrified lest they should expect him to talk.

There was the host himself, a tall, athletic young man, clad in evening dress, as also was the editor, a dyspeptic-looking gentleman named Maynard. There was the former's frail young wife, and also an elderly lady, who taught kindergarten in the settlement, and a young college student, a beautiful girl with an intense and earnest face. She only spoke once or twice while Jurgis was there — the rest of the time she sat by the table in the center of the room, resting her chin in her hands and drinking in the conversation. There were two other men, whom young Fisher had introduced to Jurgis as Mr. Lucas and Mr. Schliemann; he heard them address Adams as "Comrade," and so he knew that they were Socialists. . . .

. . . Mr. Maynard, the editor, took occasion to remark, somewhat naïvely, that he had always understood that Socialists had a cut-and-dried program for the future of civilization; whereas here were two active members of the party, who, from what he could make out, were agreed about nothing at all. Would the two, for his enlightenment, try to ascertain just what they had in common, and why they belonged to the same party? This resulted, after much debating, in the formulating of two carefully worded propositions: First, that a Socialist believes in the common ownership and democratic management of the means of producing the necessities of life; and, second, that a socialist believes that the means by which this is to be brought about is the class-conscious political organization of the wage-earners. Thus far they were at one; but no farther. To Lucas, the religious zealot, the co-operative commonwealth was the New Jerusalem, the kingdom of Heaven, which is "within you." To the other, Socialism was simply a necessary step toward a far-distant goal, a step to be tolerated with impatience. Schliemann called himself a "philosophic anarchist"; and he explained that an anarchist was one who believed that the end of human existence was the free development of every personality, unrestricted by laws save those of its own being. Since the same kind of match would light every one's fire and the same-shaped loaf of bread would fill every one's stomach, it would be perfectly feasible to submit industry to the control of a majority vote. There was only one earth, and the quantity of material things was limited. Of intellectual and moral things, on the other hand, there was no limit, and one could have more without another's having less; hence "Communism in material production, anarchism in intellectual," was the formula of modern proletarian thought. As soon as the birth agony was over, and the wounds of society had been healed, there would be established a simple system whereby each man was credited with his labor and debited with his purchases; and after that the processes of production, exchange, and consumption would go on automatically, and without our being conscious of them, any more than a man is conscious of the beating of his heart. And then, explained Schliemann, society would break up into independent, self-governing communities of mutually congenial persons; examples of which at present were clubs, churches, and political parties. After the revolution, all the intellectual, artistic, and spiritual activities of men would be cared for by such "free associations"; romantic novelists would be supported by those who liked to read romantic novels, and impressionist painters would be supported by those who liked to look at impressionist pictures — and the same with preachers and scientists, editors and actors and musicians. If any one wanted to work or paint or pray, and could find no one to maintain him, he could support himself by working part of the time. That was the case at present, the only difference being that the competitive wage system compelled a man to work all the time to live, while, after the abolition of privilege and exploitation, anyone would be able to support himself by an hour's work a day. Also the artist's audience of the present was a small minority of people, all debased and vulgarized by the effort it had cost them to win in the commercial battle; of the intellectual and artistic activities which would result when the whole of mankind was set free from the nightmare of competition, we could at present form no conception whatever.

And then the editor wanted to know upon what ground Dr. Schliemann asserted that it might be possible for a society to exist upon an hour's toil by each of its members. "Just what," answered the other, "would be the productive capacity of society if the present resources of science were utilized, we have no means of ascertaining; but we may be sure it would exceed anything that would sound reasonable to minds inured to the ferocious barbarities of Capitalism. After the triumph of the international proletariat, war would of course be inconceivable; and who can figure the cost of war to humanity — not merely the value of the lives and the material that it destroys, not merely the cost of keeping millions of men in idleness, of arming and equipping them for battle and parade, but the drain upon the vital energies of society by the war-attitude and the war-terror, the brutality and ignorance, the drunkenness, prostitution, and crime it entails, the industrial impotence and the moral deadness? Do you think that it would be too much to say that two hours of the working time of every efficient member of a community goes to feed the red fiend of war?"

And then Schliemann went on to outline some of the wastes of competition: the losses of industrial warfare; the ceaseless worry and friction; the vices — such as drink, for instance, the use of which had nearly doubled in twenty years, as a consequence of the intensification of the economic struggle; the idle and unproductive members of the community, the frivolous rich and the pauperized poor; the law and the whole machinery of repression; the wastes of social ostentation, the milliners and tailors, the hairdressers, dancing masters, chefs and lackeys. "You understand," he said, "that in a society dominated by the fact of commercial competition, money is necessarily the test of prowess, and wastefulness the sole criterion of power. So we have, at the present moment, a society with, say, thirty per cent of the population occupied in producing useless articles, and one per cent occupied in destroying them. And this is not all; for the servants and panders of the parasites are also parasites, the milliners and the jewelers and the lackeys have also to be supported by the useful members of the community. And bear in mind also that this monstrous disease affects not merely the idlers and their menials, its poison penetrates the whole social body. Beneath the hundred thousand women of the élite are a million middle-class women, miserable because they are not of the élite, and trying to appear of it in public; and beneath them, in turn, are five million farmers' wives reading 'fashion papers' and trimming bonnets, and shopgirls and serving maids selling themselves into brothels for cheap jewelry and imitation sealskin robes. And then consider that, added to this competition in display, you have, like oil on the flames, a whole system of competition in selling! You have manufacturers contriving tens of thousands of catch-penny devices, storekeepers displaying them, and newspapers and magazines filled up with advertisements of them!"

"And don't forget the wastes of fraud," put in young Fisher.

"When one comes to the ultra-modern profession of advertising," responded Schliemann — "the science of persuading people to buy what they do not want, he is in the very center of the ghastly charnel-house of capitalist destructiveness, and he scarcely knows which of a dozen horrors to point out first. But consider the waste in time and energy incidental to making ten thousand varieties of a thing for purposes of ostentation and snobbishness, where one variety would do for use! Consider all the waste incidental to the manufacture of cheap qualities of goods, of goods made to sell and deceive the ignorant; consider the wastes of adulteration — the shoddy clothing, the cotton blankets, the unstable tenements, the ground-cork life-preservers, the adulterated milk, the aniline soda-water, the potato-flour sausages —"

"And consider the moral aspects of the thing," put in the ex-preacher.

"Precisely," said Schliemann; "the low knavery and the ferocious cruelty incidental to them, the plotting and the lying and the bribing, the blustering and bragging, the screaming egotism, the hurrying and worrying. Of course, imitation and adulteration are the essence of competition — they are but another form of the phrase 'to buy in the cheapest market and sell in the dearest.' A government official has stated that the nation suffers a loss of a billion and a quarter dollars a year through adulterated foods; which means, of course, not only materials wasted that might have been useful outside of the human stomach, but doctors and nurses for people who would otherwise have been well, and undertakers for the whole human race ten or twenty years before the proper time. Then again, consider the waste of time and energy required to sell these things in a dozen stores, where one would do. There are a million or two of business firms in the country, and five or ten times as many clerks; and consider the handling and rehandling, the accounting and reaccounting, the planning and worrying, the balancing of petty profit and loss. Consider the whole machinery of the civil law made necessary by these processes; the libraries of ponderous tomes, the courts and juries to interpret them, the lawyers studying to circumvent them, the pettifogging and chicanery, the hatreds and lies! Consider the wastes incidental to the blind and haphazard production of commodities — the factories closed, the workers idle, the goods spoiling in storage; consider the activities of the stock-manipulator, the paralyzing of whole industries, the over-stimulation of others, for speculative purposes; the assignments and bank failures, the crises and panics, the deserted towns and the starving populations! Consider the energies wasted in the seeking of markets, the sterile trades, such as drummer, solicitor, billposter, advertising agent. Consider the wastes incidental to the crowding into cities, made necessary by competition and by monopoly railroad rates; consider the slums, the bad air, the disease and the waste of vital energies; consider the office buildings, the waste of time and material in the piling of story upon story, and the burrowing underground! . . .

Dr. Schliemann paused for a moment. "That was a lecture," he said with a laugh, "and yet I am only begun!"

"What else is there?" asked Maynard.

"I have pointed out some of the negative wastes of competition," answered the other. "I have hardly mentioned the positive economies of co-operation. Allowing five to a family, there are fifteen million families in this country; and at least ten million of these live separately, the domestic drudge being either the wife or a wage slave. Now set aside the modern system of pneumatic house-cleaning, and the economies of co-operative cooking; and consider one single item, the washing of dishes. Surely it is moderate to say that the dish-washing for a family of five takes half an hour a day; with ten hours as a day's work, it takes, therefore, half a million able-bodied persons — mostly women — to do the dish-washing of the country. And note that this is most filthy and deadening and brutalizing work; that it is a cause of anemia, nervousness, ugliness, and ill-temper; of prostitution, suicide, and insanity; of drunken husbands and degenerate children — for all of which things the community has naturally to pay. And now consider that in each of my little free communities there would be a machine which would wash and dry the dishes, and do it, not merely to the eye and the touch, but scientifically —sterilizing them — and do it at a saving of all of the drudgery and nine-tenths of the time! All of these things you may find in the books of Mrs. Gilman; and then take Kropotkin's *Fields, Factories, and Workshops,* and read about the new science of agriculture, which has been built up in the last ten years; by which, with made soils and intensive culture, a gardener can raise ten or twelve crops in a season, and two hundred tons of vegetables upon a single acre; by which the population of the whole globe could be supported on the soil now cultivated in the United States alone! It is impossible to apply such methods now, owing to the ignorance and poverty of our scattered farming population; but imagine the problem of providing the food supply of our nation once taken in hand systematically and rationally, by scientists! All the poor and rocky land set apart for a national timber reserve, in which our children play, and our young men hunt, and our poets dwell! The most favorable climate and soil for each product selected; the exact requirements of the community known, and the acreage figured accordingly; the most improved machinery employed, under the direction of expert agricultural chemists! I was brought up on a farm, and I know the awful deadliness of farm work; and I like to picture it all as it will be after the revolution. To picture the great potato-planting machine, drawn by four horses, or an electric motor, ploughing the furrow, cutting and dropping and covering the potatoes, and planting a score of acres a day! To picture the great potato-digging machine, run by electricity, perhaps, and moving across a thousand-acre field, scooping up earth and potatoes, and dropping the latter into sacks! To see every other kind of vegetable and fruit handled in the same way — apples and oranges picked by machinery, cows milked by electricity — things which are already done, as you may know. To picture the harvest fields of the future, to which millions of happy men and women come for a summer holiday, brought by special trains, the exactly needful number to each place! And to contrast all this with our present agonizing system of independent small farming — a stunted, haggard, ignorant man, mated with a yellow, lean, and sad-eyed drudge, and toiling from four o'clock in the morning until nine at night, working the children as soon as they are able to walk, scratching the soil with his primitive tools, and shut out from all knowledge and hope, from all the benefits of science and invention, and all the joys of the spirit — held to a bare existence by competition in labor, and boasting of his freedom because he is too blind to see his chains!"

Dr. Schliemann paused a moment. "And then," he continued, "place beside this fact of an unlimited food supply, the newest discovery of physiologists, that most of the ills of the human system are due to overfeeding! And then again, it has been proven that meat is unnecessary as a food; and meat is obviously more difficult to produce than vegetable food, less pleasant to prepare and handle, and more likely to be unclean. But what of that, so long as it tickles the palate more strongly?"

"How would Socialism change that?" asked the girl-student, quickly. It was the first time she had spoken.

"So long as we have wage slavery," answered Schliemann, "it matters not in the least how debasing and repulsive a task may be, it is easy to find people to perform it. But just as soon as labor is set free, then the price of such work will begin to rise. So one by one the old, dingy, and unsanitary factories will come down — it will be cheaper to build new; and so the steamships will be provided with stoking-machinery, and so the dangerous trades will be made safe, or substitutes will be found for their products. In exactly the same way, as the citizens of our Industrial Republic become refined, year by year the cost of slaughterhouse products will increase; until eventually those who want to eat meat will have to do their own killing — and how long do you think the custom would survive then? — To go on to another item — one of the necessary accompaniments of capitalism in a democracy is political corruption; and one of the consequences of civic administration by ignorant and vicious politicians, is that preventable diseases kill off half of our population. And even if science were allowed to try, it could do little, because the majority of human beings are not yet human beings at all, but simply machines for the creating of wealth for others. They are penned up in filthy houses and left to rot and stew in misery, and the conditions of their life make them ill faster than all the doctors in the world could heal them; and so, of course, they remain as centers of contagion, poisoning the lives of all of us, and making happiness impossible for even the most selfish. For this reason I would seriously maintain that all the medical and surgical discoveries that science can make in the future will be of less importance than the application of the knowledge we already possess, when the disinherited of the earth have established their right to a human existence."

And here the Herr Doctor relapsed into silence again. Jurgis had noticed that the beautiful young girl who sat by the center table was listening with something of the same look that he himself had worn, the time when he had first discovered Socialism. Jurgis would have liked to talk to her, he felt sure that she would have understood him. Later on in the evening, when the group broke up, he heard Mrs. Fisher say to her, in a low voice, "I wonder if Mr. Maynard will still write the same things about Socialism"; to which she answered, "I don't know — but if he does we shall know that he is a knave!" . . .

Study Guide

1. This selection can be divided into two parts:
    (a) the author's description and criticism of almost every aspect of the meat-packing industry (pp. 271–284); and
    (b) the solution he proposes — socialism — as a curative for both this particular problem and for the American economy and society as a whole (pp. 284–291).

Before you begin your analysis, take a few moments to permit yourself to enjoy a fine writer at work with his superbly written description of one aspect of the industrialization of the nation — the Chicago stockyards.

2. Note the emphasis Sinclair puts on the efficiency and the economy of operation at Durham's (a pseudonym for one of the largest meat-packing firms in the nation). Let us begin with Sinclair's evaluation of American industrial efficiency. Does he approve? Elaborate.

3. What conclusions does Sinclair come to regarding:
   (a) government health inspection;
   (b) the quality of the product produced;
   (c) labor-management relations; and
   (d) the impact of the plant on the character and the lives of its employees?

4. What does he want to tell the reader about industrial capitalism through the lives of Antanas Rudkus, Jadvyga Marcinkus, Mary Dennis, and Jonas?

5. What is the role of the government in the Durham operation? Can you see why this kind of exposé caused progressives to advocate the abandonment of *laissez faire?* Why, on the basis of what you have read, would consumers seek government controls on the meat-packing industry? Through what legislation?

6. Sinclair's socialist plea (and note that almost all the proponents of socialism are native Americans, wealthy, college-trained, well-spoken, and in the case of women, even beautiful) can be subsumed under a number of headings. Summarize Sinclair's views (through the words of Schliemann) on:
   (a) the purposes and advantages of socialism;
   (b) how socialism would be achieved;
   (c) war;
   (d) competition;
   (e) advertisements and profit;
   (f) the quality of life generally;
   (g) poverty and hunger;
   (h) private property; and
   (i) his vision of the future.

Charlotte Perkins Gilman

THE EQUALITY OF WOMEN

⊰{*1912*}⊱   THE HISTORIAN can discern three major stages in the history of American feminism: the mid-nineteenth-century struggle for basic rights (the right of married women to own and to inherit property); the early twentieth-century struggle for political equality; and the post-World War II demands for social equality. In the Progressive Era, the efforts to enhance the quality of life for women took on many forms: settlement houses, consumer leagues, temperance movements, demands for suffrage, and state laws to provide better working conditions for female employees and a minimum wage.

Charlotte Perkins Gilman (1860–1935), lecturer, author, socialist, and sociologist transcended all these movements. With more perception and sophistication than any other writer of the early twentieth century, Charlotte Gilman foresaw the enormous impact industrialism would make on the role of the woman in modern society and the alterations industrialism would bring to the relationships between the sexes. Born in New England of the illustrious Beecher family, Charlotte Gilman achieved international fame as the author of *Women and Economics* (1898), a remarkably lucid condemnation of the Victorian stereotypes of the differences between men and women and the narrow role assigned to the female sex. In this book and in her many other writings, covering a period of more than a quarter-century, Charlotte Gilman put forth several important concepts: that the common humanity shared by men and women is of greater significance than their sexual differences; that the social environment, rather than biology, determines the role of men and women in society; and that in an industrial society, women would be released from the confines of home and the rearing of children in order to make a broad human rather than a narrow feminine contribution to society. "What we have to do," she wrote, "is to recognize the woman as a human being, with her human rights and duties and to learn how to reconcile happy work with happy marriage." As Carl Degler has noted, Charlotte Perkins Gilman viewed "the woman question against the broad perspective of time, while others nibbled only at the primary and immediate issues. . . ."

Reprinted here is an essay of Gilman's published in *Harper's Weekly* in 1912. The stress, as always, is on the common human bond between male and female and the potential good to society that would accrue if women were given an opportunity to express themselves.

ARE WOMEN HUMAN BEINGS?

IN ALL wide-spread discussions where honest and able persons take opposite sides there is usually to be found some basic error in comprehension. This appears, not only in the use of terms, the same word often having different meanings to different minds, but in the grasp of the subject matter itself.

Even in friendly conversation these difficulties frequently occur. The most scholarly care in the language chosen, even in scientific treatises, does not always preclude misunderstanding. When the pressure of warm feeling is driving the words, and when the subject matter is one little understood, we are apt to descend to a mere expression of sentiment instead of an exchange of ideas.

All this is profoundly evident in the present wide — and warm — discussion of woman suffrage. On either side appear the most earnest expressions of feeling: feelings of hope, of fear, of high social devotion, of intense personal distaste; all of which are interesting as indicative of the development or limitations of the speaker.

Together with these feelings is used a strange array of arguments, some to the point, some quite beside it, some boomerangs; and these are urged with breathless earnestness and laudable perseverance, quite regardless of effect.

As social evolution has never waited for the complete enlightenment of mankind, we find the enfranchisement of women going on in all civilized countries; but since the opposition to it is strong enough to cause years of delay and a continuous outlay of organized effort, it seems worth while to point out the main error actuating that opposition.

It may seem difficult to select a major error among such a self-contradictory confusion; but under all these miscellaneous reiterated objections one governing conviction continually obtrudes itself. It colors all the utterances of the Organization Opposed to the Extension of Suffrage to Women. It exclusively dominates the grave opinions of pathologists. It is the animus of all the books written against "the woman's movement." It is the painfully visible actuating impulse of the ill-considered objections of "the man in the street," and also of the similar expressions of "the woman in the home." And, to come down to the day of small things, it is the feeling animating a leading editorial in the New York *Times,* and a peculiarly typical "Letter from the People" in that paper, called forth by the recent impressive parade of our suffragists.

This error is due to a certain arrested development of thought. It consists in seeing in women only feminine characteristics; and, conversely, seeing in all the complex functions of civilization only masculine characteristics.

Under this conception it is held, quite naturally, that women need do nothing more than fulfill their "womanly duties," *i.e.,* to be wives, mothers, and houseworkers; that for them to desire any other activities in life is to be unwomanly, unnatural, to become some sort of pervert or monster. They are spoken of as "denatured women," as "epicene," as "unsexed," as "seeking to become men." Miss Ida Tarbell in a recent magazine article describes women's professional and industrial advance as "Making a Man of Herself."

Otto Weininger, in his much-discussed book, *Sex and Character,* elaborated a theory of mixed inheritance, showing that some women inherited a proportion of masculine characteristics and some men inherited a proportion of feminine characteristics, thus explaining the undeniable phenomenon of their having many characteristics in common.

The late Mr. Grant Allen expressed this world-view in clear scientific phrase when he said that women were not only "not the human race —

they were not even half the human race, but a sub-species set apart for purposes of reproduction, merely."

The still later Mr. H. B. Marriott-Watson has put it with even more exquisite precision, saying of the American woman, "Her constitutional restlessness has caused her to abdicate those functions which alone excuse or explain her existence."

Now comes Sir Almroth Wright, M.D., in a three-column letter to the London *Times,* that letter which is said to have killed the Conciliation Bill, which was then before the House. Speaking as one long conversant with many female invalids, he rashly generalizes from his personal experience of morbid phenomena, and says, "No doctor can ever lose sight of the fact that the mind of woman is always threatened with danger from the reverberations of her physiological emergencies."

He sees, in the advance of women into wider social relations, only the perverse action of suppressed, embittered, or atrophied femininity. He sees in them, of course, nothing but femininity; that which he considers normal and admires, or which he considers abnormal and condemns. The glory of woman, according to his definition, lies "in her power of attraction, in her capacity for motherhood, and in her unswerving allegiance to the ethics which are special to her sex."

So our *Times,* of New York, in the editorial above referred to, modestly says: "One does not need to be a profound student of biology to know that some women, a very small minority, have a natural inclination to usurp the social and civic functions of men."

Simmer down this loosely gathered mass of opinion, and we find that it all resolves into the one assumption — that women have feminine functions and no others, and that social functions are masculine. Let us frankly examine these premises.

Without needing to be any more profound a student of biology than the editor of our *Times,* we must all admit that there are other functions besides the reproductive. As life spread wide upon the earth, each species developed its own means of locomotion, its means of self-defense, its means of getting a livelihood; all essential, all common to both sexes. Variations in size, in color, in intelligence, in agility, in courage, differentiate one animal from another; all essential, all common to both sexes.

Meanwhile, all creatures have some means of replenishing the earth after their kind, and we, as mammals, share in the methods of the higher orders, adding to the personal processes the vast advantage of our social processes; as in education, once wholly a maternal function, and now so largely civic and social. But while all kindred species share in the primal activities of reproduction, each is sharply distinguished from the others by its special activities in other lines.

As animals, we share in the universal distinction of sex; but as human beings, we alone possess a whole new range of faculties, vitally essential and common to both sexes.

It seems childish to insist upon so patent a fact, so simple and obvious a distinction. Yet it is precisely this simple and obvious distinction which these one-ideaed upholders of the eternal masculine utterly fail to grasp.

Consider for the moment any pair of the higher carnivora, as two leopards or two tigers. Leopards are known by their unchangeable spots, whereas tigers have stripes. Both male and female leopards have spots. Both male and female tigers have stripes. These spots and stripes have nothing to do with the sex of the animal, only with its species. The possession of eyes and ears, of hide or hoofs, of fins or scales, of fur or feathers, of four legs or two — these things are not distinctions of sex, primary or secondary; they are race distinctions, purely.

If we were to count up and to contrast the number of characteristics of sex with the number of characteristics of species, we should find at once that race distinctions far exceed sex distinctions in number and importance. Take, for example, a cow, a camel, and a whale. They all bring forth one living offspring and suckle it, the process being fairly identical. But a cow is easily distinguished from a camel and either from a whale.

Again, of two deer, the buck has a special secondary sex-distinction in his towering antlers; but his power of speed, his love of speed, is not a sex distinction but a race distinction, common to both sexes. When the doe wishes to run far and fast, she is not "unfeminine," she is not "making a buck of herself." She likes to run, not because she is a doe, but because she is a deer, just as much of a deer as he is.

This universal, glaring fact is what these sex-obsessed opponents of the normal progress of women cannot see. They see only the feminine characteristics of women, and fail to see the human ones. Yet with our species, beyond any other, the race-characteristics outnumber and outweigh all lesser distinctions.

Certain attributes we share with all matter, as weight, mass, extension; certain others with most animals, as digestion, circulation; others, again, including the reproductive processes, with the higher mammals alone; but the preponderant characteristics of humanity we share with no other creature. We, as a species, have far more conspicuous and important distinctions peculiar to ourselves than those we share with lower forms; and each and every one of these human distinctions belongs to both sexes.

The erect posture, with all its rearrangement of the internal economy, the opposable thumb and the hand's marvelous growth in varied skill; the power of speech, the whole proud range of mental development —

these are human distinctions, race distinctions, not in any sense, at any time, sex distinctions.

Yet the male of our species, from the beginning of his power of conscious thought, has arrogated to himself as part of his sex the major attributes of humanity: religion, education, government, commerce — these were for him alone. In what he has termed "his female" he has seen, and for the most part still sees, only her femininity, never her humanity.

That she should concentrate all her human faculties upon the fulfillment of her feminine functions he has held quite right and proper; that she should at any time wish to use them, not as a female, but as a human being, is to him monstrous. So absolute has been this monopolization of human functions by one sex; so complete this obsession that has persisted in considering them as sex attributes, that even the range of industries originated by women, for ages practised wholly by women, have been gradually absorbed by men, and as rapidly as they were absorbed have become "masculine."

Mere extension in method has been similarly classified: as where a woman with distaff and spindle, or foot-run wheel, was considered feminine; but to run a woolen mill must be "man's work."

Let us look at our own race history. When we were all hunters, fishers, and root-gatherers, we were men and women, just as efficiently and completely as we are now. When we kept cattle we were not any the less, or more, men and women. When we developed agriculture, we were still men and women. When we specialized in industry, we remained men and women. Men are males and women females at any time in the whole long story.

But while remaining unchanged in these respects, we have changed enormously in our social features, our common human attributes.

Specialization has given us a thousand trades, arts, crafts, and professions. Organization has multiplied our power myriad-fold. Invention and discovery have enriched and enlightened the world. Religions have changed. Governments have changed. Society evolves from age to age. All these are human processes. They belong to our race. They are common to both male and female. They have no faintest connection with any sex distinction.

As to warfare, which our ultra males are so sure to fall back on in proof of their essential dominance; warfare is not a social process at all, but a social disease, freely admitted to be most characteristic of the male. It is the instinct of sex-combat, overdeveloped and misused.

The women of our age in most countries of the same degree of development are outgrowing the artificial restrictions so long placed upon them, and following natural lines of human advance. They are specializing, because they are human. They are organizing, because they are human. They are seeking economic and political independence, because they are human. They are demanding the vote, because they are human.

Against this swelling tide stands the mere mass of inert old-world ignorance, backed by the perverse misconception of modern minds, which even science fails to illuminate.

"Go back," says this mass. "You are women. You are nothing *but* women. You are females — nothing *but* females. All these things you want to do are male things. You cannot do them without being a male. You want to be males. It is abhorrent, outrageous, impossible!"

All these adjectives and horrors would be freely granted if women really could become males — or even if they wanted to! But what needs to be hammered into these male-ridden minds is that these things the women want to do and be and have are not in any sense masculine. They do not belong to men. They never did. They are departments of our social life, hitherto arbitrarily monopolized by men, but no more made masculine by that use than the wearing of trousers by Turkish women makes trousers feminine or the wearing of corsets by German officers makes corsets masculine.

There are enough minor absurdities in the usual treatment of this subject to furnish much entertainment, as, for instance, in this same editorial in the *Times,* where it is mournfully prophesied that if women get the vote they will "play havoc with it for themselves and for society."

Is it possible that the writer does not know that women have been voting right here in this country for over forty years and are now voting in some score of States and nations the world over, with no observable "havoc" of any sort?

Even in England, where that sad pathologist, Dr. Wright, so gravely marshals his gloomy ranks of "the incomplete," "the sexually embittered," "the atrophied," "the epicene," there has been no havoc wrought by the women who have previously exercised all but the parliamentary suffrage for many years. They were just the women of England, after voting and before; neither more nor less women for going to the polls than they are more or less women for going to the theater or to the post office.

Whether in the accumulated literature of the necessarily unenlightened past, or the still accumulating literature of the wilfully unenlightened present, we find everywhere this same pervasive error, this naive assumption, which would be so insolent if it were not so absurd, that only men are human creatures, able and entitled to perform the work of the world; while women are only female creatures, able to do nothing whatever but continue in the same round of duties to which they have been so long restricted.

They darkly threaten, do these ultra male opponents, that if women persist in doing human things they will lose the respect of man — yea, more, they will lose his pecuniary support.

They should study their biology a little more profoundly. The respect of the male for the female is based on the distinction of sex, not on political or economic disability. Men respect women because they are females, not because they are weak and ignorant and defenseless.

Women will never cease to be females, but they will cease to be weak and ignorant and defenseless. They are becoming wiser, stronger, better able to protect themselves, one another, and their children. Courage, power, achievement are always respected.

As women grow, losing nothing that is essential to womanhood, but adding steadily the later qualities of humanness, they will win and hold a far larger, deeper reverence than that hitherto vouchsafed them. As they so rise and broaden, filling their full place in the world as members of society, as well as their partial places as mothers of it, they will gradually rear a new race of men, men with minds large enough to see in human beings something besides males and females.

Some such men and such women we have to-day, wise and far-seeing; quite strong enough to bear with a smile the errors of the past, the morbid views of the pathologist, the limitations of editorial profundity, and the letters from the people, as the leading minds of the world have always borne with the more backward.

Study Guide

1. This essay by Charlotte Gilman can be divided thus:
    (a) a listing of what, in her opinion, are common errors in viewing the role and function of the woman in modern society (pp. 293–295);
    (b) her reply to these views (pp. 295–298); and
    (c) her own position on the question (pp. 298–299).

Begin by summarizing the contributions each of the following authorities (cited by Gilman) make to the notion that women possess only "feminine characteristics" while men only are capable of performing "the complex functions of civilization":

    (a) Ida Tarbell;
    (b) Otto Weininger;
    (c) Grant Allen;

(d) H. B. Marriott-Watson;

(e) Sir Almroth Wright, M.D.; and

(f) the editor of the *New York Times.*

2. Charlotte Gilman attacks these views by contending that women are capable of contributing to society more than simply their ability to reproduce the species. How does she go about proving and illustrating her notion that the similarities between the human male and female outweigh the differences between them? Also, focusing on the following excerpt, amplify and illustrate how "They [her opponents] see only the feminine characteristics of women, and fail to see the human ones" (p. 296).

3. Explain and illustrate Gilman's contention that in the evolution of society, social and economic conditions rather than the sexual differences between men and women largely determined their respective roles and functions.

4. In her closing paragraphs, Gilman indicates the kind of contribution women can make to society were they to be given equality with men. Note this central facet of Gilman's thought: How the differences between the sexes are an opportunity for a *greater* contribution to society by women than a pretext for their constraint. The following quotations summarize her position:

(a) "The respect of the male for the female is based on the distinction of sex, not on political or economic disability";

(b) "Women will never cease to be females, but they will cease to be weak and ignorant and defenseless"; and

(c) "As women grow, losing nothing that is essential to womanhood, but adding steadily the later qualities of humanness, they will win and hold a far larger, deeper reverence than that hitherto vouchsafed them."

5. In retrospect: how does Gilman avoid the pitfalls of other feminists: their shrill denials that there are any distinctions between men and women and their seeming desire to ascribe masculine traits to the feminine sex? To answer this question is to understand why Charlotte Gilman commanded the respect and attention accorded her in the Progressive Era.

Theodore Roosevelt
SOCIAL JUSTICE

1910 DESPITE Theodore Roosevelt's (1858-1919) reputation as a "trust-buster" (and it was well deserved, for it was his leadership that led to the revival of the moribund Sherman Anti-Trust Act), "T.R." was not opposed in principle to large corporations or even to monopolies of some kinds. Indeed, from quite early in his career he showed a continuing and growing interest in developing the power of the federal government to control the economic affairs of the nation. Although he made use of measures like the anti-trust law, he never had much real confidence in the ability of the economy to run itself under the benevolent supervision of a government that was no more than a policeman catching and punishing flagrant wrongdoers.

However, this essential commitment of Roosevelt was not entirely clear as late as 1909, when he finished his second term as President and headed to Africa to hunt lions. But upon his return in 1910, he found himself quickly caught up in the controversy within the party between the liberals and the Old Guard. Although he honestly tried to steer a middle course, events and the increasing conservative leanings of his successor, William Howard Taft (1857-1930) pushed him steadily toward the liberal side. And as he took an increasingly liberal position, he found himself arguing more and more forcibly for a strong federal government actively intervening in the economic and social affairs of the nation. It was in a speech to a group of Civil War veterans at Osawatomie, Kansas, on August 31, 1910, that he codified the new proposals he had come to advocate, and gave his philosophy the graphic title of "The New Nationalism."

The speech was a turning point both in Roosevelt's career and in the history of the nation. Many conservative Republicans were alarmed by some of Roosevelt's proposals and by the whole tone of his remarks. He in turn was driven eventually by their rejection of his position to form the Progressive party. The whole course of national politics was disrupted by this splitting of the Republican party into liberal and conservative branches.

THE NEW NATIONALISM

WE COME here to-day to commemorate one of the epoch-making events of the long struggle for the rights of man — the long struggle for the uplift of humanity. Our country — this great Republic — means nothing unless it means the triumph of a real democracy, the triumph of popular government, and, in the long run, of an economic system under which each man shall be guaranteed the opportunity to show the best that there is in him. That is why the history of America is now the central feature of the history of the world; for the world has set its face hopefully toward our democracy; and, O my fellow citizens, each one of you carries on your shoulders not only the burden of doing well for the sake of your own country, but the burden of doing well and of seeing that this nation does well for the sake of mankind.

There have been two great crises in our country's history: first, when it was formed, and then, again, when it was perpetuated; and, in the second of these great crises — in the time of stress and strain which culminated in the Civil War, on the outcome of which depended the justification of what had been done earlier, you men of the Grand Army, you men who fought through the Civil War, not only did you justify your generation, not only did you render life worth living for our generation, but you justified the wisdom of Washington and Washington's colleagues. If this Republic had been founded by them only to be split asunder into fragments when the strain came, then the judgment of the world would have been that Washington's work was not worth doing. . . .

I do not speak of this struggle of the past merely from the historic standpoint. Our interest is primarily in the application to-day of the lessons taught by the contest of half a century ago. It is of little use for us to pay lip-loyalty to the mighty men of the past unless we sincerely endeavor to apply to the problems of the present precisely the qualities which in other crises enabled the men of that day to meet those crises. It is half melancholy and half amusing to see the way in which well-meaning people gather to do honor to the men who, in company with John Brown, and under the lead of Abraham Lincoln, faced and solved the great problems of the nineteenth century, while, at the same time, these same good people nervously shrink from, or frantically denounce, those who are trying to meet the problems of the twentieth century in the spirit which was accountable for the successful solution of the problems of Lincoln's time.

Of that generation of men to whom we owe so much, the man to whom we owe most is, of course, Lincoln. Part of our debt to him is because he forecast our present struggle and saw the way out. He said:

"I hold that while man exists it is his duty to improve not only his own conditions, but to assist in ameliorating mankind."

And again:

"Labor is prior to, and independent of, capital. Capital is only the fruit of labor, and could never have existed if labor had not first existed. Labor is the superior of capital, and deserves much the higher consideration."

If that remark was original with me, I should be even more strongly denounced as a Communist agitator than I shall be anyhow. It is Lincoln's. I am only quoting it; and that is one side; that is the side the capitalist should hear. Now, let the working man hear his side.

"Capital has its rights, which are as worthy of protection as any other rights. . . . Nor should this lead to a war upon the owners of property. Property is the fruit of labor; . . . property is desirable; is a positive good in the world."

And then comes a thoroughly Lincolnlike sentence:

"Let not him who is houseless pull down the house of another, but let him work diligently and build one for himself, thus by example assuring that his own shall be safe from violence when built."

It seems to me that, in these words, Lincoln took substantially the attitude that we ought to take; he showed the proper sense of proportion in his relative estimates of capital and labor, of human rights and property rights. Above all, in this speech, as in many others, he taught a lesson in wise kindliness and charity; an indispensable lesson to us of to-day. But this wise kindliness and charity never weakened his arm or numbed his heart. We cannot afford weakly to blind ourselves to the actual conflict which faces us to-day. The issue is joined, and we must fight or fail.

In every wise struggle for human betterment one of the main objects, and often the only object, has been to achieve in large measure equality of opportunity. In the struggle for this great end, nations rise from barbarism to civilization, and through it people press forward from one stage of enlightenment to the next. One of the chief factors in progress is the destruction of special privilege. The essence of any struggle for healthy liberty has always been, and must always be, to take from some one man or class of men the right to enjoy power, or wealth, or position, or immunity, which has not been earned by service to his or their fellows. That is what you fought for in the Civil War, and that is what we strive for now.

At many stages in the advance of humanity, this conflict between the men who possess more than they have earned and the men who have earned more than they possess is the central condition of progress. In our day it appears as the struggle of freemen to gain and hold the right of self-government as against the special interests, who twist the methods of free government into machinery for defeating the popular will. At every stage, and under all circumstances, the essence of the struggle is to equalize opportunity, destroy privilege, and give to the life and citizenship of every individual the highest possible value both to himself and to the commonwealth. That is nothing new. All I ask in civil life is what you fought for in the Civil War. I ask that civil life be carried on according to the spirit in which the army was carried on. You never get perfect justice, but the effort in handling the army was to bring to the front the men who could do the job. Nobody grudged promotion to Grant, or Sherman, or Thomas, or Sheridan, because they earned it. The only complaint was when a man got promotion which he did not earn.

Practical equality of opportunity for all citizens, when we achieve it, will have two great results. First, every man will have a fair chance to make of himself all that in him lies; to reach the highest point to which his capacities, unassisted by special privilege of his own and unhampered by the special privilege of others, can carry him, and to get for himself and his family substantially what he has earned. Second, equality of opportunity means that the commonwealth will get from every citizen the highest service of which he is capable. No man who carries the burden of the special privileges of another can give to the commonwealth that service to which it is fairly entitled.

I stand for the square deal. But when I say that I am for the square deal, I mean not merely that I stand for fair play under the present rules of the game, but that I stand for having those rules changed so as to work for a more substantial equality of opportunity and of reward for equally good service. One word of warning, which, I think, is hardly necessary in Kansas. When I say I want a square deal for the poor man, I do not mean that I want a square deal for the man who remains poor because he has not got the energy to work for himself. If a man who has had a chance will not make good, then he has got to quit. And you men of the Grand Army, you want justice for the brave man who fought, and punishment for the coward who shirked his work. Is not that so?

Now, this means that our government, National and State, must be freed from the sinister influence or control of special interests. Exactly as the special interests of cotton and slavery threatened our political integrity before the Civil War, so now the great special business interests too often control and corrupt the men and methods of government for their own profit. We must drive the special interests out of politics. That is one of our tasks to-day. Every special interest is entitled to justice — full, fair, and complete — and, now, mind you, if there were any attempt by mob-violence to plunder and work harm to the special interest, whatever it may be, that I most dislike, and the wealthy man, whomsoever he may be, for whom I have the greatest contempt, I would fight for him, and you would if you were worth your salt. He should have justice. For every special interest is entitled to justice, but not one is entitled to a vote in Congress, to a voice on the bench, or to representation in any public office. The Constitution guarantees protection to property, and we must make that promise good. But it does not give the right of suffrage to any corporation.

The true friend of property, the true conservative, is he who insists that property shall be the servant and not the master of the commonwealth; who insists that the creature of man's making shall be the servant and not the master of the man who made it. The citizens of the United States must effectively control the mighty commercial forces which they have themselves called into being.

There can be no effective control of corporations while their political activity remains. To put an end to it will be neither a short nor an easy task, but it can be done.

We must have complete and effective publicity of corporate affairs, so that the people may know beyond peradventure whether the corporations obey the law and whether their management entitles them to the confidence of the public. It is necessary that laws should be passed to prohibit the use of corporate funds directly or indirectly for political purposes; it is still more necessary that such laws should be thoroughly enforced. Corporate expenditures for political purposes, and especially such expenditures by public-service corporations, have supplied one of the principal sources of corruption in our political affairs.

It has become entirely clear that we must have government supervision of the capitalization, not only of public-service corporations, including, particularly, railways, but of all corporations doing an interstate business. I do not wish to see the nation forced into the ownership of the railways if it can possibly be avoided, and the only alternative is thoroughgoing and effective regulation, which shall be based on a full knowledge of all the facts, including a physical valuation of property. This physical valuation is not needed, or, at least, is very rarely needed, for fixing rates; but it is needed as the basis of honest capitalization.

We have come to recognize that franchises should never be granted except for a limited time, and never without proper provision for compensation to the public. It is my personal belief that the same kind and degree of control and supervision which should be exercised over public-service corporations should be extended also to combinations which control necessaries of life, such as meat, oil, and coal, or which deal in them on an important scale. I have no doubt that the ordinary man who has control of them is much like ourselves. I have no doubt he would like to do well, but I want to have enough supervision to help him realize that desire to do well.

I believe that the officers, and, especially, the directors, of corporations should be held personally responsible when any corporation breaks the law.

Combinations in industry are the result of an imperative economic law which cannot be repealed by political legislation. The effort at prohibiting all combination has substantially failed. The way out lies, not in attempting to prevent such combinations, but in completely controlling them in the interest of the public welfare. For that purpose the Federal Bureau of Corporations is an agency of first importance. Its powers, and, therefore, its efficiency, as well as that of the Interstate Commerce Commission, should be largely increased. We have a right to expect from the Bureau of Corporations and from the Interstate Commerce Commission a very high grade of public service. We should be as sure of the proper conduct of the interstate railways and the proper management of interstate business as we are now sure of the conduct and management of the national banks, and we should have as effective supervision in one case as in the other. The Hepburn Act, and the amendment to the act in the shape in which it finally passed Congress at the last session, represent a long step in advance, and we must go yet further.

There is a wide-spread belief among our people that, under the methods of making tariffs which have hitherto obtained, the special interests are too influential. Probably this is true of both the big special interests and the little special interests. These methods have put a premium on selfishness, and, naturally, the selfish big interests have gotten more than their smaller, though equally selfish, brothers. The duty of Congress is to provide a method by which the interest of the whole people shall be all that receives consideration. To this end there must be an expert tariff commission, wholly removed from the possibility of political pressure or of improper business influence. Such a commission can find the real difference between cost of production, which is mainly the difference of labor cost here and abroad. As fast as its recommendations are made, I believe in revising one schedule at a time. A general revision of the tariff almost inevitably leads to log-rolling and the subordination of the general public interest to local and special interests.

The absence of effective State, and, especially, national, restraint upon unfair money-getting has tended to create a small class of enormously wealthy and economically powerful men, whose chief object is to hold and increase their power. The prime need is to change the conditions which enable these men to accumulate power which it is not for the general welfare that they should hold or exercise. We grudge no man a fortune which represents his own power and sagacity, when exercised with entire regard to the welfare of his fellows. Again, comrades over there, take the lesson from your own experience. Not only did you not grudge, but you gloried in the promotion of the great generals who gained their promotion by leading the army to victory. So it is with us. We grudge no man a fortune in civil life if it is honorably obtained and well used. It is not even enough that it should have been gained without doing damage to the community. We should permit it to be gained only so long as the gaining represents benefit to the community. This, I know, · implies a policy of a far more active governmental interference with social and economic conditions in this country than we have yet had, but I think we have got to face the fact that such an increase in governmental control is now necessary.

No man should receive a dollar unless that dollar has been fairly earned. Every dollar received should represent a dollar's worth of service rendered — not gambling in stocks, but service rendered. The really big fortune, the swollen fortune, by the mere fact of its size acquires qualities which differentiate it in kind as well as in degree from what is possessed by men of relatively small means. Therefore, I believe in a graduated income tax on big fortunes, and in another tax which is far more easily collected and far more effective — a graduated inheritance tax on big fortunes, properly safeguarded against evasion and increasing rapidly in amount with the size of the estate. . . .

. . . Conservation means development as much as it does protection. I recognize the right and duty of this generation to develop and use the natural resources of our land; but I do not recognize the right to waste them, or to rob, by wasteful use, the generations that come after us. I ask nothing of the nation except that it so behave as each farmer here behaves with reference to his own children. That farmer is a poor creature who skins the land and leaves it worthless to his children. The farmer is a good farmer who, having enabled the land to support himself and to provide for the education of his children, leaves it to them a little better than he found it himself. I believe the same thing of a nation.

Moreover, I believe that the natural resources must be used for the benefit of all our people, and not monopolized for the benefit of the few, and here again is another case in which I am accused of taking a revolutionary attitude. People forget now that one hundred years ago there were public men of good character who advocated the nation selling its public lands in great quantities, so that the nation could get the most money out of it, and giving to the men who could cultivate it for their own uses. We took the proper democratic ground that the land should be granted in small sections to the men who were actually to till it and live on it. Now, with the water-power, with the forests, with the mines, we are brought face to face with the fact that there are many people who will go with us in conserving the resources only if they are to be allowed to exploit them for their benefit. That is one of the fundamental reasons why the special interests should be driven out of politics. Of all the questions which can come before this nation, short of the actual preservation of its existence in a great war, there is none which compares in importance with the great central task of leaving this land even a better land for our descendants than it is for us, and training them into a better race to inhabit the land and pass it on. Conservation is a great moral issue, for it involves the patriotic duty of insuring the safety and continuance of the nation. Let me add that the health and vitality of our people are at least as well worth conserving as their forests, waters, lands, and minerals, and in this great work the national government must bear a most important part.

I have spoken elsewhere also of the great task which lies before the farmers of the country to get for themselves and their wives and children not only the benefits of better farming, but also those of better business methods and better conditions of life on the farm. The burden of this great task will fall, as it should, mainly upon the great organizations of the farmers themselves. I am glad it will, for I believe they are all well able to handle it. In particular, there are strong reasons why the Departments of Agriculture of the various States, the United States Department of Agriculture, and the agricultural colleges and experiment stations should extend their work to cover all phases of farm life, instead of limiting themselves, as they have far too often limited themselves in the past, solely to the question of the production of crops. And now a special word to the farmer. I want to see him make the farm as fine a farm as it can be made; and let him remember to see that the improvement goes on indoors as well as out; let him remember that the farmer's wife should have her share of thought and attention just as much as the farmer himself.

Nothing is more true than that excess of every kind is followed by reaction; a fact which should be pondered by reformer and reactionary alike. We are face to face with new conceptions of the relations of property to human welfare, chiefly because certain advocates of the rights of property as against the rights of men have been pushing their claims too far. The man who wrongly holds that every human right is secondary to his profit must now give way to the advocate of human welfare, who rightly maintains that every man holds his property subject to the general right of the community to regulate its use to whatever degree the public welfare may require it.

But I think we may go still further. The right to regulate the use of wealth in the public interest is universally admitted. Let us admit also the right to regulate the terms and conditions of labor, which is the chief element of wealth, directly in the interest of the common good. The fundamental thing to do for every man is to give him a chance to reach a place in which he will make the greatest possible contribution to the public welfare. Understand what I say there. Give him a chance, not push him up if he will not be pushed. Help any man who stumbles; if he lies down, it is a poor job to try to carry him; but if he is a worthy man, try your best to see that he gets a chance to show the worth that is in him. No man can be a good citizen unless he has a wage more than sufficient to cover the bare cost of living, and hours of labor short enough so that after his day's work is done he will have time and energy to bear his share in the management of the community, to help in carrying the general load. We keep countless men from being good citizens by the conditions of life with which we surround them. We need comprehensive workmen's compensation acts, both State and national laws to regulate child labor and work for women, and, especially, we need in our common schools not merely education in book-learning, but also practical training for daily life and work. We need to enforce better sanitary conditions for our workers and to extend the use of safety appliances for our workers in industry and commerce, both within and between the States. Also, friends, in the interest of the working man himself we need to set our faces like flint against mob-violence just as against corporate greed; against violence and injustice and lawlessness by wage-workers just as much as against lawless cunning and greed and selfish arrogance of employers. If I could ask but one thing of my fellow countrymen, my request would be that, whenever they go in for reform, they remember the two sides, and that they always exact justice from one side as much as from the other. . . . The State must be made efficient for the work which concerns only the people of the State; and the nation for that which concerns all the people. There must remain no neutral ground to serve as a refuge for lawbreakers, and especially for lawbreakers of great wealth, who can hire the vulpine legal cunning which will teach them how to avoid both jurisdictions. It is misfortune when the national legislature fails to do its duty in providing a national remedy, so that the only national activity is the purely negative activity of the judiciary in forbidding the State to exercise power in the premises.

I do not ask for overcentralization; but I do ask that we work in a spirit of broad and far-reaching nationalism when we work for what concerns our people as a whole. We are all Americans. Our common interests are as broad as the continent. I speak to you here in Kansas exactly as I would speak in New York or Georgia, for the most vital problems are those which affect us all alike. The National Government belongs to the whole American people, and where the whole American people are interested, that interest can be guarded effectively only by the National Government. The betterment which we seek must be accomplished, I believe, mainly through the National Government.

The American people are right in demanding that New Nationalism, without which we cannot hope to deal with new problems. The New Nationalism puts the national need before sectional or personal advantage. It is impatient of the utter confusion that results from local legislatures attempting to treat national issues as local issues. It is still more impatient of the importance which springs from overdivision of governmental powers, the impotence which makes it possible for local selfishness or for legal cunning, hired by wealthy special interests, to bring national activities to a deadlock. This New Nationalism regards the executive power as the steward of the public welfare. It demands of the judiciary that it shall be interested primarily in human welfare rather than in property, just as it demands that the representative body shall represent all the people rather than any one class or section of the people.

I believe in shaping the ends of government to protect property as well as human welfare. Normally, and in the long run, the ends are the same; but whenever the alternative must be faced, I am for men and not for property, as you were in the Civil War. I am far from underestimating the importance of dividends; but I rank dividends below human character. Again, I do not have any sympathy with the reformer who says he does not care for dividends. Of course, economic welfare is necessary, for a man must pull his own weight and be able to support his family. I know well that the reformers must not bring upon the people economic ruin, or the reforms themselves will go down in the ruin. But we must be ready to face temporary disaster, whether or not brought on by those who will war against us to the knife. Those who oppose all reform will do well to remember that ruin in its worst form is inevitable if our national life brings us nothing better than swollen fortunes for the few and the triumph in both politics and business of a sordid and selfish materialism.

If our political institutions were perfect, they would absolutely prevent the political domination of money in any part of our affairs. We need to make our political representatives more quickly and sensitively responsive to the people whose servants they are. More direct action by the people in their own affairs under proper safeguards is vitally necessary. The direct primary is a step in this direction, if it is associated with a corrupt-practices act effective to prevent the advantage of the man willing recklessly and unscrupulously to spend money over his more honest competitor. It is particularly important that all moneys received or expended for campaign purposes should be publicly accounted for, not only after election, but before election as well. Political action must be made simpler, easier, and freer from confusion for every citizen. I believe that the prompt removal of unfaithful or incompetent public servants should be made easy and sure in whatever way experience shall show to be most expedient in any given class of cases.

One of the fundamental necessities in a representative government such as ours is to make certain that the men to whom the people delegate their power shall serve the people by whom they are elected, and not the special interests. I believe that every national officer, elected or appointed, should be forbidden to perform any service or receive any compensation, directly or indirectly, from interstate corporations; and a similar provision could not fail to be useful within the States.

The object of government is the welfare of the people. The material progress and prosperity of a nation are desirable chiefly so far as they lead to the moral and material welfare of all good citizens. Just in proportion as the average man and woman are honest, capable of sound judgment and high ideals, active in public affairs — but, first of all, sound in their home life, and the father and mother of healthy children whom they bring up well — just so far, and no farther, we may count our civilization a success. We must have — I believe we have already — a genuine and permanent moral awakening, without which no wisdom of legislation or administration really means anything; and, on the other hand, we must try to secure the social and economic legislation without which any improvement due to purely moral agitation is necessarily evanescent. . . . No matter how honest and decent we are in our private lives, if we do not have the right kind of law and the right kind of administration of the law, we cannot go forward as a nation. That is imperative; but it must be an addition to, and not a substitution for, the qualities that make us good citizens. In the last analysis, the most important elements in any man's career must be the sum of those qualities which, in the aggregate, we speak of as character. If he has not got it, then no law that the wit of man can devise, no administration of the law by the boldest and strongest executive, will avail to help him. We must have the right kind of character — character that makes a man, first of all, a good man in the home, a good father, a good husband — that makes a man a good neighbor. You must have that, and, then, in addition, you must have the kind of law and the kind of administration of the law which will give to those qualities in the private citizen the best possible chance for development. The prime problem of our nation is to get the right type of good citizenship, and, to get it, we must have progress, and our public men must be genuinely progressive.

Study Guide

1. Although he does not say so explicitly, Roosevelt is addressing himself to the same problem that concerned all progressives — the inequities in America and the fear that equality of opportunity was being threatened by interests and combinations stronger than the individual or even his government. You can outline the program of T.R.'s New Nationalism by dividing his speech thus:

   (a) preliminary amenities (pp. 301–304);
   (b) economics (pp. 304–307);
   (c) conservation (pp. 307–308);

(d) social welfare (pp. 308–309); and

(e) political reforms (pp. 309–311).

Starting with the first, note the many references to Civil War figures and quotations from Lincoln. Why? Note, too, the typically middle-of-the-road political position T.R. takes as between the contentions of labor and capital. What can Roosevelt's preliminary remarks tell you about the social and economic views held by middle-class Americans in the Progressive Era?

2. In his attack on "special interests," T.R. proposes a number of measures to deal with this problem. *Define precisely* his conceptualization of the problem and *outline* the solutions he offers. Do not overlook these key sentences — a basic assumption of his New Nationalism: "Combinations in industry are the result of an imperative economic law which cannot be repealed by political legislation. The effort at prohibiting all combinations has substantially failed. The way out lies, not in attempting to prevent such combinations, but in completely controlling them in the interest of the public welfare."

3. What steps does Theodore Roosevelt propose in dealing with economic inequities?

4. In his paragraphs on conservation, T.R. displays a dual concern: use of land and its distribution. Elaborate.

5. Outline the social welfare measures T.R. proposes.

6. Similarly, outline the proposals he offers for political reform.

7. In closing: what does Theodore Roosevelt's closing paragraph and his references to "moral awakening," "character," and "administrative law" tell you about the outlook and the values of the Progressive movement in which T.R. loomed so large and influential? Or, put this way: How much of a realist was Roosevelt and how much a moralist? Or was he an amalgam of both?

Woodrow Wilson

BACK TO LIBERTY

⊰{ *1913* }⊱   WHILE the need for government regulation of the economy was becoming almost daily more evident in the Progressive Era, millions of forward-looking Americans still hesitated to surrender the old, individualistic, self-reliant standards of an earlier and simpler time. These millions were ready enough to admit that society was plagued by evils and eager to see something done to correct this state of affairs. But they hoped that reform could be accomplished without abandoning traditional freedoms and without submitting to tight controls by a centralized bureaucracy. The "New Freedom" of Governor Woodrow Wilson of New Jersey perfectly suited the feelings of such people, and their support had much to do with his election to the Presidency in 1912.

In his eloquent campaign speeches, Wilson (1856–1924) hammered away at the theme that the times were out of joint and that the government must step in to put things straight. This was in line with progressive thinking. But Wilson went on to argue that once the government had rooted out the evils the old laissez-faire, free-enterprise system could function again. Thus the "new" freedom would be established. The growth of giant corporations, for example, had destroyed the "old" freedom of individuals to operate small businesses profitably. But once strict anti-trust legislation had destroyed the giants, small businessmen would again be able to operate unfettered by government controls. As another progressive described Wilson's philosophy, the New Freedom argued "that if the system of letting things alone was properly regulated and its abuses eliminated, a permanent peace would be restored to the . . . nation."

Immediately after Wilson's election, William Bayard Hale (1869–1924), a journalist who had written his official campaign biography, put together a compilation based on Wilson's speeches. This was published in 1913 as *The New Freedom*. The volume had a wide sale and a still wider influence, for it brought together in convenient form the ideas Wilson had developed piecemeal during the campaign. It is fair to say that it became the almanac and almost the Bible of the first Wilson administration.

THE NEW FREEDOM

THERE is one great basic fact which underlies all the questions that are discussed on the political platform at the present moment. That singular fact is that nothing is done in this country as it was done twenty years ago.

We are in the presence of a new organization of society. Our life has broken away from the past. The life of America is not the life that it was twenty years ago; it is not the life that it was ten years ago. We have changed our economic conditions, absolutely, from top to bottom; and, with our economic society, the organization of our life. The old political formulas do not fit the present problems; they read now like documents taken out of a forgotten age. The older cries sound as if they belonged to a past age which men have almost forgotten. Things which used to be put into the party platforms of ten years ago would sound antiquated if put into a platform now. We are facing the necessity of fitting a new social organization, as we did once fit the old organization, to the happiness and prosperity of the great body of citizens; for we are conscious that the new order of society has not been made to fit and provide the convenience or prosperity of the average man. The life of the nation has grown infinitely varied. It does not centre now upon questions of governmental structure or of the distribution of governmental powers. It centres upon questions of the very structure and operation of society itself, of which government is only the instrument. Our development has run so fast and so far along the lines sketched in the earlier day of constitutional definition, has so crossed and interlaced those lines, has piled upon them such novel structures of trust and combination, has elaborated within them a life so manifold, so full of forces which transcend the boundaries of the country itself and fill the eyes of the world, that a new nation seems to have been created which the old formulas do not fit or afford a vital interpretation of.

We have come upon a very different age from any that preceded us. We have come upon an age when we do not do business in the way in which we used to do business, — when we do not carry on any of the operations of manufacture, sale, transportation, or communication as men used to carry them on. There is a sense in which in our day the individual has been submerged. In most parts of our country men work, not for themselves, not as partners in the old way in which they used to work, but generally as employees, — in a higher or lower grade, — of great corporations. There was a time when corporations played a very minor part in our business affairs, but now they play the chief part, and most men are the servants of corporations.

You know what happens when you are the servant of a corporation. You have in no instance access to the men who are really determining the policy of the corporation. If the corporation is doing the things that it ought not to do, you really have no voice in the matter and must obey the orders, and you have oftentimes with deep mortification to co-operate in the doing of things which you know are against the public interest. Your individuality is swallowed up in the individuality and purpose of a great organization.

It is true that, while most men are thus submerged in the corporation, a few, a very few, are exalted to a power which as individuals they could never have wielded. Through the great organizations of which they are the heads, a few are enabled to play a part unprecedented by anything in history in the control of the business operations of the country and in the determination of the happiness of great numbers of people.

Yesterday, and ever since history began, men were related to one another as individuals. To be sure there were the family, the Church, and the State, institutions which associated men in certain wide circles of relationship. But in the ordinary concerns of life, in the ordinary work, in the daily round, men dealt freely and directly with one another. To-day, the everyday relationships of men are largely with great impersonal concerns, with organizations, not with other individual men.

Now this is nothing short of a new social age, a new era of human relationships, a new stage-setting for the drama of life.

In this new age we find, for instance, that our laws with regard to the relations of employer and employee are in many respects wholly antiquated and impossible. They were framed for another age, which nobody now living remembers, which is, indeed, so remote from our life that it would be difficult for many of us to understand it if it were described to us. The employer is now generally a corporation or a huge company of some kind; the employee is one of hundreds or of thousands brought together, not by individual masters whom they know and with whom they have personal relations, but by agents of one sort or another. Workingmen are marshaled in great numbers for the performance of a multitude of particular tasks under a common discipline. They generally use dangerous and powerful machinery, over whose repair and renewal they have no control. New rules must be devised with regard to their obligations and their rights, their obligations to their employers and their responsibilities to one another. Rules must be devised for their protection, for their compensation when injured, for their support when disabled.

There is something very new and very big and very complex about these new relations of capital and labor. A new economic society has sprung up, and we must effect a new set of adjustments. We must not pit power against weakness. The employer is generally, in our day, as I have said, not an individual, but a powerful group; and yet the workingman when dealing with his employer is still, under our existing law, an individual.

Why is it that we have a labor question at all? It is for the simple and very sufficient reason that the laboring man and the employer are not intimate associates now as they used to be in time past. Most of our laws were formed in the age when employer and employees knew each other, knew each other's characters, were associates with each other, dealt with each other as man with man. That is no longer the case. You not only do not come into personal contact with the men who have the supreme command in those corporations, but it would be out of the question for you to do it. Our modern corporations employ thousands, and in some instances hundreds of thousands, of men. The only persons whom you see or deal with are local superintendents or local representatives of a vast organization, which is not like anything that the workingmen of the time in which our laws were framed knew anything about. A little group of workingmen, seeing their employer every day, dealing with him in a personal way, is one thing, and the modern body of labor engaged as employees of the huge enterprises that spread all over the country, dealing with men of whom they can form no personal conception, is another thing. A very different thing. You never saw a corporation, any more than you ever saw a government. Many a workingman to-day never saw the body of men who are conducting the industry in which he is employed. And they never saw him. What they know about him is written in ledgers and books and letters, in the correspondence of the office, in the reports of the superintendents. He is a long way off from them.

So what we have to discuss is, not wrongs which individuals intentionally do, — I do not believe there are a great many of those, — but the wrongs of a system. I want to record my protest against any discussion of this matter which would seem to indicate that there are bodies of our fellow-citizens who are trying to grind us down and do us injustice. There are some men of that sort. I don't know how they sleep o' nights, but there are men of that kind. Thank God, they are not numerous. The truth is, we are all caught in a great economic system which is heartless. The modern corporation is not engaged in business as an individual. When we deal with it, we deal with an impersonal element, an immaterial piece of society. A modern corporation is a means of co-operation in the conduct of an enterprise which is so big that no one man can conduct it, and which the resources of no one man are sufficient to finance. A company is formed; that company puts out a prospectus; the promoters expect to raise a certain fund as capital stock. Well, how are they going to raise it? They are going to raise it from the public in general, some of whom will buy their stock. The moment that begins, there is formed — what? A joint stock corporation. Men begin to pool their earnings, little piles, big piles. A certain number of men are elected by the stockholders to be directors, and these directors elect a president. This president is the head of the undertaking, and the directors are its managers.

Now, do the workingmen employed by that stock corporation deal with that president and those directors? Not at all. Does the public deal with that president and that board of directors? It does not. Can anybody bring them to account? It is next to impossible to do so. If you undertake it you will find it a game of hide and seek, with the objects of your search taking refuge now behind the tree of their individual personality, now behind that of their corporate irresponsibility.

And do our laws take note of this curious state of things? Do they even attempt to distinguish between a man's act as a corporation director and as an individual? They do not. Our laws still deal with us on the basis of the old system. The law is still living in the dead past which we have left behind. This is evident, for instance, with regard to the matter of employers' liability for workingmen's injuries. Suppose that a superintendent wants a workman to use a certain piece of machinery which it is not safe for him to use, and that the workman is injured by that piece of machinery. Some of our courts have held that the superintendent is a fellow-servant, or, as the law states it, a fellow-employee, and that, therefore, the man cannot recover damages for his injury. The superintendent who probably engaged the man is not his employer. Who is his employer? And whose negligence could conceivably come in there? The board of directors did not tell the employee to use that piece of machinery; and the president of the corporation did not tell him to use that piece of machinery. And so forth. Don't you see by that theory that a man never can get redress for negligence on the part of the employer? When I hear judges reason upon the analogy of the relationships that used to exist between workmen and their employers a generation ago, I wonder if they have not opened their eyes to the modern world. You know, we have a right to expect that judges will have their eyes open, even though the law which they administer hasn't awakened.

Yet that is but a single small detail illustrative of the difficulties we are in because we have not adjusted the law to the facts of the new order.

Since I entered politics, I have chiefly had men's views confided to me privately. Some of the biggest men in the United States, in the field of commerce and manufacture, are afraid of somebody, are afraid of something. They know that there is a power somewhere so organized, so subtle, so watchful, so interlocked, so complete, so pervasive, that they had better not speak above their breath when they speak in condemnation of it.

They know that America is not a place of which it can be said, as it used to be, that a man may choose his own calling and pursue it just as far as his abilities enable him to pursue it; because to-day, if he enters certain fields there are organizations which will use means against him that will prevent his building up a business which they do not want to have built up; organizations that will see to it that the ground is cut from under him and the markets shut against him. For if he begins to sell to certain retail dealers, to any retail dealers, the monopoly will refuse to sell to those dealers, and those dealers, afraid, will not buy the new man's wares.

And this is the country which has lifted to the admiration of the world its ideals of absolutely free opportunity, where no man is supposed to be under any limitation except the limitations of his character and of his mind, where there is supposed to be no distinction of class, no distinction of blood, no distinction of social status, but where men win or lose on their merits.

I lay it very close to my own conscience as a public man whether we can any longer stand at our doors and welcome all newcomers upon those terms. American industry is not free, as once it was free; American enterprise is not free; the man with only a little capital is finding it harder to get into the field, more and more impossible to compete with the big fellow. Why? Because the laws of this country do not prevent the strong from crushing the weak. That is the reason, and because the strong have crushed the weak the strong dominate the industry and the economic life of this country. No man can deny that the lines of endeavor have more and more narrowed and stiffened; no man who knows anything about the development of industry in this country can have failed to observe that the larger kinds of credit are more and more difficult to obtain, unless you obtain them upon the terms of uniting your efforts with those who already control the industries of the country; and nobody can fail to observe that any man who tries to set himself up in competition with any process of manufacture which has been taken under the control of large combinations of capital will presently find himself either squeezed out or obliged to sell and allow himself to be absorbed.

There is a great deal that needs reconstruction in the United States. I should like to take a census of the business men,—I mean the rank and file of the business men,—as to whether they think that business conditions in this country, or rather whether the organization of business in this country, is satisfactory or not. I know what they would say if they dared. If they could vote secretly they would vote overwhelmingly that the present organization of business was meant for the big fellows and was not meant for the little fellows; that it was meant for those who are at the top and was meant to exclude those who are at the bottom; that it was meant to shut out beginners, to prevent new entries in the race, to prevent the building up of competitive enterprises that would interfere with the monopolies which the great trusts have built up.

What this country needs above everything else is a body of laws which will look after the men who are on the make rather than the men who are already made. Because the men who are already made are not going to live indefinitely, and they are not always kind enough to leave sons as able and as honest as they are.

The originative part of America, the part of America that makes new enterprises, the part into which the ambitious and gifted workingman makes his way up, the class that saves, that plans, that organizes, that presently spreads its enterprises until they have a national scope and character, — that middle class is being more and more squeezed out by the processes which we have been taught to call processes of prosperity. Its members are sharing prosperity, no doubt; but what alarms me is that they are not *originating* prosperity. No country can afford to have its prosperity originated by a small controlling class. The treasury of America does not lie in the brains of the small body of men now in control of the great enterprises that have been concentrated under the direction of a very small number of persons. The treasury of America lies in those ambitions, those energies, that cannot be restricted to a special favored class. It depends upon the inventions of unknown men, upon the originations of unknown men, upon the ambitions of unknown men. Every country is renewed out of the ranks of the unknown, not out of the ranks of those already famous and powerful and in control.

There has come over the land that un-American set of conditions which enables a small number of men who control the government to get favors from the government; by those favors to exclude their fellows from equal business opportunity; by those favors to extend a network of control that will presently dominate every industry in the country, and so make men forget the ancient time when America lay in every hamlet, when America was to be seen in every fair valley, when America displayed her great forces on the broad prairies, ran her fine fires of enterprise up over the mountainsides and down into the bowels of the earth, and eager men were everywhere captains of industry, not employees; not looking to a distant city to find out what they might do, but looking about among their neighbors, finding credit according to their character, not according to their connections, finding credit in proportion to what was known to be in them and behind them, not in proportion to the securities they held that were approved where they were not known. In order to start an enterprise now, you have to be authenticated, in a perfectly impersonal way, not according to yourself, but according to what you own that somebody else approves of your owning. You cannot begin such an enterprise as those that have made America until you are so authenticated, until you have succeeded in obtaining the good-will of large allied capitalists. Is that freedom? That is dependence, not freedom.

We used to think in the old-fashioned days when life was very simple that all that government had to do was to put on a policeman's uniform, and say, "Now don't anybody hurt anybody else." We used to say that the ideal of government was for every man to be left alone and not interfered with, except when he interfered with somebody else; and that best government was the government that did as little governing as possible. That was the idea that obtained in Jefferson's time. But we are coming now to realize that life is so complicated that we are not dealing with the old conditions, and that the law has to step in and create new conditions under which we may live, the conditions which will make it tolerable for us to live. . . .

. . . We are in a new world, struggling under old laws. As we go inspecting our lives to-day, surveying this new scene of centralized and complex society, we shall find many more things out of joint.

One of the most alarming phenomena of the time, — or rather it would be alarming if the nation had not awakened to it and shown its determination to control it, — one of the most significant signs of the new social era is the degree to which government has become associated with business. I speak, for the moment, of the control over the government exercised by Big Business. Behind the whole subject, of course, is the truth that, in the new order, government and business must be associated closely. But that association is at present of a nature absolutely intolerable; the precedence is wrong, the association is upside down. Our government has been for the past few years under the control of heads of great allied corporations with special interests. It has not controlled these interests and assigned them a proper place in the whole system of business; it has submitted itself to their control. As a result, there have grown up vicious systems and schemes of governmental favoritism (the most obvious being the extravagant tariff), far-reaching in effect upon the whole fabric of life, touching to his injury every inhabitant of the land, laying unfair and impossible handicaps upon competitors, imposing taxes in every direction, stifling everywhere the free spirit of American enterprise.

Now this has come about naturally; as we go on we shall see how very naturally. It is no use denouncing anybody, or anything, except human nature. Nevertheless, it is an intolerable thing that the government of the republic should have got so far out of the hands of the people; should have been captured by interests which are special and not general. In the train of this capture follow the troops of scandals, wrongs, indecencies, with which our politics swarm.

There are cities in America of whose government we are ashamed. There are cities everywhere, in every part of the land, in which we feel that, not the interests of the public, but the interests of special privileges, of selfish men, are served; where contracts take precedence over public interest. Not only in big cities is this the case. Have you not noticed the growth of socialistic sentiment in the smaller towns? Not many months ago I stopped at a little town in Nebraska, and while my train lingered

I met on the platform a very engaging young fellow dressed in overalls who introduced himself to me as the mayor of the town, and added that he was a Socialist. I said, "What does that mean? Does that mean that this town is socialistic?" "No, sir," he said; "I have not deceived myself; the vote by which I was elected was about 20 per cent socialistic and 80 per cent protest." It was protest against the treachery to the people of those who led both the other parties of that town.

All over the Union people are coming to feel that they have no control over the course of affairs. I live in one of the greatest States in the union, which was at one time in slavery. Until two years ago we had witnessed with increasing concern the growth in New Jersey of a spirit of almost cynical despair. Men said: "We vote; we are offered the platform we want; we elect the men who stand on that platform, and we get absolutely nothing." So they began to ask: "What is the use of voting? We know that the machines of both parties are subsidized by the same persons, and therefore it is useless to turn in either direction."

This is not confined to some of the state governments and those of some of the towns and cities. We know that something intervenes between the people of the United States and the control of their own affairs at Washington. It is not the people who have been ruling there of late.

Why are we in the presence, why are we at the threshold, of a revolution? Because we are profoundly disturbed by the influences which we see reigning in the determination of our public life and our public policy. There was a time when America was blithe with self-confidence. She boasted that she, and she alone, knew the processes of popular government; but now she sees her sky overcast; she sees that there are at work forces which she did not dream of in her hopeful youth.

Don't you know that some man with eloquent tongue, without conscience, who did not care for the nation, could put this whole country into a flame? Don't you know that this country from one end to the other believes that something is wrong? What an opportunity it would be for some man without conscience to spring up and say: "This is the way. Follow me!"—and lead in paths of destruction!

The old order changeth—changeth under our very eyes, not quietly and equably, but swiftly and with the noise and heat and tumult of reconstruction.

I suppose that all struggle for law has been conscious, that very little of it has been blind or merely instinctive. It is the fashion to say, as if with superior knowledge of affairs and of human weakness, that every age has been an age of transition, and that no age is more full of change than another; yet in very few ages of the world can the struggle for change have been so widespread, so deliberate, or upon so great a scale as in this in which we are taking part.

The transition we are witnessing is no equable transition of growth and normal alteration; no silent, unconscious unfolding of one age into another, its natural heir and successor. Society is looking itself over, in our day, from top to bottom; is making fresh and critical analysis of its very elements; is questioning its oldest practices as freely as its newest, scrutinizing every arrangement and motive of its life; and it stands ready to attempt nothing less than a radical reconstruction, which only frank and honest counsels and the forces of generous co-operation can hold back from becoming a revolution. We are in a temper to reconstruct economic society, as we were once in a temper to reconstruct political society, and political society may itself undergo a radical modification in the process. I doubt if any age was ever more conscious of its task or more unanimously desirous of radical and extended changes in its economic and political practice.

We stand in the presence of a revolution, — not a bloody revolution; America is not given to the spilling of blood, — but a silent revolution, whereby America will insist upon recovering in practice those ideals which she has always professed, upon securing a government devoted to the general interest and not to special interests.

We are upon the eve of a great reconstruction. It calls for creative statesmanship as no age has done since that great age in which we set up the government under which we live, that government which was the admiration of the world until it suffered wrongs to grow up under it which have made many of our own compatriots question the freedom of our institutions and preach revolution against them. I do not fear revolution. I have unshaken faith in the power of America to keep its self-possession. Revolution will come in peaceful guise, as it came when we put aside the crude government of the Confederation and created the great Federal Union which governs individuals, not States, and which has been these hundred and thirty years our vehicle of progress. Some radical changes we must make in our law and practice. Some reconstructions we must push forward, which a new age and new circumstances impose upon us. But we can do it all in calm and sober fashion, like statesmen and patriots.

I do not speak of these things in apprehension, because all is open and above-board. This is not a day in which great forces rally in secret. The whole stupendous program must be publicly planned and canvassed. Good temper, the wisdom that comes of sober counsel, the energy of thoughtful and unselfish men, the habit of co-operation and of compromise which has been bred in us by long years of free government, in which reason rather than passion has been made to prevail by the sheer virtue of candid and universal debate, will enable us to win through to still another great age without violence.

Study Guide

1. Read carefully, in the introduction, the distinction between Theodore Roosevelt's "New Nationalism" and Woodrow Wilson's "New Freedom." As you read this selection by Wilson, note how his views differ from those of Roosevelt. Wilson's address can be divided into the following elements:

   (a) a description of the alterations that have come into American life in recent decades (pp. 313–314);
   (b) an assessment of how these changes have affected various economic groups and their relations to one another (pp. 314–322); and
   (c) a plea for progressive "revolution."

   Begin by trying to understand Wilson's views on the central focus and problem of the Progressive Era — what Wilson terms "the presence of a new organization of society." Is this development, according to Wilson, positive or negative, temporary or permanent, superficial or profound? Answer and amplify.

2. Turning to Wilson's treatment of what today we would call the "corporate society," let us follow him as he applies this theme to employer-employee relations, to economic opportunity for the individual, to the place of government in the economy, and to the role and the power of big business. First, labor:

   (a) In what ways, according to Wilson, has the rise of corporate industry affected the workingman?
   (b) What solution does he advance for these problems?

3. In his treatment of the free-enterprise system in the United States, or as he would argue, *the lack of it,* Wilson develops "the race of life" theme — an idealized portrayal of how our capitalistic economy should function. Try to understand this, for it provides the ground for much of the legislation passed in the first two years of Wilson's administration. Observe also the distinction Wilson draws between "the men who are on the make" and "the men who are already made." Relate this to the "race of life" theme.

4. What disparities between *the ideal* and *reality* does Wilson discover in the way the government functions in the United States and, specifically, what criticism does he have of the relationship between government and big business? What sentences illustrate Wilson's point of view?

5. In closing, Wilson asks for a "revolution." On the basis of this selection and from a careful reading of its closing paragraphs, what sort of revolu-

tion do you feel Wilson has in mind — moderate or extreme, peaceful or violent? What can this tell you about the progressive outlook?

6. In retrospect: Roosevelt and Wilson are both considered important contributors to progressive thought. On the basis of these representative selections, can you make some generalizations about the political, social, and economic outlook of these men? Answer the following for assistance:

   (a) To what central development in American life are all these men addressing themselves?

   (b) What concerns do they have in common?

   (c) How are they alike in their analyses and what similarities and contrasts do you find in the solutions they advance?

   (d) Can you see with clarity the similarity between the writings of Roosevelt on one hand and the notions of Wilson on the other? Document your reply.

   (e) Which of the two would be most likely to want to return the nation to nineteenth-century ways, and why?

   (f) Which would be most likely to approve of the massive abandonment of *laissez faire* represented by the New Deal, and why?

7. And, finally, explore this statement: Despite the differences between the advocates of the New Nationalism and those of the New Freedom, their agreements vastly exceeded their differences.

Edward A. Ross

IMMIGRATION RESTRICTION

⊰⧉{*1914*}⧉⊱ ALTHOUGH ANTI-IMMIGRATION movements appeared on the American scene prior to the Civil War, it was not until the 1880's that the American people began to consider, seriously, legislation that would restrict immigration to the United States. A number of factors fostered the traditional unrestricted immigration policy of our country: the notion of America as a haven for Europe's oppressed; the need for immigrants to settle the West; and, later, the need for laborers to man the growing industrial sector of the economy. Despite social and economic tensions created by unrestricted immigration, newcomers, whether from Asia or Europe, were welcomed and looked upon as valuable assets in the development of the nation's resources and economy.

After the Civil War, in 1882, the Chinese were the first to be barred from further entry into the United States. In 1907, Japanese immigration was halted through the adoption of an informal Gentlemen's Agreement. Legislation restricting European migration came more slowly and with much more difficulty, despite the efforts of those native Americans who sought curbs of this kind as part of a national policy. Influenced by the arguments of the Immigration Restriction League, Congress passed restrictive legislation, but it was vetoed in 1897 by Grover Cleveland. Similar measures were vetoed by William Howard Taft and Woodrow Wilson. In 1917, the immigration restrictionists won their first substantial victory with the enactment of a "literacy test" requirement for entry into the United States. The ultimate victory of the restrictionists came with the passage of the Immigration Act of 1924, banning all Asiatic migrants and limiting European migration to 150,000 per year, with the bulk of the "quotas" for Europeans assigned to citizens of Northern and Western European nations.

The selection that follows is taken from *The Old World in the New,* an influential immigration restriction tract, written by the sociologist, Edward Alsworth Ross. Along with many other progressives, Ross believed in the superiority of the Anglo-Saxon peoples and was convinced that a continued policy of unrestricted immigration would harm the future of the nation. For Ross, immigration restriction — particularly of the "new" immigrants from Southern and Eastern Europe — was simply another measure, like curbs on alcohol or child labor, to improve the quality of American life. The ethnic stereotypes offered in *The Old World in the New,* along with the volume's socioeconomic arguments, were notions shared by a large number of native-born Americans in the years prior to and after World War I.

THE OLD WORLD IN THE NEW

AMERICAN BLOOD AND IMMIGRANT BLOOD

As I sought to show, . . . the conditions of settlement of this country caused those of uncommon energy and venturesomeness to outmultiply the rest of the population. Thus came into existence the pioneering breed; and this breed increased until it is safe to estimate that fully half of white Americans with native grandparents have one or more pioneers among their ancestors. Whatever valuable race traits distingush the American people from the parent European stocks are due to the efflorescence of this breed. Without it there would have been little in the performance of our people to arrest the attention of the world. Now we confront the melancholy spectacle of this pioneer breed being swamped and submerged by an overwhelming tide of latecomers from the old-world hive. In Atlanta still seven out of eight white men had American parents; in Nashville and Richmond, four out of five; in Kansas City, two out of three; and in Los Angeles, one out of two; but in Detroit, Cleveland, and Paterson one man out of five had American parents; in Chicago and New York, one out of six; in Milwaukee, one out of seven; and in Fall River, one out of nine. *Certainly never since the colonial era have the foreign-born and their children formed so large a proportion of the American people as at the present moment.* I scanned 368 persons as they passed me in Union Square, New York, at a time when the garment-workers of the Fifth Avenue lofts were returning to their homes.

Only thirty-eight of these passers-by had the type of face one would find at a county fair in the West or South. . . .

In this sense it is fair to say that the blood now being injected into the veins of our people is "sub-common." To one accustomed to the aspect of the normal American population, the Caliban type shows up with a frequency that is startling. Observe immigrants not as they come travel-wan up the gang-plank, nor as they issue toil-begrimed from pit's mouth or mill gate, but in their gatherings, washed, combed, and in their Sunday best. You are struck by the fact that from ten to twenty per cent, are hirsute, low-browed, big-faced persons of obviously low mentality. Not that they suggest evil. They simply look out of place in black clothes and stiff collar, since clearly they belong in skins, in wattled huts at the close of the Great Ice Age. These oxlike men are descendants of those *who always stayed behind*. Those in whom the soul burns with the dull, smoky flame of the pine-knot stuck to the soil, and are now thick in the sluiceways of immigration. Those in whom it burns with a clear, luminous flame have been attracted to the cities of the home land and, having prospects, have no motive to submit themselves to the hardships of the steerage.

To the practised eye, the physiognomy of certain groups unmistakably proclaims inferiority of type. I have seen gatherings of the foreign-born in which narrow and sloping foreheads were the rule. The shortness and smallness of the crania were very noticeable. There was much facial asymmetry. Among the women, beauty, aside from the fleeting, epidermal bloom of girlhood, was quite lacking. In every face there was something wrong — lips thick, mouth coarse, upper lip too long, cheek-bones too high, chin poorly formed, the bridge of the nose hollowed, the base of the nose tilted, or else the whole face prognathous. There were so many sugar-loaf heads, moon-faces, slit mouths, lantern-jaws, and goose-bill noses that one might imagine a malicious jinn had amused himself by casting human beings in a set of skew-molds discarded by the Creator.

Our captains of industry give a crowbar to the immigrant with a number nine face on a number six head, make a dividend out of him, and imagine that is the end of the matter. They overlook that this man will beget children in his image — two or three times as many as the American — and that these children will in turn beget children. They chuckle at having opened an inexhaustible store of cheap tools and, lo! the American people is being altered by all times by these tools. Once before, captains of industry took a hand in making this people. Colonial planters imported Africans to hoe in the sun, to "develop" the tobacco, indigo, and rice plantations. Then, as now, business-minded men met with contempt the protests of a few idealists against their way of "building up the country."

Those promoters of prosperity are dust, but they bequeathed a situation which in four years wiped out more wealth than two hundred years of slavery had built up, and which presents today the one unsolvable problem in this country. Without likening immigrants to negroes, one may point out how the latter-day employer resembles the old-time planter in his blindness to the effects of his labor policy upon the blood of the nation.

Immigration and Good Looks

It is reasonable to expect an early falling off in the frequency of good looks in the American people. It is unthinkable that so many persons with crooked faces, coarse mouths, bad noses, heavy jaws, and low foreheads can mingle their heredity with ours without making personal beauty yet more rare among us than it actually is. So much ugliness is at last bound to work to the surface. One ought to see the horror on the face of a fine-looking Italian or Hungarian consul when one asks him innocently, "Is the physiognomy of these immigrants typical of your people?" That the new immigrants are inferior in looks to the old immigrants may be seen by comparing, in a Labor Day parade, the faces of the cigar-makers and the garment-workers with those of the teamsters, piano-movers and steam-fitters.

Even aside from the pouring in of the ill-favored, the crossing of the heterogeneous is bound to lessen good looks among us. It is noteworthy that the beauty which has often excited the admiration of European visitors has shown itself most in communities of comparative purity of blood. New England, Virginia, and Kentucky have been renowned for their beautiful women, but not the commonwealths with a mixed population. It is in the less-heterogeneous parts of the Middle West, such as Indiana and Kansas, that one is struck by the number of comely women.

Twenty-four years ago the greatest living philosopher advised inquiring Japanese statesmen to interdict marriages of Japanese with foreigners, on the ground that the crossings of the too-unlike produce human beings with a "chaotic constitution." Herbert Spencer went on to say, "When the varieties mingled diverge beyond a certain slight degree, the result is inevitably a bad one."

Stature and Physique

Although the Slavs stand up well, our South Europeans run to low stature. A gang of Italian navvies filing along the street present, by their dwarfishness, a curious contrast to other people. The Portuguese, the

Greeks, and the Syrians are, from our point of view, undersized. The Hebrew immigrants are very poor in physique. The average of Hebrew women in New York is just over five feet, and the young women in the garment factories, although well developed, appear to be no taller than native girls of thirteen.

On the physical side the Hebrews are the polar opposite of our pioneer breed. Not only are they undersized and weak-muscled, but they shun bodily activity and are exceedingly sensitive to pain. Says a settlement worker: "You can't make boy scouts out of the Jews. There's not a troop of them in all New York." Another remarks: "They are absolute babies about pain. Their young fellows will scream with a hard lick." Students observe that husky young Hebrews on the foot-ball team lack grit, and will "take on" if they are bumped into hard. A young Ontario miner noticed that his Hebrew comrades groaned and wept over the hardships of the trail. "They kept swapping packs with me, imagining my pack must be lighter because I wasn't hollering."

Natural selection, frontier life, and the example of the red men produced in America a type of great physical self-control, gritty, uncomplaining, merciless to the body through fear of becoming "soft." To this roaming, hunting, exploring, adventurous breed what greater contrast is there than the denizens of the Ghetto? The second generation, to be sure, overtop their parents and are going in for athletics. Hebrews under Irish names abound in the prize-ring, and not long ago a sporting editor printed the item, "Jack Sullivan received a letter in Yiddish yesterday from his sister." Still, it will be long before they produce the stoical type who blithely fares forth into the wilderness, portaging his canoe, poling it against the current, wading in the torrents, living on bacon and beans, and sleeping on the ground, all for "fun" or "to keep hard."

Vitality

"The Slavs," remarks a physician, "are immune to certain kinds of dirt. They can stand what would kill a white man." The women do not have puerperal fever, as our women would under their conditions. The men violate every sanitary law, yet survive. The Slavs come from a part of the world in which never more than a third of the children have grown up. In every generation, dirt, ignorance, superstition, and lack of medical attention have winnowed out all but the sturdiest. Among Americans, two-thirds of the children grow up, which means that we keep alive many of the tenderer, who would certainly have perished in the Slavic world. There is, however, no illusion more grotesque than to suppose that our people is to be rejuvenated by absorbing these millions of hardy peasantry, that, to quote a champion of free immigration, "The new-comers in America will bring fresh, vigorous blood to a rather sterile and inbred stock." The fact is that the immigrant stock quickly loses here its distinctive ruggedness. The physicians practising among rural Poles no-tice a great saving of infant life under American conditions. Says one: "I see immigrant women and their grown daughters having infants at the same time, and the children of the former will die of the things that the children of the latter get well of. The same holds when the second gen-eration and the third bear at the same time. The latter save their children better than the former." The result is a marked softening of fiber be-tween the immigrant women and the granddaughters. Among the latter are many of a finer, but frailer, mold, who would be ruined in health if they worked in the field the third day after confinement, as grandmother did. In the old country there were very few of this type who survived infancy in a peasant family.

There is, then, no lasting revitalization from this tide of life. If our people has become weak, no transfusion of peasants will set it on its feet again; for their blood too, soon thins. The trouble, if you call it that, is not with the American people, but with the wide diffusion among us of a civilized manner of life. Where the struggle for existence is mitigated not merely for the upper quarter of society, as formerly in the Old World, but for the upper three-quarters, as in this and other democratic coun-tries, the effects of keeping alive the less hardy are bound to show. The remedy for the alleged degeneration of our stock is simple, but drastic. If we want only constitutions that can stand hardship and abuse, let us treat the young as they are treated in certain poverty-stricken parts of Russia. Since the mother is obliged to pass the day at work in distant fields, the nursling of a few months is left alone, crawling about on the dirt floor of the hut and comforting itself, when it cries from hunger, by sucking poultices of chewed bread tied to its hands and feet.

Morality

That the Mediterranean peoples are morally below the races of northern Europe is as certain as any social fact. Even when they were dirty, fero-cious barbarians, these blonds were truth-tellers. Be it pride or awkward-ness or lack of imagination or fair-play sense, something has held them back from the nimble lying of the southern races. Immigration officials find that the different peoples are as day and night in point of veracity, and report vast trouble in extracting the truth from certain brunet na-tionalities.

Some champions of immigration have become broad-minded enough to think small of the cardinal virtues. The Syrians, on Boston testimony, took "great pains to cheat the charitable societies" and are "extremely untrustworthy and unreliable." Their defender, however, after admitting their untruthfulness, explains that their lying is altruistic. If, at the fork of a road, you ask a Syrian your way, he will, in sheer transport of sympathy, study you to discover what answer will most please you. "The Anglo-Saxon variety of truthfulness," she adds, "is not a Syrian characteristic"; but, "if truthfulness includes loyalty, ready self-denial to promote a cause that seems right, the Syrian is to that extent truthful." Quoting a Syrian's admission that his fellow-merchants pay their debts for their credit's sake, but will cheat the customer, she comments, "This, however, does not seem to be exclusively a Syrian vice." To such miserable paltering does a sickly sentimentality lead. . . .

Nothing less than verminous is the readiness of the southern Europeans to prey upon their fellows. Never were British or Scandinavian immigrants so bled by fellow-countrymen as are South Italian, Greek and Semitic immigrants. Their spirit of mutual helpfulness saved them from *padrone,* "banker," and Black Hand. Among our South Italians this spirit shines out only when it is a question of shielding from American justice some cut-throat of their own race. The Greek is full of tricks to skin the greenhorn. A grocer will warn fellow-countrymen who have just established themselves in his town that he will have the police on them for violating municipal ordinances unless they buy groceries from him. The Greek mill-hand sells the greenhorn a job, and takes his chances on the foreman giving the man work. A Greek who knows a little English will get a Greek peddler arrested in order that he may get the interpreter's fee. The Greek boot-black who has freed himself from his serfdom, instead of showing up the system, starts a place of his own, and exploits his help as mercilessly as ever he was exploited.

The Northerners seem to surpass the southern Europeans in innate ethical endowment. Comparison of their behavior in marine disasters shows that discipline, sense of duty, presence of mind, and consideration for the weak are much more characteristic of northern Europeans. The southern Europeans, on the other hand, are apt, in their terror, to forget discipline, duty, women, children, everything but the saving of their own lives. In shipwreck it is the exceptional Northerner who forgets his duty, and the exceptional Southerner who is bound by it. The suicide of Italian officers on board the doomed *Monte Tabor,* the *Notice,* and the *Ajace,* is in striking contrast to the sense of responsibility of the Northerners in charge of the *Cimbria,* the *Geiser,* the *Strathcona,* and the *City of Paris.* . . . Among all nationalities the Americans bear the palm for coolness, orderly saving of life, and consideration for the weak in shipwreck, but they will lose these traits in proportion as they absorb excitable blood from southern Europe.

Natural Ability

The performance of the foreign-born and their children after they have had access to American opportunities justifies the democrat's faith that latent capacity exists all through the humbler strata of society. On the other hand, it also confirms the aristocrat's insistence that social ranks correspond somewhat with the grades of natural ability existing within a people. The descendants of Europe's lowly are to be met in all the upper levels of American society, *but not so frequently* as the descendants of those who were high or rising in the land they left. . . .

Many things have decided whether Europe should send America cream or skimmed milk. Religious or political oppression is apt to drive out the better elements. Racial oppression cannot be evaded by mere conformity; hence the emigration it sets up is apt to be representative. An unsubdued and perilous land attracts the more bold and enterprising. The seekers of homesteads include men of better stuff than the job-seekers attracted by high wages for unskilled labor. Only economic motives set in motion the sub-common people, but even in an economic emigration the early stage brings more people of initiative than the later. The deeper, straighter, and smoother the channels of migration, the lower the stratum they can tap. . . .

Oppression is now out of fashion over most of Europe, and our public lands are gone. Economic motives more and more bring us immigrants, and such motives will not uproot the educated, the propertied, the established, the well connected. The children of success are not migrating, which means that we get few scions from families of proved capacity. Europe retains most of her brains, but sends multitudes of the common and the sub-common. There is little sign of an intellectual element among the Magyars, Russians, South Slavs, Italians, Greeks, or Portuguese. This does not hold, however, for currents created by race discrimination or oppression. The Armenian, Syrian, Finnish, and Russo-Hebrew streams seem *representative,* and the first wave of Hebrews out of Russia in the eighties was superior. The Slovaks, German Poles, Lithuanians, Esthonians, and other restive subject groups probably send us a fair sample of their quality.

Race Suicide

The fewer brains they have to contribute, the lower the place immigrants take among us, and the lower the place they take, the faster they multiply. In 1890, in our cities, a thousand foreign-born women could show 565 children under five years of age to 309 children shown by a thousand native women. By 1900 the contribution of the foreign women had risen to 612, and that of the American women had declined to 296. From such figures some argue that the "sterile" Americans need the immigrants in order to supply population. It would be nearer the truth to argue that the competition of low-standard immigrants is the root cause of the mysterious "sterility" of Americans. Certainly their record down to 1830 proved the Americans to be as fertile a race as ever lived, and the decline in their fertility coincides in time and in locality with the advent of the immigrant flood. In the words of General Francis A. Walker, "Not only did the decline in the native element, as a whole, take place in singular correspondence with the excess of foreign arrivals, but it occurred chiefly in just those regions" — "in those States and in the very counties," he says elsewhere — "to which those newcomers most frequently resorted."

"Our immigrants," says a superintendent of charities, "often come here with no standards whatever. In their homes you find no sheets on the bed, no slips on the pillows, no cloth on the table, and no towels save old rags. Even in the mud-floor cabins of the poorest negroes of the South you find sheets, pillow-slips, and towels, for by serving and associating with the whites the blacks have gained standards. But many of the foreigners have no means of getting our home standards after they are here. No one shows them. They can't see into American homes, and no Americans associate with them." The Americans or Americanized immigrants who are obliged to live on wages fixed by the competition of such people must cut somewhere. If they do not choose to "live in a pig-pen and bring up one's children like pigs," they will save their standards by keeping down the size of the family. Because he keeps them clean, neatly dressed, and in school, children are an economic burden to the American. Because he lets them run wild and puts them to work early, children are an asset to the low-standard foreigner.

When a more-developed element is obliged to compete on the same economic plane with a less-developed element, the standards of cleanliness or decency or education cherished by the advanced element act on it like a slow poison. William does not leave as many children as 'Tonio, because he will not huddle his family into one room, eat macaroni off a bare board, work his wife barefoot in the field, and keep his children weeding onions instead of at school. Even moral standards may act as poison. Once the women raisin-packers at Fresno, California, were American-born. Now the American women are leaving because of the low moral tone that prevails in the working force by reason of the coming in of foreigners with lax notions of propriety. The coarseness of speech and behavior among the packers is giving raisin-packing a bad name, so that American women are quitting the work and taking the next best job. Thus the very decency of the native is a handicap to success and to fecundity.

As they feel the difficulty of keeping up their standards on a Slav wage, the older immigrant stocks are becoming sterile, even as the old Americans became sterile. In a generation complaint will be heard that the Slavs, too, are shirking big families, and that we must admit prolific Persians, Uzbegs, and Bokhariots, in order to offset the fatal sterility that attacks every race after it has become Americanized. Very truly says a distinguished economist, in praise of immigration: "The cost of rearing children in the United States is rapidly rising. In many, perhaps in most cases, it is simpler, speedier, and cheaper to import labor than to breed it." In like vein it is said that "a healthy immigrant lad of eighteen is a clear $1000 added to the national wealth of the United States."

Just so. "The Roman world was laughing when it died." Any couple or any people that does not feel it has anything to transmit to its children may well reason in such fashion. A couple may reflect, "It is simpler, speedier, and cheaper for us to adopt orphans than to produce children of our own." A nation may reason, "Why burden ourselves with the rearing of children? Let them perish unborn in the womb of time. The immigrants will keep up the population." A people that has no more respect for its ancestors and no more pride of race than this deserves the extinction that surely awaits it.

Study Guide

1. The essential thrust of this selection is twofold:
   (a) to demonstrate the differences between the "old" and the "new" immigration; and
   (b) to use this as the basis for urging upon the American people a policy of immigration restriction.

   The arguments offered by Ross are:
   (a) demographic (pp. 325–326, 331–332);
   (b) genetic and physiological (pp. 326–329);
   (c) moral (pp. 329–331);
   (d) historical (p. 331); and
   (e) socioeconomic (pp. 332–333).

Begin by summarizing, in a sentence or two, his opening demographic argument concerning the composition of the American people.

2. In the genetic and physiological arguments against the "new" immigration, Ross appears to equate the physical characteristics of the immigrants and their social behavior. How much scientific validity is there in that kind of assumption? Is there a scientific consensus on that subject today?

3. Ross's distinction between the morality of the "old" and the "new" immigration provides us with the essential ingredients for what historians call the "Anglo-Saxon myth." Draw up a list of the characteristics Ross ascribes to each of these categories. Can you relate the Anglo-Saxon bias presented in this essay to the ethnic composition of the American people in the centuries before the Civil War? If so, how?

4. From his historical analysis of the evolution of European society, Ross draws some conclusions concerning the quality of the migrants coming to the United States. Explain and assess.

5. Similarly, summarize his "race suicide" concept — a demographic argument — and the socioeconomic argument with which he closes his essay. Do you consider these to be more valid than his arguments based upon genetics and physiology? If so, why; if not, why not?

6. In retrospect: can you see how easy it would be for Ross and other progressives to translate these arguments against the "new" immigration into a belief in the inherent inferiority of American blacks? What specific arguments listed in the first question of the Study Guide are still advanced by those who advocate the inferiority of blacks and the need to segregate blacks from whites today?

Randolph Bourne
A PLURALISTIC NATION

❧{1916}❧ FROM 1815 until 1924, when Congress put permanent curbs on immigration into the United States, thirty million immigrants came to our shores. Both the sources and the volume of immigration were different before and after the turn of the century. The "old" immigrants were largely English, Scotch-Irish, Irish, and German. In the 1890's, the number of immigrants increased more than threefold and the main source of immigration shifted to Southern and Eastern Europe, bringing millions of Italians, Poles, Russo-Polish Jews, and other minorities fleeing from the Austro-Hungarian and Russian empires.

As a consequence of this "new" immigration, ethnic enclaves sprang up in the nation's cities, urban ghettoes in which the newcomers established the religious, cultural, and social institutions that would shield them from an alien environment and at the same time ease their ultimate integration into American society. Native-born Americans were of a divided mind concerning the differences between the "new" immigrants and their own way of life. Most Americans — even those who called themselves progressives — shared the views of the French immigrant Crèvecoeur who noted in 1782: "He is an American, who, leaving behind him all his ancient prejudices and manners, receives new ones from the new mode of life he has embraced, the new government he obeys, and the new rank he holds. . . . Here individuals of all races are melted into a new breed of men." The "melting-pot" theory of American society developed in the Progressive Era was a reformulation of this eighteenth-century concept.

A minority of progressives, advocates of the notion of "cultural pluralism," felt otherwise, seeing the United States as a mosaic of cultures and peoples, not a "melting pot." They urged not the hasty and often superficial Americanization of the immigrants but the preservation of their distinctive folkways. Two progressives who advocated the notion of cultural pluralism were Horace Kallen, a Harvard-trained philosopher and disciple of William James, and Randolph S. Bourne, an advocate of progressive education in the tradition of John Dewey. Kallen compared the American people to a symphony orchestra, with each ethnic group providing its "specific *timbre* and tonality." For Kallen and for Bourne, a monolithic, and perforce a purely Anglo-Saxon, culture would be both socially tyrannical and culturally sterile. The advocates of cultural pluralism before and during World War I saw the multiplicity of cultures within the United States as a singular opportunity to create what Bourne, in the selection that follows, called a "cosmopolitan" culture, rather than as a threat to the stability of American society. In "Trans-National America," the brilliant yet tragic Bourne — a deformed hunchback for most of his all-too-brief life as a result of a fall in infancy — extols the virtues of a culture and a society that transcends the boundaries of self-centered nationalism.

TRANS-NATIONAL AMERICA

No REVERBERATORY effect of the great war has caused American public opinion more solicitude than the failure of the "melting-pot." The discovery of diverse nationalistic feelings among our great alien population has come to most people as an intense shock. It has brought out the unpleasant inconsistencies of our traditional beliefs. We have had to watch hard-hearted old Brahmins virtuously indignant at the spectacle of the immigrant refusing to be melted, while they jeer at patriots like Mary Antin who write about "our forefathers." We have had to listen to publicists who express themselves as stunned by the evidence of vigorous nationalistic and cultural movements in this country among Germans, Scandinavians, Bohemians, and Poles, while in the same breath they insist that the alien shall be forcibly assimilated to that Anglo-Saxon tradition which they unquestioningly label "American."

As the unpleasant truth has come upon us that assimilation in this country was proceeding on lines very different from those we had marked out for it, we found ourselves inclined to blame those who were thwarting our prophecies. The truth became culpable. We blamed the war, we blamed the Germans. And then we discovered with a moral shock that these movements had been making great headway before the war even began. We found that the tendency, reprehensible and paradoxical as it might be, has been for the national clusters of immigrants, as they became more and more firmly established and more and more prosperous, to cultivate more and more assiduously the literatures and cultural traditions of their homelands. Assimilation, in other words, instead of washing out the memories of Europe, made them more and more intensely real. Just as these clusters became more and more objectively American, did they become more and more German or Scandinavian or Bohemian or Polish.

To face the fact that our aliens are already strong enough to take a share in the direction of their own destiny, and that the strong cultural movements represented by the foreign press, schools, and colonies are a challenge to our facile attempts, is not, however, to admit the failure of Americanization. It is not to fear the failure of democracy. It is rather to urge us to an investigation of what Americanism may rightly mean. It is to ask ourselves whether our ideal has been broad or narrow — whether perhaps the time has not come to assert a higher ideal than the "melting-pot." Surely we cannot be certain of our spiritual democracy when, claiming to melt the nations within us to a comprehension of our free and democratic institutions, we fly into panic at the first sign of their own will and tendency. We act as if we wanted Americanization to take place only on our own terms, and not by the consent of the governed. All our elaborate machinery of settlement and school and union, of social and political naturalization, however, will move with friction just in so far as it neglects to take into account this strong and virile insistence that America shall be what the immigrant will have a hand in making it, and not what a ruling class, descendant of those British stocks which were the first permanent immigrants, decide that America shall be made. This is the condition which confronts us, and which demands a clear and general readjustment of our attitude and our ideal. . . .

I

We are all foreign-born or the descendants of foreign-born, and if distinctions are to be made between us they should rightly be on some other ground than indigenousness. The early colonists came over with motives no less colonial than the later. They did not come to be assimilated in an American melting-pot. They did not come to adopt the culture of the American Indian. They had not the smallest intention of "giving themselves without reservation" to the new country. They came to get freedom to live as they wanted to. They came to escape from the stifling air and chaos of the old world; they came to make their fortune in a new land. They invented no new social framework. Rather they brought over bodily the old ways to which they had been accustomed. Tightly concentrated on a hostile frontier, they were conservative beyond belief. Their pioneer daring was reserved for the objective conquest of material resources. In their folkways, in their social and political institutions, they were, like every colonial people, slavishly imitative of the mother-country. So that, in spite of the "Revolution," our whole legal and political system remained more English than the English, petrified and unchanging, while in England law developed to meet the needs of the changing times.

It is just this English-American conservatism that has been our chief obstacle to social advance. We have needed the new peoples — the order of the German and Scandinavian, the turbulence of the Slav and Hun — to save us from our own stagnation. I do not mean that the illiterate Slav is now the equal of the New Englander of pure descent. He is raw material to be educated, not into a New Englander, but into a socialized American along such lines as those thirty nationalities are being educated in the amazing schools of Gary. I do not believe that this process is to be one of decades of evolution. The spectacle of Japan's sudden jump from mediævalism to post-modernism should have destroyed that superstition. We are not dealing with individuals who are to "evolve." We are dealing with their children, who, with that education we are about to have, will start level with all of us. Let us cease to think of ideals like democracy as magical qualities inherent in certain peoples. Let us speak, not of inferior races, but of inferior civilizations. We are all to educate and to be educated. These peoples in America are in a common enterprise. It is not what we are now that concerns us, but what this plastic next generation may become in the light of a new cosmopolitan ideal.

We are not dealing with static factors, but with fluid and dynamic generations. To contrast the older and the newer immigrants and see the one class as democratically motivated by love of liberty, and the other by mere money-getting, is not to illuminate the future. To think of earlier nationalities as culturally assimilated to America, while we picture the later as a sodden and resistive mass, makes only for bitterness and misunderstanding. There may be a difference between these earlier and these later stocks, but it lies neither in motive for coming nor in strength of cultural allegiance to the homeland. The truth is that no more tenacious cultural allegiance to the mother country has been shown by any alien nation than by the ruling class of Anglo-Saxon descendants in these American States. English snobberies, English religion, English literary styles, English literary reverences and canons, English ethics, English superiorities, have been the cultural food that we have drunk in from our mothers' breasts. . . . The unpopular and dreaded German-American of the present day is a beginning amateur in comparison with those foolish Anglophiles of Boston and New York and Philadelphia whose reversion to cultural type sees uncritically in England's cause the cause of Civilization, and, under the guise of ethical independence of thought, carries along European traditions which are no more "American" than the German categories themselves. . . .

The non-English American can scarcely be blamed if he sometimes thinks of the Anglo-Saxon predominance in America as little more than a predominance of priority. The Anglo-Saxon was merely the first immigrant, the first to found a colony. He has never really ceased to be the descendant of immigrants, nor has he ever succeeded in transforming that colony into a real nation, with a tenacious, richly woven fabric of native culture. Colonials from the other nations have come and settled down beside him. They found no definite native culture which should startle them out of their colonialism, and consequently they looked back to their mother-country, as the earlier Anglo-Saxon immigrant was looking back to his. What has been offered the newcomer has been the chance to learn English, to become a citizen, to salute the flag. And those elements of our ruling classes who are responsible for the public schools, the settlements, all the organizations for amelioration in the cities, have every reason to be proud of the care and labor which they have devoted to absorbing the immigrant. His opportunities the immigrant has taken to gladly, with almost a pathetic eagerness to make his way in the new land without friction or disturbance. The common language has made not only for the necessary communication, but for all the amenities of life.

If freedom means the right to do pretty much as one pleases, so long as one does not interfere with others, the immigrant has found freedom, and the ruling element has been singularly liberal in its treatment of the invading hordes. But if freedom means a democratic coöperation in determining the ideals and purposes and industrial and social institutions of a country, then the immigrant has not been free, and the Anglo-Saxon element is guilty of just what every dominant race is guilty of in every European country: the imposition of its own culture upon the minority peoples. The fact that this imposition has been so mild and, indeed, semi-conscious does not alter its quality. And the war has brought out just the degree to which that purpose of "Americanizing," that is, "Anglo-Saxonizing," the immigrant has failed.

For the Anglo-Saxon now in his bitterness to turn upon the other peoples, talk about their "arrogance," scold them for not being melted in a pot which never existed, is to betray the unconscious purpose which lay at the bottom of his heart. It betrays too the possession of a racial jealousy similar to that of which he is now accusing the so-called "hyphenates." Let the Anglo-Saxon be proud enough of the heroic toil and heroic sacrifices which moulded the nation. But let him ask himself, if he had had to depend on the English descendants, where he would have been living to-day. To those of us who see in the exploitation of unskilled labor the strident red *leit-motif* of our civilization, the settling of the country presents a great social drama as the waves of immigration broke over it.

Let the Anglo-Saxon ask himself where he would have been if these races had not come? Let those who feel the inferiority of the non-Anglo-Saxon immigrant contemplate that region of the States which has remained the most distinctively "American," the South. Let him ask himself whether he would really like to see the foreign hordes Americanized into such an Americanization. Let him ask himself how superior this native civilization is to the great "alien" states of Wisconsin and Minnesota, where Scandinavians, Poles, and Germans have self-consciously labored to preserve their traditional culture, while being outwardly and satisfactorily American. Let him ask himself how much more wisdom, intelligence, industry and social leadership has come out of these alien states than out of all the truly American ones. The South, in fact, while this vast Northern development has gone on, still remains an English colony, stagnant and complacent, having progressed culturally scarcely beyond the early Victorian era. It is culturally sterile because it has had no advantage of cross-fertilization like the Northern states. What has happened in states such as Wisconsin and Minnesota is that strong foreign cultures have struck root in a new and fertile soil. America has meant liberation, and German and Scandinavian political ideas and social energies have expanded to a new potency. The process has not been at all the fancied "assimilation" of the Scandinavian or Teuton. Rather has it been a process of their assimilation of us — I speak as an Anglo-Saxon. The foreign cultures have not been melted down or run together, made into some homogeneous Americanism, but have remained distinct but coöperating to the greater glory and benefit, not only of themselves but of all the native "Americanism" around them.

What we emphatically do not want is that these distinctive qualities should be washed out into a tasteless, colorless fluid of uniformity. Already we have far too much of this insipidity, — masses of people who are cultural half-breeds, neither assimilated Anglo-Saxons nor nationals of another culture. Each national colony in this country seems to retain in its foreign press, its vernacular literature, its schools, its intellectual and patriotic leaders, a central cultural nucleus. From this nucleus the colony extends out by imperceptible gradations to a fringe where national characteristics are all but lost. Our cities are filled with these half-breeds who retain their foreign names but have lost the foreign savor. This does not mean that they have actually been changed into New Englanders or Middle Westerners. It does not mean that they have been really Americanized. It means that, letting slip from them whatever native culture they had, they have substituted for it only the most rudimentary American — the American culture of the cheap newspaper, the "movies," the popular song, the ubiquitous automobile. The unthinking who survey this class call them assimilated, Americanized. The great American public school has done its work. With these people our institutions are safe. We may thrill with dread at the aggressive hyphenate, but this tame flabbiness is accepted as Americanization. The same moulders of opinion whose ideal is to melt the different races into Anglo-Saxon gold hail this poor product as the satisfying result of their alchemy.

Yet a truer cultural sense would have told us that it is not the self-conscious cultural nuclei that sap at our American life, but these fringes. It is not the Jew who sticks proudly to the faith of his fathers and boasts of that venerable culture of his who is dangerous to America, but the Jew who has lost the Jewish fire and become a mere elementary, grasping animal. It is not the Bohemian who supports the Bohemian schools in Chicago whose influence is sinister, but the Bohemian who has made money and has got into ward politics. Just so surely as we tend to disintegrate these nuclei of nationalistic culture do we tend to create hordes of men and women without a spiritual country, cultural outlaws, without taste, without standards but those of the mob. We sentence them to live on the most rudimentary planes of American life. The influences at the centre of the nuclei are centripetal. They make for the intelligence and the social values which mean an enhancement of life. And just because the foreign-born retains this expressiveness is he likely to be a better citizen of the American community. The influences at the fringe, however, are centrifugal, anarchical. They make for detached fragments of peoples. Those who came to find liberty achieve only license. They become the flotsam and jetsam of American life, the downward undertow of our civilization with its leering cheapness and falseness of taste and spiritual outlook, the absence of mind and sincere feeling which we see in our slovenly towns, our vapid moving pictures, our popular novels, and in the vacuous faces of the crowds on the city street. . . .

The war has shown us that . . . no intense nationalism of the European plan can be ours. But do we not begin to see a new and more adventurous ideal? Do we not see how the national colonies in America, deriving power from the deep cultural heart of Europe and yet living here in mutual toleration, freed from the age-long tangles of races, creeds, and dynasties, may work out a federated ideal? America is transplanted Europe, but a Europe that has not been disintegrated and scattered in the transplanting as in some Dispersion. Its colonies live here inextricably mingled, yet not homogeneous. They merge but they do not fuse.

America is a unique sociological fabric, and it bespeaks poverty of imagination not to be thrilled at the incalculable potentialities of so novel a union of men. To seek no other goal than the weary old nationalism, — belligerent, exclusive, inbreeding, the poison of which we are witnessing now in Europe, — is to make patriotism a hollow sham, and to declare that, in spite of our boastings, America must ever be a follower and not a leader of nations. . . .

III

The failure of the melting-pot, far from closing the great American democratic experiment, means that it has only just begun. Whatever American nationalism turns out to be, we see already that it will have a color richer and more exciting than our ideal has hitherto encompassed. In a world which has dreamed of internationalism, we find that we have all unawares been building up the first international nation. The voices which have cried for a tight and jealous nationalism of the European pattern are failing. From that ideal, however valiantly and disinterestedly it has been set for us, time and tendency have moved us further and further away. What we have achieved has been rather a cosmopolitan federation of national colonies, of foreign cultures, from which the sting of devastating competition has been removed. America is already the world-federation in miniature, the continent where for the first time in history has been achieved that miracle of hope, the peaceful living side by side, with character substantially preserved, of the most heterogeneous peoples under the sun. Nowhere else has such contiguity been anything but the breeder of misery. Here, notwithstanding our tragic failures of adjustment, the outlines are already too clear not to give us a new vision and a new orientation of the American mind in the world.

It is for the American of the younger generation to accept this cosmopolitanism, and carry it along with self-conscious and fruitful purpose. In his colleges, he is already getting, with the study of modern history and politics, the modern literatures, economic geography, the privilege of a cosmopolitan outlook such as the people of no other nation to-day in Europe can possibly secure. If he is still a colonial, he is no longer the colonial of one partial culture, but of many. He is a colonial of the world. Colonialism has grown into cosmopolitanism, and his motherland is no one nation, but all who have anything life-enhancing to offer to the spirit. That vague sympathy which the France of ten years ago was feeling for the world — a sympathy which was drowned in the terrible reality of war — may be the modern American's, and that in a positive and aggressive sense. If the American is parochial, it is in sheer wantonness or cowardice. His provincialism is the measure of his fear of bogies or the defect of his imagination.

Indeed, it is not uncommon for the eager Anglo-Saxon who goes to a vivid American university to-day to find his true friends not among his own race but among the acclimatized German or Austrian, the acclimatized Jew, the acclimatized Scandinavian or Italian. In them he finds the cosmopolitan note. In these youths, foreign-born or the children of foreign-born parents, he is likely to find many of his old inbred morbid problems washed away. These friends are oblivious to the repressions of that tight little society in which he so provincially grew up. He has a pleasurable sense of liberation from the stale and familiar attitudes of those whose ingrowing culture has scarcely created anything vital for his America of to-day. He breathes a larger air. In his new enthusiasms for continental literature, for unplumbed Russian depths, for French clarity of thought, for Teuton philosophies of power, he feels himself citizen of a larger world. He may be absurdly superficial, his outward-reaching wonder may ignore all the stiller and homelier virtues of his Anglo-Saxon home, but he has at least found the clue to that international mind which will be essential to all men and women of good-will if they are ever to save this Western world of ours from suicide. His new friends have gone through a similar evolution. America has burned most of the baser metal also from them. Meeting now with this common American background, all of them may yet retain that distinctiveness of their native cultures and their national spiritual slants. They are more valuable and interesting to each other for being different, yet that difference could not be creative were it not for this new cosmopolitan outlook which America has given them and which they all equally possess.

A college where such a spirit is possible even to the smallest degree, has within itself already the seeds of this international intellectual world of the future. It suggests that the contribution of America will be an intellectual internationalism which goes far beyond the mere exchange of scientific ideas and discoveries and the cold recording of facts. It will be an intellectual sympathy which is not satisfied until it has got at the heart of the different cultural expressions, and felt as they feel. It may have immense preferences, but it will make understanding and not indignation its end. Such a sympathy will unite and not divide.

Against the thinly disguised panic which calls itself "patriotism" and the thinly disguised militarism which calls itself "preparedness" the cosmopolitan ideal is set. This does not mean that those who hold it are for a policy of drift. They, too, long passionately for an integrated and disciplined America. But they do not want one which is integrated only for domestic economic exploitation of the workers or for predatory economic imperialism among the weaker peoples. They do not want one that is integrated by coercion or militarism, or for the truculent assertion of a mediæval code of honor and of doubtful rights. They believe that the most effective integration will be one which coördinates the diverse elements and turns them consciously toward working out together the place of America in the world-situation. They demand for integration a genuine integrity, a wholeness and soundness of enthusiasm and purpose which can only come when no national colony within our America feels that it is being discriminated against or that its cultural case is being prejudged. This strength of coöperation, this feeling that all who are here may have a hand in the destiny of America, will make for a finer spirit of integration than any narrow "Americanism" or forced chauvinism.

In this effort we may have to accept some form of that dual citizenship which meets with so much articulate horror among us. Dual citizenship we may have to recognize as the rudimentary form of that international citizenship to which, if our words mean anything, we aspire. We have assumed unquestioningly that mere participation in the political life of the United States must cut the new citizen off from all sympathy with his old allegiance. Anything but a bodily transfer of devotion from one sovereignty to another has been viewed as a sort of moral treason against the Republic. We have insisted that the immigrant whom we welcomed escaping from the very exclusive nationalism of his European home shall forthwith adopt a nationalism just as exclusive, just as narrow, and even less legitimate because it is founded on no warm traditions of his own. Yet a nation like France is said to permit a formal and legal dual citizenship even at the present time. Though a citizen of hers may pretend to cast off his allegiance in favor of some other sovereignty, he is still subject to her laws when he returns. Once a citizen, always a citizen, no matter how many new citizenships he may embrace. And such a dual citizenship seems to us sound and right. For it recognizes that, although the Frenchman may accept the formal institutional framework of his new country and indeed become intensely loyal to it, yet his Frenchness he will never lose. What makes up the fabric of his soul will always be of this Frenchness, so that unless he becomes utterly degenerate he will always to some degree dwell still in his native environment. . . .

Along with dual citizenship we shall have to accept, I think, that free and mobile passage of the immigrant between America and his native land again which now arouses so much prejudice among us. We shall have to accept the immigrant's return for the same reason that we consider justified our own flitting about the earth. To stigmatize the alien who works in America for a few years and returns to his own land, only perhaps to seek American fortune again, is to think in narrow nationalistic terms. It is to ignore the cosmopolitan significance of this migration. It is to ignore the fact that the returning immigrant is often a missionary to an inferior civilization.

This migratory habit has been especially common with the unskilled laborers who have been pouring into the United States in the last dozen years from every country in southeastern Europe. Many of them return to spend their earnings in their own country or to serve their country in war. But they return with an entirely new critical outlook, and a sense of the superiority of American organization to the primitive living around them. This continued passage to and fro has already raised the material standard of living in many regions of these backward countries. For these regions are thus endowed with exactly what they need, the capital for the exploitation of their natural resources, and the spirit of enterprise. America is thus educating these laggard peoples from the very bottom of society up, awaking vast masses to a new-born hope for the future. In the migratory Greek, therefore, we have not the parasitic alien, the doubtful American asset, but a symbol of that cosmopolitan interchange which is coming, in spite of all war and national exclusiveness.

Only America, by reason of the unique liberty of opportunity and traditional isolation for which she seems to stand, can lead in this cosmopolitan enterprise. Only the American — and in this category I include the migratory alien who has lived with us and caught the pioneer spirit and a sense of new social vistas — has the chance to become that citizen of the world. America is coming to be, not a nationality but a transnationality, a weaving back and forth, with the other lands, of many threads of all sizes and colors. Any movement which attempts to thwart this weaving, or to dye the fabric any one color, or disentangle the threads of the strands, is false to this cosmopolitan vision. I do not mean that we shall necessarily glut ourselves with the raw product of humanity. It would be folly to absorb the nations faster than we could weave them. We have no duty either to admit or reject. It is purely a question of expediency. What concerns us is the fact that the strands are here. We must have a policy and an ideal for an actual situation. Our question is, What shall we do with our America? How are we likely to get the more creative America — by confining our imaginations to the ideal of the melting-pot, or broadening them to some such cosmopolitan conception as I have been vaguely sketching?

The war has shown America to be unable, though isolated geographically and politically from a European world-situation, to remain aloof and irresponsible. She is a wandering star in a sky dominated by two colossal constellations of states. Can she not work out some position of her own, some life of being in, yet not quite of, this seething and embroiled European world? This is her only hope and promise. A trans-nationality of all the nations, it is spiritually impossible for her to pass into the orbit of any one. It will be folly to hurry herself into a premature and sentimental nationalism, or to emulate Europe and play fast and loose with the forces that drag into war. No Americanization will fulfill this vision which does not recognize the uniqueness of this trans-nationalism of ours. The Anglo-Saxon attempt to fuse will only create enmity and distrust. The crusade against "hyphenates" will only inflame the partial patriotism of trans-nationals, and cause them to assert their European traditions in strident and unwholesome ways. But the attempt to weave a wholly novel international nation out of our chaotic America will liberate and harmonize the creative power of all these peoples and give them the new spiritual citizenship, as so many individuals have already been given, of a world.

Is it a wild hope that the undertow of opposition to metaphysics in international relations, opposition to militarism, is less a cowardly provincialism than a groping for this higher cosmopolitan ideal? One can understand the irritated restlessness with which our proud pro-British colonists contemplate a heroic conflict across the seas in which they have no part. It was inevitable that our necessary inaction should evolve in their minds into the bogey of national shame and dishonor. But let us be careful about accepting their sensitiveness as final arbiter. Let us look at our reluctance rather as the first crude beginnings of assertion on the part of certain strands in our nationality that they have a right to a voice in the construction of the American ideal. Let us face realistically the America we have around us. Let us work with the forces that are at work. Let us make something of this trans-national spirit instead of out-lawing it. Already we are living this cosmopolitan America. What we need is everywhere a vivid consciousness of the new ideal. Deliberate headway must be made against the survivals of the melting-pot ideal for the promise of American life.

We cannot Americanize America worthily by sentimentalizing and moralizing history. When the best schools are expressly renouncing the questionable duty of teaching patriotism by means of history, it is not the time to force shibboleth upon the immigrant. This form of Americanization has been heard because it appealed to the vestiges of our sentimentalized and moralized patriotism. This has so far held the field as the expression of the new American's new devotion. The inflections of other voices have been drowned. They must be heard. We must see if the lesson of the war has not been for hundreds of these later Americans a vivid realization of their trans-nationality, a new consciousness of what America meant to them as a citizenship in the world. It is the vague historic idealisms which have provided the fuel for the European flame. Our American ideal can make no progress until we do away with this romantic gilding of the past.

All our idealisms must be those of future social goals in which all can participate, the good life of personality lived in the environment of the Beloved Community. No mere doubtful triumphs of the past, which redound to the glory of only one of our trans-nationalities, can satisfy us. It must be a future America, on which all can unite, which pulls us irresistibly toward it, as we understand each other more warmly.

To make real this striving amid dangers and apathies is work for a younger *intelligentsia* of America. Here is an enterprise of integration into which we can all pour ourselves, of a spiritual welding which should make us, if the final menace ever came, not weaker, but infinitely strong.

Study Guide

1. Bourne opens his essay by advancing two ideas:
   (a) that the war in Europe has exacerbated ethnic divisions in the United States; and
   (b) that the process of acculturation has intensified these divisions and loyalties.

   Summarize his reasoning on both these points.

2. Bourne then proceeds to develop his view of American history in order to support his pluralistic concept of American society and culture (pp. 336–341). You can follow Bourne's reasoning by defining the following:

   (a) the role and importance Bourne assigns to the Anglo-Saxon colonists and their culture;

   (b) the distinctions others make between the "old" and the "new" immigration;

   (c) Bourne's view of half-acculturated immigrants; and

   (d) his idea of the singular character of American society as compared to Europe.

3. Bourne's closing argument concerns the future of the American people — a passionate plea for an American civilization that will transcend the narrowness of the political state or geographical boundaries. You can summarize his vision of a "trans-national America" by defining Bourne's use of the following words:

   (a) "cosmopolitanism" (pp. 341–342);

   (b) "intellectual internationalism" (p. 343);

   (c) "dual citizenship" (p. 343); and

   (d) "trans-nationality" (p. 345), a reference to the title of his essay.

4. This selection by Bourne and the one by Edward A. Ross (pp. 325–333) demonstrate with great clarity the opposition of views between the two wings of the progressive movement over the future character of American society and culture. The range of differences between these two men will emerge if you define their positions on the following:

   (a) the United States as a pluralistic society and as a mosaic of cultures;

   (b) the role of the Anglo-Saxon in the history of the American nation and his future role;

   (c) the relative importance of heredity and environment in determining the social behavior of individuals and groups; and

   (d) internationalism as an ideal for the single citizen and for the American people as a whole.

5. In retrospect: consider the social and cultural history of the United States, particularly since the 1960's, with the emergence of racial pride among American blacks, the revival of ethnic folkways among the children and grandchildren of the "new" immigration, and the general resurgence of interest by other Americans in their historical and genealogical roots. Considering these developments, would you say that the United States has remained an Anglo-Saxon nation, as Ross obviously wanted it to be, a "trans-national" nation, as Bourne advocated, or a "melting-pot," as still other progressives suggested? Or consider this possibility: American society represents an amalgam of all three of these views, depending upon what aspect of America we are examining. Explore.

V. The Great Crusade and After

Woodrow Wilson

JUSTICE IN WAR AND IN PEACE

❧{*1917, 1918*}❧ DESPITE the fact that the powers of the President of the United States are carefully spelled out in the Constitution and therefore equally available to every man who holds the office, the way those powers are employed by the individual resident of the White House has a great deal to do with their practical force. "Weak" Presidents have used their authority only partially, they have employed their perquisites gingerly and unimaginatively. "Strong" ones have used their power to the full; indeed, they have often expanded the area of their authority and influence greatly simply by applying seemingly minor rights in novel and startling ways.

One of the most ingenious of our "strong" Presidents in this respect was Woodrow Wilson (1856-1924), who greatly broadened the scope of his office in a number of clever ways. One of the most important of these was also one of the simplest. Instead of following the precedent established in Jefferson's day of sending messages to the Hill by courier to be droned out by a mere clerk, he began to come in person to the Capitol where the magic of his oratory would inspire Congressmen to follow his leadership. In the process, he soon discovered, he was also able better to attract the attention of the public at large, adding greatly to the impact of his words.

Two of the most important of these personally delivered messages follow. The first, his call for a declaration of war against Germany (1917), would obviously have had a great impact in any case. But Wilson's presence at the Capitol, the depth of his feelings after his long struggle with his conscience to decide what course to follow in the crisis, clearly increased the force of his words. As he was leaving the chamber of the House of Representatives after the speech, even his bitter enemy, Henry Cabot Lodge (1850-1924), came forward to shake his hand. "Mr. President," Lodge said, "you have expressed in the loftiest manner possible the sentiments of the American people." Actually, Wilson had done more than this. By carefully distinguishing between the Kaiser's government and the German people, he made it possible to fight all-out against that government and still preserve the concept of a final peace based on fairness and magnanimity rather than on national aggrandizement and revenge.

The second message announced Wilson's famous Fourteen Points (1918) on which the postwar world was to be constructed. The impact of this speech on idealists all over the world was very great—too great, as time was to prove. For by raising their hopes for the future unrealistically high, it made their disillusionment monumental when the actual treaty ending the war had been hammered into shape. Nevertheless, the speech remains one of the most influential documents of the twentieth century. Its influence upon the settlement of both world wars was tremendous.

MESSAGE TO CONGRESS

(April 2, 1917)

Gentlemen of the Congress:

I have called the Congress into extraordinary session because there are serious, very serious, choices of policy to be made, and made immediately, which it was neither right nor constitutionally permissible that I should assume the responsibility of making.

On the third of February last I officially laid before you the extraordinary announcement of the Imperial German Government that on and after the first day of February it was its purpose to put aside all restraints of law or of humanity and use its submarines to sink every vessel that sought to approach either the ports of Great Britain and Ireland or the western coasts of Europe or any of the ports controlled by the enemies of Germany within the Mediterranean. That had seemed to be the object of the German submarine warfare earlier in the war, but since April of last year the Imperial Government had somewhat restrained the commanders of its undersea craft in conformity with its promise then given to us that passenger boats should not be sunk and that due warning would be given to all other vessels which its submarines might seek to destroy, when no resistance was offered or escape attempted, and care taken that their crews were given at least a fair chance to save their lives in their open boats. The precautions taken were meagre and haphazard enough, as was proved in distressing instance after instance in the progress of the cruel and unmanly business, but a certain degree of restraint was observed. The new policy has swept every restriction aside. Vessels of every kind, whatever their flag, their character, their cargo, their destination, their errand, have been ruthlessly sent to the bottom without warning and without thought of help or mercy for those on board, the vessels of friendly neutrals along with those of belligerents. Even hospital ships and ships carrying relief to the sorely bereaved and stricken people of Belgium, though the latter were provided with safe conduct through the proscribed areas by the German Government itself and were distinguished by unmistakable marks of identity, have been sunk with the same reckless lack of compassion or of principle.

I was for a little while unable to believe that such things would in fact be done by any government that had hitherto subscribed to the humane practices of civilized nations. International law had its origin in the attempt to set up some law which would be respected and observed upon the seas, where no nation had right of dominion and where lay the free highways of the world. By painful stage after stage has that law been built up, with meagre enough results, indeed, after all was accomplished that could be accomplished, but always with a clear view, at least, of what the heart and conscience of mankind demanded. This minimum of right the German Government has swept aside under the plea of retaliation and necessity and because it had no weapons which it could use at sea except these which it is impossible to employ as it is employing them without throwing to the winds all scruples of humanity or of respect for the understandings that were supposed to underlie the intercourse of the world. I am not now thinking of the loss of property involved, immense and serious as that is, but only of the wanton and wholesale destruction of the lives of non-combatants, men, women, and children, engaged in pursuits which have always, even in the darkest periods of modern history, been deemed innocent and legitimate. Property can be paid for; the lives of peaceful and innocent people cannot be. The present German submarine warfare against commerce is a warfare against mankind.

It is a war against all nations. American ships have been sunk, American lives taken, in ways which it has stirred us very deeply to learn of, but the ships and people of other neutral and friendly nations have been sunk and overwhelmed in the waters in the same way. There has been no discrimination. The challenge is to all mankind. Each nation must decide for itself how it will meet it. The choice we make for ourselves must be made with a moderation of counsel and a temperateness of judgment befitting our character and our motives as a nation. We must put excited feeling away. Our motive will not be revenge or the victorious assertion of the physical might of the nation, but only the vindication of right, of human right, of which we are only a single champion.

When I addressed the Congress on the twenty-sixth of February last I thought that it would suffice to assert our neutral rights with arms, our right to use the seas against unlawful interference, our right to keep our people safe against unlawful violence. But armed neutrality, it now appears, is impracticable. Because submarines are in effect outlaws when used as the German submarines have been used against merchant shipping, it is impossible to defend ships against their attacks as the law of nations has assumed that merchantmen would defend themselves against privateers or cruisers, visible craft giving chase upon the open sea. It is common prudence in such circumstances, grim necessity indeed, to endeavour to destroy them before they have shown their own intention. They must be dealt with upon sight, if dealt with at all. The German Government denies the right of neutrals to use arms at all within the areas of the sea which it has proscribed, even in the defense of rights which no modern publicist has ever before questioned their right to defend. The intimation is conveyed that the armed guards which we have placed on our merchant ships will be treated as beyond the pale of law and subject to be dealt with as pirates would be. Armed neutrality is ineffectual enough at best; in such circumstances and in the face of such pretensions it is worse than ineffectual; it is likely only to produce what it was meant to prevent; it is practically certain to draw us into the war without either the rights or the effectiveness of belligerents. There is one choice we cannot make, we are incapable of making: we will not choose the path of submission and suffer the most sacred rights of our nation and our people to be ignored or violated. The wrongs against which we now array ourselves are no common wrongs: they cut to the very roots of human life.

With a profound sense of the solemn and even tragical character of the step I am taking and of the grave responsibilities which it involves, but in unhesitating obedience to what I deem my constitutional duty, I advise that the Congress declare the recent course of the Imperial German Government to be in fact nothing less than war against the government and people of the United States; that it formally accept the status of belligerent which has thus been thrust upon it; and that it take immediate steps not only to put the country in a more thorough state of defense but also to exert all its power and employ all its resources to bring the Government of the German Empire to terms and end the war.

What this will involve is clear. It will involve the utmost practicable cooperation in counsel and action with the governments now at war with Germany, and, as incident to that, the extension to those governments of the most liberal financial credits, in order that our resources may so far as possible be added to theirs. It will involve the organization and mobilization of all the material resources of the country to supply the materials of war and serve the incidental needs of the nation in the most abundant and yet the most economical and efficient way possible. It will involve the immediate full equipment of the navy in all respects but particularly in supplying it with the best means of dealing with the enemy's submarines. It will involve the immediate addition to the armed forces of the United States already provided for by law in case of war at least five hundred thousand men, who should, in my opinion, be chosen upon the principle of universal liability to service, and also the authorization of subsequent additional increments of equal force so soon as they may be needed and can be handled in training. It will involve also, of course, the granting of adequate credits to the Government, sustained, I hope, so far as they can equitably be sustained by the present generation, by well conceived taxation.

I say sustained so far as may be equitable by taxation because it seems to me that it would be most unwise to base the credits which will now be necessary entirely on money borrowed. It is our duty, I most respectfully urge, to protect our people so far as we may against the very serious hardships and evils which would be likely to arise out of the inflation which would be produced by vast loans.

In carrying out the measures by which these things are to be accomplished we should keep constantly in mind the wisdom of interfering as little as possible in our own preparation and in the equipment of our own military forces with the duty, — for it will be a very practical duty, — of supplying the nations already at war with Germany with the materials which they can obtain only from us or by our assistance. They are in the field and we should help them in every way to be effective there.

I shall take the liberty of suggesting, through the several executive departments of the Government, for the consideration of your committees, measures for the accomplishment of the several objects I have mentioned. I hope that it will be your pleasure to deal with them as having been framed after very careful thought by the branch of the Government upon which the responsibility of conducting the war and safeguarding the nation will most directly fall.

While we do these things, these deeply momentous things, let us be very clear, and make very clear to all the world what our motives and our objects are. My own thought has not been driven from its habitual and normal course by the unhappy events of the last two months, and I do not believe that the thought of the nation has been altered or clouded by them. I have exactly the same things in mind now that I had in mind when I addressed the Senate on the twenty-second of January last; the same that I had in mind when I addressed the Congress on the third of February and on the twenty-sixth of February. Our object now, as then, is to vindicate the principles of peace and justice in the life of the world as against selfish and autocratic power and to set up amongst the really free and self-governed peoples of the world such a concert of purpose and of action as will henceforth ensure the observance of those principles. Neutrality is no longer feasible or desirable where the peace of the world is involved and the freedom of its peoples, and the menace to that peace and freedom lies in the existence of autocratic governments backed by organized force which is controlled wholly by their will, not by the will of their people. We have seen the last of neutrality in such circumstances. We are at the beginning of an age in which it will be insisted that the same standards of conduct and responsibility for wrong done shall be observed among nations and their governments that are observed among the individual citizens of civilized states.

We have no quarrel with the German people. We have no feeling toward them but one of sympathy and friendship. It was not upon their impulse that their government acted in entering this war. It was not with their previous knowledge or approval. It was a war determined upon as wars used to be determined upon in the old, unhappy days when peoples were nowhere consulted by their rulers and wars were provoked and waged in the interest of dynasties or of little groups of ambitious men who were accustomed to use their fellow men as pawns and tools. Self-governed nations do not fill their neighbour states with spies or set the course of intrigue to bring about some critical posture of affairs which will give them an opportunity to strike and make conquest. Such designs can be successfully worked out only under cover and where no one has the right to ask questions. Cunningly contrived plans of deception or aggression, carried, it may be, from generation to generation, can be worked out and kept from the light only within the privacy of courts or behind the carefully guarded confidences of a narrow and privileged class. They are happily impossible where public opinion commands and insists upon full information concerning all the nation's affairs.

A steadfast concert for peace can never be maintained except by a partnership of democratic nations. No autocratic government could be trusted to keep faith within it or observe its covenants. It must be a league of honour, a partnership of opinion. Intrigue would eat its vitals away; the plottings of inner circles who could plan what they would and render account to no one would be a corruption seated at its very heart. Only free peoples can hold their purpose and their honour steady to a common end and prefer the interests of mankind to any narrow interest of their own.

Does not every American feel that assurance has been added to our hope for the future peace of the world by the wonderful and heartening things that have been happening within the last few weeks in Russia? Russia was known by those who knew it best to have been always in fact democratic at heart, in all the vital habits of her thought, in all the intimate relationships of her people that spoke their natural instinct, their habitual attitude towards life. The autocracy that crowned the summit of her political structure, long as it had stood and terrible as was the reality of its power, was not in fact Russian in origin, character, or purpose; and now it has been shaken off and the great, generous Russian people have been added in all their naive majesty and might to the forces that are fighting for freedom in the world, for justice, and for peace. Here is a fit partner for a League of Honour.

One of the things that has served to convince us that the Prussian autocracy was not and could never be our friend is that from the very outset of the present war it has filled our unsuspecting communities and even our offices of government with spies and set criminal intrigues everywhere afoot against our national unity of counsel, our peace within and without, our industries and our commerce. Indeed it is now evident that its spies were here even before the war began; and it is unhappily not a matter of conjecture but a fact proved in our courts of justice that the intrigues which have more than once come perilously near to disturbing the peace and dislocating the industries of the country have been carried on at the instigation, with the support, and even under the personal direction of official agents of the Imperial Government accredited to the Government of the United States. Even in checking these things and trying to extirpate them we have sought to put the most generous interpretation possible upon them because we knew that their source lay, not in any hostile feeling or purpose of the German people towards us (who were, no doubt, as ignorant of them as we ourselves were), but only in the selfish designs of a Government that did what it pleased and told its people nothing. But they have played their part in serving to convince us at last that that Government entertains no real friendship for us and means to act against our peace and security at its convenience. That it means to stir up enemies against us at our very doors the intercepted note to the German Minister at Mexico City is eloquent evidence.

We are accepting this challenge of hostile purpose because we know that in such a government, following such methods, we can never have a friend; and that in the presence of its organized power, always lying in wait to accomplish we know not what purpose, there can be no assured security for the democratic governments of the world. We are now about to accept gauge of battle with this natural foe to liberty and shall, if necessary, spend the whole force of the nation to check and nullify its pretensions and its power. We are glad, now that we see the facts with no veil of false pretence about them, to fight thus for the ultimate peace of the world and for the liberation of its peoples, the German peoples included: for the rights of nations great and small and the privilege of men everywhere to choose their way of life and of obedience. The world must be made safe for democracy. Its peace must be planted upon the tested foundations of political liberty. We have no selfish ends to serve. We desire no conquest, no dominion. We seek no indemnities for ourselves, no material compensation for the sacrifices we shall freely make. We are but one of the champions of the rights of mankind. We shall be satisfied when those rights have been made as secure as the faith and the freedom of nations can make them.

Just because we fight without rancour and without selfish object, seeking nothing for ourselves but what we shall wish to share with all free peoples, we shall, I feel confident, conduct our operations as belligerents without passion and ourselves observe with proud punctilio the principles of right and of fair play we profess to be fighting for.

I have said nothing of the governments allied with the Imperial Government of Germany because they have not made war upon us or challenged us to defend our right and our honour. The Austro-Hungarian Government has, indeed, avowed its unqualified endorsement and acceptance of the reckless and lawless submarine warfare adopted now without disguise by the Imperial German Government, and it has therefore not been possible for this Government to receive Count Tarnowski, the Ambassador recently accredited to this Government by the Imperial and Royal Government of Austria-Hungary; but that Government has not actually engaged in warfare against citizens of the United States on the seas, and I take the liberty, for the present at least, of postponing a discussion of our relations with the authorities at Vienna. We enter this war only where we are clearly forced into it because there are no other means of defending our rights.

It will be all the easier for us to conduct ourselves as belligerents in a high spirit of right and fairness because we act without animus, not in enmity towards a people or with the desire to bring any injury or disadvantage upon them, but only in armed opposition to an irresponsible government which has thrown aside all considerations of humanity and of right and is running amuck. We are, let me say again, the sincere friends of the German people, and shall desire nothing so much as the early re-establishment of intimate relations of mutual advantage between us, — however hard it may be for them, for the time being, to believe that this is spoken from our hearts. We have borne with their present government through all these bitter months because of that friendship, —exercising a patience and forbearance which would otherwise have been impossible. We shall, happily, still have an opportunity to prove that friendship in our daily attitude and actions towards the millions of men and women of German birth and native sympathy who live amongst us and share our life, and we shall be proud to prove it towards all who are in fact loyal to their neighbours and to the Government in the hour of test. They are, most of them, as true and loyal Americans as if they had never known any other fealty or allegiance. They will be prompt to stand with us in rebuking and restraining the few who may be of a different mind and purpose. If there should be disloyalty, it will be dealt with with a firm hand of stern repression; but, if it lifts its head at all, it will lift it only here and there and without countenance except from a lawless and malignant few.

It is a distressing and oppressive duty, Gentlemen of the Congress, which I have performed in thus addressing you. There are, it may be, many months of fiery trial and sacrifice ahead of us. It is a fearful thing to lead this great peaceful people into war, into the most terrible and disastrous of all wars, civilization itself seeming to be in the balance. But the right is more precious than peace, and we shall fight for the things which we have always carried nearest our hearts, for democracy, for the right of those who submit to authority to have a voice in their own governments, for the rights and liberties of small nations, for a universal dominion of right by such a concert of free people as shall bring peace and safety to all nations and make the world itself at last free. To such a task we can dedicate our lives and our fortunes, everything that we are and everything that we have, with the pride of those who know that the day has come when America is privileged to spend her blood and her might for the principles that gave her birth and happiness and the peace which she has treasured. God helping her, she can do no other.

MESSAGE TO CONGRESS

(January 8, 1918)

Gentlemen of the Congress:

Once more, as repeatedly before, the spokesmen of the Central Empires have indicated their desire to discuss the objects of the war and the possible basis of a general peace. Parleys have been in progress at Brest-Litovsk between Russian representatives and representatives of the Central Powers to which the attention of all the belligerents has been invited for the purpose of ascertaining whether it may be possible to extend these parleys into a general conference with regard to terms of peace and settlement.

The Russian representatives presented not only a perfectly definite statement of the principles upon which they would be willing to conclude peace but also an equally definite program of the concrete application of those principles. The representatives of the Central Powers, on their part, presented an outline of settlement which, if much less definite, seemed susceptible of liberal interpretation until their specific program of practical terms was added. That program proposed no concessions at all either to the sovereignty of Russia or to the preferences of the populations with whose fortunes it dealt, but meant, in a word, that the Central Empires were to keep every foot of territory their armed forces had occupied — every province, every city, every point of vantage — as a permanent addition to their territories and their power.

It is a reasonable conjecture that the general principles of settlement which they at first suggested originated with the more liberal statesmen of Germany and Austria, the men who have begun to feel the force of their own people's thought and purpose, while the concrete terms of actual settlement came from the military leaders who have no thought but to keep what they have got. The negotiations have been broken off. The Russian representatives were sincere and in earnest. They cannot entertain such proposals of conquest and domination.

The whole incident is full of significance. It is also full of perplexity. With whom are the Russian representatives dealing? For whom are the representatives of the Central Empires speaking? Are they speaking for the majorities of their respective parliaments or for the minority parties, that military and imperialistic minority which has so far dominated their whole policy and controlled the affairs of Turkey and of the Balkan states which have felt obliged to become their associates in this war?

The Russian representatives have insisted, very justly, very wisely, and in the true spirit of modern democracy, that the conferences they have been holding with the Teutonic and Turkish statesmen should be held within open, not closed, doors, and all the world has been audience, as was desired. To whom have we been listening, then? To those who speak the spirit and intention of the resolutions of the German Reichstag of the 9th of July last, the spirit and intention of the Liberal leaders and parties of Germany, or to those who resist and defy that spirit and intention and insist upon conquest and subjugation? Or are we listening, in fact, to both, unreconciled and in open and hopeless contradiction? These are very serious and pregnant questions. Upon the answer to them depends the peace of the world.

But, whatever the results of the parleys at Brest-Litovsk, whatever the confusions of counsel and of purpose in the utterances of the spokesmen of the Central Empires, they have again attempted to acquaint the world with their objects in the war and have again challenged their adversaries to say what their objects are and what sort of settlement they would deem just and satisfactory. There is no good reason why that challenge should not be responded to, and responded to with the utmost candor. We did not wait for it. Not once, but again and again, we have laid our whole thought and purpose before the world, not in general terms only, but each time with sufficient definition to make it clear what sort of definite terms of settlement must necessarily spring out of them. Within the last week Mr. Lloyd George has spoken with admirable candor and in admirable spirit for the people and Government of Great Britain.

There is no confusion of counsel among the adversaries of the Central Powers, no uncertainty of principle, no vagueness of detail. The only secrecy of counsel, the only lack of fearless frankness, the only failure to make definite statement of the objects of the war, lies with Germany and her allies. The issues of life and death hang upon these definitions. No statesman who has the least conception of his responsibility ought for a moment to permit himself to continue this tragical and appalling outpouring of blood and treasure unless he is sure beyond a peradventure that the objects of the vital sacrifice are part and parcel of the very life of Society and that the people for whom he speaks think them right and imperative as he does.

There is, moreover, a voice calling for these definitions of principle and of purpose which is, it seems to me, more thrilling and more compelling than any of the many moving voices with which the troubled air of the world is filled. It is the voice of the Russian people. They are prostrate and all but helpless, it would seem, before the grim power of Germany, which has hitherto known no relenting and no pity. Their power, apparently, is shattered. And yet their soul is not subservient. They will not yield either in principle or in action. Their conception of what is right, of what is humane and honorable for them to accept, has been stated with a frankness, a largeness of view, a generosity of spirit, and a universal human sympathy which must challenge the admiration of every friend of mankind; and they have refused to compound their ideals or desert others that they themselves may be safe.

They call to us to say what it is that we desire, in what, if in anything, our purpose and our spirit differ from theirs; and I believe that the people of the United States would wish me to respond, with utter simplicity and frankness. Whether their present leaders believe it or not, it is our heartfelt desire and hope that some way may be opened whereby we may be privileged to assist the people of Russia to attain their utmost hope of liberty and ordered peace.

It will be our wish and purpose that the processes of peace, when they are begun, shall be absolutely open and that they shall involve and permit henceforth no secret understandings of any kind. The day of conquest and aggrandizement is gone by; so is also the day of secret covenants entered into in the interest of particular governments and likely at some unlooked-for moment to upset the peace of the world. It is this happy fact, now clear to the view of every public man whose thoughts do not still linger in an age that is dead and gone, which makes it possible for every nation whose purposes are consistent with justice and the peace of the world to avow now or at any other time the objects it has in view.

We entered this war because violations of right had occurred which touched us to the quick and made the life of our own people impossible unless they were corrected and the world secure once for all against their recurrence.

What we demand in this war, therefore, is nothing peculiar to ourselves. It is that the world be made fit and safe to live in; and particularly that it be made safe for every peace-loving nation which, like our own, wishes to live its own life, determine its own institutions, be assured of justice and fair dealing by the other peoples of the world as against force and selfish aggression.

All the peoples of the world are in effect partners in this interest, and for our own part we see very clearly that unless justice be done to others it will not be done to us. The program of the world's peace, therefore, is our program; and that program, the only possible program, as we see it, is this:

1. Open convenants of peace, openly arrived at, after which there shall be no private international understandings of any kind but diplomacy shall proceed always frankly and in the public view.

2. Absolute freedom of navigation upon the seas, outside territorial waters, alike in peace and in war, except as the seas may be closed in whole or in part by international action for the enforcement of international covenants.

3. The removal, so far as possible, of all economic barriers and the establishment of an equality of trade conditions among all the nations consenting to the peace and associating themselves for its maintenance.

4. Adequate guarantees given and taken that national armaments will be reduced to the lowest points consistent with domestic safety.

5. A free, open-minded, and absolutely impartial adjustment of all colonial claims, based upon a strict observance of the principle that in determining all such questions of sovereignty the interests of the populations concerned must have equal weight with the equitable claims of the government whose title is to be determined.

6. The evacuation of all Russian territory and such a settlement of all questions affecting Russia as will secure the best and freest cooperation of the other nations of the world in obtaining for her an unhampered and unembarrassed opportunity for the independent determination of her own political development and national policy and assure her of a sincere wel-

come into the society of free nations under institutions of her own choosing; and, more than a welcome, assistance also of every kind that she may need and may herself desire. The treatment accorded Russia by her sister nations in the months to come will be the acid test of their good will, of their comprehension of her needs as distinguished from their own interests, and of their intelligent and unselfish sympathy.

7. Belgium, the whole world will agree, must be evacuated and restored, without any attempt to limit the sovereignty which she enjoys in common with all other free nations. No other single act will serve as this will serve to restore confidence among the nations in the laws which they have themselves set and determined for the government of their relations with one another. Without this healing act the whole structure and validity of international law is forever impaired.

8. All French territory should be freed and the invaded portions restored, and the wrong done to France by Prussia in 1871 in the matter of Alsace-Lorraine, which has unsettled the peace of the world for nearly fifty years, should be righted, in order that peace may once more be made secure in the interest of all.

9. A readjustment of the frontiers of Italy should be affected along clearly recognizable lines of nationality.

10. The peoples of Austria-Hungary, whose place among the nations we wish to see safeguarded and assured, should be accorded the freest opportunity of autonomous development.

11. Rumania, Serbia, and Montenegro should be evacuated; occupied territories restored; Serbia accorded free and secure access to the sea; and the relations of the several Balkan states to one another determined by friendly counsel along historically established lines of allegiance and nationality; and international guarantees of the political and economic independence and territorial integrity of the several Balkan states should be entered into.

12. The Turkish portions of the present Ottoman Empire should be assured a secure sovereignty, but the other nationalities which are now under Turkish rule should be assured an undoubted security of life and an absolutely unmolested opportunity of autonomous development, and the Dardanelles should be permanently opened as a free passage to the ships and commerce of all nations under international guarantees.

13. An independent Polish state should be erected which should include the territories inhabited by indisputably Polish populations, which should be assured a free and secure access to the sea, and whose political and economic independence and territorial integrity should be guaranteed by international covenant.

14. A general association of nations must be formed under specific covenants for the purpose of affording mutual guarantees of political independence and territorial integrity to great and small states alike.

In regard to these essential rectifications of wrong and assertions of right we feel ourselves to be intimate partners of all the governments and peoples associated together against the imperialists. We cannot be separated in interest or divided in purpose. We stand together until the end.

For such arrangements and covenants we are willing to fight and to continue to fight until they are achieved; but only because we wish the right to prevail and desire a just and stable peace such as can be secured only by removing the chief provocations to war, which this program does remove.

We have no jealousy of German greatness, and there is nothing in this program that impairs it. We grudge her no achievement or distinction of learning or of pacific enterprise such as have made her record very bright and very enviable. We do not wish to injure her or to block in any way her legitimate influence or power. We do not wish to fight her either with arms or with hostile arrangements of trade if she is willing to associate herself with us and the other peace-loving nations of the world in covenants of justice and law and fair dealing.

We wish her only to accept a place of equality among the peoples of the world, — the new world on which we now live, — instead of a place of mastery.

Neither do we presume to suggest to her any alteration or modification of her institutions. But it is necessary, we must frankly say, and necessary as a preliminary to any intelligent dealings with her on our part, that we should know whom her spokesmen speak for when they speak to us, whether for the Reichstag majority or for the military party and the men whose creed is imperial domination.

We have spoken now, surely, in terms too concrete to admit of any further doubt or question. An evident principle runs through the whole program I have outlined. It is the principle of justice to all peoples and nationalities, and their right to live on equal terms of liberty and safety with one another, whether they be strong or weak.

Unless this principle be made its foundation no part of the structure of international justice can stand. The people of the United States could act upon no other principle; and to the vindication of this principle they are ready to devote their lives, their honor, and everything that they possess. The moral climax of this the culminating and final war for human liberty has come, and they are ready to put their own strength, their own highest purpose, their own integrity and devotion to the test.

Study Guide

1. Wilson's message to Congress asking for a declaration of war on Germany can be organized in this way:

   (a) historical prologue within the context of international law (pp. 352–354);

   (b) the fiscal and other implications of war (pp. 354–355);

   (c) motives for going to war (pp. 355–357); and

   (d) immediate goals and ultimate ends (pp. 357–359).

2. In order to understand Wilson's opening paragraphs, familiarize yourself, from your text, with the principal issues and incidents between the United States and Germany that led to the Sussex Pledge — a commitment by Germany to conduct only a limited form of submarine warfare. Make sure you understand, too, why in early 1917 Germany abandoned this pledge and how Wilson reacted to this from February, 1917, to the date of this address. Note the references by Wilson to "international law," "neutral rights," and "the heart and conscience of mankind." What do these phrases tell us about the context (the value-system) within which Wilson will be defining and justifying an American declaration of war on Germany? Note, for example, this sentence: "Our motive will not be revenge or the victorious assertion of the physical might of the nation, but only the vindication of right, of human right, of which we are only a single champion."

3. Wilson devotes some attention to the fiscal and manpower responsibilities (international and domestic) that the war will place on the American people. Explain.

4. Turning to the international scene, note:

   (a) Wilson's division of the world into autocratic and democratic governments;

   (b) his separation of the German government and its people;

   (c) his comments on the Russian Revolution; and

   (d) his reference to the Zimmermann affair. Elaborate on each of the above.

5. In closing, Wilson turns to two topics that will be of great importance during and after the war:

   (a) the possibility of dissent from his war aims at home; and

   (b) the *ultimate* purpose of the war.

   How does he suggest the former should be dealt with? How accurate was Wilson in this warning? As you read the paragraph of Wilson's declaration of war on Germany, pay heed to the exalted goals he sets forth for the nation and the world. Were they fulfilled? Elaborate.

6. The core of the second address, given several months before the end of World War I, is, of course, Wilson's announcement of the Fourteen Points

—his blueprint for the postwar world. Prior to that, however, Wilson comments on developments in Europe—the important negotiations between the Russian Bolshevik government and the Entente. From your text, familiarize yourself with the actions of the Soviets regarding continued participation in the war against Germany, following the successful November Revolution. Summarize Wilson's reactions to the proposals and conversations at Brest-Litovsk, his assessment of the motives of the Central Powers, and the purposes of the Bolsheviks. How accurate, in time, were these assessments?

7. Focusing on the Fourteen Points, distinguish between the first five and the last on one hand, and the remainder, on the other; the former are general principles for the conduct of international affairs, whereas the latter are recommendations for specific territorial arrangements. One historian has suggested that the Fourteen Points are simply an application in the sphere of international affairs of Wilson's progressive principles. Can you see a relationship between the Underwood Tariff and any of the Fourteen Points, or between the Clayton Act and any of the others? What domestic institution enacted during Wilson's administration would you compare to his proposal for a League of Nations? Answer and amplify.

8. How does Wilson apply the Fourteen Points to Germany? From your text ascertain whether, in truth, Wilson's notions regarding Germany were fulfilled at the Versailles Peace Conference.

Henry Cabot Lodge

AN EVIL THING WITH A HOLY NAME

❧*1919*❧ WOODROW Wilson (1856-1924) had taken the United States into the World War in order to make the world safe for democracy; quickly, as the conflict developed, he learned that victory on the battlefield would not alone accomplish this noble objective. A powerful international organization—he called it a League of Nations—would be necessary if the principles of justice were to triumph after the Central Powers had been defeated. First enunciated in his "Fourteen Points" speech of January 8, 1918, his proposal that such an organization guarantee the "political independence and territorial integrity of great and small nations alike" was developed in a series of British and American drafts and finally presented to the Versailles Peace Conference by Wilson himself in February, 1919.

Unquestionably the impact of the league idea on Americans was both heavy and favorable. As Senator Henry Cabot Lodge of Massachusetts (1850-1924), whose objections to the League of Nations proved so important in its defeat, himself confessed in a private letter: "I have no doubt that a large majority of the people of the country are very naturally fascinated by the idea of eternal preservation of the world's peace. . . . They are told that is what this league means." But the full significance of the proposed international organization was not clear to the average American in those happy days after the guns fell silent and before the difficulties of postwar readjustment had become apparent. Foes of the League soon began to point out the extent to which membership would involve surrendering America's cherished isolationism. Extremists (they were called "irreconcilables") made the most noise but it was probably the less obviously hostile, more reasonable critics who did most to swing public opinion away from the President on the League issue. And swing public opinion did, although the actual defeat of the proposal was a narrowly partisan political question settled in the Senate. The following selection from a speech delivered by Lodge in the Senate on February 28, 1919, typifies the kind of reasoning used by those opponents who objected to *Wilson's* league without rejecting offhand the whole concept of internationalism.

SPEECH IN THE SENATE

(February 28, 1919)

MR. PRESIDENT, all people, men and women alike, who are capable of connected thought abhor war and desire nothing so much as to make secure the future peace of the world. Everybody hates war. Everyone longs to make it impossible. We ought to lay aside once and for all the unfounded and really evil suggestion that because men may differ as to the best method of securing the world's peace in the future, anyone is against permanent peace, if it can be obtained, among all the nations of mankind. Because one man goes to the Capitol in Washington by one street and another man by a different street it does not follow that they are not both going to the Capitol. We all earnestly desire to advance toward the preservation of the world's peace, and difference in method makes no distinction in purpose. It is almost needless to say that the question now before us is so momentous that it transcends all party lines. Party considerations and party interests disappear in dealing with such a question as this. I will follow any man and vote for any measure which in my honest opinion will make for the maintenance of the world's peace. I will follow no man and vote for no measure which, however well intended, seem in my best judgment to lead to discussions rather than to harmony among the nations or to injury, peril, or injustice to my country. No question has ever confronted the United States Senate which equals in importance that which is involved in the league of nations intended to secure the future peace of the world. There should be no undue haste in considering it. My one desire is that not only the Senate, which is charged with responsibility, but that the press and the people of the country should investigate every proposal with the utmost thoroughness and weigh them all carefully before they make up their minds. If there is any proposition or any plan which will not bear, which will not court the most thorough and most public discussion, that fact makes it an object of suspicion at the very outset. Beware of it; be on your guard against it. Demand that those who oppose the plan now offered present arguments and reasons, based on facts and history, and that those who favor it meet objections with something more relative than rhetoric, personal denunciation, and shrill shrieks that virtue is to be preferred to vice and that peace is better than war. Glittering and enticing generalities will not serve. We must have fact, details, and sharp, clear-cut definitions. The American people cannot give too much thought to this subject, and that they shall look into it with considerate eyes is all that I desire.

In the first place, the terms of the league — the agreements which we make, — must be so plain and so explicit that no man can misunderstand them. We must, so far as it can be done by human ingenuity, have every agreement which we make so stated that it will not give rise to different interpretations and to consequent argument. Misunderstandings as to terms are not a good foundation for a treaty to promote peace. . . .

In this draft prepared for a constitution of a league of nations, which is now before the world, there is hardly a clause about the interpretation of which men do not already differ. As it stands there is serious danger that the very nations which sign the constitution of the league will quarrel about the meaning of the various articles before a twelvemonth has passed. It seems to have been very hastily drafted, and the result is crudeness and looseness of expression, unintentional, I hope. There are certainly many doubtful passages and open questions obvious in the articles which can not be settled by individual inference, but which must be made so clear and so distinct that we may all understand the exact meaning of the instrument to which we are asked to set our hands. The language of these articles does not appear to me to have the precision and unmistakable character which a constitution, a treaty, or a law ought to present. The language only too frequently is not the language of laws or statutes. The article concerning mandatories, for example, contains an argument and a statement of existing conditions. Arguments and historical facts have no place in a statute or a treaty. Statutory and legal language must assert and command, not argue and describe. I press this point because there is nothing so vital to the peace of the world as the sanctity of treaties. The suggestion that we can safely sign because we can always violate or abrogate is fatal not only to any league but to peace itself. You can not found world peace upon the cynical "scrap of paper" doctrine so dear to Germany. To whatever instrument the United States sets its hand it must carry out the provisions of that instrument to the last jot and tittle, and observe it absolutely both in letter and in spirit. If this is not done the instrument will become a source of controversy instead of agreement, of dissension instead of harmony. This is all the more essential because it is evident, although not expressly stated, that this league is intended to be indissoluble, for there is no provision for its termination or for the withdrawal of any signatory. We are left to infer that any nation withdrawing from the league exposes itself to penalties and probably to war. Therefore, before we ratify, the terms and language in which the terms are stated must be as exact and as precise, as free from any possibility of conflicting interpretations, as it is possible to make them. . . .

What I have just said indicates the vast importance of the form and the manner in which the agreements which we are to sign shall be stated. I now come to questions of substance, which seem to me to demand the most careful thought of the entire American people, and particularly of those charged with the responsibility of ratification. We abandon entirely by the proposed constitution the policy laid down by Washington in his Farewell Address and the Monroe doctrine. It is worse than idle, it is not honest, to evade, or deny this fact, and every fairminded supporter of this draft plan for a league admits it. I know that some of the ardent advocates of the plan submitted to us regard any suggestion of the importance of the Washington policy as foolish and irrelevant. Perhaps it is. Perhaps the time has come when the policies of Washington should be abandoned; but if we are to cast them aside I think that at least it should be done respectfully and with a sense of gratitude to the great man who formulated them. For nearly a century and a quarter the policies laid down in the Farewell Address have been followed and adhered to by the Government of the United States and by the American people. I doubt if any purely political declaration has even been observed by any people for so long a time. The principles of the Farewell Address in regard to our foreign relations have been sustained and acted upon by the American people down to the present moment. Washington declared against permanent alliances. He did not close the door on temporary alliances for particular purposes. Our entry in the great war just closed was entirely in accord with and violated in no respect the policy laid down by Washington. When we went to war with Germany we made no treaties with the nations engaged in the war against the German Government. The President was so careful in this direction that he did not permit himself ever to refer to the nations by whose side we fought as "allies," but always as "nations associated with us in the war." The attitude recommended by Washington was scrupulously maintained even under the pressure of the great conflict. Now, in the twinkling of an eye, while passion and emotion reign, the Washington policy is to be entirely laid aside and we are to enter upon a permanent and indissoluble alliance. That which we refuse to do in war we are to do in peace, deliberately, coolly, and with no war exigency. Let us not overlook the profound gravity of this step. . . .

But if we put aside forever the Washington policy in regard to our foreign relations we must always remember that it carries with it the corollary known as the Monroe doctrine. Under the terms of this league draft reported by the committee to the peace conference the Monroe doctrine disappears. It has been our cherished guide and guard for nearly a century. The Monroe doctrine is based on the principle of self-preservation. To say that it is a question of protecting the boundaries, the political integrity, of the American States, is not to see the Monroe doctrine. Boundaries have been changed among American States since the Monroe doctrine was enunciated. That is not the kernel of the doctrine. The real essence of that doctrine is that American questions shall be settled by Americans alone; that the Americans shall be separated from Europe and from the interference of Europe in purely American questions. That is the vital principle of the doctrine.

I have seen it said that the Monroe doctrine is preserved under article 10; that we do not abandon the Monroe doctrine, we merely extend it to all the world. How anyone can say this passes my comprehension. The Monroe doctrine exists solely for the protection of the American Hemisphere, and to that hemisphere it was limited. If you extend it to all the world, it ceases to exist, because it rests on nothing but the differentiation of the American Hemisphere from the rest of the world. Under this draft of the constitution of the league of nations, American questions and European questions and Asian and African questions are all alike put within the control and jurisdiction of the league. Europe will have the right to take part in the settlement of all American questions, and we, of course, shall have the right to share in the settlement of all questions in Europe and Asia and Africa. Europe and Asia are to take part in policing the American continent and the Panama Canal, and in return we are to have, by way of compensation, the right to police the Balkans and Asia Minor when we are asked to do so. Perhaps the time has come when it is necessary to do this, but it is a very grave step, and I wish now merely to point out that the American people ought never to abandon the Washington policy and the Monroe doctrine without being perfectly certain that they earnestly wish to do so. . . .

Two other general propositions, and I shall proceed to examine these league articles in detail. In article 10 we, in common, of course, with the other signatories and members of the projected league, guarantee the territorial integrity and the political independence of every member of the league. That means that we ultimately guarantee the independence and the boundaries, as now settled or as they may be settled by the treaty with Germany, of every nation on earth. If the United States agrees to guaranties of that sort we must maintain them. The word of the United States, her promise to guarantee the independence and the boundaries of any country, whether she does it alone or in company with other nations, whether she guarantees one country or all the countries of the world, is just as sacred as her honor — far more important than the maintenance of every financial pledge, which the people of this country would never consent to break.

I do not now say the time has not come when, in the interest of future peace, the American people may not decide that we ought to guarantee the territorial integrity of the far-flung British Empire, including her self-governing dominions and colonies, of the Balkan States, of China, or Japan, or of the French, Italian, and Portuguese colonies in Africa; but I do suggest that it is a very grave, a very perilous promise to make, because there is but one way by which such guaranties, if ever invoked, can be maintained, and that way is the way of force — whether military or economic force, it matters not. If we guarantee any country on the earth, no matter how small or how large, in its independence or its boundaries, that guarantee we must maintain at any cost when our word is once given, and we must be in constant possession of fleets and armies capable of enforcing these guarantees at a moment's notice. There is no need of arguing whether there is to be compulsive force behind this league. It is there in article 10 absolutely and entirely by the mere fact of these guaranties. The ranks of the armies and fleets of the navy made necessary by such pledges are to be filled and manned by the sons, husbands, and brothers of the people of America. I wish them carefully to consider, therefore, whether they are willing to have the youth of America ordered to war by other nations without regard to what they or their representatives desire. I would have them determine after much reflection whether they are willing to have the United States forced into war by other nations against her own will. They must bear in mind constantly that we have only one vote in the executive council, only one vote in the body of delegates, and a majority of the votes rules and is decisive.

I am not here to discuss the constitutional question of the sole right of Congress to declare war. That is a detail, as it relates only to the Constitution, which we may decide later. In my own opinion, we shall be obliged to modify the Constitution. I do not think, and I never can admit, that we can change or modify the Constitution by a treaty negotiated by the President and ratified by the Senate. I think that must be done, and can only be done, in the way prescribed by the Constitution itself, and to promise to amend our Constitution is a serious task and a doubtful undertaking.

I hope the American people will take time to consider this promise before they make it — because when it is once made it can not be broken — and ask themselves whether this is the best way of assuring perfect peace throughout the future years, which is what we are aiming at, for we all are aiming at the same object. A world's peace which requires at the outset preparations for war — for war either economic or military — in order to maintain that peace, presents questions and awakens thoughts which certainly ought to be soberly and discreetly considered.

The second general proposition to which I would call attention is this: We now in this draft bind ourselves to submit every possible international dispute or difference either to the league court or to the control of the executive council of the league. That includes immigration, a very live question, to take a single example. Are we ready to give to other nations the power to say who shall come into the United States and become citizens of the Republic? If we are ready to do this, we are prepared to part with the most precious of sovereign rights, that which guards our existence and our character as a Nation. Are we ready to leave it to other nations to determine whether we shall admit to the United States a flood of Japanese, Chinese, and Hindu labor? If we accept this plan for a league, this is precisely what we promise to do. I know that by following out all the windings of the provision for referring to the council or allowing the council to take charge of what has been called hitherto a conjusticiable question, we shall probably reach a point where it would not be possible to secure unanimous action by the league upon the question of immigration. But, Mr. President, I start with the proposition that there should be no jurisdiction in the league at all over that question; that it should be separated absolutely and entirely from any jurisdiction of the league. Are we prepared to have a league of nations — in which the United States has only one vote, which she could not cast on a dispute to which she was a party — open our doors, if they see fit, to any and all immigration from all parts of the world?

Mr. Taft has announced, in an article which appeared in the National Geographic Magazine, that the question of immigration will go before the international tribunal, and he says now that all organized labor is for the league. If American labor favors putting the restriction of immigration in the control of other nations they must have radically changed their minds and abandoned their most cherished policy. Certainly the gravity of such promises as are involved in the points I have suggested is sufficient to forbid haste. If such promises are to be given they must be given in cold blood with a full realization of what they mean and after the American people and those who represent them here have considered all that is involved with a serious care such as we have never been called upon to exercise before. We are asked to abandon the policies which we have adhered to during all our life as a Nation. We are asked to guarantee the political independence and the territorial integrity of every nation which chooses to join the league — and that means all nations as the President stated in his speech at Manchester. We are asked to leave to the decision of other nations, or to the jurisdiction of other nations, the question of what immigrants shall come to the United States. We are asked also to give up in part our sovereignty and our independence and subject our own will to the will of other nations, if there is a majority against our desires. We are asked, therefore, in a large and important degree to substitute internationalism for nationalism and an international state for pure Americanism. Certainly such things as these deserve reflection, discussion, and earnest thought.

I am not contending now that these things must not be done. I have no intention of opposing a blank negative to propositions which concern the peace of the world, which I am as anxious to see promoted as any living man can be; but I do say, in the strongest terms, that these things I have pointed out are of vast importance not only to us but to the entire world, and a mistake now in making the league of nations might result in more war and trouble than the old system in its worst days. What I ask, and all I ask, is consideration, time, and thought. . . .

. . . When the United States enters into an indissoluble permanent alliance there ought to be, as I have said, no uncertainties in the terms of the agreement. I earnestly desire to do everything that can be done to secure the peace of the world, but these articles as they stand in this proposed constitution seem to give a rich promise of being fertile in producing controversies and misunderstandings. They also make some demands which I do not believe any nation would submit to in a time of stress. Therefore this machinery would not promote the peace of the world, but would have a directly opposite effect. It would tend to increase the subjects of misunderstanding and dispute among the nations. Is it not possible to draft a better, more explicit, less dangerous scheme than the one here and now presented? Surely we are not to be shut up to this as the last and only word to take or leave.

To those who object that the criticism of this tentative draft plan of the committee of the peace conference must be not only destructive but constructive it might be said that the burden of proof lies upon those who propose, in order to establish the future peace of the world, that the United States must curtail its independence, part with a portion of its sovereignty, and abandon all the international policies which have been so successful for more than a hundred years. Those who support the present draft of the constitution for the league must demonstrate that it is an improvement before they can expect its general acceptance. But the Senate can not at this time undertake to make plans for a league; because we are in the process of negotiation, and the Senate does not begin to act until the stage of ratification is reached. At the same time there are certain constructive propositions which it would be well, I think, for the peace conference to consider. If it is said that you can preserve the Monroe doctrine by extending it, which appears to me clearly to mean its destruction and to be a contradiction in terms, then let us put three lines into the draft for the league which will preserve the Monroe doctrine beyond any possibility of doubt or question. It is easily done. Let us also have, if we enter the league, a complete exclusion from the league's jurisdiction of such questions as are involved in immigration and the right of each country to say who shall come within its borders and become citizens. This and certain other questions vital to national existence ought to be exempted from any control or jurisdiction by the league or its officials by a very few words, such as can be found in the arbitration treaties of 1907. There should be some definite provision for peaceful withdrawal from the league if any nation desires to withdraw. Lastly, let us have a definite statement in the constitution of the league as to whether the league is to have an international force of its own or is to have the power to summon the armed forces of the different members of the league. Let it be stated in plain language whether the "measures," the "recommendations," or the suggestions of the executive council are to be binding upon the members of the league and are to compel them, technically or morally, to do what the league delegates and the executive council determine to be necessary. On the question of the use of force we should not proceed in the dark. If those who support the league decline to make such simple statements as these — I mean statements in the body of the instrument, not individual statements — it is impossible to avoid the conclusion that they are seeking to do by indirection and the use of nebulous phrases what they are not willing to do directly, and nothing could be more fatal to the preservation of the world's peace than this, for every exercise of power by the executive council which the signatories to the league might fairly consider to be doubtful would lead to very perilous controversies and to menacing quarrels.

Unless some better constitution for a league than this can be drawn, it seems to me, after such examination as I have been able to give, that the world's peace would be much better, much more surely prompted, by allowing the United States to go on under the Monroe doctrine, responsible for the peace of this hemisphere, without any danger of collision with Europe as to questions among the various American States, and if a league is desired it might be made up by the Euorpean nations whose interests are chiefly concerned, and with which the United States could coöperate fully and at any time, whenever coöperation was needed. I suppose I shall make myself the subject of derision for quoting from the Farewell Address, but it states a momentous truth so admirably that I can not refrain from giving it, for I think it ought to be borne in mind. Washington says:

> Europe has a set of primary interests which to us have none or a very remote relation. Hence she must be engaged in frequent controversies the causes of which are essentially foreign to our concerns. Hence, therefore, it must be unwise in us to implicate ourselves by artificial ties in the ordinary vicissitudes of her politics or the ordinary combinations and collisions of her friendships or enmities.

It must be remembered that if the United States enters any league of nations it does so for the benefit of the world at large, and not for its own benefit. The people of the United States are a peace-loving people. We have no boundaries to rectify, no schemes, and no desire for the acquisition or conquest of territory. We have in the main kept the peace in the American hemisphere. The States of South America have grown constantly more stable, and revolutions have well-nigh disappeared in the States south of those bordering on the Caribbean. No one questions that the United States is able to prevent any conflicts in the American hemisphere which would involve the world in any way or be more than passing difficulties, which in most cases could be settled by arbitration. If we join a league, therefore, it must be with a view to maintaining peace in Europe, where all the greatest wars have originated, and where there is always danger of war, and in Asia, where serious conflicts may arise at any moment. If we join a league, of course, we have in mind the danger of European conflicts springing up in such a way as to involve us in the defense of civilization, as has just happened in the war with Germany. But such wars as that are, fortunately, rare; so rare that one has never before occurred, and when the time came we took our part; but in the main our share in any league must be almost wholly for the benefit of others. We have the right, therefore, to demand that there shall be nothing in any agreement for the maintenance of the world's peace which is likely to produce new causes of difference and dissension, or which is calculated to injure the United States, or compel from us undue sacrifice, or put us in a position where we may be forced to serve the ambitions of others. There is no gain for peace in the Americas to be found by annexing the Americas to the European system. Whatever we do there we do from almost purely altruistic motives, and therefore we are entitled to consider every proposition with the utmost care in order to make sure that it does not do us injustice or render future conditions worse instead of better than they are at present.

To me the whole subject is one of enormous difficulties. We are all striving for a like result; but to make any real advances toward the future preservation of the world's peace will take time, care, and long consideration. We can not reach our objects by a world constitution hastily constructed in a few weeks in Paris in the midst of the excitement of a war not yet ended. The one thing to do, as I said in the Senate some time ago, and that which I now wish above all others, is to make the peace with Germany — to make a peace which by its terms will prevent her from breaking out again upon the world; to exclude Turkey from Europe, strengthen Greece, and give freedom and independence to the Armenians and to the Jewish and Christian populations of Asia Minor; to erect the barrier States for the Poles, Czecho-Slovaks, and Jugo-Slavs; to take possession of the Kiel Canal; to establish the Baltic States and free them from Russia and restore Danish Schleswig to Denmark. Provision must be made for indemnities or reparation, or by whatever name we choose to call the damages to be exacted from Germany. We ought, in my judgment, to receive indemnities which would enable us to provide for the *Lusitania* claims and for the destruction of our ships by submarines — to go no further. But the enormous losses of England and Italy in shipping should be made good, either in money or in kind. Belgium must be restored and fully compensated for her terrible injuries.

Finally there is France, and the indemnities to France ought to be ample and complete. . . . We ought then to make this peace with Germany and make it at once. Much time has been wasted. The delays have bred restlessness and confusion everywhere. Germany is lifting her head again. The whining after defeat is changing to threats. She is seeking to annex nine millions of Germans in German Austria. She is reaching out in Russia and reviving her financial and commercial penetration everywhere. Her fields have not been desolated nor her factories destroyed. Germany is again threatening, and the only source of a great war is to be found in the future as in the past in Germany. She should be chained and fettered now and this menace to the world's peace should be removed at once. Whatever else we fought for certainly our first and paramount purpose was to defeat Germany. The victory over Germany is not yet complete. Let it be made so without delay.

That which I desire above everything else, that which is nearest to my heart, is to bring our soldiers home. The making of a league of nations will not do that. We can only bring our soldiers home, entirely and completely, when the peace with Germany is made and proclaimed. Let that peace be made and I can assure the world that when the treaty of peace with Germany comes in this Chamber there will be no delay in the Senate of the United States. We must bring our men back from France — the men who fought the war, the men who made the personal sacrifice. Let us get them back at once, and to that end let us have the peace made with Germany, made now, and not delay it until the complicated questions of the league of nations can be settled with the care and consideration which they demand. What is it that delays the peace with Germany? Discussions over the league of nations; nothing else. Let us have peace now, in this year of grace 1919. That is the first step to the future peace of the world. The next step will be to make sure if we can that the world shall have peace in the year 1950 or 2000. Let us have the peace with Germany and bring our boys home. . . .

Study Guide

1. The purpose of this address was to mobilize support in the Senate (and in the nation) to oppose Woodrow Wilson's proposal for a League of Nations and the United States's membership in it. The rhetoric and the substance of his argument can be partly organized in this way:

   (a) the language of the proposals for a League (pp. 367–369);
   (b) the Monroe Doctrine (pp. 369–370);
   (c) the tradition of Washington's Farewell Address (pp. 369–370);
   (d) Article 10 (pp. 370–372); and
   (e) the powers of the federal government over internal affairs (pp. 372–379).

2. The first paragraph of Lodge's address is a masterpiece of political astuteness. Explain and illustrate why.

3. What is Lodge's criticism of the language of the text? Illustrate and assess his argument.

4. In what way, according to Lodge, would the League violate the principles enunciated in Washington's Farewell Address and the Monroe Doctrine?

5. Article 10, with its commitment to a policy of collective security, is, of course, the heart of the League. Elaborate on this and outline the arguments Lodge arrays against the article.

6. What is Lodge's last "general proposition" in opposition to the League? How does this affect United States immigration policy? Can you relate this argument to Lodge's consistent advocacy of the "literacy test" for the purposes of immigration restriction? Do you understand his reference to labor's position on immigration and how he is soliciting labor's support for his position in opposition to the League?

7. In the closing portion of his address, Lodge offers a miscellany of other criticisms of the League. List them.

8. In retrospect: What do you know of Lodge's foreign policy views prior to and during World War I? Was he an opponent of our entry into the war? Was he, like Senator William E. Borah, another opponent of the League, an isolationist in foreign policy? Why, then, his intense hostility to the League? Explain.

Bruce Barton

CHRIST AS A BUSINESSMAN

❧*1925*❧ THE early twenties was pre-eminently a time when businessmen and business values ruled the United States. "The policy of the Harding administration," historian John D. Hicks says, "was to do with alacrity whatever business wanted to have done." Harding's Secretary of the Treasury Andrew Mellon, called by his admirers the greatest head of that department since Alexander Hamilton, urged Congress to eliminate all taxes on corporate profits and reduce drastically those on upper-level incomes. President Calvin Coolidge outdid even Harding in conservatism and in sympathy to the business point of view. He cut government expenses sharply; he vetoed as "socialistic" bills regulating agricultural marketing and establishing public power projects; he appointed men favorable to private enterprise to the Federal Trade Commission and other supervisory boards. He was regarded by businessmen, in Professor Hicks' words, as "the ideal President."

The pervasiveness of the business viewpoint is well illustrated by the phenomenal success of *The Man Nobody Knows* (1925), a best-selling book written by Bruce Barton, an advertising executive. Barton attempted to prove, as the following selection shows, that Jesus Christ was the prototype of the modern businessman and that by adopting His precepts and techniques, modern Americans could achieve not merely virtue but also material success.

THE MAN NOBODY KNOWS

THE little boy's body sat bolt upright in the rough wooden chair, but his mind was very busy.

This was his weekly hour of revolt.

The kindly lady who could never seem to find her glasses would have been terribly shocked if she had known what was going on inside the little boy's mind.

"You must love Jesus," she said every Sunday, "and God."

The little boy did not say anything. He was afraid to say anything; he was almost afraid that something would happen to him because of the things he thought.

Love God! Who was always picking on people for having a good time, and sending little boys to hell because they couldn't do better in a world which he had made so hard! Why didn't God take some one his own size?

Love Jesus! The little boy looked up at the picture which hung on the Sunday-school wall. It showed a pale young man with flabby forearms and a sad expression. The young man had red whiskers.

Then the little boy looked across to the other wall. There was Daniel, good old Daniel, standing off the lions. The little boy liked Daniel. He liked David, too, with the trusty sling that landed a stone square on the forehead of Goliath. And Moses, with his rod and his big brass snake. They were winners — those three. He wondered if David could whip Jeffries. Samson could! Say, that would have been a fight!

But Jesus! Jesus was the "lamb of God." The little boy did not know what that meant, but it sounded like Mary's little lamb. Something for girls — sissified. Jesus was also "meek and lowly," a "man of sorrows and acquainted with grief." He went around for three years telling people not to do things.

Sunday was Jesus' day; it was wrong to feel comfortable or laugh on Sunday.

The little boy was glad when the superintendent thumped the bell and announced: "We will now sing the closing hymn." One more bad hour was over. For one more week the little boy had got rid of Jesus.

Years went by and the boy grew up and became a business man.

He began to wonder about Jesus.

He said to himself: "Only strong magnetic men inspire great enthusiasm and build great organizations. Yet Jesus built the greatest organization of all. It is extraordinary."

The more sermons the man heard and the more books he read the more mystified he became.

One day he decided to wipe his mind clean of books and sermons.

He said, "I will read what the men who knew Jesus personally said about him. I will read about him as though he were a new historical character, about whom I had never heard anything at all."

The man was amazed.

A physical weakling! Where did they get that idea? Jesus pushed a plane and swung an adze; he was a successful carpenter. He slept outdoors and spent his days walking around his favorite lake. His muscles were so strong that when he drove the money-changers out, nobody dared to oppose him!

A kill-joy! He was the most popular dinner guest in Jerusalem! The criticism which proper people made was that he spent too much time with publicans and sinners (very good fellows, on the whole, the man thought) and enjoyed society too much. They called him a "wine bibber and a gluttonous man."

A failure! He picked up twelve men from the bottom ranks of business and forged them into an organization that conquered the world.

When the man had finished his reading he exclaimed, "This is a man nobody knows.

"Some day," said he, "some one will write a book about Jesus. Every business man will read it and send it to his partners and his salesmen. For it will tell the story of the founder of modern business."

So the man waited for some one to write the book, but no one did. Instead, more books were published about the "lamb of God" who was weak and unhappy and glad to die.

The man became impatient. One day he said, "I believe I will try to write that book, myself."

And he did.

THE EXECUTIVE

It was very late in the afternoon.

If you would like to learn the measure of a man, that is the time of day to watch him. We are all half an inch taller in the morning than at night; it is fairly easy to take a large view of things when the mind is rested and the nerves are calm. But the day is a steady drain of small annoyances, and the difference in the size of men becomes hourly more apparent. The little man loses his temper; the big man takes a firmer hold.

It was very late in the afternoon in Galilee.

The dozen men who had walked all day over the dusty roads were hot and tired, and the sight of a village was very cheering, as they looked down on it from the top of a little hill. Their leader, deciding that they had gone far enough, sent two members of the party ahead to arrange for accommodations, while he and the others sat down by the roadside to wait.

After a bit the messengers were seen returning, and even at a distance it was apparent that something unpleasant had occurred. Their cheeks were flushed, their voices angry, and as they came nearer they quickened their pace, each wanting to be the first to explode the bad news. Breathlessly they told it — the people in the village had refused to receive them, had given them blunt notice to seek shelter somewhere else.

The indignation of the messengers communicated itself to the others, who at first could hardly believe their ears. This back-woods village refuse to entertain their master — it was unthinkable. He was a famous public character in that part of the world. He had healed sick people and given freely to the poor. In the capital city crowds had followed him enthusiastically, so that even his disciples had become men of importance, looked up to and talked about. And now to have this country village deny them admittance as its guests —

"Lord, these people are insufferable," one of them cried. "Let us call down fire from Heaven and consume them."

The others joined in with enthusiasm. Fire from Heaven — that was the idea! Make them smart for their boorishness! Show them that they can't affront *us* with impunity! Come, Lord, the fire —

There are times when nothing a man can say is nearly so powerful as saying nothing. Every executive knows that instinctively. To argue brings him down to the level of those with whom he argues; silence convicts them of their folly; they wish they had not spoken so quickly; they wonder what he thinks. The lips of Jesus tightened; his fine features showed the strain of the preceding weeks, and in his eyes there was a foreshadowing of the more bitter weeks to come. He needed that night's rest, but he said not a word. Quietly he gathered up his garments and started on, his outraged companions following. It is easy to imagine his keen disappointment. He had been working with them for three years . . . would they never catch a true vision of what he was about? He had so little time, and they were constantly wasting his time. . . . He had come to save mankind, and they wanted him to gratify his personal resentment by burning up a village!

Down the hot road they trailed after him, awed by his silence, vaguely conscious that they had failed again to measure up. "And they went to another village," says the narrative — nothing more. No debate; no bitterness; no futile conversation. In the mind of Jesus the thing was too small for comment. In a world where so much must be done, and done quickly, the memory could not afford to be burdened with a petty slight.

"And they went to another village." . . .

HIS METHOD

Many leaders have dared to lay out ambitious programs, but this is the most daring of all:

"Go ye into all the world," Jesus said, "and preach the gospel *to the whole creation.*"

Consider the sublime audacity of that command. To carry Roman civilization across the then known world had cost millions of lives and billions in treasure. To create any sort of reception for a new idea or product to-day involves a vast machinery of propaganda and expense. Jesus had no funds and no machinery. His organization was a tiny group of uneducated men, one of whom had already abandoned the cause as hopeless, deserting to the enemy. He had come proclaiming a Kingdom and was to end upon a cross; yet he dared to talk of conquering all creation. What was the source of his faith in that handful of followers? By what methods had he trained them? What had they learned from him of the secrets of influencing men?

We speak of the law of "supply and demand," but the words have got turned around. With anything which is not a basic necessity the supply always precedes the demand. Elias Howe invented the sewing machine, but it nearly rusted away before American women could be persuaded to use it. With their sewing finished so quickly what would they ever do with their spare time? Howe had vision, and had made his vision come true; but he could not sell! So his biographer paints a tragic picture — the man who had done more than any other in his generation to lighten the labor of women is forced to attend the funeral of the woman he loved in a borrowed suit of clothes! . . .

What were his methods of training? How did he meet prospective believers? How did he deal with objections? By what sort of strategy did he interest and persuade?

He was making the journey back from Jerusalem after his spectacular triumph in cleansing the Temple, when he came to Jacob's Well, and being tired, sat down. His disciples had stopped behind at one of the villages to purchase food, so he was alone. The well furnished the water-supply for the neighboring city of the Samaritans, and after a little time a woman came out to it, carrying her pitcher on her shoulder. Between her people, the Samaritans, and his people, the Jews, there was a feud of centuries. To be touched by even the shadow of a Samaritan was defilement according to the strict code of the Pharisees; to speak to one was a crime. The woman made no concealment of her resentment at finding him there. Almost any remark from his lips would have kindled her anger. She would at least have turned away in scorn; she might have summoned her relatives and driven him off.

An impossible situation, you will admit. How could he meet it? How give his message to one who was forbidden by everything holy to listen? The incident is very revealing: there are times when any word is the wrong word; when only silence can prevail. Jesus knew well his precious secret. As the woman drew closer he made no move to indicate that he was conscious of her approach. His gaze was on the ground. When he spoke it was quietly, musingly, as if to himself:

"If you knew who I am," he said, "you would not need to come out here for water. I would give you living water."

The woman stopped short, her interest challenged in spite of herself; she set down the pitcher and looked at the stranger. It was a burning hot day; the well was far from the city; she was heated and tired. What did he mean by such a remark? She started to speak, checked herself and burst out impulsively, her curiosity overleaping her caution:

"What are you talking about? Do you mean to say you are greater than our father Jacob who gave us this well? Have you some magic that will save us this long walk in the sun?"

Dramatic, isn't it — a single sentence achieving triumph, arousing interest and creating desire. With sure instinct he followed up his initial advantage. He began to talk to her in terms of her own life, her ambitions, her hopes, knowing so well that each of us is interested first of all and most of all in himself. When the disciples came up a few minutes later they found an unbelievable sight — a Samaritan listening with rapt attention to the teaching of a Jew. . . .

Surely no one will consider us lacking in reverence if we say that every one of the "principles of modern salesmanship" on which business men so much pride themselves, are brilliantly exemplified in Jesus' talk and work. The first of these and perhaps the most important is the necessity for "putting yourself in step with your prospect." A great sales manager used to illustrate it in this way:

"When you want to get aboard a street car which is already in motion, you don't run at it from right angles and try to make the platform in one wild leap," he would say. "If you do, you are likely to find yourself on the floor. No. You run along beside the car, increasing your pace until you are moving just as rapidly as it is moving and in the same direction. Then you step aboard easily, without danger or jolt.

"The minds of busy men are in motion," he would continue. "They are engaged with something very different from the thought you have to present. You can't jump directly at them and expect to make an effective landing. You must put yourself in the other man's place; try to imagine what he is thinking; let your first remark be in line with his thoughts; follow it by another with which you know he will easily agree. Thus, gradually, your two minds reach a point where they can join without conflict. You encourage him to say 'yes' and 'yes' and 'that's right' and 'I've noticed that myself,' until he says the final 'yes' which is your favorable decision."

Jesus taught all this without ever teaching it. Every one of his conversations, every contact between his mind and others, is worthy of the attentive study of any sales manager. Passing along the shores of a lake one day, he saw two of the men whom he wanted as disciples. *Their* minds were in motion; their hands were busy with their nets; their conversation was about conditions in the fishing trade, and the prospects of a good market for the day's catch. To have broken in on such thinking with the offer of employment as preachers of a new religion would have been to confuse them and invite a certain rebuff. What was Jesus' approach?

"Come with me," he said, "and I will make you fishers of men."

Fishers . . . that was a word they could understand . . . fishers of men . . . that was a new idea . . . what was he driving at . . . fishers of men . . . it sounded interesting . . . well, what is it, anyway?

He sat on a hillside overlooking a fertile country. Many of the crowd who gathered around him were farmers, with their wives and sons and daughters. He wanted their interest and attention; it was important to make them understand, at the very outset, that what he had to say was nothing vague or theoretical but of direct and immediate application to their daily lives.

"A sower went forth to sow," he began, "and when he sowed some seeds fell by the wayside and the fowls came and devoured them up. . . ." Were they interested . . . *were* they? Every man of them had gone through that experience . . . the thievish crows . . . many a good day's work *they* had spoiled. . . . So this Teacher knew something about the troubles that farmers had to put up with, did he? Fair enough . . . let's hear what he has to say. . . .

. . . I propose in this chapter to speak of the advertisements of Jesus which have survived for twenty centuries and are still the most potent influence in the world.

Let us begin by asking why he was so successful in mastering public attention and why, in contrast, his churches are less so? The answer is twofold. In the first place he recognized the basic principle that all good advertising is news. He was never trite or commonplace; he had no routine. If there had been newspapers in those days, no city editor could have said, "No need to visit him to-day; he will be doing just what he did last Sunday." Reporters would have followed him every single hour, for it was impossible to predict what he would say or do; every action and word were news.

The activity begins at sunrise. Jesus was an early riser; he knew that the simplest way to live *more* than an average life is to add an hour to the fresh end of the day. At sunrise, therefore, we discover a little boat pushing out from the shore of the lake. It makes its steady way across and deposits Jesus and his disciples in Capernaum, his favorite city. He proceeds at once to the house of a friend, but not without being discovered. The report spreads instantly that he is in town, and before he can finish breakfast a crowd has collected outside the gate — a poor palsied chap among them.

The day's work is at hand.

Having slept soundly in the open air he meets the call with quiet nerves. The smile that carried confidence into even the most hopeless heart spreads over his features; he stoops down toward the sufferer.

"Be of good cheer, my son," he cries, "your sins are all forgiven."

Sins forgiven! Indeed! The respectable members of the audience draw back with sharp disapproval. "What a blasphemous phrase," they exclaim. "Who authorized him to exercise the functions of God? What right has he to decide whose sins shall be forgiven?"

Jesus sensed rather than heard their protest. He never courted controversy but he never dodged it; and much of his fame arose out of the reports of his verbal victories. Men have been elected to office — even such high office as the Presidency — by being so good-natured that they never made an enemy. But the leaders who are remembered are those who had plenty of critics and dealt with them vigorously.

"What's the objection?" he exclaimed, turning on the dissenters. "Why do you stand there and criticize? Is it easier to say, 'Thy sins be forgiven thee,' or to say, 'Arise, take up thy bed and walk?' The results are the same." Bending over the sick man again he said: "Arise, take up thy bed and go unto thine house."

The man stirred and was amazed to find that his muscles responded. Slowly, doubtingly he struggled to his feet, and with one great shout of happiness started off, surrounded by his jubilant friends. The critics had received their answer, but they refused to give up. For an hour or more they persisted in angry argument, until the meeting ended in a tumult.

Can you imagine the next day's issue of the *Capernaum News,* if there had been one?

PALSIED MAN HEALED

JESUS OF NAZARETH CLAIMS RIGHT TO

FORGIVE SINS

PROMINENT SCRIBES OBJECT

"BLASPHEMOUS," SAYS LEADING CITIZEN.

"BUT ANYWAY I CAN WALK," HEALED MAN

RETORTS.

Front page story number one and the day is still young.

One of those who had been attracted by the excitement was a tax-collector named Matthew. Being a man of business he could not stay through the argument, but slipped away early and was hard at work when Jesus passed by a few minutes before noon.

"Matthew, I want you," said Jesus.

That was all. No argument; no offer of inducements; no promise of rewards. Merely "I want you;" and the prosperous tax-collector closed his office, made a feast for the brilliant young teacher and forthwith announced himself a disciple.

* * *

PROMINENT TAX COLLECTOR JOINS

NAZARETH FORCES

MATTHEW ABANDONS BUSINESS TO PROMOTE

NEW CULT

* * *

GIVES LARGE LUNCHEON

Front page story number two.

The luncheon itself furnished the third sensation. It was not at all the kind of affair which a religious teacher would be expected to approve. Decidedly it was good-natured and noisy.

No theological test was applied in limiting the invitation. No one stood at the entrance to demand: "What is your belief regarding the birth of Jesus?" Or, "Have you or have you not been baptized?" The doors were flung wide, and, along with the disciples and the respectable folks, a swarm of publicans and sinners trooped in.

"Outrageous," grumbled the worthy folk. "Surely if this teacher had any moral standards he never would eat with such rabble."

They were shocked; but he was not. That he had condemned himself according to their formula worried him not a whit. His liking for folks overran all social boundaries; he just could not seem to remember that some people are nice people, proper people, and some are not.

"Come, come," he exclaimed to the Pharisees, "won't you ever get over nagging at me because I eat with these outsiders? Who needs the doctor most — they that are well or they that are sick?

"And here's another thing to think about," he added. "You lay so much stress on forms and creeds and occasions — do you suppose God cares about all that? What do you think he meant when he said: 'I will have mercy and not sacrifice?' Take that home and puzzle over it."

DEFENDS PUBLICANS AND SINNERS

* * *

JESUS OF NAZARETH WELCOMES THEM AT LUNCH

* * *

REBUKES PROMINENT PHARISEES

* * *

"CREEDS UNIMPORTANT," HE SAYS. "GOD WANTS

MERCY NOT SACRIFICE."

A fourth big story. You may be sure it was carried into hundreds of homes during the next few weeks, and formed the basis for many a long evening's discussion.

As the meal drew to its close there came a dramatic interruption — a ruler of the city made his way slowly to the head of the table and stood silent, bowed by the terrible weight of his grief. That morning he had sat at his daughter's bedside, clasping her frail white hand in his, watching the flutter of the pulse, trying by the force of his longing to hold that little life back from the precipice. And at last the doctors had told him that it was useless any more to hope. So he had come, this ruler, to the strange young man whose deeds of healing were the sensation of the day.

Was it too late? The ruler had thought so when he entered the door; but as he stood in that splendid presence a new thrilling conviction gripped him:

"Master, my daughter is even now dead," he exclaimed, "but come and lay your hand on her and she will live."

Jesus rose from his seat, drawn by that splendid outburst of faith and without hesitation or questioning he started for the door. All his life he seemed to feel that there was no limit at all to what he could do, if only those who beseeched him believed enough. Grasping the ruler's arm he led the way up the street, his disciples and the motley crowd hurrying along behind.

They had several blocks to travel, and before their journey was completed another interruption occurred.

A woman who had been sick for twelve years edged through the crowd, eluded the sharp eyes of the disciples and touched the hem of his garment. "For she said within herself, if I may but touch his garment, I shall be whole." . . . What an idea. . . . What a Personality his must have been to provoke such ideas. . . . "My daughter is dead, but lay your hands on her and she will live." . . . "I've been sick for twelve years; the doctors can do nothing, but if I only touch his coat I'll be all right."

. . . How can the artists possibly have imagined that a sad-faced weakling could ever inspire such amazing ideas as these!

The woman won her victory. By that touch, by his smile, by the few words he spoke, her faith rose triumphant over disease. She "was made whole from that hour."

Again he moved forward, the crowd pressing hard. The ruler's residence was now in plain sight. The paid mourners, hired by the hour, were busy about the doorway; they increased their activities as their employer came in sight — hideous wails and the dull sounding of cymbals — a horrible pretense of grief. Quickening his stride Jesus was in the midst of them.

"Give place," he cried with a commanding gesture. "The maid is not dead but sleepeth."

They laughed him to scorn. Brushing them aside he strode into the house and took the little girl by the hand. The crowd looked on dumfounded, for at the magic of his touch she opened her eyes, and sat up.

Front page stories five and six. A woman sick twelve years, and healed! A child whom the doctors had abandoned for dead, sits up and smiles! No wonder a thousand tongues were busy that night advertising his name and work. "The fame thereof went abroad into all that land," says the narrative. Nothing could keep it from going abroad. It was irresistible news!

He was advertised by his service, not by his sermons; this is the second noteworthy fact. Nowhere in the Gospels do you find it announced that:

Jesus of Nazareth Will Denounce
The Scribes and Pharisees in the
Central Synagogue
To-night at Eight O'Clock
Special Music

His preaching was almost incidental. On only one occasion did he deliver a long discourse, and that was probably interrupted often by questions and debates. He did not come to establish a theology but to lead a life. Living more healthfully than any of his contemporaries he spread health wherever he went. Thinking more daringly, more divinely, he expressed himself in thoughts of surpassing beauty, as naturally as a plant bursts into bloom. His sermons, if they may be called sermons, were chiefly explanatory of his service. He healed a lame man, gave sight to a blind man, fed the hungry, cheered the poor; and by these works he was advertised much more than by his words. . . .

These are Jesus' works, done in Jesus' name. If he were to live again, in these modern days, he would find a way to make them known — to be advertised by his service, not merely by his sermons. One thing is certain: he would not neglect the market-place. . . .

The present day market-place is the newspaper and the magazine. Printed columns are the modern thoroughfares; published advertisements are the cross-roads where the sellers and the buyers meet. Any issue of a national magazine is a world's fair, a bazaar filled with the products of the world's work. Clothes and clocks and candle-sticks; soup and soap and cigarettes; lingerie and limousines — the best of all of them are there, proclaimed by their makers in persuasive tones. That every other voice should be raised in such great market-places, and the voice of Jesus of Nazareth be still — this is a vital omission which he would find a way to correct. He would be a national advertiser today, I am sure, as he was the great advertiser of his own day. . . .

Take any one of the parables, no matter which — you will find that it exemplifies all the principles on which advertising text books are written. Always a picture in the very first sentence; crisp, graphic language and a message so clear that even the dullest can not escape it.

Ten Virgins Went Forth To Meet
A Bridegroom

A striking picture and a striking head-line. The story which follows has not a single wasted word:

> Five of the Virgins were wise, and five were foolish.
> They that were foolish took their lamps, and took no oil with them:
> But the wise took oil in their vessels with their lamps.
> While the bridegroom tarried, they all slumbered and slept.
> And at midnight there was a cry made, Behold the bridegroom cometh; go ye out to meet him.
> Then all those Virgins arose, and trimmed their lamps.
> And the foolish said unto the wise, "Give us of your oil for our lamps have gone out."
> But the wise answered, saying, "Not so; lest there be not enough for us and you; but go ye rather to them that sell, and buy for yourselves."
> And while they went to buy, the bridegroom came; and they that were ready went in with him to the marriage; and the door was shut.
> Afterward came also the other Virgins, saying, "Lord, Lord, open to me."
> But he answered and said, "Verily, I say unto you, I know you not . . ."
> Watch, therefore, for ye know neither the day nor the hour wherein the Son of man cometh.

Illustrate that with a drawing by a distinguished artist; set it up according to the best modern typography; bury it in a magazine with a hundred other pages — will it not stand out? Will it not grip the attention of even the most casual, and *make* itself read? . . .

THE FOUNDER OF MODERN BUSINESS

When Jesus was twelve years old his father and mother took him to the Feast at Jerusalem.

It was the big national vacation; even peasant families saved their pennies and looked forward to it through the year. Towns like Nazareth were emptied of their inhabitants except for the few old folks who were left behind to look after the very young ones. Crowds of cheerful pilgrims filled the highways, laughing their way across the hills and under the stars at night.

In such a mass of folk it was not surprising that a boy of twelve should be lost. When Mary and Joseph missed him on the homeward trip, they took it calmly and began a search among the relatives.

The inquiry produced no result. Some remembered having seen him in the Temple, but no one had seen him since. Mary grew frightened: where could he be? Back there in the city alone? Wandering hungry and tired through the friendless streets? Carried away by other travelers into a distant country? She pictured a hundred calamities. Nervously she and Joseph hurried back over the hot roads, through the suburbs, up through the narrow city streets, up to the courts of the Temple itself.

And there he was.

Not lost; not a bit worried. Apparently unconscious that the Feast was over, he sat in the midst of a group of old men, who were tossing questions at him and applauding the shrewd common sense of his replies. Involuntarily his parents halted — they were simple folk, uneasy among strangers and disheveled by their haste. But after all they *were* his parents, and a very human feeling of irritation quickly overcame their diffidence. Mary stepped forward and grasped his arm.

"Son, why hast thou thus dealt with us?" she demanded. "Behold thy father and I have sought thee sorrowing."

I wonder what answer she expected to receive. Did she ever know exactly what he was going to say: did any one in Nazareth quite understand this keen, eager lad, who had such curious moments of abstraction and was forever breaking out with remarks that seemed so far beyond his years?

He spoke to her now with deference, as always, but in words that did not dispel but rather added to her uncertainty.

"How is it that ye sought me?" he asked. "Wist ye not that I must be about my father's *business?*" . . .

What interests us most in this one recorded incident of his boyhood is the fact that for the first time he defined the purpose of his career. He did not say, "Wist ye not that I must practise preaching?" or "Wist ye not that I must get ready to meet the arguments of men like these?" The language was quite different, and well worth remembering. "Wist ye not that I must be about my father's *business?*" he said. He thought of his life as *business.* What did he mean by business? To what extent are the principles by which he conducted his business applicable to ours? And if he were among us again, in our highly competitive world, would his business philosophy work?

On one occasion, you recall, he stated his recipe for success. It was on the afternoon when James and John came to ask him what promotion they might expect. They were two of the most energetic of the lot, called "Sons of Thunder," by the rest, being noisy and always in the midst of some sort of a storm. They had joined the ranks because they liked him, but with no very definite idea of what it was all about; and now they wanted to know where the enterprise was heading, and just what there would be in it for them.

"Master," they said, "we want to ask what plans you have in mind for us. You're going to need big men around you when you establish your kingdom; our ambition is to sit on either side of you, one on your right hand and the other on your left."

Who can object to that attitude? If a man fails to look after himself, certainly no one will look after him. If you want a big place, go ask for it. That's the way to get ahead.

Jesus answered with a sentence which sounds poetically absurd.

"Whosoever will be great among you, shall be your minister," he said, "and whosoever of you will be the chiefest, shall be servant of all."

A fine piece of rhetoric, now isn't it? Be a good servant and you will be great; be the best possible servant and you will occupy the highest possible place. Nice idealistic talk but utterly impractical; nothing to take seriously in a common sense world. That is just what men thought for some hundreds of years; and then, quite suddenly, Business woke up to a great discovery. You will hear that discovery proclaimed in every sales convention as something distinctly modern and up to date. It is emblazoned in the advertising pages of every magazine.

Look through those pages.

Here is the advertisement of an automobile company, one of the greatest in the world. And why is it greatest? On what does it base its claim to leadership? On its huge factories and financial strength?

They are never mentioned. On its army of workmen or its high salaried executives? You might read its advertisements for years without suspecting that it had either. No. "We are great because of our service," the advertisements cry. "We will crawl under your car oftener and get our backs dirtier than any of our competitors. Drive up to our service stations and ask for anything at all — it will be granted cheerfully. We serve; therefore we grow."

A manufacturer of shoes makes the same boast in other terms. "We put ourselves at your feet and give you everything that you can possibly demand." Manufacturers of building equipment, of clothes, of food; presidents of railroads and steamship companies; the heads of banks and investment houses — *all* of them tell the same story. "Service is what we are here for," they exclaim. They call it the "spirit of modern business"; they suppose, most of them, that it is something very new. But Jesus preached it more than nineteen hundred years ago. . . .

Study Guide

1. The particular portrait of Jesus developed by Bruce Barton is concisely described in the introduction. The details can be divided thus:

    (a) the author's prologue;
    (b) Jesus's personal qualities as "an executive";
    (c) his methods; and
    (d) his career.

2. What stereotype of Jesus is the author intent on revising? Note the following sentences — central to Barton's revisionary portrait of Christianity's founder: "A failure! He picked up twelve men from the bottom ranks of business and forged them into an organization that conquered the world. . . . 'Some day,' said he [the little boy], 'some one will write a book about Jesus. Every business man will read it and send it to his partners and his salesmen. For it will tell the story of the founder of modern business.' "

3. What qualities of character does Barton ascribe to good executives, generally, and to Jesus in particular?

4. Through Barton's numerous illustrations, the methods employed by Jesus can be outlined quite simply: rapport with his audience, the ability to appear relevant and to act decisively and successfully, and literary skill. From your reading of the New Testament and from your knowledge of the teachings of Christianity, how would you assess the portrait of Christ Barton develops in this section?

5. Barton closes with a reaffirmation of his initial thesis.
   (a) Illustrate this by being able to explain his homilies on the word "business" and the word "service."
   (b) Can you accept this interpretation?
   (c) What does this selection tell you about Barton's outlook on business and business success?
   (d) What does the fact that his book was a bestseller in the 1920's tell you about the decade?

Herbert Hoover

RUGGED INDIVIDUALISM

1922 In the decade after the first World War, Herbert Hoover (1874-1964) was one of the most famous and highly regarded men in the entire world. Following a phenomenally successful career as a mining engineer, Hoover distinguished himself as an administrator and humanitarian through his work as head of the Committee for Relief in Belgium and then as United States Food Administrator. After service at the Versailles Peace Conference, he became Secretary of Commerce under Presidents Harding and Coolidge before winning the Presidency itself in 1928.

In the twenties Hoover's general view of government and society was dominant in America. The majority of the nation, tired out and disillusioned after two decades of reform and war, wanted no more of tight controls and personal sacrifices for some vaguely defined common good. Hoover, far too intelligent and too public spirited to advocate a program based on mere selfishness, developed in *American Individualism* (1922) a philosophy that suited the public's reactionary mood without completely neglecting the American tradition of progressivism and fair play. Hoover's practice as Secretary of Commerce and then as President did not measure up to the "progressive individualism" he describes in the following pages. His was a far more "rugged" and doctrinaire individualism than *American Individualism* would lead one to expect. The book, however, set the tone for the twenties. The philosophy seemed both forward looking and in the American tradition, both good for the country and good for the individual. Accepting this comfortable if somewhat glib interpretation of the American mission, the bulk of the population marched forward blithely and blindly under Hoover's leadership into the pit of the Great Depression.

AMERICAN INDIVIDUALISM

We have witnessed in this last eight years the spread of revolution over one-third of the world. The causes of these explosions lie at far greater depths than the failure of governments in war. The war itself in its last stages was a conflict of social philosophies — but beyond this the causes of social explosion lay in the great inequalities and injustices of centuries flogged beyond endurance by the conflict and freed from restraint by the destruction of war. The urgent forces which drive human society have been plunged into a terrible furnace. Great theories spun by dreamers to remedy the pressing human ills have come to the front of men's minds. Great formulas came into life that promised to dissolve all trouble. Great masses of people have flocked to their banners in hopes born of misery and suffering. Nor has this great social ferment been confined to those nations that have burned with revolutions.

Now, as the storm of war, of revolution and of emotion subsides there is left even with us of the United States much unrest, much discontent with the surer forces of human advancement. To all of us, out of this crucible of actual, poignant, individual experience has come a deal of new understanding, and it is for all of us to ponder these new currents if we are to shape our future with intelligence.

Even those parts of the world that suffered less from the war have been partly infected by these ideas. Beyond this, however, many have had high hopes of civilization suddenly purified and ennobled by the sacrifices and services of the war; they had thought the fine unity of purpose gained in war would be carried into great unity of action in remedy of the faults of civilization in peace. But from concentration of every spiritual and material energy upon the single purpose of war the scene changed to the immense complexity and the many purposes of peace.

Thus there loom up certain definite underlying forces in our national life that need to be stripped of the imaginary — the transitory — and a definition should be given to the actual permanent and persistent motivation of our civilization. In contemplation of these questions we must go far deeper than the superficials of our political and economic structure, for these are but the products of our social philosophy — the machinery of our social system.

Nor is it ever amiss to review the political, economic, and spiritual principles through which our country has steadily grown in usefulness and greatness, not only to preserve them from being fouled by false notions, but more importantly that we may guide ourselves in the road of progress.

Five or six great social philosophies are at struggle in the world for ascendency. There is the Individualism of America. There is the Individualism of the more democratic states of Europe with its careful reservations of castes and classes. There are Communism, Socialism, Syndicalism, Capitalism, and finally there is Autocracy — whether by birth, by possessions, militarism, or divine right of kings. Even the Divine Right still lingers on although our lifetime has seen fully two-thirds of the earth's population, including Germany, Austria, Russia, and China, arrive at a state of angry disgust with this type of social motive power and throw it on the scrap heap.

All these thoughts are in ferment today in every country in the world. They fluctuate in ascendency with times and places. They compromise with each other in daily reaction on governments and peoples. Some of these ideas are perhaps more adapted to one race than another. Some are false, some are true. What we are interested in is their challenge to the physical and spiritual forces of America.

The partisans of some of these other brands of social schemes challenge us to comparison; and some of their partisans even among our own people are increasing in their agitation that we adopt one or another or parts of their devices in place of our tried individualism. They insist that our social foundations are exhausted, that like feudalism and autocracy America's plan has served its purpose — that it must be abandoned.

There are those who have been left in sober doubt of our institutions or are confounded by bewildering catchwords of vivid phrases. For in this welter of discussions there is much attempt to glorify or defame social and economic forces with phrases. Nor indeed should we disregard the potency of some of these phrases in their stir to action. — "The dictatorship of the Proletariat," "Capitalistic nations," "Germany over all," and a score of others. We need only to review those that have jumped to horseback during the last ten years in order that we may be properly awed by the great social and political havoc that can be worked where the bestial instincts of hate, murder, and destruction are clothed by the demagogue in the fine terms of political idealism.

For myself, let me say at the very outset that my faith in the essential truth, strength, and vitality of the developing creed by which we have hitherto lived in this country of ours has been confirmed and deepened by the searching experiences of seven years of service in the backwash and misery of war. Seven years of contending with economic degeneration, with social disintegration, with incessant political dislocation, with all of its seething and ferment of individual and class conflict, could but impress me with the primary motivation of social forces, and the necessity for broader thought upon their great issues to humanity. And from it all I emerge an individualist — an unashamed individualist. But let me say also that I am an American individualist. For America has been steadily developing the ideals that constitute progressive individualism.

No doubt, individualism run riot, with no tempering principle, would provide a long category of inequalities, of tyrannies, dominations, and injustices. America, however, has tempered the whole conception of individualism by the injection of a definite principle, and from this principle it follows that attempts at domination, whether in government or in the processes of industry and commerce, are under an insistent curb. If we would have the values of individualism, their stimulation to initiative, to the development of hand and intellect, to the high development of thought and spirituality, they must be tempered with that firm and fixed ideal of American individualism — *an equality of opportunity*. If we would have these values we must soften its hardness and stimulate progress through that sense of service that lies in our people.

Therefore, it is not the individualism of other countries for which I would speak, but the individualism of America. Our individualism differs from all others because it embraces these great ideals: *that while we build our society upon the attainment of the individual, we shall safeguard to every individual an equality of opportunity to take that position in the community to which his intelligence, character, ability, and ambition entitle him; that we keep the social solution free from frozen strata of classes; that we shall stimulate effort of each individual to achievement; that through an enlarging sense of responsibility and understanding we shall assist him to this attainment; while he in turn must stand up to the emery wheel of competition.*

Individualism cannot be maintained as the foundation of a society if it looks to only legalistic justice based upon contracts, property, and political equality. Such legalistic safeguards are themselves not enough. In our individualism we have long since abandoned the laissez faire of the 18th Century — the notion that it is "every man for himself and the devil take the hindmost." We abandoned that when we adopted the ideal of equality of opportunity — the fair chance of Abraham Lincoln. We have confirmed its abandonment in terms of legislation, of social and economic justice, — in part because we have learned that it is the hindmost who throws the bricks at our social edifice, in part because we have learned that the foremost are not always the best nor the hindmost the worst — and in part because we have learned that social injustice is the destruction of justice itself. We have learned that the impulse to production can only be maintained at a high pitch if there is a fair division of the product. We have also learned that fair division can only be obtained by certain restrictions on the strong and the dominant. . . .

The will-o'-the-wisp of all breeds of socialism is that they contemplate a motivation of human animals by altruism alone. It necessitates a bureaucracy of the entire population, in which, having obliterated the economic stimulation of each member, the fine gradations of character and ability are to be arranged in relative authority by ballot or more likely by a Tammany Hall or a Bolshevist party, or some other form of tyranny. The proof of the futility of these ideas as a stimulation to the development and activity of the individual does not lie alone in the ghastly failure of Russia, but it also lies in our own failure in attempts at nationalized industry.

Likewise the basic foundations of autocracy, whether it be class government or capitalism in the sense that a few men through unrestrained control of property determine the welfare of great numbers, is as far apart from the rightful expression of American individualism as the two poles. The will-o'-the-wisp of autocracy in any form is that it supposes that the good Lord endowed a special few with all the divine attributes. It contemplates one human animal dealing to the other human animals his just share of earth, of glory, and of immortality. The proof of the futility of these ideas in the development of the world does not lie alone in the grim failure of Germany, but it lies in the damage to our moral and social fabric from those who have sought economic domination in America, whether employer or employee.

We in America have had too much experience of life to fool ourselves into pretending that all men are equal in ability, in character, in intelligence, in ambition. That was part of the claptrap of the French Revolution. We have grown to understand that all we can hope to assure to the individual through government is liberty, justice, intellectual welfare, equality of opportunity, and stimulation to service.

It is in maintenance of a society fluid to these human qualities that our individualism departs from the individualism of Europe. There can be no rise for the individual through the frozen strata of classes, or of castes, and no stratification can take place in a mass livened by the free stir of its particles. This guarding of our individualism against stratification insists not only in preserving in the social solution an equal opportunity for the able and ambitious to rise from the bottom; it also insists that the sons of the successful shall not by any mere right of birth or favor continue to occupy their fathers' places of power against the rise of a new generation in process of coming up from the bottom. The pioneers of our American individualism had the good sense not to reward Washington and Jefferson and Hamilton with hereditary dukedoms and fixtures in landed estates, as Great Britain rewarded Marlborough and Nelson. Otherwise our American fields of opportunity would have been clogged with long generations inheriting their fathers' privileges without their fathers' capacity for service.

That our system has avoided the establishment and domination of class has a significant proof in the present Administration in Washington. Of the twelve men comprising the President, Vice-President, and Cabinet, nine have earned their own way in life without economic inheritance, and eight of them started with manual labor.

If we examine the impulses that carry us forward, none is so potent for progress as the yearning for individual self-expression, the desire for creation of something. Perhaps the greatest human happiness flows from personal achievement. Here lies the great urge of the constructive instinct of mankind. But it can only thrive in a society where the individual has liberty and stimulation to achievement. Nor does the community progress except through its participation in these multitudes of achievements.

Furthermore, the maintenance of productivity and the advancement of the things of the spirit depend upon the ever-renewed supply from the mass of those who can rise to leadership. Our social, economic, and intellectual progress is almost solely dependent upon the creative minds of those individuals with imaginative and administrative intelligence who create or who carry discoveries to widespread application. No race possesses more than a small percentage of these minds in a single generation. But little thought has ever been given to our racial dependency upon them. Nor that our progress is in so large a measure due to the fact that with our increased means of communication these rare individuals are today able to spread their influence over so enlarged a number of lesser capable minds as to have increased their potency a million-fold. In truth, the vastly greater productivity of the world with actually less physical labor is due to the wider spread of their influence through the discovery of these facilities. And they can arise solely through the selection that comes from the free-running mills of competition. They must be free to rise from the mass; they must be given the attraction of premiums to effort.

Leadership is a quality of the individual. It is the individual alone who can function in the world of intellect and in the field of leadership. If democracy is to secure its authorities in morals, religion, and statesmanship, it must stimulate leadership from its own mass. Human leadership cannot be replenished by selection like queen bees, by divine right or bureaucracies, but by the free rise of ability, character, and intelligence.

Even so, leadership cannot, no matter how brilliant, carry progress far ahead of the average of the mass of individual units. Progress of the nation is the sum of progress in its individuals. Acts and ideas that lead to progress are born out of the womb of the individual mind, not out of the mind of the crowd. The crowd only feels: it has no mind of its own which can plan. The crowd is credulous, it destroys, it consumes, it hates, and it dreams — but it never builds. It is one of the most profound and important of exact psychological truths that man in the mass does not think but only feels. The mob functions only in a world of emotion. The demagogue feeds on mob emotions and his leadership is the leadership of emotion, not the leadership of intellect and progress. Popular desires are no criteria to the real need; they can be determined only by deliberative consideration, by education, by constructive leadership. . . .

Economic Phases

That high and increasing standards of living and comfort should be the first of considerations in public mind and in government needs no apology. We have long since realized that the basis of an advancing civilization must be a high and growing standard of living for all the people, not for a single class; that education, food, clothing, housing, and the spreading use of what we so often term non-essentials, are the real fertilizers of the soil from which spring the finer flowers of life. The economic development of the past fifty years has lifted the general standard of comfort far beyond the dreams of our forefathers. The only road to further advance in the standard of living is by greater invention, greater elimination of waste, greater production and better distribution of commodities and services, for by increasing their ratio to our numbers and dividing them justly we each will have more of them.

The superlative value of individualism through its impulse to production, its stimulation to invention has, so far as I know, never been denied. Criticism of it has lain in its wastes but more importantly in its failures of equitable sharing of the product. In our country these contentions are mainly over the division to each of his share of the comforts and luxuries, for none of us is either hungry or cold or without a place to lay his head — and we have much besides. In less than four decades we have added electric lights, plumbing, telephones, gramophones, automobiles, and what not in wide diffusion to our standards of living. Each in turn began as a luxury, each in turn has become so commonplace that seventy or eighty per cent. of our people participate in them.

To all practical souls there is little use in quarreling over the share of each of us until we have something to divide. So long as we maintain our individualism we will have increasing quantities to share and we shall have time and leisure and taxes with which to fight out proper sharing of the "surplus." The income tax returns show that this surplus is a minor part of our total production after taxes are paid. Some of this "surplus" must be set aside for rewards to saving for stimulation of proper effort to skill, to leadership and invention — therefore the dispute is in reality over much less than the total of such "surplus." While there should be no minimizing of a certain fringe of injustices in sharing the results of production or in the wasteful use made by some of their share, yet there is vastly wider field for gains to all of us through cheapening the costs of production and distribution through the eliminating of their wastes, from increasing the volume of product by each and every one doing his utmost, than will ever come to us even if we can think out a method of abstract justice in sharing which did not stifle production of the total product. . . .

But those are utterly wrong who say that individualism has as its only end the acquisition and preservation of private property — the selfish snatching and boarding of the common product. Our American individualism, indeed, is only in part an economic creed. It aims to provide opportunity for self-expression, not merely economically, but spiritually as well. Private property is not a fetich in America. The crushing of the liquor trade without a cent of compensation, with scarcely even a discussion of it, does not bear out the notion that we give property rights any headway over human rights. Our development of individualism shows an increasing tendency to regard right of property not as an object in itself, but in the light of a useful and necessary instrument in stimulation of initiative to the individual; not only stimulation to him that he may gain personal comfort, security in life, protection to his family, but also because individual accumulation and ownership is a basis of selection to leadership in administration of the tools of industry and commerce. It is where dominant private property is assembled in the hands of the groups who control the state that the individual begins to feel capital as an oppressor. Our American demand for equality of opportunity is a constant militant check upon capital becoming a thing to be feared. Out of fear we sometimes even go too far and stifle the reproductive use of capital by crushing the initiative that makes for its creation. . . .

The domination by arbitrary individual ownership is disappearing because the works of today are steadily growing more and more beyond the resources of any one individual, and steadily taxation will reduce relatively excessive individual accumulations. The number of persons in partnership through division of ownership among stockholders is steadily increasing — thus 100,000 to 200,000 partners in a single concern are not uncommon. The overwhelmingly largest portion of our mobile capi-

tal is that of our banks, insurance companies, building and loan associations, and the vast majority of all this is the aggregated small savings
of our people. Thus large capital is steadily becoming more and more a
mobilization of the savings of the small holder — the actual people themselves — and its administration becomes at once more sensitive to the
moral opinions of the people in order to attract their support. The directors and managers of large concerns, themselves employees of these great
groups of individual stockholders, or policy holders, reflect a spirit of
community responsibility.

Large masses of capital can only find their market for service or production to great numbers of the same kind of people that they employ
and they must therefore maintain confidence in their public responsibilities in order to retain their customers. In times when the products of
manufacture were mostly luxuries to the average of the people, the condition of their employees was of no such interest to their customers as
when they cater to employees in general. Of this latter, no greater proofs
need exist than the efforts of many large concerns directly dependent
upon public good will to restrain prices in scarcity — and the very general desire to yield a measure of service with the goods sold. Another
phase of this same development in administration of capital is the growth
of a sort of institutional sense in many large business enterprises. The encouragement of solidarity in all grades of their employees in the common
service and common success, the sense of mutuality with the prosperity
of the community are both vital developments in individualism. . . .

A great test of the soundness of a social system must be its ability to
evolve within itself those orderly shifts in its administration that enable
it to apply the new tools of social, economic, and intellectual progress,
and to eliminate the malign forces that may grow in the application of
these tools. When we were almost wholly an agricultural people our form
of organization and administration, both in the governmental and economic fields, could be simple. With the enormous shift in growth to
industry and commerce we have erected organisms that each generation
has denounced as Frankensteins, yet the succeeding generation proves
them to be controllable and useful. The growth of corporate organizations, of our banking systems, of our railways, of our electrical power,
of our farm coöperatives, of our trade unions, of our trade associations,
and of a hundred others indeed develops both beneficent and malign
forces. The timid become frightened. But our basic social ideas march
through the new things in the end. Our demagogues, of both radical
and standpat breed, thrive on demands for the destruction of one or
another of these organizations as the only solution for their defects, yet

progress requires only a guardianship of the vital principles of our individualism with its safeguard of true equality of opportunity in them.

Political Phases

It is not the primary purpose of this essay to discuss our political organization. Democracy is merely the mechanism which individualism invented as a device that would carry on the necessary political work of its social organization. Democracy arises out of individualism and prospers through it alone.

Without question, there exists, almost all over the world, unprecedented disquietude at the functioning of government itself. It is in part the dreamy social ferment of war emotion. It is in part the aftermath of a period when the Government was everything and the individual nothing, from which there is much stimulation to two schools of thought: one that all human ills can be cured by governmental regulation, and the other that all regulation is a sin.

During the war, the mobilization of every effort, the destruction of the normal demand and the normal avenues of distribution, required a vast excursion over the deadline of individualism in order that we might secure immediate results. Its continuation would have destroyed the initiative of our people and undermined all real progress. We are slowly getting back, but many still aspire to these supposed short cuts to the millennium.

Much of our discontent takes the form of resentment against the inequalities in the distribution of the sacrifices of war. Both silently and vocally there is complaint that while some died, others ran no risk, and yet others profited. For these complaints there is adequate justification. The facts are patent. However, no conceivable human intelligence would be able to manage the conduct of war so as to see that all sacrifices and burdens should be distributed equitably. War is destruction, and we should blame war for its injustices, not a social system whose object is construction. The submergence of the individual, however, in the struggle of the race could be but temporary — its continuance through the crushing of individual action and its equities would, if for no other reason, destroy the foundations of our civilization.

Looked at as the umpire in our social system, our Government has maintained an equality before the law and a development of legal justice and an authority in restraint of evil instincts that support this social system and its ideals so far as the imperfections of developing human institutions permit. It has gone the greatest distance of any government toward maintaining an equality of franchise; an equality of entrance to public office, and government by the majority. It has succeeded far beyond all others in those safeguards of equality of opportunity through education, public information, and the open channels of free speech and free press. It is, however, much easier to chart the course of progress to government in dealing with the abstract problems of order, political liberty, and stimulation to intellectual and moral advancement than it is to chart its relations to the economic seas. These seas are new and only partly discovered or explored.

Our Government's greatest troubles and failures are in the economic field. Forty years ago the contact of the individual with the Government had its largest expression in the sheriff or policeman, and in debates over political equality. In those happy days the Government offered but small interference with the economic life of the citizen. But with the vast development of industry and the train of regulating functions of the national and municipal government that followed from it; with the recent vast increase in taxation due to the war; — the Government has become through its relations to economic life the most potent force for maintenance or destruction of our American individualism.

The entrance of the Government began strongly three decades ago, when our industrial organization began to move powerfully in the direction of consolidation of enterprise. We found in the course of this development that equality of opportunity and its corollary, individual initiative, was being throttled by the concentration of control of industry and service, and thus an economic domination of groups builded over the nation. At this time, particularly, we were threatened with a form of autocracy of economic power. Our mass of regulation of public utilities and our legislation against restraint of trade is the monument to our intent to preserve an equality of opportunity. This regulation is itself proof that we have gone a long way toward the abandonment of the "capitalism" of Adam Smith.

Day by day we learn more as to the practical application of restrictions against economic and political domination. We sometimes lag behind in the correction of those forces that would override liberty, justice, and equality of opportunity, but the principle is so strong within us that domination of the few will not be tolerated. These restraints must keep pace with the growing complexity of our economic organization, but they need tuning to our social system if they would not take us into great dangers. As we build up our powers of production through the advancing application of science we create new forces with which men may dominate — railway, power, oil, and what not. They may produce temporary blockades upon equality of opportunity.

To curb the forces in business which would destroy equality of opportunity and yet to maintain the initiative and creative faculties of our people are the twin objects we must attain. To preserve the former we must regulate that type of activity that would dominate. To preserve the latter, the Government must keep out of production and distribution of commodities and services. This is the deadline between our system and socialism. Regulation to prevent domination and unfair practices, yet preserving rightful initiative, are in keeping with our social foundations. Nationalization of industry or business is their negation.

When we come to the practical problems of government in relation to these economic questions the test lies in two directions: Does this act safeguard an equality of opportunity? Does it maintain the initiative of our people? For in the first must lie the deadline against domination, and in the second the deadline in preservation of individualism against socialism. . . .

There are malign social forces other than our failures that would destroy our progress. There are the equal dangers both of reaction and radicalism. The perpetual howl of radicalism is that it is the sole voice of liberalism — that devotion to social progress is its field alone. These men would assume that all reform and human advance must come through government. They have forgotten that progress must come from the steady lift of the individual and that the measure of national idealism and progress is the quality of idealism in the individual. The most trying support of radicalism comes from the timid or dishonest minds that shrink from facing the result of radicalism itself but are devoted to defense of radicalism as proof of a liberal mind. . . .

The primary safeguard of American individualism is an understanding of it; of faith that it is the most precious possession of American civilization, and a willingness courageously to test every process of national life upon the touchstone of this basic social premise. Development of the human institutions and of science and of industry have been long chains of trial and error. Our public relations to them and to other phases of our national life can be advanced in no other way than by a willingness to experiment in the remedy of our social faults. The failures and unsolved problems of economic and social life can be corrected; they can be solved within our social theme and under no other system. The solution is a matter of will to find solution; of a sense of duty as well as of a sense of right and citizenship. No one who buys "bootleg" whiskey can complain of gunmen and hoodlumism.

Study Guide

1. As indicated in the introduction, this is an enlightened and somewhat appealing statement on behalf of American individualism — in contrast to the shrill and inflexible exhortations on behalf of economic individualism so characteristic of Hoover's public statements after he left office in the midst of the Great Depression in 1933. The essay can be divided in this way:

   (a) Hoover's survey of the ideological options confronting the Western nations after World War I (pp. 393–399);
   (b) a statement of the transcendent principles men (Americans) should live by (pp. 393–396); and
   (c) the application of these principles to the economic and political aspects of American life (pp. 399–404).

2. Let us begin by examining the tenor of Hoover's review of recent history.

   (a) What impression do you get of his state of mind as he surveys the developments in the United States and Europe in the past decade?
   (b) Does he appear totally complacent about the future of American capitalism or does he appear apprehensive?
   (c) Contrast the sense of urgency, and even anxiety, Hoover exudes concerning the future of the nation with the tone of optimistic certitude that pervades the selections from the prewar, Progressive Era by Theodore Roosevelt and Wilson.
   (d) What events, at home and abroad, had their impact on the temper of the nation — and are ultimately reflected in this piece by Herbert Hoover?

3. Find a sentence or two that, in your opinion, illuminate the historical and emotional context within which Hoover is operating.

4. Summarize (pp. 396–397) the unique qualities Hoover ascribes to the American variety of "individualism." How, in Hoover's opinion, has American individualism been altered over the centuries?

5. Regarding alternatives to individualism, what criticisms does Hoover level against socialistic and autocratic forms of government and those countries that retain hereditary titles and hereditary privileges?

6. Hoover's discussion of the American economy reflects the sanguine confidence of the business community in both its soundness and in the equitable manner in which the American people shared in its rewards. Note his comments on:

   (a) the standard of living;
   (b) the relationship of individualism to productivity and how this productivity has been distributed; and
   (c) the "spiritual" benefits of individualism.

7. Hoover explains democracy as a consequence (not as a cause) of individualism.

   (a) What role does Hoover assign to government in the economic system?

   (b) How would his views on this role ("To curb the forces in business which would destroy equality of opportunity and yet to maintain the initiative and creative faculties of our people are the twin objects we must attain") differ from Theodore Roosevelt or Wilson in the Progressive Era?

   (c) Contrast the above quotation on individual initiative with:

      (1) the trend toward economic consolidation in the 1920's; and

      (2) Hoover's role, as secretary of commerce, in promoting that trend.

H. L. Mencken

THE LAND OF THE BOOB

⊰❧ 1926 ❧⊱ THE BAD BOY of American letters in the 1920's was Henry Louis Mencken (1880-1956), Baltimore newspaperman, magazine editor, essayist, and lexicographer. One thing American he loved was the language, which he discussed with perception and scholarship in *The American Language,* first published in 1918 and republished with revisions and supplements several times thereafter. Most aspects of American life aroused his scorn. In the magazine *The American Mercury* and in books such as *Prejudices* (six series, 1919-1927) and *Notes on Democracy* (1926) he lambasted the low-brow middle-class public (a "booboisie" made up of *homo boobiens*), academic pomposity, the "bilge of idealism," Rotarians, Methodists, and reformers, the principles and practices of democracy, and practically all the tastes and traditions of the majority. Only for a few of the critical thinkers and writers of the time — such as Theodore Dreiser (1871-1945), Sherwood Anderson (1876-1941), and Sinclair Lewis (1885-1951) — did he ever have a good word.

His *American Mercury,* with its green cover, was seen on most American campuses in the hands of professors and students who thought of themselves as far advanced in their literary, political, and social views. In 1927 Walter Lippmann (1889-1974) referred to him as "the most powerful personal influence on this whole generation of educated people." Certainly Mencken contributed a great deal to the spirit and creed of contemporary intellectuals, who believed in social and sexual freedom, opposed the enforcement of propriety by legislation (such as the Volstead Act), smiled at conviction or commitments religious or political, enjoyed the debunking of heroes, and complained of the bad cultural consequences of mass production and the machine.

Mencken's manner, at once shocking and charming, is well illustrated by the concluding chapter from his *Notes on Democracy,* which follows.

THE FUTURE OF DEMOCRACY

WHETHER or not democrary is destined to survive in the world until the corruptible puts on incorruption and the immemorial Christian dead leap out of their graves, their faces shining and their yells resounding — this is something, I confess, that I don't know, nor is it necessary, for the purposes of the present inquiry, that I venture upon the hazard of a guess. My business is not prognosis, but diagnosis. I am not engaged in therapeutics, but in pathology. That simple statement of fact, I daresay, will be accepted as a confession, condemning me out of hand as unfit for my task, and even throwing a certain doubt upon my *bona fides*. For it is one of the peculiar intellectual accompaniments of democracy that the concept of the insoluble becomes unfashionable — nay, almost infamous. To lack a remedy is to lack the very license to discuss disease. The causes of this are to be sought, without question, in the nature of democracy itself. It came into the world as a cure-all, and it remains primarily a cure-all to this day. Any boil upon the body politic, however vast and raging, may be relieved by taking a vote; any flux of blood may be stopped by passing a law. The aim of government is to repeal the laws of nature, and re-enact them with moral amendments. War becomes simply a device to end war. The state, a mystical emanation from the mob, takes on a transcendental potency, and acquires the power to make over the father which begat it. Nothing remains inscrutable and beyond remedy, not even the way of a man with a maid. It was not so under the ancient and accursed systems of despotism, now happily purged out of the world. They, too, I grant you, had certain pretensions of an homeric gaudiness, but they at least refrained from attempts to abolish sin, poverty, stupidity, cowardice, and other such immutable realities. Mediaeval Christianity, which was a theological and philosophical *apologia* for those systems, actually erected belief in that immutability into a cardinal article of faith. The evils of the world were incurable: one put off the quest for a perfect moral order until one got to heaven, *post mortem*. There arose, in consequence, a scheme of checks and balances that was consummate and completely satisfactory, for it could not be put to a test, and the logical holes in it were chinked with miracles. But no more. To-day the Holy Saints are deposed. Now each and every human problem swings into the range of practical politics. The worst and oldest of them may be solved facilely by travelling bands of lady Ph.D.'s, each bearing the mandate of a Legislature of kept men, all unfaithful to their protectors.

Democracy becomes a substitute for the old religion, and the antithesis of it: the Ku Kluxers, though their reasoning may be faulty, are not far off the facts in their conclusion that Holy Church is its enemy. It shows all the magical potency of the great systems of faith. It has the power to enchant and disarm; it is not vulnerable to logical attack. I point for proof to the appalling gyrations and contortions of its chief exponents. Read, for example, the late James Bryce's "Modern Democracies." Observe how he amasses incontrovertible evidence that democracy doesn't work — and then concludes with a stout declaration that it does. Or, if his two fat volumes are too much for you, turn to some school reader and give a judicious perusal to Lincoln's Gettysburg Address, with its argument that the North fought the Civil War to save self-government to the world! — a thesis echoed in falsetto, and by feebler men, fifty years later. It is impossible, by any device known to philosophers, to meet doctrines of that sort; they obviously lie outside the range of logical ideas. There is, in the human mind, a natural taste for such hocus-pocus. It greatly simplifies the process of ratiocination, which is unbearably painful to the great majority of men. What dulls and baffles the teeth may be got down conveniently by an heroic gulp. No doubt there is an explanation here of the long-continued popularity of the dogma of the Trinity, which remains unstated in plain terms after two thousand years. And no doubt the dogma of Transubstantiation came under fire in the Reformation because it had grown too simple and comprehensible — because even the Scholastic philosophy had been unable to convert its plain propositions into something that could be believed without being understood. Democracy is shot through with this delight in the incredible, this banal mysticism. One cannot discuss it without colliding with preposterous postulates, all of them cherished like authentic hairs from the whiskers of Moses himself. I have alluded to its touching acceptance of the faith that progress is illimitable and ordained of God — that every human problem, in the very nature of things, may be solved. There are corollaries that are even more naïve. One, for example, is to the general effect that optimism is a virtue in itself — that there is a mysterious merit in being hopeful and of glad heart, even in the presence of adverse and immovable facts. This curious notion turns the glittering wheels of Rotary, and is the motive power of the political New Thoughters called Liberals. Certainly the attitude of the average American Liberal toward the so-called League of Nations offered superb clinical material to the student of democratic psychopathology. He began by arguing that the League would save the world. Confronted by proofs of its fraudulence, he switched to the doctrine that believing in it would save the world.

So, later on, with the Washington Disarmament Conference. The man who hopes absurdly, it appears, is in some fantastic and gaseous manner a better citizen than the man who detects and exposes the truth. Bear this sweet democratic axiom clearly in mind. It is, fundamentally, what is the matter with the United States.

As I say, my present mandate does not oblige me to conjure up a system that will surpass and shame democracy as democracy surpasses and shames the polity of the Andaman Islanders or the Great Khan — a system full-blown and perfect, like Prohibition, and ready to be put into effect by the simple adoption of an amendment to the Constitution. Such a system, for all I know, may lie outside the farthest soarings of the human mind, though that mind can weigh the stars and know God. Until the end of the chapter the ants and bees may flutter their sardonic antennae at us in that department, as they do in others: the last joke upon man may be that he never learned how to govern himself in a rational and competent manner, as the last joke upon woman may be that she never had a baby without wishing that the Day of Judgment were a week past. I am not even undertaking to prove here that democracy is too full of evils to be further borne. On the contrary, I am convinced that it has some valuable merits, not often described, and I shall refer to a few of them presently. All I argue is that its manifest defects, if they are ever to be got rid of at all, must be got rid of by examining them realistically — that they will never cease to afflict all the more puissant and exemplary nations so long as discussing them is impeded by concepts borrowed from theology. As for me, I have never encountered any actual evidence, convincing to an ordinary jury, that *vox populi* is actually *vox Dei*. The proofs, indeed, run the other way. The life of the inferior man is one long protest against the obstacles that God interposes to the attainment of his dreams, and democracy, if it is anything at all, is simply one way of getting 'round those obstacles. Thus it represents, not a jingling echo of what seems to be the divine will, but a raucous defiance of it. To that extent, perhaps, it is truly civilized, for civilization, as I have argued elsewhere, is best described as an effort to remedy the blunders and check the cruel humours of the Cosmic Kaiser. But what is defiant is surely not official, and what is not official is open to examination.

For all I know, democracy may be a self-limiting disease, as civilization itself seems to be. There are obvious paradoxes in its philosophy, and some of them have a suicidal smack. It offers John Doe a means to rise above his place beside Richard Roe, and then, by making Roe his equal, it takes away the chief usufructs of the rising. I here attempt no pretty logical gymnastics: the history of democratic states is a history of disingenuous efforts to get rid of the second half of that dilemma. There is not only the natural yearning of Doe to use and enjoy the superiority that he has won; there is also the natural tendency of Roe, as an inferior man, to acknowledge it. Democracy, in fact, is always inventing class distinctions, despite its theoretical abhorrence of them. The baron has departed, but in his place stand the grand goblin, the supreme worthy archon, the sovereign grand commander. Democratic man, as I have remarked, is quite unable to think of himself as a free individual; he must belong to a group, or shake with fear and loneliness — and the group, of course, must have its leaders. It would be hard to find a country in which such brummagem serene highnesses are revered with more passionate devotion than they get in the United States. The distinction that goes with mere office runs far ahead of the distinction that goes with actual achievement. A Harding is regarded as genuinely superior to a Halsted, no doubt because his doings are better understood. But there is a form of human striving that is understood by democratic man even better than Harding's, and that is the striving for money. Thus the plutocracy in a democratic state, tends to take the place of the missing aristocracy, and even to be mistaken for it. It is, of course, something quite different. It lacks all the essential characters of a true aristocracy: a clean tradition, culture, public spirit, honesty, honour, courage — above all, courage. It stands under no bond of obligation to the state; it has no public duty; it is transient and lacks a goal. Its most puissant dignitaries of to-day came out of the mob only yesterday — and from the mob they bring all its peculiar ignobilities. As practically encountered, the plutocracy stands quite as far from the *honnête homme* as it stands from the Holy Saints. Its main character is its incurable timorousness; it is for ever grasping at the straws held out by demagogues. Half a dozen gabby Jewish youths, meeting in a back room to plan a revolution — in other words, half a dozen kittens preparing to upset the Matterhorn — are enough to scare it half to death. Its dreams are of banshees, hobgoblins, bugaboos. The honest, untroubled snores of a Percy or a Hohenstaufen are quite beyond it.

The plutocracy, as I say, is comprehensible to the mob because its aspirations are essentially those of inferior men: it is not by accident that Christianity, a mob religion, paves heaven with gold and precious stones, *i.e.,* with money. There are, of course, reactions against this ignoble ideal among men of more civilized tastes, even in democratic states, and sometimes they arouse the mob to a transient distrust of certain of the plutocratic pretensions. But that distrust seldom arises above mere envy, and the polemic which engenders it is seldom sound in logic or impeccable in motive. What it lacks is aristocratic disinterestedness, born of aristocratic security. There is no body of opinion behind it that is, in the strictest sense, a free opinion. Its chief exponents, by some divine irony, are pedagogues of one sort or another — which is to say, men chiefly marked by their haunting fear of losing their jobs. Living under such terrors, with the plutocracy policing them harshly on one side and the mob congenitally suspicious of them on the other, it is no wonder that their revolt usually peters out in metaphysics, and that they tend to abandon it as their families grow up, and the costs of heresy become prohibitive. The pedagogue, in the long run, shows the virtues of the Congressman, the newspaper editorial writer or the butler, not those of the aristocrat. When, by any chance, he persists in contumacy beyond thirty, it is only too commonly a sign, not that he is heroic, but simply that he is pathological. So with most of his brethren of the Utopian Fife and Drum Corps, whether they issue out of his own seminary or out of the wilderness. They are fanatics; not statesmen. Thus politics, under democracy, resolves itself into impossible alternatives. Whatever the label on the parties, or the war cries issuing from the demagogues who lead them, the practical choice is between the plutocracy on the one side and a rabble of preposterous impossibilists on the other. One must either follow the New York *Times,* or one must be prepared to swallow Bryan and the Bolsheviki. It is a pity that this is so. For what democracy needs most of all is a party that will separate the good that is in it theoretically from the evils that beset it practically, and then try to erect that good into a workable system. What it needs beyond everything is a party of liberty. It produces, true enough, occasional libertarians, just as despotism produces occasional regicides, but it tries them in the same drum-head way. It will never have a party of them until it invents and installs a genuine aristocracy, to breed them and secure them.

I have alluded somewhat vaguely to the merits of democracy. One of them is quite obvious: it is, perhaps, the most charming form of government ever devised by man. The reason is not far to seek. It is based upon propositions that are palpably not true — and what is not true, as everyone knows, is always immensely more fascinating and satisfying to the vast majority of men than what is true. Truth has a harshness that alarms them, and an air of finality that collides with their incurable romanticism. They turn, in all the great emergencies of life, to the ancient promises, transparently false but immensely comforting, and of all those ancient promises there is none more comforting than the one to the effect that the lowly shall inherit the earth. It is at the bottom of the dominant religious system of the modern world, and it is at the bottom of the dominant political system. The latter, which is democracy, gives it an even higher credit and authority than the former, which is Christianity. More, democracy gives it a certain appearance of objective and demonstrable truth. The mob man, functioning as citizen, gets a feeling that he is really important to the world — that he is genuinely running things. Out of his maudlin herding after rogues and mountebanks there comes to him a sense of vast and mysterious power — which is what makes archbishops, police sergeants, the grand goblins of the Ku Klux and other such magnificoes happy. And out of it there comes too, a conviction that he is somehow wise, that his views are taken seriously by his betters — which is what makes United States Senators, fortunetellers and Young Intellectuals happy. Finally, there comes out of it a glowing consciousness of a high duty triumphantly done — which is what makes hangmen and husbands happy.

All these forms of happiness, of course, are illusory. They don't last. The democrat, leaping into the air to flap his wings and praise God, is for ever coming down with a thump. The seeds of his disaster, as I have shown, lie in his own stupidity: he can never get rid of the naïve delusion — so beautifully Christian! — that happiness is something to be got by taking it away from the other fellow. But there are seeds, too, in the very nature of things: a promise, after all, is only a promise, even when it is supported by divine revelation, and the chances against its fulfilment may be put into a depressing mathematical formula. Here the irony that lies under all human aspiration shows itself: the quest for happiness, as always, brings only *un*happiness in the end. But saying that is merely saying that the true charm of democracy is not for the democrat but for the spectator. That spectator, it seems to me, is favoured with a show of the first cut and calibre. Try to imagine anything more heroically absurd! What grotesque false pretences! What a parade of obvious imbecilities! What a welter of fraud! But is fraud amusing? Then I retire forthwith as a psychologist. The fraud of democracy, I contend, is more amusing than any other — more amusing even, and by miles, then the fraud of religion. Go into your praying-chamber and give sober thought to any of the more characteristic democratic inventions: say, Law Enforcement. Or to any of the typical democratic prophets: say, the late Archangel Bryan. If you don't come out paled and palsied by mirth then you will not laugh on the Last Day itself, when Presbyterians step out of the grave like chicks from the egg, and wings blossom from their scapulae, and they leap into interstellar space with roars of joy.

I have spoken hitherto of the possibility that democracy may be a self-limiting disease, like measles. It is, perhaps, something more: it is self-devouring. One cannot observe it objectively without being impressed by its curious distrust of itself — its apparently ineradicable tendency to abandon its whole philosophy at the first sign of strain. I need not point to what happens invariably in democratic states when the national safety is menaced. All the great tribunes of democracy, on such occasions, convert themselves, by a process as simple as taking a deep breath, into despots of an almost fabulous ferocity. Lincoln, Roosevelt and Wilson come instantly to mind: Jackson and Cleveland are in the background, waiting to be recalled. Nor is this process confined to times of alarm and terror: it is going on day in and day out. Democracy always seems bent upon killing the thing it theoretically loves. I have rehearsed some of its operations against liberty, the very cornerstone of its political metaphysic. It not only wars upon the thing itself; it even wars upon mere academic advocacy of it. I offer the spectacle of Americans jailed for reading the Bill of Rights as perhaps the most gaudily humorous ever witnessed in the modern world. Try to imagine monarchy jailing subjects for maintaining the divine right of Kings! Or Christianity damning a believer for arguing that Jesus Christ was the Son of God! This last, perhaps, has been done: anything is possible in that direction. But under democracy the remotest and most fantastic possibility is a commonplace of every day. All the axioms resolve themselves into thundering paradoxes, many amounting to downright contradictions in terms. The mob is competent to rule the rest of us — but it must be rigorously policed itself. There is a government, not of men, but of laws — but men are set upon benches to decide finally what the law is and may be. The highest function of the citizen is to serve the state — but the first assumption that meets him, when he essays to discharge it, is an assumption of his disingenuousness and dishonour. Is that assumption commonly sound? Then the farce only grows the more glorious.

I confess, for my part, that it greatly delights me. I enjoy democracy immensely. It is incomparably idiotic, and hence incomparably amusing. Does it exalt dunderheads, cowards, trimmers, frauds, cads? Then the pain of seeing them go up is balanced and obliterated by the joy of seeing them come down. Is it inordinately wasteful, extravagant, dishonest? Then so is every other form of government: all alike are enemies to laborious and virtuous men. Is rascality at the very heart of it? Well, we have borne that rascality since 1776, and continue to survive. In the long run, it may turn out that rascality is necessary to human government, and even to civilization itself — that civilization, at bottom, is nothing but a colossal swindle. I do not know: I report only that when the suckers are running well the spectacle is infinitely exhilarating. But I am, it may be, a somewhat malicious man: my sympathies, when it comes to suckers, tend to be coy. What I can't make out is how any man can believe in democracy who feels for and with them, and is pained when they are debauched and made a show of. How can any man be a democrat who is sincerely a democrat?

Study Guide

1. This is obviously a vastly different view of democratic institutions than that offered by Hoover. The disparity between Hoover's and Mencken's points of view tells us much about the fragmentation of American social thought that characterized the decade. One might start by refusing to take Mencken too seriously — though with an effort to try to understand his mordant sarcasm.

2. Along with an attack on social reformers (in his opening paragraph), Mencken lists a number of democratic beliefs — only to puncture them. Illustrate and explain.

3. Try to understand the distinction Mencken draws between the plutocracy of a democratic state and a true aristocracy (pp. 410–411) and on what grounds he prefers the latter.

4. On what basis does Mencken conclude that democracy is a "charming" form of government? On what basis is it "self-devouring"? Why does it "delight" him?

5. Perhaps Mencken can be best appreciated through some of his most intrepid assertions. Put yourself in the position of an iconoclast living in the backwash of the Progressive Era; on what grounds could you make a case for the following statements:
   (a) "For it is one of the peculiar intellectual accompaniments of democracy that the concept of the insoluble becomes unfashionable . . .";
   (b) "War becomes simply a device to end war";
   (c) "As for me, I have never encountered any actual evidence, convincing to an ordinary jury, that *vox populi* is actually *vox Dei*";
   (d) "Democratic man . . . is quite unable to think of himself as a free individual; he must belong to a group, or shake with fear and loneliness . . .";
   (e) "Its [democracy's] main character is its incurable timorousness; it is forever grasping at the straws held out by demagogues";
   (f) "Whatever the label on the parties, or the war cries issuing from the demagogues who lead them, the practical choice is between the plutocracy on the one side and a rabble of preposterous impossibilities on the other"; and

(g) "All the great tribunes of democracy, on such occasions [when the national safety is menaced], convert themselves, by a process as simple as taking a deep breath, into despots of an almost fabulous ferocity."

Franklin D. Roosevelt

FREEDOM FROM FEAR

⋇{1933}⋇ THE Great Depression of the 1930's was a worldwide phenomenon and there is a great deal to be said for the argument of Herbert Hoover (1874-1964) that nothing he could have done as President would have prevented it. It is also true that Hoover was to a large extent a "victim" of the depression; no doubt any President elected in 1928 would have been blamed for the troubles of the following years and therefore defeated in 1932.

Furthermore, it is clear that Franklin Delano Roosevelt's (1882-1945) New Deal did not provide a completely satisfactory solution for the problems of the depression. Despite all the agencies and activities, real economic recovery did not come until the economy was stimulated by the outbreak of World War II. Nevertheless, Roosevelt's election marked an important change in American history. His administration accomplished a break-through in the area of federal responsibility for the national welfare. It opened an era in which practical objectives tended to predominate over philosophical conceptions of the proper role of government in the social and economic affairs of the people.

In a very important sense the chief contribution of Roosevelt to this development was psychological. From his first hour in office his air of cheerfulness and his willingness to experiment caught the public's imagination, thus restoring confidence. Nothing demonstrates this so well as his first inaugural address, which in a moment changed the mood of the whole nation. Equally important in changing the national point of view toward the depression was his first "fireside chat." In this radio address, delivered not to a formal audience but to the people in their homes, the President (as much by his warm, confident, and confidential manner as by his ideas) convinced the public that his administration would act intelligently, fairly, imaginatively, and vigorously to solve the pressing problems of the day.

INAUGURAL ADDRESS

(March 4, 1933)

I AM CERTAIN that my fellow Americans expect that on my induction into the Presidency I will address them with a candor and a decision which the present situation of our Nation impels. This is preeminently the time to speak the truth, the whole truth, frankly and boldly. Nor need we shrink from honestly facing conditions in our country today. This great Nation will endure as it has endured, will revive and will prosper.

So, first of all, let me assert my firm belief that the only thing we have to fear is fear itself—nameless, unreasoning, unjustified terror which paralyzes needed efforts to convert retreat into advance. In every dark hour of our national life a leadership of frankness and vigor has met with that understanding and support of the people themselves which is essential to victory. I am convinced that you will again give that support to leadership in these critical days.

In such a spirit on my part and on yours we face our common difficulties. They concern, thank God, only material things. Values have shrunken to fantastic levels; taxes have risen; our ability to pay has fallen; government of all kinds is faced by serious curtailment of income; the means of exchange are frozen in the currents of trade; the withered leaves of industrial enterprise lie on every side; farmers find no markets for their produce; the savings of many years in thousands of families are gone.

More important, a host of unemployed citizens face the grim problem of existence, and an equally great number toil with little return. Only a foolish optimist can deny the dark realities of the moment.

Yet our distress comes from no failure or substance. We are stricken by no plague of locusts. Compared with the perils which our forefathers conquered because they believed and were not afraid, we have still much to be thankful for. Nature still offers her bounty and human efforts have multiplied it. Plenty is at our doorstep, but a generous use of it languishes in the very sight of the supply. Primarily this is because rulers of the exchange of mankind's goods have failed through their own stubbornness and their own incompetence, have admitted their failure, and have abdicated. Practices of the unscrupulous money changers stand indicted in the court of public opinion, rejected by the hearts and minds of men.

True they have tried, but their efforts have been cast in the pattern of an outworn tradition. Faced by failure of credit they have proposed only the lending of more money. Stripped of the lure of profit by which to induce our people to follow their leadership, they have resorted to exhortations, pleading tearfully for restored confidence. They know only the rules of a generation of self-seekers. They have no vision, and when there is no vision the people perish.

The money changers have fled from their high seats in the temple of our civilization. We may now restore that temple to the ancient truths. The measure of the restoration lies in the extent to which we apply social values more noble than mere monetary profit.

Happiness lies not in the mere possession of money; it lies in the joy of achievement, in the thrill of creative effort. The joy and moral stimulation of work no longer must be forgotten in the mad chase of evanescent profits. These dark days will be worth all they cost us if they teach us that our true destiny is not to be ministered unto but to minister to ourselves and to our fellow men.

Recognition of the falsity of material wealth as the standard of success goes hand in hand with the abandonment of the false belief that public office and high political position are to be valued only by the standards of pride of place and personal profit; and there must be an end to a conduct in banking and in business which too often has given to a sacred trust the likeness of callous and selfish wrongdoing. Small wonder that confidence lanquishes, for it thrives only on honesty, on honor, on the sacredness of obligations, on faithful protection, on unselfish performance; without them it cannot live.

Restoration calls, however, not for changes in ethics alone. This Nation asks for action, and action now.

Our greatest primary task is to put people to work. This is no unsolvable problem if we face it wisely and courageously. It can be accomplished in part by direct recruiting by the Government itself, treating the task as we would treat the emergency of a war, but at the same time, through this employment, accomplishing greatly needed projects to stimulate and reorganize the use of our natural resources.

Hand in hand with this we must frankly recognize the overbalance of population in our industrial centers and, by engaging on a national scale in a redistribution, endeavor to provide a better use of the land for those best fitted for the land. The task can be helped by definite efforts to raise the values of agricultural products and with this the power to purchase the output of our cities. It can be helped by preventing realistically the tragedy of the growing loss through foreclosure of our small homes and our farms. It can be helped by insistence that the Federal, State, and local governments act forthwith on the demand that their cost be drastically reduced. It can be helped by the unifying of relief activities which today are often scattered, uneconomical, and unequal. It can be helped by national planning for and supervision of all forms of transportation and of communications and other utilities which have a definitely public character. There are many ways in which it can be helped, but it can never be helped merely by talking about it. We must act and act quickly.

Finally, in our progress toward a resumption of work we require two safeguards against a return of the evils of the old order: there must be a strict supervision of all banking and credits and investments, so that there will be an end to speculation with other people's money; and there must be provision for an adequate but sound currency.

These are the lines of attack. I shall presently urge upon a new Congress, in special session, detailed measures for their fulfillment, and I shall seek the immediate assistance of the several States.

Through this program of action we address ourselves to putting our own national house in order and making income balance outgo. Our international trade relations, though vastly important, are in point of time and necessity secondary to the establishment of a sound national economy. I favor as a practical policy the putting of first things first. I shall spare no effort to restore world trade by international economic readjustment, but the emergency at home cannot wait on that accomplishment.

The basic thought that guides these specific means of national recovery is not narrowly nationalistic. It is the insistence, as a first consideration, upon the interdependence of the various elements in and parts of the United States — a recognition of the old and permanently important manifestation of the American spirit of the pioneer. It is the way to recovery. It is the immediate way. It is the strongest assurance that the recovery will endure.

In the field of world policy I would dedicate this Nation to the policy of the good neighbor — the neighbor who resolutely respects himself and, because he does so, respects the rights of others — the neighbor who respects his obligations and respects the sanctity of his agreements in and with a world of neighbors.

If I read the temper of our people correctly, we now realize as we have never realized before our interdependence on each other; that we cannot merely take but we must give as well; that if we are to go forward, we must move as a trained and loyal army willing to sacrifice for the good of a common discipline, because without such discipline no progress is made, no leadership becomes effective. We are, I know, ready and willing to submit our lives and property to such discipline, because it makes possible a leadership which aims at a larger good. This I propose to offer, pledging that the larger purpose will bind upon us all as a sacred obligation with a unity of duty hitherto evoked only in time of armed strife.

With this pledge taken, I assume unhesitatingly the leadership of this great army of our people dedicated to a disciplined attack upon our common problems.

Action in this image and to this end is feasible under the form of government which we have inherited from our ancestors. Our Constitution is so simple and practical that it is possible always to meet extraordinary needs by changes in emphasis and arrangement without loss of essential form. That is why our constitutional system has proved itself the most superbly enduring political mechanism the modern world has produced. It has met every stress of vast expansion of territory, of foreign wars, of bitter internal strife, of world relations.

It is to be hoped that the normal balance of Executive and legislative authority may be wholly adequate to meet the unprecedented task before us. But it may be that an unprecedented demand and need for un-delayed action may call for temporary departure from that normal bal-ance of public procedure.

I am prepared under my constitutional duty to recommend the meas-ures that a stricken Nation in the midst of a stricken world may require. These measures, or such other measures as the Congress may build out of its experience and wisdom, I shall seek, within my constitutional au-thority, to bring to speedy adoption.

But in the event that the Congress shall fail to take one of these two courses, and in the event that the national emergency is still critical, I shall not evade the clear course of duty that will then confront me. I shall ask the Congress for the one remaining instrument to meet the crisis — broad Executive power to wage a war against the emergency, as great as the power that would be given to me if we were in fact invaded by a foreign foe.

For the trust reposed in me I will return the courage and the devo-tion that befit the time. I can do no less.

We face the arduous days that lie before us in the warm courage of national unity; with the clear consciousness of seeking old and precious moral values; with the clean satisfaction that comes from the stern per-formance of duty by old and young alike. We aim at the assurance of a rounded and permanent national life.

We do not distrust the future of essential democracy. The people of the United States have not failed. In their need they have registered a man-date that they want direct, vigorous action. They have asked for disci-pline and direction under leadership. They have made me the present instrument of their wishes. In the spirit of the gift I take it.

In this dedication of a Nation we humbly ask the blessing of God. May He protect each and every one of us. May He guide me in the days to come.

Study Guide

1. This is a psychological piece and foreshadows little of the New Deal that was to follow. As you read it, ask yourself with how much of this program Hoover would have seriously disagreed. Note, therefore, the homilies, the

clichés, and the hortatory passages — and what few concrete proposals can be found. Note, too, the platitudes and the simplistic notions about what is needed in order to restore prosperity (e.g., economy in the cost of government).

2. Turning to the concrete proposals, what does F.D.R. indicate his policies will be regarding:
   (a) banking and credit;
   (b) currency; and
   (c) foreign policy — especially regarding Latin America?

3. Can you fathom from this address why Franklin Roosevelt was able to arouse so much hope in the vast majority of the American people? Explain.

THE FIRST "FIRESIDE CHAT"

AN INTIMATE TALK WITH THE PEOPLE OF THE UNITED STATES
ON BANKING, MARCH 12, 1933

I WANT to talk for a few minutes with the people of the United States about banking — with the comparatively few who understand the mechanics of banking but more particularly with the overwhelming majority who use banks for the making of deposits and the drawing of checks. I want to tell you what has been done in the last few days, why it was done, and what the next steps are going to be. I recognize that the many proclamations from state capitols and from Washington, the legislation, the Treasury regulations, etc., couched for the most part in banking and legal terms, should be explained for the benefit of the average citizen. I owe this in particular because of the fortitude and good temper with which everybody has accepted the inconvenience and hardships of the banking holiday. I know that when you understand what we in Washington have been about I shall continue to have your cooperation as fully as I have had your sympathy and help during the past week.

First of all, let me state the simple fact that when you deposit money in a bank the bank does not put the money into a safe deposit vault. It invests your money in many different forms of credit — bonds, commercial paper, mortgages and many other kinds of loans. In other words, the bank puts your money to work to keep the wheels of industry and of agriculture turning around. A comparatively small part of the money you put into the bank is kept in currency — an amount which in normal times is wholly sufficient to cover the cash needs for the average citizen. In other words, the total amount of all the currency in the country is only a small fraction of the total deposits in all of the banks.

What, then, happened during the last few days of February and the first few days of March? Because of undermined confidence on the part of the public, there was a general rush by a large portion of our population to turn bank deposits into currency or gold — a rush so great that the soundest banks could not get enough currency to meet the demand. The reason for this was that on the spur of the moment it was, of course, impossible to sell perfectly sound assets of a bank and convert them into cash except at panic prices far below their real value.

By the afternoon of March 3d scarcely a bank in the country was open to do business. Proclamations temporarily closing them in whole or in part had been issued by the Governors in almost all the States.

It was then that I issued the proclamation providing for the nationwide bank holiday, and this was the first step in the Government's reconstruction of our financial and economic fabric.

The second step was the legislation promptly and patriotically passed by the Congress confirming my proclamation and broadening my powers so that it became possible in view of the requirement of time to extend the holiday and lift the ban of that holiday gradually. This law also gave authority to develop a program of rehabilitation of our banking facilities. I want to tell our citizens in every part of the Nation that the national Congress — Republicans and Democrats alike — showed by this action a devotion to public welfare and a realization of the emergency and the necessity for speed that it is difficult to match in our history.

The third stage has been the series of regulations permitting the banks to continue their functions to take care of the distribution of food and household necessities and the payment of payrolls.

This bank holiday, while resulting in many cases in great inconvenience, is affording us the opportunity to supply the currency necessary to meet the situation. No sound bank is a dollar worse off than it was when it closed its doors last Monday. Neither is any bank which may turn out not to be in a position for immediate opening. The new law allows the twelve Federal Reserve Banks to issue additional currency on good assets and thus the banks which reopen will be able to meet every legitimate call. The new currency is being sent out by the Bureau of Engraving and Printing in large volume to every part of the country. It is sound currency because it is backed by actual, good assets.

A question you will ask is this: why are all the banks not to be reopened at the same time? The answer is simple. Your Government does not intend that history of the past few years shall be repeated. We do not want and will not have another epidemic of bank failures.

As a result, we start tomorrow, Monday, with the opening of banks in the twelve Federal Reserve Banks cities — those banks which on first examination by the Treasury have already been found to be all right. This will be followed on Tuesday by the resumption of all their functions by banks already found to be sound in cities where there are recognized clearing houses. That means about 250 cities of the United States.

On Wednesday and succeeding days banks in smaller places all through the country will resume business, subject, of course, to the Government's physical ability to complete its survey. It is necessary that the reopening of banks be extended over a period in order to permit the banks to make applications for necessary loans, to obtain currency needed to meet their requirements and to enable the Government to make common sense checkups.

Let me make it clear to you that if your bank does not open the first day you are by no means justified in believing that it will not open. A bank that opens on one of the subsequent days is in exactly the same status as the bank that opens tomorrow.

I know that many people are worrying about State banks not members of the Federal Reserve System. These banks can and will receive assistance from member banks and from the Reconstruction Finance Corporation. These State banks are following the same course as the National banks except that they get their licenses to resume business from the State authorities, and these authorities have been asked by the Secretary of the Treasury to permit their good banks to open up on the same schedule as the national banks. I am confident that the State Banking Departments will be as careful as the national Government in the policy relating to the opening of banks and will follow the same broad policy.

It is possible that when the banks resume a very few people who have not recovered from their fear may again begin withdrawals. Let me make it clear that the banks will take care of all needs — and it is my belief that hoarding during the past week has become an exceedingly unfashionable pastime. It needs no prophet to tell you that when the people find that they can get their money — that they can get it when they want it for all legitimate purposes — the phantom of fear will soon be laid. People will again be glad to have their money where it will be safely taken care of and where they can use it conveniently at any time. I can assure you that it is safer to keep your money in a reopened bank than under the mattress.

The success of our whole great national program depends, of course, upon the cooperation of the public — on its intelligent support and use of a reliable system.

Remember that the essential accomplishment of the new legislation is that it makes it possible for banks more readily to convert their assets into cash than was the case before. More liberal provision has been made for banks to borrow on these assets at the Reserve Banks and more liberal provision has also been made for issuing currency on the security of these good assets. This currency is not fiat currency. It is issued only on adequate security, and every good bank has an abundance of such security.

One more point before I close. There will be, of course, some banks unable to open without being reorganized. The new law allows the Government to assist in making these reorganizations quickly and effectively and even allows the Government to subscribe to at least a part of new capital which may be required.

I hope you can see from this elemental recital of what your Government is doing that there is nothing complex, or radical, in the process.

We had a bad banking situation. Some of our bankers had shown themselves either incompetent or dishonest in their handling of the people's funds. They had used the money entrusted to them in speculations and unwise loans. This was, of course, not true in the vast majority of our banks, but it was true in enough of them to shock the people for a time into a sense of insecurity and to put them into a frame of mind where they did not differentiate, but seemed to assume that the acts of a comparative few had tainted them all. It was the Government's job to straighten out this situation and do it as quickly as possible. And the job is being performed.

I do not promise you that every bank will be reopened or that individual losses will not be suffered, but there will be no losses that possibly could be avoided; and there would have been more and greater losses had we continued to drift. I can even promise you salvation for some at least of the sorely pressed banks. We shall be engaged not merely in reopening sound banks but in the creation of sound banks through reorganization.

It has been wonderful to me to catch the note of confidence from all over the country. I can never be sufficiently grateful to the people for the loyal support they have given me in their acceptance of the judgment that has dictated our course, even though all our processes may not have seemed clear to them.

After all, there is an element in the readjustment of our financial system more important than currency, more important than gold, and that is the confidence of the people. Confidence and courage are the essentials of success in carrying out our plan. You people must have faith;

you must not be stampeded by rumors or guesses. Let us unite in banishing fear. We have provided the machinery to restore our financial system; it is up to you to support and make it work.

It is your problem no less than it is mine. Together we cannot fail.

Study Guide

1. Familiarize yourself with the events that preceded this talk and the action taken by F.D.R. that required an explanation to the nation. Some of this is contained in the address itself.

2. Continue then and follow Roosevelt as he does the following:
   (a) offers his reasons for declaring a "bank holiday";
   (b) outlines the legislation to be passed by Congress; and
   (c) indicates the steps that the government would take in order to prevent these conditions from recurring.

3. Read the appropriate passages in your text to guide you through the details of the banking problem in 1933 and what steps were taken in 1933 and in 1935 to deal with it.

John Steinbeck
MIGRANT LABOR

1939 ALTHOUGH meteorologists had long warned that the high plains west of the 98th meridian were unsuited for ordinary agriculture because of the periodic droughts that plagued the region, American farmers repeatedly pushed out beyond that line during the "wet" phases of the weather cycle. Thus, in areas like Oklahoma and western Kansas during the "wet" 1920's, millions of acres formerly given over to natural grasses were plowed up and put to the cultivation of wheat and other grains.

Then, in the early thirties, came the inevitable arid phase, and with it high winds and blazing sun. The plow-pulverized soils, no longer held in place in dry weather by the interlaced roots of the hardy grasses, were now swept up and away in vast black clouds of dust. The region became known as the "dust bowl," and when the winds subsided and the rains came it was a barren desert, its rich humus gone, its hardpan subsoil soon gashed by ugly, rain-formed gullies.

To the horrors of the dust bowl were added, for the Western farmer, the miseries of the Great Depression, worse perhaps for him than for the industrial worker. The result was a mass migration from the plains states, some driven away by drought and erosion, others, like the protagonists in John Steinbeck's novel, by the collapse of the farm economy.

In *The Grapes of Wrath,* which was published in 1939, Steinbeck (1902–1968) captured perfectly the mood of these migrants and their pitiful plight. In the space available here it is not possible to tell even in outline the whole story of the Joad family and the other "Okies" in this novel, but the following selection fairly portrays the nature of the work and offers a few typical scenes from the Joad saga. *The Grapes of Wrath* was an immense literary and popular success, but it is also the book which best captures the spirit of the depression and the indignation and frustration of the liberals of the thirties who searched for ways and means of ending it.

THE GRAPES OF WRATH

To THE red country and part of the gray country of Oklahoma, the last rains came gently, and they did not cut the scarred earth. The plows crossed and recrossed and scattered weed colonies and grass along the sides of the roads so that the gray country and the dark red country began to disappear under a green cover. In the last part of May the sky grew pale and the clouds that had hung in high puffs for so long in the spring were dissipated. The sun flared down on the growing corn day after day until a line of brown spread along the edge of each green bayonet. The clouds appeared, and went away, and in a while they did not try any more. The weeds grew darker green to protect themselves, and they did not spread any more. The surface of the earth crusted, a thin hard crust, and as the sky became pale, so the earth became pale, pink in the red country and white in the gray country.

In the water-cut gullies the earth dusted down in dry little streams. Gophers and ant lions started small avalanches. And as the sharp sun struck day after day, the leaves of the young corn became less stiff and erect; they bent in a curve at first, and then, as the central ribs of strength grew weak, each leaf tilted downward. Then it was June, and the sun shone more fiercely. The brown lines on the corn leaves widened and moved in on the central ribs. The weeds frayed and edged back toward their roots. The air was thin and the sky more pale; and every day the earth paled.

In the roads where the teams moved, where the wheels milled the ground and the hooves of the horses beat the ground, the dirt crust broke and the dust formed. Every moving thing lifted the dust into the air: a walking man lifted a thin layer as high as his waist, and a wagon lifted the dust as high as the fence tops, and an automobile boiled a cloud behind it. The dust was long in settling back again.

When June was half gone, the big clouds moved up out of Texas and the Gulf, high heavy clouds, rain-heads. The men in the fields looked up at the clouds and sniffed at them and held wet fingers up to sense the wind. And the horses were nervous while the clouds were up. The rain-heads dropped a little spattering and hurried on to some other country.

Behind them the sky was pale again and the sun flared. In the dust there were drop craters where the rain had fallen, and there were clean splashes on the corn, and that was all.

A gentle wind followed the rain clouds, driving them on northward, a wind that softly clashed the drying corn. A day went by and the wind increased, steady, unbroken by gusts. The dust from the roads fluffed up and spread out and fell on the weeds beside the fields, and fell into the fields a little way. Now the wind grew strong and hard and it worked at the rain crust in the corn fields. Little by little the sky was darkened by the mixing dust, and the wind felt over the earth, loosened the dust, and carried it away. The wind grew stronger. The rain crust broke and the dust lifted up out of the fields and drove gray plumes into the air like sluggish smoke. The corn threshed the wind and made a dry, rushing sound. The finest dust did not settle back to earth now, but disappeared into the darkening sky.

The wind grew stronger, whisked under stones, carried up straws and old leaves, and even little clods, marking its course as it sailed across the fields. The air and the sky darkened and through them the sun shone redly, and there was a raw sting in the air. During a night the wind raced faster over the land, dug cunningly among the rootlets of the corn, and the corn fought the wind with its weakened leaves until the roots were freed by the prying wind and then each stalk settled wearily sideways toward the earth and pointed the direction of the wind.

The dawn came, but no day. In the gray sky a red sun appeared, a dim red circle that gave a little light, like dusk; and as that day advanced, the dusk slipped back toward darkness, and the wind cried and whimpered over the fallen corn.

Men and women huddled in their houses, and they tied handkerchiefs over their noses when they went out, and wore goggles to protect their eyes.

When the night came again it was black night, for the stars could not pierce the dust to get down, and the window lights could not even spread beyond their own yards. Now the dust was evenly mixed with the air, an emulsion of dust and air. Houses were shut tight, and cloth wedged around doors and windows, but the dust came in so thinly that it could not be seen in the air, and it settled like pollen on the chairs and tables, on the dishes. The people brushed it from their shoulders. Little lines of dust lay at the door sills.

In the middle of that night the wind passed on and left the land quiet. The dust-filled air muffled sound more completely than fog does. The people, lying in their beds, heard the wind stop. They awakened when the rushing wind was gone. They lay quietly and listened deep into the stillness. Then the roosters crowed, and their voices were muffled, and the people stirred restlessly in their beds and wanted the morning. They knew it would take a long time for the dust to settle out of the air. In the morning the dust hung like fog, and the sun was as red as ripe new blood. All day the dust sifted down from the sky, and the next day it sifted down. An even blanket covered the earth. It settled on the corn, piled up on the tops of the fence posts, piled up on the wires; it settled on roofs, blanketed the weeds and trees.

The people came out of their houses and smelled the hot stinging air and covered their noses from it. And the children came out of the houses, but they did not run or shout as they would have done after a rain. Men stood by their fences and looked at the ruined corn, drying fast now, only a little green showing through the film of dust. The men were silent and they did not move often. And the women came out of the houses to stand beside their men — to feel whether this time the men would break. The women studied the men's faces secretly, for the corn could go, as long as something else remained. The children stood near by, drawing figures in the dust with bare toes, and the children sent exploring senses out to see whether men and women would break. The children peeked at the faces of the men and women, and then drew careful lines in the dust with their toes. Horses came to the watering troughs and nuzzled the water to clear the surface dust. After a while the faces of the watching men lost their bemused perplexity and became hard and angry and resistant. Then the women knew that they were safe and that there was no break. Then they asked, What'll we do? And the men replied, I don't know. But it was all right. The women knew it was all right, and the watching children knew it was all right. Women and children knew deep in themselves that no misfortune was too great to bear if their men were whole. The women went into the houses to their work, and the children began to play, but cautiously at first. As the day went forward the sun became less red. It flared down on the dust-blanketed land. The men sat in the doorways of their houses; their hands were busy with sticks and little rocks. The men sat still — thinking — figuring . . .

THE OWNERS of the land came onto the land, or more often a spokesman for the owners came. They came in closed cars, and they felt the dry earth with their fingers, and sometimes they drove big earth augers into the ground for soil tests. The tenants, from their sun-beaten dooryards, watched uneasily when the closed cars drove along the fields. And at last the owner men drove into the dooryards and sat in their cars to talk out of the windows. The tenant men stood beside the cars for a while, and then squatted on their hams and found sticks with which to mark the dust.

In the open doors the women stood looking out, and behind them the children — corn-headed children, with wide eyes, one bare foot on top of the other bare foot, and the toes working. The women and the children watched their men talking to the owner men. They were silent.

Some of the owner men were kind because they hated what they had to do, and some of them were angry because they hated to be cruel, and some of them were cold because they had long ago found that one could not be an owner unless one were cold. And all of them were caught in something larger than themselves. Some of them hated the mathematics that drove them, and some were afraid, and some worshiped the mathematics because it provided a refuge from thought and from feeling. If a bank or a finance company owned the land, the owner man said, The Bank — or the Company — needs — wants — insists — must have — as though the Bank or the Company were a monster, with thought and feeling, which had ensnared them. These last would take no responsibility for the banks or the companies because they were men and slaves, while the banks were machines and masters all at the same time. Some of the owner men were a little proud to be slaves to such cold and powerful masters. The owner men sat in the cars and explained. You know the land is poor. You've scrabbled at it long enough, God knows.

The squatting tenant men nodded and wondered and drew figures in the dust, and yes, they knew, God knows. If the dust only wouldn't fly. If the top would only stay on the soil, it might not be so bad.

The owner men went on leading to their point: You know the land's getting poorer. You know what cotton does to the land; robs it, sucks all the blood out of it.

The squatters nodded they knew, God knew. If they could only rotate the crops they might pump blood back into the land.

Well, it's too late. And the owner men explained the workings and the thinkings of the monster that was stronger than they were. A man can hold land if he can just eat and pay taxes; he can do that.

Yes, he can do that until his crops fail one day and he has to borrow money from the bank.

But — you see, a bank or a company can't do that, because those creatures don't breathe air, don't eat side-meat. They breathe profits; they eat the interest on money. If they don't get it, they die the way you die without air, without sidemeat. It is a sad thing, but it is so. It is just so.

The squatting men raised their eyes to understand. Can't we just hang on? Maybe the next year will be a good year. God knows how much cotton next year. And with all the wars — God knows what price cotton will bring. Don't they make explosives out of cotton? And uniforms? Get enough wars and cotton'll hit the ceiling. Next year, maybe. They looked up questioningly.

We can't depend on it. The bank — the monster has to have profits all the time. It can't wait. It'll die. No, taxes go on. When the monster stops growing, it dies. It can't stay one size.

Soft fingers began to tap the sill of the car window, and hard fingers tightened on the restless drawing sticks. In the doorways of the sun-beaten tenant houses, women sighed and then shifted feet so that the one that had been down was now on top, and the toes working. Dogs came sniffing near the owner cars and wetted on all four tires one after another. And chickens lay in the sunny dust and fluffed their feathers to get the cleansing dust down to the skin. In the little sties the pigs grunted inquiringly over the muddy remnants of the slops.

The squatting men looked down again. What do you want us to do? We can't take less share of the crop — we're half starved now. The kids are hungry all the time. We got no clothes, torn an' ragged. If all the neighbors weren't the same, we'd be ashamed to go to meeting.

And at last the owner men came to the point. The tenant system won't work any more. One man on a tractor can take the place of twelve or fourteen families. Pay him a wage and take all the crop. We have to do it. We don't like to do it. But the monster's sick. Something's happened to the monster.

But you'll kill the land with cotton.

We know. We've got to take cotton quick before the land dies. Then we'll sell the land. Lots of families in the East would like to own a piece of land.

The tenant men looked up alarmed. But what'll happen to us? How'll we eat?

You'll have to get off the land. The plows'll go through the dooryard.

And now the squatting men stood up angrily. Grampa took up the land, and he had to kill the Indians and drive them away. And Pa was born here, and he killed weeds and snakes. Then a bad year came and he had to borrow a little money. An' we was born here. There in the door — our children born here. And Pa had to borrow money. The bank owned the land then, but we stayed and we got a little bit of what we raised.

We know that — all that. It's not us, it's the bank. A bank isn't like a man. Or an owner with fifty thousand acres, he isn't like a man either. That's the monster.

Sure, cried the tenant men, but it's our land. We measured it and broke it up. We were born on it, and we got killed on it, died on it. Even if it's no good, it's still ours. That's what makes it ours — being born on it, working it, dying on it. That makes ownership, not a paper with numbers on it.

We're sorry. It's not us. It's the monster. The bank isn't like a man.

Yes, but the bank is only made of men.

No, you're wrong there — quite wrong there. The bank is something else than men. It happens that every man in a bank hates what the bank does, and yet the bank does it. The bank is something more than men, I tell you. It's the monster. Men made it, but they can't control it.

The tenants cried, Grandpa killed Indians, Pa killed snakes for the land. Maybe we can kill banks — they're worse than Indians and snakes. Maybe we got to fight to keep our land, like Pa and Grandpa did.

And now the owner men grew angry. You'll have to go.

But it's ours, the tenant men cried. We ——

No. The bank, the monster owns it. You'll have to go.

We'll get our guns, like Grandpa when the Indians came. What then?

Well — first the sheriff, and then the troops. You'll be stealing if you try to stay, you'll be murderers if you kill to stay. The monster isn't men, but it can make men do what it wants.

But if we go, where'll we go? How'll we go? We got no money.

We're sorry, said the owner men. The bank, the fifty-thousand-acre owner can't be responsible. You're on land that isn't yours. Once over the line maybe you can pick cotton in the fall. Maybe you can go on relief. Why don't you go on west to California? There's work there, and it never gets cold. Why, you can reach out anywhere and pick an orange. Why, there's always some kind of crop to work in. Why don't you go there? And the owner men started their cars and rolled away.

The tenant men squatted down on their hams again to mark the dust with a stick, to figure, to wonder. Their sunburned faces were dark, and their sun-whipped eyes were light. The women moved cautiously out of the doorways toward their men, and the children crept behind the women, cautiously, ready to run. The bigger boys squatted beside their fathers, because that made them men. After a time the women asked, What did he want?

And the men looked up for a second, and the smolder of pain was in their eyes. We got to get off. A tractor and a superintendent. Like factories.

Where'll we go? the women asked.

We don't know. We don't know.

And the women went quickly, quietly back into the houses and herded the children ahead of them. They knew that a man so hurt and so perplexed may turn in anger, even on people he loves. They left the men alone to figure and to wonder in the dust.

After a time perhaps the tenant man looked about — at the pump put in ten years ago, with a goose-neck handle and iron flowers on the spout, at the chopping block where a thousand chickens had been killed, at the hand plow lying in the shed, and the patent crib hanging in the rafters over it.

The children crowded about the women in the houses. What we going to do, Ma? Where we going to go?

The women said, We don't know, yet. Go out and play. But don't go near your father. He might whale you if you go near him. And the women went on with the work, but all the time they watched the men squatting in the dust — perplexed and figuring.

The tractors came over the roads and into the fields, great crawlers moving like insects, having the incredible strength of insects. They crawled over the ground, laying the track and rolling on it and picking it up. Diesel tractors, puttering while they stood idle; they thundered when they moved, and then settled down to a droning roar. Snub-nosed monsters, raising the dust and sticking their snouts into it, straight down the country, across the country, through fences, through dooryards, in and out of gullies in straight lines. They did not run on the ground, but on their own roadbeds. They ignored hills and gulches, water courses, fences, houses.

The man sitting in the iron seat did not look like a man; gloved, goggled, rubber dust mask over nose and mouth, he was a part of the monster, a robot in the seat. The thunder of the cylinders sounded through the country, became one with the air and the earth, so that earth and air muttered in sympathetic vibration. The driver could not control it — straight across country it went, cutting through a dozen farms and straight back. A twitch at the controls could swerve the cat', but the driver's hands could not twitch because the monster that built the tractor, the monster that sent the tractor out, had somehow got into the driver's hands, into his brain and muscle, had goggled him and muzzled him — goggled his mind, muzzled his speech, goggled his perception, muzzled his protest. He could not see the land as it was, he could not smell the land as it smelled; his feet did not stamp the clods or feel the warmth and power of the earth. He sat in an iron seat and stepped on iron pedals. He could not cheer or beat or curse or encourage the extension of his power, and because of this he could not cheer or whip or curse or encourage himself. He did not know or own or trust or beseech the land. If a seed dropped did not germinate, it was nothing. If the young thrusting plant withered in drought or drowned in a flood of rain, it was no more to the driver than to the tractor.

He loved the land no more than the bank loved the land. He could admire the tractor — its machined surfaces, its surge of power, the roar of its detonating cylinders; but it was not his tractor. Behind the tractor rolled the shining disks, cutting the earth with blades — not plowing but surgery, pushing the cut earth to the right where the second row of disks cut it and pushed it to the left; slicing blades shining, polished by the cut earth. And pulled behind the disks, the harrows combing with iron teeth so that the little clods broke up and the earth lay smooth. Behind the harrows, the long seeders — twelve curved iron penes erected in the foundry, orgasms set by gears, raping methodically, raping without passion. The driver sat in his iron set and he was proud of the straight lines he did not will, proud of the tractor he did not own or love, proud of the power he could not control. And when that crop grew, and was harvested, no man had crumbled a hot clod in his fingers and let the earth sift past his fingertips. No man had touched the seed, or lusted for the growth. Men ate what they had not raised, had no connection with the bread. The land bore under iron, and under iron gradually died; for it was not loved or hated, it had no prayers or curses.

At noon the tractor driver stopped sometimes near a tenant house and opened his lunch: sandwiches wrapped in waxed paper, white bread, pickle, cheese, Spam, a piece of pie branded like an engine part. He ate without relish. And tenants not yet moved away came out to see him, looked curiously while the goggles were taken off, and the rubber dust mask, leaving white circles around the eyes and a large white circle around nose and mouth. The exhaust of the tractor puttered on, for fuel is so cheap it is more efficient to leave the engine running than to heat the Diesel nose for a new start. Curious children crowded close, ragged children who ate their fried dough as they watched. They watched hungrily the unwrapping of the sandwiches, and their hunger-sharpened noses smelled the pickle, cheese, and Spam. They didn't speak to the driver. They watched his hand as it carried food to his mouth. They did not watch him chewing; their eyes followed the hand that held the sandwich. After a while the tenant who could not leave the place came out and squatted in the shade beside the tractor.

"Why, you're Joe Davis's boy!"

"Sure," the driver said.

"Well, what you doing this kind of work for — against your own people?"

"Three dollars a day. I got damn sick of creeping for my dinners — and not getting it. I got a wife and kids. We got to eat. Three dollars a day, and it comes every day."

"That's right," the tenant said. "But for your three dollars a day fifteen or twenty families can't eat at all. Nearly a hundred people have to go out and wander on the roads for your three dollars a day. Is that right?"

And the driver said, "Can't think of that. Got to think of my own kids. Three dollars a day, and it comes every day. Times are changing, mister, don't you know? Can't make a living on the land unless you've got two, five, ten thousand acres and a tractor. Crop land isn't for little guys like us any more. You don't kick up a howl because you can't make Fords, because you're not the telephone company. Well, crops are like that now. Nothing to do about it. You try to get three dollars a day someplace. That's the only way."

The tenant pondered. "Funny thing how it is. If a man owns a little property, that property is him, it's part of him, and it's like him. If he owns property only so he can walk on it and handle it and be sad when it isn't doing well, and feel fine when the rain falls on it, that property is him, and some ways he's bigger because he owns it. Even if he isn't successful he's big with his property. That is so."

And the tenant pondered more. "But let a man get property he doesn't see, or can't take time to get his fingers in, or can't be there to walk on it — why, then the property is the man. He can't do what he wants, he can't think what he wants. The property is the man, stronger than he is. And he is small, not big. Only his possessions are big — and he's the servant of his property. That is so, too."

The driver munched the branded pie and threw the crust away. "Times are changed, don't you know? Thinking about stuff like that don't feed the kids. Get your three dollars a day, feed your kids. You got no call to worry about anybody's kids but your own. You get a reputation for talking like that, and you'll never get three dollars a day. Big shots won't give you three dollars a day if you worry about anything but your three dollars a day."

"Nearly a hundred people on the road for your three dollars. Where will we go?"

"And that reminds me," the driver said, "you better get out soon. I'm going through the dooryard after dinner."

"You filled in the well this morning."

"I know. Had to keep the line straight. But I'm going through the dooryard after dinner. Got to keep the lines straight. And — well, you know Joe Davis, my old man, so I'll tell you this. I got orders where there's a family not moved out — if I have an accident — you know, get too close and cave the house in a little well, I might get a couple of dollars. And my youngest kid never had no shoes yet."

"I built it with my hands. Straightened old nails to put the sheathing on. Rafters are wired to the stringers with baling wire. It's mine. I built it. You bump it down—I'll be in the window with a rifle. You even come too close and I'll pot you like a rabbit."

"It's not me. There's nothing I can do. I'll lose my job if I don't do it. And look — suppose you kill me? They'll just hang you, but long before you're hung there'll be another guy on the tractor, and he'll bump the house down. You're not killing the right guy."

"That's so," the tenant said. "Who gave you orders? I'll go after him. He's the one to kill."

"You're wrong. He got his orders from the bank. The bank told him, 'clear those people out or it's your job.'"

"Well there's a president of the bank. There's a board of directors. I'll fill up the magazine of the rifle and go into the bank."

The driver said, "Fellow was telling me the bank gets orders from the East. The orders were, 'Make the land show profit or we'll close you up.'"

"But where does it stop? Who can we shoot? I don't aim to starve to death before I kill the man that's starving me."

"I don't know. Maybe there's nobody to shoot. Maybe the thing isn't men at all. Maybe, like you said, the property's doing it. Anyway I told you my orders."

"I got to figure," the tenant said. "We all got to figure. There's some way to stop this. It's not like lightning or earthquakes. We've got a bad thing made by men, and by God that's something we can change." The tenant sat in his doorway, and the driver thundered his engine and started off, tracks falling and curving, harrows combing, and the phalli of the seeder slipping into the ground. Across the dooryard the tractor cut, and the hard, foot-beaten ground was seeded field, and the tractor cut through again; the uncut space was ten feet wide. And back he came. The iron guard bit into the house-corner, crumbled the wall, and wrenched the little house from its foundation so that it fell sideways, crushed like a bug. And the driver was goggled and a rubber mask covered his nose and mouth. The tractor cut a straight line on, and the air and the ground vibrated with its thunder. The tenant man stared after it, his rifle in his hand. His wife was beside him, and the quiet children behind. And all of them stared after the tractor. . . .

HIGHWAY 66 is the main migrant road. 66 — the long concrete path across the country, waving gently up and down on the map, from the Mississippi to Bakersfield — over the red lands and the gray lands, twisting up into the mountains, crossing the Divide and down into the bright and terrible desert, and across the desert to the mountains again, and into the rich California valleys.

66 is the path of a people in flight, refugees from dust and shrinking land, from the thunder of tractors and shrinking ownership, from the desert's slow northward invasion, from the twisting winds that howl up out of Texas, from the floods that bring no richness to the land and steal what little richness is there. From all of these the people are in flight, and they come into 66 from the tributary side roads, from the wagon tracks and the rutted country roads. 66 is the mother road, the road of flight. . . .

THE ancient overloaded Hudson creaked and grunted to the highway at Sallisaw and turned west and the sun was blinding. But on the concrete road Al built up his speed because the flattened springs were not in danger any more. From Sallisaw to Gore is twenty-one miles and the Hudson was doing thirty-five miles an hour. From Gore to Warner thirteen miles; Warner to Checotah fourteen miles; Checotah a long jump to Henrietta — thirty-four miles, but a real town at the end of it. Henrietta to Castle nineteen miles, and the sun was overhead, and the red fields, heated by the high sun, vibrated the air.

Al, at the wheel, his face purposeful, his whole body listening to the car, his restless eyes jumping from the road to the instrument panel. Al was one with his engine, every nerve listening for weakness, for the thumps or squeals, hums and chattering that indicate a change that may cause a breakdown. He had become the soul of the car.

Granma, beside him on the seat, half slept, and whimpered in her sleep, opened her eyes to peer ahead, and then dozed again. And Ma sat beside Granma, one elbow out the window and the skin reddening under the fierce sun. Ma looked ahead too, but her eyes were flat and did not see the road or the fields, the gas stations, the little eating sheds. She did not glance at them as the Hudson went by.

Al shifted himself on the broken seat and changed his grip on the steering wheel. And he sighed, "Makes a racket, but I think she's aw-right. God knows what she'll do if we got to climb a hill with the load we got. Got any hills 'tween here an' California, Ma?"

Ma turned her head slowly and her eyes came to life. "Seems to me they's hills," she said. " 'Course I dunno. But seems to me I heard they's hills an' even mountains. Big ones."

Granma drew a long whining sigh in her sleep.

Al said, "We'll burn right up if we got climbin' to do. Have to throw out some a' this stuff. Maybe we shouldn' a brang that preacher."

"You'll be glad a that preacher 'fore we're through," said Ma. "That preacher'll help us." She looked ahead at the gleaming road again.

Al steered with one hand and put the other on the vibrating gear-shift lever. He had difficulty in speaking. His mouth formed the words silently before he said them aloud. "Ma — " She looked slowly around at him, her head swaying a little with the car's motion. "Ma, you scared a goin'? You scared a goin' to a new place?"

Her eyes grew thoughtful and soft. "A little," she said. "Only it ain't like scared so much. I'm jus' a settin' here waitin'. When somepin hap-pens that I got to do somepin — I'll do it."

"Ain't you thinkin' what's it gonna be like when we get there? Ain't you scared it won't be nice like we thought?"

"No," she said quickly. "No, I ain't. You can't do that. I can't do that. It's too much — livin' too many lives. Up ahead they's a thousan' lives we might live, but when it comes, it'll on'y be one. If I go ahead on all of 'em, it's too much. You got to live ahead 'cause you're so young, but — it's jus' the road goin' by for me. An' it's jus' how soon they gonna wanta eat some more pork bones." Her face tightened. "That's all I can do. I can't do no more. All the rest'd get upset if I done any more'n that. They all depen' on me jus' thinkin' about that." . . .

Castle to Paden twenty-five miles and the sun passed the zenith and started down. And the radiator cap began to jiggle up and down and steam started to whish out. Near Paden there was a shack beside the road and two gas pumps in front of it; and beside a fence, a water faucet and a hose. Al drove in and nosed the Hudson up to the hose. As they pulled in, a stout man, red of face and arms, got up from a chair behind the gas pumps and moved toward them. He wore brown corduroys, and suspenders and a polo shirt; and he had a cardboard sun helmet, painted silver, on his head. The sweat beaded on his nose and under his eyes and formed streams in the wrinkles of his neck. He strolled toward the truck, looking truculent and stern.

"You folks aim to buy anything? Gasoline or stuff?" he asked.

Al was out already, unscrewing the steaming radiator cap with the tips of his fingers, jerking his hand away to escape the spurt when the cap should come loose. "Need some gas, mister."

"Got any money?"

"Sure. Think we're beggin'?"

The truculence left the fat man's face. "Well, that's all right, folks. He'p yourself to water." And he hastened to explain. "Road is full a people, come in, use water, dirty up the toilet, an' then, by God, they'll steal stuff an' don't buy nothin'. Got no money to buy with. Come beggin' a gallon gas to move on."

Tom dropped angrily to the ground and moved toward the fat man. "We're payin' our way," he said fiercely. "You got no call to give us a goin'-over. We ain't asked you for nothin' ."

"I ain't," the fat man said quickly. The sweat began to soak through his short-sleeved polo shirt. "Jus' he'p yourself to water, and go use the toilet if you want."

Winfield had got the hose. He drank from the end and then turned the stream over his head and face, and emerged dripping. "It ain't cool," he said.

"I don' know what the country's comin' to," the fat man continued. His complaint had shifted now and he was no longer talking to or about the Joads. "Fifty-sixty cars a folks go by ever' day, folks all movin' west with kids an' househol' stuff. Where they goin'? What they gonna do?"

"Doin' the same as us," said Tom. "Goin' someplace to live. Tryin' to get along. That's all."

"Well, I don' know what the country's comin' to. I jus' don' know. Here's me tryin' to get along, too. Think any them big new cars stops here? No, sir! They go on to them yella-painted company stations in town. They don't stop no place like this. Most folks stops here ain't got nothin'."

Al flipped the radiator cap and it jumped into the air with a head of steam behind it, and a hollow bubbling sound came out of the radiator. On top of the truck, the suffering hound dog crawled timidly to the edge of the load and looked over, whimpering, toward the water. Uncle John climbed up and lifted him down by the scruff of the neck. For a moment the dog staggered on stiff legs and then he went to lap the mud under the faucet. In the highway the cars whizzed by, glistening in the heat, and the hot wind of their going fanned into the service-station yard. Al filled the radiator with the hose.

"It ain't that I'm tryin' to git trade outa rich folks," the fat man went on. "I'm jus' tryin' to git trade. Why, the folks that stops here begs gasoline an' they trades for gasoline. I could show you in my back room the stuff they'll trade for gas an' oil: beds an' baby buggies an' pots an' pans. One family traded a doll their kid had for a gallon. An' what'm I gonna do with the stuff, open a junk shop? Why, one fella wanted to gimme his shoes for a gallon. An' if I was that kinda fella I bet I could git — " He glanced at Ma and stopped.

Jim Casy had wet his head, and the drops still coursed down his high forehead, and his muscled neck was wet, and his shirt was wet. He moved over beside Tom. "It ain't the people's fault," he said. "How'd you like to sell the bed you sleep on for a tankful a gas?"

"I know it ain't their fault. Ever' person I talked to is on the move for a damn good reason. But what's the country comin' to? That's what I wanta know. What's it comin' to? Fella can't make a livin' no more. Folks can't make a livin' farmin'. I ask you, what's it comin' to? I can't figure her out. Ever'body I ask, they can't figure her out. Fella wants to trade his shoes so he can git a hundred miles on. I can't figure her out." He took off his silver hat and wiped his forehead with his palm. And Tom took off his cap and wiped his forehead with it. He went to the hose and wet the cap through and squeezed it and put it on again. Ma worked a tin cup out through the side bars of the truck, and she took water to Granma and to Grampa on top of the load. She stood on the bars and handed the cup to Grampa, and he wet his lips, and then shook his head and refused more. The old eyes looked up at Ma in pain and bewilderment for a moment before the awareness receded again.

Al started the motor and backed the truck to the gas pump. "Fill her up. She'll take about seven," said Al. "We'll give her six so she don't spill none."

The fat man put the hose in the tank. "No, sir," he said. "I jus' don't know what the country's comin' to. Relief an' all."

Casy said, "I been walkin' aroun' in the country. Ever'body's askin' that. What we comin' to? Seems to me we don't never come to nothin'. Always on the way. Always goin' and goin'. Why don't folks think about that? They's movement now. People moving. We know why, an' we know how. Movin' 'cause they got to. That's why folks always move. Movin' 'cause they want somepin better'n what they got. An' that's the on'y way they'll ever get it. Wantin' it an' needin' it, they'll go out an' git it.

It's bein' hurt that makes folks mad to fightin'. I been walkin' aroun' the country, an' hearin' folks talk like you."

The fat man pumped the gasoline and the needle turned on the pump dial, recording the amount. "Yeah, but what's it comin' to? That's what I want ta know." . . .

ONCE California belonged to Mexico and its land to Mexicans; and a horde of tattered feverish Americans poured in. And such was their hunger for land that they took the land — stole Sutter's land, Guerrero's land, took the grants and broke them up and growled and quarreled over them, those frantic hungry men; and they guarded with guns the land they had stolen. They put up houses and barns, they turned the earth and planted crops. And these things were possession, and possession was ownership.

The Mexicans were weak and fed. They could not resist, because they wanted nothing in the world as frantically as the Americans wanted land.

Then, with time, the squatters were no longer squatters, but owners; and their children grew up and had children on the land. And the hunger was gone from them, the feral hunger, the gnawing, tearing hunger for land, for water and earth and the good sky over it, for the green thrusting grass, for the swelling roots. They had these things so completely that they did not know about them any more. . . .

And it came about that owners no longer worked on their farms. They farmed on paper; and they forgot the land, the smell, the feel it it, and remembered only that they owned it, remembered only that they gained and lost by it. And some of the farms grew so large that one man could not even conceive of them any more, so large that it took batteries of bookkeepers to keep track of interest and gain and loss; chemists to test the soil, to replenish; straw bosses to see that the stooping men were moving along the rows as swiftly as the material of their bodies could stand. Then such a farmer really became a storekeeper, and kept a store. He paid the men, and sold them food, and took the money back. And after a while he did not pay the men at all, and saved bookkeeping. These farms gave food on credit. A man might work and feed himself; and when the work was done, he might find that he owed money to the company. And the owners not only did not work the farms any more, many of them had never seen the farms they owned.

And then the dispossessed were drawn west—from Kansas, Oklahoma, Texas, New Mexico; from Nevada and Arkansas families, tribes, dusted out, tractored out. Carloads, caravans, homeless and hungry; twenty thousand and fifty thousand and a hundred thousand and two hundred thousand. They streamed over the mountains, hungry and restless — restless as ants, scurrying to find work to do — to lift, to push, to pull, to pick, to cut anything, any burden to bear, for food. The kids are hungry. We got no place to live. Like ants scurrying for work, for food and most of all for land.

We ain't foreign. Seven generations back Americans, and beyond that Irish, Scotch, English, German. One of our folks in the Revolution, an' they was lots of our folk in the Civil War — both sides. Americans.

They were hungry, and they were fierce. And they had hoped to find a home, and they found only hatred. Okies — the owners hated them because the owners knew they were soft and the Okies strong, that they were fed and the Okies hungry; and perhaps the owners had heard from their grandfathers how easy it is to steal land from a soft man if you are fierce and hungry and armed. The owners hated them. And in the towns, the storekeepers hated them because they had no money to spend. There is no shorter path to a storekeeper's contempt, and all his admirations are exactly opposite. The town men, little bankers, hated Okies because there was nothing to gain from them. They had nothing. And the laboring people hated Okies because a hungry man must work, and if he must work, if he has to work, the wage payer automatically gives him less for his work; and then no one can get more.

"We ain't no bums," Tom insisted. "We're lookin' for work. We'll take any kind a work."

The young man paused in fitting the brace to the valve slot. He looked in amazement at Tom. "Lookin' for work?" he said. "So you're lookin' for work. What ya think ever'body else is lookin' for? Di'monds? What you think I wore my ass down to a nub lookin' for?" He twisted the brace back and forth.

Tom looked about at the grimy tents, the junk equipment, at the old cars, the lumpy mattresses out in the sun, at the blackened cans on fire-blackened holes where the people cooked. He asked quietly, "Ain't they no work?"

"I don' know. Mus' be. Ain't no crop right here now. Grapes to pick later, an' cotton to pick later. We're a-movin' on, soon's I get these here valves groun'. Me an' my wife an' my kids. We heard they was work up north. We're shovin' north, up aroun' Salinas." . . . Tom said, "Back home some fellas come through with han'bills — orange ones. Says they need lots a people out here to work the crops."

The young man laughed. "They say they's three hundred thousan' us folks here, an' I bet ever' dam' fam'ly seen them han'bills."

"Yeah, but if they don' need folks, what'd they go to the trouble puttin' them things out for?"

"Use your head, why don'cha?"

"Yeah, but I wanta know."

"Look," the young man said. "S'pose you got a job a work, an' there's jus' one fella wants the job. You got to pay 'im what he asts. But s'pose they's a hunderd men." He put down his tool. His eyes hardened and his voice sharpened. "S'pose they's a hunderd men wants that job. S'pose them men got kids, an' them kids is hungry. S'pose a lousy dime'll buy a box a mush for them kids. S'pose a nickel'll buy at leas' somepin for them kids. An' you got a hunderd men. Jus' offer 'em a nickel — why, they'll kill each other fightin' for that nickel. Know what they was payin', las' job I had? Fifteen cents an hour. Ten hours for a dollar an' a half, an' ya can't stay on the place. Got to burn gasoline gettin' there." He was panting with anger, and his eyes blazed with hate. "That's why them han'bills was out. You can print a hell of a lot of han'bills with what ya save payin' fifteen cents an hour for fiel' work." . . .

The young man squatted on his heels. "I'll tell ya," he said quietly. "They's a big son-of-a-bitch of a peach orchard I worked in. Takes nine men all the year roun'." He paused impressively. "Takes three thousan' men for two weeks when them peaches is ripe. Got to have 'em or them peaches'll rot. So what do they do? They send out han'bills all over hell. They need three thousan', an' they get six thousan'. They get them men for what they wanta pay. If ya don' wanta take what they pay, goddamn it, they's a thousan' men waitin' for your job. So ya pick, an' ya pick, an' then she's done. Whole part a the country's peaches. All ripe together. When ya get 'em picked, ever'goddamn one is picked. There ain't another damn thing in that part a the country to do. An' then them owners don' want you there no more. Three thousan' of you. The work's done. You might steal, you might get drunk, you might jus' raise hell. An' besides, you don' look nice, livin' in ol' tents; an' it's a pretty country, but you stink it up. They don' want you aroun'. So they kick you out, they move you along. That's how it is." . . .

Tom said angrily, "Them peaches got to be picked right now, don't they? Jus' when they're ripe?"

" 'Course they do."

"Well, s'pose them people got together an' says, 'Let 'em rot.' Wouldn' be long 'fore the price went up, by God!"

The young man looked up from the valves, looked sardonically at Tom. "Well, you figgered out somepin, didn' you. Come right outa your own head."

"I'm tar'd," said Tom. "Drove all night. I don't wanta start no argument. An' I'm so goddam tar'd I'd argue easy. Don' be smart with me. I'm askin' you."

The young man grinned. "I didn' mean it. You ain't been here. Folks figgered that out. An' the folks with the peach orchard figgered her out too. Look, if the folks gets together, they's a leader — got to be — fella that does the talkin'. Well, first time this fella opens his mouth they grab 'im an' stick 'im in jail. An' if they's another leader pops up, why, they stick *'im* in jail."

Tom said, "Well, a fella eats in jail anyways."

"His kids don't. How'd you like to be in an' your kids starvin' to death?"

"Yeah," said Tom slowly. "Yeah."

"An' here's another thing. Ever hear a' the blacklist?"

"What's that?"

"Well, you jus' open your trap about us folks gettin' together, an' you'll see. They take your pitcher an' send it all over. Then you can't get work nowhere. An' if you got kids ———"

Tom took off his cap and twisted it in his hands. "So we take what we can get, huh, or we starve; an' if we yelp we starve."

The young man made a sweeping circle with his hand, and his hand took in the ragged tents and the rusty cars.

Tom looked down at his mother again, where she sat scraping potatoes. And the children had drawn closer. He said, "I ain't gonna take it. Goddamn it, I an' my folks ain't no sheep. I'll kick the hell outa somebody."

"Like a cop?"

"Like anybody."

"You're nuts," said the young man. "They'll pick you right off. You got no name, no property. They'll find you in a ditch, with the blood dried on your mouth an' your nose. Be one little line in the paper — know what it'll say? 'Vagrant foun' dead.' An' that's all. You'll see a lot of them little lines, 'Vagrant foun' dead.' " . . .

THE spring is beautiful in California. Valleys in which the fruit blossoms are fragrant pink and white waters in a shallow sea. Then the first tendrils of the grapes, swelling from the old gnarled vines, cascade down to cover the trunks. The full green hills are round and soft as breasts. And on the level vegetable lands are the mile-long rows of pale green lettuce And then the leaves break out on the trees, and the petals drop from the fruit trees and carpet the earth with pink and white. The centers of the blossoms swell and grow and color: cherries and apples, peaches and pears, figs which close the flower in the fruit. All California quickens with produce, and the fruit grows heavy, and the limbs bend gradually under the fruit so that little crutches must be placed under them to support the weight. . . .

And first the cherries ripen. Cent and a half a pound. Hell, we can't pick 'em for that. Black cherries and red cherries, full and sweet, and the birds eat half of each cherry and the yellowjackets buzz into the holes the birds made. And on the ground the seeds drop and dry with black shreds hanging from them.

The purple prunes soften and sweeten. My God, we can't pick them and dry and sulphur them. We can't pay wages, no matter what wages. And the purple prunes carpet the ground. And first the skins wrinkle a little and swarms of flies come to feast, and the valley is filled with the odor of sweet decay. The meat turns dark and the crop shrivels on the ground.

And the pears grow yellow and soft. Five dollars a ton. Five dollars for forty fifty-pound boxes; trees pruned and sprayed, orchards cultivated — pick the fruit, put it in boxes, load the trucks, deliver the fruit to the cannery — forty boxes for five dollars. We can't do it. And the yellow fruit falls heavily to the ground and splashes on the ground. The yellowjackets dig into the soft meat, and there is a smell of ferment and rot.

Then the grapes — we can't make good wine. People can't buy good wine. Rip the grapes from the vines good grapes, rotten grapes, wasp-stung grapes. Press stems, press dirt and rot.

But there's mildew and formic acid in the vats.

Add sulphur and tannic acid.

The smell from the ferment is not the rich odor of wine, but the smell of decay and chemicals. . . .

The decay spreads over the State, and the sweet smell is a great sorrow on the land. Men who can graft the trees and make the seed fertile and big can find no way to let the hungry people eat their produce. Men who have created new fruits in the world cannot create a system whereby their fruits may be eaten. And the failure hangs over the State like a great sorrow.

The works of the roots of the vines, of the trees, must be destroyed to keep up the price, and this is the saddest, bitterest thing of all. Carloads of oranges dumped on the ground. The people came for miles to take the fruit, but this could not be. How would they buy oranges at twenty cents a dozen if they could drive out and pick them up? And men with hoses squirt kerosene on the oranges, and they are angry at the crime, angry at the people who have come to take the fruit. A million people hungry, needing the fruit—and kerosene sprayed over the golden mountains.

And the smell of rot fills the country.

Burn coffee for fuel in the ships. Burn corn to keep warm, it makes a hot fire. Dump potatoes in the rivers and place guards along the banks to keep the hungry people from fishing them out. Slaughter the pigs and bury them, and let the putrescence drip down into the earth.

There is a crime here that goes beyond denunciation. There is a sorrow here that weeping cannot symbolize. There is a failure here that topples all our success. The fertile earth, the straight tree rows, the sturdy trunks, and the ripe fruit. And children dying of pellagra must die because a profit cannot be taken from an orange. And coroners must fill in the certificates —died of malnutrition—because the food must rot, must be forced to rot.

The people come with nets to fish for potatoes in the river, and the guards hold them back; they come in rattling cars to get the dumped oranges, but the kerosene is sprayed. And they stand still and watch the potatoes float by, listen to the screaming pigs being killed in a ditch and covered with quicklime, watch the mountains of oranges slop down to a putrefying ooze; and in the eyes of the people there is the failure; and in the eyes of the hungry there is a growing wrath. In the souls of the people the grapes of wrath are filling and growing heavy, growing heavy for the vintage. . . .

Study Guide

1. An outline of this narrative can be made in this way:
    (a) the coming of the drought (pp. 426–428);
    (b) the foreclosures (pp. 428–436);
    (c) the flight West (pp. 436–440);
    (d) the life as a migrant-laborer (pp. 440–443); and
    (e) the social commentary of an angry, sensitive, humanitarian liberal (pp. 443–445).

Before analyzing this excerpt from *The Grapes of Wrath,* read the selection through at one sitting and permit yourself to enjoy the power of Steinbeck's prose — comparable in many respects to that of Upton Sinclair.

2. After you have read this selection, go back and summarize Steinbeck's comments on the following:

(a) bankers;
(b) tenant farmers; and
(c) the mechanization of farming and those who operate the farm machinery.

What impression does the author give the reader of the consequences of the drought on the various members of the family? Describe.

3. Steinbeck's description of the desperate flight West requires no questions or commentary.

4. Similarly stark is Steinbeck's portrayal of farming in California. How does this New Deal liberal feel about:

(a) California's Mexican inhabitants;
(b) the American settlers; and
(c) the "Okies"?

5. Continue with the following:

(a) Steinbeck's description of the seasonal and economic aspects of California farming and how this affects the migrant farmers is superb. Summarize it.
(b) What comments does he make on any hopes for their organization for better conditions? What connection does this particular segment (pp. 440–443) have to the activities of Cesar Chavez on the West Coast for the last decade?

6. The selection closes with a vivid description of the waste and heartlessness of the capitalistic economy — the awful ironies of the Great Depression: hunger amidst plenty and the inability of the system to distribute the fruits of its enormous productive capacity. The following is a memorable passage: "Carloads of oranges dumped on the ground. The people came for miles to take the fruit, but this could not be. How would they buy oranges at twenty cents a dozen if they could drive out and pick them up? And men with horses squirt kerosene on the oranges, and they are angry at the crime, angry at the people who have come to take the fruit. A million people hungry, needing the fruit — and kerosene sprayed over the golden mountains."

7. In review:

(a) Marriner Eccles, one of Roosevelt's New Deal advisers, said: "You have got to take care of the unemployed or you are going to have a revolution in this country. . . ." How would the Steinbeck piece fit this observation?
(b) How would the migrants react to the following selections from F.D.R.'s first inaugural address:
(1) "Yet our distress comes from no failure or substance. . . . Nature still offers her bounty and human efforts have multiplied it";

(2) "Practices of the unscrupulous money changers stand indicted in the court of public opinion . . .";

(3) "Happiness lies not in the mere possession of money; it lies in the joy of achievement, in the thrill of creative effort"; and

(4) "This Nation asks for action, and action now."

Can you now, having read both Steinbeck and F.D.R., appreciate the latter's role as therapist for the nation during the Great Depression?

VI. Responsibilities of World Power

Charles A. Beard

THE CASE FOR ISOLATION

1940   So FAR AS foreign affairs were concerned, the years after World War I were characterized by an ardent if unrealistic effort on the part of the majority of the American people to go back to the "good old days" when the nation had been able to exist more or less comfortably isolated from the conflicts of the rest of the globe. In the rapidly shrinking modern world, this was no longer possible of course, and every foreign tremor was felt and acted upon in Washington and throughout the nation. But official policy and the speeches of most American leaders seemed to reject internationalism. Particularly, it was felt that we must not again be caught up in Europe's quarrels, we must not again fight in Europe's wars.

The rise of Hitler and Mussolini and the resulting crises when they began to extend their aggressions outside the boundaries of Germany and Italy accentuated the tendency of the majority of Americans to pursue a policy of isolation, as was seen in the passage of the Neutrality Acts of the 1930's. But finally the barbarous aggressiveness of these dictators, and of the Japanese in Asia, caused a reaction in the United States. When Hitler's invasion of Poland actually produced the Second World War which Americans had been so eager to keep out of, strong pressures developed to reverse our policy and lend active support to the Allies. As a result there was the "Great Debate" — in Congress, in the press, and at every level among the populace itself.

President Roosevelt's was the most effective of the many voices raised in favor of abandoning isolation, but the opposition was both powerful and stubborn; it resisted at every stage the steps that led to our participation in the worldwide struggle. And among the leaders of this group none was more effective than the historian Charles A. Beard (1874–1948), who brought to the battle a reputation as a scholar won through the writing of such books as his *An Economic Interpretation of the Constitution* and *The Rise of American Civilization,* a powerful and persuasive style, and a zeal and energy born of the conviction that the fate of the nation and all its traditions depended upon the preservation of the "continental Americanism" that he advocated. His *A Foreign Policy for America,* published in 1940 at the height of the controversy, made the case for isolationism as effectively as it was possible to make it. It was widely read, and very influential. Indeed, it may well be argued that it was only the force of later events, and not the counter-arguments of the internationalists, that brought defeat to the isolationist cause Beard is here defending.

A FOREIGN POLICY FOR AMERICA

THE PRIMARY foreign policy for the United States may be called for convenience Continental Americanism. The two words imply a con-

449

centration of interest on the continental domain and on building here a civilization in many respects peculiar to American life and the potentials of the American heritage. In concrete terms the words mean nonintervention in the controversies and wars of Europe and Asia and resistance to the intrusion of European or Asiatic powers, systems, and imperial ambitions into the western hemisphere. This policy is positive. It is clear-cut. And it was maintained with consistency while the Republic was being founded, democracy extended, and an American civilization developed.

So protected by foreign policy, American civilization stood in marked contrast to the semi-feudal civilizations of Europe, and the country was long regarded as an asylum for the oppressed of all lands. America, it was boasted, offered to toiling masses the example of a nation free from huge conscript armies, staggering debts, and mountainous taxes. For more than a hundred years, while this system lasted, millions of immigrants, fleeing from the wars, oppressions, persecutions, and poverty of Europe, found a haven here; and enlightened Europeans with popular sympathies rejoiced in the fortunes of the United States and in the demonstration of liberty, with all its shortcomings, made on this continent in the presence of the tyrannies of the earth.

No mere adherence to theory or tradition marked the rise and growth of continentalism. The policy was realistically framed with reference to the exigencies of the early Republic and was developed during continuous experience with the vicissitudes of European ambitions, controversies, and wars. When other policies were proposed and departures were made from the established course, continentalism remained a driving force in thought about American foreign policy.

All through the years it was associated with a conception of American civilization. In the beginning the conception was primarily concerned with forms of culture appropriate to the rising Republic; during the middle period of American history it was enlarged and enriched under the influence of democratic vistas; and, despite the spread of industrialism in the later years, its characteristic features were powerful factors in shaping the course of American events. . . .

Until near the close of the nineteenth century, the continental policy of non-interference in the disputes of European nations was followed by the Government of the United States with a consistency which almost amounted to a fixed rule. Washington had formulated it. Monroe had extended and applied it. Seward had restated and re-emphasized it. Qualified by the Monroe doctrine as to European intervention in this hemisphere, it seemed to be settled for all time as the nation celebrated the hundredth anniversary of its independence.

But the promise of undisturbed permanence was illusory, for another conception of foreign policy for America was already on the horizon. That was the conception of imperialism, world power, and active participation in the great conflicts of interests everywhere. . . .

Owing to the over-seas character of imperialist operations, naval bureaucrats, naval supply interests, and armor-plate makers naturally furnished practical considerations, while an intelligentsia was educating the people into espousing and praising the new course. As roving men, cruising around over the oceans, American naval officers had early come into contact with American merchants abroad, engaged in garnering better profits in trade than they could expect to reap at home. They saw foreign lands in the Orient and other distant places which, they thought, could be easily seized by the United States and turned into sea bases or trading posts. . . .

. . . Since the establishment of independence, the Government of the United States had given attention to commercial advantages abroad; but for nearly a century its concern with foreign trade had been a minor interest, a phase of ordinary diplomatic and consular service, not a well-organized and well-financed campaign. Washington had urged the promotion of commerce, but had quickly added "forcing nothing." Between 1813 and 1899, the Government had even employed armed coercion on numerous occasions, ranging from bombardment to open war, as a method of dealing with "backward peoples" charged with hampering commercial operations. But none of the little wars was waged in the name of colonial expansion or of trade pushing as a policy of organized force. They were regarded as "incidents" in the pursuit of commercial advantage by American nationals. They were temporary and nearly always unilateral actions which involved no permanent entanglements in the imperialistic rivalries of Europe or Asia.

By way of contrast with this commercial policy the new imperialist course of trade advancement was distinguished by six prime features: (1) emphasis on the promotion of foreign trade as a means absolutely necessary for assuring even a reasonable degree of prosperity for the United States; (2) organized, persistent, and expansive operations by the Federal Government in demanding and pressing American commercial advantages everywhere, even in the face of the most bitter rivalry; (3) systematic use of the sea power as an instrument for urging or compelling other countries to grant American "rights" claimed throughout the world; (4) addresses, messages, and agitations by politicians designed to "educate" American business men into the belief that their marginal, if not their final, hope for profitable enterprise lay in the theories and practices of imperialism; (5) the frequent substitution of cooperative action with one or more great powers for unilateral action in the prosecution and protection of American claims to trading rights, privileges, and profits; and (6) emphasis on the "moral" obligation of the United States to help other great powers in maintaining "order" and "civilizing" colored races in the "backward places" of the earth. . . .

In summary, under fine phrases, manufactured for the occasion, pleasing to the popular ear, and gratifying to national vanity, politicians in control of the Government of the United States entangled the country in numerous quarrels in Asia and Europe. They made commitments difficult, if not impossible to cancel. They carried on a campaign of agitation designed to educate the people into the belief that the new course was necessary for the very well-being of the country and at the same time made for international peace and good will. They built up in the State Department a bureaucracy and a tradition absolutely opposed to historic continentalism.

Perhaps unwittingly they prepared the way for the next stage in the development of American foreign policy. From their participation in collective world politics, from the imperialist theory of "doing good to backward peoples," it was but a step to President Wilson's scheme for permanent and open participation in European and Asiatic affairs in the alleged interest of universal peace and general welfare. . . .

The third foreign policy proposed for the United States is the internationalism which sets *world* peace as the fundamental objective for the Government in the conduct of relations with other countries. Exponents of the policy often claim a monopoly of the American peace movement and generally insist that only by following their methods can the United States obtain the blessings of peace for itself. Thus internationalism is to be distinguished sharply from the policy of keeping peace for the United States within its continental zone of interests and maintaining pacific relations elsewhere, subject to the primacy of security for American civilization and civil liberties.

Internationalism so defined is marked by specific features. It proposes to connect the United States with the European State system by permanent ties, for the accomplishment of its alleged end. It rejects the doctrine of continental independence which was proclaimed in the effort of 1776 to cut America loose from the entanglements associated with its status as a dominion of the British empire. In taking this position, internationalists also make many assumptions respecting the nature of world history and the possibilities of European politics. They assume that permanent world peace is not only desirable but is indivisible and can be obtained by the pursuit of their methods, especially if the United States will associate itself with certain nations supposed to be committed to permanent peace.

According to the internationalist hypothesis, Americans who advocate peace for the United States in the presence of European and Asiatic wars are not peace advocates in the true sense. In the internationalist view, such advocates are not contributing to peace — they are isolationists pursuing a policy which leads to armaments and wars. In internationalist literature, these peace advocates are frequently represented as selfish, cowardly, and immoral persons, who merely wish "to save their own skins," who refuse to recognize the obligations of the United States to other nations suffering not from their own follies but from the neglect of the American people. Hence there arises an apparently irreconcilable contradiction between advocates of permanent world peace and advocates of peace for the American continent and of pacific measures as constant instruments of American foreign policy.

Besides being a foreign policy for the United States, internationalism is also a basic domestic policy. It assumes that the development of industry and science has made the country more dependent for its very existence on Europe and Asia, not less dependent than when it was mainly a producer of raw materials and an importer of manufactured products. As a general proposition, internationalism holds that American economy cannot enjoy a high degree of prosperity, must indeed be in a kind of permanent crisis, unless its volume or ratio of foreign trade is increased by international agreements or by what is called "lowering trade barriers."

Under this theory nothing fundamental can be accomplished by *domestic* policies and activities in relieving the American people from the curse of poverty and unemployment, in promoting the characteristic features of American civilization, in lifting the American standard of living to a higher plane, by the fullest possible use of national resources in materials, machines, and labor, which are here in abundance. In other words, the crisis in the United States is not domestic; it is foreign; it can only be overcome, or even mitigated in any material sense, by international action, by some kind of collaboration with foreign powers.

Thus to differences over interpretations of world history, over assumptions about the possibilities of permanent world peace, over images of the world, internationalism adds irreconcilable differences over basic domestic policies; it repudiates continentalism root and branch as domestic policy and as a pacific foreign policy. . . .

As an outcome of the historical heritage, American foreign policy became a loose intermingling of conflicting elements — continentalism, imperialism, and internationalism. Each of the three programs was supported, more or less, by specific interests and portions of the intelligentsia. At every crisis in world affairs, as the running fire of debate on foreign events continued in the United States, each school manuevered for possession of the American mind and the direction of policy, through propaganda and the varied use of communication agencies. In the polls of public opinion, the winds of doctrine veered and twisted.

Yet at repeated tests, taken in formal elections and congressional battles, the principal body of that opinion was found consistently on the side of continentalism. Despite temporary victories, politicians who tried to swing the United States off its continental center of gravity toward imperialism or internationalism were never completely successful. . . .

Twice in American history the governing elite had turned the American nation away from its continental center of gravity into world adventures, ostensibly in a search for relations with the other countries or regions that would yield prosperity for American industry and a flowering of American prestige. First, in 1898; second, in 1917. But each time the main body of the people had resisted the propulsion, had found delusions in the false promises, and had returned to the continental orbit. Imperialism had failed to bring either profits, glory, or security. Internationalism had been wrecked in Versailles — by the struggle for power under the League of Nations, by the revelations of war propaganda, and by other brutal events which could not be erased from the record.

Again and again the fundamental resolve of the country against imperialism and internationalism had been revealed; in provisions for withdrawing from the Philippine area; in the surrender of specious rights to engage in trade where great nations were fighting for their lives; in neutrality acts keeping American ships and travelers out of war zones; in the refusal of Congress to transform Guam into a great naval base; in an evident unwillingness to engage in a major war over the petty commerce of China; and in persistent efforts to overcome, by domestic measures, the crisis in domestic economy, without wholesale resort to artificial devices for dumping American "surpluses" abroad, that is, giving them to foreigners.

After all the illusory adventures in policy based on the Cobden-Bright conception of "free international exchange," the American nation confronted, not a growing freedom of that kind, but a steady increase in the number of countries operating on different principles. At best free international exchange had been merely partial; and the tendencies in that direction had been reversed.

Germany, Italy, Russia, and Japan went over to controlled economies of a totalitarian character. France, Great Britain, and other powers turned in the direction of management and "regimentation." Even if the United States had labored with might and main to force commerce on these countries and widen the channels of its foreign traffic, it could have made little headway against the apparently irresistible determination of other governments — capitalist, fascist, and communist — to grapple with their problems of living by direct action at home. By sheer necessity, American civilization was turned back upon itself.

Slowly, but with increasing force, it was realized that the "foreign outlet" doctrines of imperialism and internationalism were illusions. This did not mean that foreign commerce was deprecated or deemed undesirable. Indeed such commerce was fully recognized as desirable within the limits of American needs for products not available at home. But it did mean that the potentials of buying power indispensable to keeping American industry and agriculture running at a high tempo lay right here, in the creation of new wealth at home; that three or four billions of foreign commerce were relatively small as compared with the twenty or thirty billions annually wasted in idle plants, idle labor, and idle resources at home; that the frontiers for the expansion of American enterprise were within this continent, not in the fabled Indies or on the Rhine, the Danube, or the Vistula; that all about us, right here, lay the materials for a magnificent civilization; and that the principal task was the concentration of intelligence, the cultural forces of men and women, upon the problem of putting science, technology, inventive ingenuity, private energies, and public enterprise to work in making real the vision of a civilization that rose before the mind as a goal to be attained by majestic effort on this continent, without recourse to empire or entanglements in the age-long coalitions of Europe and Asia.

This continentalism did not seek to make a "hermit" nation out of America. From the very beginning under the auspices of the early Republic, it never had embraced that impossible conception. It did not deny the obvious fact that American civilization had made use of its European heritages, was a part of western civilization, and had continuous contacts with Occidental and Oriental cultures. It did not deny the obvious fact that wars in Europe and Asia "affect" or "concern" the United States.

It did not mean "indifference" to the sufferings of Europe or China (or India or Ethiopia). In truth, in all history, no people ever poured out treasure more generously in aid of human distresses in every quarter of the globe — distresses springing from wars, famines, revolutions, persecutions, and earthquakes.

With reference to such conflicts and sufferings, continentalism merely meant a recognition of the limited nature of American powers to relieve, restore, and maintain life beyond its own sphere of interest and control — a recognition of the hard fact that the United States, either alone or in any coalition, did not possess the power to force peace on Europe and Asia, to assure the establishment of democratic and pacific governments there, or to provide the social and economic underwriting necessary to the perdurance of such governments. In respect of morality continentalists did not deny the existence of responsibilities to other nations and peoples. On the contrary they favored discharging such responsibilities, always with due regard for the physical, economic, and political limits on the powers of the United States and for the solemn obligation of protecting the Republic against misadventures headed in the direction of disaster. If this conception fell short of the selfless sacrifice required by an absolute morality, it could claim worthiness in the presence of other examples set by the family of nations.

Besides forcing a concentration of attention, energy, and intelligence on overcoming the grave economic and social crisis at home and on strengthening American civilization in all its best features, continentalism, strictly construed, meant a return to the correct and restrained diplomacy of an earlier time. The freedom of the people and the press to discuss foreign affairs and favor foreign nations, parties, factions, and causes, within the limits of neutrality laws was accepted as axiomatic. Equally axiomatic, if America was to keep its peace, was the duty of public officials, especially the President and Secretary of State, speaking in the name of the whole nation, to abstain from denouncing and abusing foreign States, good or bad, with which diplomatic relations are maintained and the United States is at peace.

Correct policy likewise commanded such public officials to avoid vain and verbose dissertations on the manners and morals of other countries; to couch protests in the language of dignity; to speak and write as briefly and courteously as possible in necessary dealings with foreign governments; to make no boasts which the army and navy could not enforce with a reasonable prospect to success; to carry on international relations with restraint, and in the subdued style of approved diplomatic usage — speaking softly, keeping the powder dry, withholding wrath except when war is intended as a last resort. Such official conduct would enable the

Government of the United States to escape innumerable hatreds abroad, offer its services and cooperation to troubled peoples with authority on proper occasions, and win respect, even affection and esteem, throughout the earth.

This policy, consistently followed by the United States, would favor, not hinder, the coming of peace to other nations of the world.

Study Guide

1. The Beard selection contains:
   (a) a historical survey of American foreign policy (pp. 449–454); and
   (b) a case for an isolationist foreign policy for the nation (pp. 454–457).

2. Beard sees American foreign policy developing in three stages: "Continental Americanism," imperialism, and internationalism. Beginning with "Continental Americanism," summarize Beard's definition of it, how the policy evolved and its major proponents. What, too, is Beard's evaluation of its effectiveness and value for the nation?

3. Contrast the above with the policy of imperialism. When did the latter evolve, who promoted it, and for what purposes? Note, by the way, that Beard contrasts a foreign policy that fosters "commercial advantage" to one of full-fledged imperialism — a distinction that parallels closely the attitude of Mark Twain and his division between the "American Game" and the "European" one on pp. 228–229. Outline the primary characteristics Beard ascribes to the policy of imperialism. What is his evaluation of this phase of American foreign policy?

4. Summarize the internationalist's basic thesis. What, according to Beard, are the overseas consequences of the internationalist foreign policy and what are some of its domestic implications?

5. The remainder of this selection consists of a brilliant critique by Beard of an internationalist foreign policy for the United States. Let us follow Beard's argument thus:
   (a) On what two occasions did the internationalists successfully determine the American posture in the world *and with what results?*
   (b) What evidence does Beard present to demonstrate how these forays abroad were repudiated by the majority of the American people?
   (c) What developments in the 1930's forced upon the United States an even stronger recognition of the need to retain an isolationist posture?

6. In his closing paragraphs, Beard — in no sense a reactionary or conservative, unlike many isolationists — carefully delimits the contours of his isolationist views in order to dispel any doubts as to his sense of humanity or his sense of realism about the United States in world affairs. Outline the precise qualifications Beard places on his isolationist position.

Franklin D. Roosevelt

AID TO BRITAIN

✢{ *1941* }✢ IN THE period between the two World Wars it was official American policy to steer clear of all foreign conflicts. The Neutrality Act of 1937, for example, forbade the shipment of arms or even the lending of money to either side in any international or civil war. However, after the outbreak of World War II and particularly after the fall of France, it became obvious to President Roosevelt (1882–1945) that the national interest called for active aid to the foes of Nazism. Nevertheless, public opinion, while divided, seemed more concerned with keeping out of the conflict than with helping the British and their allies. So strong was the anti-war feeling that in the closing days of his 1940 election campaign against Wendell Willkie (1892–1944), Roosevelt felt compelled to assure the voters: "I have said this before, but I shall say it again and again and again: Your boys are not going to be sent into any foreign wars."

But after the election, responding to a frank letter from Prime Minister Winston Churchill (1871–1965) pointing out that England had nearly exhausted her supply of dollars for the purchase of arms and was in danger of being strangled by German sub-warfare, Roosevelt decided upon the bold expedient of the "lend-lease" program. Roosevelt presented his "lend-lease" plan to Congress, in his annual message on January 6, 1941. That document, which included the so-called "Four Freedoms," completed the conversion of public opinion. Although the Lend-Lease Bill was debated hotly for some two months it finally passed both Houses of Congress with handsome majorities. Thereafter it could be assumed that the United States was committed to all-out aid to England. While American soldiers had not yet been committed to the battle, it is fair to say that active United States participation in World War II began with the passage of the Lend-Lease Act.

ANNUAL MESSAGE TO CONGRESS

(January 6, 1941)

Mr. President, Mr. Speaker, Members of the Seventy-seventh Congress:

I address you, the Members of the Seventy-seventh Congress, at a moment unprecedented in the history of the Union. I use the word "unprecedented," because at no previous time has American security been as seriously threatened from without as it is today.

Since the permanent formation of our Government under the Constitution, in 1789, most of the periods of crisis in our history have related to our domestic affairs. Fortunately, only one of these — the four-year War

Between the States — ever threatened our national unity. Today, thank God, one hundred and thirty million Americans, in forty-eight States, have forgotten points of the compass in our national unity. . . .

As long as the aggressor nations maintain the offensive, they — not we — will choose the time and the place and the method of their attack.

That is why the future of all the American Republics is today in serious danger.

That is why this Annual Message to the Congress is unique in our history.

That is why every member of the Executive Branch of the Government and every member of the Congress faces great responsibility and great accountability.

The need of the moment is that our actions and our policy should be devoted primarily — almost exclusively — to meeting this foreign peril. For all our domestic problems are now a part of the great emergency.

Just as our national policy in internal affairs has been based upon a decent respect for the rights and dignity of all nations, large and small. And the justice of morality must and will win in the end.

Our national policy is this:

First, by an impressive expression of the public will and without regard to partisanship, we are committed to all-inclusive national defense.

Second, by an impressive expression of the public will and without regard to partisanship, we are committed to full support of all those resolute peoples, everywhere, who are resisting aggression and are thereby keeping war away from our Hemisphere. By this support, we express our determination that the democratic cause shall prevail; and we strengthen the defense and the security of our own nation.

Third, by an impressive expression of the public will and without regard to partisanship, we are committed to the proposition that principles of morality and considerations for our own security will never permit us to acquiesce in a peace dictated by aggressors and sponsored by appeasers. We know that enduring peace cannot be bought at the cost of other people's freedom. . . .

New circumstances are constantly begetting new needs for our safety. I shall ask this Congress for greatly increased new appropriations and authorizations to carry on what we have begun.

I also ask this Congress for authority and for funds sufficient to manufacture additional munitions and war supplies of many kinds to be turned over to those nations which are now in actual war with aggressor nations.

Our most useful and immediate role is to act as an arsenal for them as well as for ourselves. They do not need man power, but they do need billions of dollars worth of the weapons of defense.

The time is near when they will not be able to pay for them all in ready cash. We cannot, and we will not, tell them that they must surrender, merely because of present inability to pay for the weapons which we know they must have.

I do not recommend that we make them a loan of dollars with which to pay for these weapons — a loan to be repaid in dollars.

I recommend that we make it possible for those nations to continue to obtain war materials in the United States, fitting their orders into our own program. Nearly all their matériel would, if the time ever came, be useful for our own defense.

Taking counsel of expert military and naval authorities, considering what is best for our own security, we are free to decide how much should be kept here and how much should be sent abroad to our friends who by their determined and heroic resistance are giving us time in which to make ready our own defense.

For what we send abroad, we shall be repaid within a reasonable time following the close of hostilities, in similar materials, or, at our option, in other goods of many kinds, which they can produce and which we need.

Let us say to the democracies: "We Americans are vitally concerned in your defense of freedom. We are putting forth our energies, our resources and our organizing powers to give you the strength to regain and maintain a free world. We shall send you, in ever-increasing numbers, ships, planes, tanks, guns. This is our purpose and our pledge."

In fulfillment of this purpose we will not be intimidated by the threats of dictators that they will regard as a breach of international law or as an act of war our aid to the democracies which dare to resist their aggression. Such aid is not an act of war, even if a dictator should unilaterally proclaim it so to be.

When the dictators, if the dictators, are ready to make war upon us, they will not wait for an act of war on our part. They did not wait for Norway or Belgium or the Netherlands to commit an act of war.

Their only interest is in a new one-way international law, which lacks mutuality in its observance, and, therefore, becomes an instrument of oppression.

The happiness of future generations of Americans may well depend upon how effective and how immediate we can make our aid felt. No one can tell the exact character of the emergency situations that we may be called upon to meet. The Nation's hands must not be tied when the Nation's life is in danger.

We must all prepare to make the sacrifices that the emergency — almost as serious as war itself — demands. Whatever stands in the way of speed and efficiency in defense preparations must give way to the national need.

A free nation has the right to expect full cooperation from all groups. A free nation has the right to look to the leaders of business, of labor, and of agriculture to take the lead in stimulating effort, not among other groups but within their own groups.

The best way of dealing with the few slackers or trouble makers in our midst is, first, to shame them by patriotic example, and, if that fails, to use the sovereignty of Government to save Government.

As men do not live by bread alone, they do not fight by armaments alone. Those who man our defenses, and those behind them who build our defenses, must have the stamina and the courage which come from unshakable belief in the manner of life which they are defending. The mighty action that we are calling for cannot be based on a disregard of all things worth fighting for.

The Nation takes great satisfaction and much strength from the things which have been done to make its people conscious of their individual stake in the preservation of democratic life in America. Those things have toughened the fiber of our people, have renewed their faith and strengthened their devotion to the institutions we make ready to protect.

Certainly this is no time for any of us to stop thinking about the social and economic problems which are the root cause of the social revolution which is today a supreme factor in the world.

For there is nothing mysterious about the foundations of a healthy and strong democracy. The basic things expected by our people of their political and economic systems are simple. They are:

Equality of opportunity for youth and for others.

Jobs for those who can work.

Security for those who need it.

The ending of special privilege for the few.

The preservation of civil liberties for all.

The enjoyment of the fruits of scientific progress in a wider and constantly rising standard of living.

These are the simple, basic things that must never be lost sight of in the turmoil and unbelievable complexity of our modern world. The inner and abiding strength of our economic and political systems is dependent upon the degree to which they fulfill these expectations.

Many subjects connected with our social economy call for immediate improvement.

As examples:

We should bring more citizens under the coverage of old-age pensions and unemployment insurance.

We should widen the opportunities for adequate medical care.

We should plan a better system by which persons deserving or needing gainful employment may obtain it.

I have called for personal sacrifice. I am assured of the willingness of almost all Americans to respond to that call.

A part of the sacrifice means the payment of more money in taxes. In my Budget Message I shall recommend that a greater portion of this great defense program be paid for from taxation than we are paying today. No person should try, or be allowed, to get rich out of this program; and the principle of tax payments in accordance with ability to pay should be constantly before our eyes to guide our legislation.

If the Congress maintains these principles, the voters, putting patriotism ahead of pocketbooks, will give you their applause.

In the future days, which we seek to make secure, we look forward to a world founded upon four essential human freedoms.

The first is freedom of speech and expression — everywhere in the world.

The second is freedom of every person to worship God in his own way — everywhere in the world.

The third is freedom from want — which, translated into world terms, means economic understandings which will secure to every nation a healthy peacetime life for it inhabitants — everywhere in the world.

The fourth is freedom from fear — which, translated into world terms, means a world-wide reduction of armaments to such a point and in such a thorough fashion that no nation will be in a position to commit an act of physical aggression against any neighbor — anywhere in the world.

That is no vision of a distant millennium. It is a definite basis for a kind of world attainable in our own time and generation. That kind of world is the very antithesis of the so-called new order of tyranny which the dictators seek to create with the crash of a bomb.

To that new order we oppose the greater conception — the moral order. A good society is able to face schemes of world domination and foreign revolutions alike without fear.

Since the beginning of our American history, we have been engaged in change — in a perpetual peaceful revolution — a revolution which goes on steadily, quietly adjusting itself to changing conditions — without the concentration camp or the quick-lime in the ditch. The world order which we seek is the cooperation of free countries, working together in a friendly, civilized society.

This nation has placed its destiny in the hands and heads and hearts of its millions of free men and women; and its faith in freedom under the guidance of God. Freedom means the supremacy of human rights everywhere. Our support goes to those who struggle to gain those rights or keep them. Our strength is our unity of purpose.

To that high concept there can be no end save victory.

Study Guide

1. This talk contains the essential arguments for and the provisions of lend-lease. What three principles of national policy does Roosevelt enunciate before he asks for lend-lease?

2. What reasoning does he employ to justify the lend-lease program? Summarize.

3. Turning to the home front, F.D.R. warns one group (dissenters from the war effort) and placates another (social reformers). How does he do this?

4. In closing, Roosevelt refers to and enunciates the Four Freedoms: from your text find out when and where and why they were first written. Why do you suppose he included this in his address?

5. In retrospect: Compare the address by Roosevelt with Wilson's speeches of 1917 and 1918 (pp. 352–364). How much of a parallel do you find in the position of the United States? What similarities and differences do you find in their respective justification for the need to act? How would you compare the Fourteen Points to the Four Freedoms? Which of the two men, in your opinion, is more persuasive in his arguments? Which is more exalted in the goals he offers? Answer, illustrate, and elaborate.

Harry S. Truman and *Henry L. Stimson*

THE BOMBING OF HIROSHIMA AND NAGASAKI

1945, 1947 WILLIAM L. LAURENCE, the *New York Times* reporter on special leave with the Manhattan Project, which developed the atomic bomb, described what he saw on the morning of August 6, 1945, when a single B-29 dropped the first atomic bomb ("Little Boy") on Japan in this way: "Suddenly out of the swirling purple cloud came a huge column of smoke. . . . The ten-thousand-foot column suddenly grew into a giant mushroom, with tremendous clouds of dust swirling about its base for a distance of three miles. . . . At exactly 9:15 this morning Hiroshima stood out under the clear blue sky. One tenth of a millionth of a second later . . . it had been swallowed by a cloud of swirling fire as though it has never existed. The best watches made by man still registered 9:15." The atomic bomb that was exploded over Hiroshima, one of Japan's prime industrial centers, killed 78,000 Japanese, almost all instantly, maimed a little less than half that number, and demolished an area of three miles radius and virtually all of the city's structures. The bomb ("Fat Man") dropped on Nagasaki, Japan, three days later, brought even greater destruction and human suffering. The two bombing missions ushered in the age of the atom and, at the same time, the controversial question as to whether the United States was justified in its actions.

The debate over the bombing of Japan has ensued on several levels — on strategic, diplomatic, and moral grounds. There are those who contend that Japan had already dispatched peace feelers through Russia and that a strategy of victory over Japan did not demand the bombing of the cities of a near-vanquished enemy. On diplomatic grounds, the critics of the bombing of Hiroshima and Nagasaki contend that the bombings were intended, not for the defeat of Japan, but to frighten concessions out of the Russians — which they failed to do. And, finally, there are those critics unconcerned with either strategy or diplomacy, humanitarians who feel that at the very least a warning should have been given to the Japanese before the indiscriminate bombing of defenseless men, women, and children took place. For some, this action on our part brought us into the same moral camp as the Nazis and the Japanese — our enemies in World War II.

The basic defense for the actions of the United States is contained in an article written by Henry L. Stimson for *Harper's Magazine* in 1947 on "The Decision to Use the Atomic Bomb." Stimson, as secretary of war for both Presidents Roosevelt and Harry S. Truman, played the key role in establishing the Interim Committee to advise President Truman on all facets of this new scientific and military instrument. Reprinted here is the announcement of the first bombing by Truman and Stimson's defense of that decision by Truman to bomb Japan without previous warning.

STATEMENT BY THE PRESIDENT OF THE UNITED STATES

(1945)

SIXTEEN HOURS ago an American airplane dropped one bomb on Hiroshima, an important Japanese Army base. That bomb had more power than 20,000 tons of T.N.T. It had more than two thousand times the blast power of the British "Grand Slam" which is the largest bomb ever yet used in the history of warfare.

The Japanese began the war from the air at Pearl Harbor. They have been repaid many fold. And the end is not yet. With this bomb we have now added a new and revolutionary increase in destruction to supplement the growing power of our armed forces. In their present form these bombs are now in production and even more powerful forms are in development.

It is an atomic bomb. It is a harnessing of the basic power of the universe. The force from which the sun draws its power has been loosed against those who brought war to the Far East.

Before 1939, it was the accepted belief of scientists that it was theoretically possible to release atomic energy. But no one knew any practical method of doing it. By 1942, however, we knew that the Germans were working feverishly to find a way to add atomic energy to the other engines of war with which they hoped to enslave the world. But they failed. We may be grateful to Providence that the Germans got the V–1's and the V–2's late and in limited quantities and even more grateful that they did not get the atomic bomb at all.

The battle of the laboratories held fateful risks for us as well as the battles of the air, land and sea, and we have now won the battle of the laboratories as we have won the other battles.

Beginning in 1940, before Pearl Harbor, scientific knowledge useful in war was pooled between the United States and Great Britain, and many priceless helps to our victories have come from that arrangement. Under that general policy the research on the atomic bomb was begun. With American and British scientists working together we entered the race of discovery against the Germans.

The United States had available the large number of scientists of distinction in the many needed areas of knowledge. It had the tremendous industrial and financial resources necessary for the project and they could be devoted to it without undue impairment of other vital war work. In the United States the laboratory work and the production plants, on which a substantial start had already been made, would be out of reach of enemy bombing, while at that time Britain was exposed to constant air attack and was still threatened with the possibility of invasion. For these reasons Prime Minister Churchill and President Roosevelt agreed that it was wise to carry on the project here. We now have two great plants and many lesser works devoted to the production of atomic power. Employment during peak construction numbered 125,000 and over 65,000 individuals are even now engaged in operating the plants. Many have worked there for two and a half years. Few know what they have been producing. They see great quantities of material going in and they see nothing coming out of these plants, for the physical size of the explosive charge is exceedingly small. We have spent two billion dollars on the greatest scientific gamble in history — and won.

But the greatest marvel is not the size of the enterprise, its secrecy, nor its cost, but the achievement of scientific brains in putting together infinitely complex pieces of knowledge held by many men in different fields of science into a workable plan. And hardly less marvellous has been the capacity of industry to design, and of labor to operate, the machines and methods to do things never done before so that the brain child of many minds came forth in physical shape and performed as it was supposed to do. Both science and industry worked under the direction of the United States Army, which achieved a unique success in managing so diverse a problem in the advancement of knowledge if such another combination could be got together in the world. What has been done is the greatest achievement of organized science in history. It was done under high pressure and without failure.

We are now prepared to obliterate more rapidly and completely every productive enterprise the Japanese have above ground in any city. We shall destroy their docks, their factories, and their communications. Let there be no mistake; we shall completely destroy Japan's power to make war.

It was to spare the Japanese people from utter destruction that the ultimatum of July 26 was issued at Potsdam. Their leaders promptly rejected that ultimatum. If they do not now accept our terms they may expect a rain of ruin from the air, the like of which has never been seen on this earth. Behind this air attack will follow sea and land forces in such numbers and power as they have not yet seen and with the fighting skill of which they are already well aware.

The Secretary of War, who has kept in personal touch with all phases of the project, will immediately make public a statement giving further details.

His statement will give facts concerning the sites at Oak Ridge near Knoxville, Tennessee, and at Richland near Pasco, Washington, and an installation near Santa Fe, New Mexico. Although the workers at the sites have been making materials to be used in producing the greatest destructive force in history they have not themselves been in danger beyond that of many other occupations, for the utmost care has been taken of their safety.

The fact that we can release atomic energy ushers in a new era in man's understanding of nature's forces. Atomic energy may in the future supplement the power that now comes from coal, oil, and falling water, but at present it cannot be produced on a basis to compete with them commercially. Before that comes there must be a long period of intensive research.

It has never been the habit of the scientists of this country or the policy of this Government to withhold from the world scientific knowledge. Normally, therefore, everything about the work with atomic energy would be made public.

But under present circumstances it is not intended to divulge the technical processes of production or all the military applications, pending further examination of possible methods of protecting us and the rest of the world from the danger of sudden destruction.

I shall recommend that the Congress of the United States consider promptly the establishment of an appropriate commission to control the production and use of atomic power within the United States. I shall give further consideration and make further recommendations to the Congress as to how atomic power can become a powerful and forceful influence towards the maintenance of world peace.

THE DECISION TO USE THE ATOMIC BOMB

(1947)

IN RECENT months there has been much comment about the decision to use atomic bombs in attacks on the Japanese cities of Hiroshima and Nagasaki. This decision was one of the gravest made by our government in recent years, and it is entirely proper that it should be widely discussed. I have therefore decided to record for all who may be interested my understanding of the events which led up to the attack on Hiroshima on August 6, 1945, on Nagasaki on August 9, and the Japanese decision to surrender, on August 10. . . .

It was in the fall of 1941 that the question of atomic energy was first brought directly to my attention. At that time President Roosevelt appointed a committee consisting of Vice President Wallace, General Marshall, Dr. Vannevar Bush, Dr. James B. Conant, and myself. The function of this committee was to advise the President on questions of policy relating to the study of nuclear fission which was then proceeding both in this country and in Great Britain. For nearly four years thereafter I was directly connected with all major decisions of policy on the development and use of atomic energy, and from May 1, 1943, until my resignation as Secretary of War on September 21, 1945, I was directly responsible to the President for the administration of the entire undertaking; my chief advisers in this period were General Marshall, Dr. Bush, Dr. Conant, and Major General Leslie R. Groves, the officer in charge of the project. At the same time I was the President's senior adviser on the military employment of atomic energy.

The policy adopted and steadily pursued by President Roosevelt and his advisers was a simple one. It was to spare no effort in securing the earliest possible successful development of an atomic weapon. The reasons for this policy were equally simple. The original experimental achievement of atomic fission had occurred in Germany in 1938, and it was known that the Germans had continued their experiments. In 1941 and 1942 they were believed to be ahead of us, and it was vital that they should not be the first to bring atomic weapons into the field of battle. Furthermore, if we should be the first to develop the weapon, we should have a great new instrument for shortening the war and minimizing destruction. At no time, from 1941 to 1945, did I ever hear it suggested by the President, or by any other responsible member of the government, that atomic energy should not be used in the war. All of us of course understood the terrible responsibility involved in our attempt to unlock the doors to such a devastating weapon; President Roosevelt particularly spoke to me many times of his own awareness of the catastrophic potentialities of our work. But we were at war, and the work must be done. I therefore emphasize that it was our common objective, throughout the war, to be the first to produce an atomic weapon and use it. The possible atomic weapon was considered to be a new and tremendously powerful explosive, as legitimate as any other of the deadly explosive weapons of modern war. The entire purpose was the production of a military weapon; on no other ground could the wartime expenditure of so much time and money have been justified. The exact circumstances in which that weapon might be used were unknown to any of us until the middle of 1945, and when that time came, as we shall presently see, the military use of atomic energy was connected with larger questions of national policy.

The extraordinary story of the successful development of the atomic bomb has been well told elsewhere. As time went on it became clear that the weapon would not be available in time for use in the European Theater, and the war against Germany was successfully ended by the use of what are now called conventional means. But in the spring of 1945 it became evident that the climax of our prolonged atomic effort was at hand. By the nature of atomic chain reactions, it was impossible to state with certainty that we had succeeded until a bomb had actually exploded in a full-scale experiment; nevertheless it was considered exceedingly probable that we should by midsummer have successfully detonated the first atomic bomb. This was to be done at the Alamogordo Reservation in New Mexico. It was thus time for detailed consideration of our future plans. What had begun as a well-founded hope was now developing into a reality.

On March 15, 1945 I had my last talk with President Roosevelt. . . . This conversation covered the three aspects of the question which were then uppermost in our minds. First, it was always necessary to suppress a lingering doubt that any such titanic undertaking could be successful. Second, we must consider the implications of success in terms of its long-range postwar effect. Third, we must face the problem that would be presented at the time of our first use of the weapon, for with that first use there must be some public statement.

I did not see Franklin Roosevelt again. The next time I went to the White House to discuss atomic energy was April 25, 1945, and I went to explain the nature of the problem to a man whose only previous knowledge of our activities was that of a Senator who had loyally accepted our assurance that the matter must be kept a secret from him. Now he was President and Commander-in-Chief, and the final responsibility in this as in so many other matters must be his. President Truman accepted this responsibility with the same fine spirit that Senator Truman had shown before in accepting our refusal to inform him.

I discussed with him the whole history of the project. We had with us General Groves, who explained in detail the progress which had been made and the probable future course of the work. I also discussed with President Truman the broader aspects of the subject, and the memorandum which I used in this discussion is again a fair sample of the state of our thinking at the time.

Memorandum Discussed with President Truman

April 25, 1945

1. Within four months we shall in all probability have completed the most terrible weapon ever known in human history, one bomb of which could destroy a whole city.

2. Although we have shared its development with the U.K., physically the U.S. is at present in the position of controlling the resources with which to construct and use it and no other nation could reach this position for some years.

3. Nevertheless it is practically certain that we could not remain in this position indefinitely.

a. Various segments of its discovery and production are widely known among many scientists in many countries, although few scientists are now acquainted with the whole process which we have developed.

b. Although its construction under present methods requires great scientific and industrial effort and raw materials, which are temporarily mainly within the possession and knowledge of U.S. and U.K., it is extremely probable that much easier and cheaper methods of production will be discovered by scientists in the future, together with the use of materials of much wider distribution. As a result, it is extremely probable that the future will make it possible for atomic bombs to be constructed by smaller nations or even groups, or at least by a larger nation in a much shorter time.

4. As a result, it is indicated that the future may see a time when such a weapon may be constructed in secret and used suddenly and effectively with devastating power by a wilful nation or group against an unsuspecting nation or group of much greater size and material power. With its aid even a very powerful unsuspecting nation might be conquered within a very few days by a very much smaller one. . . .

5. The world in its present state of moral advancement compared with its technical development would be eventually at the mercy of such a weapon. In other words, modern civilization might be completely destroyed.

6. To approach any world peace organization of any pattern now likely to be considered, without an appreciation by the leaders of our country of the power of this new weapon, would seem to be unrealistic. No system of control heretofore considered would be adequate to control this menace. Both inside any particular country and between the nations of the world, the control of this weapon will undoubtedly be a matter of the greatest difficulty and would involve such thoroughgoing rights of inspection and internal controls as we have never heretofore contemplated.

7. Furthermore, in the light of our present position with reference to this weapon, the question of sharing it with other nations and, if so shared, upon what terms, becomes a primary question of our foreign relations. Also our leadership in the war and in the development of this weapon has placed a certain moral responsibility upon us which we cannot shirk without very serious responsibility for any disaster to civilization which it would further.

8. On the other hand, if the problem of the proper use of this weapon can be solved, we would have the opportunity to bring the world into a pattern in which the peace of the world and our civilization can be saved.

9. As stated in General Groves' report, steps are under way looking towards the establishment of a select committee of particular qualifications for recommending action to the executive and legislative branches of our government when secrecy is no longer in full effect. The commit-

tee would also recommend the actions to be taken by the War De-
partment prior to that time in anticipation of the postwar problems. All
recommendations would of course be first submitted to the President.

The next step in our preparations was the appointment of the committee referred to in paragraph (9) above. This committee, which was
known as the Interim Committee, was charged with the function of ad-
vising the President on the various questions raised by our apparently
imminent success in developing an atomic weapon. I was its chairman,
but the principal labor of guiding its extended deliberations fell to
George L. Harrison, who acted as chairman in my absence. . . .

The discussions of the committee ranged over the whole field of atomic
energy, in its political, military, and scientific aspects. That part of its
work which particularly concerns us here relates to its recommendations
for the use of atomic energy against Japan, but it should be borne in
mind that these recommendations were not made in a vacuum. The
committee's work included the drafting of the statements which were
published immediately after the first bombs were dropped, the drafting
of a bill for the domestic control of atomic energy, and recommendations looking toward the international control of atomic energy. The
Interim Committee was assisted in its work by a Scientific Panel whose
members were the following: Dr. A. H. Compton, Dr. Enrico Fermi,
Dr. E. O. Lawrence, and Dr. J. R. Oppenheimer. All four were nuclear
physicists of the first rank; all four had held positions of great importance
in the atomic project from its inception. At a meeting with the Interim
Committee and the Scientific Panel on May 31, 1945 I urged all those
present to feel free to express themselves on any phase of the subject,
scientific or political. Both General Marshall and I at this meeting expressed the view that atomic energy could not be considered simply in
terms of military weapons but must also be considered in terms of a new
relationship of man to the universe.

On June 1, after its discussions with the Scientific Panel, the Interim
Committee unanimously adopted the following recommendations:

1. The bomb should be used against Japan as soon as possible.
2. It should be used on a dual target — that is, a military installation or
   war plant surrounded by or adjacent to houses and other buildings
   most susceptible to damage, and
3. It should be used without prior warning [of the nature of the wea-
   pon]. One member of the committee, Mr. Bard, later changed his
   view and dissented from recommendation (3).

In reaching these conclusions the Interim Committee carefully considered such alternatives as a detailed advance warning or a demonstration in some uninhabited area. Both of these suggestions were discarded as impractical. They were not regarded as likely to be effective in compelling a surrender of Japan, and both of them involved serious risks. Even the New Mexico test would not give final proof that any given bomb was certain to explode when dropped from an airplane. Quite apart from the generally unfamiliar nature of atomic explosives, there was the whole problem of exploding a bomb at a predetermined height in the air by a complicated mechanism which could not be tested in the static test of New Mexico. Nothing would have been more damaging to our effort to obtain surrender than a warning or a demonstration followed by a dud — and this was a real possibility. Furthermore, we had no bombs to waste. It was vital that a sufficient effect be quickly obtained with the few we had. . . .

. . . The ultimate responsibility for the recommendation to the President rested upon me, and I have no desire to veil it. The conclusions of the committee were similar to my own, although I reached mine independently. I felt that to extract a genuine surrender from the Emperor and his military advisers, they must be administered a tremendous shock which would carry convincing proof of our power to destroy the Empire. Such an effective shock would save many times the number of lives, both American and Japanese, that it would cost.

The facts upon which my reasoning was based and steps were taken to carry it out now follow.

U.S. POLICY TOWARD JAPAN IN JULY 1945

The principal political, social, and military objective of the United States in the summer of 1945 was the prompt and complete surrender of Japan. Only the complete destruction of her military power could open the way to lasting peace.

Japan, in July 1945, had been seriously weakened by our increasingly violent attacks. It was known to us that she had gone so far as to make tentative proposals to the Soviet government, hoping to use the Russians as mediators in a negotiated peace. These vague proposals contemplated the retention by Japan of important conquered areas and were therefore not considered seriously. There was as yet no indication of any weakening in the Japanese determination to fight rather than accept unconditional surrender. If she should persist in her fight to the end, she had still a great military force.

In the middle of July 1945, the intelligence section of the War Department General Staff estimated Japanese military strength as follows: in the home islands, slightly under 2,000,000; in Korea, Manchuria, China proper, and Formosa, slightly over 2,000,000; in French Indo-China, Thailand, and Burma, over 200,000; in the East Indies area, including the Philippines, over 500,000; in the bypassed Pacific islands, over 100,000. The total strength of the Japanese Army was estimated at about 5,000,000 men. These estimates later proved to be in very close agreement with official Japanese figures.

The Japanese Army was in much better condition than the Japanese Navy and Air Force. The Navy had practically ceased to exist except as a harrying force against an invasion fleet. The Air Force had been reduced mainly to reliance upon Kamikaze, or suicide, attacks. These latter, however, had already inflicted serious damage on our seagoing forces, and their possible effectiveness in a last ditch fight was a matter of real concern to our naval leaders.

As we understood it in July, there was a very strong possibility that the Japanese government might determine upon resistance to the end, in all the areas of the Far East under its control. In such an event the Allies would be faced with the enormous task of destroying an armed force of five million men and five thousand suicide aircraft, belonging to a race which had already amply demonstrated its ability to fight literally to the death.

The strategic plans of our armed forces for the defeat of Japan, as they stood in July, had been prepared without reliance upon the atomic bomb, which had not yet been tested in New Mexico. We were planning an intensified sea and air blockade, and greatly intensified strategic air bombing, through the summer and early fall, to be followed on November 1 by an invasion of the southern island of Kyushu. This would be followed in turn by an invasion of the main island on Honshu in the spring of 1946. The total U.S. military and naval force involved in this grand design was of the order of 5,000,000 men; if all those indirectly concerned are included, it was larger still.

We estimated that if we should be forced to carry this plan to its conclusion, the major fighting would not end until the latter part of 1946, at the earliest. I was informed that such operations might be expected to cost over a million casualties, to American forces alone. Additional large losses might be expected among our allies, and, of course, if our campaign were successful and if we could judge by previous experience, enemy casualties would be much larger than our own.

It was already clear in July that even before the invasion we should be able to inflict enormously severe damage on the Japanese homeland by the combined application of "conventional" sea and air power. The critical question was whether this kind of action would induce surrender. It therefore became necessary to consider very carefully the probable state of mind of the enemy, and to assess with accurracy the line of conduct which might end his will to resist.

With these considerations in mind, I wrote a memorandum for the President, on July 2, which I believe fairly represents the thinking of the American government as it finally took shape in action. This memorandum was prepared after discussion and general agreement with Joseph C. Grew, Acting Secretary of State, and Secretary of the Navy Forrestal, and when I discussed it with the President, he expressed his general approval.

Memorandum for the President

July 2, 1945

Proposed Program for Japan

1. The plans of operation up to and including the first landing have been authorized and the preparations for the operation are now actually going on. This situation was accepted by all members of your conference on Monday, June 18.

2. There is reason to believe that the operation for the occupation of Japan following the landing may be a very long, costly, and arduous struggle on our part. The terrain, much of which I have visited several times, has left the impression on my memory of being one which would be susceptible to a last ditch defense such as has been made on Iwo Jima and Okinawa and which of course is very much larger than either of those two areas. According to my recollection it will be much more unfavorable with regard to tank maneuvering than either the Philippines or Germany.

3. If we once land on one of the main islands and begin a forceful occupation of Japan, we shall probably have cast the die of last ditch resistance. The Japanese are highly patriotic and certainly susceptible to calls for fanatical resistance to repel an invasion. Once started in actual invasion, we shall in my opinion have to go through with an even more bitter finish fight than in Germany. We shall incur the losses incident to such a war and we shall have to leave the Japanese islands even more thoroughly destroyed than was the case with Germany. This would be due both to the difference in the Japanese and German personal character and the differences in the size and character of the terrain through which the operations will take place.

4. A question then comes: Is there any alternative to such a forceful occupation of Japan which will secure for us the equivalent of an uncon-

ditional surrender of her forces and a permanent destruction of her power again to strike an aggressive blow at the "peace of the Pacific"? I am inclined to think that there is enough such chance to make it well worthwhile our giving them a warning of what is to come and a definite opportunity to capitulate. As above suggested, it should be tried before the actual forceful occupation of the homeland islands is begun and furthermore the warning should be given in ample time to permit a national reaction to set in.

We have the following enormously favorable factors on our side — factors much weightier than those we had against Germany:

Japan has no allies.

Her navy is nearly destroyed and she is vulnerable to a surface and underwater blockade which can deprive her of sufficient food and supplies for her population.

She is terribly vulnerable to our concentrated air attack upon her crowded cities, industrial and food resources.

She has against her not only the Anglo-American forces but the rising forces of China and the ominous threat of Russia.

We have inexhaustible and untouched industrial resources to bring to bear against her diminishing potential.

We have great moral superiority through being the victim of her first sneak attack.

The problem is to translate these advantages into prompt and economical achievement of our objectives. I believe Japan is susceptible to reason in such a crisis to a much greater extent than is indicated by our current press and other current comment. Japan is not a nation composed wholly of mad fanatics of an entirely different mentality from ours. On the contrary, she has within the past century shown herself to possess extremely intelligent people, capable in an unprecedentedly short time of adopting not only the complicated technique of Occidental civilization but to a substantial extent their culture and their political and social ideas. Her advance in all these respects during the short period of sixty or seventy years has been one of the most astounding feats of national progress in history — a leap from the isolated feudalism of centuries into the position of one of the six or seven great powers of the world. She has not only built up powerful armies and navies. She has maintained an honest and effective national finance and respected position in many of the sciences in which we pride ourselves. Prior to the forcible seizure of power over her government by the fanatical military group in 1931, she had for ten years lived a reasonably responsible and respectable international life.

My own opinion is in her favor on the two points involved in this question:

> *a. I think the Japanese nation has the mental intelligence and versatile capacity in such a crisis to recognize the folly of a fight to the finish and to accept the proffer of what will amount to an unconditional surrender; and*
>
> *b. I think she has within her population enough liberal leaders (although now submerged by the terrorists) to be depended upon for her reconstruction as a responsible member of the family of nations. I think she is better in this last respect than Germany was. Her liberals yielded only at the point of the pistol and, so far as I am aware, their liberal attitude has not been personally subverted in the way which was so general in Germany.*

On the other hand, I think that the attempt to exterminate her armies and her population by gunfire or other means will tend to produce a fusion of race solidity and antipathy which has no analogy in the case of Germany. We have a national interest in creating, if possible, a condition wherein the Japanese nation may live as a peaceful and useful member of the future Pacific community.

5. It is therefore my conclusion that a carefully timed warning be given to Japan by the chief representatives of the United States, Great Britain, China, and, if then a belligerent, Russia by calling upon Japan to surrender and permit the occupation of her country in order to insure its complete demilitarization for the sake of the future peace.

This warning should contain the following elements:

> *The varied and overwhelming character of the force we are about to bring to bear on the islands.*
>
> *The inevitability and completeness of the destruction which the full application of this force will entail.*
>
> *The determination of the Allies to destroy permanently all authority and influence of those who have deceived and misled the country into embarking on world conquest.*
>
> *The determination of the Allies to limit Japanese sovereignty to her main islands and to render them powerless to mount and support another war.*
>
> *The disavowal of any attempt to extirpate the Japanese as a race or to destroy them as a nation.*
>
> *A statement of our readiness, once her economy is purged of its militaristic influence, to permit the Japanese to maintain such industries, particularly of a light consumer character, as offer no threat of aggres-*

sion against their neighbors, but which can produce a sustaining economy, and provide a reasonable standard of living. The statement should indicate our willingness, for this purpose, to give Japan trade access to external raw materials, but no longer any control over the sources of supply outside her main islands. It should also indicate our willingness, in accordance with our now established foreign trade policy, in due course to enter into mutually advantageous trade relations with her.

The withdrawal from their country as soon as the above objectives of the Allies are accomplished, and as soon as there has been established a peacefully inclined government, of a character representative of the masses of the Japanese people. I personally think that if in saying this we should add that we do not exclude a constitutional monarchy under her present dynasty, it would substantially add to the chances of acceptance.

6. Success of course will depend on the potency of the warning which we give her. She has an extremely sensitive national pride and, as we are now seeing every day, when actually locked with the enemy will fight to the very death. For that reason the warning must be tendered before the actual invasion has occurred and while the impending destruction, though clear beyond peradventure, has not yet reduced her to fanatical despair. If Russia is a part of the threat, the Russian attack, if actual, must not have progressed too far. Our own bombing should be confined to military objectives as far as possible.

It is important to emphasize the double character of the suggested warning. It was designed to promise destruction if Japan resisted, and hope, if she surrendered.

It will be noted that the atomic bomb is not mentioned in this memorandum. On grounds of secrecy the bomb was never mentioned except when absolutely necessary, and furthermore, it had not yet been tested. It was of course well forward in our minds, as the memorandum was written and discussed, that the bomb would be the best possible sanction if our warning were rejected.

THE USE OF THE BOMB

The adoption of the policy outlined in the memorandum of July 2 was a decision of high politics; once it was accepted by the President, the position of the atomic bomb in our planning became quite clear. I find that I stated in my diary, as early as June 19, that "the last chance warning ... must be given before an actual landing of the ground forces in

Japan, and fortunately the plans provide for enough time to bring in the sanctions to our warning in the shape of heavy ordinary bombing attack and an attack of S-1." S-1 was a code name for the atomic bomb.

There was much discussion in Washington about the timing of the warning to Japan. The controlling factor in the end was the date already set for the Potsdam meeting of the Big Three. It was President Truman's decision that such a warning should be solemnly issued by the U.S. and the U.K. from this meeting, with the concurrence of the head of the Chinese government, so that it would be plain that *all* of Japan's principal enemies were in entire unity. This was done, in the Potsdam ultimatum of July 26, which very closely followed the above memorandum of July 2, with the exception that it made no mention of the Japanese Emperor.

On July 28 the Premier of Japan, Suzuki, rejected the Potsdam ultimatum by announcing that it was "unworthy of public notice." In the face of this rejection we could only proceed to demonstrate that the ultimatum had meant exactly what it said when it stated that if the Japanese continued the war, "the full application of our military power, backed by our resolve, will mean the inevitable and complete destruction of the Japanese armed forces and just as inevitably the utter devastation of the Japanese homeland."

For such a purpose the atomic bomb was an eminently suitable weapon. The New Mexico test occurred while we were at Potsdam, on July 16. It was immediately clear that the power of the bomb measured up to our highest estimates. We had developed a weapon of such a revolutionary character that its use against the enemy might well be expected to produce exactly the kind of shock on the Japanese ruling oligarchy which we desired, strengthening the position of those who wished peace, and weakening that of the military party.

Because of the importance of the atomic mission against Japan, the detailed plans were brought to me by the military staff for approval. With President Truman's warm support I struck off the list of suggested targets the city of Kyoto. Although it was a target of considerable military importance, it had been the ancient capital of Japan and was a shrine of Japanese art and culture. We determined that it should be spared. I approved four other targets including the cities of Hiroshima and Nagasaki.

Hiroshima was bombed on August 6, and Nagasaki on August 9. These two cities were active working parts of the Japanese war effort. One was an army center; the other was naval and industrial. Hiroshima was the headquarters of the Japanese Army defending southern Japan and was a major military storage and assembly point. Nagasaki was a major seaport and it contained several large industrial plants of great wartime importance. We believed that our attacks had struck cities which must certainly be important to the Japanese military leaders, both Army and Navy, and we waited for a result. We waited one day.

Many accounts have been written about the Japanese surrender. After a prolonged Japanese cabinet session in which the deadlock was broken by the Emperor himself, the offer to surrender was made on August 10. It was based on the Potsdam terms, with a reservation concerning the sovereignty of the Emperor. While the Allied reply made no promises other than those already given, it implicitly recognized the Emperor's position by prescribing that his power must be subject to the order of the Allied Supreme Commander. These terms were accepted on August 14 by the Japanese, and the instrument of surrender was formally signed on September 2, in Tokyo Bay. Our great objective was thus achieved, and all the evidence I have seen indicates that the controlling factor in the final Japanese decision to accept our terms of surrender was the atomic bomb.

The two atomic bombs which we had dropped were the only ones we had ready, and our rate of production at the time was very small. Had the war continued until the projected invasion on November 1, additional fire raids of B-29's would have been more destructive of life and property than the very limited number of atomic raids which we could have executed in the same period. But the atomic bomb was more than a weapon of terrible destruction, it was a psychological weapon. In March 1945 our Air Force had launched its first great incendiary raid on the Tokyo area. In this raid more damage was done and more casualties were inflicted than was the case at Hiroshima. Hundreds of bombers took part and hundreds of tons of incendiaries were dropped. Similar successive raids burned out a great part of the urban area of Japan, but the Japanese fought on. On August 6 one B-29 dropped a single atomic bomb on Hiroshima. Three days later a second bomb was dropped on Nagasaki and the war was over. So far as the Japanese could know, our ability to execute atomic attacks, if necessary by many planes at a time, was unlimited. As Dr. Karl Compton has said, "it was not one atomic bomb, or two, which brought surrender; it was the experience of what an atomic bomb will actually do to a community, *plus the dread of many more,* that was effective."

The bomb thus served exactly the purpose we intended. The peace party was able to take the path of surrender, and the whole weight of the Emperor's prestige was exerted in favor of peace. When the Emperor ordered surrender, and the small but dangerous group of fanatics who opposed him were brought under control, the Japanese became so subdued that the great undertaking of occupation and disarmament was completed with unprecedented ease.

A PERSONAL SUMMARY

In the foregoing pages I have tried to give an accurate account of my own personal observations of the circumstances which led up to the use of the atomic bomb and the reasons which underlay our use of it. To me they have always seemed compelling and clear, and I cannot see how any person vested with such responsibilities as mine could have taken any other course or given any other advice to his chiefs.

Two great nations were approaching contact in a fight to a finish which would begin on November 1, 1945. Our enemy, Japan, commanded forces of somewhat over 5,000,000 armed men. Men of these armies had already inflicted upon us, in our breakthrough of the outer perimeter of their defenses, over 300,000 battle casualties. Enemy armies still unbeaten had the strength to cost us a million more. *As long as the Japanese government refused to surrender,* we should be forced to take and hold the ground, and smash the Japanese ground armies, by close-in fighting of the same desperate and costly kind that we had faced in the Pacific islands for nearly four years.

In the light of the formidable problem which thus confronted us, I felt that every possible step should be taken to compel a surrender of the homelands, and a withdrawal of all Japanese troops from the Asiatic mainland and from other positions, before we had commenced an invasion. We held two cards to assist us in such an effort. One was the traditional veneration in which the Japanese Emperor was held by his subjects and the power which was thus vested in him over his loyal troops. It was for this reason that I suggested in my memorandum of July 2 that his dynasty should be continued. The second card was the use of the atomic bomb in the manner best calculated to persuade that Emperor and the counselors about him to submit to our demand for what was essentially unconditional surrender, placing his immense power over his people and his troops subject to our orders.

In order to end the war in the shortest possible time and to avoid the enormous losses of human life which otherwise confronted us, I felt that we must use the Emperor as our instrument to command and compel his people to cease fighting and subject themselves to our authority through him, and that to accomplish this we must give him and his controlling advisers a compelling reason to accede to our demands. This reason furthermore must be of such a nature that his people could understand his decision. The bomb seemed to me to furnish a unique instrument for that purpose.

My chief purpose was to end the war in victory with the least possible cost in the lives of the men in the armies which I had helped to raise. In the light of the alternatives which, on a fair estimate, were open to us I believe that no man, in our position and subject to our responsibilities, holding in his hands a weapon of such possibilities for accomplishing this purpose and saving those lives, could have failed to use it and afterwards looked his countrymen in the face.

As I read over what I have written, I am aware that much of it, in this year of peace, may have a harsh and unfeeling sound. It would perhaps be possible to say the same things and say them more gently. But I do not think it would be wise. As I look back over the five years of my service as Secretary of War, I see too many stern and heartrending decisions to be willing to pretend that war is anything else than what it is. The face of war is the face of death; death is an inevitable part of every order that a wartime leader gives. The decision to use the atomic bomb was a decision that brought death to over a hundred thousand Japanese. No explanation can change that fact and I do not wish to gloss it over. But this deliberate, premeditated destruction was our least abhorrent choice. The destruction of Hiroshima and Nagasaki put an end to the Japanese war. It stopped the fire raids, and the strangling blockade; it ended the ghastly specter of a clash of great land armies.

In this last great action of the Second World War we were given final proof that war is death. War in the twentieth century has grown steadily more barbarous, more destructive, more debased in all its aspects. Now, with the release of atomic energy, man's ability to destroy himself is very nearly complete. The bombs dropped on Hiroshima and Nagasaki ended a war. They also made it wholly clear that we must never have another war. This is the lesson men and leaders everywhere must learn, and I believe that when they learn it they will find a way to lasting peace. There is no other choice.

Study Guide

1. President Harry S. Truman's "Statement" covers a number of points; some are simply fact, others are controversial. Begin by noting the size and destructiveness of the first bomb.

2. Outline Truman's history of the invention and manufacture of the bomb, noting the role of the English and the Germans. Note, too, what role Truman assigns to the Army in the production of the bomb.

3. Turning to Japan:
   (a) What policy does Truman propose the United States will carry out?
   (b) What gesture initiated at Potsdam does Truman refer to in order to justify the dropping of the bomb?

4. What does Truman foresee regarding:
   (a) other uses of atomic energy; and
   (b) sharing atomic information with other nations?
   On this last point, explain what Truman means by "under present circumstances"?

5. The article by Henry L. Stimson confirms in much greater detail the "Statement" by Truman as well as Truman's point of view on the justification for dropping the bombs. The Stimson piece can be divided thus:
   (a) his history of the steps taken to establish a policy regarding the bomb (pp. 467–471);
   (b) the recommendations of the Interim Committee (pp. 471–472);
   (c) the military condition in 1945 and the policies he recommended to President Truman (pp. 472–477); and
   (d) the action taken and a personal summation of it all (pp. 477–481).

6. Outline the steps of the development of the atomic bomb and the establishment of the Interim Committee to deal with its ramifications, and then answer the following:
   (a) What role did Stimson play in developing guidelines for the use of the bomb and, parenthetically, will this, in your opinion, influence his account?
   (b) What reason did the United States have for developing the bomb at so great a cost of men and money?
   (c) What, in summary, were Stimson's recommendations to Truman in his memorandum of April 25, 1945?

7. Turning to the Interim Committee:
   (a) Why was it established?
   (b) What were its recommendations? Outline.

8. Stimson gives his own conclusion based on his assessment of the realities of 1945 and then offers a copy of his memorandum of July 2, 1945, to President Truman. Summarize his recommendations and note that, as Stimson indicates, the warning to Japan to surrender would contain no reference to the atomic bomb.

9. Proceed by summarizing the steps then taken, using the following outline:

    (a) the warning from Potsdam;
    (b) the decision to use the bomb;
    (c) the military decision as to the sites to be bombed;
    (d) the bombings; and
    (e) the results.

10. Summarize the contentions offered by Stimson in his "Personal Summary" justifying the use of the atom bomb on Japan.

11. In retrospect, there has been a great deal of criticism of Truman and his aides for making the decision they did. Neither Truman nor Stimson, after the bombing of Hiroshima and Nagasaki, ever indicated that the United States might have erred. On the basis of this piece by Stimson, how would you assess their decision? Explore.

George F. Kennan
CONTAINMENT OF COMMUNISM

✧§{*1947*}§✧ BY THE Truman Doctrine and the Marshall Plan the United States had already begun a policy of "containing" Soviet expansion when, in July, 1947, an article rationalizing this policy appeared in the magazine *Foreign Affairs.* The title of the article was "The Sources of Soviet Conduct," and the author's name was given only as "X." Later the mysterious Mr. X was revealed as George F. Kennan (1904-   ), the head of the State Department's new policy planning staff, which was charged with the making of long-range plans for the conduct of American diplomacy. Thus the article was an authoritative exposition of official thinking. It was, indeed, an expression of the point of view behind American strategy in the "cold war." Despite differences in emphasis, this basic view continued to guide policy makers throughout the Truman and Eisenhower administrations and into the Kennedy-Johnson administration.

Kennan, a career diplomat of wide experience in Washington and abroad, was appointed ambassador to the Soviet Union in 1952. Later he devoted himself to lecturing and writing on current American policy (with which he has not always agreed) and to producing an exhaustive study of the history of the Russian Revolution.

THE SOURCES OF SOVIET CONDUCT

I

THE political personality of Soviet power as we know it today is the product of ideology and circumstances: ideology inherited by the present Soviet leaders from the movement in which they had their political origin, and circumstances of the power which they now have exercised for nearly three decades in Russia. There can be few tasks of psychological analysis more difficult than to try to trace the interaction of these two forces and the relative role of each in the determination of official Soviet conduct. Yet the attempt must be made if that conduct is to be understood and effectively countered.

It is difficult to summarize the set of ideological concepts with which the Soviet leaders came into power. Marxian ideology, in its Russian-Communist projection, has always been in process of subtle evolution. The materials on which it bases itself are extensive and complex. But the outstanding features of Communist thought as it existed in 1916 may perhaps be summarized as follows: (*a*) that the central factor in the life of man, the fact which determines the character of public life and the "physiognomy of society," is the system by which material goods are produced and exchanged; (*b*) that the capitalist system of production is a nefarious one which inevitably leads to the exploitation of the working class by the capital-owning class and is incapable of developing adequately the economic resources of society or of distributing fairly the material goods produced by human labor; (*c*) that capitalism contains the seeds of its own destruction and must, in view of the inability of the capital-owning class to adjust itself to economic change, result eventually and inescapably in a revolutionary transfer of power to the working class; and (*d*) that imperialism, the final phase of capitalism, leads directly to war and revolution.

The rest may be outlined in Lenin's own words: "Unevenness of economic and political development is the inflexible law of capitalism. It follows from this that the victory of Socialism may come originally in a few capitalist countries or even in a single capitalist country. The victorious proletariat of that country, having expropriated the capitalists and having organized Socialist production at home, would rise against the remaining capitalist world, drawing to itself in the process the oppressed classes of other countries." [1] It must be noted that there was no assumption that capitalism would perish without proletarian revolution. A final push was needed from a revolutionary proletariat movement in order to tip over the

---

[1] *Concerning the Slogans of the United States of Europe, August* 1915 (Official Soviet edition of Lenin's works).

tottering structure. But it was regarded as inevitable that sooner or later that push be given.

For fifty years prior to the outbreak of the Revolution, this pattern of thought had exercised great fascination for the members of the Russian revolutionary movement. Frustrated, discontented, hopeless of finding self-expression — or too impatient to seek it — in the confining limits of the Tsarist political system, yet lacking wide popular support for their choice of bloody revolution as a means of social betterment, these revolutionists found in Marxist theory a highly convenient rationalization for their own instinctive desires. It afforded pseudo-scientific justification for their impatience, for their categoric denial of all value in the Tsarist system, for their yearning for power and revenge and for their inclination to cut corners in the pursuit of it. It is therefore no wonder that they had come to believe implicitly in the truth and soundness of the Marxian-Leninist teachings, so congenial to their own impulses and emotions. Their sincerity need not be impugned. This is a phenomenon as old as human nature itself. It has never been more aptly described than by Edward Gibbon, who wrote in *The Decline and Fall of the Roman Empire*: "From enthusiasm to imposture the step is perilous and slippery; the demon of Socrates affords a memorable instance how a wise man may deceive himself; how a good man may deceive others, how the conscience may slumber in a mixed and middle state between self-illusion and voluntary fraud." And it was with this set of conceptions that the members of the Bolshevik Party entered into power.

Now it must be noted that through all the years of preparation for revolution, the attention of these men, as indeed of Marx himself, had been centered less on the future form which Socialism[2] would take than on the necessary overthrow of rival power which, in their view, had to precede the introduction of Socialism. Their views, therefore, on the positive program to be put into effect, once power was attained, were for the most part nebulous, visionary and impractical. Beyond the nationalization of industry and the expropriation of large private capital holdings there was no agreed program. The treatment of the peasantry, which according to the Marxist formulation was not of the proletariat, had always been a vague spot in the pattern of Communist thought; and it remained an object of controversy and vacillation for the first ten years of Communist power.

The circumstances of the immediate post-Revolution period — the existence in Russia of civil war and foreign intervention, together with the obvious fact that the Communists represented only a tiny minority of the

---

[2] Here and elsewhere in this paper "Socialism" refers to Marxist or Leninist Communism, not to liberal Socialism of the Second International variety.

Russian people — made the establishment of dictatorial power a necessity. The experiment with "war Communism" and the abrupt attempt to eliminate private production and trade had unfortunate economic consequences and caused further bitterness against the new revolutionary regime. While the temporary relaxation of the effort to communize Russia, represented by the New Economic Policy, alleviated some of this economic distress and thereby served its purpose, it also made it evident that the "capitalistic sector of society" was still prepared to profit at once from any relaxation of governmental pressure, and would, if permitted to continue to exist, always constitute a powerful opposing element to the Soviet regime and a serious rival for influence in the country. Somewhat the same situation prevailed with respect to the individual peasant who, in his own small way, was also a private producer.

Lenin, had he lived, might have proved a great enough man to reconcile these conflicting forces to the ultimate benefit of Russian society, though this is questionable. But be that as it may, Stalin, and those whom he led in the struggle for succession to Lenin's position of leadership, were not the men to tolerate rival political forces in the sphere of power which they coveted. Their sense of insecurity was too great. Their particular band of fanaticism, unmodified by any of the Anglo-Saxon traditions of compromise, was too fierce and too jealous to envisage any permanent sharing of power. From the Russian-Asiatic world out of which they had emerged they carried with them a skepticism as to the possibilities of permanent and peaceful coexistence of rival forces. Easily persuaded of their own doctrinaire "rightness," they insisted on the submission or destruction of all competing power. Outside of the Communist Party, Russian society was to have no rigidity. There were to be no forms of collective human activity or association which would not be dominated by the Party. No other force in Russian society was to be permitted to achieve vitality or integrity. Only the Party was to have structure. All else was to be an amorphous mass.

And within the Party the same principle was to apply. The mass of Party members might go through the motions of election, deliberation, decision and action; but in these motions they were to be animated not by their own individual wills but by the awesome breath of the Party leadership and the overbrooding presence of "the world."

Let it be stressed again that subjectively these men probably did not seek absolutism for its own sake. They doubtless believed — and found it easy to believe — that they alone knew what was good for society and that they would accomplish that good once their power was secure and unchallengeable. But in seeking that security of their own rule they were prepared to recognize no restrictions, either of God or man, on the character of their methods. And until such a time as that security might be achieved, they placed far down on their scale of operational priorities the comforts and happiness of the peoples entrusted to their care.

Now the outstanding circumstance concerning the Soviet regime is that down to the present day this process of political consolidation has never been completed and the men in the Kremlin have continued to be predominantly absorbed with the struggle to secure and make absolute the power which they seized in November 1917. They have endeavored to secure it primarily against forces at home, within Soviet society itself. But they have also endeavored to secure it against the outside world. For ideology, as we have seen, taught them that the outside world was hostile and that it was their duty eventually to overthrow the political forces beyond their borders. The powerful hands of Russian history and tradition reached up to sustain them in this feeling. Finally, their own aggressive intransigence with respect to the outside world began to find its own reaction; and they were soon forced, to use another Gibbonesque phrase, "to chastise the contumacy" which they themselves had provoked. It is an undeniable privilege of every man to prove himself right in the thesis that the world is his enemy; for if he reiterates it frequently enough and makes it the background of his conduct he is bound eventually to be right.

Now it lies in the nature of the mental world of the Soviet leaders, as well as in the character of their ideology, that no opposition to them can be officially recognized as having any merit or justification whatsoever. Such opposition can flow, in theory, only from the hostile and incorrigible forces of dying capitalism. As long as remnants of capitalism were officially recognized as existing in Russia, it was possible to place on them, as an internal element, part of the blame for the maintenance of a dictatorial form of society. But as these remnants were liquidated, little by little, this justification fell away; and when it was indicated officially that they had been finally destroyed, it disappeared altogether. And this fact created one of the most basic of the compulsions which came to act upon the Soviet regime: since capitalism no longer existed in Russia and since it could not be admitted that there could be serious or widespread opposition to the Kremlin springing spontaneously from the liberated masses under its authority, it became necessary to justify the retention of the dictatorship by stressing the menace of capitalism abroad.

This began at an early date. In 1924, Stalin specifically defended the retention of the "organs of suppression," meaning, among others, the army and the secret police, on the ground that "as long as there is a capitalist encirclement there will be danger of intervention with all the consequences that flow from that danger." In accordance with that theory, and from that time on, all internal opposition forces in Russia have consistently been portrayed as the agents of foreign forces of reaction antagonistic to Soviet power.

By the same token, tremendous emphasis has been placed on the original Communist thesis of a basic antagonism between the capitalist and Socialist worlds. It is clear, from many indications, that this emphasis is not founded in reality. The real facts concerning it have been confused by the existence abroad of genuine resentment provoked by Soviet philosophy and tactics and occasionally by the existence of great centers of military power, notably the Nazi regime in Germany and the Japanese Government of the late 1930's, which did indeed have aggressive designs against the Soviet Union. But there is ample evidence that the stress laid in Moscow on the menace confronting Soviet society from the world outside its borders is founded not in the realities of foreign antagonism but in the necessity of explaining away the maintenance of dictatorial authority at home.

Now the maintenance of this pattern of Soviet power, namely, the pursuit of unlimited authority domestically, accompanied by the cultivation of the semi-myth of implacable foreign hostility, has gone far to shape the actual machinery of Soviet power as we know it today. Internal organs of administration which did not serve this purpose withered on the vine. Organs which did serve this purpose became vastly swollen. The security of Soviet power came to rest on the iron discipline of the Party, on the severity and ubiquity of the secret police, and on the uncompromising economic monopolism of the state. The "organs of suppression," in which the Soviet leaders had sought security from rival forces, became in large measure the masters of those whom they were designed to serve. Today the major part of the structure of Soviet power is committed to the perfection of the dictatorship and to the maintenance of the concept of Russia as in a state of seige, with the enemy lowering beyond the walls. And the millions of human beings who form that part of the structure of power must defend at all costs this concept of Russia's position, for without it they are themselves superfluous.

As things stand today, the rulers can no longer dream of parting with these organs and suppression. The quest for absolute power, pursued now for nearly three decades with a ruthlessness unparalleled (in scope at least) in modern times, has again produced internally, as it did externally, its own reaction. The excesses of the police apparatus have fanned the potential opposition to the regime into something far greater and more dangerous than it could have been before those excesses began.

But least of all can the rulers dispense with the fiction by which the maintenance of dictatorial power has been defended. For this fiction has been canonized in Soviet philosophy by the excesses already committed in its name; and it is now anchored in the Soviet structure of thought by bonds far greater than those of mere ideology.

II

So much for the historical background. What does it spell in terms of the political personality of Soviet power as we know it today?

Of the original ideology, nothing has been officially junked. Belief is maintained in the basic badness of capitalism, in the inevitability of its destruction, in the obligation of the proletariat to assist in that destruction and to take power into its own hands. But stress has come to be laid primarily on those concepts which relate most specifically to the Soviet regime itself: to its position as the sole truly Socialist regime in a dark and misguided world, and to the relationships of power within it.

The first of these concepts is that of the innate antagonism between capitalism and Socialism. We have seen how deeply that concept has become imbedded in foundations of Soviet power. It has profound implications for Russia's conduct as a member of international society. It means that there can never be on Moscow's side any sincere assumption of a community of aims between the Soviet Union and powers which are regarded as capitalism. It must invariably be assumed in Moscow that the aims of the capitalist world are antagonistic to the Soviet regime and, therefore, to the interests of the peoples it controls. If the Soviet Government occasionally sets its signature to documents which would indicate the contrary, this is to be regarded as a tactical maneuver permissible in dealing with the enemy (who is without honor) and should be taken in the spirit of *caveat emptor*. Basically, the antagonism remains. It is postulated. And from it flow many of the phenomena which we find disturbing in the Kremlin's conduct of foreign policy: the secretiveness, the lack of frankness, the duplicity, the war suspiciousness, and the basic unfriendliness of purpose. These phenomena are there to stay, for the foreseeable future. There can be variations of degree and of emphasis. When there is something the Russians want from us, one or the other of these features of their policy may be thrust temporarily into the background; and when that happens there will always be Americans who will leap forward with gleeful announcements that "the Russians have changed," and some who will even try to take credit for having brought about such "changes." But we should not be misled by tactical maneuvers. These characteristics of Soviet policy, like the postulate from which they flow, are basic to the internal nature of Soviet power, and will be with us, whether in the foreground or the background, until the internal nature of Soviet power is changed.

This means that we are going to continue for a long time to find the Russians difficult to deal with. It does not mean that they should be considered as embarked upon a do-or-die program to overthrow our society by a given date. The theory of the inevitability of the eventual fall of capitalism has the fortunate connotation that there is no hurry about it. The forces of progress can take their time in preparing the final *coup de grâce*. Meanwhile, what is vital is that the "Socialist fatherland" — that oasis of power which has been already won for Socialism in the person of the Soviet Union — should be cherished and defended by all good Communists at home and abroad, its fortunes promoted, its enemies badgered and confounded. The promotion of premature, "adventuristic" revolutionary projects abroad which might embarrass Soviet power in any way would be an inexcusable, even a counter-revolutionary act. The cause of Socialism is the support and promotion of Soviet power, as defined in Moscow.

This brings us to the second of the concepts important to contemporary Soviet outlook. This is the infallibility of the Kremlin. The Soviet concept of power, which permits no focal points of organization outside the Party itself, requires that the Party leadership remain in theory the sole repository of truth. For if truth were to be found elsewhere, there would be justification for its expression in organized activity. But it is precisely that which the Kremlin cannot and will not permit.

The leadership of the Communist Party is therefore always right, and has been always right ever since in 1929 Stalin formalized his personal power by announcing that decisions of the Politburo were being taken unanimously.

On the principle of infallibility there rests the iron discipline of the Communist Party. In fact, the two concepts are mutually self-supporting. Perfect discipline requires recognition of infallibility. Infallibility requires the observance of discipline. And the two together go far to determine the behaviorism of the entire Soviet apparatus of power. But their effect cannot be understood unless a third factor be taken into account: namely, the fact that the leadership is at liberty to put forward for tactical purposes any particular thesis which it finds useful to the cause at any particular moment and to require the faithful and unquestioning acceptance of that thesis by the members of the movement as a whole. This means that truth is not a constant but is actually created, for all intents and purposes, by the Soviet leaders themselves. It may vary from week to week, from month to month. It is nothing absolute and immutable — nothing which flows from objective reality. It is only the most recent manifestation of the wisdom of those in whom the ultimate wisdom is supposed to reside, because they represent the logic of history. The accumulative effect of these factors is to give to the whole subordinate apparatus of Soviet power an unshakeable stubbornness and steadfastness in its orientation. This orientation can be changed at will by the Kremlin but by no other power. Once a given party line has been laid down on a given issue of current policy, the whole Soviet governmental machine, including the mechanism of diplomacy, moves inexorably along the prescribed path, like a persistent toy automobile wound up and headed in a given direction, stopping only when it meets with some unanswerable force. The individuals who are the components of this machine are unamenable to argument or reason which comes to them from outside sources. Their whole training has taught them to mistrust and discount the glib persuasiveness of the outside world. Like the white dog before the phonograph, they hear only the "master's voice." And if they are to be called off from the purposes last dictated to them, it is the master who must call them off. Thus the foreign representative cannot hope that his words will make any impression on them. The most that he can hope is that they will be transmitted to those at the top, who are capable of changing the party line. But even those are not likely to be swayed by any normal logic in the words of the bourgeois representative. Since there can be no appeal to common purposes, there can be no appeal to common mental approaches. For this reason, facts speak louder than words to the ears of the Kremlin; and words carry the greatest weight when they have the ring of reflecting, or being backed up by, facts of unchallengeable validity.

But we have seen that the Kremlin is under no ideological compulsion to accomplish its purposes in a hurry. Like the Church, it is dealing in ideological concepts which are of long-term validity, and it can afford to be patient. It has no right to risk the existing achievements of the revolution for the sake of vain baubles of the future. The very teachings of Lenin himself require great caution and flexibility in the pursuit of Communist purposes. Again, these precepts are fortified by the lessons of Russian history: of centuries of obscure battles between nomadic forces over the stretches of a vast unfortified plain. Here caution, circumspection, flexibility and deception are the valuable qualities; and their value finds natural appreciation in the Russian or the oriental mind. Thus the Kremlin has no compunction about retreating in the face of superior force. And being under the compulsion of no timetable, it does not get panicky under the necessity for such retreat. Its political action is a fluid stream which moves constantly, wherever it is permitted to move, toward a given goal. Its main concern is to make sure that it has filled every nook and cranny available to it in the basin of world power. But if it finds unassailable barriers in its path, it accepts these philosophically and accommodates itself to them. The main thing is that there should always be pressure, increasing constant pressure, toward the desired goal. There is no trace of any feeling in Soviet psychology that that goal must be reached at any given time.

These considerations make Soviet diplomacy at once easier and more difficult to deal with than the diplomacy of individual aggressive leaders like Napoleon and Hitler. On the one hand it is more sensitive to contrary force, more ready to yield on individual sectors of the diplomatic front when that force is felt to be too strong, and thus more rational in the logic and rhetoric of power. On the other hand it cannot be easily defeated or discouraged by a single victory on the part of its opponents. And the patient persistence by which it is animated means that it can be effectively countered not by sporadic acts which represent the momentary whims of democratic opinion but only by intelligent long-range policies on the part of Russia's adversaries — policies no less steady in their purpose, and no less variegated and resourceful in their application, than those of the Soviet Union itself.

In these circumstances it is clear that the main element of any United States policy toward the Soviet Union must be that of a long-term, patient but firm and vigilant containment of Russian expansive tendencies. It is important to note, however, that such a policy has nothing to do with outward histrionics: with threats or blustering or superfluous gestures of outward "toughness." While the Kremlin is basically flexible in its reaction to political realities, it is by no means unamenable to considerations of prestige. Like almost any other government, it can be placed by tactless and threatening gestures in a position where it cannot afford to yield even though this might be dictated by its sense of realism. The Russian leaders are keen judges of human psychology, and as such they are highly conscious that loss of temper and of self-control is never a source of strength in political affairs. They are quick to exploit such evidences of weakness. For these reasons, it is a *sine qua non* of successful dealing with Russia that the foreign government in question should remain at all times cool and collected and that its demands on Russian policy should be put forward in such a manner as to leave the way open for a compliance not too detrimental to Russian prestige.

III

In the light of the above, it will be clearly seen that the Soviet pressure against the free institutions of the Western world is something that can be contained by the adroit and vigilant application of counter-force at a series of constantly shifting geographical and political points, corresponding to the shifts and maneuvers of Soviet policy, but which cannot be charmed or talked out of existence. The Russians look forward to a duel of infinite duration, and they see that already they have scored great successes. It must be borne in mind that there was a time when the Communist Party represented far more of a minority in the sphere of Russian national life than Soviet power today represents in the world community.

But if ideology convinces the rulers of Russia that truth is on their side and that they can therefore afford to wait, those of us on whom that ideology has no claim are free to examine objectively the validity of that premise. The Soviet thesis not only implies complete lack of control by the West over its own economic destiny, it likewise assumes Russian unity, discipline and patience over an infinite period. Let us bring this apocalyptic vision down to earth, and suppose that the Western world finds the strength and resourcefulness to contain Soviet power over a period of ten to fifteen years. What does that spell for Russia itself?

The Soviet leaders, taking advantage of the contributions of modern technique to the arts of despotism, have solved the question of obedience within the confines of their power. Few challenge their authority; and even those who do are unable to make that challenge valid as against the organs of suppression of the state.

The Kremlin has also proved able to accomplish its purpose of building up in Russia, regardless of the interests of the inhabitants, an industrial foundation of heavy metallurgy, which is, to be sure, not yet complete but which is nevertheless continuing to grow and is approaching those of the other major industrial countries. All of this, however, both the maintenance of internal political security and the building of heavy industry, has been carried out at a terrible cost in human life and in human hopes and energies. It has necessitated the use of forced labor on a scale unprecedented in modern times under conditions of peace. It has involved the neglect or abuse of other phases of Soviet economic life, particularly agriculture, consumers' goods production, housing and transportation.

To all that, the war has added its tremendous toll of destruction, death and human exhaustion. In consequence of this, we have in Russia today a population which is physically and spiritually tired. The mass of the people are disillusioned, skeptical and no longer as accessible as they once were to the magical attraction which Soviet power still radiates to its followers abroad. The avidity with which people seized upon the slight respite accorded to the Church for tactical reasons during the war was eloquent testimony to the fact that their capacity for faith and devotion found little expression in the purposes of the regime.

In these circumstances, there are limits to the physical and nervous strength of people themselves. These limits are absolute ones, and are binding even for the cruelest dictatorship, because beyond them people cannot be driven. The forced labor camps and the other agencies of constraint provide temporary means of compelling people to work longer hours than their own volition or mere economic pressure would dictate; but if people survive them at all they become old before their time and must be considered as human casualties to the demands of dictatorship. In either case their best powers are no longer available to society and can no longer be enlisted in the service of the state.

Here only the younger generation can help. The younger generation, despite all vicissitudes and sufferings, is numerous and vigorous; and the Russians are a talented people. But it still remains to be seen what will be the effects of mature performance of the abnormal emotional strains of childhood which Soviet dictatorship created and which were enormously increased by the war. Such things as normal security and placidity of home environment have practically ceased to exist in the Soviet Union outside of the most remote farms and villages. And observers are not yet sure whether that is not going to leave its mark on the over-all capacity of the generation now coming into maturity.

In addition to this, we have the fact that Soviet economic development, while it can list certain formidable achievements, has been precariously spotty and uneven. Russian Communists who speak of the "uneven development of capitalism" should blush at the contemplation of their own national economy. Here certain branches of economic life, such as the metallurgical and machine industries, have been pushed out of all proportion to other sectors of economy. Here is a nation striving to become in a short period one of the great industrial nations of the world while it still has no highway network worthy of the name and only a relatively primitive network of railways. Much has been done to increase efficiency of labor and to teach primitive peasants something about the operation of machines. But maintenance is still a crying deficiency of all Soviet economy. Construction is hasty and poor in quality. Depreciation must be enormous. And in vast sectors of economic life it has not yet been possible to instill into labor anything like the general culture of production and technical self-respect which characterizes the skilled worker of the West.

It is difficult to see how these deficiencies can be corrected at an early date by a tired and dispirited population working largely under the shadow of fear and compulsion. And as long as they are not overcome, Russia will remain economically a vulnerable, and in a certain sense an impotent nation, capable of exporting its enthusiasms and of radiating the strange charm of its primitive political vitality but unable to back up those articles of export by the real evidences of material power and prosperity.

Meanwhile, a great uncertainty hangs over the political life of the Soviet Union. That is the uncertainty involved in the transfer of power from one individual or group of individuals to others.

This is, of course, outstandingly the problem of the personal position of Stalin. We must remember that his succession to Lenin's pinnacle of preeminence in the Communist movement was the only such transfer of individual authority which the Soviet Union has experienced. That transfer took twelve years to consolidate. It cost the lives of millions of people and shook the state to its foundations, the attendant tremors were felt all through the international revolutionary movement, to the disadvantage of the Kremlin itself.

It is always possible that another transfer of preeminent power may take place quietly and inconspicuously, with no repercussions anywhere. But again, it is possible that the questions involved may unleash, to use some of Lenin's words, one of those "incredibly swift transitions" from "delicate deceit" to "wild violence" which characterize Russian history, and may shake Soviet power to its foundations.

But this is not only a question of Stalin himself. There has been, since 1938, a dangerous congealment of political life in the higher circles of Soviet power. The All-Union Party Congress, in theory the supreme body of the Party, is supposed to meet not less often than once in three years. It will soon be eight full years since its last meeting. During this period membership in the Party has numerically doubled. Party mortality during the war was enormous, and today well over half of the Party members are persons who have entered since the last Party congress was held. Meanwhile, the same small group of men has carried on at the top through an amazing series of national vicissitudes. Surely there is some reason why the experiences of the war brought basic political changes to every one of the great governments of the West. Surely the causes of that phenomenon are basic enough to be present somewhere in the obscurity of Soviet political life, as well. And yet no recognition has been given to these causes in Russia.

It must be surmised from this that even within so highly disciplined an organization as the Communist Party there must be a growing divergence in age, outlook and interest between the great mass of Party members, only so recently recruited into the movement, and the little self-perpetuating clique of men at the top, whom most of these Party members have never met, with whom they have never conversed, and with whom they can have no political intimacy.

Who can say whether, in these circumstances, the eventual rejuvenation of the higher spheres of authority (which can only be a matter of time) can take place smoothly and peacefully, or whether rivals in the quest for

higher power will not eventually reach down into these politically imma-
ture and inexperienced masses in order to find support for their respective
claims. If this were ever to happen, strange consequences could flow for the
Communist Party: for the membership at large has been exercised only in
the practices of iron discipline and obedience and not in the arts of compromise and accommodation. And if disunity were ever to seize and para-
lyze the Party, the chaos and weakness of Russian society would be revealed in forms beyond description. For we have seen that Soviet power is
only a crust concealing an amorphous mass of human beings among
whom no independent organizational structure is tolerated. In Russia there
is not even such a thing as local government. The present generation of
Russians have never known spontaneity of collective action. If, consequently, anything were ever to occur to disrupt the unity and efficacy of the
Party as a political instrument, Soviet Russia might be changed overnight
from one of the strongest to one of the weakest and most pitiable of national societies.

Thus the future of Soviet power may not be by any means as secure as
Russian capacity for self-delusion would make it appear to the men in the
Kremlin. That they can keep power themselves, they have demonstrated.
That they can quietly and easily turn it over to others remains to be
proved. Meanwhile, the hardships of their rule and the vicissitudes of international life have taken a heavy toll of the strength and hopes of the
great people on whom their power rests. It is curious to note that the
ideological power of Soviet authority is strongest today in areas beyond
the frontiers of Russia, beyond the reach of its police power. This phenomenon brings to mind a comparison used by Thomas Mann in his great
novel *Buddenbrooks*. Observing that human institutions often show the
greatest outward brilliance at a moment when inner decay is in reality
farthest advanced, he compared the Buddenbrook family, in the days of
its greatest glamour to one of those stars whose light shines most brightly
on this world when in reality it has long since ceased to exist. And who
can say with assurance that the strong light still cast by the Kremlin on
the dissatisfied peoples of the Western world is not the powerful afterglow
of a constellation which is in actuality on the wane? This cannot be
proved. And it cannot be disproved. But the possibility remains (and in the
opinion of this writer it is a strong one) that Soviet power, like the capitalist world of its conception, bears within it the seeds of its own decay,
and that the sprouting of these seeds is well advanced.

IV

It is clear that the United States cannot expect in the foreseeable future
to enjoy political intimacy with the Soviet regime. It must continue to

regard the Soviet Union as a rival, not a partner, in the political arena. It must continue to expect that Soviet policies will reflect no abstract love of peace and stability, no real faith in the possibility of a permanent happy coexistence of the Socialist and capitalist worlds, but rather a cautious, persistent pressure toward the disruption and weakening of all rival influence and rival power.

Balanced against this are the fact that Russia, as opposed to the Western world in general, is still by far the weaker party, that Soviet policy is highly flexible, and that Soviet society may well contain deficiencies which will eventually weaken its own total potential. This would of itself warrant the United States entering with reasonable confidence upon a policy of firm containment, designed to confront the Russians with unalterable counterforce at every point where they show signs of encroaching upon the interests of a peaceful and stable world.

But in actuality the possibilities for American policy are by no means limited to holding the line and hoping for the best. It is entirely possible for the United States to influence by its actions the internal developments, both within Russia and throughout the international Communist movement, by which Russian policy is largely determined. This is not only a question of the modest measure of informational activity which this government can conduct in the Soviet Union and elsewhere, although that, too, is important. It is rather a question of the degree to which the United States can create among the peoples of the world generally the impression of a country which knows what it wants, which is coping successfully with the problems of its internal life and with the responsibilities of a World Power, and which has a spiritual vitality capable of holding its own among the major ideological currents of the time. To the extent that such an impression can be created and maintained, the aims of Russian Communism must appear sterile and quixotic, the hopes and enthusiasm of Moscow's supporters must wane, and added strain must be imposed on the Kremlin's foreign policies. For the palsied decrepitude of the capitalist world is the keystone of Communist philosophy. Even the failure of the United States to experience the early economic depression which the ravens of the Red Square have been predicting with such complacent confidence since hostilities ceased would have deep and important repercussions throughout the Communist world.

By the same token, exhibitions of indecision, disunity and internal disintegration within this country have an exhilarating effect on the whole Communist movement. At each evidence of these tendencies, a thrill of hope and excitement goes through the Communist world; a new jauntiness can be noted in the Moscow tread; now groups of foreign supporters climb on to what they can only view as the band wagon of international politics; and Russian pressure increases all along the line in international affairs.

It would be an exaggeration to say that American behavior unassisted and alone could exercise a power of life and death over the Communist movement and bring about the early fall of Soviet power in Russia. But the United States has it in its power to increase enormously the strains under which Soviet policy must operate, to force upon the Kremlin a far greater degree of moderation and circumspection than it has had to observe in recent years, and in this way to promote tendencies which must eventually find their outlet in either the break-up or the gradual mellowing of Soviet power. For no mystical, Messianic movement — and particularly not that of the Kremlin — can face frustration indefinitely without eventually adjusting itself in one way or another to the logic of that state of affairs.

Thus the decision will really fall in large measure in this country itself. The issue of Soviet-American relations is in essence a test of the over-all worth of the United States as a nation among nations. To avoid destruction the United States need only measure up to its own best traditions and prove itself worthy of preservation as a great nation.

Surely, there was never a fairer test of national quality than this. In the light of these circumstances, the thoughtful observer of Russian-American relations will find no cause for complaint in the Kremlin's challenge to American society. He will rather experience a certain gratitude to a Providence which, by providing the American people with this implacable challenge, has made their entire security as a nation dependent on their pulling themselves together and accepting the responsibilities of moral and political leadership that history plainly intended them to bear.

Study Guide

1. The selections in this chapter cover more than a quarter century of rhetoric and activity in the foreign policy area — essentially, the question of America's role in world affairs (Charles Beard and Franklin D. Roosevelt); the dropping of the atom bomb on Japan (Harry S. Truman and Henry L. Stimson); the "containment of communism" (George F. Kennan); the application of that doctrine in Southeast Asia (Lyndon B. Johnson); and an indictment of the policy of containment generally, and in Vietnam in particular (Telford Taylor).

2. The article by George Kennan contains the following:
   (a) a summary of Communist ideology (pp. 484–485);
   (b) a historical survey of its evaluation at home in Russia and abroad (pp. 485–489);

(c) an analysis of its current (post-World War II) doctrines and outlook (pp. 489–492); and

(d) a suggested posture for the United States vis-à-vis Soviet Russia (pp. 492–498).

3. Kennan provides an outline of Marxist thought in his second paragraph. Examine it and the quotation from Lenin that follows. Note this significant sentence: "It [Marxian theory] afforded pseudo-scientific justification for their impatience, for their categoric denial of all value in the Tsarist system, for their yearning for power and revenge and for their inclination to cut corners in the pursuit of it."

4. Kennan makes a thoughtful and even sympathetic effort to explain the rigidities of Soviet foreign policy abroad and its dictatorial character at home. Trace the evolution of dictatorship in Soviet Russia, as Kennan explains it, keeping in mind Kennan's emphasis on the role of Communist ideology, particular leaders, and the historical situation in which the new regime found itself. Here is a key sentence: "Now the maintenance of this pattern of Soviet power, namely, the pursuit of unlimited authority domestically, accompanied by the cultivation of the semi-myth of implacable foreign hostility, has gone far to shape the actual machinery of Soviet power as we know it today" (p. 488). What, according to Kennan, would be the future of this policy?

5. Summarize Kennan's characterization of post-1945 Soviet behavior. What two assumptions does he find dominant? What significance does he assert this has for the United States? Note the following all-important piece of advice: "In these circumstances it is clear that the main element of any United States policy toward the Soviet Union must be that of a long-term, patient but firm and vigilant containment of Russian expansive tendencies" (p. 492). Explain how and why Kennan comes to this conclusion.

6. In the third section of his essay, Kennan probes for and finds some weaknesses in the Russian system and some other hopeful signs for the West. What are they generally and what specifically does Kennan see as the problem of future leadership and social stability?

7. On the basis of the foregoing:

(a) What assumptions regarding Soviet foreign policy does Kennan suggest the United States make?

(b) What foreign policy posture does he suggest the United States adopt?

Kennan offers the American people more than a simplistic and inflexible policy of "firm containment." Based upon a careful reading of the last two pages of his essay, try to understand and define it.

8. In assessment:

(a) After reading this essay, can you understand the rationale behind the

Marshall Plan, NATO, the Truman Doctrine, SEATO, the Eisenhower Doctrine, the Bay of Pigs, and the war in Vietnam?
(b) From Kennan's essay, what credence would you give one of the principal tenets of the New Left — their charge that the cold war was initiated by the United States under the influence and leadership of men like Kennan?
(c) Would you agree that Kennan's vision could extend beyond and beneath the cold war on the basis of this passage? "Thus the decision will really fall in large measure in this country itself. The issue of Soviet-American relations is in essence a test of the over-all worth of the United States as a nation among nations. To avoid destruction, the United States need only measure up to its own best traditions and prove itself worthy of preservation as a great nation." These words were written in 1947. What are their implications for the 1960's and 1970's?

Lyndon B. Johnson

OUR DUTY IN SOUTHEAST ASIA

⟨*1965*⟩ THE UNITED STATES began to play a part in the Vietnam war as early as 1950, when the Truman administration started financing the French effort to put down Vietnamese nationalists who, under the lead of the Communist Ho Chi Minh, were struggling for independence from France. American policy makers looked upon France as a bulwark against the spread of communism in Southeast Asia. Upon the defeat and withdrawal of the French, in 1954, the Eisenhower administration committed the United States to the development of South Vietnam as a separate, non-Communist country. The Kennedy administration gave additional aid to South Vietnam, sending more than 15,000 Americans there as "military advisers." Yet the prospects for that country worsened as its people remained badly divided, its government proved weak and unstable, and its enemies stepped up their activity. By the summer of 1964 the Johnson administration was preparing for a drastic escalation of the war, but carefully kept the plans hidden from Congress and the people. Indeed, while campaigning for re-election, Lyndon B. Johnson (1908–1973) publicly repudiated the idea that we "ought to go north and drop bombs" on North Vietnam or that we ought to "get tied down in a land war in Asia." Early the next year American planes were systematically bombing North Vietnam, and on April 1, 1965, President Johnson made a decision to send combat troops to South Vietnam. He did not mention this decision when, six days later, he spoke at Johns Hopkins University on his Vietnam policy; he confined himself to presenting a justification for the American presence in that part of the world. He referred, in passing, to the fact that 400 Americans had already lost their lives there; within five years the number was to exceed 40,000.

SPEECH AT JOHNS HOPKINS UNIVERSITY,

April 7, 1965

MY FELLOW Americans: Last week 17 nations sent their views to some dozen countries having interest in Southeast Asia. We are joining these 17 countries in stating our American policy, which we believe will contribute toward peace in this area.

Tonight I want to review once again with my own people the views of your Government.

Tonight Americans and Asians are dying for a world where each people may choose its own path to change.

This is the principle for which our ancestors fought in the valleys of Pennsylvania. It is the principle for which our sons fight in the jungles of Vietnam.

Vietnam is far from this quiet campus. We have no territory there, nor do we seek any. The war is dirty and brutal and difficult. And some 400 young men — born into an America bursting with opportunity and promise — have ended their lives on Vietnam's steaming soil.

Why must we take this painful road?

Why must this nation hazard its ease, its interest and its power for the sake of a people so far away?

We fight because we must fight if we are to live in a world where every country can shape its own destiny. And only in such a world will our own freedom be finally secure.

This kind of a world will never be built by bombs and bullets. Yet the infirmities of man are such that force must often precede reason — and the waste of war, the works of peace.

We wish this were not so. But we must deal with the world as it is, if it is ever to be as we wish.

The world as it is in Asia is not a serene or peaceful place.

The first reality is that North Vietnam has attacked the independent nation of South Vietnam. Its object is total conquest.

Of course, some of the people of South Vietnam are participating in attack on their own Government. But trained men and supplies, orders and arms, flow in a constant stream from North to South. This support is the heartbeat of the war.

And it is a war of unparalleled brutality. Simple farmers are the targets of assassination and kidnapping. Women and children are strangled in the night because their men are loyal to the Government. Small and helpless villages are ravaged by sneak attacks. Large-scale raids are conducted on towns, and terror strikes in the heart of cities.

The confused nature of this conflict cannot mask the fact that it is the new face of an old enemy. It is an attack by one country upon another. And the object of that attack is a friend to which we are pledged.

Over this war — and all Asia — is another reality: the deepening shadow of Communist China. The rulers in Hanoi are urged on by Peking. This is a regime which has destroyed freedom in Tibet, attacked India and been condemned by the United Nations for aggressions in Korea. It is a nation which is helping the forces of violence in almost every continent. The contest in Vietnam is part of a wider pattern of aggressive purpose.

Why are these realities our concern? Why are we in South Vietnam?

We are there because we have a promise to keep. Since 1954 every American President has offered support to the people of South Vietnam. We have helped to build and we have helped to defend. Thus, over many years, we have made a national pledge to help South Vietnam defend its independence.

I intend to keep our promise.

To dishonor that pledge, to abandon this small and brave nation to its enemy — and to the terror that must follow — would be an unforgivable wrong.

We are also there to strengthen world order. Around the globe — from Berlin to Thailand — are people whose well-being rests, in part, on the belief they can count on us if they are attacked. To leave Vietnam to its fate would shake the confidence of all these people in the value of American commitment. The result would be increased unrest and instability, or even war.

We are also there because there are great stakes in the balance. Let no one think that retreat from Vietnam would bring an end to conflict. The battle would be renewed in one country and then another. The central lesson of our time is that the appetite of aggression is never satisfied. To withdraw from one battlefield means only to prepare for the next. We must say in Southeast Asia — as we did in Europe — in the words of the Bible: "Hitherto shalt thou come, but no further."

There are those who say that all our efforts there will be futile — that China's power is such it is bound to dominate all Southeast Asia. But there is no end to that argument until all the nations of Asia are swallowed up.

There are those who wonder why we have a responsibility for the defense of freedom in Europe. World War II was fought in both Europe and Asia, and when it ended we found ourselves with continued responsibility for the defense of freedom.

Our objective is the independence of South Vietnam, and its freedom from attack. We want nothing for ourselves — only that the people of South Vietnam be allowed to guide their own country in their own way.

We will do everything necessary to reach that objective. And we will do only what is necessary.

In recent months attacks on South Vietnam were stepped up. Thus it became necessary to increase our response and make attacks by air. This is not a change of purpose. It is a change in what we believe that purpose requires.

We do this in order to slow down aggression.

We do this to increase the confidence of the brave people of South Vietnam who have bravely borne this brutal battle for so many years and with so many casualties.

And we do this to convince the leaders of North Vietnam — and all who seek to share their conquest — of a simple fact:

We will not be defeated.

We will not grow tired.

We will not withdraw, either openly or under the cloak of a meaningless agreement.

We know that air attacks alone will not accomplish all these purposes. But it is our best and prayerful judgement that they are a necessary part of the surest road to peace.

We hope that peace will come swiftly. But that is in the hands of others beside ourselves. And we must be prepared for a long, continued conflict. It will require patience as well as bravery — the will to endure as well as the will to resist.

I wish it were possible to convince others with words of what we now find it necessary to say with guns and planes: Armed hostility is futile. Our resources are equal to any challenge. Because we fight for values and a principle, rather than territory or colonies, our patience and determination are unending.

Once this is clear, then it should also be clear that the only path for reasonable men is the path of peaceful settlement.

Such peace demands an independent South Vietnam — securely guaranteed and able to shape its own relationships to all others, free from outside interference, tied to no alliance, a military base for no other country.

These are the essentials of any final settlement.

We will never be second in the search for such a peaceful settlement in Vietnam.

There may be many ways to this kind of peace: in discussion or negotiation with the governments concerned; in large groups or in small ones; in the reaffirmation of old agreements or their strengthening with new ones.

We have stated this position over and over again 50 times and more to friend and foe alike. And we remain ready, with this purpose, for unconditional discussions.

And until that bright and necessary day of peace, we will try to keep conflict from spreading. We have no desire to see thousands die in battle — Asians or Americans. We have no desire to devastate that which the people of North Vietnam have built with toil and sacrifice. We will use our power with restraint and with all the wisdom we can command. But we will use it.

This war, like most wars, is filled with terrible irony. For what do the people of North Vietnam want? They want what their neighbors also desire: food for their hunger, health for their bodies and a chance to learn, progress for their country and an end to the bondage of material misery. And they would find all these things far more readily in peaceful association with others than in the endless course of battle.

These countries of Southeast Asia are homes for millions of impoverished people. Each day these people rise at dawn and struggle through weary hours to wrestle existence from the soil. They are often wracked by disease, plagued by hunger, and death comes early, at the age of 40.

Stability and peace do not come easily in such a land. Neither independence nor human dignity will be won by arms alone. It also requires the works of peace.

The American people have helped generously in these works.

Now there must be a much more massive effort to improve the life of man in the conflict-torn corner of the world.

The first step is for the countries of Southeast Asia to associate themselves in a greatly expanded cooperative effort for development. We would hope that North Vietnam will take its place in the common effort just as soon as peaceful cooperation is possible.

The United Nations is already actively engaged in development in this area. I would hope that the Secretary General of the United Nations could use the prestige of his great office — and his deep knowledge of Asia — to initiate, as soon as possible with the countries of the area a plan for cooperation in increased development.

For our part I will ask the Congress to join in a billion-dollar American investment in this effort when it is underway.

And I hope all other industrialized countries — including the Soviet Union — will join in this effort to replace despair with hope and terror with progress.

The task is nothing less than to enrich the hopes and existence of more than a hundred million people. And there is much to be done.

The vast Mekong River can provide food and water and power on a scale to dwarf even our own T.V.A.

The wonders of modern medicine can be spread through villages where thousands die for lack of care.

Schools can be established to train people in the skills needed to manage the process of development.

And these objectives, and more, are within the reach of a cooperative and determined effort.

I also intend to expand and speed up a program to make available our farm surplus to assist in feeding and clothing the needy in Asia. We should not allow people to go hungry and naked while our own warehouses overflow with an abundance of wheat and corn, rice and cotton.

I will very shortly name a special team of patriotic and distinguished Americans to inaugurate our participation in these programs. This team will be headed by Mr. Eugene Black, the very able former president of the World Bank.

In areas still ripped by conflict, development will not be easy. Peace will be necessary for final success. But we cannot wait for peace to begin the job.

This will be a disorderly planet for a long time. In Asia, as elsewhere, the forces of the modern world are shaking old ways and uprooting ancient civilizations. There will be turbulence and struggle and even violence. Great social change, as we see in our own country, does not always come without conflict.

We must also expect that nations will on occasion be in dispute with us. It may be because we are rich or powerful, or because we have made mistakes, or because they honestly fear our intentions. However, no nation need ever fear that we desire their land or to impose our will or to dictate their institutions.

But we will always oppose the effort of one nation to conquer another. We will do this because our own security is at stake.

But there is more to it than that. For our generation has a dream. It is a very old dream. But we have the power and the opportunity to make it real.

For centuries nations have struggled among each other. But we dream of a world where disputes are settled by law and reason. And we will try to make it so.

For most of history men have hated and killed one another in battle. But we dream of an end to war. And we will try to make it so.

For all existence most men have lived in poverty, threatened by hunger. But we dream of a world where all are fed and charged with hope. And we will help to make it so.

The ordinary men and women of North Vietnam and South Vietnam, of China and India, of Russia and America, are brave people. They are filled with the same proportions of hate and fear, of love and hope. Most of them want the same things for themselves and their families. Most of them do not want their sons to die in battle, or see the homes of others destroyed.

This can be their world yet. Man now has the knowledge — always before denied — to make this planet serve the real needs of the people who live on it.

I know this will not be easy. I know how difficult it is for reason to guide passion and love to master hate. The complexities of this world do not bow easily to pure and consistent answers.

But the simple truths are there just the same. We must try to follow them as best we can.

We often say how impressive power is. But I do not find it impressive. The guns and bombs, the rockets and warships are all symbols of human failure. They are necessary symbols. They protect what we cherish. But they are witness to human folly.

A dam built across a great river is impressive.

In the countryside where I was born, I have seen the night illuminated, the kitchens warmed and the homes heated where once the cheerless night and the ceaseless cold held sway. And all this happened because electricity came to our town along the humming wires of the Rural Electrification Administration. Electrification of the countryside is impressive.

A rich harvest in a hungry land is impressive.

The sight of healthy children in a classroom is impressive.

These — not mighty arms — are the achievements which the American nation believes to be impressive.

And — if we are steadfast — the time may come when all other nations will also find it so.

We may well be living in the time foretold many years ago when it was said: "I call heaven and earth to record this day against you, that I have set before you life and death, blessing and cursing: therefore choose life, that both thou and thy seed may live."

This generation of the world must choose: destroy or build, kill or aid, hate or understand.

We can do all these things on a scale never dreamed of before.

We will choose life. And so doing we will prevail over the enemies within man, and over the natural enemies of all mankind.

Study Guide

1. Johnson's defense of his Vietnam policy of the 1960's sums up in a single address the full range of arguments advanced in that decade by those in

and out of government who supported that policy. Let us try to follow Johnson's reasoning. What follows is an outline of his arguments; find the appropriate sentence or illustration for each:

(a) the self-determination of nations;
(b) the notion of the victim and the aggressor;
(c) the Communist menace;
(d) the "domino theory";
(e) the need to avoid another "Munich";
(f) the disinterested idealism, sense of responsibility, and power of the American people;
(g) the vision of a "New Deal" for all underdeveloped nations; and
(h) the vision of a better tomorrow through the victory of the children of light over the children of darkness.

2. To understand some of the above (e.g., Munich), consult your text; for those you fail to find there, try the library.

3. Let us place this address by Johnson in perspective with the following questions:

(a) Can you see the address of Franklin D. Roosevelt in 1941 (pp. 458–463) as setting a precedent for the Johnson address in 1965? For example: ". . . We are committed to full support of all those resolute peoples, everywhere, who are resisting aggression. . . ." Can you find other sentiments expressed by F.D.R. in 1941 that would lay the foundation for the Johnson rhetoric and actions in Indo-China in the 1960's?

(b) Or, are you of the opinion that there is no connection between the two? And what of Charles Beard's warnings? ". . . Continentalism," he wrote, "meant a recognition of the limited nature of American powers to relieve, restore, and maintain life beyond its own sphere of interest and control — a recognition of the hard fact that the United States, either alone or in any coalition, did not possess the power to force peace on Europe and Asia, to assure the establishment of democratic and pacific governments there, or to provide the social and economic underwriting necessary to the perdurance of such governments" (p. 456). On the other hand, do the actions of the Johnson administration in Vietnam fully vindicate Beard's position? Or, put this way: can they, Beard and Johnson, both be wrong?

(c) And what of the relationship between the Johnson address and Kennan's "containment" policy? Did not the Truman-Eisenhower-Kennedy-Johnson policy in Southeast Asia merely carry out Kennan's demand for "the adroit and vigilant application of counter-force at a series of constantly shifting geographical and political points . . . which cannot be charmed . . . out of existence" (p. 492)? Or was there, within Kennan's proposed policy, an option for refraining from war in Indo-China and in Vietnam? Explore.

Telford Taylor

TRAGEDY IN VIETNAM

-∰{*1970*}∰- IN THE LATE 1960's and early 1970's widespread dissatisfaction with both the apparent purposes of the American war in Vietnam and the military methods by which it was being fought led critics of the war to charge that the United States was violating in Vietnam the very principles it had helped to establish in the extraordinary trials of Nazi leaders at Nuremberg after World War II. Nazis were accused at Nuremberg of having violated the so-called laws of war, and most of them were convicted as war criminals and sentenced either to death or to long prison terms. Now, Vietnam critics charged, American policy makers and military men were committing similar crimes. Outstanding in the debate that raged over this issue was a book by Telford Taylor, *Nuremberg and Vietnam: An American Tragedy* (1970).

Taylor, a law professor at Columbia University, had been chief counsel for the prosecution at Nuremberg. In his book he summarized the history of the laws of war, explained the significance of the Nuremberg trials, and discussed the relevance of these matters to the course of the war in Southeast Asia. While Taylor was clearly critical of the war and the way the United States was conducting it, his account was judicious and his personal background gave great weight to his words. The following selection illustrates both his scholarly willingness to look at both sides of a complex question and his personal conviction that the war was truly "an American tragedy."

WAR AND PEACE

WHY WE ARE in Vietnam is today a question of mainly historical interest. We *are* there, for better or for worse, and we must deal with the situation that exists." So read the opening words of Arthur M. Schlesinger Jr.'s 1967 study of American involvement in Vietnam. But the reasons why we are in Vietnam are part of "the situation that exists," and the question — what those reasons are — is both a moral and a practical issue of great moment.

Consider the conflicting versions of our Vietnam purposes even within the White House circle. Early in 1967 Walt W. Rostow, then a close adviser to President Johnson, told a meeting of college student editors that our "intervention had been based legally on obligations under SEATO to resist aggression." His statement was immediately and publicly challenged by Richard N. Goodwin, a former assistant to Presidents Kennedy and Johnson, who declared that the United States had not acted under treaty obligations, but rather "because, in the judgment of the Presidents, American power and interests demanded it."

The same contrast is manifest in the explanations of United States policy given by Eugene V. Rostow, Walt's brother and former Under Secretary of State, in the course of a long interview with William Whitworth of the New Yorker. Speaking of American policy in India and South Vietnam, Rostow declared that "our interest is not to protect democracy as such but to deter, prevent, or defeat aggression." Then at another point he described the motivation of our intervention in Vietnam as based on the Government's being concerned about "the long-range impact a withdrawal would have on Japanese policy," and being "afraid that the enormous masses and the geographical and strategic areas of that region will fall into the hands of hostile or potentially hostile powers."

In an earlier chapter, I have stated my opinion that the courts cannot reasonably be expected to pass judgment on the legality of our Vietnam policies. But to say that the judges should not answer the question is not to deny the reality and significance of the question itself. Dean Rusk had no warrant of authority to determine for all men and all time that North Vietnam committed aggression against South Vietnam. It may be unlikely that our leaders will be called upon to answer at the bar of some future international tribunal, but there is also the bar of history. As a nation dedicated to liberty, justice and peace on earth it is surely incumbent on us to engage in hard self-scrutiny, and conform our actions, as far as humanly possible, to the principles we profess.

Are we, then, acting in Vietnam as a global policeman, under the Nuremberg principles and the United Nations Charter, to "deter, prevent or defeat aggression"? Or are we promoting "American power and interests" in Asia? Enormously different consequences would flow from the dominance of one or the other of these purposes — differences in the suitability of particular military tactics, in the weight to be given to the attitude of other nations toward our actions, and in the terms of an acceptable armistice or peace settlement.

If preservation of the American position in Southeast Asia is the governing motive, then the question whether North or South Vietnam "struck the first blow" is of only collateral significance; whichever was the more to blame, America would be equally disadvantaged by a victory for the North. . . .

Some of our other military ventures, especially in this hemisphere, have been less than simon-pure in terms of Nuremberg principles. Nevertheless, there is a deeply idealistic strain in the American interventionist tradition. In 1898, President McKinley justified the war against Spain: "In the cause of humanity and to put an end to the barbarities, bloodshed, starvation, and horrible miseries now existing" in Cuba. Thereafter, the

United States joined with other governments in denouncing the Rumanian and Russian pogroms, especially at Kishinev, and the Turkish massacres of Armenians in 1915.

The idea that a government's treatment of its own nationals can be so contrary to civilized standards as to constitute an international crime, indeed, lies at the root of the "crimes against humanity" concept of the London Charter, and of the Genocide Convention. And it was in this spirit that President Eisenhower pledged support to South Vietnam in 1954, telling President Ngo Dinh Diem that it was our purpose to "discourage any who might wish to impose a foreign ideology on your free people." In fact, the people were certainly not as "free" as the President thought; nevertheless, as Arthur Schlesinger puts it, the mood in which the Government started into Vietnam was "essentially moralistic."

To be sure, idealistic and selfish motives are not mutually exclusive, and sometimes work in conjunction. The North Korean attack against South Korea in 1950 was a far greater threat to Japan and the general American position in Asia than ever was Ho Chi Minh, and very likely the United States would have intervened whatever the Korean rights and wrongs might have been. In fact it was a clear case of aggression by North Korea, and the United Nations soon put its stamp of approval on the American action, which thus became a multilateral operation under an umbrella of international concensus.

I have already indicated my belief that one of the difficulties about applying the Nuremberg "crimes against peace" standards to our Vietnam venture is the diversity of impressions and motives that governed the many men who have influenced the course of the operation over the 16 years that it has now been under way. Things may not have looked the same to President Johnson in 1964 as they had to Eisenhower 10 years earlier; if as has been reported, Johnson was strongly moved by a desire not to be "the first American President to lose a war," one can only say that this was hardly a worthy reaction to a problem of the greatest moment to the nation, and would not be a strong defense in any forum.

Lacking the documents and testimony to establish the personal intentions of the movers and shakers in Washington, we are thrown back to the record of what the United States Government has actually *done* in Vietnam. On that record, it is difficult not to reach a harsh verdict. If the primary purpose had remained, as Eisenhower said, to protect South Vietnam from the imposition of a "foreign ideology" or, as the Rostow brothers tell us, to deter aggression, it is inconceivable that our conduct of military operations should have taken the course that it has. Whatever peace-keeping and protective intentions may have governed our initial involvement in Vietnam have by now been so completely submerged under the avalanche of death and destruction that they no longer are credible descriptions of the operation as a whole. Colonel Corson has summed up the consequences in a mordant pun: The United States in Vietnam has become an "international lethal aid society."

Why did things go wrong? Some say it is because our leaders were war criminals. Whether or not that be so, it is an unsatisfactory answer in terms of causation, for it assumes that the leaders wanted things to turn out as they have, whereas in fact it is plain that those responsible are exceedingly dissatisfied with the present consequences of their policies. Surely Lyndon Johnson would never have done what he did in 1964 and 1965 if he could have foreseen the results in 1968.

I think that Colonel Corson is much closer to the truth — or truths — in saying that "American judgment as to the effective prosecution of the war was faulty from beginning to end"; that we became "over-involved militarily in the armed forces of the present, under-involved politically in the human forces of the future"; and that in the upshot our political and military leaders alike lost sight of the old law of war that "it is a mistake, illegal and immoral, to kill people without clear military advantage in a war."

That is more enlightening on the "how" than the "why" we got off course. On the second question the record is still incomplete and cloudy, but the accounts and comments of those on the edge of the inner circle strongly indicate that there was a misfit between ends and means; that the military leaders never grasped the essentially political aims of intervention, and the political leaders neglected or were unable to police the means that the military adopted to fulfill what they conceived to be their mission.

If the objective of our Vietnam policy be stated over-simply as "to stop Communism at the 17th parallel," there were at most two ways to do that. The first, which has been our stated policy, is to gain and hold the political allegiance of the South Vietnamese to a non-Communist government, while giving them defensive assistance against any military means used by the North. The second was to ignore the South Vietnamese people, treat South Vietnam as a battlefield, and kill all the North Vietnamese or Vietcong found on or moving toward the battlefield. The sad story of America's venture in Vietnam is that the military means rapidly submerged the political ends, and the first method soon gave way to the second.

Whether or not the first method could have been successfully employed is and will remain an unanswered question. After the Second World War it worked well for us in Greece, but Vietnam is quite another place. After Ho Chi Minh's long and eventually successful struggle against the French, it is at least doubtful that any Western power — perhaps any outside power — could effectively participate in Vietnam's internecine troubles. The United States had few scholars or diplomats expert in Vietnamese institutions. Still, there were those who thought in these terms, including Roger Hilsman and Walt Rostow(!) who in 1962 "developed a cogent and comprehensive 'strategic concept for counterinsurgency' that emphasized . . . subordination of military actions to political purpose, and reliance on small scale counter guerrilla units, as opposed to conventional military formations."

According to Townsend Hoopes, the Army was strongly opposed to these projects, and it is easy to see why: The regular armed services have no capacity for such undertakings. That being so, it was a possible conclusion that Vietnam was a good place for the Army to stay out of, and that was precisely the conclusion reached in 1954 by the Chief of Army Plans, Lieut. Gen. James M. Gavin. It was his opinion that "as a military operation Vietnam made no sense," because "unless the people of the country prefer the government supported by foreign troops to the guerrillas, the mere introduction of large numbers of ground troops with modern equipment would not resolve the military conflict."

But what the Army and Air Force had, in great abundance, was mobility and firepower, and what they thought would be adequate manpower. Confronted with what appeared to be a deteriorating situation in South Vietnam, President Johnson and his advisers clutched for the means at hand without sufficiently considering their suitability for the end in view. The bankruptcy of the firepower tactic did not go unobserved. "My feeling is that you could kill every Vietcong and North Vietnamese in South Vietnam and still lose the war," said the commandant of the Marine Corps, Gen. Wallace M. Greene. "Unless we can make a success of the civic-action program, we are not going to achieve the objectives we have set." But neither Pentagon nor White House gave heed. Townsend Hoopes remained uncertain whether President Johnson "never understood the incompatibility of Westmoreland's ground strategy with his own stated political objective, i.e. to gain the political allegiance of the people of South Vietnam," or whether "he regarded the political aim as mere words and the need for military victory as the only governing reality."

However that may be, neither the President nor the Secretary of Defense, Robert McNamara, gave effective review to Westmoreland's operations. "The preferred military doctrine dictated the strategy, and the strategy determined the policy," says Hoopes, adding that "during nearly three years of steadily rising combat and casualty levels, Washington did not seriously question or modify the Westmoreland strategy of attrition." The Pentagon simply lost sight of "the truth that protection for the people against Vietcong terror had to be achieved by means that did not themselves alienate the people by causing heavy civilian casualties and wanton physical destruction."

By the summer of 1968, it had become painfully apparent that the Westmoreland fire-power tactic, apart from the moral and legal aspects, was a military failure. Heavy casualties had been inflicted on the Vietcong, but they remained undefeated. "There is considerable evidence," writes Gen. David Shoup, retired commandant of the Marine Corps, "that the National Liberation Front is in fact better organized and enjoys greater loyalty among the people of Vietnam than does the Saigon government."

Reprisal bombing attacks on villages have driven thousands of the inhabitants to refugee camps, and subjected those who stay to a fear-ridden existence. A report on refugees, done in 1968 for the Rand Corporation, reveals that "excessive misdirected bombing" had made them hostile to the Saigon Government, and served only to "knock the underpinnings from efforts to gain the support of the people." Two years yater, as American soldiers moved into Cambodia, news correspondents reported that "the pattern of Vietnam is being repeated"; that the troops were under orders to "burn everything," and that heavy bombing was driving the inhabitants into the ranks of the Vietcong.

And so in August, 1970, when newspaper headlines informed us "Americans in Vietnam Find Themselves Hated," it should have come as no surprise. "The B-52 bombing raids, the air strikes on villages where there might have been Vietcong but maybe not, the incidents of cruelty by United States troops — all these things have made many Vietnamese angry and outraged," wrote Gloria Emerson. "The Americans are hated now because they have, for so long, told the Vietnamese how to win the war. Despite such assurance, the war is a long way from being won." Now it has come to the point that Americans in Saigon can no longer walk safely alone, and are "advised to travel in pairs."

In a recent television address on the war in Southeast Asia, President Nixon coined the phrase "pitiful, helpless giant," and hotly denied that the United States, under his leadership, would play such a part. Pitiful and helpless the nation is not, but the course of events under the last three Presidents raises painful doubts whether our conduct as a nation may not have been arrogant and blind — or at best one-eyed, seeing in only one direction, and unable to perceive the lessons of the past or the trends of the present.

If an effort be made to look beneath the orders and operations and speeches and press releases for some clues to understanding the Vietnam debacle, then one must contemplate Vietnam not in isolation but in the context of the times and the many other failures and dangers that are unsettling the United States today. Most of them, I believe, can be gathered under the expression of "under-maintenance," caused by our unwillingness, despite enormous material means, to invest the time, thought and resources necessary to preserve the foundations and basic services of society. Attention is given to ever taller skyscrapers, supersonic airliners and moon landings, while we pollute the air and water and allow education, transportation, housing and health to degenerate.

Despite the billions of dollars we have spent on the Vietnam war and the incredible weight of explosives dropped on that unhappy land, our failure there is largely due to *under-maintenance.* The point is implicit in the title of Jonathan Schell's book — *The Military Half* — as explained in a concluding passage:

> Many optimistic Americans, including reporters as well as military men and civilian officials, tended to set off the destruction caused by the military effort against the construction resulting for the civil-affairs effort, seeing the two results as separate but balanced "sides" of the war; and, looking at our commitment of men and materials, they were often favorably impressed with the size of the constructive effort, almost as though it were being carried out in one country while the military effort was being carried out in another. But, of course, the two programs were being carried out in the same provinces and the same villages, and the people who received the allotments of rice were the same people whose villages had been destroyed by bombs. . . . Many of the civil-affairs officials were working exhaustingly long hours and doing the best job they could with their limited time and resources, and they could not see why the people should complain and expect more than they were getting. Many military men, for their part, were loyal only to their duty — that of conducting military operations. Having efficiently carried out the "military half," they saw it as the responsibility of the Vietnamese government and of the American civil-affairs advisers to carry out the "civilian half" by taking care of the people who had been hurt or dispossessed in the "military half." . . . But because, along with the destruction of villages, American military operations brought death to many civilians, American civil-affairs workers, no matter how well intentioned they might be, and no matter how well supplied they might someday become,

could never, from the point of view of the villagers, "balance" the sufferings caused by the military, or undo what they had done, which was
often absolute and irreversible.

The "civil half" never became "well supplied"; to paraphrase George
Orwell, some halves are larger than others, and the "military half" has
been virtually the whole. Colonel Donovan has estimated the cost of the
air war alone, to the end of 1968, at over $7-billion for bombs dropped
and aircraft lost. Over half of this sum was spent on bombing North Vietnam from early 1965 to late 1968.[1] The bombing in South Vietnam has,

[1] In August, 1969, the Air Force Chief of Staff, Gen. John P. McConnell, told the
Senate Armed Services Committee: "Every thing is operating up there [in North
Vietnam] very nearly as if it had not even been touched. I could say the repair is
75 per cent completed."

of course, been the principal cause of civilian casualties and the "generation" of refugees.

Consider, in comparison, the American investment in care for the
refugees and casualties. In the summer of 1965, a subcommittee of the
Senate Judiciary Committee, entitled "Subcommittee on Refugees" and
chaired by Senator Edward M. Kennedy, held hearings on the refugee
situation in South Vietnam, and these were followed by further investigations of both refugees and casualties in 1966 and 1967, a trip to Vietnam
by Senator Kennedy in January, 1968, and a public report by the subcommittee in May, 1968.

According to the Refugee Subcommittee's report, American financial
support for the care and resettlement of refugees amounted to approximately $100-million for the three years 1966 to 1968 inclusive. Medical
assistance for the civilian casualties total $76-million for the three years
1965 to 1967. Making generous allowance for missing figures, perhaps a
quarter of a billion dollars was devoted to civilian relief during the four
years 1965 to 1968, while military operations were at their peak. That is
less than four per cent of the cost of air operations alone during the same
period.

This parsimony in the "civil half" was observed when our own military
actions were causing conditions in the refugee camps and hospitals that
can only be described as frightful. Why? The Subcommittee found no
rational answer:

> In many respects, the subcommittee has found this Government's
> handling of the civilian casualty and health problems one of the most
> puzzling aspects of our Vietnam involvement. The needs were obvious
> from the very early stages of our military buildup in Vietnam. Equally
> obvious was the fact that the South Vietnamese were themselves in-

capable of meeting the vast demands placed upon outdated and inadequate medical facilities.

Yet for some reason this Government has been unable or unwilling to come to grips with the civilian medical situation in South Vietnam. We have talked of winning the hearts and minds of the people of South Vietnam; yet we have, we must assume by choice, chosen to meet only partially the urgent needs of the wounded, injured, and sick of this country we have sworn to help and these people we seek to protect. . . .

It is, to be sure, much more the conventional military mission to fire guns and drop bombs than to build housing and hospitals. The fundamental mistake was not the Army's, but rather the selection of the Army to do a job for which it was ill-equipped. Once it was in charge, the worst aspects of the military system surfaced, then dominated the conduct of operations. Combat command is the surest road to promotion, and the Army and Air Force were only too glad to find a new theater for military experimentation. As Colonel Donovan describes the professional consequences:

> The highly trained career officers of the Army and the other services have found the Vietnam war a frustrating but fascinating professional challenge. The very size and scope of the American military force has also generated unceasing pressures to satisfy such military demands as trying out new weapons and using the war as a military testing ground and laboratory. Helicopter assault theories, air mobile operations concepts, new helicopter types, new weapons and organizations, and counter-insurgency tactics were all ready for trial by the Army in Vietnam. It was not a life-or-death war in defense of the United States, but rather a remote and limited conflict where training and equipment could be tested and combat experience renewed or attained by the professionals. . . .

Perhaps stronger and wiser military leadership would have averted the worst of the consequences, or perhaps even advised against the entire venture, in line with the views of generals such as Ridgeway and Gavin. But the armed services no longer possess leaders of stature and influence comparable to the heros of the Second World War. In the Army, Marshall and MacArthur and their juniors such as Eisenhower and Bradley, in the Navy, King and Nimitz, in the air, Arnold, Spaatz and Doolittle wielded moral as well as doctrinal influence, derived from their seniority, achievements and manifest ability. Today there are no comparable figures. . . .

What, then, are the obligations of the young man called by draft to serve in a war that he deeply believes to be, in the old religious terminology, "unjust" — whether because we had no right to intervene in the first place, or because, in Colonel Donovan's words, our "techniques of fire and military power were immoral and were in fact destroying the people we were striving to assist"? Nuremberg, historically speaking, gives no answer. But what about Nuremberg the symbol of overriding international standards binding on individuals?

The Spanish theologians had a categorically affirmative answer to the question. "If a subject is convinced of the injustice of a war, he ought not to serve in it, even on the command of his prince," wrote Vitoria. "This is clear, for no one can authorize the killing of an innocent person. But in the case before us the enemy are innocent. Therefore they may not be killed. . . . Hence flows the corollary that subjects whose conscience is against the justice of a war may not engage in it whether they be right or wrong. This is clear for 'whatever is not of faith is sin.'" Suarez was of the same opinion.

To refuse to serve "even on the command of his prince" is a high and principled standard — too high for most men. Perhaps here the law will give some sanctuary. It is true that the Selective Service statute gives conscientious objector status only to those who are opposed to "war in any form," but today there is distinguished authority for the view that, at least in Vietnam ("a campaign fought with limited forces for limited objects with no likelihood of a battlefront within this country and without a declaration of war"), Congress cannot constitutionally require a man to do combat duty against the dictates of his conscience.

But we should not have to await an answer from the courts. Given the course the war has taken, and the depth and breadth of opposition to its conduct, it is both unwise and inhumane to compel people to serve in it against their will. For the United States, this is a new kind of war for our times — the precedents in Mexico and the Philippines are long forgotten — and one for which compulsory service should not be required.

In this respect, I believe, the views of the draft-age generation are sound, and it is only to be regretted that they have been so often pressed in a counterproductive manner. I suppose that few things have contributed more to the much-discussed "generation gap" than the circumstances that most people over 45 were more or less deeply involved in the Second World War, the purposes and waging of which they heartily approved, while no one under 25 has any meaningful recollection of any but the Vietnam war, which is widely regarded as despicable and a national calamity. One need not have been a hero to look back on military service in World War II with satisfaction if not pride, and with pleasure in feeling that one had made a contribution, however small, to a great and necessary military victory. Given these memories, American flag-burnings, Vietcong flag displays and shouts of "Ho! Ho! Ho Chi Minh!" are bound to offend deeply even those to whom the Vietnam war is an abomination. When one considers also the hundreds of thousands of families whose sons have served in Vietnam and perhaps been killed or wounded, and who have a large psychological stake in the worthwhileness of the sacrifice, bitter resentment and hostility toward the uninhibited youth demonstrators are inevitable, as is the violence that is their product.

But it is not the demonstrations that cast the shadows of doubt and cynicism across those White House posthumous awards of Medals of Honor, and the countless memorials and mournings in humbler quarters; rather it is our own record as a nation, especially since 1964. It has been well said that a people get the kind of government they deserve. The Vietnam war was not the brain-child of construction workers, or Texas oilmen, or aircraft manufacturers, or super-patriots, or paranoid heresy-hunters. The war, in the massive, lethal dimensions it acquired after 1964, was the work of highly educated academics and administrators, most of whom would fit rather easily the present Vice-President's notion of an "effete snob." It was not President Kennedy himself, but the men he brought to Washington as advisers and who stayed on with President Johnson — the Rusks, McNamaras, Bundys, and Rostows — who must bear major responsibility for the war and the course it took.

"The contest in Vietnam is a contest for the allegiance of the South Vietnamese. No foreign force can win that battle. That is why the root of the struggle has always been in the South. That is why the bombing has always been marginal in its final meaning; that is why the necessities of American politics now coincide with the necessities of the South Vietnamese future." That is how McGeorge Bundy, one-time close adviser to President Johnson, saw the matter in October, 1968, by which time he had concluded that "there is no prospect of military victory against North Vietnam by any level of U.S. military force which is acceptable," and that therefore the "burden of Vietnam" must be "lifted from our society."

Bundy was candid enough to acknowledge that "this has not always been my view," but nonetheless his recantation is oddly put. To *whom* does he wish the South Vietnamese to give "allegiance"? And are we to understand from the phrase "now coincide" that there was a time when the "necessities of American politics" did *not* coincide with the "necessities of the South Vietnamese future"? By what human calculation is bombing, and the consequent loss of life and limb, to be justified if it is "marginal in its final meaning"?

As one who until 1965 supported American intervention in Vietnam as an aggression-checking undertaking in the spirit of the United Nations Charter, I am painfully aware of the instability of individual judgment.

Nevertheless, when the nature, scale and effect of intervention changed so drastically in 1965, it is more than "puzzling" (as the Senate Refugee Subcommittee put it) that virtually no one in high authority had the capacity and inclination to perceive and articulate the inevitable consequences. How could it ever have been thought that air strikes, free-fire zones and a mass uprooting and removal of the rural population were the way to win "the allegiance of the South Vietnamese"? By what mad cerebrations could a ratio of 28 to 1 between our investments in bombing, and in relief for those we had wounded and made homeless, have even been contemplated, let alone adopted as the operational pattern?

One may well echo the acrid French epigram, and say that all this "is worse than a crime, it is a blunder" — the most costly and tragic national blunder in American history. And so it has come to this: that the anti-aggression spirit of Nuremberg and the United Nations Charter is invoked to justify our venture in Vietnam, where we have smashed the country to bits, and will not even take the trouble to clean up the blood and rubble. None there will ever thank us; few elsewhere that do not now see our America as a sort of Steinbeckian "Lennie," gigantic and powerful, but prone to shatter what we try to save. Somehow we failed ourselves to learn the lessons we undertook to teach at Nuremberg, and that failure is today's American tragedy.

Study Guide

1. Telford Taylor's indictment of American policies in Vietnam cover a number of themes:
   (a) why and how we got into the war;
   (b) our actions there; and
   (c) an assessment of it all.

2. On pp. 508–511, Taylor attempts to fathom the motives of the men who led the nation into war in Vietnam. What answers does he get from:
   (a) Arthur M. Schlesinger, Jr.;
   (b) Walt W. Rostow; and
   (c) Eugene V. Rostow?

   Why, according to Taylor, is it important to know whether the United States went to war in Vietnam for altruistic or selfish motives; or put this way, what relationship does Taylor want to establish between our *reasons* for going to war there and the *kind* of war we fought? What answer does he supply?

3. On pp. 511–516, Taylor reviews the United States military policy in Vietnam.

(a) To what general conclusion does he come?

(b) What impact has the war there had on the South Vietnamese attitudes toward Americans?

(c) Explain how Taylor employs the *"under-maintenance"* concept to criticize our military action in Vietnam.

(d) What evidence does he use from the subcommittee headed by Senator Edward M. Kennedy?

4. What are Taylor's views (pp. 516–518) on being a conscientious objector to the war in Vietnam?

5. On whom does he put the ultimate blame for the war?

6. Explain: "Somehow we failed ourselves to learn the lessons we undertook to teach at Nuremberg, and that failure is today's American tragedy."

7. Compare and contrast the attitudes expressed by President Johnson (in his Johns Hopkins speech), and Telford Taylor regarding:

(a) the menace of world communism;

(b) the commitments of the United States to other nations;

(c) domestic needs and priorities; and

(d) the consequences of the cold war and the shooting war on American society.

VII. Contemporary Domestic Concerns

Earl Warren

DESEGREGATION OF PUBLIC SCHOOLS

❧{ *1954* }❧   SOON after the ending of the Civil War and the passage of the thirteenth, fourteenth, and fifteenth amendments, it became painfully clear to believers in equal rights for the blacks that mere constitutional pronunciamentoes were insufficient to achieve the objective they sought. For a time, through the use of armed force and through new legislation, Northern friends of the blacks continued the battle, but with the passage of years interest slackened and enthusiasm declined. The Supreme Court speeded this process along in two important late-nineteenth century decisions, the Civil Rights cases (1883) and *Plessy* v. *Ferguson* (1896), which held, in effect, that the owners of restaurants, theaters, trolley cars, and other business which catered to the general public could arbitrarily exclude blacks or segregate them from white patrons, and that in interstate transportation and in education, segregation of the races was legal so long as the blacks were provided with "separate but equal" accommodations.

Two World Wars, the concentrated force of world public opinion, increasing Negro discontent, and a variety of other causes gradually made this condition more and more intolerable. Increasingly it was apparent that "separate" facilities in the South were seldom "equal"; indeed, that the mere fact of separation, being itself degrading, made equality impossible. A series of Supreme Court decisions in the 1950's indicated a growing awareness of these truths, and then, in 1954, Chief Justice Earl Warren (1891–1974) dealt a death blow to segregation in the case of *Brown* v. *Board of Education of Topeka.*

The Brown case dealt only with segregation in the public schools and of course it is obvious that many men's minds were not changed by the Chief Justice's decision. The "death" of segregation has been anything but instantaneous. Nevertheless, since 1954 the movement for real equality has been gathering force year by year. One by one the bastions of segregation have crumbled. *Brown* v. *Topeka* marks a great turning point in our history, the full significance of which no one can yet appreciate.

BROWN v. BOARD OF EDUCATION OF TOPEKA

MR. CHIEF JUSTICE WARREN: These cases come to us from the States of Kansas, South Carolina, Virginia, and Delaware. They are premised on different facts and different local conditions, but a common legal question justifies their consideration together in this consolidated opinion.

In each of the cases, minors of the Negro race, through their legal representatives, seek the aid of the courts in obtaining admission to the public schools of their community on a nonsegregated basis. In each instance, they had been denied admission to schools attended by white children under laws requiring or permitting segregation according to race. This segregation was alleged to deprive the plaintiffs of the equal protection of the laws under the Fourteenth Amendment. In each of the cases other than the Delaware case, a three-judge federal district court denied relief to the plaintiffs on the so-called "separate but equal" doctrine announced by this Court in *Plessy vs. Ferguson,* 163 U.S. 537. Under that doctrine, equality of treatment is accorded when the races are provided substantially equal facilities, even though these facilities be separate. In the Delaware case, the Supreme Court of Delaware adhered to that doctrine, but ordered that the plaintiffs be admitted to the white schools because of their superiority to the Negro schools.

The plaintiffs contend that segregated public schools are not "equal" and cannot be made "equal," and that hence they are deprived of the equal protection of the laws. Because of the obvious importance of the question presented, the Court took jurisdiction. Argument was heard in the 1952 Term, and reargument was heard this Term on certain questions propounded by the Court.

Reargument was largely devoted to the circumstances surrounding the adoption of the Fourteenth Amendment in 1868. It covered exhaustively consideration of the Amendment in Congress, ratification by the states, then existing practices in racial segregation, and the views of proponents and opponents of the Amendment. This discussion and our own investigation convince us that, although these sources cast some light, it is not enough to resolve the problem with which we are faced. At best, they are inconclusive. The most avid proponents of the post-War Amendments undoubtedly intended them to remove all legal distinctions among "all persons born or naturalized in the United States." Their opponents, just as certainly, were antagonistic to both the letter and the spirit of the Amendments and wished them to have the most limited effect. What others in Congress and the state legislatures had in mind cannot be determined with any degree of certainty.

An additional reason for the inconclusive nature of the Amendment's history, with respect to segregated schools, is the status of public education at that time. In the South, the movement toward free common schools, supported by general taxation, had not yet taken hold. Education of white children was largely in the hands of private groups. Education of Negroes was almost nonexistent, and practically all of the race were illiterate. In fact, any education of Negroes was forbidden by law in some states. Today, in contrast, many Negroes have achieved outstanding success in the arts and sciences as well as in the business and professional world. It is true that public school education at the time of the Amendment had advanced further in the North, but the effect of the Amendment on Northern States was generally ignored in the congressional debates. Even in the North, the conditions of public education did not approximate those existing today. The curriculum was usually rudimentary; ungraded schools were common in rural areas; the school term was but three months a year in many states; and compulsory school attendance was virtually unknown. As a consequence, it is not surprising that there should be so little in the history of the Fourteenth Amendment relating to its intended effect on public education.

In the first cases in this Court construing the Fourteenth Amendment, decided shortly after its adoption, the Court interpreted it as proscribing all state-imposed discriminations against the Negro race. The doctrine of "separate but equal" did not make its appearance in this Court until 1896 in the case of *Plessy v. Ferguson, supra,* involving not education but transportation. American courts have since labored with the doctrine for over half a century. In this Court, there have been six cases involving the "separate but equal" doctrine in the field of public education. In *Cunning v. County Board of Education,* 175 U.S. 528, and *Gong Lum v. Rice,* 275 U.S. 78, the validity of the doctrine itself was not challenged. In more recent cases, all on the graduate school level, inequality was found in that specific benefits enjoyed by white students were denied to Negro students of the same educational qualifications. *Missouri ex rel. Gaines v. Canada,* 305 U.S. 337; *Sipuel v. Oklahoma,* 332 U.S. 631; *Sweatt v. Painter,* 339 U.S. 629; *McLaurin v. Oklahoma State Regents,* 339 U.S. 637. In none of these cases was it necessary to re-examine the doctrine to grant relief to the Negro plaintiff. And in *Sweatt v. Painter, supra,* the Court expressly reserved decision on the question whether *Plessy v. Ferguson* should be held inapplicable to the public education.

In the instant cases, that question is directly presented. Here, unlike *Sweatt v. Painter,* there are findings below that the Negro and white schools involved have been equalized, or are being equalized, with respect to buildings, curricula, qualifications and salaries of teachers, and other "tangible" factors. Our decision, therefore, cannot turn on merely a comparison of these tangible factors in the Negro and white schools involved in each of the cases. We must look instead to the effect of segregation itself on public education.

In approaching this problem, we cannot turn the clock back to 1868 when the Amendment was adopted, or even to 1896 when *Plessy v. Ferguson* was written. We must consider public education in the light of its full development and its present place in American life throughout the

Nation. Only in this way can it be determined if segregation in public schools deprives these plaintiffs of the equal protection of the laws.

Today, education is perhaps the most important function of state and local governments. Compulsory school attendance laws and the great expenditures for education both demonstrate our recognition of the importance of education to our democratic society. It is required in the performance of our most basic public responsibilities, even service in the armed forces. It is the very foundation of good citizenship. Today it is a principal instrument in awakening the child to cultural values, in preparing him for later professional training, and in helping him to adjust normally to his environment. In these days, it is doubtful that any child may reasonably be expected to succeed in life if he is denied the opportunity of an education. Such an opportunity, where the state has undertaken to provide it, is a right which must be made available to all on equal terms.

We come then to the question presented: Does segregation of children in public schools solely on the basis of race, even though the physical facilities and other "tangible" factors may be equal, deprive the children of the minority group of equal educational opportunities? We believe that it does.

In *Sweatt v. Painter, supra,* in finding that a segregated law school for Negroes could not provide them equal educational opportunities, this Court relied in large part on "those qualities which are incapable of objective measurement but which makes for greatness in a law school." In *McLaurin v. Oklahoma State Regents, supra,* the Court, in requiring that a Negro admitted to a white graduate school be treated like all other students, again resorted to intangible considerations: ". . . his ability to study, to engage in discussions and exchange views with other students, and, in general, to learn his profession." Such considerations apply with added force to children in grade and high schools. To separate them from others of similar age and qualifications solely because of their race generates a feeling of inferiority as to their status in the community that may affect their hearts and minds in a way unlikely ever to be undone. The effect of this separation on their educational opportunities was well stated by a finding in the Kansas case by a court which nevertheless felt compelled to rule against the Negro plaintiffs:

> Segregation of white and colored children in public schools has a detrimental effect upon the colored children. The impact is greater when it has the sanction of the law; for the policy of separating the races is usually interpreted as denoting the inferiority of the negro group. A sense of inferiority affects the motivation of a child to learn. Segregation with the

sanction of law, therefore, has a tendency to [retard] the education and mental development of negro children and to deprive them of some of the benefits they would receive in a racial[ly] integrated school system.

Whatever may have been the extent of psychological knowledge at the time of *Plessy v. Ferguson,* this finding is amply supported by modern authority. Any language in *Plessy v. Ferguson* contrary to this finding is rejected.

We conclude that in the field of public education the doctrine of "separate but equal" has no place. Separate educational facilities are inherently unequal. Therefore, we hold that the plaintiffs and others similarly situated for whom the actions have been brought are, by reasons of the segregation complained of, deprived of the equal protection of the laws guaranteed by the Fourteenth Amendment. This disposition makes unnecessary any discussion whether such segregation also violates the Due Process Clause of the Fourteenth Amendment.

Because these are class actions, because of the wide applicability of this decision, and because of the great variety of local conditions, the formulation of decrees in these cases presents problems of considerable complexity. On reargument, the consideration of appropriate relief was necessarily subordinated to the primary question — the constitutionality of segregation on public education. We have now announced that such segregation is a denial of the equal protection of the laws. . . .

Study Guide

1. Dominating the thirty years since World War II has been the problem of racial justice: the judicial decision to desegregate the schools (*Brown* v. *Topeka*); a nonviolent black response (Martin Luther King) and a militant one (S.N.C.C. Position Paper). Additionally there have appeared spokesmen for the poor (Michael Harrington) and for women (NOW).

2. We begin with the decision of the Supreme Court in the *Brown* v. *Board of Education* case of 1954. The introduction will provide you with the necessary historical background for understanding this landmark in American judicial history. Warren's decision includes:
    (a) a summary of the facts and the issue (pp. 523–524);
    (b) the arguments (pp. 524–526); and
    (c) the Court's decision (pp. 526–527).

3. Start by asking the following: What are the facts in the case and what is the issue? What did the plaintiffs contend and on what constitutional grounds? Look up the "equal-protection" clause of the Fourteenth Amend-

ment in the United States Constitution (usually found at the back of a text).

4. What is Warren's conclusion concerning the relevance of the intentions of the framers of the Fourteenth Amendment? What comments does he have on *Plessy* v. *Ferguson?* How does *Brown* v. *Board of Education* differ from *Sweatt* v. *Painter?* Explain.

5. On what grounds does Warren arrive at his decision; i.e., what is the essential question, as far as he is concerned, and the only answer? Here are the key sentences: "Does segregation of children in public schools solely on the basis of race, even though the physical facilities and other 'tangible' factors may be equal, deprive the children of the minority group of equal educational opportunities? We believe that it does."

6. What is the decision of the Court regarding the application of *Plessy* v. *Ferguson* to education?

7. Can you find parallels between the sociological arguments advanced by Warren for declaring school segregation unconstitutional and those of Charles Sumner in 1872 (pp. 29–41)? Explore and amplify.

Martin Luther King, Jr.

A WAY OUT FOR BLACK AMERICANS

⊰{1958}⊱   ON THE evening of December 1, 1955, Mrs. Rosa Parks of Montgomery, Alabama, left the downtown department store where she was employed as a seamstress and boarded a Cleveland Avenue bus. Being a black, she dutifully took a seat toward the rear, immediately behind the section reserved for white passengers. Soon, however, as homeward-bound workers and shoppers crowded aboard, the white section of the bus became filled, and then, following long-established regulations, the driver ordered Mrs. Parks and three other blacks to give up their places. The others complied but Mrs. Parks refused to move. As a result, upon the driver's complaint, she was arrested.

Previously other blacks had rebelled against the Montgomery ordinance segregating city buses, but the case of Mrs. Parks was different. She was a woman of impeccable reputation, widely known in the community for her work in the National Association for the Advancement of Colored People. So, too, the times were different. The local blacks' long-smothered hopes for improving their lot had been revived by the then-recent Supreme Court decision in the case of *Brown* v. *Topeka,* pointing toward the desegregation of public schools. In any case, a handful of leading blacks hurriedly organized a boycott of the buses to protest against segregation and Mrs. Parks's arrest. The response was immediate and enthusiastic; when the buses rolled on Monday morning, December 5, scarcely a black in the community was aboard. Soon newspapers all over the land were headlining the Montgomery "bus strike." With amazing self-discipline and orderliness, the blacks of Montgomery held to their refusal to ride on segregated buses for over a year. Finally, after a Supreme Court decision outlawing the segregation ordinance, their fight was won.

Among the leaders in this long struggle was a young Baptist minister named Martin Luther King, Jr. (1929–1968). It was King who turned the movement from a militant boycott into a crusade, and he did so by stressing passive resistance as a general device for protesting the mistreatment of the black race. His book describing the struggle, *Stride Toward Freedom,* attracted wide notice and played a major role on the development of the "sit in" technique that has been used so effectively in the drive to desegregate lunch counters and other public facilities in the South. In the following selection from that book, the Reverend Mr. King explains how he came to espouse the philosophy of passive resistance.

PILGRIMAGE TO NONVIOLENCE

OFTEN the question has arisen concerning my own intellectual pilgrimage to nonviolence. In order to get at this question it is necessary to go back to my early teens in Atlanta. I had grown up abhorring not only segregation but also the oppressive and barbarous acts that grew out of it. I had passed spots where Negroes had been savagely lynched, and had watched the Ku Klux Klan on its rides at night. I had seen police brutality with my own eyes, and watched Negroes receive the most tragic injustice in the courts. All of these things had done something to my growing personality. I had come perilously close to resenting all white people.

I had also learned that the inseparable twin of racial injustice was economic injustice. Although I came from a home of economic security and relative comfort, I could never get out of my mind the economic insecurity of many of my playmates and the tragic poverty of those living around me. During my late teens I worked two summers, against my father's wishes — he never wanted my brother and me to work around white people because of the oppressive conditions — in a plant that hired both Negroes and whites. Here I saw economic injustice firsthand, and realized that the poor white was exploited just as much as the Negro. Through these early experiences I grew up deeply conscious of the varieties of injustice in our society.

So when I went to Atlanta's Morehouse College as a freshman in 1944 my concern for racial and economic justice was already substantial. During my student days at Morehouse I read Thoreau's *Essay on Civil Disobedience* for the first time. Fascinated by the idea of refusing to coöperate with an evil system, I was so deeply moved that I reread the work several times. This was my first intellectual contact with the theory of nonviolent resistance.

Not until I entered Crozer Theological Seminary in 1948, however, did I begin a serious intellectual quest for a method to eliminate social evil. Although my major interest was in the fields of theology and philosophy, I spent a great deal of time reading the works of the great social philosophers. I came early to Walter Rauschenbusch's *Christianity and the Social Crisis,* which left an indelible imprint on my thinking by giving me a theological basis for the social concern which had already grown up in me as a result of my early experiences. Of course there were points at which I differed with Rauschenbusch. I felt that he had fallen victim to the nineteenth-century "cult of inevitable progress" which led him to a superficial optimism concerning man's nature. Moreover, he came perilously close to identifying the Kingdom of God with a particular social and economic system — a tendency which should never befall the Church. But in spite of these shortcomings Rauschenbusch had done a great service for the Christian Church by insisting that the gospel deals with the whole man, not only his soul but his body; not only his spiritual well-being but his material well-being. It has been my conviction ever since reading Rauschenbusch that any religion which professes to be concerned about the souls of men and is not concerned about the social and economic conditions that scar the soul, is a spiritually moribund religion only waiting for the day to be buried. It well has been said: "A religion that ends with the individual, ends."

After reading Rauschenbusch, I turned to a serious study of the social and ethical theories of the great philosophers, from Plato and Aristotle down to Rousseau, Hobbes, Bentham, Mill, and Locke. All of these masters stimulated my thinking — such as it was — and, while finding things to question in each of them, I nevertheless learned a great deal from their study.

During the Christmas holidays of 1949 I decided to spend my spare time reading Karl Marx to try to understand the appeal of communism for many people. For the first time I carefully scrutinized *Das Kapital* and *The Communist Manifesto.* I also read some interpretive works on the thinking of Marx and Lenin. In reading such Communist writings I drew certain conclusions that have remained with me as convictions to this day. First I rejected their materialistic interpretation of history. Communism, avowedly secularistic and materialistic, has no place for God. This I could never accept, for as a Christian I believe that there is a creative personal power in this universe who is the ground and essence of all reality — a power that cannot be explained in materialistic terms. History is ultimately guided by spirit, not matter. Second, I strongly disagreed with communism's ethical relativism. Since for the Communist there is no divine government, no absolute moral order, there are no fixed, immutable principles; consequently almost anything — force, violence, murder, lying — is a justifiable means to the "millennial" end. This type of relativism was abhorrent to me. Constructive ends can never give absolute moral justification to destructive means, because in the final analysis the end is preëxistent in the mean. Third, I opposed communism's political totalitarianism. In communism the individual ends up in subjection to the state. True, the Marxist would argue that the state is an "interim" reality which is to be eliminated when the classless society emerges; but the state is the end while it lasts, and man only a means to that end. And if any man's so-called rights or liberties stand in the way of that end, they are simply swept aside. His liberties of expression, his freedom to vote, his freedom to listen to what news he likes or to choose his books are all restricted. Man becomes hardly more, in communism, than a depersonalized cog in the turning wheel of the state.

This deprecation of individual freedom was objectionable to me. I am convinced now, as I was then, that man is an end because he is a child of God. Man is not made for the state; the state is made for man. To deprive man of freedom is to relegate him to the status of a thing, rather than elevate him to the status a person. Man must never be treated as a means to the end of the state, but always as an end within himself.

Yet, in spite of the fact that my response to communism was and is negative, and I considered it basically evil, there were points at which I found it challenging. The late Archbishop of Canterbury, William Temple, referred to communism as a Christian heresy. By this he meant that communism had laid hold of certain truths which are essential parts of the Christian view of things, but that it had bound up with them concepts and practices which no Christian could ever accept or profess. Communism challenged the late Archbishop and it should challenge every Christian — as it challenged me — to a growing concern about social justice. With all of its false assumptions and evil methods, communism grew as a protest against the hardships of the underprivileged. Communism in theory emphasized a classless society, and a concern for social justice, though the world knows from sad experience that in practice it created new classes and a new lexicon of injustice. The Christian ought always to be challenged by any protest against unfair treatment of the poor, for Christianity is itself such a protest, nowhere expressed more eloquently than in Jesus' words: "The Spirit of the Lord is upon me, because he hath anointed me to preach the gospel to the poor; he hath sent me to heal the brokenhearted, to preach deliverance to the captives, and recovering of sight to the blind, to set at liberty them that are bruised, to preach the acceptable year of the Lord."

I also sought systematic answers to Marx's critique of modern bourgeois culture. He presented capitalism as essentially a struggle between the owners of the productive resources and the workers, whom Marx regarded as the real producers. Marx interpreted economic forces as the dialectical process by which society moved from feudalism through capitalism to socialism, with the primary mechanism of this historical movement being the struggle between economic classes whose interests were irreconcilable. Obviously this theory left out of account the numerous and significant complexities — political, economic, moral, religious, and psychological — which played a vital role in shaping the constellation of institutions and ideas known today as Western civilization. Moreover, it was dated in the sense that the capitalism Marx wrote about bore only a partial resemblance to the capitalism we know in this country today.

But in spite of the shortcomings of his analysis, Marx had raised some basic questions. I was deeply concerned from my early teen days about the gulf between superfluous wealth and abject poverty, and my reading of Marx made me ever more conscious of this gulf. Although modern American capitalism had greatly reduced the gap through social reforms, there was still need for a better distribution of wealth. Moreover, Marx had revealed the danger of the profit motive as the sole basis of an economic system: capitalism is always in danger of inspiring men to be more concerned about making a living than making a life. We are prone to judge success by the index of our salaries or the size of our automobiles, rather than by the quality of our service and relationship to humanity — thus capitalism can lead to a practical materialism that is as pernicious as the materialism taught by communism.

In short, I read Marx as I read all of the influential historical thinkers — from a dialectical point of view, combining a partial yes and a partial no. In so far as Marx posited a metaphysical materialism, an ethical relativism, and a strangulating totalitarianism, I responded with an unambiguous "no"; but in so far as he pointed to weaknesses of traditional capitalism, contributed to the growth of a definite self-consciousness in the masses, and challenged the social conscience of the Christian churches. I responded with a definite "yes."

My reading of Marx also convinced me that truth is found neither in Marxism nor in traditional capitalism. Each represents a partial truth. Historically capitalism failed to see the truth in collective enterprise and Marxism failed to see the truth in individual enterprise. Nineteenth-century capitalism failed to see that life is social and Marxism failed and still fails to see that life is individual and personal. The Kingdom of God is neither the thesis of individual enterprise nor the antithesis of collective enterprise, but a synthesis which reconciles the truths of both.

During my stay at Crozer, I was also exposed for the first time to the pacifist position in a lecture by Dr. A. J. Muste. I was deeply moved by Dr. Muste's talk, but far from convinced of the practicability of his position. Like most of the students of Crozer, I felt that while war could never be a positive or absolute good, it could serve as a negative good in the sense of preventing the spread and growth of an evil force. War, horrible as it is, might be preferable to surrender to a totalitarian system — Nazi, Fascist, or Communist.

During this period I had about despaired of the power of love in solving social problems. Perhaps my faith in love was temporarily shaken by the philosophy of Nietzsche. I had been reading parts of *The Genealogy of Morals* and the whole of *The Will to Power*. Nietzsche's glorification of power — in his theory all life expressed the will to power — was an outgrowth of his contempt for ordinary morals. He attacked the whole of the Hebraic-Christian morality — with its virtues of piety and humility, its otherworldliness and its attitude toward suffering — as the glorification of weakness, as making virtues out of necessity and impotence. He looked to the development of a superman who would surpass man as man surpassed the ape.

Then one Sunday afternoon I traveled to Philadelphia to hear a sermon by Dr. Mordecai Johnson, president of Howard University. He was there to preach for the Fellowship House of Philadelphia. Dr. Johnson had just returned from a trip to India, and, to my great interest, he spoke of the life and teachings of Mahatma Gandhi. His message was so profound and electrifying that I left the meeting and bought a half-dozen books on Gandhi's life and works.

Like most people, I had heard of Gandhi, but I had never studied him seriously. As I read I became deeply fascinated by his campaigns of non-violent resistance. I was particularly moved by the Salt March to the Sea and his numerous fasts. The whole concept of "Satyagraha" (*Satya* is truth which equals love, and *agraha* is force; "Satyagraha," therefore, means truth-force or love force) was profoundly significant to me. As I delved deeper into the philosophy of Gandhi my skepticism concerning the power of love gradually diminished, and I came to see for the first time its potency in the area of social reform. Prior to reading Gandhi, I had about concluded that the ethics of Jesus were only effective in individual relationship. The "turn the other cheek" philosophy and the "love your enemies" philosophy were only valid, I felt, when individuals were in conflict with other individuals; when racial groups and nations were in conflict a more realistic approach seemed necessary. But after reading Gandhi, I saw how utterly mistaken I was.

Gandhi was probably the first person in history to lift the love ethic of Jesus above mere interaction between individuals to a powerful and effective social force on a large scale. Love for Gandhi was a potent instrument for social and collective transformation. It was in this Gandhian emphasis on love and nonviolence that I discovered the method for social reform that I had been seeking for so many months. The intellectual and moral satisfaction that I failed to gain from the utilitarianism of Bentham and Mill, the revolutionary methods of Marx and Lenin, the social-contracts theory of Hobbes, the "back to nature" optimism of Rousseau, and the superman philosophy of Nietzsche, I found in the nonviolent resistance philosophy of Gandhi. I came to feel that this was the only morally and practically sound method open to oppressed people in their struggle for freedom.

But my intellectual odyssey to nonviolence did not end here. During my last year in theological school, I began to read the works of Reinhold Niebuhr. The prophetic and realistic elements in Niebuhr's passionate style and profound thought were appealing to me, and I became so enamored of his social ethics that I almost fell into the trap of accepting uncritically everything he wrote.

About this time I read Niebuhr's critique of the pacifist position. Niebuhr had himself once been a member of the pacifist ranks. For several years, he had been national chairman of the Fellowship of Reconciliation. His break with pacifism came in the early thirties, and the first full statement of his criticism of pacifism was in *Moral Man and Immoral Society*. Here he argued that there was no intrinsic moral difference between violent and nonviolent resistance. The social consequences of the two methods were different, he contended, but the differences were in degree rather than kind. Later Niebuhr began emphasizing the irresponsibility of relying on nonviolent resistance when there was no ground for believing that it would be successful in preventing the spread of totalitarian tyranny. It could only be successful, he argued, if the groups against whom the resistance was taking place had some degree of moral conscience, as was the case in Gandhi's struggle against the British. Niebuhr's ultimate rejection of pacifism was based primarily on the doctrine of man. He argued that pacifism failed to do justice to the reformation doctrine of justification by faith, substituting for it a sectarian perfectionism which believes "that divine grace actually lifts men out of the sinful contradictions of history and establishes him above the sins of the world."

At first, Niebuhr's critique of pacifism left me in a state of confusion. As I continued to read, however, I came to see more and more the shortcomings of his position. For instance, many of his statements revealed that he interpreted pacifism as a sort of passive nonresistance to evil expressing naïve trust in the power of love. But this was a serious distortion. My study of Gandhi convinced me that true pacifism is not nonresistance to evil, but nonviolent resistance to evil. Between the two positions, there is a world of difference. Gandhi resisted evil with as much vigor and power as the violent resister, but he resisted with love instead of hate. True pacifism is not unrealistic submission to evil power, as Niebuhr contends. It is rather a courageous confrontation of evil by the power of love, in the faith that it is better to be the recipient of violence than the inflicter of it, since the latter only multiplies the existence of violence and bitterness in the universe, while the former may develop a sense of shame in the opponent, and thereby bring about a transformation and change of heart.

In spite of the fact that I found many things to be desired in Niebuhr's philosophy, there were several points at which he constructively influenced my thinking. Niebuhr's great contribution to contemporary theology is that he has refuted the false optimism characteristic of a great segment of Protestant liberalism, without falling into the anti-rationalism of the continental theologian Karl Barth, or the semi-fundamentalism of other dialectical theologians. Moreover, Niebuhr has extraordinary insight into human nature, especially the behavior of nations and social groups. He is keenly aware of the complexity of human motives and of the relation between morality and power. His theology is a persistent reminder of the reality of sin on every level of man's existence. These elements in Niebuhr's thinking helped me to recognize the illusions of a superficial optimism concerning human nature and the dangers of a false idealism. While I still believed in man's potential for good, Niebuhr made me realize his potential for evil as well. Moreover, Niebuhr helped me to recognize the complexity of man's social involvement and the glaring reality of collective evil.

Many pacifists, I felt, failed to see this. All too many had an unwarranted optimism concerning man and leaned unconsciously toward self-righteousness. It was my revolt against these attitudes under the influence of Niebuhr that accounts for the fact that in spite of my strong leaning toward pacifism, I never joined a pacifist organization. After reading Niebuhr, I tried to arrive at a realistic pacifism. In other words, I came to see the pacifist position not as sinless but as the lesser evil in the circumstances. I felt then, and I feel now, that the pacifist would have a greater appeal if he did not claim to be free from the moral dilemmas that the Christian nonpacifist confronts.

The next stage of my intellectual pilgrimage to nonviolence came during my doctoral studies at Boston University. Here I had the opportunity to talk to many exponents of nonviolence, both students and visitors to the campus. Boston University School of Theology, under the influence of Dean Walter Muelder and Professor Allen Knight Chalmers, had a deep sympathy for pacifism. Both Dean Muelder and Dr. Chalmers had a passion for social justice that stemmed, not from a superficial optimism, but from a deep faith in the possibilities of human beings when they allowed themselves to become co-workers with God. It was at Boston University that I came to see that Niebuhr had overemphasized the corruption of human nature. His pessimism concerning human nature was not balanced by an optimism concerning divine nature. He was so involved in diagnosing man's sickness of sin that he overlooked the cure of grace.

I studied philosophy and theology at Boston University under Edgar S. Brightman and L. Harold DeWolf. Both men greatly stimulated my thinking. It was mainly under these teachers that I studied personalistic philosophy — the theory that the clue to the meaning of ultimate reality is found in personality. This personal idealism remains today my basic philosophical position. Personalism's insistence that only personality — finite and infinite — is ultimately real strengthened me in two convictions: it gave me metaphysical and philosophical grounding for the idea of a personal God, and it gave me a metaphysical basis for the dignity and worth of all human personality.

Just before Dr. Brightman's death, I began studying the philosophy of Hegel with him. Although the course was mainly a study of Hegel's monumental work, *Phenomenology of Mind,* I spent my spare time reading his *Philosophy of History* and *Philosophy of Right.* There were points in Hegel's philosophy that I strongly disagreed with. For instance, his absolute idealism was rationally unsound to me because it tended to swallow up the many in the one. But there were other aspects of his thinking that I found stimulating. His contention that "truth is the whole" led me to a philosophical method of rational coherence. His analysis of the dialectical process, in spite of its shortcomings, helped me to see that growth comes through struggle.

In 1954 I ended my formal training with all of these relatively divergent intellectual forces converging into a positive social philosophy. One of the main tenets of this philosophy was the conviction that nonviolent resistance was one of the most potent weapons available to oppressed people in their quest for social justice. At this time, however, I had merely an intellectual understanding and appreciation of the position, with no firm determination to organize it in a socially effective situation.

When I went to Montgomery as a pastor, I had not the slightest idea that I would later become involved in a crisis in which nonviolent resistance would be applicable. I neither started the protest nor suggested it. I simply responded to the call of the people for a spokesman. When the protest began, my mind, consciously or unconsciously, was driven back to the Sermon on the Mount, with its sublime teachings on love, and the Gandhian method of nonviolent resistance. As the days unfolded, I came to see the power of nonviolence more and more. Living through the actual experience of the protest, nonviolence became more than a method to which I gave intellectual assent; it became a commitment to a way of life. Many of the things that I had not cleared up intellectually concerning nonviolence were now solved in the sphere of practical action.

Since the philosophy of nonviolence played such a positive role in the Montgomery Movement, it may be wise to turn to a brief discussion of some basic aspects of this philosophy.

First, it must be emphasized that nonviolent resistance is not a method for cowards; it does resist. If one uses this method because he is afraid or merely because he lacks the instruments of violence, he is not truly nonviolent. This is why Gandhi often said that if cowardice is the only alternative to violence, it is better to fight. He made this statement conscious of the fact that there is always another alternative; no individual or group need submit to any wrong, nor need they use violence to right the wrong; there is the way of nonviolence resistance. This is ultimately the way of the strong man. It is not a method of stagnant passivity. The phrase "passive resistance" often gives the false impression that this is a sort of "do-nothing method" in which the resister quietly and passively accepts evil. But nothing is further from the truth. For while the nonviolent resister is passive in the sense that he is not physically aggressive toward his opponent, his mind and emotions are always active, constantly seeking to persuade his opponent that he is wrong. The method is passive physically, but strongly active spiritually. It is not passive non-resistance to evil, it is active nonviolent resistance to evil.

A second basic fact that characterizes nonviolence is that it does not seek to defeat or humiliate the opponent, but to win his friendship and understanding. The nonviolent resister must often express his protest through noncoöperation or boycotts, but he realizes that these are not ends themselves; they are merely means to awaken a sense of moral shame in the opponent. The end is redemption and reconciliation. The aftermath of nonviolence is the creation of the beloved community, while the aftermath of violence is tragic bitterness.

A third characteristic of this method is that the attack is directed against forces of evil rather than against persons who happen to be doing the evil. It is evil that the nonviolent resister seeks to defeat, not the persons victimized by evil. If he is opposing racial injustice, the nonviolent resister has the vision to see that the basic tension is not between races. As I like to say to the people in Montgomery: "The tension in this city is not between white people and Negro people. The tension is, at bottom, between justice and injustice, between the forces of light and the forces of darkness. And if there is a victory, it will be victory not merely for fifty thousand Negroes, but a victory for justice and the forces of light. We are out to defeat injustice and not white persons who may be unjust."

A fourth point that characterizes nonviolent resistance is a willingness to accept suffering without retaliation, to accept blows from the opponent without striking back. "Rivers of blood may have to flow before we gain our freedom, but it must be our blood," Gandhi said to his countrymen. The nonviolent resister is willing to accept violence if necessary, but never to inflict it. He does not seek to dodge jail. If going to jail is necessary, he enters it "as a bridegroom enters the bride's chamber."

One may well ask: "What is the nonviolent resister's justification for this ordeal to which he invites men, for this mass political application of the ancient doctrine of turning the other cheek?" The answer is found in the realization that unearned suffering is redemptive. Suffering, the nonviolent resister realizes, has tremendous educational and transforming possibilities. "Things of fundamental importance to people are not secured by reason alone, but have to be purchased with their suffering," said Gandhi. He continues: "Suffering is infinitely more powerful than the law of the jungle for converting the opponent and opening his ears which are otherwise shut to the voice of reason."

A fifth point concerning nonviolent resistance is that it avoids not only external physical violence but also internal violence of spirit. The nonviolent resister not only refuses to shoot his opponent but he also refuses to hate him. At the center of nonviolence stands the principle of love. The nonviolent resister would contend that in the struggle for human dignity, the oppressed people of the world must not succumb to the temptation of becoming bitter or indulging in hate campaigns. To retaliate in kind would do nothing but intensify the existence of hate in the universe. Along the way of life, someone must have sense enough and morality enough to cut off the chain of hate. This can only be done by projecting the ethic of love to the center of our lives.

In speaking of love at this point, we are not referring to some sentimental or affectionate emotion. It would be nonsense to urge men to love their oppressors in an affectionate sense. Love in this connection means understanding, redemptive good will. Here the Greek language comes to our aid. There are three words for love in the Greek New Testament. First, there is *eros*. In Platonic philosophy *eros* meant the yearning of the soul for the realm of the divine. It has now come to a sort of aesthetic or romantic love. Second, there is *philia* which means intimate affection between personal friends. *Philia* denotes a sort of reciprocal love; the person loves because he is loved. When we speak of loving those who oppose us, we refer to neither *eros* nor *philia;* we speak of a love which is expressed in the Greek word *agape*. *Agape* means understanding, redeeming good will for all men. It is an overflowing love which is purely spontaneous, unmotivated, groundless, and creative. It is not set in motion by any quality or function of its object. It is the love of God operating in the human heart.

Agape is disinterested love. It is a love in which the individual seeks not his own good, but the good of his neighbor (1 Cor. 10:24). *Agape* does not begin by discriminating between worthy and unworthy people, or any qualities people possess. It begins by loving others *for their sakes*. It is an entirely "neighbor-regarding concern for others," which discovers the neighbor in every man it meets. Therefore, *agape* makes no distinction between friend and enemy; it is directed toward both. If one loves an individual merely on account of his friendliness, he loves him for the sake of the benefits to be gained from the friendship, rather than for the friend's own sake. Consequently, the best way to assure oneself that Love is disinterested is to have love for the enemy-neighbor from whom you can expect no good in return, but only hostility and persecution.

Another basic point about *agape* is that it springs from the *need* of the other person — his need for belonging to the best in the human family. The Samaritan who helped the Jew on the Jericho Road was "good" because he responded to the human need that he was presented with. God's love is eternal and fails not because man needs his love. St. Paul assures us that the loving act of redemption was done "while we were yet sinners" — that is, at the point of our greatest need for love. Since the white man's personality is greatly distorted by segregation, and his soul is greatly scarred, he needs the love of the Negro. The Negro must love the white man, because the white man needs his love to remove his tensions, insecurities, and fears.

Agape is not a weak, passive love. It is love in action. *Agape* is love seeking to preserve and create community. It is insistence on community even when one seeks to break it. *Agape* is a willingness to sacrifice in the interest of mutuality. *Agape* is a willingness to go to any length to restore community. It doesn't stop at the first mile, but it goes the second mile to restore community. It is a willingness to forgive, not seven times, but seventy times seven to restore community. The cross is the eternal expression of the length to which God will go in order to restore broken community. The resurrection is a symbol of God's triumph over all the forces that seek to block community. The Holy Spirit is the continuing community creating reality that moves through history. He who works against community is working against the whole of creation. Therefore, if I respond to hate with a reciprocal hate I do nothing but intensify the cleavage in broken community. I can only close the gap in broken community by meeting hate with love. If I meet hate with hate, I become depersonalized, because creation is so designed that my personality can only be fulfilled in the context of community. Booker T. Washington was right: "Let no man pull you so low as to make you hate him." When he pulls you that low he brings you to the point of working against community; he drags you to the point of defying creation, and thereby becoming depersonalized.

In the final analysis, *agape* means a recognition of the fact that all life is interrelated. All humanity is involved in a single process, and all men are brothers. To the degree that I harm my brother, no matter what he is doing to me, to that extent I am harming myself. For example, white men often refuse federal aid to education in order to avoid giving the Negro his rights; but because all men are brothers they cannot deny Negro children without harming their own. They end, all efforts to the contrary, by hurting themselves. Why is this? Because men are brothers. If you harm me, you harm yourself.

Love, *agape,* is the only cement that can hold this broken community together. When I am commanded to love, I am commanded to restore community, to resist injustice, and to meet the needs of my brothers.

A sixth basic fact about nonviolent resistance is that it is based on the conviction that the universe is on the side of justice. Consequently, the believer in nonviolence has deep faith in the future. This faith is another reason why the nonviolent resister can accept suffering without retaliation. For he knows that in his struggle for justice he has cosmic companionship. It is true that there are devout believers in nonviolence who find it difficult to believe in a personal God. But even these persons believe in the existence of some creative force that works for universal wholeness. Whether we call it an unconscious process, an impersonal Brahman, or a Personal Being of matchless power and infinite love, there is a creative force in this universe that works to bring the disconnected aspects of reality into a harmonious whole.

Study Guide

1. This essay contains two sections: the first is an autobiographical narrative of how King came to a philosophy of nonviolence (pp. 529–537), and the second half is a statement of that position (pp. 537–541). Trace King's reading and reasoning through his assessments of and his relationships to Thoreau, Rauschenbusch, Marx, Nietzsche, Gandhi, Niebuhr, and Brightman by answering the following:

   (a) From your text, find out when and why Thoreau wrote *Civil Disobedience*. Why would this piece appeal to young King?

   (b) Summarize what in the social gospel of Walter Rauschenbusch attracted King.

   (c) Obviously, King disagrees with the notions of Marx. Outline his objection to communism as a social philosophy. What, however, in Marx's writings does King find worth salvaging?

   (d) Why did Nietzsche's philosophy unnerve King momentarily?

   (e) In the life and career of Gandhi, King found a source of inspiration and social reform. Explain. Similarly, what did he learn from the writings of Rheinhold Niebuhr and Edgar S. Brightman?

   (f) Summarize the position King came to as he began his ministry in Atlanta.

2. Outline King's philosophy of nonviolence.

   (a) What distinctions does King draw between *eros, philia,* and *agape*?

   (b) What are the implications of *agape* according to King?

Student Nonviolent Coordinating Committee

BLACK POWER

❈{ *1966* }❈   A DECISIVE shift in the black revolution occurred in the mid-1960's. The nonviolence preached by Martin Luther King, so evident in the sit-in movement earlier in the decade, began to give way to violent protest.

In the summer months, blacks in city ghettoes rioted against the slum conditions that neither the Civil Rights Act nor the war on poverty had altered. Bloody upheavals in New York's Harlem in 1964 and in the Watts district of Los Angeles in 1965 began a pattern of destruction that was repeated summer after summer in cities across the nation.

A new militancy also entered into the civil rights movement. Black racists, notably the Black Muslims and the followers of Malcolm X, had originally been shunned by civil rights leaders. But in May 1966 Stokely Carmichael (1941–   ), a native of Trinidad who had lived both in segregated Harlem and a white neighborhood in the Bronx, gained control of the Student Nonviolent Coordinating Committee. Carmichael was a student at Howard University when he joined the movement in 1961, and over the next five years he participated in the Southern sit-in campaigns, going to jail twenty-seven times, once for forty-five days in the Mississippi state penitentiary. In June 1966 Carmichael came forward with the Black Power slogan during demonstrations in Mississippi as he warned blacks that they could never rely on whites in their struggle for freedom. He was the prime mover in preparing the following position paper adopted by S.N.C.C. in early August 1966.

POSITION PAPER

THE MYTH that the Negro is somehow incapable of liberating himself, is lazy, etc., came out of the American experience. In the books that children read, whites are always "good" (good symbols are white), blacks are "evil" or seen as savages in movies, their language is referred to as a "dialect," and black people in this country are supposedly descended from savages.

Any white person who comes into the movement has these concepts in his mind about black people if only subconsciously. He cannot escape them because the whole society has geared his subconscious in that direction.

Miss America coming from Mississippi has a chance to represent all of America, but a black person from either Mississippi or New York will never represent America. So that white people coming into the movement cannot relate to the black experience, cannot relate to the word "black," cannot relate to the "nitty gritty," cannot relate to the experience that brought such a word into being, cannot relate to chitterlings, hog's head cheese, pig feet, hamhocks, and cannot relate to slavery, because these things are not a part of their experience. They also cannot relate to the black religious experience, nor to the black church unless, of course, this church has taken on white manifestations.

Negroes in this country have never been allowed to organize themselves because of white interference. As a result of this, the stereotype has been reinforced that blacks cannot organize themselves. The white psychology that blacks have to be watched, also reinforces this stereotype. Blacks, in fact, feel intimidated by the presence of whites, because of their knowledge of the power that whites have over their lives. One white person can come into a meeting of black people and change the complexion of that meeting, whereas one black person would not change the complexion of that meeting unless he was an obvious Uncle Tom. People would immediately start talking about "brotherhood," "love," etc.; race would not be discussed.

If people must express themselves freely, there has to be a climate in which they can do this. If blacks feel intimidated by whites, then they are not liable to vent the rage that they feel about whites in the presence of whites — especially not the black people whom we are trying to organize, i.e., the broad masses of black people. A climate has to be created whereby blacks can express themselves. The reason that whites must be excluded is not that one is anti-white, but because the efforts that one is trying to achieve cannot succeed because whites have an intimidating effect. Qfttimes the intimidating effect is in direct proportion to the amount of degradation that black people have suffered at the hands of white people.

It must be offered that white people who desire change in this country should go where that problem (of racism) is most manifest. The problem is not in the black community. The white people should go into white communities where the whites have created power for the express [purpose] of denying blacks human dignity and self-determination. Whites who come into the black community with ideas of change seem to want to absolve the power structure of its responsibility of what it is doing, and saying that change can come only through black unity, which is only the worst kind of paternalism. This is not to say that whites have not had an important role in the movement. In the case of Mississippi, their role was very key in that they helped give blacks the right to organize, but that role is now over, and it should be.

People now have the right to picket, the right to give out leaflets, the right to vote, the right to demonstrate, the right to print.

These things which revolve around the right to organize have been accomplished mainly because of the entrance of white people into Mississippi, in the summer of '64. Since these goals have now been accomplished, their (whites') role in the movement has now ended. What does it mean if black people, once having the right to organize, are not allowed to organize themselves? It means that blacks' ideas about inferiority are being reinforced. Shouldn't people be able to organize themselves? Blacks should be given this right. Further (white participation) means in the eyes of the black community that whites are the "brains" behind the movement and blacks cannot function without whites. This only serves to perpetuate existing attitudes within the existing society, i.e., blacks are "dumb," "unable to take care of business," etc. Whites are "smart," the "brains" behind everything.

How do blacks relate to other blacks as such? How do we react to Willie Mays as against Mickey Mantle? What is our response to Mays hitting a home run against Mantle performing the same deed? One has to come to the conclusion that it is because of black participation in baseball. Negroes still identify with the Dodgers because of Jackie Robinson's efforts with the Dodgers. Negroes would instinctively champion all-black teams if they opposed all-white or predominantly white teams. The same principle operates for the movement as it does for baseball: a mystique must be created whereby Negroes can identify with the movement.

Thus an all-black project is needed in order for the people to free themselves. This has to exist from the beginning. This relates to what can be called "coalition politics." There is no doubt in our minds that some whites are just as disgusted with this system as we are. But it is meaningless to talk about coalition if there is no one to align ourselves with, because of the lack of organization in the white communities. There can be no talk of "hooking up" unless black people organize blacks and white people organize whites. If these conditions are met then perhaps at some later date — and if we are going in the same direction — talks about exchange of personnel, coalition, and other meaningful alliances can be discussed.

In the beginning of the movement, we had fallen into a trap whereby we thought that our problems revolved around the right to eat at certain lunch counters or the right to vote, or to organize our communities. We have seen, however, that the problem is much deeper. The problem of this country, as we had seen it, concerned all blacks and all whites (and therefore) if decisions were left to the young people, then solutions would be arrived at. But this negates the history of black people and whites. We have dealt stringently with the problem of "Uncle Tom," but we have not yet gotten around to Simon Legree. We must ask ourselves who is the real villain? Uncle Tom or Simon Legree? Everybody knows Uncle Tom but who knows Simon Legree?

So what we have now (in S.N.C.C.) is a closed society. A clique. Black people cannot relate to S.N.C.C., because of its unrealistic, nonracial atmosphere; denying their experiences of America as a racist society. In contrast, S.C.L.C. [the Rev. Martin Luther King, Jr.'s Southern Christian Leadership Conference] has a staff that at least maintains a black façade.

The front office is virtually all-black, but nobody accuses S.C.L.C. of being racist.

If we are to proceed toward true liberation, we must cut ourselves off from white people. We must form our own institutions, credit unions, co-ops, political parties, write our own histories.

To proceed further let us make some comparisons between the Black Movement of the (early) 1900's and the movement of the 1960's — the N.A.A.C.P. [the National Association for the Advancement of Colored People] with S.N.C.C. Whites subverted the Niagara movement [the forerunner of the N.A.A.C.P.] which, at the outset, was an all-black movement. The name of the new organization was also very revealing, in that it pre-supposed blacks have to be advanced to the level of whites. We are now aware that the N.A.A.C.P. has grown reactionary, is controlled by the black power structure itself, and stands as one of the main roadblocks to black freedom. S.N.C.C., by allowing the whites to remain in the organization, can have its efforts subverted in the same manner, i.e., through having them play important roles such as community organizers, etc. Indigenous leadership cannot be built with whites in the positions they now hold.

These facts do not mean that whites cannot help. They can participate on a voluntary basis. We can contract work out to them, but in no way can they participate on a policy-making level.

The charge may be made that we are "racists," but whites who are sensitive to our problems will realize that we must determine our own destiny.

In an attempt to find a solution to our dilemma, we propose that our organization (S.N.C.C.) should be black-staffed, black-controlled and black-financed. We do not want to fall into a similar dilemma that other civil rights organizations have fallen. If we continue to rely upon white financial support we will find ourselves entwined in the tentacles of the white power complex that controls this country. It is also important that a black organization (devoid of cultism) be projected to our people so that it can be demonstrated that such organizations are viable.

More and more we see black people in this country being used as a tool of the white liberal establishment. Liberal whites have not begun to address themselves to the real problem of black people in this country; witness their bewilderment, fear and anxiety when nationalism is mentioned concerning black people. An analysis of their (white liberal) reaction to the word alone (nationalism) reveals a very meaningful attitude of whites of any ideological persuasion toward blacks in this country. It means previous solutions to black problems in this country have been made in the interests of those whites dealing with these problems and not in the best interests of black people in this country. Whites can only subvert our true search and struggle for self-determination, self-identification, and liberation in this country. Re-evaluation of the white and black roles must NOW take place so that whites no longer designate roles that black people play but rather black people define white people's roles.

Too long have we allowed white people to interpret the importance and meaning of the cultural aspects of our society. We have allowed them to tell us what was good about our Afro-American music, art and literature. How many black critics do we have on the "jazz" scene? How can a white person who is not a part of the black psyche (except in the oppressor's role) interpret the meaning of the blues to us who are manifestations of the songs themselves?

It must also be pointed out that on whatever level of contact that blacks and whites come together, that meeting or confrontation is not on the level of the blacks but always on the level of the whites. This only means that our everyday contact with whites is a reinforcement of the myth of white supremacy. Whites are the ones who must try to raise themselves to our humanistic level. We are not, after all, the ones who are responsible for a genocidal war in Vietnam; we are not the ones who are responsible for neocolonialism in Africa and Latin America; we are not the ones who held a people in animalistic bondage over 400 years. We reject the American dream as defined by white people and must work to construct an American reality defined by Afro-Americans.

One of the criticisms of white militants and radicals is that when we view the masses of white people we view the over-all reality of America, we view the racism, the bigotry, and the distortion of personality, we view man's inhumanity to man; we view in reality 180 million racists. The sensitive white intellectual and radical who is fighting to bring about change is conscious of this fact, but does not have the courage to admit this. When he admits this reality, then he must also admit his involvement because he is a part of the collective white America. It is only to the extent that he recognizes this that he will be able to change his reality.

Another concern is how does the white radical view the black community and how does he view the poor white community in terms of organizing. So far, we have found that most white radicals have sought to escape the horrible reality of America by going into the black community and attempting to organize black people while neglecting the organization of their own people's racist communities. How can one clean up someone else's yard when one's own yard is untidy? Again we feel that S.N.C.C. and the civil rights movement in general is in many aspects similar to the anti-colonial situations in the African and Asian countries. We have the whites in the movement corresponding to the white civil servants and missionaries in the colonial countries who have worked with the colonial people for a long period of time and have developed a paternalistic attitude toward them. The reality of the colonial people taking over their own lives and controlling their own destiny must be faced. Having to move aside and letting this natural process of growth and development take place must be faced.

These views should not be equated with outside influence or outside agitation but should be viewed as the natural process of growth and development within a movement; so that the move by the black militants and S.N.C.C. in this direction should be viewed as a turn toward self-determination.

It is very ironic and curious how aware whites in this country can champion anti-colonialism in other countries in Africa, Asia, and Latin America, but when black people move toward similar goals of self-determination in this country they are viewed as racists and antiwhite by these same progressive whites. In proceeding further, it can be said that this attitude derives from the overall point of view of the white psyche as it concerns the black people. This attitude stems from the era of the slave revolts when every white man was a potential deputy or sheriff or guardian of the state. Because when black people got together among themselves to work out their problems, it became a threat to white people, because such meetings were potential slave revolts.

It can be maintained that this attitude or way of thinking has perpetuated itself to this current period and that it is part of the psyche of white people in this country whatever their political persuasion might be. It is part of the white fear-guilt complex resulting from the slave revolts. There have been examples of whites who stated that they can deal with black fellows on an individual basis but become threatened or menaced by the presence of groups of blacks. It can be maintained that this attitude is held by the majority of progressive whites in this country.

A thorough re-examination must be made by black people concerning the contributions that we have made in shaping this country. If this re-examination and re-evaluation is not made, and black people are not given their proper due and respect, then the antagonisms and contradictions are going to become more and more glaring, more and more intense until a national explosion may result.

When people attempt to move from these conclusions it would be faulty reasoning to say they are ordered by racism, because, in this country and in the West, racism has functioned as a type of white nationalism when dealing with black people. We all know the habit that this has created throughout the world and particularly among nonwhite people in this country.

Therefore any re-evaluation that we must make will, for the most part, deal with identification. Who are black people, what are black people; what is their relationship to America and the world?

It must be repeated that the whole myth of "Negro citizenship," perpetuated by the white elite, has confused the thinking of radical and progressive blacks and whites in this country. The broad masses of black people react to American society in the same manner as colonial peoples react to the West in Africa, and Latin America, and had the same relationship — that of the colonized toward the colonizer.

Study Guide

1. In this Student Nonviolent Coordinating Committee document two objectives are attained:
   (a) a denial of historical stereotypes of the blacks; and
   (b) a delineation of the dimensions of black nationalism.

2. Begin by summarizing the S.N.C.C. comments on the meaning of color (black and white) in the American historical and social experience (pp. 542–544), and then take up the following:
   (a) What disadvantages accrued to the blacks as a consequence of white participation in the civil rights movement? Were there any advantages at all? What should the future role of whites in the movement be?
   (b) What impact will the exodus of whites from black organizations have on the latter and their members?
   (c) How does S.N.C.C., in contrast to the Southern Christian Leadership Conference, epitomize the problem of the integration of blacks and whites?
   (d) What future role does S.N.C.C. assign to whites who want to work in the movement?

3. In a single paragraph, the statement comes to its central thesis: "Re-evaluation of the white and black roles must NOW take place. . . ." Absorb the meaning of the entire paragraph, for it introduces and serves as the basic assumption for what follows (pp. 546–548).
   (a) What are some of the aesthetic (e.g., musical and literary) implications of the alteration of roles S.N.C.C. is demanding?
   (b) What other positive implications will recognition of the separation of the races produce?

4. In review:
   (a) Summarize the core of this statement and its full meaning for the black and white communities.
   (b) Explore the nuances and the validity of the following:
       (1) "Any white person . . . cannot escape them [negative myths about the Negro] because the whole society has geared his subconscious in that direction."
       (2) "Negroes in this country have never been able to organize themselves because of white interference."
       (3) "We have dealt stringently with the problem of 'Uncle Tom,' but we have not yet gotten around to Simon Legree."
       (4) "If we are to proceed toward true liberation, we must cut ourselves off from white people."
       (5) "The charge may be made that we are 'racists.' . . ."
       (6) "Too long have we allowed white people to interpret the importance and meaning of the cultural aspects of our society."
       (7) "A thorough re-examination must be made by black people concerning the contributions that we have made in shaping this country."

5. In historical retrospect:
   (a) Compare and contrast the attitudes expressed in this statement with those of Martin Luther King.
   (b) Proceed then to relate the views of Stokely Carmichael and King to another pair of black leaders — Booker T. Washington and W. E. B. DuBois, whose statements on the problems of the blacks at the turn of the century will be found on pp. 67–75 and 237–249. Although the terms and the subjects touched upon by Washington and DuBois differ somewhat from the topics taken up by King and Carmichael, all four men are dealing with a single problem: how to live as a member of a black minority in white America. Drawing up a spectrum of black nationalism (or militancy), where would you place each of these four men and why?
   (c) And finally: Do you attach any significance to the fact that both Carmichael and DuBois were reared and largely educated in the North (at Harvard, for that matter) while Washington and King were basically Southerners? Explore.

Michael Harrington

THE INVISIBLE POOR

◄{ *1962* }► IN THESE times when discussions of the problem of poverty in the United States figure so prominently in the newspapers and magazines and in the deliberations of local, state, and national legislatures, it is easy to forget how startling — even shocking — was the impact of Michael Harrington's exposé of the phenomenon of poverty in the midst of plenty when it first appeared in 1962 in *The Other America.* The rapid expansion of the economy after World War II had accustomed people to look at the statistics of production and living standards nationally, and to draw smug comparisons between conditions in the parlous days of the "Great Depression" and the new era of prosperity and growth. Harrington was a youthful reformer, well known among liberal Catholic groups, and a former editor of *The Catholic Worker. The Other America* won him a national reputation and made him a powerful force. His moving, scathingly critical, yet fact-filled, scholarly analysis caused, or at least dramatically advanced, a fundamental shift in liberal opinion, and triggered a political and social movement that is still in full course. Not merely did he demonstrate that millions of Americans were desperately, even hopelessly, poor; he also explained why so many of his well-meaning countrymen did not even know that these poor people existed.

THE INVISIBLE LAND

THERE IS a familiar America. It is celebrated in speeches and advertised on television and in the magazines. It has the highest mass standard of living the world has ever known.

In the 1950's this America worried about itself, yet even its anxieties were products of abundance. The title of a brilliant book was widely misinterpreted, and the familiar America began to call itself "the affluent society." There was introspection about Madison Avenue and tail fins; there was discussion of the emotional suffering taking place in the suburbs. In all this, there was an implicit assumption that the basic grinding economic problems had been solved in the United States. In this theory the nation's problems were no longer a matter of basic human needs, of food, shelter, and clothing. Now they were seen as qualitative, a question of learning to live decently amid luxury.

While this discussion was carried on, there existed another America. In it dwelt somewhere between 40,000,000 and 50,000,000 citizens of this land. They were poor. They still are.

To be sure, the other America is not impoverished in the same sense as those poor nations where millions cling to hunger as a defense against starvation. This country has escaped such extremes. That does not change the fact that tens of millions of Americans are, at this very moment, maimed in body and spirit, existing at levels beneath those necessary for human decency. If these people are not starving, they are hungry, and sometimes fat with hunger, for that is what cheap foods do. They are without adequate housing and education and medical care.

The Government has documented what this means to the bodies of the poor, and the figures will be cited throughout this book. But even more basic, this poverty twists and deforms the spirit. The American poor are pessimistic and defeated, and they are victimized by mental suffering to a degree unknown in Suburbia.

This book is a description of the world in which these people live; it is about the other America. Here are the unskilled workers, the migrant farm workers, the aged, the minorities, and all the others who live in the economic underworld of American life. In all this, there will be statistics, and that offers the opportunity for disagreement among honest and sincere men. I would ask the reader to respond critically to every assertion, but not to allow statistical quibbling to obscure the huge, enormous, and intolerable fact of poverty in America. For, when all is said and done, that fact is unmistakable, whatever its exact dimensions, and the truly human reaction can only be outrage. As W. H. Auden wrote:

> Hunger allows no choice
> To the citizen or the police;
> We must love one another or die.

I

The millions who are poor in the United States tend to become increasingly invisible. Here is a great mass of people, yet it takes an effort of the intellect and will even to see them.

I discovered this personally in a curious way. After I wrote my first article on poverty in America, I had all the statistics down on paper. I had proved to my satisfaction that there were around 50,000,000 poor in this country. Yet, I realized I did not believe my own figures. The poor existed in the Government reports; they were percentages and numbers in long, close columns, but they were not part of my experience. I could prove that the other America existed, but I had never been there.

My response was not accidental. It was typical of what is happening to an entire society, and it reflects profound social changes in this nation. The other America, the America of poverty, is hidden today in a way that it never was before. Its millions are socially invisible to the rest of us. No wonder that so many misinterpreted Galbraith's title and assumed that "the affluent society" meant that everyone had a decent standard of life. The misinterpretation was true as far as the actual day-to-day lives of two-thirds of the nation were concerned. Thus, one must begin a description of the other America by understanding why we do not see it.

There are perennial reasons that make the other America an invisible land.

Poverty is often off the beaten track. It always has been. The ordinary tourist never left the main highway, and today he rides interstate turnpikes. He does not go into the valleys of Pennsylvania where the towns look like movie sets of Wales in the thirties. He does not see the company houses in rows, the rutted roads (the poor always have bad roads whether they live in the city, in towns, or on farms), and everything is black and dirty. And even if he were to pass through such a place by accident, the tourist would not meet the unemployed men in the bar or the women coming home from a runaway sweatshop.

Then, too, beauty and myths are perennial masks of poverty. The traveler comes to the Appalachians in the lovely season. He sees the hills, the streams, the foliage — but not the poor. Or perhaps he looks at a run-down mountain house and, remembering Rousseau rather than seeing with his eyes, decides that "those people" are truly fortunate to be living the way they are and that they are lucky to be exempt from the strains and tensions of the middle class. The only problem is that "those people," the quaint inhabitants of those hills, are undereducated, underprivileged, lack medical care, and are in the process of being forced from the land into a life in the cities, where they are misfits.

These are normal and obvious causes of the invisibility of the poor. They operated a generation ago; they will be functioning a generation hence. It is more important to understand that the very development of American society is creating a new kind of blindness about poverty. The poor are increasingly slipping out of the very experience and consciousness of the nation.

If the middle class never did like ugliness and poverty, it was at least aware of them. "Across the tracks" was not a very long way to go. There were forays into the slums at Christmas time; there were charitable organizations that brought contact with the poor. Occasionally, almost everyone passed through the Negro ghetto or the blocks of tenements, if only to get downtown to work or to entertainment.

Now the American city has been transformed. The poor still inhabit the miserable housing in the central area, but they are increasingly isolated from contact with, or sight of, anybody else. Middle-class women coming in from Suburbia on a rare trip may catch the merest glimpse of the other America on the way to an evening at the theater, but their children are segregated in suburban schools. The business or professional man may drive along the fringes of slums in a car or bus, but it is not an important experience to him. The failures, the unskilled, the disabled, the aged, and the minorities are right there, across the tracks, where they have always been. But hardly anyone else is.

In short, the very development of the American city has removed poverty from the living, emotional experience of millions of middle-class Americans. Living out in the suburbs, it is easy to assume that ours is, indeed, an affluent society.

This new segregation of poverty is compounded by a well-meaning ignorance. A good many concerned and sympathetic Americans are aware that there is much discussion of urban renewal. Suddenly, driving through the city, they notice that a familiar slum has been torn down and that there are towering, modern buildings where once there had been tenements or hovels. There is a warm feeling of satisfaction, of pride in the way things are working out: the poor, it is obvious, are being taken care of.

The irony in this . . . is that the truth is nearly the exact opposite to the impression. The total impact of the various housing programs in postwar America has been to squeeze more and more people into existing slums. More often than not, the modern apartment in a towering building rents at $40 a room or more. For, during the past decade and a half, there has been more subsidization of middle- and upper-income housing than there has been of housing for the poor.

Clothes make the poor invisible too: America has the best-dressed poverty the world has ever known. For a variety of reasons, the benefits of mass production have been spread much more evenly in this area than in many others. It is much easier in the United States to be decently dressed than it is to be decently housed, fed, or doctored. Even people with terribly depressed incomes can look prosperous.

This is an extremely important factor in defining our emotional and existential ignorance of poverty. In Detroit the existence of social classes became much more difficult to discern the day the companies put lockers in the plants. From that moment on, one did not see men in work clothes on the way to the factory, but citizens in slacks and white shirts. This process has been magnified with the poor throughout the country. There are tens of thousands of Americans in the big cities who are wearing shoes, perhaps even a stylishly cut suit or dress, and yet are hungry. It is not a matter of planning, though it almost seems as if the affluent society had given out costumes to the poor so that they would not offend the rest of society with the sight of rags.

Then, many of the poor are the wrong age to be seen. A good number of them (over 8,000,000) are sixty-five years of age or better; an even larger number are under eighteen. The aged members of the other America are often sick, and they cannot move. Another group of them live out their lives in loneliness and frustration: they sit in rented rooms, or else they stay close to a house in a neighborhood that has completely changed from the old days. Indeed, one of the worst aspects of poverty among the aged is that these people are out of sight and out of mind, and alone.

The young are somewhat more visible, yet they too stay close to their neighborhoods. Sometimes they advertise their poverty through a lurid tabloid story about a gang killing. But generally they do not disturb the quiet streets of the middle class.

And finally, the poor are politically invisible. It is one of the cruelest ironies of social life in advanced countries that the dispossessed at the bottom of society are unable to speak for themselves. The people of the other America do not, by far and large, belong to unions, to fraternal organizations, or to political parties. They are without lobbies of their own; they put forward no legislative program. As a group, they are atomized. They have no face; they have no voice.

Thus, there is not even a cynical political motive for caring about the poor, as in the old days. Because the slums are no longer centers of powerful political organizations, the politicians need not really care about their inhabitants. The slums are no longer visible to the middle class, so much of the idealistic urge to fight for those who need help is gone. Only the social agencies have a really direct involvement with the other America, and they are without any great political power. . . .

THE TWO NATIONS

THE UNITED STATES in the sixties contains an affluent society within its borders. Millions and tens of millions enjoy the highest standard of life the world has ever known. This blessing is mixed. It is built upon a peculiarly distorted economy, one that often proliferates pseudo-needs rather than satisfying human needs. For some, it has resulted in a sense of spiritual emptiness, of alienation. Yet a man would be a fool to prefer hunger to satiety, and the material gains at least open up the possibility of a rich and full existence.

At the same time, the United States contains an underdeveloped nation, a culture of poverty. Its inhabitants do not suffer the extreme privation of the peasants of Asia or the tribesmen of Africa, yet the mechanism of the misery is similar. They are beyond history, beyond progress, sunk in a paralyzing, maiming routine.

The new nations, however, have one advantage: poverty is so general and so extreme that it is the passion of the entire society to obliterate it. Every resource, every policy, is measured by its effect on the lowest and most impoverished. There is a gigantic mobilization of the spirit of the society: aspiration becomes a national purpose that penetrates to every village and motivates a historic transformation.

But this country seems to be caught in a paradox. Because its poverty is not so deadly, because so many are enjoying a decent standard of life, there are indifference and blindness to the plight of the poor. There are even those who deny that the culture of poverty exists. It is as if Disraeli's famous remark about the two nations of the rich and the poor had come true in a fantastic fashion. At precisely that moment in history where for the first time a people have the material ability to end poverty, they lack the will to do so. They cannot see; they cannot act. The consciences of the well-off are the victims of affluence; the lives of the poor are the victims of a physical and spiritual misery.

The problem, then, is to a great extent one of vision. The nation of the well-off must be able to see through the wall of affluence and recognize the alien citizens on the other side. And there must be vision in the sense of purpose, of aspiration: if the word does not grate upon the ears of a gentile America, there must be a passion to end poverty, for nothing less than that will do. . . .

I

. . . Poverty in America forms a culture, a way of life and feeling. It is crucial to generalize this idea, for it profoundly affects how one moves to destroy poverty.

The most obvious aspect of this interrelatedness is in the way in which the various subcultures of the other America feed into one another. This is clearest with the aged. There the poverty of the declining years is, for some millions of human beings, a function of the poverty of the earlier years. If there were adequate medical care for everyone in the United States, there would be less misery for old people. It is as simple as that. Or there is the relation between the poor farmers and the unskilled workers. When a man is driven off the land because of the impoverishment worked by technological progress, he leaves one part of the culture of poverty and joins another. If something were done about the low-income farmer, that would immediately tell in the statistics of urban unemployment and the economic underworld. The same is true of the

Negroes. Any gain for America's minorities will immediately be translated into an advance for all the unskilled workers. One cannot raise the bottom of a society without benefiting everyone above.

Indeed, there is a curious advantage in the wholeness of poverty. Since the other America forms a distinct system within the United States, effective action at any one decisive point will have a "multiplier" effect; it will ramify through the entire culture of misery and ultimately through the entire society.

Then, poverty is a culture in the sense that the mechanism of impoverishment is fundamentally the same in every part of the system. The vicious circle is a basic pattern. It takes different forms for the unskilled workers, for the aged, for the Negroes, for the agricultural workers, but in each case the principle is the same. There are people in the affluent society who are poor because they are poor; and who stay poor because they are poor.

To realize this is to see that there are some tens of millions of Americans who are beyond the welfare state. Some of them are simply not covered by social legislation: they are omitted from Social Security and from minimum wage. Others are covered, but since they are so poor they do not know how to take advantage of the opportunities, or else their coverage is so inadequate as not to make a difference.

The welfare state was designed during that great burst of social creativity that took place in the 1930's. As previously noted its structure corresponds to the needs of those who played the most important role in building it: the middle third, the organized workers, the forces of urban liberalism, and so on. At the worst, there is "socialism for the rich and free enterprise for the poor," as when the huge corporation farms are the main beneficiaries of the farm program while the poor farmers get practically nothing; or when public funds are directed to aid in the construction of luxury housing while the slums are left to themselves (or become more dense as space is created for the well-off).

So there is the fundamental paradox of the welfare state: that it is not built for the desperate, but for those who are already capable of helping themselves. As long as the illusion persists that the poor are merrily freeloading on the public dole, so long will the other America continue unthreatened. The truth, it must be understood, is the exact opposite. The poor get less out of the welfare state than any group in America.

This is, of course, related to the most distinguishing mark of the other America: its common sense of hopelessness. For even when there are programs designed to help the other Americans, the poor are held back by their own pessimism. . . .

III

If research makes it clear that a basic attack upon poverty is necessary, it also suggests the kind of program the nation needs.

First and foremost, any attempt to abolish poverty in the United States must seek to destroy the pessimism and fatalism that flourish in the other America. In part, this can be done by offering real opportunities to these people, by changing the social reality that gives rise to their sense of hopelessness. But beyond that (these fears of the poor have a life of their own and are not simply rooted in analyses of employment chances), there should be a spirit, an élan, that communicates itself to the entire society.

If the nation comes into the other America grudgingly, with the mentality of an administrator, and says, "All right, we'll help you people," then there will be gains, but they will be kept to the minimum; a dollar spent will return a dollar. But if there is an attitude that society is gaining by eradicating poverty, if there is a positive attempt to bring these millions of the poor to the point where they can make their contribution to the United States, that will make a huge difference. The spirit of a campaign against poverty does not cost a single cent. It is a matter of vision, of sensitivity.

Let me give an example to make this point palpable. During the Montgomery bus boycott, there was only one aim in the Negro community of that city: to integrate the buses. There were no speeches on crime or juvenile delinquency. And yet it is reported that the crime rate among Negroes in Montgomery declined. Thousands of people had been given a sense of purpose, of their own worth and dignity. On their own, and without any special urging, they began to change their personal lives; they became a different people. If the same élan could invade the other America, there would be similar results.

Second, this book is based upon the proposition that poverty forms a culture, an interdependent system. In case after case, it has been documented that one cannot deal with the various components of poverty in isolation, changing this or that condition but leaving the basic structure intact. Consequently, a campaign against the misery of the poor should be comprehensive. It should think, not in terms of this or that aspect of poverty, but along the lines of establishing new communities, of substituting a human environment for the inhuman one that now exists.

Here, housing is probably the basic point of departure. If there were the funds and imagination for a campaign to end slums in the United States, most of the other steps needed to deal with poverty could be integrated with it. The vision should be the one described in the previous chapter: the political, economic, and social integration of the poor with the rest of the society. The second nation in our midst, the other America, must be brought into the Union.

In order to do this, there is a need for planning. It is literally incredible that this nation knows so much about poverty, that it has made so many inventories of misery, and that it has done so little. The material for a comprehensive program is already available. It exists in congressional reports and the statistics of Government agencies. What is needed is that the society make use of its knowledge in a rational and systematic way. As this book is being written, there are proposals for a Department of Urban Affairs in the Cabinet (and it will probably be a reality by the time these words are published). Such an agency could be the coordinating center for a crusade against the other America. In any case, if there is not planning, any attempt to deal with the problem of poverty will fail, at least in part.

Then there are some relatively simple things that could be done, involving the expansion of existing institutions and programs. Every American should be brought under the coverage of social security, and the payments should be enough to support a dignified old age. The principle already exists. Now it must be extended to those who need help the most. The same is true with minimum wage. The spectacle of excluding the most desperate from coverage must come to an end. If it did, there would be a giant step toward the elimination of poverty itself.

In every subculture of the other America, sickness and disease are the most important agencies of continuing misery. The New York *Times* publishes a list of the "neediest cases" each Christmas. In 1960 the descriptions of personal tragedy that ran along with this appeal involved in the majority of cases the want of those who had been struck down by illness. If there were adequate medical care, this charity would be unnecessary.

Today the debate on medical care centers on the aged. And indeed, these are the people who are in the most desperate straits. Yet it would be an error of the first magnitude to think that society's responsibility begins with those sixty-five years of age. As has been pointed out several times, the ills of the elderly are often the inheritance of the earlier years. A comprehensive medical program, guaranteeing decent care to every American, would actually reduce the cost of caring for the aged. That, of course, is only the hardheaded argument for such an approach. More importantly, such a program would make possible a human kind of existence for everyone in the society.

And finally, it must be remembered that none of these objectives can be accomplished if racial prejudice is to continue in the United States. Negroes and other minorities constitute only 25 per cent of the poor, yet their degradation is an important element in maintaining the entire culture of poverty. As long as there is a reservoir of cheap Negro labor, there is a means of keeping the poor whites down. In this sense, civil-rights legislation is an absolutely essential component in any campaign to end poverty in the United States.

In short, the welfare provisions of American society that now help the upper two-thirds must be extended to the poor. This can be done if the other Americans are motivated to take advantage of the opportunities before them, if they are invited into the society. It can be done if there is a comprehensive program that attacks the culture of poverty at every one of its strong points.

But who will carry out this campaign? . . . There is no place to look except toward the Federal Government. And indeed, even if there were alternate choices, Washington would have to play an important role, if only because of the need for a comprehensive program and for national planning. But in any case there is no argument, for there is only one realistic possibility: only the Federal Government has the power to abolish poverty.

In saying this, it is not necessary to advocate complete central control of such a campaign. Far from it. Washington is essential in a double sense: as a source of the considerable funds needed to mount a campaign against the other America, and as a place for coordination, for planning, and the establishment of national standards. The actual implementation of a program to abolish poverty can be carried out through myriad institutions, and the closer they are to the specific local area, the better the results. There are, as has been pointed out already, housing administrators, welfare workers, and city planners with dedication and vision. They are working on the local level, and their main frustration is the lack of funds. They could be trusted actually to carry through on a national program. What they lack now is money and the support of the American people.

There is no point in attempting to blueprint or detail the mechanisms and institutions of a war on poverty in the United States. There is information enough for action. All that is lacking is political will.

Thus the difficult, hardheaded question about poverty that one must answer is this: Where is the political will coming from? The other America is systematically underrepresented in the Government of the United States. It cannot really speak for itself. The poor, even in politics, must always be the object of charity (with the major exception of the Negroes, who, in recent times, have made tremendous strides forward in organization).

Indeed, part of the invisibility of poverty in American life is a result of party structure. Since each major party contained differences within itself greater than the differences between it and the other party, politics in the fifties and early sixties tended to have an issueless character. And where issues were not discussed, the poor did not have a chance. They could benefit only if elections were designed to bring new information to the people, to wake up the nation, to challenge, and to call to action.

In all probability there will not be a real attack on the culture of poverty so long as this situation persists. For the other America cannot be abolished through concessions and compromises that are almost inevitably made at the expense of the poor. The spirit, the vision that are required if the nation is to penetrate the wall of pessimism and despair that surrounds the impoverished millions cannot be produced under such circumstances.

What is needed if poverty is to be abolished is a return of political debate, a restructuring of the party system so that there can be clear choices, a new mood of social idealism.

These, then, are the strangest poor in the history of mankind.

They exist within the most powerful and rich society the world has ever known. Their misery has continued while the majority of the nation talked of itself as being "affluent" and worried about neuroses in the suburbs. In this way tens of millions of human beings became invisible. They dropped out of sight and out of mind; they were without their own political voice.

Yet this need not be. The means are at hand to fulfill the age-old dream: poverty can now be abolished. How long shall we ignore this underdeveloped nation in our midst? How long shall we look the other way while our fellow human beings suffer? How long?

Study Guide

1. The selections from Michael Harrington's *The Other America* contain the following themes:
   (a) the invisible character of American poverty (pp. 550–554);
   (b) its culture (pp. 554–556);
   (c) a program for the eradication of poverty (pp. 557–559); and
   (d) the politics of the problem (pp. 559–560).

2. Harrington introduces his first theme thus: "The millions who are poor in the United States tend to become increasingly invisible." He then proceeds to offer a number of reasons for this state of affairs. Outline the reasons — those that have always prevailed and those that prevail in our generation.

3. Turning to Harrington's assessment of poverty in the United States, how does he account for the permanence of poverty, or what he describes as poverty's "vicious circle" or its culture"?

4. On "the culture of poverty":
   (a) What does Harrington mean by the phrase? Explain and illustrate.
   (b) Why has the welfare state of the New Deal, according to Harrington, not helped the poor?

5. Turning to Harrington's solutions to the problem of poverty, what value does he place on:
   (a) attitude;
   (b) comprehensiveness;
   (c) housing;
   (d) planning;
   (e) social security and medical care; and
   (f) race prejudice?

6. What roles does Harrington assign to the federal government in attacking the poverty problem?

7. Summarize Harrington's assessment of the political prospects for dealing with the problem.

8. In retrospect: To what extent has our nation fulfilled Harrington's plea since the publication of his book in 1962?

National Organization for Women
THE LIBERATION OF WOMEN

❊ 1966, 1967 ❊ THE SOCIAL and political consensus enjoyed by middle-class Americans in the decades after 1945 was first shattered by the justifiable rebellion of the blacks over their lot and then, with less obvious justification, by the radical and the young. The last to rebel were the women of America, triggering a movement that, in the opinion of some, may bring about a more fundamental alteration in the mores and institutions of our country than all of the other protest movements of the 1960's and 1970's. Feminist movements were not new in American history. Prior to the Civil War, women sought to obtain basic civic and economic rights and in the late nineteenth century they continued to fight for the right to education, property rights, and the right to vote.

During the Progressive Era, these demands were joined with a concern over working conditions for women and, for a minority of feminists, a desire to redefine the social role of women. This latter trend, along with a stress on the psychological dimensions of their plight, has been the central concern of the Women's Liberation Movement of the 1960's and 1970's.

A host of economic inequities in the business and professional world provided a realistic backdrop to "women's lib" — quite apart from the sociopsychological thrust of the movement. "Women's lib" leaders pointed to the tiny percentage of women represented in the legal and medical professions and on university faculties (in almost all instances a smaller proportion than in the early decades of the century), the small representation of women in politics, and the lowly, even menial, positions women were consigned to in the nation's burgeoning corporate structures. Despite lip service to equal pay for equal work, there was abundant evidence that women received a lower rate of pay for work no less skilled or no less arduous than that performed by their male counterparts.

In response to both economic discrimination and to an "identity" crisis growing out of an increasing tension between the university training and aspirations of women and the subsequent domestic role most often assigned to them, hundreds of "women's lib" movements came into existence by 1970. Some feminists drew attention to "sexism," the subservient relationship of women to men, by the adoption of a new life style — refusing to permit men to open doors for them or to light their cigarettes or by stripping off their clothes in protest against a campus lecture in favor of the pro-male *Playboy* philosophy. Others, particularly the middle-class women affiliated with the National Organization for Women (NOW) focused on more tangible inequities. NOW succeeded in obtaining a ban on discriminatory want-ads and in getting the Equal Employment Opportunity Commission to enforce the 1964 Civil Rights Act prohibiting discrimination against women as well as blacks. Additionally, they have advocated day-care centers for the children of working mothers and other programs designed to improve the conditions of life and work for the American woman.

Reprinted here are the Statement of Purpose drawn up by the National Organization for Women (NOW) at their organizing conference in 1966 and the Bill of Rights adopted one year later.

STATEMENT OF PURPOSE

(ADOPTED AT THE ORGANIZING CONFERENCE IN WASHINGTON, D.C., OCTOBER 29, 1966)

WE, MEN AND WOMEN who hereby constitute ourselves as the National Organization for Women, believe that the time has come for a new movement toward true equality for all women in America, and toward a fully equal partnership of the sexes, as part of the world-wide revolution of human rights now taking place within and beyond our national borders.

The purpose of NOW is to take action to bring women into full participation in the mainstream of American society now, exercising all the privileges and responsibilities thereof in truly equal partnership with men.

We believe the time has come to move beyond the abstract argument, discussion and symposia over the status and special nature of women which have raged in America in recent years; the time has come to confront, with concrete action, the conditions that now prevent women from enjoying the equality of opportunity and freedom of choice which is their right, as individual Americans, and as human beings.

NOW is dedicated to the proposition that women, first and foremost, are human beings, who, like all other people in our society, must have the chance to develop their fullest human potential. We believe that women can achieve such equality only by accepting to the full the challenges and responsibilities they share with all other people in our society, as part of the decision-making mainstream of American political, economic, and social life.

We organize to initiate or support action, nationally, or in any part of this nation, by individuals or organizations, to break through the silken curtain of prejudice and discrimination against women in government, industry, the professions, the churches, the political parties, the judiciary, the labor unions, in education, science, medicine, law, religion, and every other field of importance in American society.

Enormous changes taking place in our society make it both possible and urgently necessary to advance the unfinished revolution of women toward true equality, now. With a life-span lengthened to nearly 75 years it is no longer either necessary or possible for women to devote the greater part of their lives to childrearing; yet childbearing and rearing — which continue to be a most important part of most women's lives — still are used to justify barring women from equal professional and economic participation and advance.

Today's technology has reduced most of the productive chores which women once performed in the home and in mass-production industries based upon routine unskilled labor. This same technology has virtually eliminated the quality of muscular strength as a criterion for filling most jobs, while intensifying American industry's need for creative intelligence. In view of this new industrial revolution created by automation in the mid-twentieth century, women can and must participate in old and new fields of society in full equality — or become permanent outsiders.

Despite all the talk about the status of American women in recent years, the actual position of women in the United States has declined, and is declining, to an alarming degree throughout the 1950's and 1960's. Although 46.4% of all American women between the ages of 18 and 65 now work outside the home, the overwhelming majority — 75% — are in routine clerical, sales, or factory jobs, or they are household workers, cleaning women, hospital attendants. About two-thirds of Negro women workers are in the lowest paid service occupations. Working women are becoming increasingly — not less — concentrated on the bottom of the job ladder. As a consequence full-time women workers today earn on the average only 60% of what men earn, and that wage gap has been increasing over the past twenty-five years in every major industry group. In 1964, of all women with a yearly income, 89% earned under $5,000 a year; half of all full-time year round women workers earned less than $3,690; only 1.4% of full-time year round women workers had an annual income of $10,000 or more.

Further, with higher education increasingly essential in today's society, too few women are entering and finishing college or going on to graduate or professional school. Today, women earn only one in three of the B.A.'s and M.A.'s granted, and one in ten of the Ph.D's.

In all the professions considered of importance to society, and in the executive ranks of industry and government, women are losing ground. Where they are present it is only a token handful. Women comprise less than 1% of federal judges; less than 4% of all lawyers; 7% of doctors. Yet women represent 51% of the U.S. population. And, increasingly, men are replacing women in the top positions in secondary and elementary schools, in social work, and in libraries — once thought to be women's fields.

Official pronouncements of the advance in the status of women hide not only the reality of this dangerous decline, but the fact that nothing is being done to stop it. The excellent reports of the President's Commission on the Status of Women and of the State Commissions have not been fully implemented. Such Commissions have power only to advise. They have no power to enforce their recommendations; nor have they the freedom to organize American women and men to press for action on them. The reports of these commissions have, however, created a basis upon which it is now possible to build.

Discrimination in employment on the basis of sex is now prohibited by federal law, in Title VII of the Civil Rights Act of 1964. But although nearly one-third of the cases brought before the Equal Employment Opportunity Commission during the first year dealt with sex discrimination and the proportion is increasing dramatically, the Commission has not made clear its intention to enforce the law with the same seriousness on behalf of women as of other victims of discrimination. Many of these cases were Negro women, who are the victims of the double discrimination of race and sex. Until now, too few women's organizations and official spokesmen have been willing to speak out against these dangers facing women. Too many women have been restrained by the fear of being called "feminist."

There is no civil rights movement to speak for women, as there has been for Negroes and other victims of discrimination. The National Organization for Women must therefore begin to speak.

WE BELIEVE that the power of American law, and the protection guaranteed by the U.S. Constitution to the civil rights of all individuals, must be effectively applied and enforced to isolate and remove patterns of sex discrimination, to ensure equality of opportunity in employment and education, and equality of civil and political rights and responsibilities on behalf of women, as well as for Negroes and other deprived groups.

We realize that women's problems are linked to many broader questions of social justice; their solution will require concerted action by many groups. Therefore, convinced that human rights for all are indivisible, we expect to give active support to the common cause of equal rights for all those who suffer discrimination and deprivation, and we call upon other organizations committed to such goals to support our efforts toward equality for women.

WE DO NOT ACCEPT the token appointment of a few women to high-level positions in government and industry as a substitute for a serious continuing effort to recruit and advance women according to their individual abilities. To this end, we urge American government and industry to mobilize the same resources of ingenuity and command with which they have solved problems of far greater difficulty than those now impeding the progress of women.

WE BELIEVE that this nation has a capacity at least as great as other nations, to innovate new social institutions which will enable women to enjoy true equality of opportunity and responsibility in society, without conflict with their responsibilities as mothers and homemakers. In such innovations, America does not lead the Western world, but lags by decades behind many European countries. We do not accept the traditional assumption that a woman has to choose between marriage and motherhood, on the one hand, and serious participation in industry or the professions on the other. We question the present expectation that all normal women will retire from job or profession for 10 to 15 years, to devote their full time to raising children, only to re-enter the job market at a relatively minor level. This, in itself, is a deterrent to the aspirations of women, to their acceptance into management or professional training courses, and to the very possibility of equality of opportunity or real choice, for all but a few women. Above all, we reject the assumption that these problems are the unique responsibility of each individual woman, rather than a basic social dilemma which society must solve. True equality of opportunity and freedom of choice for women require such practical and possible innovations as a nationwide network of child-care centers, which will make it unnecessary for women to retire completely from society until their children are grown, and national programs to provide retraining for women who have chosen to care for their own children full-time.

WE BELIEVE that it is an essential for every girl to be educated to her full potential of human ability as it is for every boy — with the knowledge that such education is the key to effective participation in today's economy and that, for a girl as for a boy, education can only be serious where there is expectation that it will be used in society. We believe that American educators are capable of devising means of imparting such expectations to girl students. Moreover, we consider the decline in the proportion of women receiving higher and professional education to be evidence of discrimination. This discrimination may take the form of quotas against the admission of women to colleges and professional schools; lack of encouragement by parents, counselors, and educators; denial of loans or fellowships; or the traditional or arbitrary procedures in graduate and professional training geared in terms of men, which inadvertently discriminate against women. We believe that the same serious attention must be given to high school dropouts who are girls as to boys.

WE REJECT the current assumptions that a man must carry the sole burden of supporting himself, his wife, and family, and that a woman is automatically entitled to lifelong support by a man upon her marriage, or that marriage, home, and family are primarily woman's world and responsibility — hers to dominate — his to support. We believe that a true partnership between the sexes demands a different concept of marriage, an equitable sharing of the responsibilities of home and children and of the economic burdens of their support. We believe that proper recognition should be given to the economic and social value of homemaking and child care. To these ends, we will seek to open a re-examination of laws and mores governing marriage and divorce, for we believe that the current state of "half-equality" between the sexes discriminates against both men and women, and is the cause of much unnecessary hostility between the sexes.

WE BELIEVE that women must now exercise their political rights and responsibilities as American citizens. They must refuse to be segregated on the basis of sex into separate-and-not-equal ladies' auxiliaries in the political parties, and they must demand representation according to their numbers in the regularly constituted party committees — at local, state, and national levels — and in the informal power structure, participating fully in the selection of candidates and political decision-making, and running for office themselves.

IN THE INTERESTS OF THE HUMAN DIGNITY OF WOMEN, we will protest, and endeavor to change, the false image of women now prevalent in the mass media, and in the texts, ceremonies, laws, and practices of our major social institutions. Such images perpetuate contempt for women by society and by women for themselves. We are similarly opposed to all policies and practices — in church, state, college, factory, or office — which, in the guise of protectiveness, not only deny opportunities but also foster in women self-denigration, dependence, and evasion of responsibility, undermine their confidence in their own abilities and foster contempt for women.

NOW WILL HOLD ITSELF INDEPENDENT OF ANY POLITICAL PARTY in order to mobilize the political power of all women and men intent on our goals. We will strive to ensure that no party, candidate, president, senator, governor, congressman, or any public official who betrays or ignores the principle of full equality between the sexes is elected or appointed to office. If it is necessary to mobilize the votes of men and women who believe in our cause, in order to win for women the final right to be fully free and equal human beings, we so commit ourselves.

WE BELIEVE that women will do most to create a new image of women by *acting* now, and by speaking out in behalf of their own equality, freedom, and human dignity — not in pleas for special privilege, nor in enmity toward men, who are also victims of the current, half-equality between the sexes — but in an active, self-respecting partnership with men. By so doing, women will develop confidence in their own ability to determine actively, in partnership with men, the conditions of their life, their choices, their future, and their society.

BILL OF RIGHTS

(1967)

I. Equal Rights Constitutional Amendment

II. Enforce Law Banning Sex Discrimination in Employment

III. Maternity Leave Rights in Employment and in Social Security Benefits

IV. Tax Deduction for Home and Child Care Expenses for Working Parents

V. Child Day Care Centers

VI. Equal and Unsegregated Education

VII. Equal Job Training Opportunities and Allowances for Women in Poverty

VIII. The Right of Women to Control Their Reproductive Lives
WE DEMAND:

I. That the U.S. Congress immediately pass the Equal Rights Amendment to the Constitution to provide that "Equality of rights under the law shall not be denied or abridged by the United States or by any State on account of sex," and that such then be immediately ratified by the several States.

II. That equal employment opportunity be guaranteed to all women, as well as men, by insisting that the Equal Employment Opportunity Commission enforces the prohibitions against racial discrimination.

III. That women be protected by law to ensure their rights to return to their jobs within a reasonable time after childbirth without loss of seniority or other accrued benefits, and be paid maternity leave as a form of social security and/or employee benefit.

IV. Immediate revision of tax laws to permit the deduction of home and child-care expenses for working parents.

V. That child-care facilities be established by law on the same basis as parks, libraries, and public schools, adequate to the needs of children from the pre-school years through adolescence, as a community resource to be used by all citizens from all income levels.

VI. That the right of women to be educated to their full potential equally with men be secured by Federal and State legislation, eliminating all discrimination and segregation by sex, written and unwritten, at all levels of education, including colleges, graduate and professional schools, loans and fellowships, and Federal and State training programs such as the Job Corps.

VII. The right of women in poverty to secure job training, housing, and family allowances on equal terms with men, but without prejudice to a parent's right to remain at home to care for his or her children; revision of welfare legislation and poverty programs which deny women dignity, privacy, and self-respect.

VIII. The right of women to control their own reproductive lives by removing from the penal code laws limiting access to contraceptive information and devices, and by repealing penal laws governing abortion.

Study Guide

1. The NOW Statement of Purpose contains a series of criticisms of the status of women in the United States and a series of demands that would correct these inequities. Begin with the first by summarizing the disabilities suffered by women in the following areas:

(a) occupations and wages;
(b) schooling; and
(c) the professions.

2. What evidence is there of job discrimination and what link does the Statement want to make between discrimination in employment on the basis of sex and other forms of discrimination?

3. What, according to NOW, is the status of women in the United States as compared to that of women in other countries?

4. Turning to remedies, what alterations and/or other improvements are sought by NOW in the following:
(a) the professions;
(b) the relationships between husband and wife in the home; and
(c) the media?

5. How does NOW propose to proceed in order to secure the liberation of women generally and the fulfillment of these goals specifically?

6. In retrospect: How does this critique of American mores regarding women and the changes demanded compare to the views set forth in the progressive period by Charlotte Perkins Gilman (pp. 292–299)? Compare and contrast.

7. Outline the Bill of Rights.

8. Explain how this program grows out of the analysis of the problem as formulated in the Statement of Purpose.

Richard M. Nixon

THE WATERGATE AFFAIR

✾*1973, 1972* ✾   IF EVER words may be said to have "made" American history, those of President Richard M. Nixon, broadcast over television to millions of citizens and recorded surreptitiously in the White House certainly did so. The Watergate affair, surely one of the most bizarre and indeed foolishly unnecessary crises in the history of any nation, has been discussed and analyzed by hundreds of observers and critics. What happened — the burglary of Democratic party headquarters at the Watergate complex in Washington, D. C., in June, 1972, by representatives of the Republican Committee to Reelect the President — is well known. However, why this was done remains obscure.

The event did not affect the result of the presidential election of 1972, which Nixon won by a huge majority. But the trial of the burglars and Congressional investigations of the incident led to charges that members of the Nixon administration and possibly the President himself had participated in the affair and had then attempted to conceal their involvement. Ultimately, as everyone knows, the release of taped conversations between Nixon and his close advisers showed the extent of this involvement and the nature of the concealment. But what most appalled the nation and forced Nixon to resign the presidency in disgrace was the discovery that the President had not only tried to obscure his administration's role in the burglary but had also lied directly to the American people. The first of the following excerpts is from Nixon's television address of April 30, 1973. The second, the notorious "smoking gun" conversation between Nixon and H. R. Haldeman, White House chief of staff, is from a tape recording of June 23, 1972, which Nixon released on August 5, 1974, after the Supreme Court ordered him to do so.

PRESIDENTIAL TELEVISION ADDRESS

(1973)

I WANT to talk to you tonight from my heart on a subject of deep concern to every American.

In recent months, members of my Administration and officials of the Committee for the Re-election of the President — including some of my closest friends and most trusted aides — have been charged with involvement in what has come to be known as the Watergate affair. These include charges of illegal activity during and preceding the 1972 Presidential election and charges that responsible officials participated in efforts to cover up that illegal activity.

The inevitable result of these charges has been to raise serious questions about the integrity of the White House itself. Tonight I wish to address those questions.

Last June 17, while I was in Florida trying to get a few days' rest after my visit to Moscow, I first learned from news reports of the Watergate break-in. I was appalled at this senseless, illegal action, and I was shocked to learn that employees of the Re-election Committee were apparently among those guilty. I immediately ordered an investigation by appropriate government authorities. On September 15, as you will recall, indictments were brought against seven defendants in the case.

As the investigations went forward, I repeatedly asked those conducting the investigation whether there was any reason to believe that members of my Administration were in any way involved. I received repeated assurances that there were not. Because of these continuing reassurances — because I believed the reports I was getting, because I had faith in the persons from whom I was getting them — I discounted the stories in the press that appeared to implicate members of my Administration or other officials of the campaign committee.

Until March of this year, I remained convinced that the denials were true and that the charges of involvement by members of the White House staff were false. The comments I made during this period, and the comments made by my Press Secretary on my behalf, were based on the information provided to us at the time we made those comments. However, new information then came to me which persuaded me that there was a real possibility that some of these charges were true, and suggesting further that there had been an effort to conceal the facts both from the public, from you, and from me.

As a result, on March 21, I personally assumed the responsibility for coordinating intensive new inquiries into the matter, and I personally ordered those conducting the investigations to get all the facts and to report them directly to me, right here in this office.

I again ordered that all persons in the Government or at the Re-election Committee should cooperate fully with the FBI, the prosecutors and the Grand Jury. I also ordered that anyone who refused to cooperate in telling the truth would be asked to resign from government service. And, with ground rules adopted that would preserve the basic constitutional separation of powers between the Congress and the Presidency, I directed that members of the White House staff should appear and testify voluntarily under oath before the Senate Committee investigating Watergate.

I was determined that we should get to the bottom of the matter, and that the truth should be fully brought out — no matter who was involved.

At the same time, I was determined not to take precipitate action, and to avoid, if at all possible, any action that would appear to reflect on innocent people. I wanted to be fair. But I knew that in the final analysis, the integrity of this office — public faith in the integrity of this office — would have to take priority over all personal considerations.

Today, in one of the most difficult decisions of my Presidency, I accepted the resignations of two of my closest associates in the White House — Bob Haldeman, John Ehrlichman — two of the finest public servants it has been my privilege to know.

I want to stress that in accepting these resignations, I mean to leave no implication whatever of personal wrongdoing on their part, and I leave no implication tonight of implication on the part of others who have been charged in this matter. But in matters as sensitive as guarding the integrity of our democratic process, it is essential not only that rigorous legal and ethical standards be observed, but also that the public, you, have the total confidence that they are both being observed and enforced by those in authority and particularly by the President of the United States. They agreed with me that this move was necessary in order to restore that confidence.

Because Attorney General Kleindienst — though a distinguished public servant, my personal friend for 20 years, with no personal involvement whatever in this matter — has been a close personal and professional associate of some of those who are involved in this case, he and I both felt that it was also necessary to name a new Attorney General.

The Counsel to the President, John Dean, has also resigned.

As the new Attorney General, I have today named Elliot Richardson, a man of unimpeachable integrity and rigorously high principle. I have directed him to do everything necessary to ensure that the Department of Justice has the confidence and trust of every law abiding person in this country.

I have given him absolute authority to make all decisions bearing upon the prosecution of the Watergate case and related matters. I have instructed him that if he should consider it appropriate, he has the authority to name a special supervising prosecutor for matters arising out of the case.

Whatever may appear to have been the case before — whatever improper activities may yet be discovered in connection with this whole sordid affair — I want the American people, I want you to know beyond the shadow of a doubt that during my terms as President, justice will be pursued fairly, fully, and impartially, no matter who is involved. This office is a sacred trust and I am determined to be worthy of that trust.

Looking back at the history of this case, two questions arise:

How could it have happened?

Who is to blame?

Political commentators have correctly observed that during my 27 years in politics, I have always previously insisted on running my own campaigns for office.

But 1972 presented a very different situation. In both domestic and foreign policy, 1972 was a year of crucially important decisions, of intense negotiations, of vital new directions, particularly in working toward the goal which has been my overriding concern throughout my political career — the goal of bringing peace to America and peace to the world.

That is why I decided, as the 1972 campaign approached, that the Presidency should come first and politics second. To the maximum extent possible, therefore, I sought to delegate campaign operations, and to remove the day-to-day campaign decisions from the President's office and from the White House. I also, as you recall, severely limited the number of my own campaign appearances.

Who, then, is to blame for what happened in this case?

For specific criminal actions by specific individuals, those who committed those actions, must, of course, bear the liability and pay the penalty.

For the fact that alleged improper actions took place within the White House or within my campaign organization, the easiest course would be for me to blame those to whom I delegated the responsibility to run the campaign. But that would be a cowardly thing to do.

I will not place the blame on subordinates — on people whose zeal exceeded their judgment, and who may have done wrong in a cause they deeply believed to be right.

In any organization, the man at the top must bear the responsibility. That responsibility, therefore, belongs here, in this office. I accept that. And I pledge to you tonight, from this office, that I will do everything in my power to ensure that the guilty are brought to justice, and that such abuses are purged from our political processes in the years to come, long after I have left this office. . . .

. . . I love America. I deeply believe that America is the hope of the world, and I know that in the quality and wisdom of the leadership America gives lies the only hope for millions of people all over the world, that they can live their lives in peace and freedom. We must be worthy of that hope, in every sense of the word. Tonight, I ask for your prayers to help me in everything that I do throughout the days of my Presidency to be worthy of their hopes and of yours.

God bless America and God bless each and every one of you.

TRANSCRIPTS OF WHITE HOUSE CONVERSATIONS

(June 23, 1972)

MEETING I (10:04–11:39 A.M.)

HALDEMAN: Now, on the investigation, you know the Democratic break-in thing, we're back in the problem area because the FBI is not under control, because [Director Patrick] Gray doesn't exactly know how to control it and they have — their investigation is now leading into some productive areas . . . They've been able to trace the money — not through the money itself — but through the bank sources — the banker. And it goes in some directions we don't want it to go. Ah, also there have been some [other] things — like an informant came in off the street to the FBI in Miami who was a photographer or has a friend who is a photographer who developed some films through this guy [Bernard] Barker and the films had pictures of Democratic National Committee letterhead documents and things. So it's things like that that are filtering in. [Attorney General John] Mitchell came up with yesterday, and [Presidential Counsel] John Dean analyzed very carefully last night and concludes, concurs now with Mitchell's recommendation that the only way to solve this, and we're set up beautifully to do it . . . is for us to have [CIA Assistant Director Vernon] Walters call Pat Gray and just say, "Stay to hell out of this — this is ah, [our] business here. We don't want you to go any further on it." That's not an unusual development, and ah, that would take care of it.

PRESIDENT: What about Pat Gray — you mean Pat Gray doesn't want to?

HALDEMAN: Pat does want to. He doesn't know how to, and he doesn't have any basis for doing it. Given this, he will then have the basis. He'll call [FBI Assistant Director] Mark Felt in, and the two of them — and Mark Felt wants to cooperate because he's ambitious —

PRESIDENT: Yeah.

HALDEMAN: He'll call him in and say, "We've got the signal from across the river to put the hold on this." And that will fit rather well because the FBI agents who are working the case, at this point, feel that's what it is.

PRESIDENT: This is CIA? They've traced the money? Who'd they trace it to?

HALDEMAN: Well they've traced it to a name, but they haven't gotten to the guy yet.

PRESIDENT: Would it be somebody here?

HALDEMAN: Ken Dahlberg.

PRESIDENT: Who the hell is Ken Dahlberg?

HALDEMAN: He gave $25,000 in Minnesota and, ah, the check went directly to this guy Barker.

PRESIDENT: It isn't from the Committee though, from [Finance Chairman Maurice] Stans?

HALDEMAN: Yeah. It is. It's directly traceable and there's some more through some Texas people that went to the Mexican bank which can also be traced to the Mexican bank — they'll get their names today.

PRESIDENT: Well, I mean, there's no way — I'm just thinking if they don't cooperate, what do they say? That they were approached by the Cubans? That's what Dahlberg has to say, the Texans too.

HALDEMAN: Well, if they will. But then we're relying on more and more people all the time. That's the problem and they'll [i.e., the FBI] stop if we could take this other route.

PRESIDENT: All right.

HALDEMAN: And you seem to think the thing to do is get them to stop?

PRESIDENT: Right, fine.

HALDEMAN: They [Mitchell and Dean] say the only way to do that is from White House instructions. And it's got to be to [CIA Director Richard] Helms and to — ah, what's his name. . . . ? Walters.

PRESIDENT: Walters.

HALDEMAN: And the proposal would be that [presidential adviser John] Ehrlichman and I call them in, and say, ah —

PRESIDENT: All right, fine. How do you call him in — I mean you just — well, we protected Helms from one hell of a lot of things.

HALDEMAN: That's what Ehrlichman says.

PRESIDENT: Of course; this [Howard] Hunt [business.] That will uncover a lot of things. You open that scab there's a hell of a lot of things and we just feel that it would be very detrimental to have this thing go any further. This involves these Cubans, Hunt, and a lot of hanky-panky that we have nothing to do with ourselves. Well what the hell, did Mitchell know about this?

HALDEMAN: I think so. I don't think he knew the details, but I think he knew.

PRESIDENT: He didn't know how it was going to be handled though — with Dahlberg and the Texans and so forth? Well who was the asshole that did? Is it [G. Gordon] Liddy? Is that the fellow? He must be a little nuts!

HALDEMAN: He is.

PRESIDENT: I mean he just isn't well screwed on is he? Is that the problem?

HALDEMAN: No, but he was under pressure, apparently, to get more information, and as he got more pressure, he pushed the people harder.

PRESIDENT: Pressure from Mitchell?

HALDEMAN: Apparently. . . .

PRESIDENT: All right, fine, I understand it all. We won't second-guess Mitchell and the rest. Thank God it wasn't [special counsel Charles] Colson.

HALDEMAN: The FBI interviewed Colson yesterday. They determined that would be a good thing to do. To have him take an interrogation, which he did, and the FBI guys working the case concluded that there were one or two possibilities — one, that this was a White House (they don't think that there is anything at the Election Committee) they think it was either a White House operation and they had some obscure reasons for it — non-political, or it was a — Cuban [operation] and [involved] the CIA. And after their interrogation of Colson yesterday, they concluded it was not the White House, but are now convinced it is a CIA thing, so the CIA turnoff would —

PRESIDENT: Well, not sure of their analysis, I'm not going to get that involved. I'm (unintelligible).

HALDEMAN: No, sir, we don't want you to.

PRESIDENT: You call them in.

HALDEMAN: Good deal.

PRESIDENT: Play it tough. That's the way they play it and that's the way we are going to play it. . . .

MEETING 2 (1:04–1:13 P.M.)

PRESIDENT: O.K. . . . Just say (unintelligible) very bad to have this fellow Hunt, ah, he knows too damned much. . . . If it gets out that this is all involved, the Cuba thing, it would be a fiasco. It would make the CIA look bad, it's going to make Hunt look bad, and it is likely to blow the whole Bay of Pigs thing which we think would be very unfortunate — both for CIA, and for the country, at this time, and for American foreign policy. Just tell him to lay off. Don't you [think so]?

HALDEMAN: Yep. That's the basis to do it on. Just leave it at that. . . .

Study Guide

1. These two excerpts encapsulate much of what we now know of Nixon's role in the Watergate affair:

    (a) his early involvement (pp. 573–576); and
    (b) his public disclaimers — for more than a year — of any direct knowledge of the Watergate events (pp. 570–573).

    Turn your attention to the first excerpt, Nixon's address to the nation on April 30, 1973, and summarize the precise involvement — and blame — he is willing to ascribe to the following persons:

    (a) himself;
    (b) H. R. Haldeman and John Ehrlichman; and
    (c) John Dean.

    Nixon obviously has different feelings toward Haldeman and Ehrlichman on the one hand and toward Dean on the other. Explain why, referring to your text, if necessary.

2. How does Nixon account for his lack of involvement in the planning of the 1972 presidential campaign? How then would you reconcile this argument with this statement: "In any organization, the man at the top must bear responsibility." Can you find other contradictions of a similar sort in this address?

3. Let us assume for a moment that this address had been given in a uni-

versity speech class. What grade (A, B, C, D, or F) — in terms of an effective public address — would you assign to Nixon and *on what grounds?*

4. Turning from the April 30 address to the Nixon-Haldeman conversations of June 23, 1972, you can grasp the essence of the conversation between these two men by defining how they proposed to use the following men and institutions:

(a) Bernard Baker and the Cubans;
(b) Patrick Gray and Mark Felt of the Federal Bureau of Investigation;
(c) Vernon Walters and Richard Helms of the Central Intelligence Agency;
(d) Kenneth Dahlberg; and
(e) Maurice Stans and "the Texas people."

Identify, too, their relationship to and assessments of

(a) Howard Hunt;
(b) G. Gordon Liddy; and
(c) John Mitchell and Charles Colson.

For some of these, you may, again, need to refer to your textbook.

5. Some final questions:

(a) For what reason would the June 23 conversations between Nixon and Haldeman be called "the smoking gun"?
(b) On which of the following three grounds, in *your* opinion, would these conversations justify impeachment: treason, bribery, or the obstruction of justice. Document your selection of one, two, or all three.
(c) And, finally, what contradictions can you find between the facts that emerge from the "smoking gun" conversation of June 23, 1972, and Nixon's address of April 30, 1973?

To the student:

We, as publishers, realize that one way to improve education is to improve textbooks. We also realize that you, the student, have a large role in the success or failure of textbooks. Although teachers choose books to be used in the classroom, if the students do not buy and use books, those books are failures.

Usually only the teacher is asked about the quality of a text; his opinion alone is considered as revisions are written or as new books are planned. Now, Little, Brown would like to ask you about this book: how you liked or disliked it; why it was successful or dull; if it taught you anything. Would you fill in this form and return it to us at: Little, Brown and Co., History Department, College Division, 34 Beacon St., Boston, Mass. 02106. It is your chance to directly affect the publication of future textbooks.

Book title: _____   School: _____

Course title: _____   Course enrollment: _____

1. Did you like the book? _____

2. CONTENT: Was it too easy? _____

   Did you read all the selections? _____

   Which did you like most? _____

   Which did you like least? _____

(over)

3. Were the study questions helpful? _____

   How should they be changed? _____

   _____

4. INTRODUCTIONS: Are they useful? _____

   How should they be changed? _____

   _____

5. Do you feel the professor should continue to assign this book next year?

   _____

6. Will you keep this book for your library? _____

7. Please add any comments or suggestions on how we might improve this book, in either content or format.

   _____

   _____

   _____

   _____

   _____

8. May we quote you, either in promotion for this book, or in future publishing ventures? _____ yes _____ no

   date _____   signature _____